THE ART OF THE POSSIBLE

Documents on Great Power Diplomacy, 1814–1914

...In this country we demand from everyone who holds an office—for instance in the judiciary, for someone serving as a sergeant or in some other capacity—that he passes exams, an internship, difficult tests. But when it comes to [discussing] politics at the highest level: anyone can dabble in that; everyone feels that he has a calling; and, in a field so open to any talent, nothing is easier than asserting, as long as it is done with a straight face, anything at all. But to have any hope of refuting such assertions, one must—as is well known—write an entire book, except: the one who made the remark still refuses to be convinced....

—Bismarck in the Prussian Legislature (Upper House), 21 December 1863, *GW,* 10:200

As to our foreign policy—I hardly dare to open the subject with you. If I took your gloomy view, I should commence immediate enquiries as to the most painless form of suicide. But I think you listen too much to the soldiers. No lesson seems to be so deeply inculcated by the experience of life as that you never should trust in experts. If you believe the doctors nothing is wholesome: if you believe the theologians nothing is innocent: if you believe the soldiers nothing is safe....

—Salisbury to Lytton, 15 June 1877, in Lady Gwendolen Cecil, *Life of . . . Salisbury*
(London, 1921), 2:145

...Foreign policy is essentially a matter of saying what you are going to do.... Foreign policy is displayed in discussion—either in parliament or with foreigners....

—A. J. P. Taylor, "The Traditions of British Foreign Policy," in *Europe: Grandeur and Decline* (New York, 1967), 233

THE ART OF THE POSSIBLE:

DOCUMENTS ON GREAT POWER DIPLOMACY, 1814–1914

RALPH R. MENNING

THE McGRAW-HILL COMPANIES, INC.

New York St. Louis San Francisco Auckland Bogotá Caracas
Lisbon London Madrid Mexico City Milan Montreal New Delhi
San Juan Singapore Sydney Tokyo Toronto

McGraw-Hill

A Division of The **McGraw·Hill** Companies

THE ART OF THE POSSIBLE:
Documents on Great Power Diplomacy, 1814–1914

This book is printed on acid-free paper.

1 2 3 4 5 6 7 8 9 0 DOC DOC 9 0 9 8 7 6 5

ISBN 0-07-041574-9

This book was set in Garamond Book and Optima by Graphic World, Inc.
The editor was Leslye Jackson;
the text designer was Joan Greenfield;
the production supervisor was Leroy A. Young.
The cover was designed by Christopher Brady.
Project supervision was done by Editorial Services of New England, Inc.
R. R. Donnelley & Sons Company was printer and binder.

Library of Congress Catalog Card Number: 95-81699

About the Author

Ralph R. Menning has taught history and international relations at Brown, the University of Montana, Heidelberg College, and the University of Toledo. He has lectured to Model United Nations conferences, Smithsonian study groups, professional and civic associations, and students at all levels. Their questions and enthusiasm motivated him to write this book.

A graduate of the UN International School, Yale, and Brown, Professor Menning has been a fellow of the Institut für Europäische Geschichte in Mainz and has studied public international law at the Hague Academy. His articles and reviews have appeared in *Central European History,* the *Austrian History Yearbook,* and other journals. He has contributed to several reference works, including the American Historical Association's *Guide to Historical Literature,* and is about to complete a study of the First Moroccan and Bosnian crises, *The Concert Wrecked: Britain, Germany, and the Politics of Global Confrontation, 1906–1909.* He lives in Toledo, Ohio.

For Carol

Table of Contents

1. Foundations of the "1815 System" 1

1.1 Metternich's Statesmanship—1.2 Castlereagh's Mission to the Continent—1.3 The Question of Maritime Rights—1.4 Treaty of Chaumont, 1 March 1814—1.5 The Abdication of Napoleon—1.6 The French and Overseas Settlements, 1814—1.7 The Alliance Strained: The Saxon-Polish Crisis—1.8 The Slave Trade Condemned—1.9 The "One Hundred Days," February to July 1815—1.10 Final Act of the Congress of Vienna, 9 June 1815—1.11 Holy Alliance, 26 September 1815—1.12 Second Peace of Paris, 20 November 1815—1.13 Quadruple Alliance, 20 November 1815

2. The "1815 System" in Operation: Fissures and Adjustments 28 1815-1839

2.1 Metternich on England and Russia—2.2 Congress of Aix-la-Chapelle—2.3 Intermediary Bodies and the European Equilibrium: The German Confederation—2.4 Intervention Debated: Conferences of Troppau and Laibach—2.5 Intervention Deemed Ill Advised: Castlereagh on the Greek Insurrection—2.6 Intervention Tolerated: Canning and the French "War" against Spain—2.7 The Monroe Doctrine, 1823—2.8 Intermediary Bodies and the European Equilibrium: The Neutrality of Belgium—2.9 Metternich on the Zollverein

3. The Eastern Question, 1774-1841 45

3.1 Treaty of Kuchuk-Kainarji, 10/21 July 1774—3.2 The Straits Question in the Napoleonic Era—3.3 The European Concert Reinvented: St. Petersburg Protocol and Treaty of London—3.4 Polignac's Scheme—3.5 Peace of Adrianople—3.6 Settlement of the Greek Question—3.7 The Straits Question, 1833-1838—3.8 To the Brink of European War and Back: The Second Mohammed Ali Crisis, 1838-1841—

11.   *The Narrowing Margin, 1905–1914* 315

12.   *The Collapse of Diplomacy, July 1914* 393

List of Abbreviations

BD George P. Gooch and Harold V. Temperley (eds.), *British Documents on the Origins of the War, 1898–1914,* 11 vols. (London, 1925–1938)*

Bourne Kenneth Bourne, *The Foreign Policy of Victorian England, 1830–1902* (Oxford, 1970)

CTS Clive Parry (ed.), *The Consolidated Treaty Series, 1648–1919,* 231 vols. (Dobbs Ferry, NY, 1969–1986)

D'Angeberg Comte d'Angeberg [pseud. for Jakob Leonhard Chodzko] (ed.), *Le Congrès de Vienne et les traités de 1815,* 2 vols. (Paris, 1863)

DD Karl Kautsky, Count Max Montgelas, and Walter Schücking (eds.), *Die Deutschen Dokumente zum Kriegsausbruch 1914* (Berlin, 1919; 1922)

DDF *Documents diplomatiques français, 1871–1914,* 1st Series: *1871–1900,* 16 vols. (Paris, 1929–1959); 2nd Series: *1901–11,* 14 vols. (Paris, 1930–1955); 3rd Series: *1911–14,* 11 vols. (Paris, 1929–1936)*

FO Foreign Office files, Public Record Office, London

GP Johannes Lepsius, Albrecht Mendelssohn Bartholdy, and Friedrich Thimme (eds.), *Die Grosse Politik der europäischen Kabinette, 1871–1914,* 40 vols. in 54 (Berlin, 1922–1927)*

GW Otto von Bismarck, *Die gesammelten Werke,* ed. by H. von Petersdorff et al., 15 vols. (Berlin, 1924–1935)*

*References are to document rather than page numbers.

HP   Normal Rich and M. H. Fisher (eds.), *The Holstein Papers,* 4
                       vols. (Cambridge, 1956–1963), and *Die geheimen Papiere
                       Friedrich von Holsteins,* 4 vols. (Göttingen, 1956–1963)*

Hertslet   Edward Hertslet (ed.), *The Map of Europe by Treaty,* 4 vols.
                       (London, 1877–1891; reprint: 1969)

Hertslet II   Edward Hertslet (ed.), *The Map of Africa by Treaty,* 3 vols. (3rd
                       rev. ed., London, 1909; reprint, 1967)

Hertslet III   Godfrey E. P. Hertslet (ed.), *Treaties, etc., between Great Britain
                       and China and between China and Foreign Powers,* 2 vols. (3rd
                       ed., London, 1908)

Hurewitz   *The Middle East and North Africa in World Politics: A Docu-
                       mentary Record,* 2nd ed., vol. 1: *European Expansion,
                       1535–1914* (New Haven: Yale University Press, 1975), comp.,
                       trans., and ed. by J. C. Hurewitz, © J. C. Hurewitz.

Hurst   Michael Hurst (ed.), *Key Treaties for the Great Powers,
                       1814–1914,* 2 vols. (New York, 1972)

OeU   Ludwig Bittner and Hans Uebersberger (eds.), *Oesterreich-
                       Ungarns Aussenpolitik von der Bosnischen Krise 1908 bis zum
                       Kriegsausbruch 1914,* 9 vols. (Vienna, 1930)*

PA   German Foreign Ministry Archives, Bonn

Parl. Deb.   *Hansard's Parliamentary Debates*

PP   *Parliamentary Papers*

Pribram   Alfred Pribram (ed.), *The Secret Treaties of Austria-Hungary,
                       1879–1914,* 2 vols. (Cambridge, MA, 1920)

QV   Reginald, Viscount Esher and George Earl Buckle (eds.), *The
                       Letters of Queen Victoria,* 1st Series: *1837–61,* 3 vols. (London,
                       1907); 2nd Series: *1862–85,* 3 vols. (London, 1926–1928); 3rd
                       Series: *1885–1901,* 3 vols. (London, 1930–1932)

Reichstag   [German parliament,] *Stenographische Berichte über die Ver-
                       handlungen des Reichstags*

SP   *British and Foreign State Papers,* 170 vols. (London,
                       1841–1968)

Temperley and Penson Harold Temperley and Lillian M. Penson, *Foundations of British
                       Foreign Policy from Pitt (1792) to Salisbury (1902)* (Cambridge,
                       1938; reprint: New York, 1966)

ZI   Otto Hoetzsch et al. (trans. and eds.), *Die internationalen
                       Beziehungen im Zeitalter des Imperialismus. Dokumente aus
                       den Archiven der zarischen und der provisorischen Regierung,
                       1878–1917,* 3rd Series [1911–1916], 10 vols. (Berlin,
                       1930–1942)*

Preface

As this book took shape, I could not check for long the impulse to badger friends and colleagues, even recent acquaintances, with requests for help of every kind. Had it not been for their patience and their willingness to set aside their own work to humor me, the book would not have been possible. I thank them all for their generosity.

For their suggestions and advice, I am particularly indebted to Robert Berkhofer, III, Owen Bradley, James Chastain, Phil Harner, Holger Herwig, Ned Newman, Nancy Perry, Merle Rife, and Ann Pottinger Saab. I have benefited greatly from the expertise of my former colleagues at the University of Montana, especially Paul Gordon Lauren and Richard Drake, and from that of Glenn Ames, Sally Hadden, William Hoover, and Robert Freeman Smith at the University of Toledo. Michael Jakobson freely gave his time to translate several passages from and into Russian. Without assistance from Anna Miller, the French prose of Wilhelm von Humboldt would be a mystery still. My wife, Carol Bresnahan Menning, translated the bulk of the documents from French and Italian sources.

In Bonn, Dr. Maria Keipert and the staff of the German foreign ministry archives offered kind hospitality and once again gave me invaluable help. I wish to thank Leopold Kammerhofer of the Haus-, Hof- und Staatsarchiv for patiently dealing with an avalanche of questions. Nancy Rubenstein and her coworkers in the interlibrary loan office of Beeghley Library processed a mountain of requests, many of them as outlandish as they were exasperating. My friends and former students Michael Groomes, Kim Pace, Linville Taggart, and Christine Utick bore with good cheer the drudgery of a thousand tasks, and I am obliged to Sabine Pagel and Katja Wüstenbecker for scouring the university libraries at Heidelberg and Marburg for a range of rare items.

Paul Schroeder took time from a busy schedule to read a draft of the first eight chapters; his extensive commentaries gave me a sense of perspective and saved me from many a blunder. Linda Frey, Marsha Frey, and Norman Rich slogged through the entire manuscript, persevered even when I imposed on them what I thought were new and improved versions, and were still kind enough to offer constant encouragement and moral support. But this book would have never come into being had it not been for my wife, who brought to her many and various roles—as translator, researcher, editor extraordinaire, sounding board—the discerning eye of someone who has been through it all before. I am not sure that I can devise an adequate form of repayment, but dedicating this book to her might just be a small step in the right direction.

I would also like to express my thanks for the many useful comments and suggestions provided by the following reviewers: Darwin Bostick, Old Dominion University; George Giacomini, Santa Clara University; Robert Herzstein, University of South Carolina; John Hill, Immaculata College; H. Peter Krosby, SUNY, Albany; Herbert Rothfeder, East Carolina University; Thomas Sakmyster, University of Cincinnati; William Scott, Duke University; Daniel Silverman, Penn State University; and Marla Stone, Occidental College.

A summer grant from the University of Montana first gave me the time to think about the basic scheme of this book. My editors at McGraw-Hill—David Follmer, Pam Gordon, Nancy Blaine, and Leslye Jackson—have been models of patience and understanding, and more than once gave me the confidence to proceed. Finally, Lauren Byrne of Editorial Services of New England, Inc., piloted this project through the production stage with sound judgment and a steady hand. I am grateful to them all.

Ralph R. Menning

Acknowledgments

Material from the Royal Archives, Windsor, is reprinted by gracious permission of Her Majesty Queen Elizabeth II. I wish to thank Prince Ferdinand von Bismarck for permission to use passages from Otto von Bismarck's *Gesammelte Werke,* and the Earl of Selborne for extracts from *The Crisis of British Power: The Imperial and Naval Papers of the Second Earl of Selborne, 1895–1910,* ed. by D. George Boyce. I am grateful to the following authors for allowing me to quote from their works: Winfried Baumgart (ed.), *Akten zur Geschichte des Krimkriegs,* Series 1: *Österreichische Akten,* vol. 1 (Munich, 1980), © Winfried Baumgart; *The Middle East and North Africa in World Politics: A Documentary Record,* 2nd ed., vol. 1: *European Expansion, 1535–1914* (New Haven, 1975), comp., trans., and ed. by J. C. Hurewitz, copyright © J. C. Hurewitz; Denis Mack Smith (ed.), *The Making of Italy, 1796–1870* (New York, 1968), © Denis Mack Smith; John C. G. Röhl (ed.), "An der Schwelle zum Weltkrieg: Eine Dokumentation über den Kriegsrat vom 8. Dezember 1912," in *Militärgeschichtliche Mitteilungen* 10 (1977), 77–134, © John C. G. Röhl.

Thanks are also due the American Historical Association for permission to quote from Robert A. Kann, "Emperor William II and Archduke Francis Ferdinand in Their Correspondence," in *American Historical Review* 57 (1951/52) and from Paul Knaplund (ed.), "Letters from the Berlin Embassy," from the *Annual Report of the American Historical Association for the Year 1942,* vol. 2. Selections from the correspondence of Wilhelm II in the Brandenburgisches-Hohenzollern'sches Hausarchiv are courtesy of the Geheimes Staatsarchiv of the Stiftung Preussischer Kulturbesitz. Excerpts from *Rassegna storica del Risorgimento* 26 (1939) and Alberto M. Ghisalberti (ed.), *Lettere di Felice Orsini* appear with permission from the Istituto per la storia del Risorgimento Italiano; extracts from Sergio Camerani and Gaetano Arfé (eds.), *Carteggi di Bettino Ricàsoli* are reprinted with kind permission from the Istituto storico Italiano per l'età moderna e contemporanea. I am grateful to the Japan Foundation for allowing use of excerpts from *Kenkenroku: A Diplomatic Record of the Sino-Japanese War, 1894–95,* ed. by Gordon Mark Berger; the Kommission für bayerische Landesgeschichte bei der Bayerischen Akademie der Wissenschaften for Anton Chroust (ed.), *Gesandtschaftsberichte aus München;* the Royal Historical Society for vol. 25 of *Camden Fourth Series,* "The Diary of Edward Goschen, 1900–1914," ed. C.H.D. Howard; the Südost-Institut at the University of Munich for Karl Nehring (ed.), *Flugblätter und Flugschriften der ungarischen Revolution von 1848/49;* the Van Riebeeck Society, Cape Town, for Phyllis Lewsen (ed.), *Selections from the Correspondence of J.X. Merriman.* Crown copyright is reproduced with the permission of the Controller of HMSO. Selections from the *Documents diplomatiques français* are reproduced with authorization from the Ministère français des Affaires Etrangères.

The following publishers have granted permission to quote from works under copyright: Athlone Press for Rose L. Greaves, *Persia and the Defense of India, 1884–1892. A Study in the Foreign Policy of the Third Marquess of Salisbury,* © 1959; Verlag Berger for F. R. Bridge, "Izvolsky, Aehrenthal, and the End of the Austro-Russian Entente, 1906–8," in *Mitteilungen des österreichischen Staatsarchivs* 29 (1976), 315–62; Harald Boldt Verlag for Deutsche Geschichtsquellen, vol. 50/I, *Briefwechsel Hertling-Lerchenfeld,* ed. by Ernst Deuerlein, © 1973, and Deutsche Geschichtsquellen, vol. 52/III, *Philipp Eulenburgs politische Korrespondenz,* ed. by John C.G. Röhl, © 1983; Cambridge University Press for W.K. Hancock and Jean van der Poel (eds.), *Selections from the Smuts Papers,* vol. 1, © 1966, for Robert J. Kerner "Russia's New Policy in the Near East," in *Cambridge Historical Journal* 5 (1937), for Norman Rich and M.H. Fisher (eds.), *The Holstein Papers,* © 1956-1965, and for A. W. Ward and G. P. Gooch (eds.), *Cambridge History of British Foreign Policy,* © 1923. Extracts from H.V. Temperley and Lillian M. Penson (eds.), *Foundations of British Foreign Policy from Pitt (1792) to Salisbury (1902),* © 1938, are reprinted with kind permission of Frank Cass and Company, Ltd., London. The translation of Tocqueville's speech of 18 October 1849 is from J.P. Mayer (ed.), *The Recollections of Alexis de Tocqueville,* copyright © 1949 by Columbia University Press. I wish to thank Droste Verlag, Düsseldorf, for permission to quote from Volker R. Berghahn and Wilhelm Deist (eds.), *Rüstung im Zeichen der willhelminischen Weltpolitik. Grundlegende Dokumente, 1890–1914,* © 1988; Walter de Gruyter & Co., for Wilhelm von Humboldt, *Gesammelte Schriften,* ed. by Bruno Gebhardt, vols. 11 and 12, © 1903 and 1968; HarperCollins Publishers, Ltd., for *The Political Diaries of C.P. Scott,* ed. by Trevor Wilson, © 1970; Harvard University Press for Etling Morison et al. (eds.), *The Letters of Theodore Roosevelt,* © 1951–54. Excerpts from *Winston S. Churchill: Companion Volume II, Part 3,* by Randoph S. Churchill, copyright © 1969 by C & T Publications, are reprinted by permission of Houghton Mifflin Company (all rights reserved). Vittorio Klostermann Verlag has kindly granted permission to quote from Lothar Wickert (ed.), *Theodor Mommsen—Otto Jahn Briefwechsel, 1842–1868,* © 1962; W. Kohlhammer GmbH for Ernst R. Huber (ed.), *Dokumente zur deutschen Verfassungsgeschichte,* © 1964, 1979, and 1991; Hutchinson, Ltd., for Georges Bonnin (ed.), *Bismarck and the Hohenzollern Candidature for the Spanish Throne,* © 1959; John Murray (Publishers), Ltd., for Edward David (ed.), *Inside Asquith's Cabinet: From the Diaries of Charles Hobhouse,* © 1977; Nauka Publishers, Moscow, for *Dnevnik P.A. Valueva,* © 1961; Oxford University Press for Dudley W.R. Bahlmann (ed.), *The Diary of Sir Walter Hamilton,* © 1972, for H.C.G. Matthew (ed.), *The Gladstone Diaries,* vol. 11, ©1990, for Kenneth Bourne, *The Foreign Policy of Victorian England,* © 1970, for Agatha Ramm (ed.), *The Political Correspondence of Mr. Gladstone and Lord Granville, 1876–1886,* © 1962, and for B.H. Sumner, *Russia and the Balkans,* © 1937. Extracts from "Fachoda (1898)," in *Revue d'histoire diplomatique* 69 (1955) are reprinted with permission from Edition A. Pedone. The passages from Obruchev's memorandum of 7/19 May 1892, from George F. Kennan, *The Fateful Alliance: France, Russia, and the Coming of the First World War,* © 1984, appear with permission of Random House. Permission has been granted by the editors of the *Slavonic and East European Review* to reproduce extracts from volume 26 (1948); no. 66, pp. 303-8 and pp. 309-13; and volume 62 (1984), no. 4, pp. 556-57. Excerpts from Richard Metternich's report of 22 February 1863 are reprinted from the translation in *Distaff Diplomacy: The Empress Eugénie and the Foreign Policy of the Second Empire* by Nancy Nichols Barker, copyright © 1967, courtesy of the University of Texas Press. I am grateful to Vandenhoeck & Ruprecht,

Göttingen, for use of the excerpts from Karl-Kietrich Erdmann (ed.), *Kurt Riezler. Tagebücher, Aufsätze, Dokumente,* © 1972, and to S.F. Vanni for Howard Marraro (ed.), *Diplomatic Relations between the United States and the Kingdom of the Two Sicilies,* © 1952.

Ralph R. Menning

Introduction: The Art of the Possible

The purpose of any collection of primary sources is to convey a sense of immediacy: to impart to the reader a "you-were-there" atmosphere by allowing him or her to look over the shoulder, so to speak, of the leading characters as they take pen in hand. The reader of the present work can follow statesmen and politicians as they take a stand, force an issue, flim-flam a reluctant monarch, beat a retreat, disguise their underlying motives from parliamentary scrutiny, or scramble for cover. Embedded in their style are their motives, sympathies and antipathies, perspective, good judgment (or lack thereof). But language and style do more than simply mirror personality: Castlereagh's prolixity, Palmerston's bombast, Bismarck's pithiness, the diatribes of Napoleon III or Wilhelm II derive their real significance from what they suggest about these figures' realism, their focus and assumptions, the quality of their leadership.

In diplomacy, language and style are the building blocks of compromise or confrontation, the ingredients on which the outcome of many a negotiation or maneuver may hinge, the essence of a perpetual game of defining and redefining the bounds of the possible. Of course, geography, fiscal or other constraints, technological advances, and mobilization schedules impose limits on what the most accomplished practitioner of the art of the possible can achieve. But the power of words should not be underestimated: a verbal conjuring trick may outwit an ally or an adversary, while a misstep may well turn one into the other.

This book was motivated in part by my belief that the politics of the nineteenth century is of more than antiquarian interest for the student of modern international relations. A recital of arguments might begin with the suggestion that the past should be studied for its own sake. Second, familiarity with the nineteenth century (by which diplomatic historians generally mean the years between Napoleon's defeat in 1814 and the outbreak of the First World War in 1914) is a prerequisite for understanding the twentieth. The demons of this century—total war, mechanized butchery on an unprecedented scale, national (and class) hatreds so intense that previous outbursts pale in comparison—were set free by the First World War, a conflagration unleashed by politicians and diplomats who paradoxically shared a premonition that a war among the Great Powers would end the international and social order as they knew it. If we measure the importance of events by the consequences that they generate, then the inability (or refusal?) of the Great Powers in 1914 to settle their differences peaceably continues to take pride of place as one of the most spectacular failures ever. Long after the guns fell silent, the legacy of the July crisis of 1914 continued to poison international relations: the determination of the victorious Allies to hold Germany responsible for having caused the First World War, the German attempt to refute this charge, and the ensuing battle for the hearts and minds of the public permeated the political climate of the 1920s and 1930s. Understanding the inter-war years means having to understand the widespread revulsion, particularly in Britain, against the sins of July 1914 and against the brinkmanship which characterized the many crises of the pre-World War I decade. Those in Britain who made the Anglo-German naval agreement of 1935 and those who denounced the Franco-Soviet pact of the same year merely thought they had learned from the lessons of history that unchecked arms races and peace-time alliances were catalysts of war.

But there are even more compelling reasons for investigating nineteenth-century interna-tional politics. The nineteenth century, with its two long periods of peace among the Great Powers (1815–1853 and 1871–1914), contrasts sharply with the era of the world wars of the twentieth. Yet it speaks to a range of issues that have surfaced in the post-cold war world. This is not to propose that history repeats itself. On the contrary, the suggestion that there are links between the nineteenth century and the present calls for a reminder that comparisons over time are fraught with danger. But the nineteenth-century record enriches our understanding of subjects as diverse as the functioning of a multipolar, as opposed to a bipolar, state system; the aging and fraying of alliances; the decay of multinational states; the assault of ideologies, promising deliverance and utopia, on the status quo; the setting of priorities and the making of choices in an environment of political and economic constraints. Anyone interested in today's headlines on the origins of ethnic conflict in the Caucasus or the Balkans, on the illogic of Africa's borders, on the relationship of Russia to China or to the Muslim world, or on the com-patibility of a united Germany with the European equilibrium will find that these issues simply cannot be understood without an appreciation of their nineteenth-century roots.

It is only fair for an author to share with his readers his biases at the outset, and here I would like to mention several which have influenced me in the compilation of this volume. Writers on international affairs often use the term "national interest" as if it were an objective or independent agent. But definitions of the "national interest" evolve over time, are trans-formed in reaction to new circumstances, or vary with the individuals charged with the mak-ing of policy. One of the goals of this book is to show how, for the principal Great Powers over the course of the nineteenth century, the definition of the "national interest" changed and what (or who) was responsible for these changes. This approach, in its turn, demands a good hard look at the fashion, still wide-spread in many college texts, of reducing the history of other countries to a dozen or so well-worn images which are continually evoked to the ex-clusion of everything else. I am reluctant to accept that outcomes are preordained because of a genetic disposition for "British," "French," or "German" statesmen to act in certain ways: the shorthand "British" to describe the policies of both Palmerston and Salisbury, or "German" to explain the views of Humboldt, Bismarck, and Bülow, does little to advance our understand-ing but does obscure crucial differences in temperament, approach, and outlook.

History would be easier to understand if all spectacular events had spectacular causes. Alas, great events are often set into motion by trivial occurrences, and the student of interna-tional relations is frequently surprised to discover the picayune surroundings that attended the birth of policies later extolled by historians as "guiding principles" or "diplomatic systems." The Three Emperors' League or the Reinsurance Treaty is often invoked, but who—apart from the professional historian—remembers the specific circumstances to which these instruments responded? The milestone remains—frozen in time, yanked out of its context—but the road leading up to it lies concealed in a dense fog of forgetfulness. Part of the purpose of this book is to recall some of these details and to draw attention to their importance. In trying to strike a balance between the particular and the general, I have been sparing in my use of the word "system" (though I occasionally use "systemic" to suggest a bird's-eye perspective); the only true "system"with which this book deals, and which was consciously conceived as such, was the one established by the alliances and peace treaties of 1814–1815.

Moreover, I hope that these readings will assist students as they "do" history, as they test the theories of historians against the written record, as they develop their own hypotheses. It has been said in jest that a tragedy is a beautiful theory killed by an ugly fact, and perhaps the ultimate test of the usefulness of the documents here is whether they corroborate, counter, or even damage well-established generalizations: how do they speak to the idea that the Great Powers between 1820 and 1848 divided into two camps, the "liberal west" and the "autocratic east"; to the notion that the unification of Germany was the result of profound and irresistible forces; to the assertion that nineteenth–century Russian foreign policy was a relentless drive to warm-water ports; to the orthodoxy that Germany planned or willed the First World War?

The published documents dealing with the international relations of the Great Powers in the nineteenth century, never mind the archival holdings, run in the hundreds of thousands of items, and it would be folly to pretend that these vast records can be condensed to a single, definitive volume. Most documents here have been chosen because there is widespread agreement that they are essential to an understanding of nineteenth-century Great Power politics (and, indeed, modern international relations); others, because they offer capsule descriptions or "snapshots" of larger vistas. Some were selected on the basis of more eccentric criteria—to demonstrate dissent from within the ranks, to supply a corrective to present-day reductionism and prejudices, or to show that a result celebrated as inevitable by posterity was very much in doubt until the last moment. In a few cases, I have not been able to resist the temptation to include documents because of their literary charm.

Throughout, I have given preference to sources that are immediate to the events under consideration. Such documents—correspondence, diaries, memoranda, speeches, instructions, the treaties themselves—are the ones that either set matters in motion or constitute spontaneous reactions. I have largely shunned autobiographies, for there is no reason to believe that the memories of statesmen are less defective than our own, and the few exceptions that I have made tend to prove this point. But some passages in this book have been deliberately chosen because they contain references to events treated earlier; these seem particularly apt as they reflect an effort on the part of the principals of this story to interpret the events at hand in light of the "lessons of history."

The vast majority of documents in this book are drawn from published collections, though many appear in English translation for the first time. Some documents come from my own work in the archives. By and large, procuring many of the documents reproduced here has been something of an education: given the frequency with which they are cited by scholars, I thought them far more accessible than they actually are. As this volume progressed, the challenge (and frustration) of locating some of these supposedly well-known sources itself became a justification for the book. It strikes me as ironic, and not a little incongruous, that on one hand we demand that our students become more cosmopolitan, that they increase their knowledge of international relations, or that they make informed judgments on the diplomacy of imperialism or the origins of the First World War, while on the other hand the sources—particularly those in languages other than English—remain hidden away in a handful of research libraries.

Each of the chapters is introduced by a note placing that chapter in a larger context. Within chapters, each document or cluster of documents is preceded by a headnote. The purpose of these headnotes is to explain the background events, to raise questions or interpretive difficulties specific to each document, to refer the reader to the scholarly debates which it may have generated, and to provide a point of departure for discussion or independent research. In some instances, the notes seek to alert the reader to documents that have acquired importance or notoriety because of what they do not explicitly say, because of the issues which they skirt, because of their omissions. The notes stop short of summarizing the document, of giving away too much of its substance, so as not to interfere with the reader's process of discovery.

The bibliographical essay at the end of this book focuses on primary sources; each of the chapter notes concludes with a short list of further readings in the secondary literature. For reasons of space, these suggestions are brief: they are limited to recent titles or earlier works with extensive bibliographies. Readers interested in fuller coverage should consult Section 47 ("International Relations, 1815–1920") of the American Historical Association's *Guide to Historical Literature* (Oxford, 1995) or the bibliographies in Norman Rich, *Great Power Diplomacy, 1814–1914* (McGraw-Hill, 1992); Paul W. Schroeder, *The Transformation of European Politics, 1763–1848* (Oxford, 1994); and A. J. P. Taylor, *The Struggle for Mastery in Europe, 1848–1918* (Oxford, 1954).

For the sake of readability, I have modified capitalization and spelling and have added or deleted commas in some documents. Such interventions have not, I hope, altered the meaning of these texts.

CHAPTER 1

Foundations of the "1815 System"

The documents in this chapter show how the Allies harmonized their aims during the final campaigns against Napoleon, how they developed the principles which guided their search for peace, and how the postwar political order became anchored in the treaties of 1814–1815.

One measure of the importance of the 1814–1815 treaties, and one reason for studying them, is their long hold on the international politics of the nineteenth century. The Treaty of Chaumont of March 1814 and the Quadruple Alliance of November 1815 laid the foundation for the Concert of Europe, the informal postwar grouping of the European Great Powers. The concert, it is true, was increasingly marred by dissonances when Allied unity crumbled in the 1820s over issues such as the revolts in Spain, Naples, and Greece. But most statesmen accepted for several more decades the fundamental assumptions on which the concert was predicated: that each Great Power had a legitimate role to play in the international order, that all the Great Powers were entitled to interests (prestige, influence, control or possession of certain strategic territories), that a threat to one of them threatened them all, and that, in a confrontation amongst them, the risks by far outweighed the benefits.

Even more resilient than the political foundations of the 1815 settlement were its territorial provisions. The breakup of the United Netherlands in 1830 and Austria's annexation of the Republic of Cracow in 1846 modified the borders of 1815, but otherwise these borders survived the 1848 revolutions and were shattered only, between 1859 and 1866, by the unification of Italy and by the destruction of the German Confederation.

There is no reason to doubt the architects of the 1815 settlement in their determination to prevent a return to the chaos of the Napoleonic era. But it has long been fashionable to ask whether the peacemakers aimed to restore the *ancien régime* (and looked, for their guiding ideals, to the period before the French revolution) or whether they instead hoped to create a new order entirely. The answer lies embedded in the documents excerpted in this chapter—in the terms of the treaties of alliance which the Allies concluded among themselves, in the stipulations of their peace treaties with France, and in the territorial provisions of the Final Act of the Congress of Vienna.

In one respect at least, the 1814–1815 settlement differed from the peace treaties of the seventeenth and eighteenth centuries: it proved far more durable. The usual explanations are that, after a generation of warfare, an exhausted public yearned for peace; and that, over the next three decades, the opponents of the new order were disorganized and had only sporadic access to power. But explaining the longevity of the peace in merely negative terms, in terms of an absence of a successful challenge, may overlook the principal reason for the relative success of the 1815 settlement—its architecture. Previous treaties, in their preambles and initial articles, also pledged their signatories to eternal peace and good neighborliness, but the language of the post-Napoleonic peace went well beyond these ritual incantations and pointedly referred to the lessons of history, as these were understood by the principals of the tale. In its repudiation of past practices, the 1815 settlement sought to restructure the very premises on which the foreign relations of the Great Powers had hitherto been based. Earlier and later settlements derived their legitimacy from abstractions (the divine right of kings, "self-determination," "making the world safe for democracy" all come to mind), but in 1815 the terms and provisions of the treaties themselves became the building blocks of the new international order, the standard by which future actions would be justified and measured, the new legitimacy.

GENERAL READING: Owen Connelly, *Blundering to Glory: Napoleon's Military Campaigns* (Wilmington, 1987); Edward V. Gulick, *Europe's Classical Balance of Power* (Ithaca, 1955); Enno E. Kraehe, *Metternich's German Policy*, 2 vols. (Princeton, 1963–1983); Paul W. Schroeder, *The Transformation of European Politics, 1763–1848* (Oxford, 1994); Paul R. Sweet, *Wilhelm von Humboldt: A Biography*, 2 vols. (Columbus, OH, 1980); Charles K. Webster, *The Foreign Policy of Castlereagh, 1812–15* (London, 1931)

1.1   METTERNICH'S STATESMANSHIP

Humboldt to Friedrich Wilhelm III, 17 February 1811

In 1809, Austria's renewed defeat at the hands of Napoleon demonstrated that, if only for the interim, the survival of the Habsburg monarchy hinged on a policy of accommodating the French emperor. The architect of this policy was Count Clemens von Metternich, the new Austrian foreign minister.

A native of the Rhineland and son of an Austrian diplomat, Metternich had used his marriage to the granddaughter and heiress of Prince Anton Kaunitz (Austrian chancellor, 1753–1792) to gain access to the highest circles of Viennese society and to accelerate his career. He served as minister to Saxony (1801 to 1803) and subsequently as Austrian ambassador in Berlin (1803 to 1805) and Paris (1806 to 1809). Upon becoming foreign minister, Metternich's first project was to engineer the marriage of Marie Louise, daughter of the Austrian Emperor Francis I, to Napoleon. This dynastic tie revived a well-tried Habsburg tradition (summed up by the quip, dating from the *ancien régime*, "others wage wars, but you, o happy Austria, marry"). Marriage into Europe's most distinguished ruling house gave Napoleon the legitimacy which he craved; in return, the dynastic alliance might assure Austria of a modicum of protection from the caprices of the French emperor.

That Metternich had little room to maneuver was readily apparent. More difficult to fathom were his aims. If Metternich's long-term goal was a reduction of French power, he was wise not to proclaim this intention openly—perhaps the strongest card in his hand was to leave others guessing. Metternich's predicament was well captured by Wilhelm von Humboldt, a noted linguist and founder of the University of Berlin, who had just been appointed Prussian ambassador to Vienna. In a carefully crafted report to his monarch, Humboldt contrasted Metternich with Count Philipp Stadion, whose policies had led Austria into the adventure of 1809. This may have been a device to draw attention to the less savory side of Metternich's character, but Humboldt may also have intended the comparison as a warning to the war party in Berlin that, in moments of military weakness, honesty and forthrightness could be dangerous liabilities. Humboldt's assessment of Metternich was remarkably perspicacious: in March 1812, the Austrian minister accepted a French subsidy to outfit an Austrian auxiliary corps of thirty thousand for Napoleon's campaign against Russia in exchange for a French territorial guarantee of Austria. Characteristically, Metternich tempered his support for France with an assurance to Tsar Alexander I that this army was raised for appearances only and that it would evade battle.

Humboldt to Friedrich Wilhelm III, 17 February 1811

. . . The great influence which this minister [Metternich] has, and will continue to have for a long time, in my opinion, makes it necessary, in order to judge the future behavior of the Court of Vienna, to try to form insofar as possible a fair idea of his character and his way of thinking. I say, "insofar as possible," because I regard as difficult if not impossible deciphering his real character and predicting what he would be capable or incapable of doing in the exigencies of the moment—which have a great hold on him.

As Count von Metternich is personally known to Your Majesty and his minister, I do not need to say that he is an extremely cold and reserved man whenever he wants to be, [but] with an obvious facility and natural tendency to chat and to tell stories, a man having absolute control over himself, never seeming to be carried away by any sentiment, never giving a trace of what he is thinking, but being very careful to show in all his facial expressions the same impassivity. His conduct then can only be based on premeditated calculations.

One of his favorite subjects of conversation is to argue against excitement and passionate outbursts; and as often as I have heard him discuss specific examples, I have never heard him argue anything other than the advantage or disadvantage that one or the other position can offer. With this character, he has become the successor of a man who—mistaking his own abilities and charging himself with a task far beyond them—caused great misfortune to his country; who never followed anything other than the impulse of his feelings; who was carried away by the excitement inspired in him by noble and patriotic principles; who was never accustomed to conduct himself according to simple calculations of particular interest and of whom even those who did not know him well could say with certainty that whatever the circumstances and whatever the dangers with which he was threatened, he would never have done what was contrary to his way of thinking and of acting . . . .

I do not believe Count Metternich ever capable of sacrificing the interests of his master to his own; and in examining his entire ministry, I see nothing that justifies the fear that he could without dire cause renounce the independence of Austria . . . . But one cannot deny . . . that it is also very unfortunate that he inspires so little confidence in the firmness and immutability of his principles, which are [otherwise] appealing; while he rejects the imputation [*idée*] that, having the talent to get used to and to accommodate himself to anything, he knows better how to conduct himself as circumstances require rather than according to principles . . . .

The goal of his ministry will thus be, I dare almost to guarantee, rather to preserve the status quo and to consolidate it further. But should one want to adopt the completely opposite approach, if the circumstances require or seem to require, one will not need to remove him from his position, as would be the case with a man with a pronounced and steady character.

In truth the Austrian monarchy needs a vigorous man, endowed with courage and the necessary talents, totally devoted to the care of saving his country and reuniting thus the confidence of the nation and of the Court. But this man does not seem to exist at the present, and Count Metternich, himself playing only the role of a temporizer adept at politics, seems to me preferable to many of those who could easily succeed him.

—Wilhelm von Humboldt, *Gesammelte Schriften* (Berlin, 1903; reprint, 1968), 11:3

1.2   CASTLEREAGH'S MISSION TO THE CONTINENT

Castlereagh's Instructions, 26 December 1813 ●
Castlereagh to Liverpool, 22 January 1814

By late December 1813, the armies of the Fourth Coalition were poised to carry the war against Napoleon to France itself. The Duke of Wellington's Peninsular Army had reached Bayonne, Holland had risen in insurrection against its French occupiers, the Prussian general Gebhard von Blücher was about to cross the Rhine, and an Austrian army had passed through the Swiss canton of Basel to enter eastern France. Both Tsar Alexander I and Metternich accompanied the Allied armies in the field.

Joining the Allied headquarters was Lord Castlereagh, the first British foreign secretary to travel to the continent to conduct summit diplomacy in person. Castlereagh's mission was motivated by two considerations. First, the prestige of his rank would make it impossible for Britain to be by-passed in the highest Allied councils. Second, his presence at headquarters eliminated the risk of misrepresentation of his views by subordinates and allowed him to exercise close control over British policy.

The tasks awaiting Castlereagh were formidable. The treaties which held together the Fourth Coalition outlined the political goals of the alliance only in the most general terms. The details of the peace settlement in Central Europe and Italy in turn depended on whether the Allies could persuade Napoleon to accept a negotiated peace (and, if so, on what or whose terms), or whether a peace settlement with France would be possible only after Napoleon's military defeat and ouster.

Reproduced below are extracts from Castlereagh's instructions, which he wrote himself, and from one of his first dispatches after his arrival at headquarters in Basel. The first excerpt sketches British goals within the alliance; the second weighs the options available to the Allies in their dealings with France.

a)   *Castlereagh's Instructions, 26 December 1813*

. . . Lord Castlereagh . . . is to Endeavour to Establish a Clear and definite understanding with the Allies, not only on all Matters of Common Interest, but upon such Points, as are likely to be discussed with the Enemy, so that the Several Allied Powers may in their Negotiations with France act in perfect Concert, and together maintain one Common Interest.

If Call'd on for an Explanation of the views of his Gov[ernmen]t as to Terms of Peace, and the sacrifice of Conquests, which G[rea]t Britain is disposed to make for the general Interest, he is to State, that with respect to the latter, It must in a great Measure be governed by the Nature of the Conditions with respect to the Continent, which the Allied Powers may be Enabled to obtain from the Enemy.

If the Maritime Power of France shall be restricted within due bounds by the Effectual Establishment of Holland—The [Iberian] Peninsula and Italy in Security, and Independence, G[rea]t Britain consistent with her own Security may then be induced to apply the greater proportion of her Conquests to promote the general Interests. If on the Contrary the arrangement should be defective in any of these Points, G[rea]t Britain must secure a proportionable share of those Conquests to render her secure against France.

If Call'd on for more detailed Explanation he may State, that the objects sine Quâ Non upon which G[rea]t Britain can venture to divest herself of her Conquests in any material degree are, 1st the Absolute Exclusion of France from any Naval Establishment on the Scheldt, and Especially at Antwerp and 2ndly The Security of Holland being adequately provided for under the House of Orange by a Barrier, which shall at least Include Juliers and Antwerp as well as Maastricht with a Suitable Arrondisement of Territory in Addition to Holland as it stood in 1792. It being understood that Wesel [on the Lower Rhine] shall also be in the hands of one of the Allied Powers.

It must be understood that the Monarchies of the Peninsula must also be Independent under their Legitimate Sovereigns. Their Dominions at least in Europe being guaranteed against attack by France. The Allied Powers to take Engagements to this Effect, and to Stipulate the Amount of Succours to be actually furnished in such Case.

If none acceptable to the Continental Powers G[rea]t Britain will be prepared to confine the Casus foederis to the Continent, being nevertheless bound to afford the Stipulated Succours, provided Holland and the Peninsula shall be secured.

In consideration of such an Arrangement for Holland and the Peninsula, G[rea]t Britain will be disposed to Stipulate for the Restitution of the Conquests made from France as Enumerated in the Margin and in this view to render them available for the purposes of Negotiation.

Malta[1] Always being understood to Remain British, The Mauritius and Bourbon

---

[1]Captured from the Knights of St. John by a French army in 1798, occupied by Britain in 1800. In article 10 of the 1802 Treaty of Amiens, Britain promised to restore the island to the Knights of St. John but evaded implementation of this article. Cf. article 7 of the Paris Peace, Document 1.6 below.

[Réunion][2]—Guadeloupe and the [Îles des] Saintes[3] cannot be restored to France. The Mauritius is retained as being when in the hands of an Enemy a most Injurious Naval station to our Indian Commerce, whilst it is of little Comparative Value to France. Guadeloupe is insisted upon as a debt of Honor to Sweden.

If by the Success of the Allied Arms Holland and the Peninsula shall be secured as above, the Conquests specified in the Margin may then be applied to Compensate other demands which our Continental Allies may have to bring forward.

If the Restoration of Guadeloupe should be made a point Sine Qua Non by France and consequently of War with Sweden, the Latter Power might in an Ultimatum be compensated by Bourbon, or a Dutch Colony, Holland in that Case taking Bourbon.

Holland being secured by a Barrier as above, the Dutch Colonies as Specified in the Margin to be restored to Holland—

The Cape of Good Hope is excepted,[4] as a Position connected with the Security of our Empire in the East, but in lieu of this Colony G[rea]t Britain to appropriate Two Million Sterling to be applied towards the Improvement of the Dutch Barrier [along the northern border with France].

With respect to the Danish Conquests, It is proposed they should (with the Exception of Heligoland) be made Instrumental to the Execution of our Engagements to Sweden.

In all Communications on the Expediency of Peace, the same Course to be pursued as heretofore—viz to Evince a desire to Conform as far as possible to the general Interests of the Continent—To give to the Allies the most unequivocal Assurances of a firm determination to support them in Contending for an Advantageous Peace and to avoid everything that might countenance a Suspicion that G[rea]t Britain was Inclined to push them forward in the War for [her] own purposes.

The Utmost Exertions to be used to prevent any relaxation in the Military Operations, whilst Negotiations are pending . . . .

If the Barrier for Holland should not be secured to the Extent propose[d], . . . Britain . . . will in that Case have no other alternative than to preserve her Colonial Conquests as a Counterpoise to the dominion of the Enemy and on these grounds to withhold those Cessions which she would otherwise be prepared to make to France . . . .

In any Arrangement of Italy, the Military Line of the Alps, and the Roads lately open'd in the direction of Italy to be particularly attended to.

With respect to the Internal Arrangement of Italy, It is highly Expedient that the King of Sardinia should be restored, perhaps receiving Genoa in Exchange for Savoy.

[2]Mauritius and Réunion had been captured by the British navy in 1810. Cf. article 8 of the Paris peace, Document 1.6 below.

[3]The Anglo-Swedish treaty of subsidy of 3 March 1813 provided for the transfer of the Guadeloupe archipelago, including the Saintes, to Sweden, but the Treaty of Paris (Document 1.6) returned the islands to France. An Anglo-Swedish treaty of 13 August 1814 indemnified Sweden with monies to be raised from the Dutch possessions acquired by England. *Hertslet's Commercial Treaties* (London, 1840), 1:337–45.

[4]As was Ceylon, which had become a British colony under article 5 of the 1802 Treaty of Amiens.

[5]Joachim Murat (who had ruled in Naples since 1808 as King Gioacchino Napoleone) did conclude an agreement with Austria on 11 January 1814. Austria promised to intercede on behalf of Murat and also to secure for him *"un acte de renonciation"* of Bourbon claims to the mainland. D'Angeberg, 1:83–87. Murat was thus the only one of Napoleon's satellite kings to retain his throne after the campaigns of 1813–1814. But plagued by doubts about Austria's willingness to abide by the agreement, he joined Napoleon after the latter's return from Elba. After the battle of Waterloo, Murat tried to reclaim his Neapolitan throne; he was now, however, regarded as a rebel. Arrested by troops loyal to the Neapolitan Bourbons, Murat was executed on 13 October 1815.

If Austria Connects herself with Murat,[5] the Sicilian Family [Neapolitan Bourbons] to have Tuscany and Elba. The Pope to be restored to the Estates of the Church. The Milanese, Modena, Parma, Plascentia etc to be subject to discussion.[6]

The Prince Regent's Mediation, if solicited by the Allies in the Arrangement of the Internal Affairs of Germany, to be afforded.

G[rea]t Britain to declare her readiness, should a General Peace be signed, to Sign a Separate Peace with the United States of America on the *Status Quo Ante Bellum*, without Involving in such Treaty any decisions upon the Points in dispute at the Commencement of Hostilities . . . .

The Five Millions Subsidy may be granted under the following Provisos. 1st: Reserve as to sending Home the Russian Fleet;[7] 2ndly: The accepting, if required, a proportion of the Same in Credit Bills; 3rdly: The signing of such Engagements and Especially with respect to Holland and the Peninsula, as may Justify both to the British Publick and the allies so great an Exertion in favor of the three powers.

The Treaty of Alliance not to terminate with the War, but to Contain defensive Engagements with eventual obligations to support the Powers attack'd by France, with a certain extent of Stipulated Succours.

The *Casus Foederis* to be an Attack by France on the European Dominions of any one of the Contracting Parties.

Spain and if possible Holland to be included as Contracting Parties . . . .

—Temperley and Penson, 29–34

b)   ***Castlereagh to Liverpool,*[8] *22 January 1814***

. . . what occurred to me on the four alternatives to be looked to as to the government of France. 1st., Buonaparte, 2nd., a French general, suppose Bernadotte,[9] 3rd., a regency,[10] 4th., the Bourbons. I represented the 2nd. and 3rd. as both peculiarly objectionable, not stable in themselves but likely to lead to some new change—in the meantime calculated to create dissension by appearing to throw an undue weight on the one case into the scale of Russia, on the other case of Austria, perhaps in both exciting jealousy rather than giving real power. I represented that if Austria refused to reassume the imperial crown in order to avoid unconstitutional and odious authority, she ought doubly to deprecate a state of things, in which an Austrian regency in France would be involving her in endless jealousies and embarrassments. Prince

---

[6]Compare Castlereagh's program for Italy with article 93 of the Final Act of the Congress of Vienna, Document 1.9 below.

[7]In October 1807, Russia had protested Britain's attack on neutral Denmark with a declaration of war. The Russian Mediterranean fleet was subsequently captured by the British navy in the Tagus estuary in 1808 (cf. Documents 1.3 and 3.2). The Anglo-Russian conflict was brought to a close in June 1812, only weeks before Napoleon's invasion of Russia.

[8]Robert, Earl of Liverpool (1770–1828). English prime minister, 1812–1827.

[9]Jean-Baptiste Bernadotte (1763–1844). Marshal of France (1804), elected prince royal of Sweden as successor to the childless Charles XIII (1810), ruled as Charles XIV John (1818–1844). In 1814, Tsar Alexander I was rumored to support Bernadotte's bid for the *French* throne.

[10]For Napoleon's infant son (1811–1832), king of Rome (1811–1814) and later duke of Reichstadt (1818–1832). A regency would have given Empress Marie Louise, and hence the Austrian court, ample opportunity to play a role in French politics.

Metternich entered fully into this reasoning and said of the four alternatives he thought it was that which Austria should most deprecate.

With respect to the second, we considered it too objectionable to be very formidable . . . .

He represented that the 1st. and the 4th. alternatives had the advantage of leading to no discussion among ourselves. In the first place we agreed in forcing the best possible peace upon Buonaparte and in preserving it by a defensive union when made. In the last the Government of France would devolve to its ancient and legitimate sovereigns unconnected equally with any of the Allies, and likely to be too weak for years to molest any of them.

Prince Metternich admitted . . . he could not hesitate to prefer the Bourbons, but that he would not interfere to decide what belonged to France to regulate.

—Charles K. Webster, *British Diplomacy, 1813–1815* (London, 1921), 137–38

1.3   THE QUESTION OF MARITIME RIGHTS

Castlereagh to Cathcart, 5 July 1813 ●
Congress of Châtillon: Protocol of 4 February 1814

That maritime rights (search and seizure on the high seas, the rights of vessels flying neutral flags, the laws of blockade) were not a fit subject for discussion among the Allies or at a future peace congress was stressed again and again by Castlereagh in the inter-Allied negotiations of 1813. From his point of view, why should Britain concede out of its free will the very same positions for which it had risked confrontation with the Armed Neutrality Leagues of 1780–1783 and 1800–1801, which lay at the heart of the Anglo-Russian war of 1807–1812, and which led to war with the United States in 1812?

How central this issue was to Britain's national interest, and its bearing on the war of 1812, emerges from the documents below.[11] Featured here are, first, a passage from draft instructions intended for the British ambassador to the tsar in early July 1813; and second, an extract from the proceedings of the Congress of Châtillon, where Allied representatives met with the French foreign minister, Armand de Caulaincourt, between 4 February and 19 March 1814 in a last attempt to explore a settlement with Napoleon.

a)   *Castlereagh to Cathcart,[12] 5 July 1813*

There is only one other point on which I feel it necessary to caution Your Lordship, which is with regard to America . . . . I am afraid this [Russian] tender of mediation, which, on a question of maritime right, cannot be listened to by Great Britain, however kindly and liberally intended, will have had the unfortunate effect of protracting the war with the United States . . . .

Your Lordship will be enabled to satisfy the [Russian] Emperor that, if this is a subject on which the mediation of an ally cannot be accepted, it is still less a question

---

[11]For other classic illustrations of this point, see also Documents 10.1, 11.15, 11.16b.
[12]Sir William Schaw Cathcart (1755–1843). British ambassador in St. Petersburg, 1812–1820.

that we could consent to discuss in a general Congress:—however ready the Prince Regent will be at all times to treat for Peace with America, and for a settlement of all differences.

Your Lordship will, under all these circumstances, press the Emperor of Russia in the strongest manner not to push his personal interference on this point further:—and as the Maritime Question is one which Buonaparte will endeavour to bring before a Congress, principally in the hope of creating disunion between Great Britain and her Allies, you will use your utmost endeavours to persuade His Imperial Majesty that every consideration of Policy should determine Him pointedly to discountenance a design so mischievously calculated to promote the views of France.

—FO 181/10; Wilhelm Oncken, *Österreich und Preussen im Befreiungskriege* (Berlin, 1879), 2:702–5

b)   *Congress of Châtillon: Protocol of 4 February 1814*

The plenipotentiaries of the Allied Courts declare as follows:

That the Allied Courts adhere to the declaration of the British government stating:

That all discussion of maritime rights would be contrary to the practices observed to this point in negotiations of the nature of the present ones; that Great Britain not demand from other nations nor accord them any concession relative to rights that she regards as reciprocally obligatory and of a nature not to have to be regulated except by the Law of Nations, except where those same rights have been modified by special conventions between particular states;

That as a result the Allied Courts would regard the insistence of France on this subject as contrary to the goal of the meeting of the plenipotentiaries, and as tending to pose an obstacle in the reestablishment of peace.

On receiving this declaration, His Most Excellent Monsieur, the Duke of Vicenza,[13] replied that France's intention was never to ask anything contrary to the Law of Nations, and that he had no other observation to make . . . . The plenipotentiaries view thereupon this declaration as an acceptance.

—D'Angeberg, 1:105–6

1.4   ✗TREATY OF CHAUMONT, 1 MARCH 1814

In concluding the Treaty of Chaumont, the Allies left their options open. They may have wished to speed along the negotiations still underway at Châtillon, or, frustrated with the lack of progress at these meetings, they may have already looked beyond Châtillon to dealing with a France without Napoleon. Whatever the motive, the treaty is instructive less for its clauses on how the Allies should continue the war than for its vision of the postwar order. Its text should therefore be examined for glimpses of the Allies' collective intent and of the ideals

---

[13]Armand de Caulaincourt, duke of Vicenza (1773–1827). French foreign minister, November 1813–March 1814.

underpinning the Allied cause. Particularly significant in light of later events (cf. Document 2.3) is the pledge, written into the preamble, "of maintaining against every attempt the order" envisaged by the treaty.

[Preamble:] [Their Majesties] . . . having transmitted to the French Government proposals for concluding a General Peace, and being desirous, should France refuse the conditions therein contained, to draw closer the ties which unite them for the vigorous prosecution of a War undertaken for the salutary purpose of putting an end to the miseries of Europe, of securing its future repose, by reestablishing a just equilibrium [*équilibre*], and being at the same time desirous, should the Almighty bless their pacific intentions, to fix the means of maintaining against every attempt the order of things which shall have been the happy consequence of their efforts, have agreed to sanction by a solemn Treaty, signed separately by each of the 4 Powers with the 3 others, this twofold engagement . . . . :

Art. 1: The High Contracting Parties above named solemnly engage by the present Treaty, and in the event of France refusing to accede to the conditions of Peace now proposed, to apply all the means of their respective States to the vigorous prosecution of the war against that Power, and to employ them in perfect concert, in order to obtain for themselves and for Europe a General Peace, under the protection of which the rights and liberties of all nations may be established and secured . . . .

Art. 2: The High Contracting Parties reciprocally engage not to negotiate separately with the common enemy, nor to sign Peace, Truce nor Convention but with common consent. They, moreover, engage not to lay down their arms until the object of the war, mutually understood and agreed upon, shall have been attained.

Art. 3: In order to contribute in the most prompt and decisive manner to fulfil this great object, His Britannic Majesty engages to furnish a Subsidy of £5,000,000 for the service of the year 1814, to be divided in equal proportions amongst the three Powers . . . .

Art. 5: The High Contracting Powers, reserving to themselves to concert together, on the conclusion of a peace with France, as to the means best adapted to guarantee to Europe, and to themselves reciprocally the continuance of the Peace, have also determined to enter, without delay, into defensive engagements for the protection of their respective States in Europe against every attempt which France might make to infringe the order of things resulting from such Pacification.

Art. 6: To effect this, they agree that in the event of one of the High Contracting Parties being threatened with an attack by France, the others shall employ their most strenuous efforts to prevent it, by friendly interposition.

Art. 7: In the case of these endeavors proving ineffectual, the High Contracting Parties promise to come to the immediate assistance of the Power attacked, each with a body of 60,000 men . . . .

Art. 16: The present Treaty of Defensive Alliance having for its object to maintain the equilibrium of Europe, to secure the repose and independence of its States, and to prevent the invasions which during so many years have desolated the world, the High Contracting Parties have agreed to extend the duration of it to 20 years to take date from the day of its signature; and they reserve to themselves to concert upon its ulterior prolongation, 3 years before its expiration, should circumstances require it . . . .

Secret Articles: 1: The reestablishment of the balance among the Powers and a just repartition of forces among them being the goal of the present war, Their Imperial and Royal Majesties commit themselves to direct all their efforts towards the real establishment of the following system in Europe, viz.: [i] Germany composed of sovereign princes united by a federal tie that may assure and guarantee the independence of Germany. [ii] The Swiss Federation in its ancient borders and independent, placed under the guarantee of the Great Powers of Europe, including France. [iii] Italy divided into independent states between [*intermédiaires*] the Austrian possessions in Italy, and France. [iv] Spain governed by King Ferdinand VII, in its ancient borders. [v] Holland, a free and independent state, under the sovereignty of the Prince of Orange with an increase of territory and the establishment of an appropriate frontier.

2: The High Contracting Parties . . . invite to accede to the present treaty of defensive alliance the monarchies of Spain and of Portugal, Sweden, and His Royal Highness the Prince of Orange, and to admit to it other sovereigns and states as circumstances warrant.

3: Considering the need that may exist after the conclusion of a definitive peace treaty with France to keep in the field, for a certain time, forces sufficient to safeguard the arrangements that the Allies must make among themselves for the stabilization of the condition of Europe, the High Allied Powers have decided to come to an agreement to act together, not only on the necessity, but on the number and the distribution of forces to keep mobilized, as circumstances require . . . .

—*SP*, 1:121–29; secret articles in F. Martens, *Recueil des traités et conventions conclus par la Russie avec les puissances étrangères, publié d'ordre du ministère des affaires étrangères* (St. Petersburg, 1876), 3:163–65

1.5   THE ABDICATION OF NAPOLEON

Treaty of Fontainebleau, 11 and 12 April 1814

With the Allied armies in Paris, further resistance by Napoleon had become pointless. The terms for his abdication were drafted by the principal Allies (but not Britain)[14] in Paris and sent to Napoleon's headquarters in Fontainebleau for his signature. After a melodramatic but half-hearted attempt at suicide, Napoleon signed.

Treaty of Fontainebleau, 11 and 12 April 1814

Art. 1: The Emperor Napoleon renounces for himself, his successors and descendants, as for each member of his family, all rights of sovereignty and authority both over the French Empire and the Kingdom of Italy and over all other lands.

---

[14]Having been at war with France for the duration of the French Empire, Britain had no treaty relationship with Napoleon as emperor of the French and hence was alone among the major powers in not recognizing him or the Empire.

Art. 2: Their Majesties the Emperor Napoleon and the Empress Marie-Louise shall retain their titles and social perquisites [*qualités*] for the rest of their lives. The mother, brothers, sisters, nephews and nieces of the emperor shall likewise retain, wherever they shall be, the titles of princes of his family.

Art. 3: The island of Elba, chosen by His Majesty the Emperor Napoleon for the place of his residence, will constitute, during his lifetime, a separate principality that will be possessed by him in full sovereignty and proprietorship. An annual revenue of 2 million francs in income in the Great Book [of the Public Debt] of France will be given, moreover, to the Emperor Napoleon to dispose of as he likes, of which one million revert to the empress.

—D'Angeberg, 1:148

1.6   THE FRENCH AND OVERSEAS SETTLEMENTS, 1814

Peace of Paris, 30 May 1814 • *Anglo-Dutch Convention, 13 August 1814*

The peace treaty with France was a triumph for moderation. It also rested on a hard-nosed calculation. The Allies needed to treat with a peaceable and stable France, for which a restored Bourbon dynasty seemed to offer the best guarantee. But Louis XVIII owed his throne to the Allies and perhaps to the savvy of Talleyrand, not to his own exertions. He thus depended on the Allies to help him win over the nation, or at least secure its acquiescence to Bourbon rule. Propping up the stature of the French monarchy was in the Allies' interest; the sole question was how they should underwrite this face-lift with only a minimum cost to themselves. The Allies found that the cheapest coin with which to pay was, first, to give their blessing to the Constitutional Charter promulgated by Louis and, second, to enhance the image of the monarchy by granting Bourbon France a lenient peace.

The treaty of Paris of 30 May 1814 settled most of the colonial issues among the powers. An additional item of crucial importance to Britain was transacted in an Anglo-Dutch convention ten weeks later. The two instruments afford one measure of the success of Castlereagh's diplomacy, and it is highly instructive to compare the features of these treaties to the aims which he had set for himself in December 1813 (Document 1.2).

a)   *Peace of Paris, 30 May 1814*

[Preamble:] H.M. the King of the United Kingdom of Great Britain and Ireland, and his Allies on the one part, and H.M. the King of France and of Navarre on the other part, animated by an equal desire to terminate the long agitation of Europe, and the sufferings of mankind, by a permanent Peace, founded upon a just repartition of force between its States, and containing in its stipulations the pledge of its durability; and his Britannic Majesty, together with his Allies, being unwilling to require of France, now that, replaced under the paternal government of her Kings, she offers the assurance of security and stability to Europe, the conditions and guarantees which they had with regret demanded from her former Government, Their said Majesties have named Plenipotentiaries to discuss, settle and sign a Treaty of Peace and Amity . . . .

Art. 2: The Kingdom of France retains its limits entire, as they existed on the 1st of January, 1792 . . . .

Art. 7: The Island of Malta and its Dependencies shall belong in full right and Sovereignty to His Britannic Majesty.

Art. 8: His Britannic Majesty, stipulating for himself and his Allies, engages to restore to His Most Christian Majesty [of France], within the term which shall hereafter be fixed, the colonies, fisheries, factories, and establishments of every kind which were possessed by France on the 1st of January, 1792, in the Seas and on the continents of America, Africa, and Asia; with the exception, however, of the Islands of Tobago and St. Lucia, and of the Isle of France [Mauritius] and its dependencies, especially Rodrigues and Les Séchelles . . . and also the portion of St. Domingo ceded to France by the Treaty of Basel, and which His Most Christian Majesty restores in full right and sovereignty to His Catholic Majesty.

Art. 9: His Majesty the King of Sweden and Norway . . . consents that the Island of Guadaloupe be restored to His Most Christian Majesty, and gives up all the rights he may have acquired over that island . . . .

Art. 15: . . . Antwerp shall for the future be solely a commercial port.

Art. 16: The High Contracting Parties, desirous to bury in entire oblivion the dissensions which have agitated Europe, declare and promise that no Individual, of whatever rank or condition he may be, in the Countries restored and ceded by the present Treaty, shall be prosecuted, disturbed, or molested, in his Person or Property, under any pretext whatsoever, either on account of his conduct or political opinions, his attachment either to any of the Contracting Parties, or to any Government which has ceased to exist, or for any other reason, except for Debts contracted towards individuals, or acts posterior to the date of the present Treaty.

Art. 17: The native inhabitants and aliens of whatever nation and condition they may be, in those countries which are to change sovereigns . . . shall be allowed a period of six years, reckoning from the exchange of the ratifications, for the purpose of disposing of their property, if they think fit, whether it be acquired before or during the present war, and retiring to whatever country they may choose.

Art. 18: The Allied Powers desiring to offer His Most Christian Majesty a new proof of their anxiety to arrest, as far as is in their power, the bad consequences of the disastrous epoch fortunately terminated by the present peace, renounce all sums which their governments claim from France, whether on account of contracts, supplies, or any other advances whatsoever to the French government, during the different wars which have taken place since 1792 . . . .

Art. 19: The French government engages to liquidate and pay all debts it may be found to owe in countries beyond its own territory, on account of contracts, or other formal engagements between individuals, or private establishments, and the French authorities, as well for supplies, as in satisfaction of legal engagements . . . .

Art. 32: All the powers engaged on either side of the present war, shall, within the space of two months, send plenipotentiaries to Vienna, for the purpose of regulating, in general congress, the arrangements which are to complete the provisions of the present treaty . . . .

[Separate and Secret Articles] 2. . . . The King of [Piedmont-]Sardinia shall return to the possession of his ancient Dominions . . . .

3. The establishment of a just equilibrium in Europe requiring that Holland should be so constituted as to be enabled to support her independence through her own resources, the countries comprised between the Sea, the frontiers of France, and the Meuse shall be given up for ever to Holland . . . .

—Hurst, 1:1–21; *SP*, 1:151–73; *CTS*, 63:171–97 [French and English]

b)   *Anglo-Dutch Convention, 13 August 1814*

Art. 1: His Britannic Majesty engages to restore to the Prince Sovereign of the United Netherlands . . . the Colonies, Factories, and Establishments which were possessed by Holland at the commencement of the late war, viz., on the 1st of January 1803, in the Seas and on the Continents of America, Africa, and Asia; with the exception of the Cape of Good Hope and the Settlements [in Guayana] of Demerara, Esquibo, and Berbice . . . . [15]

—*Hertslet's Commercial Treaties* (London, 1840), 1:359–69

1.7   THE ALLIANCE STRAINED: THE SAXON-POLISH CRISIS

Anglo-Austrian-French Treaty, 3 January 1815 •
Talleyrand to Louis XVIII, 19 January and 1 February 1815

The peace process was well advanced even before the Congress of Vienna assembled in September 1814: peace with France had been restored, overseas and colonial questions had been settled, all discussion of maritime rights had been banished from the Allied agenda. Thus Britain had already realized many of its goals, whereas Austria, Russia, and particularly Prussia depended on the congress to confirm, and even define, their gains.

The primary task of the Congress of Vienna was the political and territorial reorganization of Central Europe and Italy. Above all, the congress needed to implement the principles developed by the Allies during the campaign of 1813–1814. Rather than prescribing specific terms, these principles were more in the nature of general guidelines. For instance, Prussia was to be restored to the "statistic, geographic, and financial proportions" of 1806, but not necessarily its 1806 borders.[16]

Prussia in the borders of 1806 had included Warsaw and western Poland. In 1807, by the terms of the Treaty of Tilsit, Napoleon sealed his victory over Prussia by forcing it to cede these territories, now reconstituted as the Grand Duchy of Warsaw. The crown of the grand duchy went to Frederick Augustus, King of Saxony—a curious throwback to the years 1697–1763 when the electors of that German state also governed the Kingdom of Poland in personal union. If anything, Napoleon's revival of this dynastic arrangement persuaded contemporaries to view the issues of Poland and Saxony as linked.

Tsar Alexander's desire to rule as King of Poland led to his suggestion at the Congress of Vienna that Prussia relinquish its claims to western Poland and be compensated by being allowed to annex Saxony. This proposal, readily accepted by the Prussian monarch, seemed all the more reasonable given the fact that the Saxon king Frederick Augustus had failed to desert

---

[15]Britain thus only returned the Antilles, portions of Guayana, the Dutch forts on the Gold Coast, and the Dutch East Indies.

[16]Article 1 of the Treaty of Kalisch and Breslau (Russia and Prussia, 27 February 1813). Similar assurances were contained in the Treaty of Reichenbach (Britain and Prussia, 14 June 1813) and the Treaties of Teplitz (Austria and Russia with Prussia, 9 September 1813). Similarly, Austria induced Bavaria to join the Fourth Coalition in exchange for an Allied promise to secure for it its gains under Napoleon by maintaining its size but not necessarily its borders (Treaty of Ried, 8 October 1813). Texts in D'Angeberg, 1:1–2; 9–10; 50n; 56–60.

Napoleon in time, had been captured by the Allies, and could now be made to pay the price for his loyalty to the Napoleonic cause. With a nod to the principle of monarchical solidarity, Frederick Augustus might be compensated with the Grand Duchy of Luxemburg.[17]

This plan was immediately opposed by Britain and Austria because it was about to extend Russian power even farther into Central Europe and would have eliminated an important midsize state. Metternich's objections may have been fueled by the sentimental reflection that Saxony had been a traditional ally of Austria and had served as an important counterweight to Prussia in the eighteenth-century intra-German balance of power.

The Saxon-Polish crisis came closer to jeopardizing the wartime alliance than any other issue at the Congress of Vienna. When Prussia intimated that it would not rule out war to gain possession of all of Saxony, the impending showdown gave the French negotiator, Charles-Maurice de Talleyrand, the opportunity to play a decisive role. Castlereagh and Metternich bought his support on the Saxon-Polish issue in exchange for France's admittance to the deliberations amongst the principal Allies—France was thus upgraded to a full-fledged partner of the Big Four and a prospective signatory of the congress's Final Act. The new Anglo-Austrian-French combination chose the vehicle of a defensive, and supposedly secret, alliance to impress its point of view on Russia and Prussia. This tactic succeeded once the terms of the alliance leaked out: Prussia retreated, retaining Polish-speaking Posen and Gnesen, and contented itself with two-fifths of Saxony, leaving Frederick Augustus to rule the remainder of his amputated but sovereign state.

a)   ***Anglo-Austrian-French Treaty, 3 January 1815***

. . . [Their Majesties] seeing . . . it necessary . . . to provide for the means of repelling all aggression to which their own possessions, or those of one of them, should find themselves exposed in contempt of the propositions that they believed it their duty to make and to support by a common accord and through the principle of justice and equity; and having nothing else in their heart than the fulfilment of the dispositions of the Treaty of Paris in a manner as appropriate as possible to its true goals and spirit; have, to these ends, resolved to make among themselves a solemn convention, and to conclude a defensive alliance . . . .

Art. 1: . . . If . . . the possessions of any of [the contracting parties] were to be attacked, they agree and oblige themselves to consider this an attack on all three, to make common cause among themselves and to assist each other mutually to repel such aggression with all the force stipulated hereafter.

Art. 2: If in the circumstances stipulated above . . . one of the High Contracting Parties finds itself threatened by one or several Powers, the two other parties shall, by friendly intervention, attempt, as far as possible, to prevent the aggression.

Art. 3: In the case where their efforts to prevent it shall be ineffective, the High Contracting Parties promise to come immediately to the help of the attacked Power; each of them with a corps of one hundred fifty thousand men . . . .

---

[17]Variations on this theme continued to surface in French diplomacy. See Document 3.4 and Palmerston's insinuation that Talleyrand promoted the candidacy of the King of Saxony for the Belgian throne in 1831. Temperley and Penson, 91; Bourne, 217.

MAP 1   EUROPE IN 1815

	Prussia
	Bavaria
	Other German states
	Austrian Empire
	Ottoman Empire
	German Confederation

Art. 5: The location of the countries that might become a theater of war or other circumstances raising the possibility that England may encounter difficulties in providing, within the fixed time, the stipulated aid in the form of English troops and maintaining them on a war footing, His Britannic Majesty reserves the right to furnish his contingent to the requesting Power in foreign troops at England's expense, or to pay annually to the said Power a sum of money calculated at the rate of 20 pounds sterling for each infantryman, and 30 pounds sterling for each cavalryman until the stipulated aid has been rendered . . . .

Art. 10: The High Contracting Parties . . . agree in the case, may God forbid it, that war should break out, to consider the Treaty of Paris as having the force to regulate, at the peace, the nature, extent and borders of their respective possessions . . . .

Art. 13: . . . The High Contracting Parties agree that . . . if the territories of His Majesty the King of Hanover or the territories of His Highness the sovereign Prince of the United Provinces, including those which find themselves actually under his administration, should be attacked, [the Parties] shall be obliged to act to repulse that aggression as if it had taken place against one of their own territories.

—D'Angeberg, 1:589–91

b)   Talleyrand to Louis XVIII, 19 January and 1 February 1815

[19 January 1815:] . . .Unfortunately, Lord Castlereagh . . . has on all questions of military topography, and even on the simplest matters of continental geography, such imperfect notions, I may say, such utter ignorance, that while it is necessary to prove the smallest details to him, it is extremely difficult to convince him of them. It is said that an Englishman who was here in Prince Kaunitz's time, retailed a number of absurdities respecting the German states, and that Prince Kaunitz, instead of amusing himself by refuting them, exclaimed in a tone of the greatest surprise, "It is really marvellous how ignorant the English are!" How often have I had occasion to mentally make the same observation during my conferences with Lord Castlereagh!

[1 February 1815:] Nothing seemed more irrevocably settled than the fate of Saxony when we arrived here. Prussia demanded the whole of it for herself, and Russia backed her up. Lord Castlereagh had completely abandoned her, and so had Austria, except as regards some minor frontier arrangements. Your Majesty alone took up the defence of Saxony; you alone maintained the principles of right. You had to overcome all kinds of influences; the spirit of coalition which was very strong, and what was perhaps more difficult, the self-esteem of all the Great Powers, who by their pretensions, declarations and concessions had so far compromised themselves as to make it almost impossible for them to recede without shame; but by noble opposition to an injustice, all but accomplished, Your Majesty has gained the glory of overcoming all these obstacles, and not only have you triumphed over them, but the coalition has been dissolved, and Your Majesty has come to an understanding with two of the greatest powers, which may perhaps, later on, save Europe from the dangers which menace it, through the ambition of some of the states. Saxony, which was a third-rate power, will continue to be so . . . [,] interpose[d] between Prussia and Austria and between Russia and Bavaria.

—Duc de Broglie (ed.), *Memoirs of the Prince de Talleyrand*
(London, n.d.), 3:15–16, 30

1.8   # THE SLAVE TRADE CONDEMNED

Annex XV to the Final Act of the Congress of Vienna, 8 February 1815 ●
Anglo-American ("Webster-Ashburton") Treaty, 9 August 1842

Domestic legislation in Denmark, Britain, and the United States prohibited individuals from taking part in the overseas slave trade as of 1802, 1808, and 1809, respectively. Napoleon, after his return from Elba, forbade the participation of French citizens. In the meantime, the peace settlements of 1814–1815 had begun to translate the growing revulsion against the slave trade into international commitments: article X of the Treaty of Ghent somewhat lamely pledged Britain and the United States to continue "their efforts to promote its entire abolition";[18] annex XV to the Final Act of the Congress of Vienna, excerpted here, employed more vigorous language but contained important reservations; and an additional article, appended to the Second Peace of Paris (cf. Document 1.12), called on the British and French governments "without loss of time" to bring about the "entire and definitive abolition" of the slave trade. The major holdouts were the governments of Spain and Portugal, which followed suit only in 1820. The performance of the international community may be judged from the fact that the Allies, at the Verona Conference in November 1822, again found it necessary to condemn the slave trade. Nor did the wording of the Anglo-American ("Webster-Ashburton") treaty of 1842 leave any doubt about the failure of the powers to implement their resolve. Of course, it should be borne in mind that these commitments banned the slave *trade*, not slavery itself.

a)   ***Annex XV to the Final Act of the Congress of Vienna,***
                          8 February 1815

The plenipotentiaries of the Powers that signed the Treaty of Paris of 30 May 1814, meeting in conference, have taken into consideration that the trade known under the name of traffic of blacks from Africa has been seen by enlightened men of all times as repugnant to humanitarian principles and to universal morality . . .

that, by a separate article of the last treaty of Paris, Great Britain and France have committed themselves to a joint effort to have pronounced at the Congress of Vienna, by all the powers of Christendom, the universal and definitive abolition of the commerce in blacks;

that the plenipotentiaries assembled in this Congress know no better way to honor their mission, fulfil their duty and exhibit the principles that guide their august sovereigns, than in working to achieve this goal, and in proclaiming, in the name of their sovereigns, the vow to put an end to a calamity that has for so long desolated Africa, degraded Europe and afflicted mankind . . . .

. . . [H]owever honorable their goal, they will not pursue it without fair arrangements for the interests, customs and predispositions of their subjects . . . : as a result, the determination of the period of time in which this traffic ought universally to stop will be a matter of negotiation among the Powers; with the understanding that no appropriate means will be neglected in order to assure and to speed the process; and that the reciprocal determination to act contracted by the present declaration among

---

[18]For example, the Anglo-Swedish convention of 3 March 1813 (separate article 4) and article 8 of the Anglo-Dutch convention of 13 August 1814 were far more precise.

the sovereigns who have taken part will not be considered as fulfilled until their combined efforts are crowned with complete success.

—D'Angeberg, 1:726–27

b) Anglo-American ("Webster-Ashburton") Treaty, 9 August 1842

. . . Art. 9: Whereas, notwithstanding all efforts which may be made on the coast of Africa for suppressing the slave-trade, the facilities for carrying on that traffic and avoiding the vigilance of cruisers, by the fraudulent use of flags and other means, are so great, and the temptations for pursuing it, while a market can be found for slaves, so strong, as that the desired result may be long delayed unless all markets be shut against the purchase of African negroes, the parties to this treaty agree that they will unite in all becoming representations and remonstrances with any and all Powers within whose dominions such markets are allowed to exist, and that they will urge upon all such Powers the propriety and duty of closing such markets effectually, at once and forever.

—Hurst, 1:266–67

1.9   THE "ONE HUNDRED DAYS," FEBRUARY–JULY 1815

Declaration of the Signatories of the Treaty of Paris, 13 March 1815 •
Maistre to Rossi, 10 April 1815

Napoleon's decision, on 26 February 1815, to leave Elba and return to France violated the Treaty of Fontainebleau. The Allies' first official reaction to this breach of treaty came in the communiqué excerpted here. On 25 March 1815, the Allies renewed the Treaty of Chaumont. Napoleon was not deterred: he had entered Paris on 20 March to a tumultuous welcome and now dedicated himself to raising and organizing an army, presumably in the hope that, after a succession of victories, he could force the Allies to the bargaining table. Thus began the road that would lead him to his defeat at Waterloo on 18 June.

Napoleon's popularity testified to the fact that the Bourbons, eleven months after their return, had not won the nation over. One of the most eloquent explanations for their failure came from Joseph de Maistre, chiefly remembered by posterity as an apologist for divine right monarchy and the legitimist principle. But for the Allies, too, the unpopularity of the Bourbons posed a dilemma which spoke, uncomfortably, to the collapse of the Allied expectation that a moderate peace would strengthen the Bourbon monarchy and enhance the image of Louis XVIII.

a)   Declaration of the Signatories of the Treaty of Paris, 13 March 1815

The Powers declare . . . that Napoleon Bonaparte has placed himself outside civil and social relations, and that, as the enemy and disturber of public tranquility, he is declared a public outlaw.

. . . [F]irmly resolved to maintain intact the Treaty of Paris of 30 May 1814 . . . they shall use every means and rejoin their efforts so that general peace, the desire of Europe and the constant goal of their labors, not be endangered anew, and to protect it against every attempt which threatens to plunge peoples once again into the disorder and unhappiness of revolutions.

—D'Angeberg, 2:913

b)   *Maistre[19] to Rossi,[20] 10 April 1815*

. . . For twenty-five years, the French have been deprived of their legitimate masters. One must add to that at least another ten or twelve years; since, before that age, man does not know himself. To anyone in France younger than 40—that is to say: the entire army and half the nation—the Bourbons are about as well known as the Heraclids[21] or the Ptolemies.[22] Since 1789, no moral and religious instruction, no nobility, no priesthood, no moral grandeur of any kind; war and nothing but war . . . . In the colleges, the academies, the theater, the church, as in the guardhouse, the French have heard speak of none but Bonaparte . . . .

—*Oeuvres Complètes de Joseph de Maistre* (Lyon, 1886), 13:57

1.10   FINAL ACT OF THE CONGRESS OF VIENNA, 9 JUNE 1815

The Final Act of the Congress of Vienna dealt primarily with the territorial and political reorganization of Poland (articles 1–14), Germany (articles 15–64), the Netherlands (articles 65–73), Switzerland (articles 74–84), Piedmont-Sardinia (articles 85–92), Austria (articles 93–97), the central Italian states (articles 98–104), and Portugal (articles 104–7). A last section established a legal regime for international rivers. Fifteen annexes amplified the treaty; another two dealt with the slave trade (see Document 1.8) and questions of diplomatic protocol. The passages reprinted here recapitulate some of the more important provisions of the Final Act. They also help answer the question whether the congress aimed at a restoration or whether it created a new political order.

Art. 1. The Duchy of Warsaw, with the exception of the provinces and districts which are otherwise disposed of by the following Articles, is united to the Russian Empire. It shall be irrevocably attached to it by its Constitution, and be possessed by His Majesty the Emperor of all the Russias, his heirs and successors in perpetuity. His Imperial Majesty reserves to himself to give to this State, enjoying a distinct administration, the interior improvement which he shall judge proper . . . .The Poles, who are respective

---

[19]Joseph de Maistre (1765–1821). Philosopher and religious thinker; minister of Piedmont-Sardinia in St. Petersburg, 1803–1817.
    [20]Count Rossi. Minister of Piedmont-Sardinia in Vienna.
    [21]Mythical Greek dynasty on the Peloponnesus, descended from Heracles.
    [22]Hellenistic dynasty in Egypt, 323–330 B.C.

subjects of Russia, Austria, and Prussia, shall obtain a Representation and National Institutions, regulated according to the degree of political consideration, that each of the Governments to which they belong shall judge expedient and proper to grant them . . . .

Art. 4: The Town of Cracow, with its Territory, is declared to be forever a Free, Independent, and strictly Neutral City, under the protection of Austria, Russia, and Prussia . . . .

Art. 9: . . . [N]o asylum shall be afforded in the free town and territory of Cracow to fugitives, deserters, and persons under prosecution, belonging to the country of either of the High Powers aforesaid; and in the event of the demand of their surrender by the competent authorities, such individuals shall be arrested and given up without delay . . . .

Art. 53: The Sovereign Princes and Free Towns of Germany under which denomination, for the present purpose, are comprehended their Majesties the Emperor of Austria, the Kings of Prussia, of Denmark, and of the Netherlands—that is to say: the Emperor of Austria and the King of Prussia, for all their possessions which anciently belonged to the German [Holy Roman] Empire; the King of Denmark, for the Duchy of Holstein; and the King of the Netherlands, for the Grand Duchy of Luxemburg—establish among themselves a perpetual Confederation, which shall be called "The German Confederation."

Art. 54: The object of this Confederation is the maintenance of the external and internal safety of Germany, and of the Independence and Inviolability of the Confederated States . . . .

Art. 86: The States which constituted the former republic of Genoa,[23] are united in perpetuity to those of His Majesty the King of Sardinia . . . .

Art. 93: In pursuance of the Renunciations agreed upon by the Treaty of Paris of the 30th May, 1814, the Powers who sign the present Treaty, recognise His Majesty the Emperor of Austria, his heirs and successors, as legitimate Sovereign of the Provinces and Territories which had been ceded, either wholly or in part, by the Treaties of Campo-Formio of 1797, of Lunéville of 1801, of Pressburg of 1805, by the additional Convention of Fontainebleau of 1807, and by the Treaty of Vienna of 1809; the possession of which provinces and territories His Imperial and Royal Apostolic Majesty obtained in consequence of the last war; such as, Istria, Austrian as well as heretofore Venetian,[24] Dalmatia, the ancient Venetian Isles of the Adriatic, the Mouths of the Cattaro, the City of Venice, with its waters, as well as all the other provinces and districts of the formerly Venetian States of the Terra Firma upon the left bank of the Adige [Etsch], the Duchies of Milan and Mantua, the Principalities of Brixen and Trent, the County of Tyrol, the Vorarlberg, the Austrian Friaul, the ancient Venetian Friaul, the territory of Montefalcone, the Government and Town of Trieste, Carniola, Upper Carinthia, Croatia on the right of the Save, Fiume and the Hungarian Littorale, and the District of Castua . . . .

Art. 98: . . . the Archduke Francis [IV] d'Este[-Habsburg], his heirs and successors, shall possess, in full sovereignty, the Duchies of Modena, Reggio, and Mirandola . . . .

Art. 100: . . . the Archduke Ferdinand [III] of Austria is re-established, himself, his heirs and successors . . . in the Grand Duchy of Tuscany . . . .

---

[23]France disestablished the Republic of Genoa in 1796.
[24]Venice and its possessions were absorbed by Austria at Campo Formio in 1797.

Art. 104: . . . King Ferdinand IV, his heirs, and successors, is restored to the throne of Naples, and His Majesty is acknowledged by the Powers as King of the Two Sicilies . . . .

Annex IX: Art. 13: There shall be Assemblies of the States in all the countries belonging to the [German] Confederation.

Art. 14: In order to secure to the ancient [E]states of the Empire, mediatised[25] in 1806, and in the subsequent years, the enjoyment of equal rights in all countries belonging to the Confederation . . . the Confederated States establish the following principles:

. . . B. The heads of these Houses are to form the principal class of the States in the countries to which they belong: they, as well as their families, are to be included in the number of the most privileged persons, particularly in respect to taxes.

C. . . . Among the[ir] rights . . . are specially included: . . . 3) the privilege of being . . . exempt from all military conscription for themselves and families; 4) the exercise of civil and criminal jurisdiction, in the First Instance and, if the possessions are sufficiently extensive, in the Second Instance, the exercise of the forest jurisdiction, of the local police, and of the inspection of churches, schools, and charitable institutions, the whole conformably to the laws of the country to which they remain subject . . . .

Art. 16: The different Christian sects in the countries and territories of the Germanic Confederation shall not experience any difference in the enjoyment of civil and political rights. The Diet shall consider of the means of effecting, in the most uniform manner, an amelioration in the civil state of those who profess the Jewish religion in Germany, and shall pay particular attention to the measures by which the enjoyment of civil rights shall be secured and guaranteed to them in the Confederated States, upon condition, however, of their submitting to all the obligations imposed upon other citizens. In the mean time, the privileges already granted to this sect by any particular State shall be secured to them.

Annex XIa: The Powers . . . having acknowledged that the general interest demands that the Helvetic States [cantons] should enjoy the benefit of a perpetual Neutrality; and wishing, by territorial restitutions and cessions, to enable it [Switzerland] to secure its Independence and maintain its Neutrality: . . . Declare, That as soon as the Helvetic Diet shall have duly and formally acceded to the stipulations contained in the present Instrument, an Act shall be prepared, containing the acknowledgment and the guarantee, on the part of all the Powers, of the perpetual Neutrality of Switzerland, in her new frontiers . . . .

—Hertslet, 1:208–74; Hurst, 1:30–96

1.11   THE HOLY ALLIANCE, 26 SEPTEMBER 1815

The Holy Alliance, 26 September 1815 ●
Reply of the Prince Regent of Great Britain, 6 October 1815

In September 1815, Tsar Alexander I presented the Austrian emperor and the king of Prussia with a proposal for an alliance. Its purpose was to put the relations among the signatories on

[25]Mediatization was the process by which, between 1801 and 1806, almost one hundred German princes lost their status as sovereign rulers. Their territories were amalgamated into other German states (particularly Bavaria, Baden, Württemberg, and the Hessian principalities).

a new footing. Metternich, for all of his disparaging remarks then or later, at the time thought Alexander's draft important enough to warrant some fundamental revisions. In the process, he transformed both the tenor and the intent of the tsar's text. A comparison between the earlier and final versions of the Holy Alliance should answer the question whether it was the sinister instrument for the maintenance of the status quo which nineteenth-century liberals, Whigs, and nationalists alleged. In any case, those powers—which, after 1820, proposed to meet threats to the status quo with armed intervention—justified their measures not with reference to the Holy Alliance but to other treaties.

Of Europe's sovereigns, only the pope, the sultan (who, as a non-Christian monarch, was not invited), and the prince regent of England did not accede to the Holy Alliance. The reasons why the British cabinet and the prince regent declined the invitation are detailed in the second document below.

The text here renders the Holy Alliance in its final form. Words or phrases from Alexander's draft that were deleted from the final version appear in brackets. Metternich's additions or alterations are in italics.

a)   ***The Holy Alliance, 26 September 1815***

In the name of the Most Holy Indivisible Trinity. Their Majesties the Emperor of Austria, the King of Prussia, and the Emperor of Russia, having, in consequence of the great events which have marked the course of the three last years in Europe, and especially of the [multiple] blessings which it has pleased Divine Providence to shower down upon those States which place their confidence and their hope on it alone, acquired the intimate conviction [that the course previously adopted] *of the necessity of settling the course to be observed* by the Powers in their reciprocal relations [ought to be fundamentally changed, in that it is urgent to work towards substituting for it an order of affairs founded uniquely] on the sublime truths which the Holy Religion of Our Saviour teaches;

They solemnly declare that the present Act has no other object than to publish, in the face of the whole world their fixed resolution, both in the administration of their respective States, and in their political relations with every other Government, to take for their sole guide [for the future] the precepts of that Holy Religion, namely, the precepts of Justice, Christian Charity, and Peace, which, far from being applicable only to private concerns [as has been thought up to now], must have an immediate influence on the councils of Princes, and guide all their steps, as being the only means of consolidating human institutions and remedying their imperfections. In consequence, Their Majesties have agreed on the following Articles:

Art. 1: In conformity with the words of the Holy Scriptures, which command all men to consider each other as brethren, the [subjects of the three contracting parties] *three contracting Monarchs* will remain united by the bonds of a true *and indissoluable* fraternity, and considering each other as fellow countrymen, they will, on all occasions and in all places, lend each other aid and assistance; [it will also be thus for the respective armies, which will in the same manner see themselves only as comprising the same army, called upon] *and, regarding themselves towards their subjects and armies as fathers of families, they will lead them, in the same spirit of fraternity with which they are animated*, to protect Religion, Peace, and Justice.

Art. 2: *In consequence*, the sole principle of force, whether between the said Governments or between their Subjects, shall be that of doing each other reciprocal service, and of testifying by unalterable good will the mutual affection with which they ought to be animated, to consider themselves all as members [of the same nation under the title of Christian nation] *of one and the same Christian nation*; the three allied Princes looking on themselves as merely delegated by Providence to govern [three provinces of that same nation] *three branches of the One family*, namely, Austria, Prussia, and Russia, thus confessing that the Christian world [in essence one] *of which they and their people form a part*, has *in reality* no other Sovereign than Him to whom alone power really belongs, because in Him alone are found all the treasures of love, science, and infinite wisdom, that is to say, *God*, our Divine Saviour, the Word of the Most High, the Word of Life. Their Majesties consequently recommend to their people with the most tender solicitude, as the sole means of enjoying that Peace which arises from a good conscience, and which alone is durable, to strengthen themselves every day more and more in the principles and exercise of the duties which the Divine Saviour has taught to mankind.

Art. 3: All the [States] *Powers* who shall choose solemnly to avow the sacred principles which have dictated the present Act, and shall acknowledge how important it is for the happiness of nations, too long agitated, that these truths should henceforth exercise over the destinies of mankind all the influence which belongs to them, will be received with equal ardor and affection into this Holy Alliance . . . .

—Werner Näf, *Zur Geschichte der Heiligen Allianz* (Berne, 1928), 31–33

b) *Reply of the Prince Regent of Great Britain, 6 October 1815*

As the forms of the British Constitution, which I am called upon to administer in the name and on behalf of the King, my father, preclude me from acceding formally to this Treaty, in the shape in which it has been presented to me, I adopt this course of conveying to the august Sovereigns who have signed it, my entire concurrence in the principles they have laid down . . . . [I]t will be always my earnest endeavour to regulate my conduct . . . by these sacred maxims, and to co-operate with my august Allies in all measures which may be likely to contribute to the peace and happiness of mankind.

—Hertslet, 1:320; Hurst, 1:99

1.12 SECOND PEACE OF PARIS, 20 NOVEMBER 1815

In drawing up the Second Peace of Paris, the Allies clearly intended that the outpouring of support for Napoleon upon his return to France should not go unpunished. More stringent than the First Peace (Document 1.6), this second treaty with France still represented a triumph of moderation (and undeniably so if it is compared to the settlements that Napoleon had imposed on his vanquished foes). The principal differences between the two peace treaties lie in their territorial provisions, in the financial terms of the Second Peace, and in the measures taken to ensure French compliance.

Art. 1: The Frontiers of France shall be the same as they were in the year 1790, save and except the modifications . . . which are detailed in the present Article . . . .

Art. 4: The pecuniary part of the Indemnity to be furnished by France to the Allied Powers is fixed at the sum of 700,000,000 francs. The modes, the periods, and the guarantees for the payment of this sum shall be regulated by a Special Convention . . . .

Art. 5: The state of uneasiness and of fermentation, which after so many violent convulsions, and particularly after the last catastrophe, France must still experience, notwithstanding the paternal intentions of her King, and the advantages secured to every class of his subjects by the Constitutional Charter, requiring, for the security of the neighbouring States, certain measures of precaution and of temporary guarantee, it has been judged indispensable to occupy, during a fixed time, by a corps of Allied Troops certain military positions along the frontiers of France, under the express reserve, that such occupation shall in no way prejudice the Sovereignty of His Most Christian Majesty, nor the state of possession, such as it is recognized and confirmed by the present Treaty. The number of these troops shall not exceed 150,000 men . . . . The utmost extent of the duration of this military occupation is fixed at 5 years. It may terminate before that period if, at the end of 3 years, the Allied Sovereigns, . . . shall agree to acknowledge that the motives which led them to that measure have ceased to exist. But whatever may be the result of this deliberation, all the Fortresses and Positions occupied by the Allied troops shall, at the expiration of 5 years, be evacuated without further delay . . . .

—Hertslet, 1:342–50; Hurst, 1:128–34

1.13   THE QUADRUPLE ALLIANCE, 20 NOVEMBER 1815

On the same day that the Allies concluded the Second Peace of Paris with France, they renewed the alliance among themselves. The seven bilateral treaties of this Quadruple Alliance resembled—and explicitly referred to—the earlier Treaty of Chaumont (cf. Document 1.4), which had been disrupted by the Saxon-Polish crisis (Document 1.7) but was revived after the return of Napoleon from Elba (Document 1.9). One implicit continuity between the Treaty of Chaumont and the Quadruple Alliance can be found in the new alliance's expansion, in article 6, of the commitment undertaken in article 5 of the earlier treaty. But, unlike the Treaty of Chaumont, the Quadruple Alliance did not specify the duration of the pact. Another principal difference between the two instruments was the conspicuous absence in the Quadruple Alliance of any reference to secondary powers.

Whether the articles of the Quadruple Alliance lived up to the intentions outlined in its preamble became the subject of considerable controversy among the signatories in the postwar period (cf. Documents 2.2 and 2.4). For the time being, the treaty defined the obligations of the signatories (1) in case of an outright French attack and (2) in the event of another revolution in France.

[Preamble:] The purpose of the Alliance concluded at Vienna the 25th day of March, 1815, having been happily attained by the re-establishment in France of the order of things which the last criminal attempt of Napoleon Bonaparte had momentarily subverted; Their Majesties . . . considering that the repose of Europe is essentially interwoven with the confirmation of the order of things founded on the maintenance of the [French] Royal Authority and of the Constitutional Charter, and wishing to employ all their means to prevent the general Tranquility (the object of the wishes of mankind and the constant end of their efforts) from being again disturbed; desirous moreover to draw closer the ties which unite them for the common interests of their people, have resolved to give to the principles solemnly laid down in the Treaties of Chaumont of the 1st March, 1814, and of Vienna of the 25th March, 1815, the application the most analogous to the present state of affairs, and to fix beforehand by a solemn treaty the principles which they propose to follow, in order to guarantee Europe from dangers by which she may still be menaced . . . .

Art. 2: The High Contracting Parties, having engaged in the war which has just terminated, for the purpose of maintaining inviolably the Arrangements settled at Paris last year, for the safety and interest of Europe, have judged it advisable to renew the said Engagements by the present Act, and to confirm them as mutually obligatory . . . . And as the same revolutionary principles which upheld the last criminal usurpation, might again, under other forms, convulse France, and thereby endanger the repose of other States; under these circumstances, the High Contracting Parties solemnly admitting it to be their duty to redouble their watchfulness for the tranquility and interests of their people, engage, in case so unfortunate an event should again occur, to concert amongst themselves, and with His Most Christian Majesty, the measures which they may judge necessary to be pursued for the safety of their respective States, and for the general Tranquility of Europe.

Art. 3: . . . [U]niformly disposed to adopt every salutary measure calculated to secure the Tranquility of Europe by maintaining the order of things re-established in France, they [the signatories] engage, in case the said body of [occupation] troops should be attacked or menaced with an attack on the part of France, that the said powers should be again obliged to place themselves on a war establishment against that Power . . . .

Art. 5: The High Contracting Parties . . . declare, moreover, that even after the expiration of this measure [the occupation], the said engagements shall remain in full force and vigor . . . .

Art. 6: To facilitate and secure the execution of the present Treaty, and to consolidate the connections which at the present moment so closely unite the Four Sovereigns for the happiness of the world, the High Contracting Parties have agreed to renew their Meetings at fixed periods, either under the immediate auspices of the Sovereigns themselves, or by their respective Ministers, for the purpose of consulting upon their common interests, and for the consideration of the measures which at each of those periods shall be considered the most salutary for the repose and prosperity of Nations, and for the maintenance of the Peace of Europe.

—Hertslet, 1:372–75; Hurst, 1:121–24

CHAPTER 2

The "1815 System" in Operation: Fissures and Adjustments, 1815–1839

That wartime coalitions do not long survive the defeat of the common enemy is a truism borne out by our century. The 1815 system was no exception. By the early 1820s, challenges on the European periphery—in Spain, Naples, and Ottoman Greece—eroded Allied unity. The concert was further shaken by the death of Castlereagh, one of its leading architects, and the appointment of a successor who openly scorned the notion of collective security.

GENERAL READING: Timothy E. Anna, *Spain and the Loss of America* (Lincoln, NE, 1983); Ernest R. May, *The Making of the Monroe Doctrine* (Cambridge, MA, 1975); Paul W. Schroeder, *Metternich's Diplomacy at its Zenith, 1820–1823* (1962; reprint: Austin, 1977); Paul W. Schroeder, *The Transformation of European Politics, 1763–1848* (Oxford, 1994); Charles K. Webster, *The Foreign Policy of Castlereagh, 1815–1822* (London, 1925); Harold W. V. Temperley, *The Foreign Policy of Canning, 1822–27* (1925; reprint: Hamden, CT, 1966); Daniel Thomas, *The Guarantee of Belgian Neutrality in European Politics* (Kingston, RI, 1983)

2.1   METTERNICH ON ENGLAND AND RUSSIA

Metternich to Esterhazy, 26 March 1817

Dividing the European powers into two groups—the "liberal west," consisting of Britain and France, and the "autocratic east" of the three "northern courts" of Vienna, St. Petersburg, and Berlin—may be a convenient shorthand. Proponents of this view assume that a country's foreign policy is shaped primarily by its constitutional structure. But even on constitutional grounds, the dichotomy of the "liberal west" and "autocratic east" is of only limited value. The British parliament and the French chamber were based on the narrowest of franchises, and the governments of Regency England and Restoration France were aristocratic oligarchies, hardly representative of the new industrial wealth in either country, never mind the population at large.

Second, this view exaggerates the differences between Britain and Austria just as it exaggerates the commonalities between Austria and Russia. Metternich's instructions to the

Austrian ambassador in London of 26 March 1817 provide an interesting corrective. The extract below concludes a long litany of complaints about Russia's alleged aims both in the Mediterranean and vis-à-vis the Ottoman Empire and caps an effort by Metternich to resuscitate the spirit of the Anglo-French-Austrian combination of January 1815 (Document 1.7). But Castlereagh evaded Metternich's overture. His initiative spurned, Metternich now had little choice but to seek some form of accommodation with Russia.

Metternich to Esterhazy,[1] 26 March 1817

. . . The most secure moral safeguard, the only one that I believe useful to propose today to counter the inclinations—more marked daily—of the Emperor of Russia, seems to me to be found in the most genuine convergence [*réunion la plus franche*] of outlooks and interests among us, England, Prussia, and France. If M. Castlereagh objects that all the means of direct and immediate action are today beyond the reach of Great Britain, it will not be difficult for you, *mon Prince*, to prove to the Minister that Austria finds itself in a much more vexing and constrained position. Our intentions, as a result, cannot go so far as to include physical intervention [*opérations matérielles*]: we are far from calling for a coalition. But the more we feel how much our physical means are circumscribed for the present, the more we are convinced that we should place ourselves in a strong moral position . . . . Now this goal—the only one we aim for and pursue as long as the Emperor Alexander keeps on his mask—can only be achieved by the means that we propose. But to attain it, the English government must open up and trust in us more than it does ordinarily; and it must furnish us with evidence that it has finally seen that it is erroneous to believe that one can control the Emperor Alexander's opinion and direct his will by flattering his whims, and by showing him so much deference that virtually none is left for other courts. . . .

—Haus-, Hof- und Staatsarchiv (Vienna): England, Diplomatische
Korrespondenz 159; Instruction no. 4 of 26 March 1817

2.2   CONGRESS OF AIX-LA-CHAPELLE

Allied Convention with France, 9 October 1818 • Castlereagh's Memorandum,
October 1818 • Allied Note to the Duc de Richelieu, 4 November 1818 •
Protocol of the Five-Power Conference, 15 November 1818

Acting both on article 5 of the Second Peace of Paris (Document 1.12) and on article 6 of the Quadruple Alliance (Document 1.13), the Allies met in Aix-la-Chapelle (German: Aachen) in September 1818. On that occasion, the Allies agreed to withdraw their occupation forces from France, accept a reduction in the French indemnity, and invite France to participate in their councils. The meeting at Aix inspired Castlereagh to reflect on the purposes of the postwar European system and the obligations of the Great Powers. In these observations can be found the germ of Castlereagh's position vis-à-vis the continental powers in subsequent years.

---

[1]Paul Anton, Prince Esterhazy (1786–1866). Austrian ambassador in London, 1814–1842.

a)   *Allied Convention with France, 9 October 1818*

Art. 1: The troops composing the Army of Occupation shall be withdrawn from the territory of France by the 30th of November next, or sooner, if possible. . . .

—Hertslet, 1:557–60; Hurst, 1:141

b)   *Castlereagh's Memorandum, October 1818*

. . . These transactions [the Act of Vienna and the Paris peace treaties] to which all the States of Europe (with the exception of the Porte), are at this day either signing or acceding parties, may be considered as the great charte, by which the territorial system of Europe, unhinged by the events of war and revolution, has been again restored to order . . . . There is no doubt that a breach of the covenant by any one State is an injury, which all the other States may, if they shall think fit, either separately or collectively resent, but the treaties do not impose, by express obligation, the doing so as a matter of positive obligation . . . . The only safe principle is that of the law of nations—that no State has a right to endanger its neighbours by its internal proceedings, and that if it does, provided they exercise a sound discretion, their right of interference is clear . . . . The problem of an universal alliance for the peace and happiness of the world has always been one of speculation and of hope, but it has never yet been reduced to practice, and if an opinion may be hazarded from its difficulty, it never can; but you may in practice approach towards it, and perhaps the design has never been so far realized as in the last four years. . . .

—Charles K. Webster, *The Congress of Vienna, 1814–1815* (1919; reprint: London, 1965), 187–93

c)   *Allied Note to the Duc de Richelieu,[2] 4 November 1818*

. . . the French government has fulfilled, with the most scrupulous and honourable punctuality, all the clauses of the Treaties and Conventions of the 20th November [1815]; . . . The undersigned . . . invite His Excellency to take part in their present and future deliberations, consecrated to the maintenance of the peace, the treaties on which it is founded, the rights and mutual relations established or confirmed by these treaties, and recognised by all the European powers. . . .

—Hertslet, 1:564–66; Hurst, 1:143–44

d)   *Protocol of the Five-Power Conference, 15 November 1818*

. . . [T]he Courts . . . declare . . . 3) That France, associated with other powers by the restoration of the legitimate monarchical and constitutional power, engages henceforth to concur in the maintenance and consolidation of a System which has given

---

[2]Armand du Plessis, Duc de Richelieu (1766–1822). French prime minister, 1815–1818; 1820–1821.

peace to Europe, and which can alone insure its duration; 4) That if, for the better attaining the above declared object, the Powers which have concurred in the present Act, should judge it necessary to establish particular meetings, . . . the time and place of these meetings shall, on each occasion, be previously fixed by means of diplomatic communications; and that in the case of these meetings having for their object affairs specially connected with the interests of the other States of Europe, they shall only take place in pursuance of a formal invitation on the part of those States as the said affairs may concern, and under the express reservation of their right of direct participation therein. . . .

—Hurst, 1:147

2.3 INTERMEDIARY BODIES AND THE EUROPEAN EQUILIBRIUM: THE GERMAN CONFEDERATION

Memorandum by Humboldt, 30 September 1816 •
Statute of the German Confederation, May 1820

Of the various territorial arrangements in the modern history of German-speaking lands, the German Confederation (1815–1866) was one of the more enduring; yet the scholarly literature on it remains sparse. An Allied war aim (Document 1.4) and subject of extensive discussion at the Congress of Vienna, the German Confederation was endowed with its ultimate constitutional form only in 1820. Those articles of the Final Act that regulated the conduct and obligations of its members vis-à-vis one another now breathed the spirit of Metternich's repressive Carlsbad Decrees of the preceding year. Other articles reproduced below defined the confederation's role in the European equilibrium; the excerpts here have been chosen with an eye to later events (Documents 2.9, 4.13, and 8.6).

a) *Memorandum by Humboldt, 30 September 1816*

. . . One must never forget the true and real purpose of the Confederation in European politics. This purpose is to ensure tranquillity. The entire conception of the Confederation has been calculated with an eye to maintaining the equilibrium through natural gravity. This would be entirely counteracted if there were introduced into the ranks of European states a new collective state in addition to those larger German states which already exist . . . . No one could then prevent Germany, as Germany, from becoming an aggressive state, which no true German can want. . . .

—Wilhelm von Humboldt, *Gesammelte Schriften*, op. cit., 12:77

b) *Statute of the German Confederation, May 1820*

Art. 1: The German Confederation is a union according to international law of the Sovereign Princes and Free Towns of Germany, for the preservation of the independence and inviolability of the States comprised in it, and for maintaining the internal and external security of Germany.

Art. 2: As to its internal relations, this Union consists of a community of States independent of each other, with reciprocal and equal rights and obligations stipulated by Treaties. As to its external relations, it constitutes a collective Power, bound together in political unity. . . .

Art 5: The Confederation is established as an indissoluble Union, and therefore none of its Members can be at liberty to secede from it. . . .

Art 25: . . . [The Confederation] may co-operate for the preservation or restoration of tranquillity [in member states], in case of the resistance of subjects against their Government, in that of an open revolt, or dangerous movements in several States of the Confederation.

Art. 26: When the internal tranquillity of a Confederate State is immediately endangered by the resistance of subjects to the authorities, and the spreading of the seditious movements is to be feared, or when an actual revolt has broken out, and the Government of the country, after having exhausted all constitutional and legal means, calls for the assistance of the Confederation, the Diet[2a] is bound to cause the most prompt assistance to be given for the reestablishment of order. . . .

Art. 35: The Confederation has the right, as a Collective Power, to declare war, to make peace, to contract alliances, and to conclude other Treaties. According, however, to the object of the Confederation expressed in Article 2 of the Federal Act, it only exercises this right for its own defence. . . .

Art. 36: . . . no individual State of the Confederation can be injured by a foreign Power, without the injury affecting at the same time, and to an equal degree, the whole of the Confederation. On the other hand, the individual States of the Confederation are bound on their side not to give any cause for such injuries, and not to do any to foreign States. In case a foreign State should complain to the Diet of any injury inflicted on it by a Member of the Confederation, and this complaint should prove to be well founded, the Diet is bound to require the Member that has given cause for the complaint to make prompt and satisfactory reparation, and to unite with this requisition, according to the circumstances, such measures as may prevent in time any further consequences injurious to peace. . . .

Art. 46: If a State of the Confederation, having possessions beyond the limits of the Confederation, enters into a war in its position as a European Power, such a war, so long as it does not affect the relations and obligations of the Confederation, remains quite foreign to it. . . .

—Hurst, 1:149–67; Hertslet, 1:636–57

2.4 INTERVENTION DEBATED: CONFERENCES OF TROPPAU AND LAIBACH

Austro-Neapolitan Treaty, 12 June 1815 • *Castlereagh's State Paper, 5 May 1820*
• *Troppau Conference: Austro-Prussian-Russian Circular, 8 December 1820* •
Metternich to Rechberg, 31 December 1820 • *Castlereagh Circular, 19 January
1821* • *Laibach Conference: Austro-Prussian-Russian Circular, 12 May 1821*

Spanish army units awaiting passage from the port of Cadiz to the Spanish colonies in Latin America revolted in January 1820. By March, the insurgents prevailed on the Bourbon King

[2a]A permanent conference of ambassadors which represented German princes and towns and met in Frankfurt.

Ferdinand VII to restore the liberal constitution of 1812, which he had suspended six weeks after his return to Spain in March 1814. A similar outbreak in the Bourbon Kingdom of the Two Sicilies followed in July 1820; in Naples, the revolutionaries pressured King Ferdinand IV to adopt a constitution patterned on the Spanish model.

The revolutions in Spain and Naples soon became a subject of controversy among the Great Powers: Did these insurrections pose a threat to the postwar order? Could a mandate to intervene be construed from the wording of the 1815 treaties? from their intent? from neither? If there was a mandate for intervention, what should be its form—diplomatic or military? unilateral or multilateral?

The issue was first broached by Tsar Alexander in April 1820, several weeks before the outbreak of the Neapolitan revolution. Castlereagh's state paper of 5 May defined the response of the British government and represented a further evolution of his thoughts, first set down in the aftermath of the congress at Aix (Document 2.2). Metternich thought of the revolution in Spain as too far away to pose any danger to Austrian interests. Naples, a crucial part of the Austrian glacis in Italy, was a different matter: this revolution might spread to other Italian states. If only for political reasons, Austria should act preemptively; moreover, intervention could be justified with reference to Austria's treaty rights in Naples. Indeed, Mettternich was proven right when Piedmontese revolutionaries in March 1821 also demanded the Spanish constitution for this northern Italian state.

In response to the events in Naples, the Austrian, Russian, and Prussian monarchs, together with their ministers, convened at Troppau in Austrian Silesia in December 1820. The protocol of the Troppau conference—which had been attended by British and French observers without plenipotentiary powers—prompted Castlereagh to restate the British position on intervention on 19 January 1821. The Troppau powers met at a follow-up conference in Laibach (Ljubljana) between January and May 1821; selected passages from this conference's final communiqué constitute the last excerpt below.

a)   *Austro-Neapolitan Treaty, 12 June 1815*

[Secret Articles:] . . . Art. 2: . . . it is understood by the two High Contracting Parties that, in reestablishing the government of the kingdom, His Majesty the King of the Two Sicilies [= Naples and Sicily] will not agree to any change whatsoever which is incompatible either with ancient monarchical institutions or with the principles adopted by His Imperial and Royal Apostolic Majesty for the governance of his Italian provinces. . . .

—*CTS*, 65:14–17

b)   *Castlereagh's State Paper, 5 May 1820*

. . . In this Alliance as in all other human arrangements, nothing is more likely to impair or even destroy its real utility, than any attempt to push its duties and obligations beyond the Sphere which its original conception and understood principles will warrant:—It was an union for the reconquest and liberation of a great proportion of the continent of Europe from the military dominion of France, and having subdued the conqueror it took the state of possession as established by the Peace under the protection of the Alliance:—It never was however intended as an Union for the Government of the World, or for the superintendence of the internal affairs of other states . . . . We shall be found in our place when actual danger menaces the System of Europe, but this country cannot, and will not, act upon abstract and speculative principles of precaution. . . .

—A.W. Ward and G.P. Gooch (eds.), *Cambridge History of British Foreign Policy* (Cambridge, 1923), 2:623–33

c)   *Troppau Conference: Austro-Prussian-Russian Circular, 8 December 1820*

. . . The Powers have exercised an undeniable right in concerting together upon means of safety against those States in which the overthrow of a Government caused by revolution could only be considered as a dangerous example, which could only result in an hostile attitude against constitutional and legitimate governments. The exercise of this right became still more urgent when those who had placed themselves in that position sought to communicate to neighboring States the misfortune into which they had themselves plunged, and to propagate revolution and confusion around them. . . .

There is nothing new in the system followed by Austria, Prussia, and Russia; it rests upon the same maxims as those which served as the bases of the treaties upon which the Alliance of the European states was founded. . . .

—Hertslet, 1:658–61

d)   *Metternich to Rechberg,[2b] 31 December 1820*

. . . Any catastrophe such as that of Naples presents different periods, whether regarded from a domestic or a foreign point of view. The revolt breaks out; it is indubitable and evident; it is the beginning of a conflagration; if they are in good order, take your fire-engines there; ask no questions; do not hesitate; extinguish the fire; success will be certain. Do not take empty fire-engines, but let them be well-filled.

Then comes the second period. The revolt takes the appearance of reform. A feeble sovereign swears to put a knife to his throat. A chorus of liberals and radicals join in his hymns; the sovereign is praised to the skies; and the people seem to adore him. Milk and honey are to flow in all the veins of the State abandoned to anarchy; tyrants alone could hinder the development of so fine a work! . . . Our fire-engines were not full in July, otherwise we should have set to work immediately. In the second period, it did not seem to us that our neutral attitude was sufficient; the Naples affair threatened Italy, Austria, Europe equally. It is therefore for the latter to declare itself in principle with us. We take upon ourselves the material part. . . .

—Metternich, *Memoirs* (London, 1881), 3:444–50

[2b]Alois, Count Rechberg (1766–1849). Bavarian foreign minister, 1817–1825.

e)   *Castlereagh Circular, 19 January 1821*

. . . The King has felt himself obliged to decline becoming a party to the measures in question. These measures embrace two different objects:—1st, the establishment of certain General Principles for the regulation of the future political conduct of the Allies in the cases therein described:—2ndly, The proposed mode of dealing, under these principles, with the existing affairs of Naples.

The system of measures proposed under the former head, if to be reciprocally acted upon, would be in direct repugnance to the fundamental laws of this country.—But even if this decisive objection did not exist, the British government would nevertheless regard the principles on which these measures rest, to be such as could not be safely admitted as a system of international law. They are of the opinion that their adoption would inevitably sanction, and, in the hands of less beneficent monarchs, might hereafter lead to a much more frequent and extensive interference in the internal transactions of States, than they are persuaded is intended by the august parties from whom they proceed, or can be reconcileable either with the general interest, or with the efficient authority and dignity, of independent sovereigns. They do not regard the alliance as entitled, under existing treaties, to assume, in their character as allies, any such general powers. . . .

With respect to the particular case of Naples, the British government, at the very earliest moment, did not hesitate to express their strong disapprobation of the mode and circumstances, under which that revolution was understood to have been effected; but they, at the same time, expressly declared to the several Allied courts, that they should not consider themselves as either called upon, or justified, to advise an interference on the part of this country: they fully admitted, however, that other European states, and especially Austria and the Italian powers, might feel themselves differently circumstanced; . . . it should be clearly understood that no government can be more prepared than the British Government is, to uphold the right of any State or States to interfere, where their own immediate security or essential interests are seriously endangered by the internal transactions of another State.—But as they regard the assumption of such right, as only to be justified by the strongest necessity, and to be limited and regulated thereby, they cannot admit that this right can receive a general and indiscriminate application to all revolutionary movements, without reference to their immediate bearing upon some particular State or States, or be made prospectively the basis of an alliance. . . . *Intervene when it physically threatens GBP*

—Hertslet, 1:664–66

f)   *Laibach Conference: Austro-Prussian-Russian Circular,*
12 May 1821

. . . At the very same time at which their [the Allied sovereigns'] generous determination was being accomplished in the Kingdom of Naples, a rebellion, if possible, of a more odious character, broke out in Piedmont. . . . Destined simply to fight against and repel rebellion, the Allied forces, far from upholding any exclusive interest, came to the assistance of subdued peoples, and they considered it as coming in support of their liberty, and not as an attack against their independence. From that moment war ceased; from that moment the States which the revolt had overtaken, became friendly states towards the powers who had never looked for anything but their tranquillity and their prosperity. . . .

—Hertslet, 1:667–69

2.5   INTERVENTION DEEMED ILL ADVISED: CASTLEREAGH ON THE GREEK INSURRECTION

Castlereagh to Bagot, 28 October 1821

Five months after the formal close of the Laibach conference, Metternich met Castlereagh in Hanover on the occasion of George IV's first visit, as monarch, to his German kingdom (it will be recalled that the kings of England, between 1714 and 1837, also ruled Hanover). The main topic of conversation between the two statesmen was how to restrain Tsar Alexander I from intervening on behalf of the Greek insurrection against Ottoman rule in the Peloponnesus.

At Hanover, Castlereagh and Metternich found themselves in broad agreement. Their concurrence once again raises the question whether the dichotomy "liberal west"/"autocratic east" is in fact a useful shorthand for the international politics of the 1820s, or whether it underestimates Austro-Russian differences and downplays the ability of Austria and Britain to cooperate, at least for as long as Castlereagh was at the Foreign Office.

Castlereagh's summary of his conversations with Metternich, excerpted below, does reveal one interesting inconsistency: his (questionable) reference to the scope of the "1815 system," as it might pertain to the Ottoman Empire, should be contrasted with the views he had expressed on this subject in October 1818 (Document 2.2).

Castlereagh to Bagot,[3] 28 October 1821

. . . I cannot, therefore, reconcile it to my sense of duty to embark in a scheme for a new modelling of the position of the Greek population in those countries at the hazard of all the destructive confusion and disunion which such an attempt may lead to, not only within Turkey but in Europe. I am by no means persuaded, were the Turks even miraculously to be withdrawn (what it would cost of blood and suffering forcibly to expel them I now dismiss from my calculations) that the Greek population, as it now subsists or is likely to subsist for a course of years, could frame from their own materials a system of government less defective either in its external or internal character, and especially as the question regards Russia, than that which at present unfortunately exists. I cannot, therefore, be tempted, nor even called upon in moral duty under loose notions of humanity and amendment, to forget the obligations of existing Treaties, to endanger the frame of long established relations, and to aid the insurrectionary efforts now in progress in Greece, upon the chance that it may, through war, mould itself into some scheme of government, but at the certainty that it must in the meantime, open a field for every ardent adventurer and political fanatic

[3]Sir Charles Bagot (1781–1843). British ambassador in St. Petersburg, 1820–1824.

in Europe to hazard not only his own fortune, but what is our province more anxiously to watch over, the fortune and destiny of that system to the conservation of which our latest solemn transactions with our Allies have bound us. . . .

—Charles K. Webster, *The Foreign Policy of Castlereagh, 1815–1822:*
Britain and the European Alliance (London, 1925), 376–77

2.6   INTERVENTION TOLERATED: CANNING AND THE FRENCH "WAR" AGAINST SPAIN

Canning to Stuart, 31 March 1823 ●
Canning in the House of Commons, 28 April 1823 and 3 February 1824

There was little love lost between Castlereagh and George Canning (the two men had fought a duel in 1809), but Canning was offered the Foreign Office after Castlereagh's suicide in August 1822. His first test as foreign secretary came when the Congress of Verona (October–December 1822) failed to harmonize Allied policy on the ongoing crisis in Spain. Casting aside the objections of both Metternich and Canning, France in early 1823 declared war on the constitutional government in Spain, avowedly to restore the monarchical rule of King Ferdinand VII. Canning, perhaps because he refused to coordinate his policy with Metternich, could not prevent the French measure. But he defined the limits of what Britain was prepared to tolerate and, despite his own assertions to the contrary, continued to distrust French assurances as to the objective of the intervention. Whether Canning's message to the French foreign minister in early April 1823—to use the words of his biographer—constituted "practically an ultimatum" is best for the reader to decide. Canning's dispatch articulated British policy not just on Spain proper, but on the related question of the Spanish colonies in Latin America.

After the French forces crossed into Spain, Canning's speeches in parliament, for all their verbal flourish and braggadocio, sounded a defensive tone. The two speeches excerpted here give considerable insight into his political credo; in the second one, he found himself almost arguing against his own political convictions in trying to counter an attack on him by Sir Henry Peter Brougham, one of the most prominent Whigs in parliament. Brougham had portrayed Canning's foreign policy as acquiescing to the "conspiracy" of France in Spain and Austria in Italy, placing England in a position in which it had been "kicked by a herd of despots, . . . duped and cajoled."

a)   *Canning to Stuart,[4] 31 March 1823*

The repeated disavowal, by His Most Christian Majesty's Government, of all views of ambition and aggrandizement, forbids the suspicion of any design on the part of France, to establish a permanent military occupation of Spain; or to force His Catholick Majesty into any measures, derogatory to the independence of his Crown, or to his existing relations with other Powers. . . .

With respect to the Provinces in America, which have thrown off their allegiance to the Crown of Spain, time and the course of events appear to have substantially decided their separation from the Mother Country; although the formal recognition of

[4]Sir Charles Stuart (1779–1845). British ambassador in Paris, 1815–1830.

those Provinces, as Independent States, by His Majesty, may be hastened or retarded by various external circumstances . . . . Disclaiming in the most solemn manner any intention of appropriating to Himself the smallest portion of the late Spanish possessions in America, His Majesty is satisfied that no attempt will be made by France, to bring under her dominion any of those possessions, either by conquest, or by cession, from Spain.

This frank explanation upon the points on which perhaps alone the possibility of any collision of France with Great Britain can be apprehended in a War between France and Spain, your Excellency will represent to M. de Chateaubriand, as dictated by an earnest desire to be enabled to preserve, in that War, a strict and undeviating Neutrality: a Neutrality not liable to alteration towards either Party, so long as the Honour and just Interests of Great Britain are equally respected by both.

—*SP* 10:64–70; Temperley, *Foreign Policy of Canning,* op. cit., 84–85

b)   ***Canning in the House of Commons, 28 April 1823***
and 3 February 1824

[28 April 1823:] . . . Sir, it is as true in politics, as in mechanics, that the test of skill and of success is to achieve the greatest purpose with the least power. . . . it appears that there was to be no joint declaration against Spain; and it was, it seems, generally understood at Verona, that the instructions given to His Majesty's Plenipotentiary, by the liberal—I beg pardon, to be quite accurate I am afraid I must say, the radical—Foreign Minister of England, were the cause. . . . The immediate object of England, therefore, was to hinder the impress of a joint character to be affixed to the war—if war there must be—with Spain; to take care that the war should not grow out of an assumed jurisdiction of the Congress; to keep within reasonable bounds that predominating areopagitical spirit, which the memorandum of the British Cabinet of May 1820 describes as "beyond the sphere of the original conception, and understood principles of the alliance,"—"an alliance never intended as a union for the government of the world, or for the superintendence of the internal affairs of other states." And this, I say, was accomplished. . . .

. . . I contemplate, I confess, with fearful anxiety, the peculiar character of the war in which France and Spain are engaged, and the peculiar direction which that character may possibly give to it. I was—I still am—an enthusiast for national independence; but I am not—I hope I never shall be—an enthusiast in favour of revolution. And yet how fearfully are those two considerations intermingled, in the present contest between France and Spain! This is no war for territory, or for commercial advantages. It is unhappily a war of principle. France has invaded Spain from enmity to her new institutions. Supposing the enterprise of France not to succeed, what is there to prevent Spain from invading France, in return, from hatred of the principle upon which her invasion had been justified?

No man can witness with more delight than I do the widening diffusion of political liberty. Acknowledging all the blessings which we have long derived from liberty ourselves, I do not grudge to others a participation in them. I would not prohibit other nations from kindling their torches at the flame of British freedom. But let us not deceive ourselves. The general acquisition of free institutions is not necessarily a security for general peace. I am obliged to confess that its immediate tendency is the other way . . . . In truth, long intervals of profound peace are much more readily to be found under settlements of a monarchical form. Did the republic of Rome, in the whole career of her existence, enjoy an interval of peace of as long duration as that which this country enjoyed under the administration of Sir Robert Walpole?[5]—and that interval, be it remembered, was broken short through the instigation of popular feeling. I am not saying that this is right or wrong—but that it is so. . . .

[3 February 1824:] . . . What was to be done, he wished to know, with Austria, in the view of the hon. and learned gentleman? How was the gap which her absence would leave to be filled after we had lost her? Were we to abolish her as a power, or to take up arms against her, because her internal arrangements did not meet our approval? This was surely too absurd and extravagant a proposition to be listened to. Let us rather maintain all our external relations . . . without examining too minutely into the abuses which may exist in foreign governments . . . .

—R. Therry, *The Speeches of the Rt. Hon. George Canning* (London, 1836), 5:52–135; *Parl. Debates*, New Series, 10:78

2.7   THE MONROE DOCTRINE, 1823

Canning to Rush, 20 August 1823 • Monroe's Message to Congress, 2 December 1823 • Canning to Vaughan, 18 February 1826 • Canning in the House of Commons, 12 December 1826 • Covenant of the League of Nations, 28 April 1919

President Monroe's message to Congress had its roots in American apprehensions that Russia would extend its claims to much of the Oregon coast,[6] that Britain harbored designs on Cuba, and that France might spearhead an attempt on behalf of the Holy Alliance powers to restore Spanish rule on the Latin American mainland.

As early as August 1823, Canning had broached with the American minister in London the subject of a bilateral Anglo-American declaration on the fledgling Latin American republics—already recognized by the United States, though not yet by Britain. While Monroe inclined toward a joint Anglo-American stand, his secretary of state, John Quincy Adams, prevailed with his view that if there were to be a declaration, it should have a uniquely American imprint.

Canning was thus preempted. He now feared that, unless Britain extended diplomatic recognition to the new republics, the United States would come to enjoy a monopoly on the affections of Latin America. He overcame the resistance of the die-hard Tories in the cabinet and a recalcitrant monarch only gradually; they finally gave way in December 1824. Canning claimed his share of the glory when the Commons, on 12 December 1826, debated British

---

[5](1676–1745). First Lord of the Treasury (prime minister), 1714–1717; 1720–1742. In 1734, Walpole justified British neutrality in the War of the Polish Succession by telling Queen Caroline: "Madam, there are 50,000 men slain this year in Europe, and not one Englishman." John Croker (ed.), *Memoirs of the Reign of George II . . . by John, Lord Hervey* (Philadelphia, 1848), 1:334. Britain's neutrality facilitated a Franco-Spanish victory over Austria.

[6]For Alexander I's ukase of 4/16 September 1821 and the Russo-American convention of 5 April 1824, see Basil Dmytryshyn et al. (eds.), *The Russian American Colonies: A Documentary Record, 1798–1867* (Portland, OR, 1989), 339–52 and 383–85.

policy in the face of a Spanish threat to Portugal. Using this occasion to take a swipe at the continental powers, Canning saw fit not to mention the fact that nine months earlier he had been educated to the uses of the European concert, albeit in the Near East (cf. Document 3.3).

A unilateral proclamation pure and simple, the Monroe Doctrine was not a treaty, agreement, law, or contract of any kind. As a result, the legality of actions undertaken in its name was feeble. Grover Cleveland and Theodore Roosevelt sought to overcome this defect (cf. Documents 10.6 and 10.22), but, as is evident from the last excerpt below, it was Woodrow Wilson who outdid all his predecessors in giving the Monroe Doctrine stature and standing in international law.

a)   ***Canning to Rush,[7] 20 August 1823***

. . . Is not the moment come when our governments might understand each other as to the Spanish-American Colonies? . . .

1. For ourselves we have no disguise. We conceive the recovery of the Colonies by Spain, to be hopeless. 2. We conceive the question of the Recognition of them as Independent States, to be one of time and circumstances. 3. We are, however, by no means disposed to throw any impediment in the way of an arrangement between them and the mother country by amicable negotiation. 4. We aim not at the possession of any portion of them ourselves. 5. We could not see any portion of them transferred to any other Power, with indifference.

If these opinions and feelings are, as I firmly believe them to be, common to your government with ours, why should we hesitate mutually to confide them to each other, and to declare them in the face of the world? . . .

—Stanislaus Murray Hamilton (ed.), *The Writings of James Monroe* (New York, 1902), 6:365–66

b)   ***Monroe's Message to Congress, 2 December 1823***

. . . the American continents, by the free and independent condition which they have assumed and maintain, are henceforth not to be considered as subjects for future colonization by any European powers . . . . In the wars of the European powers in matters relating to themselves we have never taken any part, nor does it comport with our policy so to do. It is only when our rights are invaded or seriously menaced that we resent injuries or make preparation for our defense. With the movements in this hemisphere we are of necessity more immediately connected, and by causes which must be obvious to all enlightened and impartial observers . . . . We owe it, therefore, to candor and to the amicable relations existing between the United States and those powers to declare that we should consider any attempt on their part to extend their system to any portion of this hemisphere as dangerous to our peace and safety. With the existing colonies or dependencies of any European power we have not interfered

[7]Richard Rush (1780–1859). Acting secretary of state, 1817; American minister at the Court of St. James, 1817–1825.

and shall not interfere. But with the Governments who have declared their independence and maintained it, and whose independence we have, on great consideration and on just principles, acknowledged, we could not view any interposition for the purpose of oppressing them, or controlling in any other manner their destiny by any European power in any other light than as the manifestation of an unfriendly disposition toward the United States. In the war between those new Governments and Spain we declared our neutrality at the time of their recognition, and to this we have adhered, and shall continue to adhere . . . . It is impossible that the allied powers should extend their political system to any portion of either continent without endangering our peace and happiness; nor can anyone believe that our southern brethren, if left to themselves would adopt it of their own accord. It is equally impossible therefore that we should behold such interposition in any form with indifference. . . .

—James D. Richardson (ed.), *A Compilation of the Messages and Papers of the Presidents* (Washington, 1899), 2:207–20

c)   ***Canning to Vaughan,*** [8] ***18 February 1826***

The avowed pretension of the United States to put themselves at the head of the confederacy of all the Americans and to sway that Confederacy against Europe is not a pretension identified with our interests, or one that we can countenance or tolerate. It is, however, a pretension which there is no use in contesting in the abstract, but we must not say anything that seems to admit the principle.

—Temperley, *Foreign Policy of Canning*, op. cit., 158

d)   ***Canning in the House of Commons, 12 December 1826***

. . . If France occupied Spain, was it necessary, in order to avoid the consequences of that occupation, that we blockade Cadiz? No. I looked another way. I sought materials of compensation in another hemisphere. Contemplating Spain, such as our ancestors had known her, I resolved that if France had Spain, it should not be Spain "with the Indies." I called the New World into existence, to redress the balance of the Old [great cheering]. . . .

—Therry, *Speeches*, op. cit., 6:110–12

e)   ***Covenant of the League of Nations, 28 April 1919***

Art. 21: Nothing in this Covenant shall be deemed to affect the validity of international engagements, such as treaties of arbitration or regional understandings like the Monroe Doctrine, for securing the maintenance of the peace.

---

[8] Charles Richard Vaughan (1774–1849). British minister in Washington, 1825–1835.

2.8   INTERMEDIARY BODIES AND THE EUROPEAN EQUILIBRIUM: THE NEUTRALITY OF BELGIUM

Convention of Austria, Britain, France, Prussia,
and Russia with Belgium, 14 December 1831 • Treaty of Austria,
Britain, France, Prussia, and Russia with Belgium, 19 April 1839 •
Minute by Hardinge, 15(?) November 1908

The secession of Belgium from the United Netherlands was the first territorial revision of the Vienna settlement. Although all Great Powers recognized Belgium by November 1831, the Dutch government could not be moved to do the same. An Anglo-French and a Franco-Belgian convention of October and November 1832, respectively, provided for an Anglo-French blockade of the Dutch coast and for the entry of French forces into Belgium to enforce the treaty of 1831, that is, to sweep Dutch troops out of their remaining strongholds. An armistice was concluded by May 1833, but the King of the Netherlands withheld his recognition of Belgium for five more years; subsequent foot-dragging by the Belgian government over the financial clauses of the separation delayed the settlement for another year.

In April 1839, three treaties—between the Great Powers and the Netherlands; between the Great Powers and Belgium; and between Belgium and the Netherlands—finally settled the question. The terms of the 1839 treaties, notwithstanding some financial and commercial adjustments, were essentially the same as those of the 1831 treaty.

The problem of Belgian neutrality became acute again during the Franco-German war of 1870 (cf. Document 8.14), as many of the initial military operations took place near the Franco-Belgian border. After the outbreak of hostilities, France and the North German Confederation concluded separate self-denying treaties with England in which the signatories pledged to respect the neutrality of Belgium for the duration of the war; these treaties, if nothing else, made clear the importance which Britain attached to the maintenance of the status quo (cf. also Document 12.14).[9]

The powers' guarantee of Belgium did not prescribe specific measures in the event Belgian neutrality was violated. In essence, each party was free to choose its form of reprisal—a point of view amply confirmed in 1908 by the minute of Sir Charles Hardinge, then permanent under-secretary in the Foreign Office.

a)   *Convention of Austria, Britain, France, Prussia, and Russia with Belgium, 14 December 1831*

. . . Art. 4: The Fortresses of Belgium, which are not mentioned in Article 1 of the present Convention as destined to be dismantled, shall be maintained: His Majesty the King of the Belgians engages to keep them constantly in good order.

—Hertslet, 2:881–84; Hurst, 1:216

[9]Texts of Anglo-North German and Anglo-French treaties of, respectively, 9 and 11 August 1870 in Hurst, 1:455–58.

b)   ***Treaty of Austria, Britain, France, Prussia, and***
Russia with Belgium, 19 April 1839

Art. 1: [Their Majesties] declare, that the Articles hereunto annexed, and forming the tenor of the Treaty concluded this day between His Majesty the King of the Belgians and His Majesty the King of the Netherlands . . . are considered as having the same force and validity as if they were textually inserted in the present Act, and that they are thus placed under the Guarantee of their said Majesties. . . .

Annex [bilateral Dutch-Belgian treaty]: . . . Art. 7: Belgium, within the limits specified in articles 1, 2, and 4, shall form an Independent and perpetually Neutral State. It shall be bound to observe such Neutrality towards all other States. . . .

—Hertslet, 2:979–98; Hurst, 1:250, 242

c)   ***Minute by Hardinge,[10] 15(?) November 1908***

. . . whether we could be called upon to carry out our obligation and to vindicate the neutrality of Belgium in opposing its violation must necessarily depend on our policy at the time and circumstances of the moment. Supposing that France violated the neutrality of Belgium in a war against Germany, it is, under present circumstances, doubtful whether England or Russia would move a finger to maintain Belgian neutrality, which [sic] if the neutrality of Belgium were violated by Germany it is probable that the converse would be the case.

—BD, 8:311

2.9   ## METTERNICH ON THE ZOLLVEREIN

Metternich to Emperor Francis I, June 1833

Prussia's corrugated borders and numerous exclaves made the levying of import duties and the interdiction of smuggling difficult, if not impossible, tasks. To eliminate these inefficiencies, Prussia in 1819 began to forge a customs union with some of its German neighbors. Over the next decade, this entity absorbed several similar ventures among smaller German states. In 1833, it received a major boost with the accession of Saxony and the integration of the Bavaria-Württemberg common market; it now styled itself Deutscher Zollverein (German customs union). The one German state that Prussia did not woo, and in the 1850s would consistently block from joining, was Austria.

The formation of the Zollverein provided the backdrop for Metternich's memorandum, excerpted below. He sensed that the mere fact of association binds states to one another; he

[10]Sir Charles Hardinge (1858–1944). Permanent under-secretary in the Foreign Office, 1906–1910; 1916–1920.

saw that Prussia would acquire not only economic but political leverage—if only by denying Austria that cozy feeling which comes with being part of a group. But he may have overstated his case. Participants in economic associations will guard with zeal their *political* sovereignty—the present-day track record of the European Union illustrates that economic ties do not automatically blossom into political union. In the Austro-Prussian war of 1866 (Document 8.6), particularism rather than membership in the Zollverein decided the line-up of German states: the majority of Prussia's economic partners sided with Austria, not Prussia.

Metternich to Emperor Francis I, June 1833

. . . for the German Confederation, but particularly for Austria, this Prussian Zollverein is a most disadvantageous, pernicious phenomenon. . . .

. . . Within the Confederation, a smaller unit is formed, truly a state within a state, which will soon become accustomed to give priority to its own goals, and will respect the goals and purposes of the Confederation only in so far as they can be reconciled with the former. Given time, Prussian leadership, and the development of common interests, the members [of the Zollverein] will coalesce into a more or less compact body. . . .

Prussia will strive to weaken the influence of Austria at the princely courts locked into this network, using every diplomatic stratagem and seducing them with material benefits; will try to loosen their ties to us; will accustom them to look, with both fear and hope, only to Berlin; and will, finally, seek to stigmatize Austria as a foreign country [*Ausland*], which, in commercial terms, we have indeed become vis-à-vis these states—and which conforms to an image Prussian writers find so fashionable and pursue with such enthusiasm. . . .

—Richard von Metternich and Alfons von Klinkowström (eds.),
Aus Metternichs nachgelassenen Papieren (Vienna, 1881), 5:502–19

CHAPTER 3

The Eastern Question, 1774–1841

Frederick II, King in Prussia from 1740 to 1786, once characterized the eighteenth-century contests of Austria and Russia against the Ottoman Empire as the wars of the one-eyed against the blind.[1] If anything, these wars revealed the weakness of the Ottoman state, a tottering giant which at the onset of the nineteenth century still stretched across parts of three continents—from the Balkans to Basra, from Batoum to Benghazi. The decrepitude of the empire—together with the attempts of the Great Powers to deal with or exploit this condition—became known in the vocabulary of European diplomacy as the Eastern Question. In the first half of the nineteenth century, the three components of the Eastern Question were the search for an international legal regime for the Turkish Straits; the emergence of Greek and Balkan nationalisms; and the bid of Mohammed Ali Pasha of Egypt, the sultan's most important vassal, to topple his overlord.

GENERAL READING: M. S. Anderson, *The Eastern Question, 1774–1923* (London, 1966); Nina Athanas-soglou-Kallmyer, *French Images from the Greek War of Independence, 1820–30* (New Haven, 1989); Marie Bennigsen Broxup (ed.), *The North Caucasus Barrier: The Russian Advance towards the Muslim World* (New York, 1992); John Shelton Curtiss, *The Russian Army under Nicholas I, 1825–1855* (Durham, NC, 1965); Allan Cunningham, *Anglo-Ottoman Encounters in the Age of Revolution*, 2 vols. (London, 1993); Roderic H. Davison, "The Treaty of Kuchuk Kaynardja: A Note on its Italian Text," *International History Review* 10 (1988): 611–21; John H. Gleason, *The Genesis of Russophobia in Great Britain* (Cambridge, MA, 1950); J. C. Hurewitz (ed.), *The Middle East and North Africa in World Politics: A Documentary Record*, vol. 1: *European Expansion, 1535–1914* (New Haven, 1975); Edward Ingram, *Britain's Persian Connection, 1798–1828* (Oxford, 1993)

3.1   TREATY OF KUCHUK-KAINARJI, 10/21 JULY 1774

The peace of Kuchuk-Kainarji ended the third Russo-Ottoman war (1768–1774) of the eighteenth century and superseded all earlier treaties between the two countries (except for a convention on Azov concluded in 1700). Of immediate import were the clauses, not reproduced here, on the evacuation of occupied Ottoman territory in the Aegean and the Danubian Principalities, on the removal of the Crimea from direct Ottoman control, and on the unhindered access of Russian merchant vessels to the Black Sea, the Danube, and the Straits. But with the passage of time, these provisions were dwarfed by other features of the treaty. Relying on a broad interpretation of the articles excerpted below, Tsar Nicholas I (1825–1855) asserted that

[1] *Oeuvres de Frédéric le Grand* (Berlin, 1846–1857), 6:23–24.

the Russian government derived from the treaty a mandate for the protection of the Greek Orthodox church in the Ottoman Empire (cf. Documents 3.5c and 5.2b).

... Art. 7: The Sublime Porte [= Ottoman government] promises to protect constantly the Christian religion and its churches, and it also allows the Ministers of the Imperial Court of Russia to make, upon all occasions, representations, as well in favour of the new church at Constantinople, of which mention will be made in Article 14, as on behalf of its officiating ministers, promising to take such representations into due consideration, as being made by a confidential functionary of a neighbouring and sincerely friendly Power. . . .

Art. 14: After the manner of the other Powers, permission is given to the High Court of Russia, in addition to the chapel built in the Minister's residence, to erect in one of the quarters of Galata, in the street called Bey Oglu, a public church of the Greek ritual, which shall always be under the protection of the Ministers of that Empire, and secure from all coercion and outrage. . . .

Art. 16: The Empire of Russia restores to the Sublime Porte the whole of Bessarabia. . . . Similarly the Empire of Russia restores to the Sublime Porte the two Principalities of Wallachia and Moldavia, together with all the fortresses, cities, towns, villages, and all which they contain, and the Sublime Porte receives them upon the following conditions, solemnly promising to keep them religiously. . . .

2. To obstruct in no manner whatsoever the free exercise of the Christian religion, and to interpose no obstacle to the erection of new churches and to the repairing of the old ones, as has been done heretofore. . . .

10. The Porte likewise permits that, according as the circumstances of these two Principalities may require, the Ministers of the Imperial Court of Russia resident at Constantinople may remonstrate in their favour; and promises to listen to them with all the attention which is due to friendly and respected Powers.

Art. 17: The Empire of Russia restores to the Sublime Porte all the islands of the [Greek] Archipelago which are under its dependence, and the Sublime Porte, on its part, promises. . . .

2. That the Christian religion shall not be exposed to the least oppression any more than its churches, and that no obstacle shall be opposed to the erection or repair of them; and also that the officiating ministers shall neither be oppressed nor insulted. . . .

—PP 1854, 72:133–41 [French]; Hurewitz, 1:93–101

3.2   THE STRAITS QUESTION IN THE NAPOLEONIC ERA

Russo-Ottoman Secret Treaty, 23 December 1798/3 January 1799 • Secret Articles of Russo-Ottoman Treaty of 11/23 September 1805 • Anglo-Ottoman Treaty of Peace, 5 January 1809 • Russo-Ottoman Peace of Bucharest, 16/28 May 1812

Whether the Turkish Straits were to be open or closed to the passage of foreign warships is a problem best understood not in the abstract but in the overall context of the Eastern Question, first in the Napoleonic era and, subsequently, during the Egyptian crises of the 1830s (cf. Document 3.7).

The Russo-Ottoman treaty of 1799 was concluded against the background of Napoleon's invasion of Egypt and the Anglo-Austrian-Russian War of the Second Coalition against France. Its most visible result was the joint Russo-Turkish capture of the Ionian Islands[2] in March 1799. In a similar vein, the short-lived Russo-Turkish treaty of 1805 promoted the aims of the Third Coalition against Napoleon.

Between 1806 and 1809, the Near Eastern policies of the powers were anarchic: the Ottoman Empire found itself in a three-cornered war with Russia (as of December 1806) and Britain (as of January 1807). The Dardanelles treaty of 1809 restored peace between Britain and Turkey, but the Russo-Ottoman conflict continued until 1812, running parallel to the Anglo-Russian war of 1807–1812. Whether the Russo-Ottoman peace of 1812 did in fact refer to the Straits is best left for the reader to decide.

a)   *Russo-Ottoman Secret Treaty,*
23 December 1798/3 January 1799

Art. 3: . . . His Majesty the Emperor of All the Russias . . . promises that the passage of his fleet and the free communication of the warships from the Black Sea into the White [Marmara and/or Mediterranean] Sea via the Canal of Constantinople, as well as the return of the said fleet to the Russian ports of the Black Sea . . . may not establish the right or serve as a pretext for claiming future free passage of war vessels through the Canal . . .

—Hurewitz, 1:128–32

b)   *Secret Articles of Russo-Ottoman Treaty of*
11/23 September 1805

Art. 1: . . . the Sublime Porte shall for the duration of such a war [against France], facilitate the passage through the Canal of Constantinople of warships and military transports that his Majesty the Emperor may be obliged to send into the Mediterranean. . . .

Art. 4: . . . the Ottoman Porte, for the duration of the presence of Russian troops in the territory of the Septinsular Republic [of the Ionian Islands], shall facilitate the passage through the Canal of Constantinople of Russian warships destined to replace the naval forces in the said islands or to supply and relieve the troops stationed there. . . .

—Hurewitz, 1:165–67

[2]Retained by France in the Treaty of Campo Formio (October 1797); reorganized as a Russo-Ottoman condominium (the "Septinsular Republic") after 1799; restored to France by the 1807 Treaty of Tilsit; occupied by British forces after the conclusion of the Anglo-Ottoman peace of January 1809; British protectorate, 1814; incorporated into Greece, 1864. The Russian presence in the Ionian Islands from 1799 to 1807 justified the presence of a Russian fleet ("Senyavin's Squadron") in the Mediterranean.

c)   *Anglo-Ottoman Treaty of Peace, 5 January 1809*

. . . Art. 11: As ships of war have at all times been prohibited from entering the Canal of Constantinople, viz. in the Straits of the Dardanelles and of the Black Sea, and as the ancient regulation of the Ottoman Empire is in future to be observed by every Power in time of peace, the Court of Great Britain promises on its part to conform to this principle . . .

—Hurewitz, 1:189–91; Sir Robert Adair, *The Negotiations for the Peace of the Dardanelles in 1808–9* (London, 1845), 1:118–23

d)   *Russo-Ottoman Peace of Bucharest, 16/28 May 1812*

. . . Art. 3: . . . [W]ith the exception of those articles which, as a result of the passage of time, have suffered some change. . . [,] the two High Contracting Parties promise faithfully and solemnly to observe not only the present Treaty but all prior treaties. . . .

Art. 8: . . . the Sublime Porte shall, at the request of the Serbians, grant them the same advantages as those enjoyed by the subjects of the islands of the Archipelago[3] and other parts of their provinces and shall also give them a proof of its magnanimity in leaving to them the care of their country's internal administration. . . .

—Hurewitz, 1:194–97

3.3   THE EUROPEAN CONCERT REINVENTED: ST. PETERSBURG PROTOCOL AND TREATY OF LONDON

Anglo-Russian St. Petersburg Protocol, 4 April 1826 ●
Sultan Mahmud II to Mohammed Ali Pasha, May 1826 ●
Anglo-Russian-French Treaty of London, 6 July 1827

Canning's boast of December 1826 that he "called the New World into existence to redress the balance of the Old" (Document 2.7d) is the one phrase by which he is most likely to be remembered. Like all sound bites, this one too is misleading. For all of his public contempt for the European concert, Canning had begun to appreciate its uses in the Greek question. In the Greek war for independence, Canning, like Castlereagh before him (Document 2.5), feared the ever-present danger of Russia's intervention on behalf of its coreligionists against the Ottoman Empire.

By 1825, the Greek war had moved into a new stage: Mohammed Ali Pasha, the sultan's Egyptian vassal, had responded to his overlord's plea for help. After "pacifying" Cyprus, Crete, and the Cyclades, the Egyptian army contained the insurrection on the Peloponnesus (Morea). The most visible symbol of its success was the reduction of the Greek stronghold of Missolonghi and its submission in late April 1826.

---

[3]Cf. Treaty of Kuchuk-Kainarji, Art. 17 (Document 3.1).

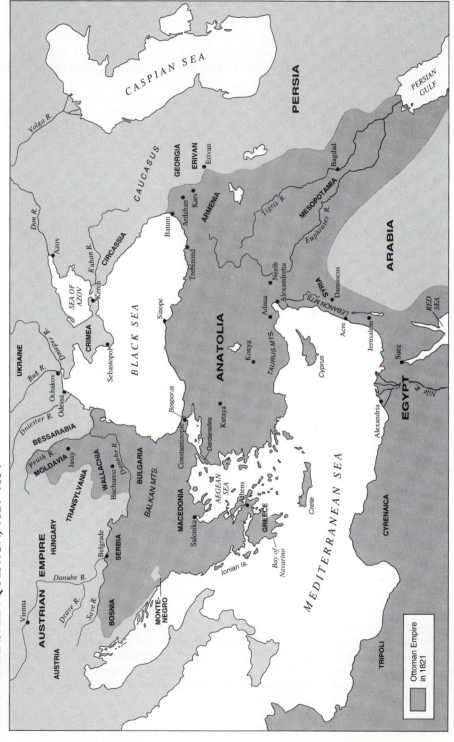

MAP 2   THE EASTERN QUESTION, 1821–1854

Ottoman Empire in 1821

The Egyptian victories again raised the question whether Russia would allow the Ottoman-Egyptian force to crush the insurrection or whether it would intervene on behalf of the Greeks. Canning found neither scenario particularly appealing: the suppression of the revolt would expose him to the wrath of the philhellene luminaries of the age, while an autonomous Greek entity established as the result of Russian intervention was likely to become a Russian outpost on the Mediterranean.

Tsar Nicholas I was less susceptible to the legitimist arguments that had persuaded his predecessor not to take up arms to assist the Greeks. But if Russia could no longer be expected to remain as passive as in former years, then Canning's objective was to chain Russia to a British go-slow policy, his method to propose an Anglo-Russian mediation. He seemed to have attained this goal with an Anglo-Russian protocol, signed in St. Petersburg shortly before the fall of Missolonghi. Upon closer inspection, however, the protocol proved defective—the wording of article 3 could be construed to preserve Russia's freedom of action after all. Canning managed to remedy this flaw in the trilateral Anglo-French-Russian Treaty of London, which came closer to his original aim. But there was a price: the Treaty of London contemplated military measures which, if ill defined, went further than anything stipulated by the St. Petersburg protocol. Canning did not live to see the consequences. Shortly after the conclusion of the Treaty of London on 6 July 1827, he succumbed to illness and died on 8 August 1827.

After Missolonghi, Sultan Mahmud II ignored the Anglo-Russian request to mediate the conflict. Instead, he sought to buy off Russia by affirming the special privileges of Moldavia, Wallachia, and Serbia in the Convention of Akkerman (September 1826).[4] With both the Greeks and the Great Powers seemingly at bay, Mahmud ordered the massacre of the Janissaries, whom he had identified as the principal obstacle to the modernization of the Ottoman Empire and who in 1808 had ended the reformist impulses of his predecessor, Selim III, by having him dethroned and strangled.

But Mahmud's delicate balancing act soon began to unravel. A combined English, French, and Russian fleet, enforcing the additional article of the Treaty of London, annihilated the Ottoman and Egyptian navies at Navarino on 20 October 1827. The Porte responded by denouncing the Convention of Akkerman. In so doing, it committed suicide for fear of death: a Russian declaration of war was now all but inevitable. The Russian army crossed the Danube in June 1828 and, by August of the following year, had moved within striking distance of Constantinople.

a)   *Anglo-Russian St. Petersburg Protocol, 4 April 1826*

. . . Art. 1: . . . the Greeks should enjoy a complete liberty of Conscience, entire freedom of Commerce, and should, exclusively, conduct their own internal Government. Greece should be a Dependency of that [Ottoman] Empire, and the Greeks should pay to the Porte an annual Tribute, the amount of which should be permanently fixed by common consent. They should be exclusively governed by authorities to be chosen and named by themselves, but in the nomination of which authorities the Porte should have a certain influence. In order to effect a complete separation between individuals of the two nations, and to prevent the collisions which must be the necessary consequences of a contest of such duration, the Greeks should purchase the Property of Turks. . . .

[4]Text in Hurst, 1:169–79.

Art. 3: If the Mediation offered by His Britannic Majesty should not have been accepted by the Porte, and whatever may be the nature of the relations between His Imperial Majesty [the Tsar] and the Turkish Government, His Britannic Majesty and His Imperial Majesty will still consider the terms of the Arrangement specified in Article 1 of this Protocol, as the basis of any reconciliation to be effected by their intervention, whether in concert or separately, between the Porte and the Greeks; and they will avail themselves of every favourable opportunity to exert their influence with both parties, in order to effect this reconciliation on the above-mentioned basis. . . .

—Hertslet, 1:741–43

b)   *Sultan Mahmud II to Mohammed Ali Pasha of Egypt,*
May 1826

. . . It is with the greatest joy that the Sultan learned the news of the taking of the fortress of Missolonghi, the stronghold of the rebels, which occurred after a fierce siege by land and by sea. . . . The 2,750 pairs of ears of the rebels killed in the battle of Missolonghi have been presented to the Sultan. The zeal displayed by Mohammed Ali Pasha in the suppression of the revolts of Crete and Peloponnesus has greatly pleased the Sultan, who will never forget the distinguished services rendered by him [Mohammed Ali] to the Empire and to Islam, and who as a sign of his heartfelt gratitude, sends him a ceremonial cloak of sable, embroidered with brocade, and a scimitar with a pommel of inlaid diamonds. . . .

—Haim Nahoum, *Recueil de firmans impériaux ottomans adressés
aux valis et aux khédives d'Égypte* (Cairo, 1934), 148

c)   *Anglo-Russian-French Treaty of London, 6 July 1827*

. . . Art. 5: The Contracting Powers will not seek, in these Arrangements, any augmentation of territory, any exclusive influence, or any commercial advantage for their subjects, which those of every other nation may not equally obtain. . . .

Additional Article: In case the Ottoman Porte should not, within the space of one month, accept the Mediation which is to be proposed to it, the High Contracting Parties agree upon the following measures:

I.   . . . the High Contracting Parties . . . shall . . . [establish] commercial relations with the Greeks, and . . . [send] to and [receive] from them, for this purpose, Consular Agents, provided there shall exist in Greece authorities capable of supporting such relations.

II.   If, within the said term of one month, the Porte does not accept the Armistice proposed . . . or if the Greeks refuse to carry it into execution, the High Contracting Powers shall declare to either of the Contending Parties which may be disposed to continue hostilities, or to both of them, if necessary, that the said High Powers intend to exert all the means which circumstances may suggest to their prudence, for the purpose of obtaining the immediate effects of the Armistice of which they desire the execution, by preventing, as far as possible, all collision between the Contending

Parties, and in consequence, immediately after the above-mentioned declaration, the High Powers will, jointly, exert all their efforts to accomplish the object of such Armistice, without, however, taking any part in the hostilities between the Two Contending Parties. . . . [T]he High Contracting Powers will, consequently, transmit to the Admirals commanding their respective squadrons in the Levant conditional Instructions in conformity to the arrangements above declared.

 III. Finally, if, contrary to all expectation, these measures do not prove sufficient . . . the High Contracting Powers will . . . discuss and determine the future measures which it may become necessary to employ. . . .

—Hertslet, 1:769–76

3.4   POLIGNAC'S SCHEME

Polignac to Mortemart, September 1829

One of the wildest schemes for the wholesale revision of the 1815 settlement was hatched by the Duc de Polignac in the course of the Russo-Turkish war of 1828–1829. Appointed to head a cabinet of ultraroyalists in August 1829, Polignac hoped to deflect the increasing unpopularity of his sovereign by scoring a success in foreign policy. Polignac's ministry took office just as Russia's army had moved within striking distance of Constantinople, a development that seemed to presage the unraveling of the Ottoman Empire and thus presented an opportunity of the first order for France. France could exact a high price for its support of Russia in the destruction of the Ottoman Empire: just as in 1807, a Franco-Russian alliance might rearrange the map of Europe. This expectation was dashed with the Russian decision in favor of a lenient peace (cf. Document 3.5). Polignac, however, continued his search for a *coup de théâtre*. His first impulse was to sponsor an Egyptian invasion of Algiers. When this overture was turned aside by Mohammed Ali, Polignac dispatched a French expedition instead, thereby inaugurating the French colonization of the Maghreb.

Polignac to Mortemart,[5] September 1829

. . . Once the Turkish Empire has been destroyed in Europe, no cabinet [in Europe] could even consider reestablishing it. . . . In a reorganization combined with the resulting dismemberment of the Ottoman Empire, France wants for its part the Belgian provinces of Holland up to the Meuse-Rhine line, and to recover in Alsace the border taken away in 1815. Russia will surely be interested in our acquiring what will give us new means to resist the ascendancy of a neighboring power which is of no less concern to it than to ourselves.

 If Saxony is given up to Prussia, the preservation of the principles of legitimacy, the kind of solidarity that exists between the ruling houses, and the dignity of the king demand that the prince who rules in Dresden will receive compensation elsewhere: the Prussian provinces situated between the Rhine and the Meuse, set up as a kingdom, can furnish it. Some section of this territory that is more extended and populated than that of Saxony will be detached for Bavaria.

---

[5]Casimir, Duc de Mortemart (1787–1875). French ambassador in St. Petersburg, 1828–1830; 1831–1833.

Prussia would find a rich compensation for this cession in obtaining for itself the Dutch provinces from the North Sea up to the Rhine: this acquisition would make it a maritime power, which should correspond equally with the views of France and Russia.

The Dutch colonies could be assigned in this arrangement to England, as at least part of its share. The king of the Low Countries will go to rule at Constantinople; his empire would be formed of the Turkish possessions in Europe; one would detach from it cessions to make to Russia, the same as with Serbia and Bosnia which would be given to Austria to serve as a counterweight to the new acquisitions of its powerful neighbor.

The Russian acquisitions could consist, in Europe, of Wallachia and Moldavia. This power would increase its territory in Asia as well: in this area rather than in Europe it would be important to invite [Russia] to expand.

Without claiming that these bases of an arrangement be exactly those which ought to be adopted . . . one should seek as much as possible to reach agreement on them. . . . The king will have, within three months, if necessary, an army of more than 200,000 men available to enforce his rights or to guarantee the execution of the arrangements to which he has consented.

It should not be necessary to remind Your Highness that this dispatch is completely confidential. It is best that you keep it completely to yourself, and not file it in the embassy archives, so that no trace of it exists in Russia and you may discuss it with me yourself after your return to France. . . .

—Theodor Schiemann, *Geschichte Russlands unter Kaiser Nikolaus I.* (Berlin, 1908), 2:511–19

3.5   **PEACE OF ADRIANOPLE**

Report of the Tsar's Special Committee on the Affairs of Turkey,
4/16 September 1829 ● *Treaty of Adrianople, 2/14 September 1829*

Russian armies had never before penetrated as far into the Ottoman Empire as during the Russo-Turkish war of 1828–1829. When peace was finally concluded at Adrianople, they were within striking distance of the capital of the Ottoman state. Yet the peace was remarkably lenient. Its provisions pertaining to the Danubian principalities, Serbia, Greece, and the Caucasus are excerpted below. The clauses on the Caucasus rounded out Russian gains made at the expense of Persia in the far harsher Peace of Turkmanchai (February 1828).[6] At Turkmanchai, Persia ceded Armenia, agreed to the exclusion from the Caspian of all warships other than Russian, and accepted a commercial treaty granting extraterritoriality to Russian subjects in Persia. The cumulative effect of both treaties, Turkmanchai and Adrianople, was to transform what had been a patchwork of Russian possessions and client states in the Caucasus into a contiguous whole, but Russian armies spent another decade and a half "pacifying" the newly acquired mountaineer populations, many of which—such as Circassians, Chechens, and Abkhazians—were Muslim.

The terms of the Peace of Adrianople flowed logically from recommendations made to Tsar Nicholas by a special committee on the future of the Ottoman Empire, which included the Russian foreign minister, Count Charles Robert Nesselrode.

[6]Text in Hurewitz, 1:231–37. For the 1813 Treaty of Gulistan, see ibid., 197–99.

MAP 3   THE TURKISH STRAITS

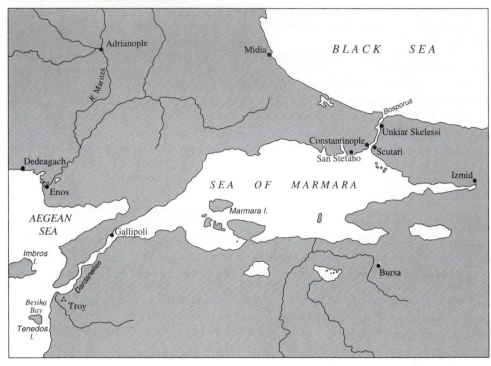

a)   Report of the Tsar's Special Committee on the Affairs of Turkey, 4/16 September 1829

. . . the committee recognizes: that the advantages of the maintenance of the Ottoman Empire in Europe are superior to the disadvantages which it presents; that its fall consequently would be contrary to the true interests of Russia. . . . In case a revolution in Constantinople would result in either the ascent to the throne of one of the sons of the Sultan and the establishment of a regency or a change in dynasty, the Committee is of the opinion that neither one nor the other of these events would be contrary to Russia's interests, as [either] would prolong the existence of the Ottoman Empire, and it could even become favorable to us in placing on the throne a Sovereign less opinionated than the Sultan Mahmud, and one less an enemy of the Russian government. . . . And if on the other hand revolution should break out in Constantinople and lead to a general upheaval, of which the consequence will be confusion and anarchy in the capital as well as in the provinces, such an event can only be seen as the signal for the fall of the Ottoman Empire. If this catastrophe, which we have consciously sought to prevent by every means within our power, actually occurs, as in the event that the Sultan, having fled to Asia, continues to resist our propositions and to divest himself [*se dépouilleroit*] of his European states, it would become vital to adopt certain provisional arrangements. . . .

1. that European Turkey be militarily occupied by Russian armies, in such a way that the fate of the lands that make it up not be definitively determined;
2. that this occupation be of a particularly imposing nature;
3. that to this effect Constantinople, the castles of the Bosporus, and those of the Dardanelles have Russian garrisons. . . .
7. As to the diplomatic course to follow, the Committee recognized that it would be contrary to all the principles of a sane policy, to fix arbitrarily and without the agreement of the principal Powers, the order of things that ought to replace the Ottoman Empire in Europe. . . .

> —Robert J. Kerner, "Russia's New Policy in the Near East after the Peace of Adrianople; Including the Text of the Protocol of 16 September 1829," *Cambridge Historical Journal* 5 (1937): 280–90

b)   *Treaty of Adrianople, 2/14 September 1829*

. . . Art. 4: . . . [T]he two High Contracting Powers have. . . taken into consideration the necessary means for opposing insurmountable obstacles to the incursions and depredations which, up to the present time, have been practised by the frontier tribes, and which have so often compromised the relations of amity and good fellowship between the two Empires. . . . [T]hose [territories] which are situated to the north and east of the said line, towards Georgia, Imeritia, and Gouriel, as well as the whole of the coast of the Black Sea, from the south of the Kuban as far as the port of St. Nicholas inclusively, shall remain in perpetuity under the dominion of the Empire of Russia. . . .

Art. 5: The Principalities of Moldavia and Wallachia . . . shall preserve all the privileges and immunities which have been granted to them either by their Capitulations, or by the Treaties concluded between the two Empires, or by the Hatt-i-Sherifs promulgated at different times. In consequence whereof, they shall enjoy the free exercise of their Worship, perfect security, an independent national Government, and full liberty of Commerce. . . .

Art. 8: . . . The Sublime Porte, by way of reparation for these losses and injuries, shall pay to the Imperial Court of Russia, within the course of 18 months, at periods which shall hereafter be agreed upon, the sum of 1,500,000 ducats of Holland. . . .

Art. 9: The prolongation of the War to which the present Treaty of Peace happily puts an end, having occasioned the Imperial Court considerable expenses, the Sublime Porte acknowledges the necessity of offering it a suitable indemnification. . . .

Art. 10: In declaring its entire adhesion to the stipulations of the Treaty concluded at London on the 24th June/6th July, 1827, between Russia, Great Britain, and France, the Sublime Porte equally accedes to the Act entered into on the 10th/22nd of March, 1829. . . .[7]

[Separate Act #2:] Art. 3: . . . In consequence of this stipulation [Art. 9 above], it is agreed and determined that the said Indemnity shall be fixed at 10,000,000 of ducats of Holland. . . . [T]he Imperial Court of Russia shall consent to receive on account of the sum above mentioned compensations in kind. . . .

> —Hertslet, 2:814–31; Hurst, 1:188–203

[7]Cf. Document 3.6.

3.6   **SETTLEMENT OF THE GREEK QUESTION**

London Protocol, 22 March 1829 • *London Protocol, 3 February 1830*

In article 10 of the Treaty of Adrianople, the Porte accepted the recommendations of the Anglo-French-Russian London Protocol of 22 March 1829 for ending the Greek insurgency. These, however, were remarkably vague about the legal status of the new Greek entity. The protocol repeatedly referred to the Greek "state," but also stipulated that this "state" should remain tributary to the Porte. A new protocol, drawn up almost a year later, was far more definitive. Its provisions, moreover, aimed to prevent Greece from becoming a satellite of any of the three signatories. In keeping with article 3, the powers offered the Greek throne to Otto of Bavaria (a payback of sorts for the outspoken philhellenism of his father, Ludwig I). When this first reign in the turbulent history of the modern Greek monarchy ended in failure, the three powers installed a Danish line in 1863.[8]

Of the Aegean islands, only the Cyclades were included in the new Greek state, and the Greek population of the Ottoman Empire by far outnumbered the Greek population of Greece itself. On the other hand, Greece—as a result of its territorial expansion of 1881 and 1912–1913—acquired a sizable Muslim population, most of which was transferred to Turkey after the Greco-Turkish war of 1921–1923. A small Muslim minority remains to this day in Eastern Thrace.

a)   ***London Protocol, 22 March 1829***

. . . All the provinces situated south of that line [Arta-Volo] shall be comprised in the new Greek State. . . . It shall be proposed to the Ottoman Porte, in the name of the three Courts, that the Greeks shall pay to it an annual Tribute. . . .

—Hertslet, 2:804–7

b)   ***London Protocol, 3 February 1830***

Art. 1: Greece shall form an independent state, and shall enjoy all rights, political, administrative, and commercial attached to complete independence. . . .

Art. 3: The Greek government shall be monarchical, and hereditary according to the order of primogeniture. It shall be confided to a Prince, who shall not be capable of being chosen from among those families reigning in the States that signed the Treaty of the 6th July, 1827, and shall bear the title of Sovereign Prince of Greece. . . .

Art. 5: . . . The Act of amnesty by the Porte shall proclaim, that no Greek in the whole extent of its dominions shall be liable to be deprived of his property, or in any way disturbed, in consequence of the part which he may have taken in the insurrection of Greece. The Act of amnesty of the Greek government shall proclaim the

[8]Anglo-French-Russian treaty with Bavaria of 7 May 1832 in Hertslet, 2:893; Anglo-French-Russian treaty with Denmark of 13 July 1863 in Hertslet, 2:1539, 1563–64; Hurst, 1:410–13.

same principle in favor of all the Mussulmans or Christians who may have taken part against its cause; . . . Mussulmans who may be desirous of continuing to inhabit the territories and islands allotted to Greece, shall preserve their properties therein, and invariably enjoy, with their families, perfect security. . . .

Art. 8: . . . No troops belonging to one of the Contracting Powers shall be allowed to enter the territory of the new Greek State, without the consent of the two other Courts who signed the Treaty [of 6 July 1827]. . . .

—Augustus Oakes and R. B. Mowat (eds.), *The Great European Treaties of the Nineteenth Century* (Oxford, 1921), 120–23

3.7   THE STRAITS QUESTION, 1833–1838

Treaty of Unkiar-Skelessi, 26 June/8 July 1833 ● *Austro-Russian Convention of Münchengrätz, 18 September 1833* ● *Palmerston to William Temple, 7 October 1833* ● *Nesselrode on the Regime of the Straits, 16/28 January 1838* ● *Churchill and Stalin at the Potsdam Conference, 22 July 1945*

Preoccupied with franchise reform at home, the Portuguese civil war, and the Belgian revolution, Britain was caught off guard when Mohammed Ali attacked the sultan in 1832. After the Egyptian victory at Koniah in Asia Minor, the road to Constantinople essentially lay open to Mohammed Ali's army. Only Russia offered military assistance to the endangered Ottoman dynasty: it disembarked fifteen thousand troops on the Asiatic side of the Bosporus in April 1833 and succeeded in negotiating the Treaty of Unkiar-Skelessi before returning this force to Russia in July. The Austro-Russian convention of Münchengrätz (September 1833) reflected continuing Russian anxiety over the threat posed by Mohammed Ali and sought to anticipate a range of contingencies. While Palmerston, British foreign secretary since 1830, knew the text of Unkiar-Skelessi, he had only a vague notion of what had come to pass at Münchengrätz. Nonetheless, he was quick to impute to Russia the most sinister motives.

Translated into political shorthand, the term "closure of the Straits" stood for the British desire to deny Russian warships access to the Mediterranean. Beginning in the 1820s, British statesmen were prone to ascribe to Russia a single-minded drive to obtain warm-water ports. They argued that Ottoman entanglements during the Napoleonic wars (cf. Document 3.2) and during the Mohammed Ali crises of the 1830s were exploited by Russia to strengthen its legal position in the Straits. The reality may have been more complex. The fact that the Peace of Bucharest did not refer to the Straits can be attributed to Russia's desire to extricate itself from its war with the Ottoman Empire in order to face Napoleon. In concluding the Treaty of Adrianople (cf. Document 3.5), however, Russia was under no such constraint. Nor did the Treaty of Unkiar-Skelessi, except in the separate article quoted below, refer to the Straits.

Russian policy, like that of all powers, depended on who or which faction was in charge at what moment in time. As evinced by the treaties of Unkiar-Skelessi and Münchengrätz, Nesselrode preferred a subtle approach. Certainly he was well aware of the advantages offered by the status quo: the closure of the Straits, by also barring the British navy from the Black Sea, offered Russia a modicum of security along its southern coastline. That Palmerston was not alone in—willfully?—misinterpreting Nesselrode's diplomacy or Russia's legal rights is evident from the last excerpt below.

a)   Treaty of Unkiar-Skelessi, 26 June/8 July 1833

. . . Art. 3: In consequence of the principle of conservation and mutual defence, which is the basis of the present Treaty of Alliance, and by reason of a most sincere desire of securing the permanence, maintenance, and entire Independence of the Sublime Porte, His Majesty the Emperor of All the Russias, in the event of circumstances occurring which should again determine the Sublime Porte to call for the naval and military assistance of Russia, although, if it please God, that case is by no means likely to happen, engages to furnish, by land and by sea, as many troops and forces as the two High Contracting Parties may deem necessary. It is accordingly agreed, that in this case the Land and Sea Forces, whose aid the Sublime Porte may call for, shall be held at its disposal. . . .

Art. 5: . . . it has been agreed to fix its [the Treaty's] duration at 8 years from the day of the exchange of the Imperial Ratifications. . . .

[Separate Article:] . . . [T]he Sublime Ottoman Porte, in place of the aid which it is bound to furnish [to Russia] in case of need, according to the principle of reciprocity of the Patent Treaty, shall confine its action in favour of the Imperial Court of Russia to closing the Strait of the Dardanelles, that is to say, to not allowing any Foreign Vessels of War to enter therein under any pretext whatsoever.

—Hertslet, 2:925–28; Hurewitz, 1:252–53; Hurst, 1:225–28

b)   Austro-Russian Convention of Münchengrätz,
18 September 1833

. . . Art. 2: . . . the two Imperial Courts undertake to oppose in common any combination affecting the independence of sovereign authority in Turkey, whether by the establishment of a provisional regency, or by a complete change of dynasty. If either of these situations should occur, the two High Contracting Parties will not only refuse to recognize such an order of things but will also consult immediately. . . .

[Separate and Secret Articles:] 1. The High Contracting Parties intend to apply specifically to the Pasha of Egypt the stipulations of Article 2 of today's Convention, and they undertake in common expressly to prevent the authority of the Pasha of Egypt from extending, directly or indirectly, to the European provinces of the Ottoman Empire. . . .

—Hurewitz, 1:254–55

c)   Palmerston to William Temple,[9] 7 October 1833

. . . What have been the subjects of discussion at . . . Münchengrätz seems [sic] to be gradually getting out. . . . An eventual partition of Turkey between Austria and Russia

---

[9]William Temple (1788–1856). Palmerston's younger brother; British minister to Naples, 1833–1856.

is thought to be one of the topics; and this seems to me very probable. It is needless to say that England and France would oppose this to the utmost of their means, and I think we should be able, with the assistance of Mohammed Ali, to offer a strong barrier against the accomplishment of this project. . . .

—Bourne, 221–23; Henry Lytton Bulwer, *The Life of Henry John Temple, Viscount Palmerston* (London, 1870–1874), 2:169–70

d)   **Nesselrode on the Regime of the Straits, 16/28 January 1838**

. . . [W]e should not, as I have already observed, have any positive right to insist on this passage [of Russian naval vessels through the Straits]. In refusing our demand the Porte would base its action on the [principle of] strict execution of the treaties. It would be legally within its rights. We would have no basis for objecting to its refusal. But, however circumspectly [the Porte's refusal] might be phrased, it is no less true that in the eyes of Europe such a refusal would injure Russia's dignity. We should suffer a double disadvantage: on the one hand, perceptible injury would have been done to our influence; on the other hand, a grievance would have been created and a motive provoked for a misunderstanding that could not fail to react in a trying manner on our direct relations with Turkey.

In the second case, admitting that the Sultan grants us passage, England and France in their turn would rapidly seize this pretext to demand the Porte's permission to send several warships into the Black Sea. England would profit more from this circumstance. . . .

. . . Assuming, on the other hand, that the Sultan, ceding to the maritime powers, might grant them passage, we should be destroying with our own hands the barrier that constitutes our security; we should be losing an ally faithful until now and we should hand Turkey over to the influence of England and France. . . . [T]o maintain instead of destroying this political and moral barrier that the Dardanelles establishes between us and the maritime powers in the Orient seems to be a faithful expression of the thought and wishes of Your Majesty. . . .

—Hurewitz, 1:262–65; Philip E. Mosely, *Russian Diplomacy and the Opening of the Eastern Question in 1838 and 1839* (Cambridge, MA, 1934), 141–47 [French]

e)   **Churchill and Stalin at the Potsdam Conference, 22 July 1945**

. . . [Churchill:] . . . Quite a different question is raised when Russia asks for a military base and asks that no powers be permitted to participate in the control of the Straits but Russia and Turkey. I am quite certain that Turkey will never agree to this.

[Stalin:] Similar treaties existed between Turkey and Russia at other times.

[Churchill:] What times do you refer to?

[Stalin:] In 1805 and 1833. . . .

—Foreign Relations of the United States: The Conference of Berlin, 1945 (Washington, 1960), 2:267

3.8   TO THE BRINK OF EUROPEAN WAR AND BACK: THE SECOND MOHAMMED ALI CRISIS, 1838–1841

Anglo-Ottoman Commercial Treaty (Balta Liman), 16 August 1838 • Helmuth von Moltke on the Battle of Nesib, 12 July 1839 • Thiers's Draft for Louis Philippe's Opening of the Chamber, 8 October 1840 • Précis of a Conversation between Louis Philippe and Thiers, 15 October 1840 • Thiers in the French Chamber, 27 November 1840 • Five-Power ("Straits") Convention with the Ottoman Empire, 13 July 1841

Sultan Mahmud II regarded the Convention of Kutaiah (May 1833)—in which he bestowed Syria plus the right to collect taxes in Adana in Asia Minor on Mohammed Ali—as no more than a cease-fire with his unruly vassal. By 1839, Mahmud resumed the war, perhaps in the belief that the ongoing contest with Mohammed Ali interfered with his program for modernizing the Ottoman Empire, perhaps because he expected the backing of the European powers in a renewed showdown with the pasha. But he overestimated his resources: at Nesib on the Euphrates, Mohammed Ali's son Ibrahim inflicted a devastating defeat on the Ottoman forces. Adding to the catastrophe, the Ottoman fleet deserted to Alexandria.

Nonetheless, Mahmud may have calculated correctly in his anticipation of British support. Still suspicious of the Treaty of Unkiar-Skelessi, Palmerston welcomed any opportunity to shoulder Russia aside in Constantinople. Moreover, the British government had just concluded a highly favorable commercial treaty with the Ottoman Empire. An Ottoman victory would bring about its implementation in Egypt and henceforth the dismantling of the Egyptian state monopolies, incompatible with the treaty, that Mohammed Ali had set up in the 1820s.

The liberal ministry of Adolphe Thiers in France saw things rather differently. Thiers regarded Egypt as an outpost of French influence, perhaps even as a complement in the eastern Mediterranean to the French presence in Algeria. Confident of an Egyptian victory after the battle of Nesib, Thiers hoped to expand French influence by siding with Mohammed Ali. He thus refused to join the other Great Powers in their collective stand against the pasha, which they articulated in the Treaty of London (July 1840) and its annexes. In article 3, the signatories pledged unspecified "measures" against Mohammed Ali; in article 4, they committed themselves to "the ancient rule of the Ottoman Empire, in virtue of which it has in all times been prohibited for Ships of War of Foreign Powers to enter the Straits of the Dardanelles and of the Bosporus."[10] At the heart of the treaty, however, lay a graduated ultimatum: if Mohammed Ali accepted within ten days, the sultan would invest him and, thereafter, his male descendants with Egypt and Acre. After the tenth day, Acre was no longer part of the offer; after the twentieth day, the offer would be withdrawn altogether.

With his troops enjoying the battlefield advantage and the Thiers ministry ready to take up the cudgels on his behalf, Mohammed Ali saw no reason to comply. But when British agents reignited the Druze revolt against Egyptian rule in the Lebanon mountains and the British navy landed English and Austrian marines behind Egyptian lines, the Egyptian position became untenable. Ibrahim bowed to military necessity and ordered the evacuation of Syria.

Thiers had insinuated that he was prepared to risk a European war in support of Mohammed Ali. This calculation only made sense if Mohammed Ali could hold his own, thereby compelling the other powers to divide their forces between a Middle Eastern and a European theater of war. But the Egyptian withdrawal from Syria made this expectation illusory. It also sealed the fate of his ministry: Louis Philippe, unwilling to back a cause so

---

[10]Text, with annexes, in Hurst, 1:252–58; Hurewitz, 1:271–75; *CTS*, 90:285ff.

uncertain of success, refused to deliver the address for the opening of the French chamber which Thiers had composed for him. Unable to carry the king, Thiers resigned and preferred to salvage his reputation with a fiery speech from the floor of the chamber.

The fall of Thiers and the return of a more conciliatory ministry under François Guizot allowed France to rejoin the European concert. Its climb-down was rewarded by its accession to the Treaty of London, now renamed the Straits Convention of 1841.

a)   *Anglo-Ottoman Commercial Treaty (Balta Liman),* *16 August 1838*

Art. 1: All rights, privileges, and immunities which have been conferred on the subjects or ships of Great Britain by the existing Capitulations and Treaties, are confirmed now and forever, except in as far as they may be specifically altered by the present Convention: and it is moreover expressly stipulated, that all rights, privileges, or immunities which the Sublime Porte now grants, or may hereafter grant to the ships and subjects of any other foreign power, or which may suffer the ships and subjects of any other foreign power to enjoy, shall be equally granted to, and exercised and enjoyed by, the subjects and ships of Great Britain.

Art. 2: . . . the Sublime Porte formally engages to abolish all monopolies of agricultural produce, or of any articles whatsoever, as well as *Permits* from the local Governors. . . . [A]ny attempt to compel the subjects of Her Britannic Majesty to receive such *Permits* from the local Governors, shall be considered an infraction of Treaties. . . .

Art. 6: It is agreed by the Turkish Government, that the regulations established in the present Convention shall be general throughout the Turkish Empire, whether Turkey in Europe or Turkey in Asia, in Egypt, or other African possessions belonging to the Sublime Porte, and shall be applicable to all the subjects, whatever their description, of the Ottoman dominions: and the Turkish Government also agrees not to object to other foreign Powers settling their trade upon the basis of this present Convention.

—*PP 1839*, 50:291–95; Hurewitz, 1:265–66

b)   *Helmuth von Moltke*[11] *on the Battle of Nesib, 12 July 1839*

. . . Since the Convention of Kutaiah, the weapons had fallen silent in these lands. All [outside] parties determinedly requested the Porte and Mohammed Ali to content themselves with the existing status quo—without reflecting on whether this state of affairs was tenable or durable or whether in the long run it would not ruin both. Similar to the manner in which two substances in chemistry can neutralize one another, all of Turkey's strength was absorbed by Egypt; all of Egypt's by Turkey; and both states [sic] were brought to the brink of ruin. The Danube, Schumla, Constantinople

[11]Helmuth von Moltke (1800–1891) left the Danish for the Prussian army in 1822. Prussian military adviser in the Ottoman Empire, 1836–1839; chief of the Prussian general staff, 1858–1888.

were without defenders; Alexandria and Cairo were manned by invalids—while in a remote corner of Kurdistan and Syria mighty armies confronted one another. All large concentrations of men are unnatural: in civilized countries they are difficult and costly, in countries such as these, murderous and, in the long run, insufferable. The pressure under which these unfortunate provinces labored for years was terrible, but the whole empire sighed under the burden of having to maintain a large army in far-away regions for no reason except that a powerful neighbor also had an army in the field there. In seven years, at least fifty thousand men were recruited and buried here, a hundred million [piasters?] were wasted unproductively and the harvest of entire provinces was consumed only because the opponent did the same. . . . There can be no question that Sultan Mahmud was irrevocably determined to put an end to these conditions by going to war: large new sacrifices were made, no expenditure was too much, decorations and promotions were lavishly doled out, the strength of the units was forcibly increased, the artillery was reequipped, stocks were replenished, and each demand of the commanding general complied with. To mollify the European embassies, [the Porte] in the meantime officially assured them of its peaceful intentions. . . . indeed I think that in Europe no one had a real understanding of the true situation. . . .

—Helmuth von Moltke, *Briefe über Zustände und Begebenheiten in der Türkei aus den Jahren 1835 bis 1839* (1841; reprint, Cologne, 1968)

c)   *Thiers's Draft for Louis Philippe's Opening of the Chamber, 8 October 1840*

Just as the last session [of the assembly] was finishing, a treaty was signed between the Ottoman Porte, England, Austria, Prussia, and Russia to settle the differences between the sultan and the viceroy of Egypt. This important act, done without the participation of France, could in its execution lead to dangerous consequences. France should anticipate these and prepare itself to face all eventualities. My government has taken as its responsibility all measures authorized by the law that this new situation requires. France, which continues sincerely to hope for peace, remains faithful to the policy which you have more than once supported with striking approval. Zealous of assuring the independence and the integrity of the Ottoman Empire, she believes these goals reconcilable with the existence of the viceroy of Egypt, himself having become one of the necessary elements of the power of that empire. It is in balancing all rights, in respecting all interests, that one can set up in the Orient the bases of a lasting arrangement. But the events which are developing could lead to the gravest consequences. The measures taken up to this point by my government thus can no longer suffice. They thus must be completed by new measures, for which the agreement of the two Chambers was necessary. I was obliged to convoke them. They will think as do I that France, which has not been the first to consign the peace of the world to the fortune of arms, should hold itself ready to act the day that she believes the European equilibrium to be seriously threatened. . . . Gentlemen, I want to count more than ever on your patriotic support. You want France to be strong and great, as do I. No sacrifice will be too dear to keep it where it belongs in the world. It does not want to decline. France is strongly attached to peace, but will not buy it at a price unworthy of itself; and your king, who has staked his glory on preserving it [France's place] in the world, wishes to leave intact to his son this sacred trust of independence and national honor that the French revolution has placed in his hands.

—Charles de Rémusat, *Mémoires de ma vie* (Paris, 1858–1867), 3:482–84

d) *Précis of a Conversation between Louis Philippe and Thiers, 15 October 1840*

[Louis Philippe:] . . . When I built up our armaments, I had hoped to frighten off England; but today I see that my arms have not had that effect on Lord Palmerston. On the contrary, I believe that he wants war. My role, therefore, is to step back, to halt my armaments, because, I repeat, at all costs do I want to avoid war. I would rather suffer any fate than to arrive at that extreme.

[Thiers:] But, Sire, you most certainly will not allow France to be humiliated!

[Louis Philippe:] France be humiliated! My dear minister, that's the language of the newspapers. All right, I have such a horror of war that I would rather suffer anything than to reach that point. . . . You don't know this country; in its heart of hearts, it doesn't want war and if we undertake one, we will all be lost: you, me, my children, my family, my wife, your wife, your mother-in-law!

[Thiers:] But, Sire, consider also the internal dangers if you adopt this course.

[Louis Philippe:] I know—you are going to tell me, aren't you, that someone will take a shot at me. . . . All right! Providence has spared me five times, it will spare me again. And anyway, I would rather meet my end that way than at the hands of a foreigner. . . .

—Henri Malo (ed.), *Mémoires de Madame* [Eurydice] *Dosne* (Paris, 1928), 1:215

e)   *Thiers in the French Chamber, 27 November 1840*

. . . Gentlemen, the word "war" is a terrible one to utter; and as a man who has been active in his country's politics and who may still be called back to them, even though not desiring it, I would never have uttered this terrible word "war" had the situation not been extremely grave. Europe had believed that we would allow the treaty to be executed in its entirety [commotion]. The English minister had said that France, after having shown its ill disposition, would shut itself up and accede [lively exclamations].

Let them condemn me, let them exclude me from power forever, I resign myself to that voluntarily; but, when I see my country thus humiliated, I cannot contain the feelings that oppress me, and I cry out: "Whatever happens, let us know ourselves to be the men our fathers were, and let us ensure that France does not descend from the rank that it has always occupied in Europe" [lively support from the left; prolonged acclamation].

—Adolphe Thiers, *Discours parlementaires*, ed. Calmon (Paris, 1879), 5:297

f)   *Five-Power ("Straits") Convention with the Ottoman Empire, 13 July 1841*

Art. 1: His Highness the Sultan, on the one part, declares that he is firmly resolved to maintain for the future the principle invariably established as the ancient rule of his Empire, and in virtue of which it has at all times been prohibited for the Ships of War of Foreign Powers to enter the Straits of the Dardanelles and of the Bosporus; and that, so long as the Porte is at Peace, His Highness will admit no Foreign Ships of War into the said Straits. And their Majesties [of Britain, Austria, the French, Prussia, and Russia] . . . , on the other part, engage to respect this determination of the Sultan, and to conform themselves to the principle above declared. . . .

—Hertslet, 2:1024–26; Hurst, 1:259–61

3.9   AFTERMATH OF THE 1840 CRISIS: THE REBIRTH OF GERMAN NATIONALISM

Bourgoing to Guizot, 27 June 1841 •
Hoffmann's "Song of the Germans," 28 August 1841

Thiers's apparent willingness to provoke a European crisis and the combative tone of the Paris press unleashed in the German states a storm of popular indignation against France. If there had indeed been a war, much of the fighting would have taken place along the Rhine or in the Rhineland, and so this river became a metaphor for Germanness and for resistance to France. The song "The German Rhine" by Nikolaus Becker, a law clerk from Bonn, with its refrain "they shall not have it, the free German Rhine," summarized the passions of the day. It inspired a flood of similar exertions, though some authors had the temerity to point out that the Rhine, while German, was not necessarily free. The war of words was fanned further by the eagerness with which French poets took up the cudgels for their homeland: of particular note was an effort by Alfred de Musset, leading off with the inflammatory *"nous l'avons eu, votre Rhin allemand"* (which could be loosely rendered as "we have enjoyed its favors, your German Rhine").

Amidst the general outpouring of sentiment, Heinrich Hoffmann penned his "Song of the Germans." Like the Austrian anthem, it was set to Joseph Haydn's melancholy "Emperor Quartet." Though embraced by the public, the "Song of the Germans" did not become the national anthem until 1922 (the third stanza, not reproduced here, still serves this purpose); the Prussian anthem continued to be "Hail to Thee in the Victor's Laurels" to the tune of "God Save the King" (or, for that matter, "America").

a)   *Bourgoing[12] to Guizot, 27 June 1841*

. . . For nearly 50 years we have been singing the Marseillaise and have been inspired to great deeds. The Germans, on the other hand, need to consolidate a national spirit

---

[12]Paul de Bourgoing (1791–1864). French minister in Munich, 1835–1848.

which is only of a recent vintage, and nothing tends more to unite them against us than those threats and injuries which we direct to the people of Germany and through which we sanction anew the pretension towards national unity. . . . The creation of a Germanic nationality is one of the most important facts of our century. . . .

—Anton Chroust (ed.), *Gesandtschaftsberichte aus München* (1935–1951),
1st Series: *Berichte der französischen Gesandten, 1816–48*, 4:255–57

b) Heinrich Hoffmann's[13] "Song of the Germans," 28 August 1841

Deutschland, Deutschland über alles,	Germany, Germany above everything,
über alles in der Welt,	above everything in the world
wenn es stets zum Schutz und Trutze	whenever, to protect and defy,
brüderlich zusammenhält,	it sticks together, brotherly,
von der Maas bis an die Memel	from the Meuse to the Njemen
von der Etsch bis an den Belt—	from the Adige to [Jutland] Sound—
Deutschland, Deutschland etc. . . .	Germany, Germany etc. . . .

3.10 PALMERSTON ON THE PURPOSES OF BRITISH POLICY

*Urquhart in the House of Commons, 23 February 1848 • Palmerston
in the House of Commons, 1 March 1848 • Palmerston in the
House of Commons, 25 June 1850*

The Russian pacification of the Caucasus in the 1830s and 1840s proceeded without interference from the other Great Powers. In Britain, however, Russia's methods (along with its suppression of the Polish revolution of 1830) became fodder for a parliamentary and press campaign stoked by David Urquhart, a former secretary in the Constantinople embassy and member of parliament between 1847 and 1852. Not content to accuse Palmerston of acquiescing in Russia's conduct, Urquhart claimed that Palmerston was in fact a Russian agent and, pursuing this romantic fantasy to the fullest, tried to initiate impeachment proceedings against him in the House of Commons.

On 23 February and 1 March 1848, Palmerston stood his ground in two convoluted speeches. His defense culminated in a seemingly timeless definition of Britain's national interest; indeed, he has been cited approvingly by Whig historians ever since. It was easy then (and it is easy now) to be blinded by the brilliance of Palmerston's rhetorical maneuver: he side-stepped Urquhart's argument; he served up generalities which suggested that the issue was settled and that there was no need to probe deeper; he wrapped himself in the flag.

Palmerston may well have been right in claiming that there are constants which shape a country's foreign policy. He also understood that casting political decisions in the mantle of the national interest sanctifies and legitimizes these decisions and, conversely, discredits the

[13]Heinrich Hoffmann ("von Fallersleben"; 1798–1874). Medievalist and librarian; professor of literature at the University of Breslau, 1830–1842. Stigmatized as a nationalist agitator by the Prussian government and fired from his teaching position.

options that are not pursued. But in response to Palmerston it might be argued that the national self-interest is self-evident only on the rarest of occasions. Even when this is so, politicians face a bewildering range of options as they search for the policy that best seems to meet its requirements: generally, the issue is not whether but *how* to promote the national interest. By refusing to engage the issue on this level and by focusing instead on the constants in British foreign policy, Palmerston reduced a complex issue to a few facile generalizations. In effect, he smothered the one legitimate question which lay at the heart of Urquhart's bluster: Who is to define the national interest, and who is to decide which policy is best suited to advance it?

Whether Palmerston's actions followed his words, however, is debatable. In 1850, he ordered a naval demonstration off the Greek port of Piraeus to enforce the wildly exaggerated claims of Don Pacifico, a British subject of Portuguese descent, against Greece. In this instance, Palmerston alienated the French and Russian governments (cf. Document 3.6b, article 8) as well as a broad spectrum within his own party; he also earned a sharp rebuke from the queen. But once again, Palmerston managed to cover his tracks with honeyed words.

a)   *Urquhart in the House of Commons, 23 February 1848*

. . . [D]uring seventeen years I have stood opposed to the noble Lord, attempting to rescue—contemptuously as you may treat the assertion—England from his hands. . . . I speak to you not in your political but in your judicial character, as the chief of the Grand Inquest of the Nation. . . . When you raise a ministry to office, the Foreign Office falls to an individual who has not been selected by peculiar qualifications, and who does not depend for the support of this House upon the peculiar merits which he has displayed, or the success which he has attained in his own department; he depends entirely upon the aggregate of opinion which favors the party to which he belongs, or to which he professes to adhere. . . . [B]y your functions of inquisitors into the conduct of ministers, I appeal to you not to deny inquiry. . . .

—*Parl. Debates*, 3rd Series, 96:1230–37

b)   *Palmerston in the House of Commons, 1 March 1848*

. . . I hold with respect to alliances that England is a power sufficiently strong, sufficiently powerful, to steer her own course, and not to tie herself as an unnecessary appendage to the policy of any other government. I hold that the real policy of England—apart from questions which involve her particular interests, political or commercial—is to be the champion of justice and right; pursuing that course with moderation and prudence, not becoming the Quixote of the world, but giving the weight of her moral sanction and support wherever she thinks that justice is, and wherever she thinks that wrong has been done. . . . We have no eternal allies, and we have no perpetual enemies. Our interests are eternal and perpetual. . . . It is our duty not to pass too harsh a judgement upon others, because they do not exactly see things in the same light as we see; and it is our duty not lightly to engage this country in the frightful responsibilities of war, because from time to time we may find this or that power disinclined to concur with us in matters where their opinion and ours may fairly differ. . . .

—*Parl. Debates*, 3rd Series, 97:122

c)   *Palmerston in the House of Commons, 25 June 1850*

. . . [The question is] whether the principles on which the policy of Her Majesty's Government has been conducted, and the sense of duty which has led us to think ourselves bound to afford protection to our fellow subjects abroad, are proper and fitting guides for those who are charged with the Government of England; and whether, as the Roman, in days of old, held himself free from indignity, when he could say *"Civis Romanum sum"* ["I am a Roman citizen"]; so also a British subject, in whatever land he may be, shall feel confident that the watchful eye and the strong arm of England, will protect him against injustice and wrong.

—*Parl. Debates*, 3rd Series, 112:444

CHAPTER 4

The Revolutions of 1848–1849

When the revolutions of 1848–1849 finally burnt themselves out, not a single European border had changed. For those who advocated the destruction of the "1815 system" in Italy and Germany and the creation of national states in its stead, the events of 1848–1849 were a lesson in failure. This lesson, however, created powerful legacies in its own right: unlikely to repudiate their ultimate goal, Italian, German, or Hungarian nationalists were nonetheless unlikely to try again methods that had led to disaster the first time. Unrepentant nationalists would have to search for different means to accomplish their objectives and, in this sense, the failures of 1848–1849 shaped the future by ruling out a repetition of the past.

But the events of 1848–1849 did not vanish without at least leaving a trace: Prussia, Austria, and Piedmont-Sardinia now had constitutions and legislatures; France, with a nephew of the great Napoleon at the helm, reemerged as a major player in Italy; Russia, the only continental power unscathed by revolution (aside from a minor rising in Poland), appeared to have become the arbiter of Central and Eastern Europe.

GENERAL READING: James Chastain (ed.), *Encyclopedia of the 1848 Revolutions* (New York, forthcoming); [on France:] James Chastain, *The Liberation of Sovereign Peoples: The French Foreign Policy of 1848* (Athens, OH, 1988); Lawrence C. Jennings, *France and Europe in 1848: A Study of French Foreign Affairs in Time of Crisis* (Oxford, 1973); [on "Germany":] Frank Eyck, *The Frankfurt Parliament, 1848–1849* (New York, 1968); Günter Wollstein, *Das "Grossdeutschland" der Paulskirche: Nationale Ziele in der bürgerlichen Revolution* (Düsseldorf, 1977); [on Hungary:] Istvan Deak, *The Lawful Revolution: Louis Kossuth and the Hungarians, 1848–1849* (New York, 1979); Ian W. Roberts, *Nicholas I and the Russian Intervention in Hungary* (New York, 1991); [on Italy:] Frank J. Coppa, *The Origins of the Italian Wars of Independence* (London, 1990); Alan Sked, *The Survival of the Habsburg Empire. Radetzky, the Imperial Army and the Class War 1848* (London, 1979); A. J. P. Taylor, *The Italian Problem in European Diplomacy, 1848–1849* (Manchester, 1934)

4.1   LAMARTINE ON THE PURPOSES OF REVOLUTIONARY POLICY

Lamartine's "Manifesto to Europe," 7 March 1848

Before 1848, the literary reputation of Alphonse de Lamartine rested on his elegiac poetry and a romanticized *Histoire des Girondins* (1847). But when he was appointed foreign minister of the French revolutionary government in February 1848, he was no newcomer to politics: minor assignments in the French foreign service had taken him to Naples and Florence; in 1829, he refused an appointment in the Polignac ministry. Elected to the French chamber in 1834, he became an increasingly vocal opponent of the July monarchy in its last years.

When the Paris mob burst into the chamber on 24 February 1848, Lamartine's oratory helped seal the fate of the July monarchy and assured him of a leading role in the provisional government, which was to prepare elections for a constituent assembly. His first major act as foreign minister came within the week. In a circular to French missions abroad, Lamartine sought to explain the objectives of the new republican regime. This "masterpiece of contradiction," as it has been characterized by one scholar,[1] reflected the ambivalence of the long-time critic in the wings who is suddenly thrust onto center stage. On one hand, he needed to play to the revolutionary constituencies in Paris; on the other, he wanted to keep the Great Powers at bay by reassuring them that the new French republic would not follow in the footsteps of its predecessor of 1792. Lamartine need not have worried, as the spread of the Paris revolution to the German states and to northern Italy immobilized Prussia and Austria. But he soon discovered that his rhetoric had galvanized a large circle of emigrés in Paris—who hoped that France would put itself at the head of a crusade for the liberation of their oppressed homelands.

Lamartine's "Manifesto to Europe," 7 March 1848

. . . War, therefore, is not now the principle of the French republic, as it was the fatal and glorious necessity of the republic of 1792. . . . It is not the country but liberty, which is exposed to the greatest danger in time of war. War is almost invariably a dictatorship. Soldiers are regardless of civil institutions and laws. Storms tempt ambition; glory dazzles patriotism. The prestige of a victorious name veils the design against national sovereignty. The republic doubtless desires glory, but she desires it for herself, and not for Caesars and Napoleons. . . .

The convictions of the men who govern France at the present moment is this: it will be fortunate for France should war be declared against her, and should she be thus constrained to augment her power and her glory, in spite of her moderation; but terrible will be the responsibility to France should the republic itself declare war without being provoked thereto! . . .

The treaties of 1815 have no longer any lawful existence in the eyes of the French republic; nevertheless, the territorial limits circumscribed by those treaties are facts which the republic admits as a basis, and as a starting point, in her relations with foreign nations.

But if the treaties of 1815 have no existence save as facts to be modified by common consent, and if the republic openly declares that her right and mission are to arrive regularly and pacifically at those modifications,—the good sense, the moderation, the conscience, the prudence of the republic exist, and they afford to Europe a surer and more honorable guarantee than the words of those treaties, which have so frequently been violated or modified by Europe itself. . . .

. . . [I]f Switzerland . . . ; if the independent states of Italy should be invaded; if limits or obstacles should be opposed to their internal changes; if there should be any

[1] William L. Langer, *Political and Social Upheaval, 1832–1852* (New York, 1969), 337.

armed interference with their right of allying themselves together for the purpose of consolidating an Italian nation—the French republic would think itself entitled to take up arms in defense of those lawful movements for the improvement and the nationality of states. . . . It proclaims itself the intellectual and cordial ally of popular rights and progress, and of every legitimate development of institutions among nations who may be desirous of maintaining the same principles as her own. . . .

—Alphonse de Lamartine, *History of the French Revolution of 1848* (London, 1852), 278–85

4.2   *L'ITALIA FARÀ DA SÉ*

Charles Albert's Proclamation to Lombardy and Venetia, 23 March 1848

On 18 March, only five days after the outbreak of the Viennese revolution, Milan rose against Austrian rule. Anticipating an Austrian move to quell the revolt, the leaders of the Milan revolt appealed to Piedmont-Sardinia for assistance. The initial success of the rising, together with the fact that by 22 March Austrian authority had also crumbled in Venice, augured well for a Piedmontese venture against Austria. Even so, such an attempt was not without risk, as the Austrian army retired in relatively good order to the quadrilateral of fortifications straddling the border between Lombardy and Venetia.

King Charles Albert of Piedmont-Sardinia had just weathered a revolt in his own state by granting a constitution and a parliament. The new parliament could be expected to clamor for the expulsion of Austria from northern Italy and was likely to provoke another domestic crisis unless he heeded the appeal from Milan. This prospect decided the issue. In a royal proclamation to the inhabitants of Lombardy and Venetia, Charles Albert invoked a phrase, later abstracted to *"l'Italia farà da sé"* (Italy can do it on its own), which came to embody the expectations and hopes of the Italian national movement of 1848–1849.

Charles Albert's Proclamation to Lombardy and Venetia, 23 March 1848

. . . We, out of love for our common race, understanding as we do what is now happening, and supported by public opinion, hasten to associate ourselves with the unanimous admiration which Italy bestows on you.

Peoples of Lombardy and Venetia, our arms, which were concentrating on your frontier when you forestalled events by liberating your glorious Milan, are now coming to offer you in the latter phases of your fight the help which a brother expects from a brother, and a friend from a friend.

We will support your just desires, confident as we are in the help of that God who is manifestly on our side; of the God who has given Pius IX[2] to Italy; of God whose helpful hand has wonderfully enabled Italy to rely on her own strength [*fare da sé*]. . . .

—Denis Mack Smith (ed.), *The Making of Italy, 1796–1870* (New York, 1968), 148

[2]At the time of his election in 1846, Pope Pius IX was considered a liberal hopeful. Cf. Document 4.12.

4.3   ARNIM RESPONDS TO LAMARTINE

Arnim's Manifesto, 17 March 1848 • *Circourt to Lamartine, 31 March 1848*

Responding to the March 1848 revolution in Berlin, King Friedrich Wilhelm IV appointed Ludolf Camphausen to the prime ministership and Heinrich von Arnim-Suckow as foreign minister. Only a few days before his appointment, Arnim published a pamphlet (by itself highly unorthodox behavior for a Prussian career diplomat) which established his liberal credentials and which may have brought him to the king's attention in the first place. Arnim sketched a vision of a united Germany forged by an all-German parliament, convened in Berlin; moreover, this united Germany would champion the reconstitution of Poland.

A Polish rising in the Prussian Grand Duchy of Posen had indeed come on the heels of the revolution in Berlin. Though a royal decree of 24 March vaguely promised a "national reorganization" for Posen, the ongoing disturbances in this province dominated the first days of the Camphausen-Arnim ministry. This question transcended Prussian domestic politics because of its implications for Russo-Prussian relations and because of the interest taken in it by Prince Adam Czartoryski, a former foreign minister of Tsar Alexander I, now a Polish exile in Paris, and a possible candidate for the crown of a reconstituted Poland. Apparently on 25 March, one of Czartoryski's agents contacted the new Prussian ministry with an offer of a Franco-Prussian alliance for the reestablishment of Poland. Arnim's response was reported to Paris by Lamartine's envoy to Berlin, Adolphe de Circourt, himself married to a Polish aristocrat.

As in 1830, the Polish cause at first engendered widespread sympathy in Germany. But the initial enthusiasm was soon dampened by local frictions between the Polish majority and the German minority in Posen. These were aggravated by the decision of the Frankfurt Parliament in July 1848 to seat delegates from Posen and to include much of the province in Germany even though it had not been part of the German Confederation. The debates on Posen in the spring and summer of 1848 were among the most tortuous in the Frankfurt Parliament, forcing this body to wrestle with the principles by which it should establish the borders of Germany. The Prussian legislature in October 1848 added to the confusion: it defied the Frankfurt Parliament by voting to exclude Posen from "Germany."

a)   *Arnim's Manifesto, 17 March 1848*

. . . These days, domestic and foreign policy are inseparably intertwined everywhere, but particularly in Prussia. . . . The aim—which the King, despite his selflessness, is destined by providence to attain—this high aim is: the unity of Germany with, through, and in Prussia, or, in other words: the expansion and elevation of Prussia to [become] Germany. . . . Today, the sole remaining question is this: should Germany attain this goal in the guise of a constitutional monarchy or that of a confederated republic? Should there be a German Reich with princes and a sovereign? or a United States of Germany with a president?

It goes without saying that there is nothing Germany can expect from Austria and from the Diet [of the German Confederation]. The trust [in them] is gone. . . .

The condition of Poland today can no longer be reconciled with public opinion and European peace, nor with the European balance and a healthy policy. The King would bring about complications and dangers for Prussia and Germany in the near future if he did not take up the reconstitution of Poland as an aim of his policy.

Common sense suggests the necessity and freedom to bow [to this fact]. It is a question of preventing one's own house from catching fire, of preventing conflict with France, with the armed revolution, with the principle of the inviolability of national rights, with the generally held views of the age. The sacrifice which Prussia would have to make is in no proportion to what it would gain: to start with, the bond of peace with England and France and a barrier against Russia.

When, because of Poland, serious dangers—emanating from Paris or London or from Poland itself—threaten to disturb the peace, Prussia should openly declare to the four [Great] Powers its readiness, in the interest of calm and the European balance, to proffer its hand for the reconstitution of the independence of the old Poland, under the condition of [its] perpetual neutrality, and to enter into the necessary peaceful negotiations with neighboring states on this important subject.

—Anonymous [Heinrich von Arnim-Suckow], *Die politische Denkschrift vom 17. März 1848 über die französische Februar-Revolution und ihre Folgen für Deutschland* (Berlin, 1848), 13–15; 21–22

b)   ***Circourt to Lamartine, 31 March 1848***

. . . The Grand Duchy [of Posen] will become the site of the reunion of almost the entire Polish emigration; it is morally impossible that in these deeds and in the manifestations which will follow, the Russian government will not see indirect aggression, hostility against its principles, an imminent danger to its interests. . . . In this case, what will France do? What will England do?. . . What does it [the Prussian cabinet] expect, or rather what does it hope for from you?

Two things: first, a solemn declaration of alliance and political solidarity insofar as the reconstruction of the Polish nationality is concerned; that would give it moral support of appreciable worth. Second, eventually, if it shall ask you, to send a French squadron to the Baltic as a diversion; two ships with our flag would be enough to make a notable show of force and of confidence to the Polish national party and to its German auxiliaries. . . .

But when the French, English and German nations find themselves united in a common enterprise, legitimate in its goal, and practicable by means of the enormous force at the disposal of such a combination, the fear of war in the west and center of Europe would disappear; credit will reestablish itself; the passions that boil up in the breast of the Latin and Germanic nations, finding an honorable and natural outlet, would cease to shake the foundations of society . . . .

—Adolphe de Circourt, *Souvenirs d'une mission à Berlin en 1848* (Paris, 1908), 1:325–28

4.4   ## A EUROPEAN NECESSITY: PALACKY ON THE HABSBURG MONARCHY

Palacky to the Committee of Fifty, 11 April 1848 •
Manifesto of the Slav Congress, 12 June 1848

The demand for a constitutional and united Germany figured prominently in the March 1848 revolutions in the German states. A largely self-styled preparliament, meeting in Frankfurt, formed a Committee of Fifty to organize elections to an all-German assembly. These elections were to take place throughout the German Confederation and in Schleswig, East Prussia, West Prussia, and the "German" parts of Posen. As Bohemia was part of the confederation, the Committee of Fifty invited Frantisek Palacky, a well-known Czech nationalist and author of a multivolume *History of Bohemia* (published in German before its translation into Czech) to join its deliberations. Extracts from Palacky's reply appear below.

Palacky was the principal organizer of a Slav congress that assembled in Prague between 2 and 12 June. The congress was intended as a Slavic counterweight to German influence and Magyar constitutional privileges in the Habsburg monarchy but fell short of this goal. It instead revealed strong disagreements among Czechs, Poles, Slovaks, and Croats—differences which a final communiqué, excerpted below, sought to paper over. Just as the congress wound up its business, an insurrection divided Prague on social rather than national lines. It was put down by troops loyal to the governor of Bohemia, Prince Windischgrätz, who thus handed the old order its first victory.

a)   *Palacky to the Committee of Fifty, 11 April 1848*

. . . I am unable, gentlemen, to accept your invitation. . . . I am not a German—at least I do not feel myself to be one—and you would assuredly not desire to call me in to join you as a mere assentor, a "yes-man" without a mind or will of his own; for in that case I should at Frankfurt either have to deny my true feelings and appear in false colors, or if it came to that point, raise my voice loudly in opposition. . . .

The second reason which prevents me from taking part in your deliberations is the fact that, according to all I have so far learned of your aims and intentions as publicly proclaimed, it is your irrevocable desire and purpose to undermine Austria as an independent empire and indeed to make her impossible for all time to come—an empire whose preservation, integrity, and consolidation is, and must be, a great and important matter not only for my own nation but also for the whole of Europe, indeed, for humanity and civilization itself . . . .

You know that in the south-east of Europe, along the frontiers of the Russian Empire, there live many nations widely differing in origin, in language, in history and morals—Slavs, Wallachians, Magyars and Germans, not to speak of Turks and Albanians—none of whom is sufficiently powerful itself to bid successful defiance to the superior neighbor on the East for all time. They could only do so if a close and firm tie bound them all together as one. The vital artery of such a union of nations is the Danube. The focus of power of such a union must never be diverted far from this river, if the union is to be effective and to remain so. Assuredly, if the Austrian state had not existed for ages, it would have been a behest for us in the interests of Europe and indeed of humanity to endeavor to create it as soon as possible. . . .

Metternich did not fall merely because he was the greatest foe of liberty but also because he was the bitterest, the most determined, enemy of all the Slavonic races in Austria. When I direct my gaze beyond the frontiers of Bohemia, natural and historical considerations constrain me to turn, not to Frankfurt but to Vienna, to seek there the center which is fitted and predestined to ensure and defend the peace, the liberty, and the rights of my nation. . . .

As to the establishment of a republic in the German Reich—this is a matter wholly outside my competence, so that I have no desire even to express my opinion on it. I must, however, reject expressly and emphatically in advance the idea of a republic within the frontiers of the Austrian Empire. Think of the Austrian Empire divided up into sundry republics, some considerable in size and others small—what a delightful basis for a universal Russian monarchy!. . .

—*Slavonic and East European Review* 26 (1948), 303–8

b)   *Manifesto of the Slav Congress, 12 June 1848*

. . . we have proposed to the Austrian Emperor, under whose constitutional rule the majority of us live, that the imperial state be converted into a federation of nations all enjoying equal rights. . . . In any case we are determined to ensure for our nationality in Austria, by all the means available to us, a full recognition of the same rights in the state as the German and Magyar nations already enjoy. . . .

The enemies of our nationality have succeeded in terrifying Europe with the bogy of political Panslavism which, they have declared, threatens to destroy all that has been won anywhere for freedom, enlightenment, and humanity. . . .

We protest against the arbitrary partition of territories such as has been desired to carry out of late especially in Poznan [Posen]; we look to the Governments of Prussia and Saxony to abandon the systematic denationalization of the Slavs in Lusatia, in Poznan, and in East and West Prussia, which they have carried on up till now; we demand of the Hungarian ministry that without delay they cease to employ inhuman and violent methods against the Slavonic peoples in Hungary, in particular the Serbs, the Croats, the Slovaks, and Ruthenians, and that the national rights which are their due shall be fully assured them as speedily as possible. Finally, we hope that a callous policy will no longer be an obstacle to our kinsmen in Turkey, but that they will be enabled to give free play to their national aspirations. . . .

—*Slavonic and East European Review* 26 (1948), 309–13

4.5   A EUROPEAN NECESSITY, IF RETOOLED: PALMERSTON ON THE HABSBURG MONARCHY

Palmerston to King Leopold of the Belgians, 15 June 1848 •
Schwarzenberg to Werner, 4 December 1848

The revolution in northern Italy appealed to Palmerston's ideological outlook: he therefore was quick to judge the success of the revolt not to be just in Britain's national interest but also in Austria's. Needless to say, successive Austrian governments remained unconvinced that the loss of Austria's position in Italy was really to its benefit. They were, however, too cowed to contradict Palmerston openly.

Once Prince Felix Schwarzenberg formed a new ministry in November 1848, Austrian policy began to breathe a new spirit. Schwarzenberg himself lost no time in announcing that he was loath to accept Palmerston's guidance. Ultimately, the issue was decided not by rhetoric but on the battlefied: King Charles Albert's decision in March 1849 to resume

Piedmont's war against Austria ended in military disaster; the battle of Novara thereby also sealed the fate of Palmerston's north Italian scheme.

a)   ***Palmerston to King Leopold of the Belgians,***
15 June 1848

. . . As to poor Austria, every person who attaches value to the maintenance of a balance of power in Europe must lament her present helpless condition; and every man gifted with ever so little foresight must have seen, for a long time past, that feebleness and decay were the inevitable consequences of Prince Metternich's system of government: though certainly no one could have expected that the rottenness within would so soon and so completely have shown itself without. Lord Bacon says that a man who aims at being the only figure among ciphers is the ruin of an age: and so it has been with Metternich. . . . The wonder is, not that the accumulated pressure should at last have broke the barrier and have deluged the country, but that his artificial impediments should have produced stagnation so long.

I cannot regret the expulsion of the Austrians from Italy. I do not believe, Sire, that it will diminish the real strength nor impair the real security of Austria as a European Power. . . . I should wish to see the whole of Northern Italy united into one kingdom, comprehending Piedmont, Genoa, Lombardy, Venice, Parma, and Modena; and Bologna would, in that case, sooner or later unite itself either to that state or to Tuscany. Such an arrangement of Northern Italy would be most conducive to the peace of Europe, by interposing between France and Austria a neutral state strong enough to make itself respected, and sympathising in its habits and character neither with France nor with Austria; while, with reference to the progress of civilization, such a state would have great advantages, political, commercial, and intellectual. . . .

—Evelyn Ashley (ed.), *The Life of Henry John Temple, Viscount Palmerston: 1846–65*
(London, 1876), 1:97–98

b)   ***Schwarzenberg to Werner,[3] 4 December 1848***

. . . Truthfully, my dear Baron, Lord Palmerston regards himself a little too much as the arbiter of Europe's destinies. For our part, we are not at all disposed to bestow on him the role of Providence in our affairs. We never impose our advice on him regarding Irish affairs; let him spare himself the trouble of imposing his on the issue of Lombardy. If the notes, dispatches, and verbal communications that he showers on us are to be believed, one would have to say that nothing weighs on him more than the happiness and well-being of our Empire: he finds Austria crumbling and he envisions but one hope of health for her: that is the dismemberment of the Monarchy. . . . I tell you that we are tired of these eternal insinuations, of that tone, so protective and didactic, so insulting, always unwelcome. We have decided to tolerate it no longer. . . . We will uphold the basis of the treaties, we shall not cede an inch of

[3]Joseph von Werner (1791–1871). Under-secretary in the Austrian foreign ministry, 1849–1859.

terrain. If Lord Palmerston doesn't like it, tough for him. Lord Palmerston reminds us of the Hummelauer project;[4] let us make him see that we know no Hummelauer projects. . . .

—HHSta, PA VIII-27,40–45; Vittorio Barbieri, "I tentativi di mediazione anglo-francesi durante la guerra del '48," *Rassegna Storica del Risorgimento* 26:1 (1939), 721

4.6   "GERMANY" BETRAYED? THE MALMÖ ARMISTICE

Theodor Mommsen to Otto Jahn, 5 August 1848 • *Jacob Grimm to Wilhelm Grimm, 3 September 1848* • *Friedrich Engels in the* Neue Rheinische Zeitung, *8 September and 10 September 1848* • *Friedrich Hebbel for the* Augsburger Allgemeine Zeitung, *19 September 1848*

The legal status of the so-called Elbe Duchies, Schleswig and Holstein, was so complex that Palmerston once quipped that only three men understood it—one who took the secret with him to his grave, one who had gone mad, and he himself, who had forgotten it. The two duchies had been ruled since 1460 in "personal union"[5] by Danish monarchs (themselves descendants of the north German house of Oldenburg) and were, according to their medieval constitution, "inseparable in perpetuity." Holstein was a member of the German Confederation; Schleswig—though its southern two-thirds was predominantly German—was not.

The Schleswig-Holstein crisis of the mid-nineteenth century can be described as a clash of Danish and German nationalisms, but its root cause lay in the fact that the succession in the duchies was limited to the male line while the law of succession in Denmark proper provided for descent through the female line as well. This constitutional difference was not unusual—the personal unions of Britain with Hanover and of Holland with Luxemburg were dissolved in 1837 and 1890, respectively, because of similar divergencies. On the death of the childless Danish King Frederick VII (acceded in January 1848, died in March 1863), Denmark and the duchies were expected to devolve on members of different branch lines. To prevent this event from taking place (and acting under intense pressure from Schleswig Danes and the Danish nationalist-revolutionary movement), Frederick promised in March 1848 to introduce the Danish constitution (and hence the Danish order of succession) to Schleswig.

In reaction, the provincial diets of Schleswig and Holstein immediately formed a provisional government and asked to be recognized by the Frankfurt preliminary parliament. The Frankfurt body not only admitted Schleswig but also urged the German states to send troops to defend the duchies. In response to this appeal, Prussian forces occupied the duchies and launched an invasion of the Jutland peninsula, prompting Denmark to retaliate with a devastatingly effective blockade of German coasts.

In this conflict, Denmark received token military assistance from Sweden-Norway and, more important, the diplomatic support of Britain and Russia, neither of which cherished the prospect of Prussian influence so close to the Danish straits. Under pressure from both powers

---

[4]Carl von Hummelauer (1790 [1791?]–1874), official in the Austrian foreign ministry. In May 1848, Schwarzenberg's predecessor, Johann von Wessenberg, sent Hummelauer to London to seek British mediation in the Lombardo-Venetian crisis. Palmerston rejected Hummelauer's offer of autonomy for both provinces but accepted a second plan in which Hummelauer proposed independence for Lombardy and autonomy for Venetia. This second offer, however, failed to win the approval of the British cabinet, and Hummelauer, his mission a failure, returned to Vienna in June 1848.

[5]A dynastic arrangement in which the same monarch governed two or more territories, each according to its own constitutional laws and through its own institutions.

and without consulting the Frankfurt Parliament, Prussia signed a seven-month armistice in the Swedish port of Malmö on 28 August.

The Malmö armistice exposed the fact that the Frankfurt Parliament could be ignored at will and was powerless to act on its own. After rancorous debates on whether or not to accept the armistice, it bowed to the inevitable and acquiesced on 16 September. Delegates and commentators alike were well aware that the parliament's authority had suffered a sharp blow from which it was unlikely to recover. But the Malmö armistice also assured that the Schleswig-Holstein question in its various manifestations (national, diplomatic, naval) was seared into the consciousness of the German left.

The voices quoted here cover the spectrum from reformist liberal to communist. Theodor Mommsen wrote for a paper in his native Schleswig, was appointed professor of Roman law at the University of Leipzig later in 1848 (only to be dismissed in 1850), and went on to receive the 1902 Nobel prize in literature for his *Roman History*. The brothers Grimm, best known for their compilation of folk tales, had both been fired from the University of Göttingen in 1837 for their liberal views; once elected to the Frankfurt Parliament, Jacob distinguished himself for his attack on aristocratic privilege. Friedrich Engels, together with Karl Marx, edited the *Neue Rheinische Zeitung*. Friedrich Hebbel, a native of Holstein, was a distinguished realist playwright and literary editor of the Vienna paper *Oesterreichische Reichszeitung*. One of the ironies of this tale is that his career, like that of Mommsen, had been launched by a Danish royal grant.

a)   ***Theodor Mommsen to Otto Jahn,[6] 5 August 1848***

... It is a fantasy world here in Frankfurt. While war and unrest wreak havoc elsewhere and the beams of the thousand-year old structure are groaning, the leisurely parliamentary idyll takes its course and the various disturbances are only conversation pieces. It is a laboratory writ large; the parliament proceeds and does not allow itself to be disturbed, like Archimedes in Syracuse. The way the deputies tell it, now that they have taken care of the Schleswig and Posen questions: if only the Italian one could be settled, everything will be fine. That Limburg, Hanover, Prussia take no notice of their decrees, that no German state will raise the monies and soldiers which they have already voted (neither the 6 million dollars [Taler] for the fleet nor the new levy of 300,000 troops) simply does not figure in the discussion: that is a question of no concern to the National Assembly. ...

—Lothar Wickert (ed.), *Theodor Mommsen—Otto Jahn. Briefwechsel, 1842–1868*
(Frankfurt, 1962), 72–73

b)   ***Jacob Grimm to Wilhelm Grimm, 3 September 1848***

... You can imagine the unhappy impression produced here by the cease-fire concluded just now, and tomorrow we will have an acrimonious session. Considerations of honor really should supersede everything else, and honor and power would have compensated for any material losses in the Baltic. I fail to understand how the king

---

[6]Otto Jahn (1813–1869). Professor of classics at Leipzig; biographer of Mozart.

could ratify such a treaty which once again puts Prussia into stern opposition to our German unity. Some here think that it is possible to continue the war even without Prussia. At the very moment when combative south Germans have gone to Schleswig [to fight], such a dishonorable bargain is struck! . . . How can Germany put trust in Prussia, which on this occasion did not make the necessary sacrifice and which, in its momentary discomfort, allowed itself to be led astray to gamble away the honor of the fatherland?! All Europe will be looking on with glee. . . .

—Wilhelm Schoof and Jörn Göres (eds.), *Unbekannte Briefe der Brüder Grimm* (Bonn, 1960), 385–86

c)   *Friedrich Engels in the* **Neue Rheinische Zeitung,**
8 September and 10 September 1848

[8 September 1848:] . . . Should [the Frankfurt Parliament] refuse to go along with the cease-fire, then we will have a European war, the break between Prussia and Germany, new revolutions, the disintegration of Prussia, and the real unity of Germany. . . . But wouldn't the representatives of the bourgeoisie in Frankfurt rather accept any humiliation . . . than expose themselves to new turmoil which will endanger the rule of their class in Germany?

[10 September 1848:] . . . And who has been on the side of Denmark since the beginning? The three most counter-revolutionary powers in Europe: Russia, England, and the Prussian government. The Prussian government has, for as long as it could get away with it, carried on a phony war. . . . Prussia, England, and Russia are the three powers which most fear the German revolution and its first outcome: German unity—Prussia, because, as a result, it will cease to exist; England, because the German market will no longer be there for it to exploit; Russia, because consequently democracy will advance to the Vistula, and even as far as the Dvina and the Dnjepr. Prussia, England, and Russia have conspired against Schleswig-Holstein, against Germany, and against the revolution.

The war which might result from decisions taken in Frankfurt would be a war of Germany against Prussia, England, and Russia . . . .—a war against the three Great Powers of the counter-revolution, a war in which Prussia will really be fused into Germany, which will make the alliance with Poland an unavoidable necessity, which will immediately bring about the freeing of Italy . . . a war which will put the fatherland in danger and will save it because it will make Germany's victory dependent on the victory of democracy.

—Karl Marx/Friedrich Engels, *Werke* (Berlin [East], 1956–1968), 5:389, 397

d)   *Friedrich Hebbel for the* **Augsburger Allgemeine Zeitung,**
19 September 1848[7]

. . . I have always considered the Schleswig-Holstein issue to be the barometer of our German efforts for unity. This much seems to be clear: whoever is indifferent to this

---

[7]Published on 25 September.

matter has no interest in bringing about a united Germany. Here in Vienna one is indifferent, indifferent to an unbelievable degree. At the very least, one might have expected the disregard of the central authority, and therewith the humiliation of the Austrian prince who heads it, to elicit a reaction–but no. . . .[8]

—Friedrich Hebbel, *Sämtliche Werke* (Berlin, 1904), 10:122–23

4.7   **"GERMANY" AND AUSTRIA**

*Constitutional Draft of the Frankfurt Parliament, 19 October 1848 ● The
Debate on Articles 2 and 3, October 1848 ● Program of the Schwarzenberg
Ministry as Announced in the Austrian (Kremsier) Reichstag, 27 November 1848*

As a result of the Czech boycott (Document 4.4) of the elections to the Frankfurt Parliament, the Habsburg lands were underrepresented in that body. But when the parliament's constitutional committee submitted its draft to the assembly at large, the debate on its first three articles was dominated by Austrians. At issue was whether the united Germany should (1) exclude the Austrian empire; (2) include it in its entirety; or (3) include only its historically "German" lands, thereby leaving open the future of its other provinces. On 28 October 1848, the parliament adopted article 2 by 340 to 76 votes; it rejected the minority amendment by 375 to 38.

The Schwarzenberg government made clear its attitude as it took office in November 1848.

a)   ***Constitutional Draft of the Frankfurt Parliament,
19 October 1848***

Art. 1, § 1: The German Reich consists of the territory of the hitherto existing German Confederation. The status of the Duchy of Schleswig and the definition of the border in the Grand Duchy of Posen are still to be determined. . . .

Art. 2, § 2: No part of the German Reich should be combined with non-German lands in a single state. (Minority report: Addition to § 2: "Insofar as the circumstances of Austria do not permit execution of article 2 and the paragraphs derived therefrom, the unity and power of Germany shall be attained through the closest union [*Anschluss*] of Austria to Germany by means of an international alliance between the Reich executive power and the Austrian government").

§ 3: If a German land and a non-German land have the same head of state, then the relationship between both lands shall be based solely on the principles of a personal union.

§ 4: The head of state of a German land connected to a non-German land by a personal union, must either reside in his German land or must appoint [in a constitutional manner][9] a regency to which appointment is open only to Germans. (Minority report: Addition to § 4: "The head of state of a German land connected to a

[8]The Habsburg Archduke John (1782–1859), an uncle of the Austrian emperor, had been elected provisional "head of state" *(Reichsverweser)* by the Frankfurt Parliament on 28 June.
[9]These words were inserted by amendment on 31 October 1848. Wigard, *Stenographischer Bericht,* 4:2959.

non-German land by a personal union cannot move non-German troops into his lands except during a war involving the Reich and by order of the Reich executive").

—Franz Wigard (comp.), *Stenographischer Bericht über die Verhandlungen der deutschen constituirenden Nationalversammlung* (Frankfurt, 1848), 4:2717

b)   *The Debate on Articles 2 and 3, October 1848*

[21 October] Alfred von Arneth[10]: . . . Gentlemen, the Austrian is and wants to remain German; he has in the past proven his German identity [*Gesinnung*] more than many other German tribes. But neither does he want to see Austria torn apart, he does not want to see Austria destroyed; he wants the continued existence of Austria in and with Germany. No, gentlemen, if it is a matter of formally incorporating all of Austria including its non-German provinces, then I think there would only be few German-Austrians who would oppose such a fusion of their fatherland in Germany. We think that the dismemberment of Austria is of no benefit to Germany; we believe that it is in Germany's interest to hinder the emergence on Germany's eastern border of new independent states, be they Magyar or Slav, which would indubitably result from a separation of the non-German provinces from Austria. . . . I who have been sent here to participate in the drafting of a German constitution, I who have been sent here to work for its implementation in the German-Austrian provinces, I am supposed to approve the phrase [in the minority report] which, because it provides for a bond in international law, separates our common fatherland into two parts, a phrase which, if approved, will lead to a departure of the Austrian deputies from the parliament! Because how could we Austrians continue to sit in a parliament which has nothing further to do with Austria except to conclude international treaties? No, gentlemen, we are Germans as much as you! Austria has always been German and will, if you give it the opportunity which you have in your hands, always remain German. . . .

[24 October] Heinrich Reitter[11]: . . . Gentlemen! If you do not want to exert yourselves on behalf of the Germans in Austria, if you do not want to give your support to this constituency, they will nonetheless not cease to be Germans. If we do not get help here, we will look after ourselves, and we will stay Germans in our intuition and with our feelings [bravo! on the left].

[28 October] Christian Friedrich Wurm[12]: . . . We know the mission of the Austrian state, we know why the imperial crown has remained with the Habsburg dynasty; and when the danger emanating from the Turks had passed with the Treaty of Kuchuk-Kainarji, the danger from the Russians began—between the two, the larger evil. Austria stood at its post until this last decade. If Austria can no longer be at its post, I cannot deny the danger, the great danger, inherent in the consequences. Thus, gentlemen, it is all the more necessary that a strong and unified Germany be created to guard against this danger. . . .

—Wigard, op. cit., 4:2779–81, 2814, 2906

[10](1819–1897). Austrian member (Vienna), Casino-Partei/Pariser Hof (right center). Biographer of Eugene of Savoy and Maria Theresa; appointed director of the Austrian imperial archives in 1868.

[11](1816–1906). Austrian member (Prague), Westendhall (moderate left).

[12](1803–1859). Member for Württemberg, Württemberger Hof/Augsburger Hof (left center).

c) **Program of the Schwarzenberg Ministry as Announced in the Austrian (Kremsier) Reichstag, 27 November 1848**

Gentlemen! The great calling which is incumbent upon us together with the peoples [of the monarchy] is the creation of a new bond which shall unite all lands and tribes of the monarchy in one great body politic. This point of view will guide this ministry in the German question. Germany will not derive its greatness from the dismemberment of the monarchy, or its strengthening through the weakening of the monarchy. Austria's continued existence as a unitary state is a German and a European necessity. . . .

—Ernst Rudolf Huber, *Dokumente zur deutschen Verfassungsgeschichte* (Stuttgart, 1964), 1:360

4.8   AN "EMPEROR OF THE GERMANS"?

Friedrich Wilhelm IV to Bunsen, December 1848

The attitude of the Schwarzenberg ministry in Austria (preceding document) sounded the death knell to any effort by the Frankfurt Parliament to include Austria in the German state envisioned by it. The Frankfurt Parliament now changed tack: it abandoned a "large German" (*"grossdeutsch"*) state in favor of a "small German" (*"kleindeutsch"*) solution—one that, in its main features, excluded Austria and stipulated that the King of Prussia serve as "Emperor of the Germans." In March 1849, having adopted its constitution, the parliament dispatched a delegation to Berlin to offer the crown to King Friedrich Wilhelm IV. It was refused.

Months earlier and unbeknownst to the parliament, Friedrich Wilhelm IV had already reached his decision. The reasons which he gave in the letter excerpted here smack of an atavistic romanticism strangely out of place in an industrial age (and reveal a deep hatred for the notion of popular sovereignty) but address a question pivotal to the existence of any state: the legitimacy of its executive. Moreover, it took no special gift of prophecy to predict that the other German princes would hardly be content with the subordinate role assigned to them by the Frankfurt constitution. Nor could Austria's opposition be in doubt. Austria, as the events of 1849–1850 (Document 4.13) would demonstrate, in all likelihood was able to count on the support of Russia, the power which in the years 1848–1849 proved the mainstay of the monarchical order.

The Frankfurt constitution went through one last permutation. After Friedrich Wilhelm's refusal of the crown, the Prussian cabinet, by-passing the Frankfurt Parliament, initiated negotiations among the German governments to accept the Frankfurt constitution. Though twenty-eight smaller states were prepared to adhere, Austria, Bavaria, Württemberg, and Saxony rejected the Prussian initiative. The Prussian government now demanded the resignation of deputies representing Prussian electoral districts in Frankfurt. This the Frankfurt Parliament was not prepared to concede, arguing that its members derived their mandate not from governments but from their electorate. Nonetheless, many members from Prussian districts chose to leave. These resignations, together with the departure of Austrian members earlier on, decimated the parliament's moderate wing. It was thus easy for the Prussian government to stigmatize the remaining "rump parliament" as a radical assembly and to demand its dissolution. Spontaneous risings in Saxony, the Prussian Rhineland, the Bavarian Palatinate, and Baden on behalf of the parliament were gunned down by Prussian troops.

Friedrich Wilhelm IV to Bunsen,[13] *December 1848*

. . . I want the princes' approval of neither *this* election nor *this* crown. Do you understand the words emphasized here? For you I want to shed light on this as briefly and brightly as possible. First, *this* crown is no crown. The crown which a Hohenzoller[14] could accept, *if* circumstances *permitted*, is not one *made* by an assembly sprung from a revolutionary seed in the genre of the crown of cobble stones of Louis Philippe[15]—even if this assembly was established with the sanction of princes . . . but one which bears the stamp of God, one which makes [the individual] on whom it [the crown] is placed, after his anointment, a "divine right" monarch—just as it has elevated more than 34 princes to Kings of the Germans by divine right and just as it bonds the last of these to his predecessors. The crown worn by Ottonians,[16] Staufens,[17] Habsburgs can of course also be worn by a Hohenzoller; it honors him overwhelmingly with the luster of a thousand years. But *this* one, to which you regrettably refer, overwhelmingly dishonors [its bearer] with its smell of the gunpowder of the 1848 revolution—the silliest, dumbest, worst, though—thank God!—not the most evil of this century. Such an imaginary headband, baked out of dirt and the letters of the alphabet, is supposed to be welcome to a legitimate divine right king: to put it more precisely, to the King of Prussia who is blessed with a crown which may not be the oldest but, of all those which have never been stolen, is the most noble? . . . I will tell you outright: if the thousand-year old crown of the German nation which has lain dormant for 42 years[18] should be bestowed again, it will be *I* and my equals who will bestow it. And woe to those who assume [powers] to which they have no title.

—Leopold von Ranke (ed.), *Aus dem Briefwechsel Friedrich Wilhelms IV. mit Bunsen*
(Leipzig, 1874), 148–49

4.9   THE HUNGARIAN DECLARATION OF INDEPENDENCE, 19 APRIL 1849

In the Habsburg empire, the fiercest and most protracted resistance to the reestablishment of the status quo ante came from the Hungarian government (itself a constitutional novelty granted to Hungary in March 1848 by an increasingly desperate imperial court). In December 1848, the Hungarian government, in a clear act of defiance, did not recognize the succession

---

[13]Christian von Bunsen (1791–1860). Prussian diplomat and theologian; informal adviser to Friedrich Wilhelm IV; minister in London, 1845–1854.

[14]The Prussian royal house.

[15]An allusion to the July 1830 revolution in France and the establishment of the July monarchy.

[16]German kings, 919–1002; in 962, Otto I revived the Roman Empire in the west.

[17]German kings and Roman emperors, 1056–1268. The designation "Holy Roman Empire" was coined in the reign of Frederick I ("Barbarossa").

[18]A reference to the dissolution of the Holy Roman Empire in 1806.

of Franz Joseph to the Hungarian throne; in the meantime, its armies successfully prevented imperial forces from restoring Austrian rule. Up to this point, the Hungarian parliament had not disavowed the union of the Austrian and Hungarian crowns. It took this step only when it learned that the Schwarzenberg ministry had asked for—and received—Russian military assistance in crushing Hungary's resistance.

How "modern" was the Hungarian declaration of independence? Published as a pamphlet in all major European languages, it appealed to the "public opinion of the world"; but it left no doubt that independent Hungary would claim and defend the traditional (i.e., medieval) borders of the Kingdom of Hungary, encompassing substantial non-Magyar populations. Croats, Romanians, and Slovaks were hence served notice that self-determination did not apply to them.

. . . And as if these sins of the House of Austria were not enough... it turned to the Russian tsar for help and brought—violating all international law and ignoring the protests of the Ottoman Porte and all European consuls in Bucharest—Russian armies from Wallachia into Transylvania to devastate the Hungarian nation. . . .

We have recounted in simple historical truth the long and unparalleled list of transgressions of the House of Habsburg-Lorraine. Appealing to the judgment of eternal God and the public opinion of the world, we say that there is no possibility of reaching an accommodation [*Ausgleichung*] with this treasonous House: we owe it to our fatherland, to justice, to morality, to honor, to Europe, and to the interests of civilization to ban this treasonous ruling House from the throne of the Hungarian kings. We deliver it to the judgment of God, of public opinion, of morality, and of honor. . . .

Hungary with Transylvania, as by law united, and with all of its parts and provinces is declared a free, sovereign and independent European realm, indivisible in its unity and inviolable in its integrity. . . .

—from German-language facsimile in Karl Nehring (ed.), *Flugblätter und Flugschriften der ungarischen Revolution von 1848/49* (Munich, 1977), 57–68

4.10 PALMERSTON AND THE HUNGARIAN REVOLUTION

Palmerston in the House of Commons, 21 July 1849 • *Palmerston to Ponsonby, 9 September 1849* • *Palmerston to Ponsonby, 6 October 1849*

Like the insurrections against Austrian rule in northern Italy, the revolution in Hungary appealed to Palmerston's Whig sentiments. But in this instance, he drew a different conclusion: the success of the revolution would retard rather than advance Britain's national interest.

When Austrian and Russian armies crushed the Hungarian secessionist movement between June and August 1849, Britain could do little more than posture. Unable to dissuade Austria from taking repressive measures in the aftermath of the Hungarian rebellion, Palmerston salvaged one modest success: he ensured that the sultan turned aside an Austro-Russian demand for the extradition of Hungarian and Polish revolutionaries who had fled to Ottoman territory.

a)   ***Palmerston in the House of Commons, 21 July 1849***

. . . It is of the utmost importance to Europe, that Austria should remain great and powerful; but it is impossible to disguise from ourselves that, if the war is to be fought out, Austria must thereby be weakened, because, on the one hand, if the Hungarians should be successful, and their success should end in the entire separation of Hungary from Austria, it will be impossible not to see that this will be such a dismemberment of the Austrian empire as will prevent Austria from continuing to occupy the great position she has hitherto held among European Powers. If, on the other hand, the war being fought out to the uttermost, Hungary should by superior forces be entirely crushed, Austria in that battle will have crushed her own right arm. . . .

—*Parl. Debates*, 3rd Series, 107:811–12

b)   ***Palmerston to Ponsonby,*[19]** ***9 September 1849***

. . . The Austrians are really the greatest brutes that ever called themselves by the undeserved name of civilised men. . . . The rulers of Austria (I call them not statesmen or stateswomen) have now brought their country to this remarkable condition, that the Emperor holds his various territories at the goodwill and pleasure of three external Powers. He holds Italy just as long as and no longer than France chooses to let him have it. The first quarrel between Austria and France will drive the Austrians out of Lombardy and Venice. He holds Hungary and Galicia just as long as and no longer than Russia chooses to let him have them. The first quarrel with Russia will detach those countries from the Austrian crown. He holds his German provinces by a tenure dependent, in a great degree, upon feelings and opinions which it will be very difficult for him and his ministers either to combine with or to stand out against. The remedy against these various dangers which are rapidly undermining the Austrian empire would be generous conciliation; but instead of that, the Austrian Government know no method of administration but what consists in flogging, imprisoning, and shooting. "The *Austrians* know no argument but force."

—Ashley, *Palmerston*, 1: 139–41

c)   ***Palmerston to Ponsonby, 6 October 1849***

. . . What could Austria hope to gain by a war with Turkey, supported, as she [Turkey] would be, by England and France? Austria would lose her Italian provinces, to which she seems to attach such undue value, and she never would see them again. . . . Pray do what you can to persuade the Austrian Government to allow these Hungarians . . . to leave Turkey. . . .

—Ashley, *Palmerston*, 1:154–55

[19]John, Viscount Ponsonby (1770–1855). British ambassador in Vienna, 1846–1850.

4.11   LOUIS NAPOLEON ON THE NAPOLEONIC IDEAS

The Napoleonic Ideas, 1839

After the death of Napoleon's son in 1832, Charles Louis Napoleon Bonaparte became the principal Bonapartist claimant. Nephew of the great Napoleon and third son of Louis Bonaparte—Napoleon's younger brother and satellite king of Holland (1806–1810)—Louis Napoleon after the collapse of the empire settled with his mother in northern Switzerland (his contemporaries claimed to notice a Swiss-German inflection in his speech). His activities belied the stolidity of his Swiss citizenship: he participated in the rising of the Romagna against the papal government in 1831, headed a coup against the July monarchy in 1836, traveled to the United States, and found a home in England, where in 1839 he published *The Napoleonic Ideas*. Translated into six languages and selling about 500,000 copies in France alone, *The Napoleonic Ideas* became a best-seller by any standard.

Louis Napoleon's literary fame at first did not translate into political success. A second coup attempt against the government of Louis Philippe in 1840, with a dramatically staged landing on the coast near Boulogne, earned him little more than arrest by the local village gendarme and incarceration in the northern French fortress of Ham. During his imprisonment, he authored several tracts on social and economic questions before the inattentiveness of his jailors, or, more precisely, his disguise in women's clothing, allowed him to escape. But in December 1848, Louis Napoleon handily won election to the presidency of the Second Republic. In imitation of his uncle's decision to elevate himself to Consul for Life (1802) and Emperor of the French (1804), Louis Napoleon staged a coup d'état against the republican constitution on 2 December 1851 to become president for life. Exactly one year later he had himself proclaimed Napoleon III, Emperor of the French. Both dates had been carefully chosen to coincide with the anniversary of the battle of Austerlitz, his uncle's spectacular triumph over a joint Austro-Russian army on 2 December 1805.

The Napoleonic Ideas, *1839*

. . . Men of liberty, ye who rejoiced in the fall of Napoleon, lamentable indeed was your error! How many years must still pass away, how many struggles and sacrifices must there be, before you again reach the point to which Napoleon brought you!

And you, statesmen of the Congress of Vienna, who have made yourselves masters of the world on the wreck of the Empire, your part might have been a noble part, but you did not comprehend it! In the name of liberty, and even of license, you aroused the nations against Napoleon; you placed him under the ban of Europe, as a despot and a tyrant; you proclaimed that you had delivered the nations and secured their repose. For a moment they believed you; but nothing solid can be built upon a lie and a blunder! Napoleon had closed the gulf of revolutions; that gulf, when you overthrew him, you reopened. . . .

Here, then, again let us ask, who are the greatest statesmen: those who founded a system which is crumbling away on all sides, despite their omnipotence; or those who founded a system which survives their defeat, and which springs anew from their ashes?

The Napoleonic ideas, then, bear the character of ideas which regulate the movement of societies, since they advance of their own force, though deprived of their author. . . . [T]he system of the Emperor . . . will reconstruct itself: sovereigns and people, all will aid to reestablish it, because every man will see in it a guarantee of order, of peace, and of prosperity. . . .

Let us repeat in conclusion: the Napoleonic idea is not an idea of war, but a social, industrial, commercial idea—an idea of humanity. . . .

—The Political and Historical Works of Louis Napoleon Bonaparte (London, 1852), 1:343–49

4.12   THE DEMISE OF THE ROMAN REPUBLIC

Mazzini to de Lesseps, 18 May 1849 •
Tocqueville in the French Chamber, 18 October 1849

The evocation of the Napoleonic legend was not without its pitfalls—for all its glory, the Napoleonic empire had ended on the road to Waterloo, and even the most assiduous promoter of the legend had to come to terms with the question of whether the final outcome did not have its roots in systemic or structural flaws. Louis Napoleon for one was not blind to this paradox, and he certainly wanted to avoid the missteps that, in his view, had proved the undoing of his uncle. In foreign policy, the lessons of history seemed to suggest that a neo-Napoleonic program would succeed only if it were tolerated by England. In French domestic politics, it was in Louis Napoleon's interest to repudiate the antagonism between church and state which had clouded the history of the First Empire.

In November 1848, Pope Pius IX had fled the revolution in Rome. A newly elected Roman assembly on 9 February 1849 "guarantee[d] . . . the independent exercise of [the pope's] spiritual power" but otherwise declared papal government at an end and proclaimed a republic in its stead. Seizing this opportunity to improve his standing with French Catholic opinion, Louis Napoleon persuaded the French parliament to vote the funds for sending a French expeditionary army to Rome. Those who on ideological grounds deplored the confrontation of two fledgling republics were assured that the population of Rome would prefer to treat with French rather than Austrian, Neapolitan, or Spanish troops.

By sheer coincidence, the Roman question brought together an unlikely cast of principals. The Roman republic was administered by a triumvirate headed by the nationalist philosopher Giuseppe Mazzini. Its military defense lay in the hands of Giuseppe Garibaldi. The French ministry's man on the spot, Ferdinand de Lesseps, and the new foreign minister himself, Alexis de Tocqueville, are better known to posterity for activities other than their involvement in the Roman question.

Probably dispatched to play for time as the French expeditionary corps awaited reinforcements, de Lesseps was under the illusion that the purpose of his mission was to find a peaceful resolution of the conflict. He reached a compromise with Mazzini on 31 May 1849, only to have its terms disavowed by the French commander, General Nicolas Oudinot. Oudinot's troops seized the city, thereby inaugurating a French presence in Rome which, with the exception of a brief interval in 1867, lasted until 1870.

In restoring the temporal authority of the pope, French forces returned to power a regime notorious throughout Europe for its misgovernment. Tocqueville had taken office in June 1849 reluctant to assume any responsibility for the sending of the French expeditionary army. But when the new papal administration turned a deaf ear to French entreaties to liberalize, Tocqueville was thrust into the position of having to defend his government's policy in a raucous session of the French chamber. His explanations were unpersuasive. They are interesting, however, for Tocqueville's views of the now defunct Roman republic and its principal authors.

a)   ***Mazzini to de Lesseps, 18 May 1849***

. . . There is in the heart of this people one resolute determination, and that is the downfall of the temporal power invested in the Pope, the hatred of priestly government under whatever attenuated or indirect form it may present itself. I say hatred, not of individuals, but of the government. . . . Remember that a return to the past means neither more nor less than organized disorder, a renewal of the struggle of secret societies, the uprising of anarchy in the heart of Italy, the inoculation of vengeance into a people which is only desirous of forgetting, a brand of discord permanently implanted in the midst of Europe, the program of the extreme parties supplanting the orderly Republican Government of which we are now the organs.

This surely cannot be desired by France, by her government, by the nephew of Napoleon; especially in the presence of the double invasion of the Neapolitans and Austrians. . . .

—Ferdinand de Lesseps, *Recollections of Forty Years* (London, 1887), 1:24–30

b)   ***Tocqueville in the French Chamber, 18 October 1849***

[Tocqueville:] . . . I hope that our requests will be granted. I cherish this hope because I have faith in the word and the character of Pius IX, because in heeding our appeal he will be carrying out his great design—referred to by M. de Corcelles[20]—to reconcile liberty with religion and to continue to play the lofty part he has so gloriously begun [ironical laughter on the left], this great part which has aroused so much enthusiasm and won him such noble support when at his first steps the whole of Europe acclaimed his efforts and on all sides, on this very tribune, eloquent voices called out to him: "Courage, Holy Father, Courage" [shouts on the left].

[A Member:] That is M. Thiers.

[Many Voices:] Yes! Yes! Hear! Hear!

[Tocqueville:] I believe, therefore, that our plea will be heard. Some of the limitations introduced in the amnesty have already been removed or modified in a sense that is extremely favourable to those to whom it applies. In any case, so far as it is possible to tell at present, this Roman revolution which began with violence and murder . . . [commotion on the left, shouts of: "No, no, that is a libel";—on the right: "Yes, yes, quite true, hear! Hear!"].

[Tocqueville:] . . . which began with violence and murder [renewed clamor and interpolations on the left].

[Testelin:[21]] You lie! [Oh! Oh!]

[President of the Chamber:] M. Testelin [renewed shouts of Order! Order!] Wait, Gentlemen, please.—[Then turning to the extreme left]. M. Testelin, I have heard many interruptions from this side; but they were simultaneous and I was waiting for

[20]Claude Tircuy de Corcelles (1802–1892). French minister to the papal government.
[21]Achille Testelin (1814–1891). Journalist; radical member from the Département du Nord; proscribed during the Second Empire. Resistance against the repressive measures of the Second Empire was particularly strong in the Nord, perhaps because of the easy availability of Belgian pamphlets and newspapers (cf. Document 7.1).

the moment when I should be able to recognize an individual voice saying things that deserved censure. The word you have used is an insult and I call you to order.

[Testelin:] I submit [on the right and in the centre: Order! Order!].

[President:] Instead of submitting you go on. For the second time I call you to order, the fact to be entered in the verbatim record [on the right: Hear! Hear! Censure!; on the left excited shouts and turbulence].

[Duprat:[22]] [rises and addresses the President, but in the midst of the uproar it is impossible to hear what he says. Several members of the extreme left appear for a moment on the point of leaving the Chamber].

[President:] M. Duprat, you are not called upon to speak. Please sit down and be silent [Duprat sits down and calm is restored].

[Tocqueville:] I have the profoundest contempt for such insults and I repeat that one thing is certain up to the present and that is that this revolution which began with violence and bloodshed . . . [renewed shouts on the left: It is not true].

[Many Voices:] It is true. Hear! Hear!

[Tocqueville:] . . . which continued in the midst of violence and folly, has up to the present cost no man his liberty, his goods or his life for political reasons. That is the truth. When I remember—without wishing to allude to any particular incident—the more or less tragic events to which the restoration of former powers has given rise in recent times in Italy and elsewhere in Europe, when I think of all this I feel justified in declaring here and now that those whom we have defeated should thank Heaven . . . [outcry on the left. On the right: Why, obviously!] . . . I say that those we have defeated must thank Heaven that it was the arm of France that struck them and not that of another [lively applause on the right and in the centre]. Gentlemen, I have said all I have to say. I have explained in the midst of interruptions which were, to say the least, uncalled for and certainly improper, the ideas and actions of French diplomacy. France and the Assembly will be the judges [on the left: Yes! Yes! on the right: Hear! Hear! Lively applause from many sides]. . . .

—*Moniteur Universelle*, 19 October 1849, 3211, or Alexis de Tocqueville, *Oeuvres complètes: Écrits et discours politiques* (Paris, 1990), 3:363–65; translation in J. P. Mayer (ed.), *The Recollections of Alexis de Tocqueville* (New York, 1949), 343–45

4.13   PRUSSIA'S "HUMILIATION" AT OLMÜTZ

Schwarzenberg to Prokesch-Osten, 26 October 1850 • *Convention of Olmütz, 29 November 1850* • *Bismarck in the Prussian Legislature, 3 December 1850* • *Bismarck in his Memoirs, 1898*

In May and June 1849, Prussian pressure had caused the Frankfurt Parliament to be disbanded. Prussia had since sought to group the German princes in a league (the "Erfurt union") dominated by itself but from which Austria remained excluded. For its part, Austria in May 1850 tried to reactivate the Diet of the German Confederation. In this endeavor it could rely on the support of Bavaria, Württemberg, and an increasing number of midsize German states; Prussia and its dwindling number of supporters, however, continued to boycott the diet.

The Austro-Prussian crisis came to a head over the question of Holstein and Hesse-Kassel. In his capacity as Duke of Holstein (cf. Documents 4.6 and 4.14), King Frederick VII of

---

[22]Pascal Duprat (1815–1885). Journalist; member for the moderate left; exiled from 1852 to 1869.

Denmark invoked the diet's support for the restoration of his rule in this province. The diet complied on 25 October 1850. Similarly, the Elector of Hesse-Kassel (whose state formed a geographical wedge between the western provinces of Prussia and the bulk of its territories) appealed to the diet for support against his uncooperative parliament on the basis of articles 25 and 26 of the Vienna Act of 1820 (cf. Document 2.3). On 26 October 1850, the diet ordered federal troops to enforce the elector's authority. Prussia declared the diet's intervention unconstitutional and garrisoned the military roads across Hesse-Kassel, which connected both parts of Prussia, thereby preventing the advance of the federal forces to the city of Kassel.

The showdown over Hesse-Kassel brought Prussia and Austria to the brink of armed confrontation; in fact, Prussian and federal troops exchanged fire near Fulda on 8 November. But, for all practical purposes, the issue had already been decided: in a meeting in Warsaw on 26 October, Schwarzenberg had secured Russia's support for the Austrian position. Facing the prospect of an Austro-Russian coalition in the German question, Prussia now had little choice but to back down.

Meeting in the Moravian town of Olmütz on 29 November, the prime ministers of Austria and Prussia settled their differences, but essentially on Austria's terms. Implicit in their agreement was Prussia's recognition of the reconstituted German Confederation, its membership in this institution, and its abandonment of any separate Prussian-led league of German princes.

In time, the "humiliation" of Olmütz became a symbol of Prussia's fortunes at their nadir—a point hammered home by nationalist writers during and after the unification of Germany. But in December 1850, the most vigorous defense of the Olmütz convention came from Otto von Bismarck, then a member of the Prussian legislature. Insofar as Bismarck had enjoyed a political reputation at all, it was for his ultraroyalist outlook and his eccentricities. But his speech in the legislature of 3 December 1850 on the Olmütz convention catapulted him into the limelight; above all, it identified him as a champion of cooperation with Austria. Bismarck thus became a logical choice for the post of Prussian minister to the Diet of the German Confederation in Frankfurt, an appointment which was offered, and which he accepted, in July 1851. One of the ironies of this tale is that, fifteen years later, it was Bismarck, now Prussian prime minister, who was the driving force behind the demolition of the German Confederation and the expulsion of Austria from Germany.

a)   *Schwarzenberg to Prokesch-Osten,*[23] *26 October 1850*

Yesterday and today I had rather extensive conversations with the Russian Tsar and Count Nesselrode on the subject of the German matter or, put more correctly, our relationship with Prussia. . . . In the Hessian question, the right of the Confederation to render the assistance which has been demanded of it is recognized completely. Prussia is denied any objection and certainly any physical hindrance of the measures to be taken by the Confederation. Should this lead to a conflict or a war, Prussia alone will be saddled with the responsibility and there will be a declaration in Berlin that Russia, sharing the views of Austria, will remain neutral as long as other foreign (i.e., non-German) governments will not intervene on behalf of Prussia. The declarations on the Danish matter are supposed to be even more definitive. The intervention of the Confederation is recognized as a right and even a duty and [it is] declared that any

---

[23]Anton Prokesch von Osten (1795–1875). Austrian minister in Berlin, 1849–1852.

attempt to hinder the effectiveness of the Confederation in the pacification of Holstein will bring about the active intervention of Russia, e.g. the advance of a Russian army into Prussia. . . .

—Huber, *Dokumente*, 1:574–75

b)   *Convention of Olmütz, 29 November 1850*

. . . 1. The Governments of Austria and Prussia declare that it is their intention to bring about the final and definitive settlement of the affairs of Electoral Hesse [= Hesse-Kassel] and Holstein, by the common decision of all the German governments. . . .

3. . . . both in Electoral Hesse and in Holstein, there should be established a legal state of things conformable with the fundamental laws of the [German] Confederation . . . : A) in Electoral Hesse, Prussia will pose no impediment to the action of the troops [of the Confederation] called in by the Elector . . . ; B) . . . Austria and Prussia will send to Holstein . . . joint commissioners . . . in the name of the Confederation. . . .

—Hertslet, 2:1143-45; Hurst, 1:289–90

c)   *Bismarck in the Prussian Legislature, 3 December 1850*

. . . Nowadays, why do great states wage war? The only healthy basis of a great state— and this is what sets it apart from a small state—is its egotism and not some romantic notion. It is not dignified for a great state to quarrel on behalf of a matter that does not correspond to its interests. Accordingly, gentlemen, show me a goal worthy of a war and I will support you. It is too easy for a statesman, either in his ministry or in the legislature, to follow the popular winds, to beat the war drum—while warming himself in front of his fireplace and delivering thundering speeches in this forum, and leaving the question up to the foot-soldier who bleeds to death in the snows whether or not his "system" will succeed. Nothing is easier than that. But woe to the statesman who at this time does not find a reason for the war, a reason which will still be unimpeachable after its conclusion. I am convinced that you will, in a year's time, view differently the questions with which we are now occupied—after you examine them retrospectively through a long perspective of battlefields and fire, misery and deprivation, of a hundred thousand corpses and a debt of a hundred million. Will you then have the courage to visit the farmer on his ruined plot, the cripple who has been shot to pieces, the father who has lost his child, in order to say: you have suffered much, but: rejoice with us! the constitution of the [Erfurt] union is saved! [amusement]. . .

Prussia's honor, in my opinion, does not mean that everywhere in Germany Prussia needs to play the part of Don Quixote ready to defend miffed parliamentary celebrities who think that their local constitution is endangered. . . . [I]t is a strange form of unity which . . . in its pursuit of German honor causes the fulcrum of the German question to be placed in Warsaw and Paris. Picture an armed confrontation in Germany in which both sides are about equally powerful: then the intervention even of powers of lesser import than Russia or France can be decisive. . . .

—GW, 10:101–10

d)   ***Bismarck in his Memoirs, 1898***

. . . The fundamental error of the Prussian policy . . . was that people fancied they could attain—through publicist, parliamentary, or diplomatic hypocrisies—results which could really be had only through a fight or through the readiness for a fight; results which, however, in our wishful thinking, we hoped would be handed to us to reward us for our virtuous moderation, for our rhetorical displays of 'German sentiment.' In a later day these became known as 'moral conquests'; it was the hope that others would do for us what we dared not do for ourselves.

—Otto von Bismarck, *Gedanken und Erinnerungen* (Stuttgart, 1898) 1:77

4.14   NATIONALISM DENIED: THE SCHLESWIG-HOLSTEIN SETTLEMENT, 1852

Prussian Précis of the Austro-Prussian Negotiations with Denmark,
30 December 1851 • *London Protocol, 8 May 1852* • *Act of Renunciation by*
the Duke of Augustenburg, 30 December 1852

The Malmö armistice of 28 August 1848 (cf. Document 4.6) ushered in a season of inconclusive diplomatic wrangling. Denmark's renunciation of the armistice in February 1849 sounded the death knell for various mediation proposals (including one by Palmerston that had been accepted by the Frankfurt Parliament). The Frankfurt Parliament did not survive long enough to witness the conclusion of a second Prusso-Danish armistice (July 1849) and preliminary peace (July 1850), concluded without prejudice to the legal claims of the various parties. These were finally resolved—or so it was thought—in the London Protocol of 8 May 1852.

Signed by the Great Powers, Sweden, and Denmark, the London Protocol completely ignored the nationalist passions that had set the Schleswig-Holstein question into motion in the first place. A dynastic settlement pure and simple, the protocol showed once again the longevity of rights accrued even under the *ancien régime*—a powerful demonstration of the importance of positivist law in an age clamoring for the recognition of natural rights. But by giving legal standing to the Great Powers and Sweden, the London Protocol also assured that any future dispute over the implementation of the agreement would not be limited to Denmark, the duchies, and the German Confederation.

The last document reproduced below imparts a similar, almost medieval, flavor. In it, the Duke of Augustenburg, the claimant to the duchies who had been excluded from the succession by the London settlement, renounced his claim. The obligations which he assumed for himself and his successors are spelled out here; in exchange, the King of Denmark assumed all outstanding debts on the properties transferred and, in addition, paid the duke an indemnity.

Finally, it should be noted that Russia's position in the Schleswig-Holstein crisis was dictated not only by Russia's strategic interests in the Danish straits (Document 4.6) but also by dynastic considerations. Tsar Nicholas's daughter Alexandra had married Frederick VII (before his accession to the throne) and died shortly thereafter in childbirth. Moreover, Nicholas was not only head of the Romanovs but—through his direct descent from Charles-Frederick of

Holstein-Gottorp—the highest-ranking member of this family as well and therewith titular head of the Danish royal clan.

a)   *Prussian Précis of the Austro-Prussian Negotiations with Denmark, 30 December 1851*

. . . 6. The Royal Danish Government will agree with the German powers [Prussia and Austria] that the Duchy of Schleswig will continue to exist as a separate part of the Danish monarchy, to be incorporated neither constitutionally nor administratively in the Kingdom of Denmark. . . .

7. . . . the Royal Danish government has no intention of introducing in the Duchies of Holstein and Lauenburg, or in the Duchy of Schleswig, the constitution or the electoral laws currently in force in the Kingdom of Denmark. . . .

—*Danske Tractater efter 1800* (Copenhagen, 1877), 1st Series, 1:271–72

b)   *London Protocol, 8 May 1852*

[Preamble:] [Their Majesties] taking into consideration that the maintenance of the integrity of the Danish monarchy, as connected with the general interests of the European equilibrium [*équilibre européen*] is of high importance to the preservation of peace, and that an arrangement by which the succession to the whole of the dominions now united under the scepter of His Majesty, the King of Denmark, should devolve upon the male line, to the exclusion of females, would be the best means of securing the integrity of that monarchy, have resolved, at the invitation of His Danish Majesty, to conclude a treaty, in order to give to the arrangements relating to such order of succession an additional pledge of stability by an act of European acknowledgment. . . .

Art. 3: It is expressly understood that the reciprocal rights and obligations of His Majesty the King of Denmark, and of the German Confederation, concerning the Duchies of Holstein and Lauenburg, rights and obligations established by the Federal Act of 1815, and by the existing Federal Right, shall not be affected by the present treaty. . . .

—Hurst, 1:293–96; *SP* 42:13–17 [French]

c)   *Act of Renunciation by the Duke of Augustenburg, 30 December 1852*

We, Christian August . . . 1) cede and transfer on behalf of Ourselves, Our heirs, and descendants all Our rights to the Augustenburg ducal estates and possessions on Alsen Island and on the mainland of the Duchy of Schleswig . . . to Your Royal Majesty, the King of Denmark . . . ; 2) in addition commit Ourselves to take Our future residence for Ourselves and Our family outside of Your Majesty's realm and lands, wherein We and Our descendants will naturally neither want to acquire nor be allowed to acquire landed property; and vouch and promise for Ourselves and Our family, on Our princely word and honor, to do nothing which could disturb or endanger the calm in Your Royal Majesty's realms and lands; and to oppose in no way past or future decisions of Your Royal Majesty pertaining to the order of succession for all lands presently united under Your Majesty's scepter or the future organization of Your monarchy. . . .

—Danske Tractater, 1st Series, 1:289–90

CHAPTER 5

The European Concert Wrecked: The Crimean War

In the English-speaking world, the politics and diplomacy of the Crimean War are remembered chiefly for the role played by Palmerston and Stratford in promoting the anti-Russian hysteria that gripped much of the reading public in England, with the goal of bringing England into a war against Russia over the Eastern Question. Summing up this view, the Scottish historian Robert W. Seton-Watson wrote, "The Crimean War has come to be regarded by most historians as the most unnecessary in the history of modern Europe: and even if this is too sweeping a verdict, it will remain beyond all question as the classic proof that in foreign policy the voice of the people is not necessarily the voice of God, and that an ill-informed and excitable public opinion can plunge a country into a war no less effectually than a dictator or a crowned autocrat."[1]

The Crimean War can also be approached from a different angle. It can be seen as a consequence of the breakdown of the European concert, as an object lesson of what can happen when statesmen's collective assumptions about the purpose of the state "system" (its objectives and the limits which it places on the behavior of individual members) collapse. The consensus about what was desirable and what was possible had, since 1815, succeeded in containing other crises and had kept Great Power rivalries from flaring into shooting wars. But what brought on its breakdown in 1853–1854? In the view of a foremost student of this subject, "concert diplomacy did not . . .fail because it was worn out, no longer adequate to the task; it failed because it was prevented from succeeding, its basic principles repudiated and its fundamental rules broken."[2] From this vantage point, the origins of the war are best explored through the questions: Who or which power provoked the initial crisis and for what reason? Who escalated the crisis and why? And, finally, who intended war and for what purpose?

When analyzed from hindsight—that is, from the perspective of its results—the Crimean War looms as the watershed in the diplomatic history of the nineteenth century. Russia, in defeat, focused its energies on domestic issues and preferred expansion in Central and East Asia to a resolute policy in Europe. Britain, painfully aware of the

---

[1] *Britain in Europe, 1789–1914. A Survey of Foreign Policy* (Cambridge, 1937), 359.
[2] Paul W. Schroeder, *Austria, Great Britain, and the Crimean War: The Destruction of the European Concert* (Ithaca, 1972), 408.

disproportion between its efforts and the meager results obtained, lost its taste for military entanglements on the European continent. The war's principal victim, however, was not one of the belligerents, but Austria—the one state that in the past had depended most on the functioning of the 1815 system, on the tolerance (and, occasionally, the active support) of at least one of the powers on Europe's flanks. Pressured by Britain and France, Austria drifted more and more into the western camp, disrupting in the process the Austro-Russian alliance on which its own survival had been predicated in 1848–1849. As the Austro-Russian cooperation of the years 1876–1877 and 1897–1907 would show, this relationship was not irretrievably doomed. But it was unlikely that Russia, after the Crimean War, would again rush to the rescue of its neighbor, offer its support to buttress Austria's position in Italy, or help decide in Austria's favor the Austro-Prussian contest for primacy in Germany.

GENERAL READING: Winfried Baumgart, *The Peace of Paris 1856. Studies in War, Diplomacy and Peacemaking* (Santa Barbara, 1981); Ann Pottinger Saab, *The Origins of the Crimean Alliance* (Charlottesville, 1977); Norman Rich, *Why the Crimean War? A Cautionary Tale* (1985; reprint: McGraw-Hill, 1992); Paul W. Schroeder, *Austria, Great Britain, and the Crimean War: The Destruction of the European Concert* (Ithaca, 1972)

5.1   THE QUARREL OVER THE HOLY PLACES

Thouvenel to Cintrat, 9 December 1851 ● *Buol to Leiningen, 22 January 1853*

If Louis Napoleon's purpose was to dismantle the 1815 system, then the most effective method was not to take it head on but to choose a more circuitous route. The Ottoman Empire was neither a signatory to—nor was it covered by—the 1815 treaties, and it was here, in the murky waters of the Eastern Question, that Louis Napoleon might find the means for driving a wedge between the Great Powers.

An opportunity for so doing was afforded by championing the claims of the Catholic church in the Holy Land. French support for the Roman church had the additional merit of playing well with Catholic opinion in France, but it was foreseeable that any rights granted by the Porte to Catholic institutions would create a ripple effect: they would come at the expense of the Greek Orthodox church and might therefore lead to a Russian counterdemonstration. Russian intervention on behalf of the Orthodox church in the Ottoman Empire, in its turn, might stoke the suspicions of other powers, suspicions that had already been aroused by the increase in Russia's stature resulting from its military intervention in Hungary (cf. Document 4.9), the exercise of Russian diplomatic pressure in the German (cf. Document 4.13) and Schleswig-Holstein questions (cf. Document 4.14), and Russia's occupation of Moldavia and Wallachia between 1848 and 1851.

The purpose of the French action was clearly evident to the French minister in Munich, Édouard Thouvenel, who was about to return to Paris to head the political department in the French foreign ministry.[3] It was equally apparent to the new Austrian foreign minister, Karl von Buol.[4] His instructions to Christian von Leiningen,[5] excerpted below, are of interest for this

---

[3](1818–1866). French counselor, then minister, in Athens, 1845–1850; ambassador in Constantinople, 1855–1860; foreign minister, 1860–1862.

[4](1797–1865). Buol was both prime and foreign minister, 1852–1859.

[5]Christian Franz, Count Leiningen (1812–1856).

reason, but also because Leiningen was an Austrian general who had just been dispatched on a special mission to Constantinople to pressure the Porte on behalf of the prince-bishop of Montenegro. The irony here is that the Leiningen mission, and Leiningen's success in Constantinople, may well have signaled to Tsar Nicholas I that the way to do business in the Ottoman Empire was to send a high-ranking officer to thump the table.

a)   ***Thouvenel to Cintrat,[6] 9 December 1851***

. . . What then is the meaning of this quarrel that we stirred up in Constantinopel?. . . I know the East and I assure you that Russia will not give in. For it [Russia] this represents a question of life and death and it is to be hoped that one knows this full well in Paris in case one wishes to push the affair to the limit. . . .

—Édouard Thouvenel, *Nicolas Ier et Napoleon III. Les préliminaires de la guerre de Crimée, 1852–54, d'après les papiers inédits de M. Thouvenel* (Paris, 1891), 1–2

b)   ***Buol to Leiningen, 22 January 1853***

. . . The question then is not what the Porte should do, but: what is it capable of doing? And one should ponder a further question: what is the purpose of a demand which goes beyond the capacity of the party to which it is addressed? . . .

Whenever the long negotiations about the Holy Places touched on questions of essence, the Porte has behaved in as conciliatory and understanding a manner as only possible, but whenever questions of form were involved, its dealings have frequently not been straightforward. Its point of departure—and from its perspective, a correct one—has been the equality of the Christian denominations and it has, albeit in vain, done everything in its power to secure peace for this religion of peace in its original home. But it has, yielding to outside pressures, given to all sides assurances which contradict one another and which were, consequently, quickly exposed and which could not be fulfilled to the satisfaction of any of the parties. Differing degrees of fear—fear that sometimes waxes, sometimes wanes—are mirrored in these oral and written assurances. . . .

If in this question the Emperor of the French does not recognize the limits of what can be attained, if he will therefore pressure the helpless Porte into making promises which it cannot keep without offending Russia, then we have to draw the conclusion that France is working to bring about a rupture between the Ottoman Empire and its powerful neighbor. . . . It will be difficult to give the Porte any advice

---

[6]Pierre Cintrat (b. 1793). Director of the French foreign ministry archives, 1849–1866.

because its ability to satisfy both sides depends less on the Porte itself than on the willingness of both of these parties to declare themselves satisfied. . . .

—Winfried Baumgart et al. (eds.), *Österreichische Akten zur Geschichte des Krimkriegs* (Munich, 1980), 1:10

5.2   THE ABERDEEN AND SEYMOUR CONVERSATIONS

Nesselrode Memorandum, 3 December 1844 ●
Seymour to Russell, 22 January 1853 ●
Russell to Seymour, 9 February 1853

Tsar Nicholas I visited Britain in 1844. His extensive conversations with the foreign secretary, Lord Aberdeen, had as their main focus the future of the Ottoman Empire. After the tsar's return to Russia, Nesselrode sent a summary of the talks to Aberdeen. Aberdeen indicated that Nesselrode's synopsis indeed captured the essence of the talks, but carefully refrained from saying that he or the cabinet endorsed the modus procedendi suggested by the tsar—a nuance that may have been lost on the Russian ruler.

The very same subject—the future of the Ottoman Empire—inspired the tsar to bare his soul to the British ambassador, Sir George Hamilton Seymour, nine years later. The tsar was visibly displeased by the Franco-Ottoman convention of December 1852 that promoted Catholic rights at the Church of the Holy Sepulcher in Jerusalem and the Church of the Nativity in Bethlehem. Nicholas's distrust of the parvenu French emperor was outweighed only by his fear that France's gains had come at the expense of the Orthodox church and had, however indirectly, damaged Russia's standing at the Porte.

Nicholas may have expected that his views would get a favorable hearing in London as Aberdeen had become prime minister in December 1852. But the tsar may have overestimated Aberdeen's strength in his own cabinet: his foreign secretaries, in quick succession, were the Earl of Russell and the Earl of Clarendon, whose views on foreign affairs in general and Russia in particular hewed more closely to Palmerston's than Aberdeen's. Be that as it may, the tsar gave himself more latitude in his conversations with Seymour than tact or prudence warranted. Seymour for one suspected that the tsar was motivated less by solicitude for the condition of the Ottoman Empire than by a desire to hasten its collapse. Nor was the tsar's allusion to the Treaty of Kuchuk-Kainarji (it was unclear whether he referred solely to the Christians of the Danubian Principalities or to Turkey's entire Christian population) likely to remove British doubts. Russell initially took note—albeit with a touch of sarcasm—of the tsar's view of Russian treaty rights in the Ottoman Empire, but Nicholas's interpretation soon became unpalatable to the English cabinet.

a)   ***Nesselrode Memorandum, 3 December 1844***

. . . The object for which Russia and England will have to come to an understanding may be expressed in the following manner:

1. To seek to maintain the existence of the Ottoman Empire in its present state, so long as that political combination shall be possible.

2. If we foresee that it must crumble to pieces, to enter into previous concert as to everything relating to the establishment of a new order of things, intended to replace that which now exists, and in conjunction with each other. . . .

—Hurewitz, 1:291–92; *PP 1854*, 71:865–68

b)   *Seymour to Russell, 22 January 1853*

. . . His Majesty said . . . [o]n the contrary, my country is so vast, so happily circumstanced in every way, that it would be unreasonable for me to desire more territory. . . .

Well, in that Empire [Turkey], there are several millions of Christians whose interests I am called upon to watch over (*surveiller*), while the right of doing so is secured to me by Treaty. I may truly say that I make a moderate and sparing use of my right, and I will freely confess that it is one which is attended with obligations occasionally very inconvenient; but I cannot recede from the discharge of a distinct duty. Our religion, as established in this country, came to us from the East, and there are feelings, as well as obligations, which never must be lost sight of.

Now Turkey, in the condition which I have described, has by degrees fallen into such a state of decrepitude that, as I told you the other night, eager as we are for the prolonged existence of the man (and that I am as desirous as you can be for the continuance of his life, I beg you to believe), he may suddenly die upon our hands (*nous rester sur le bras*); we cannot resuscitate what is dead; if the Turkish Empire falls, it falls to rise no more; and I put it to you, therefore, whether it is not better to be provided beforehand for a contingency, than to incur the chaos, confusion, and the certainty of an European war, all of which must attend the catastrophe if it should occur unexpectedly, and before some ulterior system has been sketched; this is the point to which I am desirous that you should call the attention of your Government. . . .

[I]t is of the greatest importance that we should understand one another, and not allow events to take us by surprise; "Now I desire to speak to you as a friend and as a *gentleman*; if England and I arrive at an understanding on this matter, as regards the rest, it matters little to me; it is indifferent to me what others do or think. Frankly then, I tell you plainly, that if England thinks of establishing herself one of these days at Constantinople, I will not allow it. I do not attribute this intention to you, but it is better on these occasions to speak plainly; for my part, I am equally disposed to take the engagement not to establish myself there as proprietor that is to say; for as occupier, I do not say: it might happen that circumstances, if no previous provision were made, if everything should be left to chance, might place me in the position of occupying Constantinople."

. . . To render my meaning more clear I [Seymour] said further: I can only repeat, Sir, that in my opinion, Her Majesty's Government will be indisposed to make certain arrangements connected with the downfall of Turkey, but it is possible that they may be ready to pledge themselves against certain arrangements which might, in that event, be attempted. . . .

I would now submit to Your Lordship that this overture cannot with propriety pass unnoticed by Her Majesty's Government. . . . If, then, the proposal were to remain unanswered, a decided advantage would be secured to the Imperial Cabinet, which, in the event of some great catastrophe taking place in Turkey, would be able to point to proposals made to England, and which, not having been responded to, left the Emperor at liberty, or placed him under the necessity, of following his own line of policy in the East. . . .

—Hurewitz, 1:299–301; *PP 1854*, 71:837–40

c)   *Russell to Seymour, 9 February 1853*

. . . [I]t would hardly be consistent with the friendly feelings towards the Sultan which animate the Emperor of Russia, no less than the Queen of Great Britain, to dispose beforehand of the provinces under his dominion. . . . An agreement thus made . . .would not be very long a secret; and while it would alarm and alienate the Sultan, the knowledge of its existence would stimulate all his enemies to increased violence and more obstinate conflict. They would fight with the conviction that they must ultimately triumph; while the Sultan's generals and troops would feel that no immediate success could save their cause from final overthrow. Thus would be produced and strengthened that very anarchy which is now feared, and the foresight of the friends of the patient would prove the cause of his death. . . .

The more the Turkish government adopts the rules of impartial law and equal administration [for his Christian subjects], the less will the Emperor of Russia find it necessary to apply that exceptional protection which His Imperial Majesty has found so burdensome and inconvenient, though no doubt prescribed by duty and sanctioned by treaty. . . .

—Hurewitz, 1:301–3; Bourne, 313–16; *PP 1854*, 71:840–42

5.3   THE MENSHIKOV MISSION AND THE VIENNA NOTE

Nesselrode to Menshikov, 28 January/9 February 1853 ●
Vienna Note, 31 July 1853

To counteract the Franco-Ottoman convention and to restore Russian prestige, the tsar—following the example set by Austria (Document 5.1)—dispatched a special mission to Constantinople. Its object was to state Russian grievances and, by way of remedy, to demand a formal treaty embodying Russia's rights. Whether the value of such an instrument would have lain chiefly in its symbolism or whether the act of concluding a treaty would in itself have expanded Russia's rights can of course be debated. In any event, the question became moot when the tsar's envoy, Prince Menshikov, found the Ottoman government intractable.

The Porte continued to stonewall even when faced by a Russian threat (carried out by early July) to occupy Moldavia and Wallachia. To Russia, the Danubian Principalities were a familiar territory: it had extensive treaty rights in these Ottoman provinces (cf. Documents 3.1 and 3.5), had suppressed a rising there in 1848, and had evacuated the last of its forces only in 1851. But a Russian move against the principalities in the context of the crisis of 1853, even if justified with reference to Russia's treaty rights, could not but escalate the Russo-Turkish conflict.

MAP 4   *THE CRIMEAN WAR*

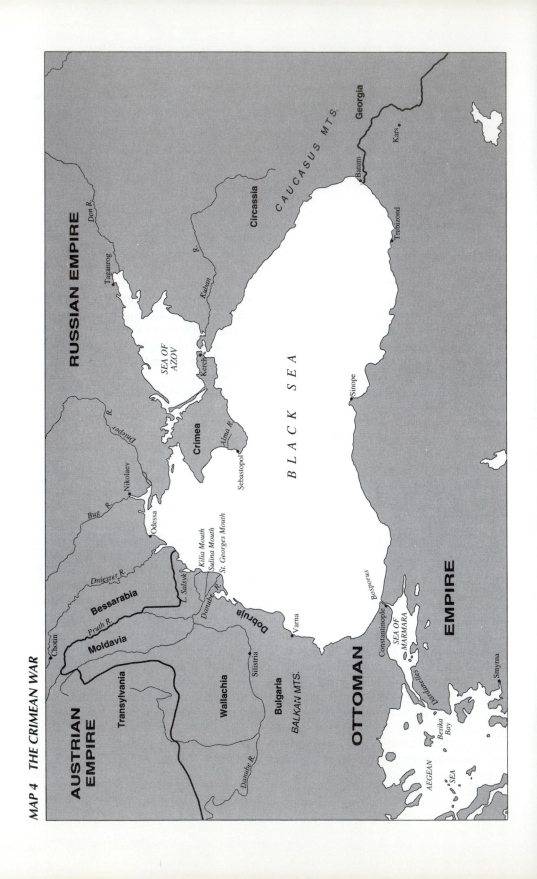

RUSSIAN EMPIRE

AUSTRIAN EMPIRE

Don R.

Taganrog

SEA OF AZOV

Kuban R.

R.

Dnieper R.

Nikolaev

Bug R.

Odessa

Dniester R.

Bessarabia

Prut R.

Moldavia

Chotin

Transylvania

L. Salsyk

Kilia Mouth
Sulina Mouth
St. Georges Mouth

Danube R.

Danube R.

Wallachia

Bulgaria

Silistria

BALKAN MTS.

Dobruja

Crimea

Alma R.

Sebastopol

Kerch

Varna

CAUCASUS MTS.

Circassia

Georgia

Kars

Batum

Trebizond

Sinope

BLACK SEA

Bosporus

Constantinople

SEA OF MARMARA

Dardanelles

OTTOMAN

EMPIRE

Smyrna

Besika Bay

AEGEAN SEA

Led by Austria, the four remaining Great Powers searched for a diplomatic solution to the Russo-Ottoman crisis. The language of the Vienna Note, drafted in consultation with Russia, seemed to offer such a solution. Russia accepted the note under the proviso that the Porte should consent to it without reservations, alterations, or amendments. For their part, the Great Powers instructed their ambassadors in Constantinople to secure the Porte's acceptance of the note.

The Vienna Note is a telling case study in the importance of form. The note envisaged a unilateral declaration that the sultan was to address to the Russian government. Any obligations spelled out in the declaration emanated solely from the Ottoman Empire; consequently, Russia had only the slimmest legal standing in the event of a dispute over its implementation.

Both the form and the language of the note were a far cry from Russia's original demands. One measure of the climb-down that Nicholas was now prepared to accept is the contrast between the wording of the Vienna Note on one hand and, on the other, the tsar's remarks to Seymour (preceding document) or his government's instructions to Menshikov.

a)   *Nesselrode to Menshikov, 28 January/9 February 1853*

. . . 5) that after all that has taken place recently at Constantinople and at Jerusalem, and after the retraction of solemn and repeated promises which the Ottoman government had made to us, the Imperial [Russian] Cabinet will consider neither new published *firmans* nor a declared arrangement as a sufficient guarantee unless these measures, agreed upon and understood [*arrêté*] by the Ottoman ministry and Your Excellency, shall be made into a patent or secret separate act entitled *convention* or *sened*, having the force and validity of a treaty. . . .

In other times and under other circumstances a resolution would have been much more easily obtained; today Turkey is for us an enemy much more vexing than dangerous. . . .

—A. M. Zaionchkovskii, *Vostochnaya Voina, 1853–56gg.*, supp. vol. 1: *Prilocheniya* (St. Petersburg, 1908), 371–74

b)   *Vienna Note, 31 July 1853*

His Majesty the Sultan, having nothing more at heart than to reestablish between himself and His Majesty the Emperor of Russia the relations of good neighbourhood and perfect understanding which have been unfortunately impaired by recent and painful complications, has diligently endeavoured to discover the means of obliterating the traces of those differences, and a sovereign *iradé* dated ____[7] having made known to him the Imperial decision, he is happy to be able to communicate it to his Excellency the Ambassador of Russia (or to his Excellency Count Nesselrode).

If the Emperors of Russia have at all times evinced their active solicitude for the maintenance of the immunities and privileges of the orthodox Greek Church in

[7]It should be remembered that one of the purposes of the Vienna Note was to secure said *iradé*. As of yet, it did not exist; hence, the date was left blank.

the Ottoman Empire, the Sultans have never refused again to confirm them by solemn acts testifying their ancient and constant benevolence towards their Christian subjects. His Majesty the Sultan, Abdul-Mejid, now reigning, inspired with the same dispositions, and being desirous of giving to His Majesty the Emperor of Russia a personal proof of his most sincere friendship, and of his hearty desire to consolidate the ancient relations of good neighbourhood and thorough understanding existing between the two States, has been solely influenced by his unbounded confidence in the eminent qualities of his august friend and ally, and has been pleased to take into serious consideration the representations which His Excellency Prince Menshikov conveyed to him.

The Undersigned has in consequence received orders to declare by the present note that the Government of His Majesty the Sultan will remain faithful to the letter and to the spirit of the Treaties of [Kuchuk] Kainardji and Adrianople relative to the protection of the Christian religion, and that His Majesty considers himself bound in honour to cause to be observed for ever, and to preserve from all prejudice either now or hereafter, the enjoyment of the spiritual privileges which have been granted by His Majesty's august ancestors to the orthodox Eastern Church, and which are maintained and confirmed by him; and moreover, in a spirit of exalted equity, to cause the Greek rite to share in the advantages granted to the other Christian rites by Convention or special arrangement. . . .

—PP 1854, 71ii:25–27 [new pagination: 457–59]

5.4   RUSSIA'S RETREAT AFFIRMED: THE OLMÜTZ PROJECT

Austro-Russian Draft, 28 September 1853 •
Colloredo to Buol, 6 October 1853

But the Porte did turn down the Vienna Note. It may have done so in the belief that the British government's support for the note had been lukewarm to begin with and hence that, if the Ottoman government persisted in its opposition to the note, it could detach Britain from the other three mediating powers (France, Austria, and Prussia). It may have been strengthened in this belief by the British ambassador in Constantinople, Lord Stratford de Redcliffe. Stratford's biographer assures us that his hero, in his own words, did his " '*official* best in support of the Vienna Note,' " but this does raise the question of what he did unofficially.[8]

Once the Porte rejected the Vienna Note, the Russian government—making good on the reservations with which it had accepted the note—no longer considered itself bound by it. But Buol, the Austrian foreign minister, tried one more time to bridge the widening gap between Russia and Britain. A meeting with the tsar and Nesselrode at Olmütz gave him his opportunity. Buol claimed that he had to "wrest every word from the Tsar," but in the final analysis the Russian emperor proved willing to resolve the Russo-Turkish conflict through diplomatic means. As the second document here shows, this time the obstacle was the British cabinet.

---

[8]Emphasis in original. Stratford to Clarendon, 20 August 1853, in Stanley Lane-Poole, *The Life of . . .Stratford Canning* (London, 1888), 2:295.

In any case, it is unlikely that the Olmütz project would have deterred the Porte: on 4 October, the Ottoman government, in the expectation of British and French backing, declared war on Russia.

a)   ***Austro-Russian Draft, 28 September 1853***

In recommending unanimously to the Sublime Porte the adoption of the Vienna Note, the Courts of Austria, France, England and Prussia are imbued with the conviction that this document does not infringe on the sovereign rights and the dignity of His Majesty the Sultan.

This conviction is based on the positive assurances that the cabinet of St. Petersburg gave regarding the intentions that motivate His Majesty the Emperor of Russia in his demand for a general guarantee of the religious immunities accorded by the Sultans to the Greek church within their Empire.

It is evident from these assurances that in asking, by virtue of the principle put forth in the treaty of [Kuchuk] Kainardji, that the Greek rite and clergy continue to enjoy their spiritual privileges under the aegis of their Sovereign the Sultan, the Emperor demands nothing contrary to the independence and the rights of the Sultan, nothing that suggests an intention to interfere in the internal affairs of the Ottoman Empire. What the Emperor of Russia wishes is the strict maintenance of the religious status quo of his rite, that is: a complete equality of rights and immunities between the Greek church and the other Christian communities subject to the Porte, [and] by consequence the enjoyment, on the part of the Greek church, of the privileges already accorded to those communities. He does not expect any revival of privileges of the Greek church that have fallen into disuse over time, or any administrative changes, but asks that the Sultan let it take part in all the privileges which he will in the future accord to other Christian rites.

The Imperial Cabinet of Austria as a result does not doubt that the Sublime Porte . . . will accept the adoption pure and simple of the Vienna Note. This acceptance, which would assure the Ottoman government of new evidence of the sympathy and support of the Powers which have advised it, offers it in one stroke a way both quick and honorable of effecting its open reconciliation with the Empire of Russia, a reconciliation that so many important interests call for seriously.

—Baumgart (ed.), Akten, op. cit., 1st Series, 1:176

b)   ***Colloredo[9] to Buol, 6 October 1853***

The Foreign Secretary has just told me that the British cabinet will not adopt the Olmütz Note as a means for getting the Vienna Note signed by the Ottoman Porte. He considers impossible obtaining or even proposing its signature.

—Baumgart (ed.), Akten, op. cit., 1st Series, 1:185

[9]Franz, Count Colloredo-Wallsee (1799–1859). Austrian ambassador in London, 1852–1856.

5.5   # PALMERSTON'S AND STRATFORD'S WAR AIMS

Memorandum by Palmerston, 19 March 1854 • *Palmerston in the House of Commons, 8 June 1855* • *Stratford to Clarendon, 13 September 1855*

Even before the expiration (on 25 April 1854) of Anglo-French ultimata to Russia, Palmerston sketched his objectives for an impending war against the tsarist empire. This catalogue of war aims was intended for his colleagues in the cabinet. In his public pronouncements, Palmerston preferred vague generalities and continued to do so even after assuming the prime ministership in February 1855. When his parliamentary critics charged in June 1855 that he was needlessly prolonging the war, Palmerston argued that a return to the status quo ante was unacceptable. But Palmerston avoided any specific public statement of war aims beyond insisting that Russia accept "limitations" on its power in the Black Sea. His speech was notable for its review of the course of Russian expansion and for a reference to the "natural line" of Russia's boundaries. He did not say, however, whether the object of the war was to return Russia to this "natural line," nor did he explain to his audience his method of discerning how "nature" determined the borders of states.

The fall of Sevastopol, Russia's principal fortified port on the Crimea, created the military preconditions for a peace in which Russia had to accept restrictions on its military and naval power in the Black Sea. But for Stratford de Redcliffe this was not enough. He still hoped for a wider war that would allow the Allies to wrest even further concessions from Russia.

a)   ## Memorandum by Palmerston, 19 March 1854

My beau ideal of the result of the war which is about to begin with Russia is as follows: Aaland and Finland restored to Sweden. Some of the German provinces of Russia on the Baltic ceded to Prussia. A substantive Kingdom of Poland reestablished as a barrier between Germany and Russia. Wallachia and Moldavia and the mouths of the Danube given to Austria. Lombardy and Venice set free from Austrian rule and either made independent States or incorporated with Piedmont. The Crimea, Circassia and Georgia wrested from Russia, the Crimea and Georgia given to Turkey, and Circassia either independent or connected with the Sultan as Suzerain. Such results it is true could be accomplished only by a combination of Sweden, Prussia and Austria, with England, France, and Turkey, and such results presuppose great defeats of Russia. But such results are not impossible and should not be wholly discarded from our thoughts.

—Lord John Russell, *Later Correspondence*, ed. by George Peabody Gooch (London, 1925), 2:160–61

b)   ## Palmerston in the House of Commons, 8 June 1855

. . . It is not necessary for me to go into the systematic extension of territory which had marked the policy of Russia for some time. It would be easy for me to trace her encroachments from the eastern shores of Asia to Central Asia by the Caspian Sea; her encroachments on Armenia to the Danube; on Poland, towards Norway and the Arctic Sea; to show how on every point of her immense circumference she has always been looking for extension, and how in every treaty that she has made with her neighbors she has ever sought to fix her boundary, not where nature had placed it, but beyond its natural line, in order to obtain a post which would either further extend her dominion, or assist her in making an aggression at a future time, or lay the ground for future demands. . . .

The right hon. Gentleman has thrown out certain suggestions, some of which, no doubt, are deserving of consideration, with respect to the arrangements for the future protection of Turkey, and one of those suggestions was that the Principalities should be declared neutral. There certainly are instances in Europe of such propositions, and it has been agreed by treaty that Belgium and Switzerland should be declared neutral; but I am not disposed to attach very much importance to such engagements, for the history of the world shows that when a quarrel arises, and a nation makes war, and thinks it is advantageous to traverse with its army such neutral territory, the declarations of neutrality are not apt to be very religiously respected. . . .

I say that the intention of Russia to partition Turkey is as manifest as the sun at noonday, and it is to prevent that [that] we are carrying on the war. . . . Let no man imagine that if Russia gets possession of Turkey, and if that gigantic power, like a colossus, had one foot upon the Baltic and another upon the Mediterranean, the great interests of this country will not be perilled—let not the peace-at-all-price imagine for a moment that their trade and their commerce would not be deeply injured. . . .

—*Parl. Debates*, 3rd Series, 138:1741–56

c)   ***Stratford to Clarendon,*[10] *13 September 1855***

In justice the Russians have no indulgence to expect from us. Having reduced the Russia of accumulated power, we have to guard against the Russia of prospective growth. This, I imagine might be effected by interposing a barrier of independent neutrals along the whole frontier. The Principalities are already better than independent. The remaining part of the line seems to offer more difficulty as to the arrangement in peace than to acquisition in war.

This, on the side of Georgia, would open a noble field for British valour and energy next year, after the ground shall have been tried by Omar Pasha this autumn, and the results, if successful, would be in their character compensatory as to our military credit in Europe, and highly influential as to our political power in Asia. It may be presumed that Russia is not yet quite prepared to accept such terms of peace. But Russia must be losing her self-confidence from day to day, and in a nation of superstitious slaves, when devotion is puzzled, and fear of authority relaxed, to say nothing of pressure on trade and property, the spirit of resistance declines rapidly, and the moral preparation for peace on any terms makes progress in proportion. A bold advance from Eupatoria, or some other well-selected point, would probably be attended with success beyond our expectation; but to produce its full effect the Russians ought not to be allowed time for looking about them and recovering their breath.

I abstain from pushing the speculation further, and I have already betrayed my conviction that enough is done or in progress even now to secure a complete satisfaction on the Four Points;[11] but surely our title to more solid guarantees and a more

[10]George Villiers, Earl of Clarendon (1800–1870). Foreign secretary, February 1853 to February 1858; October 1865 to April 1866; December 1868 to June 1870.
[11]Next document.

perfect settlement grows naturally out of a larger amount of hazard, sacrifice and success on our side.

—Stanley Lane-Poole, *Life of the Right Honourable Stratford Canning* (London, 1888), 2:413–14

5.6   OFFICIAL ALLIED AIMS: THE VIENNA FOUR POINTS, 8 AUGUST 1854

Westmorland to Buol, 8 August 1854

The Vienna Four Points were incorporated in a mutual exchange of notes among the British, French, and Austrian governments. Their purpose was to set forth the war aims of the Allies (and Austria) and to establish a basis for peace negotiations.

Point one stipulated the surrender of specific Russian treaty rights in the Ottoman Empire. Point two, though vague about the measures to be taken, applied to a strategic but small territory. Russia had already conceded point four in principle by agreeing to the Vienna Note.

The stumbling block, however, was the wording of point three. How was "the balance of power in Europe" to be measured, defined, quantified? What criteria or principles, beyond those spelled out in the three other points, needed to be applied for the balance to be reestablished?

These questions go to the heart of a conceptual problem. The balance of power was not self-evident. It did not operate automatically, nor could it be impartially defined.[12] Instead, its definition depended on one or more powers purporting to speak on its behalf. But those who invoked the balance found it to their advantage to portray it as an independent agent, a mechanism that reflected the workings of a higher principle. To be seen as acting on behalf of the balance conferred a claim to the moral high ground; it could also provide a convenient smoke screen for one's real motives.

The reference to the balance of power in point three was rendered even more ambiguous by the final paragraph of the British note. The refusal to state terms with precision gave Britain the option to revise or even increase its demands at a later date: the very elasticity of this formula could easily accommodate additional war aims without impairing the moral authority of the Allies. As demonstrated in Document 5.5, this was indeed part of Palmerston's and Stratford's calculations.

The extract here is from the British précis of the Vienna negotiations, submitted by the British ambassador to the Austrian government.

Westmorland[13] to Buol, 8 August 1854

. . . it results from the confidential communications which have taken place between the Courts of Vienna, Paris, and London . . .that the 3 powers are equally of opinion that the relations of the Sublime Porte with the Imperial Court of Russia cannot be re-established on solid and durable bases

---

[12]On this point, see A. J. P. Taylor, "The Traditions of British Foreign Policy," in *Europe: Grandeur and Decline* (New York, 1967).

[13]John Fane, Earl of Westmorland (1784–1859). British ambassador in Vienna, 1851–1855.

1. If the Protectorate hitherto exercised by the Imperial Court of Russia over the Principalities of Wallachia, Moldavia, and Serbia, be not discontinued for the future; and if the Privileges accorded by the Sultans to those Provinces, dependent on their Empire, be not placed under the Collective Guarantee of the Powers, in virtue of an Arrangement to be concluded with the Sublime Porte, and the stipulations of which should at the same time regulate all questions of detail.

2. If the Navigation of the Danube at its mouths be not freed from all obstacle, and made subject to the application of the principles established by the Acts of the Congress of Vienna.

3. If the Treaty of the 13th July, 1841[14] be not revised in concert by all the High Contracting Parties in the interest of the Balance of Power in Europe.

4. If Russia does not cease to claim the right of exercising an official Protectorate over the subjects of the Sublime Porte, to whatever rite they may belong, and if France, Austria, Great Britain, Prussia, and Russia, do not mutually assist each other in obtaining from the original action of the Ottoman Government the confirmation and the observance of the Religious Privileges of the different Christian communities, and in turning to account, for the common interest of their co-religionists, the generous intentions manifested by His Majesty the Sultan, without any prejudice resulting therefrom to his dignity and the Independence of his Crown.

The Undersigned is moreover authorised to declare that the Government of Her Majesty the Queen of Great Britain, while reserving to themselves the right of making known, at a suitable time, the particular conditions which they may attach to the conclusion of peace with Russia, and of modifying the general Guarantees above specified in such manner as the continuance of hostilities may render necessary, are resolved not to discuss and not to take into consideration any proposition from the cabinet of St. Petersburg which should not imply on its part a full and entire adhesion to the principles on which they are already agreed with the Governments of His Majesty the Emperor of Austria and of His Majesty the Emperor of France.

—Hertslet, 2:1216–17

5.7   THE PARIS PEACE SETTLEMENT

Firman of Sultan Abdul Mejid, 18 February 1856 • "General Treaty,"
30 March 1856 • Anglo-French-Russian Convention on the Aaland Islands,
30 March 1856 • Anglo-French-Austrian Guarantee of the Ottoman Empire,
15 April 1856 • Declaration on Maritime Law, 16 April 1856

The Paris peace consisted of a cluster of treaties and conventions. Mutual evacuations of occupied territory, border rectifications in Bessarabia, the neutralization of the Black Sea, the establishment of a Danube commission, and the rights of the Porte in Serbia and the Danubian Principalities all fell under the purview of a "general treaty." Appended to this "general treaty" were several additional agreements: a Russo-Ottoman convention limiting the naval forces that both powers could maintain as coastal patrols in the Black Sea; an affirmation of the closure of the Straits laid down by the Convention of 1841, exempting from this rule only light vessels for the Danube patrol and those supplying the Constantinople missions; an Anglo-French-Austrian guarantee of the Ottoman Empire, signed 15 April 1856; a convention

[14]Document 3.8f.

among Britain, France, and Russia on the Aaland islands (one of the few territorial provisions of nineteenth-century treaty law still in effect today). The "general treaty" also took note of an imperial firman, issued on 18 February 1856, reaffirming the privileges and immunities of the non-Muslim communities in the Ottoman Empire. One measure taken by the congress was unrelated to the Crimean War: the powers assembled at Paris issued a declaration on maritime law, eventually acceded to by all powers with major maritime interests except the United States.

Two pivotal questions, which might be answered on the basis of the excerpts that follow here, are: first, whether the settlement lived up to the war aims of the Allies (Document 5.6) as well as those of Palmerston and Stratford (Document 5.5); second, how the settlement promoted the dual pledge, contained in the preamble of the general treaty, to effect an enduring pacification of the east and to eliminate the conditions which had led to war in the first place.[15] Finally, the reader should be alerted to the novelty item in article 24 of the general treaty. Even though tempered by the preceding article, article 24 offered lip service to an almost revolutionary notion: that of self-determination, a concept studiously ignored in other recent pacifications (cf. Documents 4.13 and 4.14).

a)   *Firman of Sultan Abdul Mejid, 18 February 1856*

. . . All the privileges and spiritual immunities granted by my ancestors *ab antiquo*, and at subsequent dates, to all Christian communities or other non-Mussulman persuasions established in my empire, under my protection, shall be confirmed and maintained. . . .

Proceedings shall be taken for a reform in the constitution of the provincial and communal councils in order to insure fairness in the choice of the deputies of the Mussulman, Christian, and other communities and freedom of voting. . . .

—Hertslet, 2:1243–49; Hurewitz, 1: 315–18; *PP 1856*, 61:430–36

b)   *"General Treaty," 30 March 1856*

Their Majesties . . .animated by the desire of putting an end to the calamities of War, and wishing to prevent the return of the complications which occasioned it . . .by securing, through effectual and reciprocal guarantees, the Independence and Integrity of the Ottoman Empire [have agreed:] . . .

Art. 7: [Their Majesties] . . .declare the Sublime Porte admitted to participate in the advantages of the Public Law and System (*concert*) of Europe. Their Majesties engage, each on his part, to respect the Independence and the Territorial Integrity of the Ottoman Empire; Guarantee in common the strict observance of that engagement; and will, in consequence, consider any act tending to its violation as a question of general interest. . . .

Art. 9: His Imperial Majesty the Sultan having, in his constant solicitude for the welfare of his subjects, issued a Firman, which while ameliorating their condition

[15]The reader wishing to measure the success of these provisions might turn to Documents 8.14, 9.3 through 9.11, and 10.8.

without distinction of Religion or of Race, records his generous intentions towards the Christian population of his Empire, and wishing to give a further proof of his sentiments in that respect, has resolved to communicate to the Contracting Parties the said Firman, emanating spontaneously from his Sovereign will. The Contracting Powers recognise the high value of this communication. It is clearly understood that it cannot, in any case, give to the said Powers the right to interfere, either collectively or separately, in the relations of His Majesty the Sultan with his subjects, nor in the Internal Administration of his Empire.

Art. 10: The Convention of 13th of July, 1841, which maintains the ancient rule of the Ottoman Empire relative to the Closing of the Straits of the Bosporus and of Dardanelles, has been revised by common consent. . . .

Art. 11: The Black Sea is Neutralised; its Waters and its Ports, thrown open to the Mercantile Marine of every Nation, are formally and in perpetuity interdicted to the Flag of War, either of the Powers possessing its Coasts, or of any other Power. . . .

Art. 13: The Black Sea being Neutralised according to the terms of Art. 11, the maintenance or establishment upon its Coast of Military-Maritime Arsenals becomes alike unnecessary and purposeless. . . .

Art. 17: A [Danube] Commission . . ., which shall be permanent: 1. Shall prepare Regulations of Navigation and River Police; 2. Shall remove the impediments, of whatever nature they may be, which still prevent the application to the Danube of the Arrangements of the Treaty of Vienna; 3. Shall order and cause to be executed the necessary Works throughout the whole course of the River; and 4. Shall, after the dissolution of the European Commission, see to maintaining the Mouths of the Danube and the neighbouring parts of the Sea in a navigable state. . . .

Art. 20: . . .His Majesty the Emperor of All the Russias consents to the rectification of his Frontier in Bessarabia. . . .

Art. 23: . . .a Special Commission [for the principalities], as to the composition of which the High Contracting Powers will come to an understanding among themselves, shall assemble, without delay, at Bucharest, together with a Commissioner of the Sublime Porte. The business of this Commission shall be to investigate the present state of the Principalities, and to propose bases for their future organization.

Art. 24: His Majesty the Sultan promises to convoke immediately in each of the two Provinces a Divan ad hoc, composed in such a manner as to represent most closely the interests of all classes of society. These Divans shall be called upon to express the wishes of the people in regard to the definitive organization of the Principalities. An Instruction from the Congress shall regulate the relations between the Commission and these Divans. . . .

Art. 27: If the Internal Tranquillity of the Principalities should be menaced or compromised . . . [n]o armed Intervention can take place without previous agreement between . . . [the] Powers.

Art. 28: The Principality of Serbia shall continue to hold of the Sublime Porte, in conformity with the Imperial *Hats* [proclamations] which fix and determine its Rights and Immunities, placed henceforward under the Collective Guarantee of the Contracting Powers. . . .

Art. 30: His Majesty the Emperor of all the Russias and His Majesty the Sultan maintain in its integrity the state of their possessions in Asia, such as it legally existed before the rupture. . . .

—Hertslet, 2:1250–65; Hurst, 1: 317–28

c)   *Anglo-French-Russian Convention on the Aaland Islands, 30 March 1856*

Art. 1: His Majesty the Emperor of All the Russias . . .declares that the Aaland Islands shall not be fortified, and that no military or naval establishment shall be maintained or created there. . . .

—Hertslet, 2:1272–73; Hurst, 1:333

d)   *Anglo-French-Austrian Guarantee of the Ottoman Empire, 15 April 1856*

. . . Art. 2: Any infraction of the stipulations of the said Treaty [of Paris of 30 March] will be considered by the Powers signing the present treaty as a *casus belli*. . . .

—Hertslet, 2:1280–81; Hurst, 1:337

e)   *Declaration on Maritime Law, 16 April 1856*

Considering:

That Maritime Law, in time of War, has long been the subject of deplorable disputes;

That the uncertainty of the law and of the duties in such a matter, gives rise to differences of opinion between Neutrals and Belligerents which may occasion serious difficulties, and even conflicts;

That it is consequently advantageous to establish a uniform doctrine on so important a point . . .the Plenipotentiaries . . .have adopted the following solemn Declaration:

1. Privateering is, and remains abolished;

2. The Neutral Flag covers Enemy's Goods, with the exception of Contraband of War;

3. Neutral goods, with the exception of Contraband of War, are not liable to capture under Enemy's Flag;

4. Blockades, in order to be binding, must be effective, that is to say, maintained by a force sufficient really to prevent access to the coast of the enemy. . . .

The present Declaration is not and shall not be binding, except between those Powers who have acceded, or shall accede, to it.

—Hertslet, 2:1282–83

CHAPTER 6

Varieties of Mid-Century Imperialism

What distinguished the imperialism of the mid-nineteenth century—outside of the Eastern Question—from earlier and later varieties was its marginal impact on the relations of the Great Powers toward one another. But its impact on the societies of East, Southeast, and Central Asia was devastating. Outgunned by superior firepower, these had little choice but to bow to the demands of the European and American intruders.

GENERAL READING: Peter Ward Fay, *The Opium War, 1840–42* (Chapel Hill, 1975); Dietrich Geyer, *Russian Imperialism: The Interaction of Domestic and Foreign Policy, 1869–1914* (New Haven, 1987); Gerald S. Graham, *The China Station: War and Diplomacy, 1830–60* (Oxford, 1978); Daniel R. Headrick, *The Tools of Empire: Technology and European Imperialism in the Nineteenth Century* (Oxford, 1981); Firuz Kazemzadeh, *Russia and Britain in Persia, 1864–1914* (New Haven, 1968); David MacKenzie, *The Lion of Tashkent: The Career of General M. G. Cherniaev* (Athens, GA, 1974)

6.1   TREATY OF NANKING, 29 AUGUST 1842

The Peace of Nanking ended the Opium War (1839–1842) on British terms. By forcing China to abandon its traditional policy of dealing with the sea powers solely through the port of Canton, the treaty revolutionized not only the pattern of seaborne trade in East Asia but the entire Chinese regulatory system for contacts with the outside world. Ironically, the treaty text glossed over the principal cause of the war—the illegal import to China of opium from British India. Opium was mentioned in the treaty text only once, in the context of the indemnifications extorted from China.

Anglo-Chinese Treaty of Nanking, 29 August 1842

. . . Art. 2: His Majesty the Emperor of China agrees, that British subjects, with their families and establishments, shall be allowed to reside, for the purpose of carrying on their mercantile pursuits, without molestation or restraint, at the cities and towns of Canton, Amoy, Foochowfoo, Ningpo, and Shanghai. And Her Majesty the Queen of Great Britain, &c., will appoint Superintendents, or Consular Officers, to reside at each of the above named cities or towns, to be the medium of communication between the Chinese authorities and the said merchants, and to see that the just duties and other dues of the Chinese Government, as hereafter provided for, are duly discharged by Her Britannic Majesty's subjects.

Art. 3: It being obviously necessary and desirable that British subjects should have some port at which they may careen and refit their ships, when required, and keep stores for that purpose, His Majesty the Emperor of China cedes to Her Majesty the Queen of Great Britain, &c., the Island of Hong Kong, to be possessed in perpetuity by Her Britannic Majesty, her heirs and successors. . . .

Art. 4: The Emperor of China agrees to pay the sum of 6,000,000 dollars, as the value of the Opium which was delivered up at Canton in the month of March, 1839, as a ransom for the lives of Her Britannic Majesty's Superintendent and subjects, who had been imprisoned and threatened with death by the Chinese High Officers. . . .

Art. 7: It is agreed, that the total amount of 21,000,000 dollars, described in the 3 preceding Articles, shall be paid as follows. . . .

> —China. The Maritime Customs, *Treaties, Conventions, etc. between China and Foreign States*
> (1917; reprint: New York, 1973), 1:351–56; Hurst, 1:268–72

6.2   EXTRATERRITORIALITY AND MOST-FAVORED-NATION STATUS

Anglo-Chinese "General Regulations of Trade," 22 July/8 October 1843 •
Anglo-Chinese Supplementary Treaty (Hoomun Chai), 8 October 1843

An Anglo-Chinese agreement on "General Regulations of Trade" fulfilled China's pledge, in article 10 of the Treaty of Nanking, to establish a "Tariff of Export and Import Customs and other Dues." But the General Regulations went further: they also granted British subjects nearly complete immunity from local jurisdiction in China. A subsequent commercial treaty, to which the General Regulations were annexed, conferred most-favored-nation status on British trade. Noticeably absent from either document was a provision for reciprocity, a fact that made these instruments, from a moral as well as a legal point of view, "unequal treaties." These agreements introduced into East Asia a form of commercial and treaty law which had evolved, since the sixteenth century, from the interactions of the western maritime powers with Indian rajahs and Middle Eastern rulers. But once concluded, the Anglo-Chinese agreements of 1843 inspired imitation: within a year, they had become a template for similar treaties between China and the United States and between China and France.[1]

By the 1860s, China had been compelled to extend most-favored-nation status and extraterritoriality to all European maritime powers; within another generation, the western scramble for ever more extensive rights, concessions, and exemptions brought the Celestial Empire to the brink of collapse.[2] Although the western powers relinquished much of the substance of their treaty rights in China in the late 1920s, Britain and the United States held on to the vestiges until well into World War II. A formal termination of British and American extraterritorial rights came only in January 1943, a century after their inception.

[1] Texts in Hunter Miller (ed.), *Treaties and Other International Acts of the United States of America* (Washington, D.C., 1934), 4:109; Maritime Customs, *Treaties*, op. cit., 1:677–712 (United States and China); and ibid., 1:771–813 (France and China).
[2] Cf. Documents 10.5, 10.10, and 10.25.

a) ***Anglo-Chinese "General Regulations of Trade,"***
22 July/8 October 1843

. . . Art. 13: Whenever a British subject has reason to complain of a Chinese, he must first proceed to the Consulate and state his grievance. The Consul will thereupon inquire into the merits of the case, and do his utmost to arrange it amicably. In like manner, if a Chinese has reason to complain of a British subject, he shall no less listen to his complaint and endeavor to settle it in a friendly manner. If an English merchant has occasion to address the Chinese authorities, he shall send such address through the Consul, who will see that the language is becoming; and if otherwise, will direct it to be changed, or will refuse to convey the address. If unfortunately any disputes take place of such a nature that the Consul cannot arrange them amicably, then he shall request the assistance of a Chinese officer that they may together examine into the merits of the case, and decide it equitably. Regarding the punishment of English criminals, the English government will enact the laws necessary to attain that end, and the Consul will be empowered to put them into force; and regarding the punishment of Chinese criminals, these will be tried and punished by their own laws. . . .

—Maritime Customs, *Treaties*, op. cit., 1:383–89

b) ***Anglo-Chinese Supplementary Treaty (Hoomun Chai),***
8 October 1843

. . . Art. 6: It is agreed that English merchants and others residing at or resorting to the Five Ports to be opened shall not go into the surrounding country. . . . [S]hould any persons whatever infringe the stipulations of this article and wander away into the country, they shall be seized and handed over to the British consul for suitable punishment. . . .

Art. 8: The Emperor of China having been graciously pleased to grant to all foreign countries whose subjects or citizens have hitherto traded at Canton the privilege of resorting for purposes of trade to the other four ports of Fuchow, Amoy, Nigpo, and Shanghai, on the same terms as the English, it is further agreed, that should the Emperor thereafter, from any cause whatever, be pleased to grant additional privileges or immunities to any of the subjects or citizens of such foreign countries, the same privileges and immunities will be extended to and enjoyed by British subjects; but it is to be understood that demands or requests are not, on this plea, to be unnecessarily brought forward.

—Maritime Customs, *Treaties*, op. cit., 1:390–99

6.3　　　　　　　　　　THE "OPENING" OF JAPAN

Japanese American ("Perry's") Treaty of Kanagawa, 31 March 1854 ●
Japanese-American ("Townsend Harris") Treaty of Edo, 29 July 1859

Dutch and Chinese traders in Nagasaki maintained the only contacts between Japan and the outside world which were licensed by the shogunate. The arrival of the American

Commodore Matthew C. Perry in Edo (Tokyo) Bay in July 1853 brought this system to an end. Perry's objectives were to secure Japanese assistance for American vessels in distress and to institutionalize a commercial relationship. On this occasion, Perry succeeded only in having a letter from President Millard Fillmore brought to the attention of the emperor. By Japanese standards, this in itself was a revolutionary event. It fanned the debate between the regional lords and the shogunate about the advisability of increased foreign contacts, but Perry himself forced the issue when he returned with seven warships in February 1854. In concluding the Treaty of Kanagawa, Perry had to settle for less than unrestricted trade (article 7). Nor did the treaty establish extraterritoriality for American citizens in the two treaty ports.

These defects from the American point of view were remedied by the Japanese-American ("Townsend Harris") Treaty of Edo of 29 July 1858. In concluding his treaty, Harris benefited from the Japanese fear that Britain and France, after their joint military expedition against China (Document 6.4), would turn on Japan—a fear that helps explain the language of article 2. But the Townsend Harris treaty was not designed to buffer Japan against the predatory practices of the west. Within six months, it had become the model for similar treaties between Japan and the Netherlands, Russia, Britain, and France; it was thus to Japan what the 1843 Anglo-Chinese commercial treaty was to China. When Japan adopted a constitution in 1889 (itself patterned after the German constitution of 1867–1871) and western-style legal codes one year later, the juridical provisions of the Townsend Harris treaty and its offspring were no longer tenable. In 1894, Britain became the first power to relinquish extraterritoriality (Document 10.5a); the United States followed suit on 22 November 1894.[3]

a)   *Japanese-American ("Perry's") Treaty of Kanagawa, 31 March 1854*

. . . Art 7: It is agreed that ships of the United States resorting to the ports open to them, shall be permitted to exchange gold and silver coin and articles of goods for other articles of goods, under such regulations as shall be temporarily established by the Japanese government for that purpose. It is stipulated, however, that the ships of the United States shall be permitted to carry away whatever articles they are unwilling to exchange. . . .

Art. 9: It is agreed that if at any future day the government of Japan shall grant to any other nation or nations privileges and advantages which are not herein granted to the United States, and the citizens thereof, that these same privileges and advantages shall be granted likewise to the United States, and to the citizens thereof, without any consultation or delay.

Art. 10: Ships of the United States shall be permitted to resort to no other ports in Japan but Shimoda and Hakodate unless in distress or forced by stress of weather. . . .

—Hunter Miller (ed.), *Treaties and Other International Acts of the United States of America* (Washington, 1942), 6:164

---

[3]Text in Bevans, 9:387–96.

b) *Japanese-American ("Townsend Harris") Treaty of Edo, 29 July 1859*

. . . Art. 2: The President of the United States, at the request of the Japanese government, will act as a friendly mediator, in such matters of difference, as may arise between the government of Japan, and any European power. . . .

Art. 6: Americans, committing offences against Japanese, shall be tried in American consular courts, and when guilty, shall be punished according to American law. Japanese, committing offences against Americans, shall be tried by the Japanese authorities, and punished according to Japanese law. The consular courts shall be open to Japanese creditors, to enable them, to recover their just claims, against American citizens, and the Japanese courts shall in like manner be open to American citizens, for their recovery of their just claims, against Japanese. . . .

—Miller, op. cit., 7: 955

6.4   THE WESTERN POWERS AND RUSSIA IN CHINA, 1858–1860

Russo-Chinese Treaty of Aigun, 16/28 May 1858 • Anglo-Chinese Treaty of Tientsin, 26 June 1858 • Anglo-Chinese Treaty of Peking, 24 October 1860 • Russo-Chinese Treaty of Peking, 2/14 November 1860

In the 1850s and 1860s, the Chinese empire was on the verge of disintegration. The exact number of casualties incurred in the wake of the fifteen-year T'ai P'ing rebellion (1850–1864) will never be known, but this event has been reckoned as the largest bloodletting in human history. At the same time, the Nien Fei bandits (1853–1868) denied the imperial government effective control of much of the eastern coastal provinces, while Muslim secessionists (1855–1873) in Yunan broke away from central authority.

Superimposed on this civil strife was an Anglo-French war against China (1856–1860). In 1858, the Allied capture of the Taku fort outside of Tientsin (Tianjin) persuaded the imperial government to conclude peace. In treaties with France and Britain, China opened further treaty ports, several of them located hundreds of miles inland along the Yangtze River. But when the Chinese government sought to evade the terms of the Tientsin treaties, Britain and France resumed the war. In this second phase of the conflict, the Allies advanced to Peking. After Allied troops burned the Summer Palace—an event seared into the Chinese consciousness as the ultimate humiliation of the Ch'ing dynasty—and were otherwise in control of Peking, the imperial government used the Russian minister, Count Nicholas Ignatiev, as an intermediary in negotiations with the Allied commanders. The new peace, enshrined in the Anglo-Chinese and Franco-Chinese conventions of Peking, confirmed the earlier treaties of Tientsin, increased the indemnity from two to eight million taels (approximately six million dollars), and opened a further port. Ignatiev, for his part, commanded a high price for his services: he secured from the Chinese government a significant revision of the earlier Russo-Chinese Treaty of Aigun.

a)   ***Russo-Chinese Treaty of Aigun, 16/28 May 1858***

Art. 1: The left bank of the Amur river, from the Argun river up to the mouth of the Amur, will belong to the empire of Russia, and its right bank, down to the Ussuri river, will belong to the Chinese empire; the territories and places situated between the Ussuri and the sea, just as at present, will be held in common by the Chinese empire and the empire of Russia, until the border between the two states is determined.

—William Frederick Mayers (ed.), *Treaties between the Empire of China and Foreign Powers* (1877; reprint: Taipei, 1966), 100

b)   ***Anglo-Chinese Treaty of Tientsin, 26 June 1858***

. . . Art. 3: His Majesty the Emperor of China hereby agrees, that the Ambassador, Minister, or other Diplomatic Agent, so appointed by Her Majesty the Queen of Great Britain, may reside, with his family and establishment, permanently at the capital, or may visit it occasionally, at the option of the British government. He shall not be called upon to perform any ceremony derogatory to him as representing the Sovereign of an independent nation, on a footing of equality with that of China. . . .

Art. 10: British merchant ships shall have authority to trade upon the Great River [Yang-tze]. The Upper and the Lower Valley of the river being, however, disturbed by outlaws, no port shall be for the present open to trade, with the exception of Chinkiang, which shall be opened in a year from the date of the signing of this Treaty. So soon as peace shall have been restored, British vessels shall also be admitted to trade at such ports as far as Hankow, not exceeding three in number. . . .

Art. 11: In addition to the cities and towns of Canton, Amoy, Foochow, Ningpo, and Shanghai, opened by the Treaty of Nanking, it is agreed that British subjects may frequent the cities and ports of Newchwang, Tangchow, Taipeh, Swatow and Kiungchow. . . .

Art. 47: British merchant vessels are not entitled to resort to other than the ports of trade declared open by this Treaty. . . .

Art. 51: It is agreed, that henceforth the character "I" (barbarian) shall not be applied to the Government or subjects of Her Britannic Majesty in any Chinese official document issued by the Chinese authorities in the capital or the provinces. . . .

—Mayers (ed.), *Treaties*, 11ff.; Hurst, 1:343–58

c)   ***Anglo-Chinese Treaty of Peking, 24 October 1860***

. . . Art. 4: It is agreed that . . . His Imperial Majesty the Emperor of China shall open the port of Tientsin to trade. . . .

Art. 6: . . . His Imperial Majesty the Emperor of China agrees to cede to Her Majesty the Queen of Great Britain and Ireland, and to Her heirs and successors, to have and to hold, as a dependency of Her Majesty's colony of Hong Kong, that portion of the township of Kowloon. . . .

—Maritime Customs, *Treaties*, op. cit., 1:430–34; Hurst, 1:404–8

d)   ***Russo-Chinese Treaty of Peking, 2/14 November 1860***

Art. 1: To corroborate and elucidate Article 1 of the Treaty concluded in the city of Aigun on 16 May 1858 . . . it is established: . . . The lands situated on the eastern (right) bank of these rivers [the Ussuri and the Son'gatcha] belong to the Russian empire and on the western (left) bank to the Empire of China. . . .Along this line, equally, the lands situated to the east belong to the Empire of Russia and those to the west to the Empire of China. . . .

—Mayers (ed.), *Treaties*, 105ff.

6.5   NAPOLEONIC WORLD POLICY, I: TREATY OF SAIGON

Treaty of Saigon, 5 June 1862

The France of Napoleon III pursued an ambitious world policy. In the South Pacific, it rounded off the July monarchy's gains by annexing New Caledonia in 1853. Using the murder of a French missionary as a pretext, France joined Britain in the Chinese wars of 1856–1860 (cf. preceding document). In 1860–1861 a massacre of Christians in Syria led to the dispatch of a French expeditionary force; though a self-denying protocol estopped France from making territorial acquisitions, it took a leading role in establishing Mt. Lebanon as a separate Ottoman province with a Christian governor and a heavily Christian provincial administration. In Indochina, the Treaty of Saigon of 1862, excerpted below, created the nucleus of a French colonial empire. In the same year, France acquired Obock, located on the Red Sea coast north of Djibouti. "The beach of Kotonou" on the Dahomey coast was ceded to France in 1864. In the western hemisphere, French troops landed in Veracruz in December 1861—ostensibly to collect outstanding debts, but in reality to take advantage of the American Civil War to create a French satellite state in Mexico (cf. Document 8.3).

Given this reckless pursuit of prestige and protectorates, it is ironic that the Second Empire's most enduring accomplishment overseas—the construction of the Suez Canal—owed more to the entrepreneurial skills of Ferdinand de Lesseps than to the belated patronage of Napoleon III. British opposition to the canal caused Napoleon to deny official support to de Lesseps's struggling enterprise until the early 1860s, when it became clear that the canal would be built with or without Napoleon's support. The case of the Suez Canal is perhaps the exception to an article of faith that Napoleon otherwise observed religiously: to pursue his overseas projects not in opposition to Britain but in concert with it. The military cooperation of the Crimean War was continued in China; the Mexican expedition of 1861 began as a trilateral Franco-British-Spanish venture. In the Syrian expedition of 1860, it was British suspicion, aroused by the French annexation of Nice and Savoy (cf. Document 7.5), that caused Napoleon to abjure any territorial ambition.

The Treaty of Saigon, excerpted below, concluded a joint Franco-Spanish expedition against the central Vietnamese kingdom of Annam, itself tributary to China. The treaty gave

France a sizable bridgehead in Indochina: in 1864, France claimed a protectorate over Cambodia, in 1874 over Tonkin, and in 1884 over Annam itself (Treaty of Hué). The last of these aggrandizements led to war with China. In the course of this conflict, French forces occupied Taiwan and the Pescadores Islands. The Chinese government, to secure the evacuation of its territory, had little choice but to recognize the new status quo in Indochina.

Treaty of Saigon, 5 June 1862

. . . Art. 2: The subjects of the two nations of France and Spain shall be able to practice the Christian religion in the kingdom of Annam, and the subjects of that kingdom, without distinction, who shall wish to embrace Christianity shall be able to do so freely and without constraint; but those who have no desire to do so shall not be forced to become Christians.

Art. 3: The three entire provinces of Bien Hoa, Gia Dinh and Dinh Tuong (Mitto), as well as the island of Pulo Condor, are wholly ceded by this Treaty to His Majesty the Emperor of the French in full sovereignty. In addition, French merchants shall be able freely to trade and to come and go [*circuler*] on ships, of whatever type, in the great river of Cambodia [Mekong] and in all the branches of this river; the same will hold true for French warships sent in surveillance on this same river or its branches.

Art. 4: . . . [I]f a foreign nation should wish, either by provocation, or by a Treaty, to have ceded to itself part of Annamite territory . . . this cession shall be sanctioned only by consent of the Emperor of the French.

Art. 5: The subjects of the Empire of France and of the Kingdom of Spain shall freely trade in the three ports of Tourane, Balat and Quang An. Annamite subjects may equally trade freely in the ports of France and Spain, always in conformity with the rule of established law. If a foreign country undertakes commerce with the Kingdom of Annam, the subjects of that foreign country shall not enjoy greater protection than that of France or Spain, and if the said foreign country obtains a concession in the Kingdom of Annam, it may not be a concession greater than those accorded to France or Spain. . . .

Art. 8: The King of Annam shall pay as an indemnity the sum of four million dollars within the period of ten years. . . . [In the event of] the Kingdom of Annam having no dollars, the dollar shall be set at a value of seventy-two hundredths of a taël....

—Georg Friedrich Martens, *Nouveau recueil général* (Göttingen, 1861 [sic]), [1st Series] 17:169–73

6.6   RUSSIA IN CENTRAL ASIA

Gorchakov's Circular to Russian Missions, 21 November/3 December 1864 •
Diary Entry by Peter Alexandrovitch Valuev, 20 July/1 August 1865 •
Russo-Khivan Peace, 12/24 August 1873 • *Russo-Bukharan Treaty of Friendship, 28 September/10 October 1873*

Between Russian Turkestan in the north and Persia and Afghanistan in the south lay the Muslim khanates of Khiva, Kokand, Bukhara, and Merv. The latter three bordered on Afghanistan in that order, east to west. Northern Kokand fell to a Russian army in 1865; its principal city, Tashkent, became the provincial capital of Russian Turkestan. The last remnants of Kokand were absorbed into this province in February 1876. Merv was annexed to Russian Trans-Caspia (governed from Tiflis) in March 1884. Khiva and Bukhara retained a semblance of autonomy as Russian protectorates, though their treaty relationships with Russia were not identical. The decision against outright annexation may have been prompted by budgetary considerations, by interbureaucratic wrangling between Tashkent and Tiflis, or perhaps by the wish to camouflage from Britain the real extent of Russia's penetration of Central Asia.

Ever since the late 1820s, Russia feared the extension of English influence into Afghanistan and the khanates. These fears were reciprocated, in London and Calcutta, by British apprehensions that Central Asia would fall under Russian dominion. The phrase "great game" to describe the Anglo-Russian rivalry in Central Asia had in fact been coined by Arthur Conolly, a British officer captured and executed by the Emir of Bukhara in 1842. The mutual apprehensions had somewhat subsided in the aftermath of the Crimean War, but they were revived by the Russian expansion of the 1860s (cf. Document 8.5h). In a circular to Russian diplomatic missions abroad, Russia's foreign minister, Prince Alexander Gorchakov, emphasized that the motive for Russia's drive into Central Asia lay in the open frontier along Russia's southern steppes rather than in the fear of renewed English machinations. Although the Russian advances of the 1860s were met by little more than British paper protests, the annexation of Kokand caused a flutter in Anglo-Russian relations, while that of Merv in 1884 and the subsequent Russian threat to western Afghanistan caused a full-blown crisis (Document 9.22).

a)   ***Gorchakov's Circular to Russian Missions,***
21 November/3 December 1864

. . . The situation of Russia in Central Asia is that of all civilized states which have come into contact with nomadic, barbarian peoples without concrete institutions. The security of borders and of commerce demands in such cases that the civilized state should have a certain preponderance over its neighbors. At first their incursions and raids are to be turned back. To bring these to an end, it is necessary to more or less bring about the submission of the border population. Once this goal has been accomplished, the inhabitants of the border will take up calmer and more sedentary habits, but are now likely to be disturbed by tribes farther afield. The state is under an obligation to protect the former and to discipline the latter. From this springs the necessity of distant, costly, repeated expeditions against an enemy whose [lack of] organization makes him essentially impregnable. Each step forward leads to new steps; each difficulty solved to new difficulties. But there is no way back because the Asiatics would interpret that as weakness. They respect only perceptible and tangible force. . . .This is the fate of all states in the same conditions. The United States in America, France in Africa, Holland in its colonies, England in India—all, not because of ambition but because of necessity, allowed themselves to be pulled inexorably forward on this path where the greatest difficulty is the ability to stand still. . . .

—*PP 1873*, 75:2, 70–75 [new pagination: 788–93]

b)   ***Diary Entry by Peter Alexandrovitch Valuev,[4]***
                          20 July/1 August 1865

... Tashkent was taken by General Cherniaev. Why ask why? Moreover, General Kryzhanovskii, acting on the instructions of Cherniaev, requests by telegraph [permission] to halt all caravans from Bukhara: goods, etc. The ministry of finance and the ministry of war are puzzled. There is something erotic in everything happening on the distant periphery of our empire. Amur, Ussuri—now Tashkent.

                          —*Dnevnik P. A. Valueva* (Moscow, 1961), 2:60–61

c)   ***Russo-Khivan Peace, 12/24 August 1873***

Art. 1: Saiyid Muhammad Rahim Bohadur Khan acknowledges himself to be the obedient servant of the Emperor of All the Russias. He renounces the right to maintain direct and friendly relations with neighboring rulers and khans and to conclude with them any commercial or other treaties; he will not undertake any military actions against them without the knowledge and permission of the supreme Russian authority in Central Asia. . . .

                —*CTS* 146:345–50; trans. in Seymour Becker, *Russia's Protectorates in Central Asia:*
                          Bukhara and Khiva, 1865–1924 (Cambridge, MA, 1968), 316–18

d)   ***Russo-Bukharan Treaty of Friendship,***
                          28 September/10 October 1873

... Art. 15: In order to maintain an uninterrupted, direct relationship with the supreme Russian authority in Central Asia, the emir of Bukhara will appoint from among his retinue an agent to act as his permanent envoy and plenipotentiary in Tashkent. This plenipotentiary will live in Tashkent in the emir's house and at the emir's expense.

   Art. 16: The Russian government may likewise have its own permanent representative in Bukhara at the court of His High Eminence the Emir. The Russian plenipotentiary in Bukhara, like the emir's envoy in Tashkent, will live in the house of, and at the expense of, the Russian government.

[4](1814–1890). Russian minister of the interior, 1861–1868; minister of agriculture, 1872–1879; chairman of the council of ministers, 1877–1881. Cf. also the diary entry by Count Dimitri Alexeievitch Miliutin (Russian minister of war, 1861–1881), sometime between 1864 and 1867: "[One] does not need to ask the English ministers for forgiveness for any of our forward movements. They act pretty unceremoniously towards us—conquering whole kingdoms, taking foreign cities and islands—and we don't ask why they do that either." *Dnevnik D. A. Miliutina,* 2 vols. (Moscow, 1947–1949), 1:35. See Geyer, *Russian Imperialism,* 89.

Art. 17: To please his Majesty the Emperor of All the Russias, and for the greater glory of His Imperial Majesty, His High Eminence the Emir Saiyid Muzaffar has decreed that henceforth and for all time the shameful trade in human beings, which is contrary to the laws of humanity, is abolished within the borders of Bukhara. In accordance with this decree, Saiyid Muzaffar shall at this time circulate to all his beys strict orders to the following effect: if, despite the emir's injunction about the end of the slave trade, slaves should be brought from neighboring countries to Bukharan frontier towns for sale to Bukharan subjects, said slaves will be taken from their masters and immediately set free. . . .

—*CTS* 146:431ff.; *SP* 65:467ff.; trans. in Becker, *Russia's Protectorates*, 319–21

CHAPTER 7

The "1815 System" Shattered: The Unification of Italy, 1856–1866

Only from hindsight does the unification of Italy appear as a foregone conclusion. The primary obstacle was Austria—its possession of Lombardy and Venetia; its control of the central Italian states of Parma, Modena, and Tuscany; and its troop deployments in the Papal Romagna made it a formidable bulwark of the status quo. But the French garrison in much of the remainder of the Papal States—in Latium and in Rome itself—stood no less in the way of a united Italy. Both the pope, propped up as he was by the forces of these two great powers, and the King of the Two Sicilies could be expected to offer fierce resistance to any diminution of their sovereign rights.

Nor can the relationship among the three principals of the *risorgimento*—the Italian national movement—be described as one of all sweetness and light. Their differences of opinion centered not on whether to strive for a united Italy, but on the constitutional structure of the new Italian state. Count Camillo Benso di Cavour, Piedmontese prime minister from 1852 to 1859 and again from 1860 to his death in the next year, thought it sufficient to graft Piedmontese institutions onto the remainder of the peninsula: his monarch, Victor Emmanuel II of Piedmont-Sardinia, became King of Italy; the Piedmontese parliament was expanded to become the Italian parliament; the narrow Piedmontese suffrage became the electoral law for all of Italy; Piedmontese administrators swarmed into central and southern Italy, to bring with them the blessings of efficient local government.

The new realities bore little resemblance to the ideals of the two other major figures of the *risorgimento.* In the 1830s, Piedmontese courts had rewarded the republican and revolutionary enthusiasm of Giuseppe Mazzini (1805–1872) and Giuseppe Garibaldi (1807–1882) by trying them in absentia and sentencing them to death. Both spent most of the 1830s and 1840s in exile; both were heroes of the Roman republic of 1849; both returned to exile after its collapse. More at home in the library of the British Museum and the editorial offices of the journals that he published, Mazzini seemed to have little in common with Garibaldi, who had honed his skills as a guerrilla leader in the brushfire wars of Latin America. But neither was willing to compromise his republican beliefs, and both greeted with grave reservations the establishment of the new Italian monarchy, which, in its turn, did its utmost to deny them access to political office and power.

In the unification of Italy, Great Power politics meshed with regional issues—that is, concerns specific to the Italian peninsula. The Franco-Piedmontese war of 1859 against Austria led to a purely "Italian" phase that revolved around the fate of the Central Italian states. Piedmont's annexation of these states prompted Napoleon III to demand compen-

MAP 5   THE UNIFICATION OF ITALY

sations for France. The transfer of the Piedmontese districts of Nice and Savoy to France was followed by a second "Italian" stage in the unification process, namely the destruction of the Kingdom of the Two Sicilies and the dismemberment of the Papal States.

How complete was the new Italian state from the vantage point of Italian nationalism? Venetia continued to be governed by Austria until the latter's defeat at the hands of a Prusso-Italian alliance in 1866. While the war of 1866 in its Italian theater is usually remembered for Austria's surrender of Venetia, it should also be borne in mind that farther-reaching Italian aims (i.e., the recovery of other ex-Venetian territories in the Adriatic) were stymied by Austria's destruction of the Italian fleet at Lissa. Farther south, the French garrison in Rome and the surrounding province of Latium assured the survival of the Papal States in the 1860s; however, the withdrawal of these troops in the course of the Franco-German war of 1870 allowed Italy to annex both Latium and Rome and to reduce papal authority to the Vatican. After 1870, the existence of Italian-speaking populations outside of Italy's borders, primarily in the Habsburg monarchy (in the Trentino, Trieste, and a number of Dalmatian cities), inspired a popular agitation on behalf of *Italia irredenta*—"unredeemed Italy"—supposedly clamoring to be made part of the Italian state. Largely for fear that official support for such claims might inspire an Austrian war of revenge which Italy would have to face alone, Italian governments consistently shied away from backing the demands of the irredentist lobby.

GENERAL READING: Arnold Blumberg, *A Carefully Planned Accident: The Italian War of 1859* (Selinsgrove, 1990); Frank J. Coppa, *The Origins of the Italian Wars of Independence* (London, 1992); Richard Elrod, "Austria and the Venetian Question, 1860–66," *Central European History* 4 (1971), 149–71; Denis Mack Smith, *Cavour and Garibaldi, 1860: A Study in Political Conflict* (Cambridge, 1954), *The Making of Italy, 1796–1870* (New York, 1968), *Italy and its Monarchy* (New Haven, 1989)

7.1   THE ITALIAN ISSUE AT THE PARIS PEACE CONGRESS

Protocol of the 22nd Session of the Paris Peace Congress, 8 April 1856 •
Cavour to Rattazzi, 9 April 1856

The lessons of 1848–1849, at least as they were interpreted by Cavour, were that the realities of power politics had proven wrong the slogan *Italia farà da sé* (Document 4.2). If Piedmont-Sardinia wanted to oust Austria from the Italian peninsula, it could do so only with the assistance of a foreign power. Acting on this insight, Cavour demanded that Piedmont join the western powers in the Crimean War. He expected that the Piedmontese commitment of troops would translate into a place for Piedmont at the peace conference, where, in turn, he would find a chance to pillory the status quo in Italy.

In the twenty-second session of the Congress of Paris on 8 April 1856, the French and British foreign ministers gave Cavour an opening. But they, as well as Cavour, soon found themselves entangled in a web of contradictions. The French foreign minister felt free to castigate the Papal and Neapolitan governments but complained bitterly that the Belgian press dared criticize Napoleon III's domestic repression. Cavour was similarly frustrated in his attempt to capture the moral high ground: his censure of the Austrian occupation of the Papal Romagna lost much of its forcefulness when one of the Austrian representatives countered that Piedmont, after all, occupied part of Monaco. The defensive pose that Cavour struck at the congress, however, should be measured against the far more forthright account of his intentions in the second excerpt below.

a)   Protocol of the 22nd Session of the Paris Peace Congress, 8 April 1856

[Walewski:[1]] . . . observes that the Pontifical States are equally in an abnormal state; that the necessity for not leaving the country to anarchy had decided France as well

[1]Alexandre Colonna, Count Walewski (1810–1868). Illegitimate son of Napoleon I; French foreign minister, 1855–1860; minister of police, 1860–1868.

as Austria to comply with the demand of the Holy See by causing Rome to be occupied by her troops while the Austrian troops occupied the Legations [Romagna] . . . . The title eldest son of the church which is the boast of the Sovereign of France makes it a duty for the Emperor to afford aid and support to the Sovereign Pontiff; the tranquillity of the Roman States and that of the whole of Italy affects too closely the maintenance of social order in Europe for France not to have an overbearing interest in securing it by all the means in her power. . . . Count Walewski asks himself if it is not to be desired that certain Governments on the Italian Peninsula, by well-devised acts of clemency, and by rallying to themselves minds gone astray and not perverted, should put an end to a system which is directly opposed to its object and which, instead of reaching the enemies of public order, has the effect of weakening the Governments, and of furnishing partisans to popular faction. In his opinion it would render a signal service to the Government of the Two Sicilies, as well as to the cause of order in the Italian Peninsula, to enlighten that Government as to the false course in which it is engaged. . . .

The first Plenipotentiary of France then says that he must call the attention of the Congress to a subject which, although more particularly affecting France, is not the less of great interest for all the Powers of Europe. He considers it superfluous to state that there are every day printed in Belgium publications the most insulting, the most hostile against France and her government; that revolt and assassination are openly advocated in them. . . . [A]ll these publications are so many implements of war directed against the repose and tranquillity of France by the enemies of social order, who, relying on the impunity which they find under the shelter of the Belgian legislation, retain the hope of eventually realizing their culpable designs. . . .

[Clarendon:[2]] . . . is of the opinion that it must doubtless be admitted in principle that no government has the right to interfere in the internal affairs of other states, but he considers there are cases in which the exception to this rule becomes equally a right and a duty. The Neapolitan Government seems to him to have conferred this right, and to have imposed this duty upon Europe; and as the Governments represented in the Congress are all equally desirous to support the monarchical principle and to repel revolution, it is a duty to lift up the voice against a system which keeps up revolutionary ferment among the masses instead of seeking to moderate it. "We do not wish," he says, "that peace should be disturbed, and there is no peace without justice; we ought then to make known to the King of Naples the wish of the Congress for the amelioration of his system of Government—a wish which cannot remain without effect—and require of him an amnesty in favor of the persons who have been condemned or who are imprisoned without trial for political offences. . . ."

[Buol:[3]] It would be impossible for him, indeed, to discuss the internal situation of independent States which are not represented at the Congress. The Plenipotentiaries have received no other commission than to apply themselves to the affairs of the Levant, and they have not been convened for the purpose of making known to independent Sovereigns wishes in regard to the internal organization of their states; the full powers deposited among the acts of the Congress prove this. . . .

The first plenipotentiary of Sardinia [Cavour] states that the occupation of the Roman states by the Austrian troops assumes every day more of a permanent

[2]George Villiers, fourth Earl of Clarendon (1800–1870). British foreign secretary, 1853–1858; 1865–1866; 1868–1870.
[3]Karl von Buol (1797–1865). Austrian prime and foreign minister, 1852–1859.

character; that it has lasted seven years, and that, nevertheless, no indication appears which would lead to the supposition that it will cease at a more or less early period; that the causes which gave rise to it are still in existence; that the state of the country which they occupy is assuredly not improved, and that in order to be satisfied of this it is enough to remark that Austria considers herself to be obliged to maintain, in its utmost severity, the state of siege at Bologna, although it dates from the occupation itself. He observes that the presence of Austrian troops in the Legations and in the Duchy of Parma destroys the balance of power in Italy and constitutes a real danger for Sardinia. The Plenipotentiaries of Sardinia, he says, deem it, therefore, a duty to point out to the attention of Europe a state of things so abnormal as that which results from the indefinite occupation of a great part of Italy by Austrian troops. As regards the question of Naples, Count Cavour shares entirely the opinions expressed by Count Walewski and the Earl of Clarendon. . . .

Baron Hübner,[4] on his part, says that the first Plenipotentiary of Sardinia has spoken only of the Austrian occupation and kept silence in regard to that of France; that nevertheless the two occupations took place at the same time and with the same object. . . . He remarks that in Italy it is not only the Roman States which are occupied by foreign troops; that the communes of Menton and of Roquebrune, forming part of the Principality of Monaco, have been for the last eight years occupied by Sardinia, and that the only difference which exists between the two occupations is that the Austrians and the French were invited by the Sovereign of the country, while the Sardinian troops entered the territory of the Prince of Monaco contrary to his wishes and maintain themselves therein notwithstanding the remonstrances of the Sovereign of the country.

In reply to Baron Hübner, Count Cavour says that he is desirous that the French occupation should cease as well as the Austrian, but that he cannot help considering the one as being far more dangerous than the other for the independent states of Italy. He adds that a small corps d'armée at a great distance from France is menacing for no one; whereas it is very alarming to see Austria resting on Ferrara and on Placentia, the fortifications of which she is enlarging contrary to the spirit if not to the letter of the Treaties of Vienna and extending herself along the Adriatic as far as Ancona. . . .

—*PP 1856*, 61:137–42

b)   *Cavour to Rattazzi,[5] 9 April 1856*

. . . [In] yesterday's session of the Congress, the Italian question came up. . . . As we went out, I told him [Clarendon]: "My Lord, you see we have nothing to hope for from mere diplomacy; we shall have to resort to other means, at least over Naples." He replied: "We must deal with Naples, and soon." As we parted, I added that I would like another word with him about it; and I think I can then put to him that we should place a bomb under King Bomba.[6] . . .

[4]Joseph Alexander von Hübner (1811–1892). Austrian minister in Paris, 1849–1859.
[5]Urbano Rattazzi (1810–1873). Piedmontese minister of justice, 1853–1858; interior, 1859–1860. Italian prime minister, 1862, 1867.
[6]Ferdinand II (1810–1859), King of the Two Sicilies, 1800–1859. Earned sobriquet "Bomba" for his methods in quelling the Sicilian revolution of 1849.

Italy cannot be left as it is. Napoleon is quite sure about this; and, as diplomacy is useless, we shall have to adopt extra-legal means. Though moderate in my views, I incline to favor extreme and audacious methods. In the nineteenth century, audacity is often the best policy. It helped Napoleon; perhaps it will help us. . . .

—[Camillo Benso di Cavour,] *Cavour e l'Inghilterra. Carteggio con V. E. d'Azeglio* (Bologna, 1933), 1:442; translation from Denis Mack Smith, *The Making of Italy, 1796–1870* (New York, 1968), 204

7.2   ORSINI'S PLOT AGAINST NAPOLEON III, 14 JANUARY 1858

Orsini to Napoleon III, 11 February 1858

In 1849, Felice Orsini participated in the defense of the Roman republic against the French army which had been dispatched by the government of Louis Napoleon to restore the pope to his capital (Document 4.12). Orsini's dislike of Napoleon III may have stemmed from the events of 1849 and there can be no doubt that the purpose of his plot to assassinate the French emperor was to draw attention to the cause of Italian nationalism. Orsini's bombs, hurled at the emperor's carriage, missed Napoleon but killed six and wounded about forty bystanders. During Orsini's trial, his attorney, Jules Favre, created a sensation when he revealed that his client had written to the emperor from prison. The letter was published in the official *Moniteur* on 27 February. It accomplished everything Orsini had set out to do. In the words of the Austrian ambassador: "Orsini is the hero of the hour. The Empress is completely beside herself, she spends her time crying and appeals to Emperor's sense of mercy to save the life of this miscreant." Eugénie was not alone in her tears. As Orsini was led off to his execution, the ambassador found that "the beautiful people here are infatuated by the dignity, the devotion, the spirituality of the murderer Orsini. Particularly noticed was the nobility of his demeanor when he pulled back his dense pitch-black hair from the nape of his neck before giving himself up to the executioner."[7]

Orsini to Napoleon III, 11 February 1858

. . . I shall submit without asking for mercy; however, I will never humiliate myself before he who murders the nascent liberty of my unhappy fatherland. So long as Italy is enslaved, death for me is welcome.

Though my end is near, I want nonetheless to make the last efforts to see to the freeing of Italy for whose independence I have always faced every kind of danger and sacrifice, and which was the constant goal of all my passions. And I intend to express this thought of mine with the following words which I address to Your Imperial Majesty.

Because of the actual political condition of Europe, it is at present in your power to make Italy independent or to keep it the slave of Austria and of every other species

[7]Joseph Alexander von Hübner, *Neuf ans de souvenirs* (Paris, 1904), vol. 2, entries for 28 February and 13 March 1858. Hübner's views corresponded to those of the British ambassador. See F. A. Wellesley (ed.), *Secrets of the Second Empire* (New York, 1929), 159–60.

of foreigner. Do I mean perhaps with these words that French blood be shed for the Italians? No, they do not ask that of you: they ask that France not intervene against them; they ask that France not permit that any nation intervene in the future, and perhaps imminent, struggles of Italy against Austria. Now this point Your Imperial Majesty can resolve to bring about: on Your will the happiness or the unhappiness of my country depends, as does the life or death of a nation to which Europe owes to a great degree its civilization.

As a simple individual, I dare to raise my feeble voice from my prison to Your Majesty to beg you to give back to Italy that independence which its sons lost in 1849 through a blow from the French.

Remember, Your Majesty, that the Italians (and among them my father himself) willingly shed blood for Napoleon the Great wherever he chose to lead them; remember that they were faithful up to his fall; remember that so long as Italy is not made independent, the tranquility of Europe and of Your Majesty is only a dream.

—Albert M. Ghisalberti (ed.), *Lettere di Felice Orsini* (Rome, 1936), 254–55

7.3   AGGRESSIVE WAR HATCHED: PLOMBIÈRES

Cavour to Victor Emmanuel II, 24 July 1858 ● *Clotilde to Cavour, 12 August 1858*

The meeting of Napoleon III and Cavour in the Alsatian spa of Plombières was deliberately kept out of the public eye. Napoleon's ministers were conspicuous for their absence; the certainty that there would be no protocol, minutes, or official notes allowed the imagination of the summiteers to roam freely. This was all the more understandable given the delicacy of the subject at hand. The meeting laid the groundwork for the reorganization of Italy and plotted the Franco-Piedmontese war against Austria that would bring about the new territorial and political order. The principles agreed upon at Plombières were embodied in a formal alliance which, together with a military and a financial convention, was concluded in January 1859 and backdated to 12 December 1858.[8] Not specifically mentioned in the alliance but discussed at length at Plombières was a further device to cement the bonds between France and Piedmont. This was the marriage of Victor Emmanuel II's fifteen-year-old daughter Clotilde to Prince Jérôme Napoleon ("Plon-Plon"), a cousin of the emperor. But Plon-Plon's sexual exploits, very much the talk of the town in Paris, were not likely to endear him to Victor Emmanuel as a prospective son-in-law. Cavour's report on what had transpired at Plombières thus needed to allay the doubts of a skeptical father. His arguments must have been germane to his task: the marriage took place on 30 January 1859, Clotilde thus becoming the first casualty of the Plombières war plot.

a)   *Cavour to Victor Emmanuel II, 24 July 1858*

. . . [Napoleon III] began by saying that he had decided to support Piedmont with all his power in a war against Austria, provided that the war was undertaken for a non-

[8]Text in *Carteggio Cavour-Nigra*, 1:311–15.

revolutionary end which could be justified in the eyes of diplomatic circles—and still more in the eyes of French and European public opinion. . . .

He observed that the grievances we put forward in 1856[9] had not been sufficient to make France and England intervene in our favor, and they would still not appear to justify an appeal to arms. . . . My position now became embarrassing because I had no other precise proposal to make. The Emperor came to my aid, and together we set ourselves to discussing each state in Italy, seeking grounds for war. It was very hard to find any. . . .

. . . [W]hat would be the objective of the war? The Emperor readily agreed that it was necessary to drive the Austrians out of Italy once and for all, and to leave them without an inch of territory south of the Alps or west of the Isonzo. But how was Italy to be organized for that? . . . The valley of the Po, the Romagna, and the Legations would form a kingdom of Upper Italy under the House of Savoy. Rome and its immediate surroundings would be left to the Pope. The rest of the Papal States, together with Tuscany, would form a kingdom of central Italy. The Neapolitan frontier would be left unchanged. These four Italian states would form a confederation like the German Confederation, the presidency of which would be given to the pope to console him for losing the best part of his estates. . . .

The Emperor asked me what France would get, and whether Your Majesty would cede Savoy and the county of Nice. . . .

The Emperor counts positively on England's neutrality; he advised me to make every effort to influence opinion in that country to compel the government (which is a slave to public opinion) not to side with Austria. He counts, too, on the antipathy of the Prince [Regent] of Prussia towards the Austrians to keep Prussia from deciding against us. As for Russia, Alexander has repeatedly promised not to oppose Napoleon's Italian projects. . . . [H]e is ready to provide us with whatever munitions we need, and to help us negotiate a loan in Paris. . . .

The Emperor answered that he was very eager for the marriage of his cousin with Princess Clotilde. . . . "[Prince] Napoleon," he added, "is much better than his reputation; he is a *frondeur,* he loves to be contrary, but he is witty as well as sensible, and he is warmhearted." All this is true. . . . [T]hat his heart is good is irrefutably proved by his constancy toward both friends and mistresses. A man without heart would not have left Paris amid the pleasures of carnival time to make a last visit to Rachel[10] who was dying at Cannes, especially when they had separated four years earlier. . . .

I do not hesitate to declare my most profound convictions that to accept the alliance but refuse the marriage would be an immense political error which could bring grave misfortunes upon Your Majesty and our country. . . .

Despite all this, I realize that Your Majesty may still hesitate and fear to compromise the future of your beloved daughter. But would she be more tranquil tied to an ancient princely family? History shows that princesses may be condemned to a sad life when they marry in accordance with propriety and ancient customs. . . .

—[Camillo Benso di Cavour,] *Il carteggio Cavour-Nigra dal 1858 al 1861,* (Bologna, 1926), 1:103–14; translation from Mack Smith, *Making of Italy,* 238–47

[9]See Document 7.1.
[10]Elisa-Rachel Félix had died on 3 January 1858. Besides Plon-Plon, her circle of Napoleonic lovers had included Walewski and Louis Napoleon himself.

b)   ***Clotilde to Cavour, 12 August 1858***

. . . I have already given it a great deal of thought, but this matter of my marriage to Prince Napoleon is very serious and it is, above all, completely at odds with my own ideas. I also know, *mon cher Comte,* that it could perhaps be beneficial to the future of a nation like ours and especially to the King, my father. . . . I will think it over and I hope that the Lord will truly guide me with his infallible will; for now, I place everything in His hands. . . .

—*Carteggio Cavour-Nigra,* op. cit., 1:126

7.4   **AGGRESSIVE WAR ABORTED: THE VILLAFRANCA ARMISTICE**

Armistice of Villafranca, 11 July 1859 ●
Treaty of Zurich (Austro-French), 10 November 1859

The frightful carnage between the French and Austrian armies at Solferino gave Napoleon III an impetus to bring the Franco-Piedmontese war against Austria to an early end. The emperor's resolve was hastened by the knowledge that the British government opposed any French territorial aggrandizement. Moreover, the news that Prussia planned to mobilize its forces and was considering an "armed mediation" did not augur well for France. Ironically, the prospect of Prussian mobilization was no less unsettling for Austria. What appeared, on the surface of things, as a boon would surely carry with it a price that Austria was reluctant to pay. Faced with the desire of both emperors to extricate themselves from the war, Piedmont, incapable of continuing hostilities on its own, had no choice but to acquiesce.

In concluding the Villafranca armistice, Napoleon's fear of further complications outweighed any sense of obligation to the letter of the Franco-Piedmontese alliance. The difference between what had been promised at Plombières (and in the alliance of January 1859) and what was accomplished at Villafranca caused Cavour to resign but also allowed Piedmont to abrogate its part of the Franco-Piedmontese bargain, namely the cession of Nice and Savoy to France.

The terms of the Villafranca armistice were elaborated by three interlocking peace treaties, signed at Zurich in November 1859. Neither the trilateral Austro-French-Piedmontese treaty nor the Franco-Piedmontese treaty referred to the rights of the Central Italian princes who had abandoned their thrones during the war. Only article 19 of the Austro-French instrument addressed this important issue, but in language far less direct than the Villafranca armistice.

a)   ***Armistice of Villafranca, 11 July 1859***

. . . His Majesty the Emperor of Austria and His Majesty the Emperor of the French . . .:
. . . favour the creation of an Italian Confederation. This Confederation shall be under the honorary Presidency of the Holy Father.

The Emperor of Austria cedes to the Emperor of the French his rights over Lombardy, with the exception of the Fortresses of Mantua and Peschiera. . . .

The Emperor of the French shall present the ceded Territory to the King of [Piedmont-] Sardinia.

Venetia shall form part of the Italian Confederation, remaining, however, subject to the Crown of the Emperor of Austria.

The Grand Duke of Tuscany and the Duke of Modena return to their States, granting a General Amnesty.

The two Emperors shall request the Holy Father to introduce in his States some indispensable reforms.

Full and complete Amnesty is granted on both sides to persons compromised on the occasion of the recent events in the territories of the belligerents.

—Hertslet, 2:1374–75; Hurst, 1:375–6

b)   *Treaty of Zurich (Austro-French), 10 November 1859*

. . . Art. 19: As the Territorial Delimitations of the Independent States of Italy, who took no part in the late War, can be changed only with the sanction of the Powers who presided at their formation and recognised their existence, the Rights of the Grand Duke of Tuscany, of the Duke of Modena, and of the Duke of Parma, are expressly reserved for the consideration of the High Contracting Parties. . . .[11]

—Hertslet, 2:1380–91; Hurst, 1:383

7.5   LEGITIMACY BY TREATY DEEMED INSUFFICIENT: BRITISH VIEWS ON THE CHANGES IN CENTRAL AND NORTHERN ITALY

Russell to Bloomfield, 7 July 1859 • *Queen Victoria to Russell, 13 July 1859*
• *Memorandum for the Cabinet by Palmerston, 5 January 1860* •
Queen Victoria to Russell, 11 January 1860 • *Russell in the Commons,*
26 March 1860

Article 19 of the Austro-French treaty of Zurich could be interpreted as calling for an outright restoration of the Central Italian princes or, failing this, for the convening of a general congress to deliberate their fate. But neither scenario got under way: newly elected assemblies in Parma, Modena, Tuscany, and the Romagna clamored for union with Piedmont and barred the reestablishment of the Central Italian princes (in case of the Romagna, the pope).

In a memorandum to the cabinet of 5 January 1860, Palmerston (who had returned to the prime ministership in June 1859) outlined his vision of British policy if a congress assembled. The congress never materialized; in any event, the cabinet refused to go along with Palmerston's recommendations. But these offer an astounding picture of rhetoric running amuck, of Palmerston's ability to believe what he wanted to believe even if his notions flew in the face

[11]See Document 1.9, articles 98 and 100.

of principles that he usually propagated as virtue incarnate: it is difficult to see how an Anglo-French-Piedmontese alliance against Austria—alienated as it was from Russia and Prussia and, by Palmerston's own admission, beset by domestic dangers—would serve the European balance of power.

The strength of Palmerston's convictions on this occasion might be measured against his conduct two months later. After France's acquisition of Nice and Savoy from Piedmont (Document 7.6), Russell elaborated in the Commons why this scheme might jeopardize Anglo-French relations. His remarks were endorsed by Palmerston in a conversation with the French ambassador the next day. By July 1862, Palmerston's reversal was complete: the Austrian ambassador in London reported on 13 July 1862 that Palmerston "would like an alliance with us more than anyone."[12]

Not prepared to defend the sanctity of the 1815 settlement in Central Italy, Palmerston and Russell bemoaned the fading away, in Nice and Savoy, of the strategic Alpine border imposed on France as part of that same settlement. Unlike Queen Victoria, they were not bothered by the fact that the selective upholding of international treaties is unlikely to inspire confidence in the practitioner of foreign policy. The stage was thus set for another row over the control of foreign policy, and also over the different principles that should animate the nation's conduct of foreign affairs.

a)   *Russell to Bloomfield,*[13] *7 July 1859*

. . . it is the firm persuasion of Her Majesty's Government that an Italy in which the people should be "free citizens of a great country" would strengthen and confirm the balance of power.

The independence of States is never so secure as when the sovereign authority is supported by the attachment of the people.

Every one knows that Rome and the Legations have been much worse governed by the Pope's ministers than Lombardy by Austrian archdukes, and that it would be a partial and unsatisfactory arrangement which struck down the rule of the latter, and left the former in all its deformity.

—Bourne, 340–44

b)   *Queen Victoria to Russell, 13 July 1859*

. . . The Emperor Napoleon, by his military successes, and after great apparent moderation, or prudence immediately after them, has created for himself a most formidable position of strength in Europe. It is remarkable that he has acted towards Austria now just as he did towards Russia after the fall of Sevastopol; and if it was our lot then to be left alone to act the part of the extortioner whilst he acted that of the generous victor, the Queen is doubly glad that we should not now have fallen into the trap, to

---

[12]Temperley and Penson, 205.
[13]John, Baron Bloomfield (1802–1879). British ambassador in Berlin, 1851–1860.

ask Austria (as friends and neutrals) for concessions which he was ready to waive. He will now probably omit no occasion to cajole Austria as he has done to Russia, and turn her spirit of revenge upon Prussia and Germany—the Emperor's probable next victims. Should he thus have rendered himself the master of the entire continent, the time may come for us either to obey or to fight him with terrible odds against us. This has been the Queen's view from the beginning of this complication and events have hitherto wonderfully supported them. How Italy is to prosper under the Pope's presidency, whose misgovernment of his own small portion of it was the ostensible cause of the war, the Queen is at a loss to conceive. . . .

—*QV*, 1st Series, 3:452–53

c)   *Memorandum for the Cabinet by Palmerston, 5 January 1860*

. . . There can be no reasonable doubt, therefore, that both France and [Piedmont-]Sardinia would unite with England in maintaining the principle that the Italians should be secured against foreign compulsion, and should be left free to determine, according to their own will, what shall be their future political condition. . . .

[This] triple alliance, while it would be honourable to England (I might say, the only course that would be honourable to England), would secure the continuance of peace in Italy, and thereby avert one danger to the general peace of Europe.

But it is said we cannot trust the Emperor Napoleon, and when we had entered into this triple alliance, he would throw us over and make some arrangement of his own without consulting us. It is no doubt true that such was the course pursued by Austria during the war which ended in 1815. Austria took our subsidies, bound herself by treaty not to make peace without our concurrence, sustained signal defeat in battle, and precipitately made peace without our concurrence. But on what occasion has the Emperor Napoleon so acted? On none. He differed with us about certain conditions and the interpretation of certain conditions of the treaty of peace with Russia, but the points in dispute were settled substantially in conformity with our views. There is no ground for imputing to him bad faith in his conduct towards us as allies. But it is said that he has not steadiness of purpose, and the agreement of Villafranca is a proof of this. That agreement was certainly much short of the declarations of intention with which he began the war, but he had great difficulties of many kinds to contend with in further carrying on the war; and though we, as lookers-on, may think, and perhaps rightly, that if he had persevered those difficulties would have faded away, yet there can be no doubt that he thought them at the time real; and he is not the only instance of a sovereign or a general who has at the end of a war or a campaign accepted conditions of peace less full and complete than what he expected or demanded when hostilities began. . . .

[I]f . . . the Congress should be given up . . . the necessity of coming to an agreement with France and Sardinia would be stronger still. In that case matters would have to be settled by diplomatic negotiation or by force of arms and in either way an agreement between England, France, and [Piedmont-]Sardinia would carry into effect the objects which such an agreement might have in view. . . .

. . . [Austria's] provinces are all of them ready to boil over with discontent, and some parts of her territory like Hungary are only waiting for a renewal of the war to break out into rebellion, her army dissatisfied with recent military arrangements, and her Emperor universally disliked and extensively despised. This is not the condition in which Austria would be likely to run her head against a coalition of England, France and Sardinia. . . .

—Bourne, 354-59; Ashley, *Life of...Palmerston*, 2:174–80

d)   *Queen Victoria to Russell, 11 January 1860*

The Queen . . . was much relieved by finding a proposal to call upon France and Austria not to interfere in Italy substituted for the former one implying war on our part for the defence of the Provisional Governments of Central Italy. . . . Austria has reversionary rights in Tuscany and Modena,[14] Sardinia has no rights at all, if a desire for acquisition is not to be considered as one. . . .

—*QV*, 1st Series, 3:488–89

e)   *Russell in the Commons, 26 March 1860*

. . . [S]uch an act as the annexation of Savoy is one that will lead a nation so warlike as the French to call upon its government from time to time to commit other acts of aggression. . . . [T]he peace of Europe is a matter dear to this country, and that settlement and that peace cannot be assured if it is liable to perpetual interruption—to constant fears, to doubts and rumors with respect to the annexation of this one country, or the union and junction of that other; but that the powers of Europe, if they wish to maintain that peace, must respect each other's rights, must respect each other's limit, and, above all, restore and not disturb that commercial confidence which is the result of peace. . . .

—*Parl. Debates*, 3rd Series, 157:1258

7.6   THE NEW LEGITIMACY DISPUTED: GARIBALDI AND CHENAL ON THE TRANSFER OF NICE AND SAVOY

Garibaldi, Cavour, and Chenal in the North Italian Parliament, 12 April 1860

The situation in Central Italy (preceding Document) had remained in flux until Cavour returned to the prime ministership in January 1860. His goal was to annex Central Italy to Piedmont, his method a series of plebiscites held between 10 and 12 March. The voting, predictably, yielded huge majorities in favor of union. This exercise in self-determination, Cavour hoped, would lend legitimacy to the transaction and silence the objections of the powers.

---

[14]Modena and Tuscany were Austrian secundogenitures (i.e., ruled by branch lines of the house of Habsburg-Lorraine); articles 98 and 100 of the Vienna General Act affirmed Austrian rights to determine the succession in these states in the event their ruling houses became extinct.

But Napoleon III, resuscitating the spirit of Plombières, demanded Nice and Savoy as compensation for Piedmont's gains. Pressured by Napoleon, Cavour, in a treaty dated 24 March 1860, surrendered both territories to France—on the condition that the new North Italian parliament, to be elected on 25 March, would legitimize the cession.[15] Thus emerged a further complication for Cavour: representing Nice in the newly elected chamber was the city's most famous son, Giuseppe Garibaldi. Speaking in parliament on 12 April, Garibaldi scorned the proposed act of territorial self-immolation. While the subsequent debate on the floor of the legislature captured the emotional gulf dividing him and his followers from Cavour, its intellectual highlight was provided by Agricola Chenal, a seven-term member for Savoy, who, speaking in his native French (!), similarly objected to being reduced to a pawn in Cavour's game with Napoleon.

But these efforts were to no avail. Plebiscites in Nice (15 April) and Savoy (25 April) yielded huge majorities for France; the North Italian parliament ratified the cession on 29 May. Garibaldi did not await the outcome: leading his "Thousand," he sailed for Sicily on 5 May to support an insurrection against that island's Bourbon ruler (cf. Document 7.7).

Garibaldi, Cavour, and Chenal in the North Italian Parliament, 12 April 1860

[Garibaldi:] Gentlemen, article 5 of the *Statuto* [constitution of 4 March 1848] says: "Treaties that bring about a change in the territory of the [Italian] state will not take effect unless the Chambers have agreed to them."
The implication of this article of the basic law is that any initiative leading to a reduction [in size] of the state, before this reduction has been sanctioned by the Chamber, is contrary to the law. That one part of the state votes for separation before the Chamber has decided if this separation ought to take place, before it has decided if there ought to be a vote, and how to vote to initiate the separation itself, is an unconstitutional act. This, gentlemen, is the issue of Nice insofar as constitutionality is concerned that I place before the wise judgment of the Chamber. . . .

[Cavour:] The honorable deputy Garibaldi has condemned the Treaty of 24 March as unconstitutional, as well as contrary to the law of nations, and as based on a policy that can be fatal to our country, and which should be rejected by all civilized peoples. . . . For the time being, in the political arena, I will limit myself to this single statement, namely that the cession of Nice and Savoy was a necessary condition for the pursuit of that political road which in a short period of time has led to Milan, to Florence, to Bologna [lively signs of approval]. We are convinced of one thing, namely that one could in fact reject the treaty of 24 March, but it was impossible to do so without making a mistake which for us would have been inevitably fatal. It was impossible to reject the treaty and to pursue the same policy; not only would past victories be placed in manifest danger, but the future of the country as well! [commotion]. . .

[Chenal:] . . . Can a nation or even a part of a nation be ceded for the benefit of another? Who would dare to uphold that idea? Italian honor can only repudiate such a barbarous tradition from the most evil days of feudalism. If a people is its own master, if it is master of its destiny and its territory, then no one has the power to make it an object of barter, to dispose of it like a commodity, to liken it to merchandise. The

[15]Text of Franco-Piedmontese treaty in Hurst, 1:402–4.

same language, the confluence of several rivers, a more-or-less open border are not enough to legitimize the annexation of one people by another. . . . [Otherwise,] from the point of view of commonality of language, Alsace ought to be returned to Germany. . . . If the trade in blacks is immoral, is the trade in whites any less so? If popular sovereignty is accepted, recognized here as a sacred principle, if Central Italy has been called to freely dispose of its own destiny, to vote freely for its annexation to Piedmont, the principle invoked in that case, recognized as sacred, cannot be contradicted when it comes to my country. . . . Italy is free to abandon Savoy, to break all association with it; but beyond that, it does not follow that it has the right to dispose of Savoy's destiny: Italy should leave Savoy to be its own master, should allow it its own initiative. . . . The day that this Chamber cedes Savoy to France is the day that the Chamber will have denied its own principles. It will have undertaken retrogressive policy; will have ratified what the Congress of Vienna did; will have sanctioned the deeds of the powerful against the weak; will have denied its own independence. Let it beware! Politics is often subject to the most bitter vicissitudes. . . .

[Speaker:] The proposal of deputy Chenal is the following: "I ask that Savoy be free to vote either to remain part of Piedmont, or to be annexed to France, or to Switzerland, whichever it shall prefer. I insist above all that serious consideration be given to the two northern districts of Savoy, which are in an exceptional position, should they decide that it is in their interest to vote for annexation by Switzerland."

[Cavour:] Gentlemen, if we follow this advice [with passion], I believe we will be betraying the nation itself [hear, hear! bravo!]. It is unimportant that *ministers* compromise both in domestic politics and in foreign affairs; it is unimportant that *ministers* draw onto their heads potent enmities; but it would be a great loss, irreparable if these hatreds, if these enmities fell upon the representatives of the nation [hear, hear! bravo!]. The ministers in a constitutional country should know how to sacrifice themselves for the general interest [bravo! hear, hear!] and never [forcefully] so long as we are ministers, will we hide behind the vote of parliament to cover up our responsibility [applause].

[Garibaldi:] . . . I would always have preferred to uphold the dignity of my country rather than to throw myself into the vasselage of France [bravo! bravo! from the gallery]. . . .

Whether my fatherland is French or not, honorable deputies, does not take much understanding of history to be able to show. Many know well that I would perhaps be better at picking up a rifle—if you pardon the expression—than debating in the presence of these most honorable men, wise and learned in every branch of knowledge; nonetheless, I know something about the history of my country. I know for example that my fellow citizens throughout their past have always fought against the French. . . .

—*Atti del Parlamento italiano*, Camera dei deputati, sessione del 1860, 1 [O.S. 65]:84–104

7.7   THE DESTRUCTION OF THE KINGDOM OF THE TWO SICILIES AND THE DISMEMBERMENT OF THE PAPAL STATES

Russell to Queen Victoria, 30 April 1860 ● *Queen Victoria to Russell, 30 April 1860* ● *Cavour in the Italian Senate, 16 October 1860* ● *Circular by Casella, 19 October 1860*

After his confrontation with Garibaldi on the floor of the North Italian parliament, Cavour was delighted to deflect the energies of the irascible adventurer elsewhere. Cavour was far from disconsolate to see Garibaldi, with his force of the "Thousand," sail for Sicily to support a local insurrection against the Bourbon ruler of Naples-Sicily. Not only would Garibaldi be out of Cavour's way, but his prospects might founder in the political quicksands of the Italian south. Contrary to all expectations, Garibaldi's forces took Sicily by storm, crossed the Strait of Messina for the mainland, and routed the Neapolitan army. In Sicily, Garibaldi owed his success to the hostility of the island's population toward their Neapolitan rulers; in Calabria, to mass desertions; in both, to the popular expectation that he was the harbinger of social reform. In the areas under his sway, Garibaldi established himself as dictator on behalf of Victor Emmanuel. Not content to rest on these laurels, he signaled his intention to take his forces into the portion of the Papal States garrisoned by French troops. Cavour, ostensibly anxious to prevent a major crisis with France, now had his opportunity: he ordered the Piedmontese army to cross the Papal States to enter Naples to intercept and neutralize Garibaldi. The former kingdom of the Two Sicilies was thus joined to northern Italy. Once ensconced in the Papal States, the Piedmontese army was in a position to annex Umbria and the Marches (the Papal Romagna, it will be recalled, had been incorporated into Piedmont earlier that year). Reduced to Latium and Rome, Pius IX lost three-quarters of the Papal States to the new Italian kingdom.

Cavour's boasts, in the third excerpt below, might be measured against the fact that, although Garibaldi had been accorded a tumultuous welcome, the Piedmontese administrators who followed in his wake were not greeted with similar enthusiasm. Indeed, the realization in the Italian south that union with the north was no panacea for the social ills of the *mezzogiorno* soon led to widespread insurgencies. Now that the shoe was on the other foot, the new national government contemptuously dismissed the rebels as "brigands" but was unable to master the situation until well into the 1870s. To complete the role reversal, the insurgents—no doubt to enhance their own legitimacy—claimed that the goal of the rising was to restore the Bourbons.

a) *Russell to Queen Victoria, 30 April 1860*

Lord John Russell . . . is sorry he cannot agree that there would be any moral wrong in assisting to overthrow the Government of the King of the Two Sicilies. The best writers on International Law consider it a merit to overthrow a tyrannical government, and there have been few governments so tyrannical as that of Naples. Of course the King of Sardinia has no right to assist the people of the Two Sicilies unless he was asked by them to do so, as the Prince of Orange was asked by the best men in England to overthrow the tyranny of James II—an attempt which has received the applause of all our great public writers, and is the origin of our present form of government.

—*QV*, 1st Series, 3:505–6

b) *Queen Victoria to Russell, 30 April 1860*

The Queen has received Lord John Russell's letter and trusts he will see, upon further reflection, that the case before us is not one in which the Revolution of 1688, and the advent of William III called to the Throne, can be appealed to as a parallel. . . . [N]o public writer nor the International Law will call it morally right that one state should abet revolution in another, not with the disinterested object of defending a suffering people against tyranny, but in order to extinguish that State and make it "an acquisition" of its own. If William III had made England a province of Holland, he would not have received the applause Lord John quotes. . . .

—*QV*, 1st Series, 3:506

c)   *Cavour in the Italian Senate, 16 October 1860*

. . . I do not know if the means adopted to accomplish this great deed are perfectly regular, but I do know that the undertaking [*scopo*] is holy, and that the undertaking perhaps will justify whatever might be irregular in the means [approval]. Even in these provinces [Umbria and the Marches], gentlemen, we have not brought revolution and disorder. We are there to establish good government, legality, and morality. Whatever allegations there may be to the contrary, I proclaim with certainty—and what I say will be confirmed by the impartial voice of Liberal and enlightened Europe—that no war has ever been conducted with greater generosity, magnanimity, and justice. . . .

. . . I believe [Rome] to be destined to become the noble capital of the reborn Italy. I am not ignorant of the difficulties. . . . I firmly believe that this principle [of freedom of conscience] will reconcile him [Pope Pius IX] with modern society; and that in a few years there will be a transformation in relations between religious and civil society; that this transformation will yield an easy solution to a great problem, namely the coexistence in Rome of the august head of the Catholic religion and the center of government of the reborn Italy. . . .

—Isaaco Artom and Alberto Blanc (eds.), *Il Conte Cavour in Parlamento* (Florence, 1868), 1:625–29

d)   *Circular by Casella,[16] 19 October 1860*

. . . H. M. [of Naples-Sicily] was living, as every Sovereign, under the protection of the law of nations, under the guardianship of public right. And, confiding in the word of the King of Sardinia, he could not expect that he would come at the head of his army to invade and take possession of his States, without declaration of war and when Ministers were still accredited at the two courts. . . .

The example of the Two Sicilies will demonstrate to the world that it is lawful to trample on every sentiment of loyalty and of justice in order to carry first revolution into the territory of a friendly Sovereign and then to take possession of his states in a time of complete peace, without regard to any right or to any treaty, destroying the most legitimate interests and setting at nought the public opinion of Europe. . . .

—Howard R. Marraro (ed.), *Diplomatic Relations between the United States and the Kingdom of the Two Sicilies: Instructions and Dispatches, 1816–1861* (New York, 1952), 2:742–43

[16]Francesco Casella (1819–1894). Minister of state of the Kingdom of the Two Sicilies.

7.8   # THE VENETIAN QUESTION, 1866*

Blome to Mensdorff, 20 May 1866 ● *Franco-Austrian Treaty, 12 June 1866* ●
Ricàsoli to Visconti Venosta, 12 July 1866

Austria spread itself thin in its determination to hold on to its position both in northern Italy and in Germany. The Austrian refusal to yield in either created an opportunity for its opponents, Prussia and Italy, to find common ground.[17] Almost in desperation, Austria flung itself into the arms of France, which hoped to play the part of the laughing third in the bargain.

The documents below are interesting in that they illustrate the rewards that the various parties hoped to snatch from a war. They show the extent of Austria's aims in Germany and Italy's in the Adriatic, and they leave little doubt that France was well poised to take advantage of any territorial changes in the map of Germany, even though these were not specified.

Prussia was at war with Austria and its German allies by 16 June 1866; Italy honored its alliance with Prussia by declaring war on Austria on 20 June.

a)   ### Blome[18] to Mensdorff,[19] 20 May 1866

To no statement do I subscribe to more completely than to the two sentences in Your Excellency's kind letter of yesterday: 1) if one could have delayed the decisive showdown until Napoleon's death and the crises thereafter, then this would have been worth a small sacrifice; 2) other powers will prevent us from harvesting the fruits of this victory, and this war may only be the first in a series of wars. The postponement of the crisis had always been my goal, and in this vein I advocated an understanding with Prussia last summer. But retrospective regrets are of no use. Bismarck has not permitted us to await Napoleon's exit; he has purposefully provoked the crisis. Now it is important to stride forward, unless we simultaneously want to lose our position in Germany and in Italy. The fruits of victory may be small in material terms, but we require the moral [uplift]; the embarrassments of Magenta and Solferino[20] have to be undone; Austria's will has to be revived. If there is then a series of wars rather than a long peace, this too has its positive aspects: namely to keep the revolution at bay. . . .

—Heinrich Ritter von Srbik (ed.), *Quellen zur deutschen Politik Oesterreichs* (1938; reprint: Osnabrück, 1967), 5:2760

b)   ### Franco-Austrian Treaty, 12 June 1866

Art. 1: If war breaks out in Germany, the French government will observe towards Austria absolute neutrality and will make every effort to make Italy subscribe to the same attitude.

---

* The excerpts in this subsection are equally pertinent to Chapter 8.
[17] For text of Prusso-Italian treaty of 8 April 1866, see Document 8.6.
[18] Gustav, Count Blome (1829–1906). Austrian minister in Munich.
[19] Alexander, Count Mensdorff (1813–1871). Austrian foreign minister, 1864–1866.
[20] Cf. Document 7.4.

Art. 2: If Austria is victorious in Germany, it will cede Venetia to the French government when it concludes peace. If it is victorious in Italy, it pledges not to change in that [Lombardo-Venetian] kingdom the status quo ante bellum except by agreement with France.

Art. 3: If the events of the war should change the relationships among the German powers, the Austrian government pledges to reach agreement with the French government before sanctioning any territorial revisions which would change the European equilibrium.

Additional Note: . . . 6: If Austria is victorious in Germany, the French government will sanction all territorial acquisitions by Austria, provided that this not disturb the European equilibrium, in establishing an Austrian hegemony which would unite Germany under a single authority.

7: In case of territorial revisions, the Austrian government, exercising the rights of sovereignty of those Princes of the Imperial House who have been dispossessed,[21] may demand for them compensations anywhere except in Italy.

—Heinrich Oncken, *Die Rheinpolitik Kaiser Napoleons III* (1926; reprint, Osnabrück, 1967), 1:147

c)   Ricàsoli[22] to Visconti Venosta,[23] 12 July 1866

. . . It is absolutely necessary for the King [of Italy] to order this occupation [of the Tirol] with regular troops. The fleet should be supplied with marines because it is important to occupy Istria, which is Italian territory and should be ours. Garibaldi and the volunteers should be sent with at least 40,000 soldiers to Croatia to wage war and insurrection in those Austrian provinces and thus [we can] reestablish our military position relative to Prussia. . . . We must have Istria, and it is thus urgent to supply the fleet with sufficient marines. . . .

—Sergio Camerani and Gaetano Arfé (eds.), *Carteggi di Bettino Ricàsoli* (Rome, 1967), 22:358

[21]An allusion to the former rulers of Modena and Tuscany. See Documents 7.4 and 7.5.
[22]Bettino Ricàsoli (1809–1880). Italian prime minister, 1861–1862; 1866–1867.
[23]Emilio Visconti Venosta (1829–1914). Italian foreign minister 1863–1864; 1866–1867; 1873–1876; 1896–1898; 1900–1901.

CHAPTER 8

Central Europe Reorganized, 1862-1871

The unification of Germany and its immediate consequences outside of Germany—the restructuring of the Habsburg monarchy in 1867 and the collapse of the French Second Empire in 1870—spawned controversies that still raged a century later. By and large, these debates have revolved around the policies of Otto von Bismarck, prime minister of Prussia from 1862 to 1890 and German chancellor from 1871 to 1890. Historians have disagreed on whether Bismarck was a planner or an opportunist; a militarist or a dedicated advocate of civilian leadership; a German nationalist or, first and foremost, a servant of the Prussian state. Since the 1960s, historians of modern Germany have asked whether the structural flaws of Bismarck's edifice were responsible for the disasters of the twentieth century—World War I and, ultimately, the Nazi dictatorship. Finally, the question has been raised whether the history of the German unification can (or should) be written as part of Bismarck's biography or whether the social and economic currents of the day were inexorably moving in this direction anyhow—a hypothesis possibly motivated by the unspoken assumption that the result would have been a kinder, gentler Germany.

One point on which most scholars seem to agree is that Bismarck, like Cavour before him, practiced Realpolitik.[1] This word can be translated as the "politics of realism" or the "politics of expediency" or even as "Machiavellianism." In the works of many English and American historians, Realpolitik connotes a hard-nosed, perhaps ruthless, approach to politics. But the term "politics of realism" also conjures up other qualities: an awareness, by its practitioners, of the constraints acting on them; the pursuit of attainable, hence limited, goals; an appreciation that political fortunes can change at barely a moment's notice—the imponderabilia of politics, to use one of Bismarck's favorite terms.

The history of the unification of Germany can be written from many different perspectives, but a central feature of this process was the wars of 1864, 1866, and 1870-1871. In 1864, Austria and Prussia fought Denmark; in 1866, Prussia defeated Austria and its German allies; and in 1870-1871, Prussia, now joined by the southern German states, not only brought down Napoleon III's French Empire but also thwarted

---

[1]The term was probably coined by Ludwig von Rochau, a disillusioned supporter of liberal causes during the 1848 revolutions, in the title of his book, *Grundsätze der Realpolitik* (1853).

French armies hastily raised by a provisional government of national defense. It has been argued in each of these three cases that Bismarck deliberately fomented war. But this version of events errs in suggesting that the outcome was preordained; it moreover denies Bismarck's diplomacy the ability to keep open as many options as possible, the very elasticity which was its hallmark. But if Bismarck did not plan war, neither did he shy away from it. Once begun, each of these wars served a specific purpose. In 1864, Denmark's reopening of the Schleswig-Holstein question gave Bismarck his opportunity to cater to German nationalism and to steal a march on Austria. The war of 1866 was fought to exclude Austria from Germany and to destroy the German Confederation, the organization that in the past had proved the principal obstacle to Prusssian influence in Germany. The French declaration of war on Prussia in 1870 silenced the antiunion sentiment in the German south, while the military victories of the German armies in France created their own logic, namely the suggestion that the joint effort on the battlefield ought to culminate in political unity.

GENERAL READING: [on Bismarck:] Lothar Gall, *Bismarck*, 2 vols. (Boston, 1986); Andreas Kaernbach, *Bismarcks Konzepte zur Reform des Deutschen Bundes* (Göttingen, 1992); George O. Kent, *Bismarck and His Times* (Carbondale, IL,1978); Otto Pflanze, *Bismarck and the Unification of Germany*, vol. 1 (1963; rev. ed., Princeton, 1990); A. J. P. Taylor, *Bismarck* (New York, 1955); [on France:] Nancy N. Barker, *Distaff Diplomacy* (Austin, 1967) and "Monarchy in Mexico," *Journal of Modern History* 48 (1976), 51–68; Ann Pottinger [Saab], *Napoleon III and the German Crisis* (Cambridge, MA, 1966); [on 1870:] S. William Halperin, "Origins of the Franco-Prussian War Revisited," *Journal of Modern History* 45 (1973), 83–91; Michael Howard, *The Franco-Prussian War* (1961; reprint, New York, 1990); Eberhard Kolb, *Der Weg aus dem Krieg* (Munich, 1989); [systemic:] Werner E. Mosse, *The European Powers and the German Question, 1848–71* (1958; reprint: New York, 1981); Paul W. Schroeder, "The Lost Intermediaries," *International History Review* 6 (1984), 1–27

8.1   THE PREMISES OF REALPOLITIK

*Bismarck to Manteuffel, 26 April 1856 • Bismarck to Gerlach, 11 May 1857 •
Bismarck's Iron-and-Blood Statement in the Prussian Legislature,
30 September 1862*

In a roundabout manner, the Prussian constitutional conflict of the early 1860s was an outgrowth of the Italian war of 1859. The fear—unwarranted, as it turned out—that France would launch a northern campaign against the German Confederation had led Prussia to mobilize its forces. The woeful inefficiencies which attended this event did not escape the notice of Prince Wilhelm (regent, 1858–1861; king, 1861–1888), whose long army career had left him particularly susceptible to any sign of military weakness. Seeking a remedy, Wilhelm proposed a reorganization of the army and, to realize it, asked the Prussian legislature for the necessary budgetary appropriations. This request immediately came under attack from Liberal members of parliament who, in their campaign against the measure, scuttled two successive ministries.

In a last attempt to resolve the governmental gridlock in his favor, Wilhelm appointed Bismarck prime minister, a move aptly characterized by one historian as the "desperate act of a distraught king."[2] While Bismarck's task was to secure passage of the budget, his tactics were to circumvent the Liberals' resistance by an appeal to their nationalism. In an appear-

[2]Theodore S. Hamerow, *The Social Foundations of German Unification, 1858–1871: Struggles and Accomplishments* (Princeton, 1972), 2:158.

ance before the budget committee which attracted instant attention, Bismarck sought to rede-fine the issue, shifting the question of the army reform from a Prussian to a German context. But he had gone too far, and, within minutes, found himself in a confrontation with Rudolf Vir-chow, the spokesman for the Progressive party.

Virchow had consistently denounced the army bill as a stalking horse for the expansion of royal prerogative. His stature as one of Europe's leading scientists—he was professor of pathology at the University of Berlin—in itself made him a power to be reckoned with, but what mattered here was that the Progressive party, with nearly 40 percent of the seats in the Prussian legislature, was the largest single grouping in that body. Bismarck had found his match; he now spent much of the remainder of this session trying to cover his tracks.

Historians are in broad agreement that Bismarck promoted a new brand of conservatism that looked for inspiration to the future and not the past. But they differ in their assessment of his methods, and he is variously described as the nineteenth-century Machiavellian for whom the ends justified the means; the political opportunist pure and simple; or the perspicacious practitioner of a policy free from ideological or personal preferences.

Bismarck no doubt would have preferred the latter description; certainly his correspon-dence of the 1850s casts him as the anti-ideologue par excellence. Even if one allows for the possibility that in these letters he postured for posterity, they create a context for his famous statement in the budget committee of the Prussian legislature in 1862. They show his eight years (1851 to 1859) as Prussian ambassador to the German Confederation to be a formative experience in which he became increasingly convinced that Austria stood in the way of Prus-sia's aims in Germany. The second document below reveals what would necessarily be one of the consequences of this new conviction—the growing rift between him and his ultraconserv-ative supporters at the Prussian court. The first excerpt is taken from a lengthy analysis of the impact of the Paris peace (Document 5.7) on Prussia's and Austria's position in the European system; it too affords a measure of the man and his method.

a)   ***Bismarck to Manteuffel,[3] 26 April 1856***

...Forgive me for these conjectures about [future] wars and alliances, all of which still belong to the realm of dreams. But my assessment of the present is conditioned by the prospects which the future may hold out. . . .

—*GW*, 2:152

b)   ***Bismarck to Gerlach,[4] 11 May 1857***

... The news from Berlin is that at court I am called a Bonapartist. This is an injustice. In 1850 our opponents accused me of a treasonous inclination towards Austria and

[3]Otto von Manteuffel (1805–1882), Prussian conservative. Foreign and prime minister, 1850–1858.
[4]Leopold von Gerlach (1790–1861), Prussian conservative and legitimist. Friend of Prince Wilhelm and Friedrich Wilhelm IV; promoter of Bismarck's early career. Headed the so-called "camarilla," a non-constitutional kitchen cabinet at the court of Friedrich Wilhelm in the 1850s.

we were called the Viennese in Berlin; later [during the Crimean War] it was found that we smelled of Russia leather and we were called the cossacks on the River Spree. Then I always replied to the question whether I was pro-Russian or for the western powers by answering "I am Prussian"; and my ideal for the practitioner of foreign affairs is freedom from prejudice, of making decisions unencumbered by impressions of distaste or preference for foreign states and their monarchs. As far as other countries are concerned, in my life I have had sympathies only for England and its inhabitants and I have not been able to free myself entirely from this sentiment; but these people do not want to be loved by us. It would make no difference to me whether our troops fired on the French, Russians, English, or Austrians provided that there would be convincing proof that so doing would be in the interest of a healthy and well thought-out Prussian policy. . . .

—*GW*, 14i:648

c)   ***Bismarck's Iron-and-Blood Statement in the Prussian Legislature, 30 September 1862***

[Bismarck:] . . . Germany does not look up to Prussia's liberalism but to its power. Bavaria, Württemberg, Baden may indulge in liberalism, and still no one will assign to them the part Prussia [is destined to play]. Prussia must gather its strength and must harness it for the right opportunity—which has already been missed several times. The Vienna treaties did not endow Prussia with borders favorable to a healthy body politic. Not by speeches and majorities will the great questions of the day be decided—that was the great mistake of 1848 and 1849—but by iron and blood. . . .

[Virchow:] . . . If the minister interprets the constitution in the manner in which he has . . . then conditions will deteriorate so that they will resemble those already existing in other German states.[5] How anyone, under such circumstances, can conceive of [simultaneously] wanting to solve the great questions of power politics is flabbergasting. . . .

[Bismarck:] . . . He must protest against [the imputation] that he was seeking foreign conflicts to overcome domestic difficulties: that would be frivolous. He was not looking for trouble. He was speaking of conflicts which we will not be able to avoid even though we may have no desire to provoke them.

—Horst Kohl (ed.), *Die Reden des Ministerpräsidenten von Bismarck-Schönhausen im Preussischen Landtage, 1862–1865* (Stuttgart, 1892), 29–31

8.2   EMPRESS EUGÉNIE SEES THE FUTURE, FEBRUARY 1863

Richard Metternich to Rechberg, 22 February 1863

In a parlor conversation that soon turned political, Empress Eugénie conjured up for the Austrian ambassador to Paris, Prince Richard Metternich, a vision of possibilities that was as un-

---

[5]An allusion to the ongoing constitutional conflict in Hesse-Kassel, by then in its third decade.

fettered as it was reckless. Escapism, boredom, and ambition may have all played a role in prompting Eugénie's remarks, but she was also driven by a desire to put the Austro-French relationship on a better footing. Widespread sympathy in France for the Polish revolution of 1863 and, consequently, disgust with its suppression by Russian armies made impossible the continuation of the Franco-Russian entente that Napoleon III had so assiduously cultivated since the Crimean War. Cooperation with Austria seemed to offer an alternative; the question was how and where and under what circumstances France and Austria might pursue their partnership.

Richard Metternich to Rechberg,[6] 22 February 1863

The Empress announced to me that . . . the Emperor thought of nothing but the entente between Austria, France and England, an entente which could lead to the solution of all affairs, to the consolidation of His dynasty and to the happiness of the world. . . .

I permitted myself to observe to Her Majesty that I did not deserve the flattering assurances She addressed to me, but that in any case I thought that I could repeat everything She told me without fear of displeasing my Sovereign Master. "As for the rest, you know, Madame," I added, "that if truly You betray all Your secrets, that in itself is a fact of such importance, for were Your plans the overthrow of the world, their revelation would have an inestimable value for those to whom You are willing to confide them, as at least we shall be warned."

Smiling, the Empress said: "To make you understand what I would like, the ideal of my policy, we must have a map!" . . . Her Majesty . . . explained to me for more than an hour the utopian but very curious plan which enthuses Her.

I could not possibly follow in all its details the peregrination of the Empress as the crow flies (what a flight and what a bird!) and I arrive immediately at what seemed to me the positive goal. . . .

Russia: driven back in the East and sparingly rewarded for the loss of Poland and the provinces which composed it by a compensation in Turkish Asia.

Poland: reconstituted with an [Austrian] Archduke as King, if we wish, but better yet with the King of Saxony reasserting his dynastic rights in compensation for the cession of his kingdom to Prussia.

Prussia: would cede Posen to Poland, Silesia to Austria and the left bank of the Rhine to France but would obtain Saxony, Hanover and the duchies North of the Main River.

Austria: would cede Venetia to Piedmont, a part of Galicia (Lemberg and Cracow) to Poland, would take a long line of new frontiers across Serbia along the Adriatic, Silesia and all she would like South of the Main.

France: would cede nothing! but would take the left bank of the Rhine sparing Belgium on account of England unless that power would leave her Brussels and Ostend etc., etc., in order to take Antwerp.

[6]Johann Bernhard, Count Rechberg (1806–1899). Austrian prime minister, 1859–1860; foreign minister, 1859–1865. Son of Alois, Count Rechberg (cf. Document 2.3).

Italy: Piedmont would have Lombardy, Venetia, Tuscany, Parma, Piacenza, Bologna and Ferrara; but would restore the Two Sicilies to the King of Naples who would round out the Pope.

Turkey: abolished for reason of public benefit and Christian morality [it] would let itself be partitioned, ceding its Asiatic possessions to Russia; the shore of the Adriatic to Austria; Thessaly, Albania and Constantinople to Greece; the Principalities as an independent enclave to a native Prince. The Kings and Princes dispossessed in Europe would go to civilize and monarchize the beautiful American republics which would follow the example of Mexico.

There is the plan of the Empress and I beg You, *M. le Comte*, please do not consider it a joke. I believe the Empress and even the Emperor are well convinced of the possibility and of the necessity of realizing it some day. Let us put to one side the Napoleonic fantasies and permit me to examine the situation seriously from the point of view of our real interests, . . . were it only to lead the Emperor to pledge himself to us in the Eastern question! . . . I am pleased that we are not tête-à-tête [with France] for the moment, and I encourage with all my might the idea of a triple entente, because I foresee that English policy can be a great help to us.

—Hermann Oncken, *Die Rheinpolitik Kaiser Napoleons III. von 1863 bis 1870* (1926; reprint: Osnabrück, 1967), 1:3–6; trans. from Barker, *Distaff Diplomacy*, op. cit., 215–18

8.3   NAPOLEONIC WORLD POLICY, II: MIRAMAR CONVENTION

Napoleon III to Ferdinand Max, 18 March 1864 • *Franz Joseph to Ferdinand Max, 22 March 1864* • *Miramar Convention, 10 April 1864*

A host of arguments seemed to speak for the dispatch of a French expeditionary force to intervene on behalf of the conservative faction in the Mexican civil war: the overthrow of the anticlerical Juarez regime would curry favor with French Catholics; access to Mexican silver would prop up French bimetallism; the claims of French bondholders would be enforced. Major foreign complications were not expected, as the United States' preoccupation with its own civil war would prevent application of the Monroe Doctrine.

Nonetheless, it was ironic that Napoleon III, who understood well the importance of (pseudo)democratic credentials for nineteenth-century rulers, would contemplate the establishment of a French-sponsored *monarchy* in Mexico. To cement his relationship with Austria, Napoleon hoped to cast in the role of satellite king the Austrian archduke Ferdinand Max, a brother of Emperor Franz Joseph. The archduke's interest was keen: he was left unfulfilled by previous appointments as viceroy of Lombardy-Venetia and head of the Austrian navy; his wife Charlotte, daughter of King Leopold of the Belgians, similarly had a weakness for the trappings of power and thus became susceptible to Eugénie's blandishments. With little more to go on than the fact that New Spain had once been a Habsburg dominion and the assurance of Mexican conservatives that he would be welcome, Ferdinand Max proved a willing collaborator in Napoleon's scheme. But even the start-up price was high. Franz Joseph, acting as head of the house of Habsburg, posed onerous conditions. Napoleon too was revealed as a shrewd businessman. Of particular interest are the monetary provisions of the convention (named after his Adriatic estate of Miramar) which established Ferdinand Max as Emperor Maximilian of Mexico.

a)   *Napoleon III to Ferdinand Max, 18 March 1864*

... I beg you always to rely upon my friendship, and to be assured that I appreciate at their true value the lofty sentiments which prompt Your Royal Highness to accept the throne of Mexico. To regenerate a people and to found an empire on principles which reason and morality approve is a fine mission worthy to arouse a noble ambition.

You may be sure that my support will not fail you in the accomplishment of the task which you are undertaking with so much courage....

—Egon Caesar Count Corti, *Maximilian and Charlotte of Mexico,* 2 vols.
(1928, reprint: Hamden, CT 1968), 332–33

b)   *Franz Joseph to Ferdinand Max, 22 March 1864*

Sir, my dear brother, Archduke Ferdinand Max! Since, according to the information I have received, you are disposed to accept the throne of Mexico which has been offered to you, and to found an empire there, God helping you, I find myself compelled, as Supreme Head of the House of Austria, and after the most mature and earnest consideration of the duties which are incumbent upon me as sovereign, to notify you that I can grant my consent to this grave and momentous act of state only on condition that you previously draw up and solemnly confirm the deed of which I enclose a copy, renouncing your and your heirs' rights of succession and inheritance in Austria. Should you be unable to consent to this, and prefer to refuse the crown of Mexico which is offered you, I would take it upon myself to notify foreign countries of your refusal, and in particular the Imperial Court of France.

—Corti, *Maximilian and Charlotte,* op. cit., 333–34

c)   *Miramar Convention, 10 April 1864*

Art. 2: ... The French troops shall gradually evacuate Mexico as H.M. the Emperor of Mexico shall be able to reorganize the troops necessary to take their place....

Art. 7: So long as the needs of the French army corps will require, every two months a service of transports between France and the port of Vera Cruz shall be maintained; the expense of this service, fixed at the sum of 400,000 francs per journey, including return, shall be borne by the Mexican government and paid in Mexico.

Art. 8: The naval stations supported by France in the Antilles and in the Pacific Ocean shall frequently send ships to show the French flag in the Mexican ports.

Art. 9: The cost of the French expedition to Mexico, to be reimbursed by the Mexican government, is fixed at the sum of 270,000,000 francs from the time of the expedition to July 1, 1864. This sum shall bear interest at 3 percent a year.

Art. 10: The indemnity to be paid to France by the Mexican government for the pay and support of the army corps from July 1, 1864, shall be fixed at the rate of 1,000 francs per year per man.

Art. 11: The Mexican government shall at once remit to the French government the sum of 66,000,000 francs in loan securities at par. . . .

Art. 14: The Mexican government agrees to indemnify French subjects for the grievances unduly suffered by them and which caused the expedition. . . .

—Percy F. Martin, *Maximilian in Mexico* (New York, 1914), 442–47

8.4   BISMARCK'S LEVER: THE SCHLESWIG-HOLSTEIN QUESTION

Austro-Prussian Alliance, 16 January 1864 • *Treaty of Vienna, 30 October 1864* • *Austro-Prussian Convention of Gastein, 14 August 1865*

In November 1863, the Danish monarchy introduced the Danish constitution in Schleswig. This effort violated the London settlement of 1852 (Document 4.14) and reopened the Schleswig-Holstein question. It also gave Bismarck his opportunity. Vis-à-vis England and Russia, he posed as the champion of treaty law; within Germany, he now had the means to shift the attention of the public (and the Prussian legislature) from the constitutional conflict in Prussia to a larger German issue, to tap into German national sentiment, and to cast Prussia as a far stauncher supporter of German causes than Austria.

In the aftermath of the Austro-Prussian war against Denmark, the Schleswig-Holstein issue entered yet another phase. Ceded to Austria and Prussia, the two duchies became a lever in Bismarck's strategy to compel Austria either to grant to Prussia a form of equality within Germany or to acknowledge Prussia as the preponderant power in north Germany. Disputes between Berlin and Vienna on how to administer and eventually dispose of their condominium over the duchies kept a permanent low-level crisis simmering, though the Austro-Prussian Gastein convention of August 1865, which allocated Holstein to Austria and Schleswig to Prussia, seemed to suggest that the two German powers were still capable of compromise.

Whether Bismarck was in fact a nationalist and how far he was prepared to go on behalf of German national sentiment are questions best answered with reference to his handling of the claims of Frederick, Duke of Augustenburg. The duke's father, it will be recalled (Document 4.14c), had relinquished his claims to Schleswig and Holstein as part of the overall settlement of this question in 1852. Once Denmark violated the premise of the settlement (i.e., the constitutional separation of Denmark from the two duchies), the elder duke no longer considered the act of renunciation to be binding on his son. The son proclaimed himself "Frederick VIII" of a sovereign principality of Schleswig-Holstein (an entity which, however, existed only in his imagination and that of his supporters); his cause was espoused by the German Confederation and, in a throwback to 1848–1849, by German nationalists. These facts constitute the background to the question posed at the beginning of this paragraph. The question itself should be evaluated in light of articles 4 and 5 of the Austro-Prussian alliance, article 3 of the Treaty of Vienna, and article 1 of the Gastein convention.

a)   *Austro-Prussian Alliance, 16 January 1864*

[Art.] 4:...In the event of an occupation of Schleswig by Federal or Prussian or Austrian forces, the two powers will not allow [popular] demonstrations to influence the settlement of the succession question. . . . The authority of the King of Denmark will be suspended. [Attempts] by Danish authorities to project influence, or demonstrations by a part of the population on behalf of Denmark will not be tolerated, nor will any attempts by the Augustenburg or democratic lobby [*Partei*], from outside or from within the territories, to exercise a political presence.

[Art.] 5:...In the event that hostilities in Schleswig nullify the existing treaty arrangements between the German Powers and Denmark, the courts of Prussia and Austria reserve to themselves the determination of the future status of the Duchies by mutual agreement only. In this event, they will consult further to reach agreement. They will anyhow decide the succession question in the Duchies in no other [manner] than by mutual agreement.

—Huber, *Dokumente*, 2:165–67

b)   *Treaty of Vienna, 30 October 1864*

... Art. 3: His Majesty the King of Denmark renounces all his Rights over the Duchies of Schleswig, Holstein, and Lauenburg in favour of Their Majesties the King of Prussia and the Emperor of Austria and agrees to recognize the dispositions which Their said Majesties shall make with reference to those Duchies. . . .

—Hurst, 1:418–21

c)   *Austro-Prussian Convention of Gastein, 14 August 1865*

Their Majesties . . . have become convinced that the Co-Sovereignty which has hitherto existed in the Territories ceded by Denmark in the Treaty of Peace of 30th October, 1864, leads to untoward results, which at the same time endanger both the good understanding between their Governments and the Interests of the Duchies. Their Majesties have therefore resolved for the future not to exercise in common the Rights which have accrued to them by Article 3 of the above-mentioned Treaty, but to divide the exercise thereof geographically until a further agreement may be made.

Art. 1: The exercise of the Rights . . . shall, without prejudice to the continuance of those rights of both Powers to the whole of both Duchies, pass to His Majesty the Emperor of Austria as regards the Duchy of Holstein, and to His Majesty the King of Prussia as regards the Duchy of Schleswig. . . .

Art. 7: Prussia is entitled to make the Canal that is to be cut between the North Sea and the Baltic, through the Territory of Holstein. . . .

Art. 9: . . . the Emperor of Austria cedes to . . . the King of Prussia . . . the Duchy of Lauenburg; and in return the Royal Prussian Government binds itself to pay to the Austrian Government the sum of 2,500,000 Danish rix-dollars. . . .

—Hurst, 1:421–25

8.5   BRITAIN AND THE SCHLESWIG-HOLSTEIN CRISIS: THE ROOTS OF ANTI-PRUSSIANISM

Bismarck on Britain, 5 July 1862 • Palmerston in the House of Commons, 23 July 1863 • Crown Princess Victoria of Prussia to Queen Victoria, 13 April 1864 • Palmerston to Apponyi, 1 May 1864 • Queen Victoria to Clarendon, 17 May 1864 • Palmerston to Gladstone, 3 July 1864 • Queen Victoria to King Leopold I of the Belgians, 3 August 1865 • Palmerston to Russell, 13 September 1865 • Clarendon to Queen Victoria, 31 March 1866

Ever since Waterloo (and even through the Schleswig-Holstein crisis of 1848–1852), British governments regarded Prussia as something of a nonentity among the Great Powers—a view confirmed by the Paris peace conference of 1856, which admitted Prussia to its deliberations late and only because Prussia had been a signatory to the Straits Convention of 1841 (Document 3.8). The renewed crisis over Schleswig-Holstein of 1863–1866 jolted British statesmen out of their complacency. The emergence of Prussia as a major player in European affairs created its own problems, but these were intertwined with the very issues that had haunted British policy during the Italian crisis of 1859–1860. The Schleswig-Holstein problem raised once again the question of whether or how to intervene and, if so, on behalf of what political or legal principle: the balance of power? the defense of treaty rights? the desires of the local population (which were to be ascertained how and by whom)?

The Schleswig-Holstein question, like the earlier crises over Italy, opened deep rifts between Queen Victoria and her ministry. But it also set members of the royal family at odds with one another. Queen Victoria's mother and husband were Saxe-Coburgs; consequently, she was partial to the "German" cause but sensitive to the suspicions of Prussia harbored by the minor German princes. Her attitude thus differed from that of the Prince of Wales (the later Edward VII), whose outlook was largely shaped by his wife, the former Princess Alexandra of Denmark. The politics of marriage similarly influenced Queen Victoria's oldest daughter, Crown Princess Victoria of Prussia. Elated by the Austro-Prussian victory over Denmark, the younger Victoria temporarily forgot her deeply ingrained distaste for her new home and denounced the very same English institutions with which she could normally find no fault.

All of Palmerston's bluster and blandishments (the Schleswig-Holstein crisis gave him yet another opportunity to threaten war) were in vain. Neither the crown nor the cabinet, each for reasons of its own, was keen on intervention. But the importance of the Schleswig-Holstein crisis lay not in the debate on intervention, but in that it shaped in the British "official mind" an attitude toward Prussia (and, ultimately, Prussian-led Germany) which would prove a heavy mortgage on the future relationship between these two powers.

a)   *Bismarck on Britain, 5 July 1862*

[to Roon:[7]] Just came back from London. People there are much better informed about China and Turkey than about Prussia. . . .

[to Johanna von Bismarck:] . . . It was quite nice there, but the English ministers know less about Prussia than about Japan and Mongolia, nor are they smarter than ours. . . .

—*GW*, 14ii:871, 872

b)   *Palmerston in the House of Commons, 23 July 1863*

. . . I am satisfied with all reasonable men in Europe, including those in France and Russia, in desiring that the independence, the integrity, and the rights of Denmark may be maintained. We are convinced—I am convinced at least—that if any violent attempt were made to overthrow those rights and interfere with that independence, those who made the attempt would find in the result, that it would not be Denmark alone with which they would have to contend. . . .

—*Parl. Debates*, 3rd Series, 172:1252

c)   *Crown Princess Victoria of Prussia to Queen Victoria, 13 April 1864*

. . . The continual meddling and interfering of England in other peoples' affairs has become so ridiculous abroad that it almost ceases to annoy. But to an English heart it is no pleasant sight to see the dignity of one's country so compromised and let down—its influence so completely lost. The highly pathetic, philanthropic, and virtuous tone in which all the attacks against Prussia are made has something intensely ludicrous about it. The English would not like, if they were engaged in a war, to be dictated to in a pompous style, how they were to conduct it; indeed I am sure they would not stand such interference. Why should we then be supposed to submit to it? . . .

—*QV*, 2nd Series, 1:171

---

[7]Albrecht von Roon (1803–1879). Prussian minister of war, 1859–1873; prime minister, 1873.

d)   *Palmerston to Apponyi,*[8] *1 May 1864*

... I consider the passage of an Austrian squadron through our [sic] Channel and past our ports, to give help in a war which we strongly condemn, as an insult to England, and I am resolved, for my part, to leave the Cabinet rather than suffer such an affront. I am convinced that the country shares my views in this respect, for I flatter myself that I can divine the instincts and opinions of my countrymen. It is generally thought, and especially in Germany, that England is cowardly [*poltronne*], that it wishes to avoid war at any price; you can easily be deceived. You know the price I attach to good relations with Austria; but if you enter the Baltic a struggle is inevitable, and that means war. . . . [W]e can do you much harm. There are ports in the Adriatic and Baltic and there are other enemies who only wait for the opportunity to fall upon Austria. All this deserves to be seriously considered, and I thought it more loyal to warn you in a friendly way. . . .

—Haus–, Hof– und Staatsarchiv, PA VIII/64 No. 42C, 26-37; Temperley and Penson, 269–70

e)   *Queen Victoria to Clarendon, 17 May 1864*

It strikes the Queen that it would be very useful, if Lord Clarendon would take an opportunity of ... cautioning the Prince of Wales against violent abuse of Prussia; for [it] is fearfully dangerous for the heir to Her throne to take up one side violently, while he is bound by so many ties of blood to Germany, and only quite lately, by marriage, to Denmark. The Queen knows it is not easy where one's feelings are strongly moved; but if one is determined to act only in a spirit of justice and conciliation (would to God that this country had done so from the very beginning!), one can keep clear of violent partisanship, and one's own sympathies and affections never can interfere with one's duty. In the interest of this country, above all, but also in the interest of Denmark, it is most essential that the Prince of Wales should understand this.

—*QV*, 2nd Series, 1:190

f)   *Palmerston to Gladstone, 3 July 1864*

... It would be well not to be too hard upon the Danes. It is true that they were wrong in the beginning and have been wrong in the end, but they have been most unjustly used by the Germans and the sympathies of the majority of the House and in the nation are Danish.

—Philip Guedalla (ed.), *Gladstone and Palmerston, 1851–1865* (New York, 1928; reprint, 1971), 290

[8]Rudolph, Count Apponyi (1812–1876). Austrian ambassador at the Court of St. James, 1856–1872.

g)   *Queen Victoria to King Leopold I of the Belgians, 3 August 1865*

. . . In Germany things look rather critical and threatening. Prussia seems inclined to behave as atrociously as possible, and as she *always has done*! Odious people the Prussians are, *that* I *must* say.

—*QV*, 2nd Series, 1:271

h)   *Palmerston to Russell, 13 September 1865*

. . . Prussia is too weak as she now is ever to be honest or independent in her action, and, with a view to the future, it is desirable that Germany, in the aggregate, should be strong, in order to control those two ambitious and aggressive powers, France and Russia, that press upon her west and east. As to France, we know how restless and aggressive she is, and how ready to break loose for Belgium, for the Rhine, for anything she would be likely to get without too great an exertion. As to Russia,[9] she will, in due time, become a power almost as great as the old Roman Empire. She can become mistress of all Asia, except British India, whenever she chooses to take it, and, when enlightened arrangements have made her revenue proportioned to her territory and railways shall have abridged distances, her command of men will become enormous, her pecuniary means gigantic, and her power of transporting armies over great distances most formidable. Germany ought to be strong in order to resist Russian aggression, and a strong Prussia is essential to German strength. Therefore, though I heartily condemn the whole of the proceedings of Austria and Prussia about the Duchies, I own that I should rather see them incorporated with Prussia than converted into an additional asteroid in the system of Europe.

—Gooch (ed.), *Lord John Russell. Later Correspondence*, 2:314–15; Ashley, *Life of . . . Palmerston*, 2:270–72

i)   *Clarendon to Queen Victoria, 31 March 1866*

. . . [I]n the present state of Ireland, and the menacing aspect of our relations with the United States, the military and pecuniary resources of England must be husbanded with the utmost care. . . .

—*QV*, 2nd Series, 1:314–15

[9]Cf. Document 6.6a.

LEGEND

■ Kingdom of Prussia, 1866

■ Acquired by Prussia after Austro-Prussian War, 1866

⋮ South German states, 1866

▨ Austria within Confederation, 1815-1866

▥ Austrian possessions outside Confederation, 1815-1866

— Boundary of German Confederation, 1866

NORTH SEA

JUTLAND PENINSULA

DENMARK

Copenhagen

Malmö

Düppel

SCHLESWIG

Flensburg

Schleswig

Elbe R.

Kiel

North Sea-Baltic Canal (1895)

Heligoland

HOLSTEIN

Rostock

Stralsund

Lübeck

Wismar

LAUEN-BURG

MECKLENBURG-SCHWERIN

Strelitz

Oder R.

Emden

Hamburg

Groningen

NETHERLANDS

Amsterdam

Utrecht

Rotterdam

OLDEN-BURG

Bremen

HANOVER

Hanover

Weser R.

Elbe R.

Magdeburg

BRANDENBURG

Berlin

ANHALT

Wittenberg

Kottbus

Osnabrück

LIPPE

Pyrmont

BRUNSWICK

Münster

WESTPHALIA

WALDECK

Göttingen

HESSE-KASSEL

Kassel

Lagensalza

Leipzig

Elbe R.

Dresden

Wesel

Rhine R.

Düsseldorf

Cologne

Aachen

LIMBURG

Calais

Ghent

Brussels

Lille

BELGIUM

Liège

Namur

Arras

RHINE PROVINCE

Ems

NASSAU

to HESSE-D.

Gotha

Erfurt

Weimar

THURINGIAN STATES

SAXONY

Plauen

Eger

LUXEMBURG

Sedan

Moselle R.

Meuse R.

Frankfurt

Mainz

HESSE-DARMSTAD

Würzburg

Main R.

Bamberg

Nürnberg

BOHEMIA

Pilsen

Moldau R.

Reims

Paris

Verdun

Metz

Seine R.

PALATINATE (BAV.)

Saarbrücken

Landau

Heidelberg

BAVARIA

Regensburg

Passau

Linz

LORRAINE (Annexed, 1871)

Strassburg

BADEN

WÜRTTEMBERG

Stuttgart

Ulm

Danube R.

Augsburg

Inn R.

VOSGES MTS.

ALSACE (Annexed 1871)

Mühlhausen

Freiburg

Munich

HOHENZOLLERN-SIGMARINGEN

Salzburg

FRANCE

Basel

Zürich

Rhine R.

Innsbruck

SALZBURG

Gastein

AUSTRIA

Besançon

Berne

SWITZERLAND

TYROL

Bozen

CARINTHIA

Klagenfurt

Geneva

Sitten

A L P S

Adige R.

Trent

Udine

CARNIOLA

Trieste

SAVOY (To France, 1860)

KINGDOM OF SARDINIA

Milan

LOMBARDY (To Piedmont, 1859)

Verona

VENETIA (To Italy, 1866)

Venice

Rhône R.

MAP 6   THE GERMAN CONFEDERATION, THE HABSBURG EMPIRE, AND THE UNIFICATION OF GERMANY

154

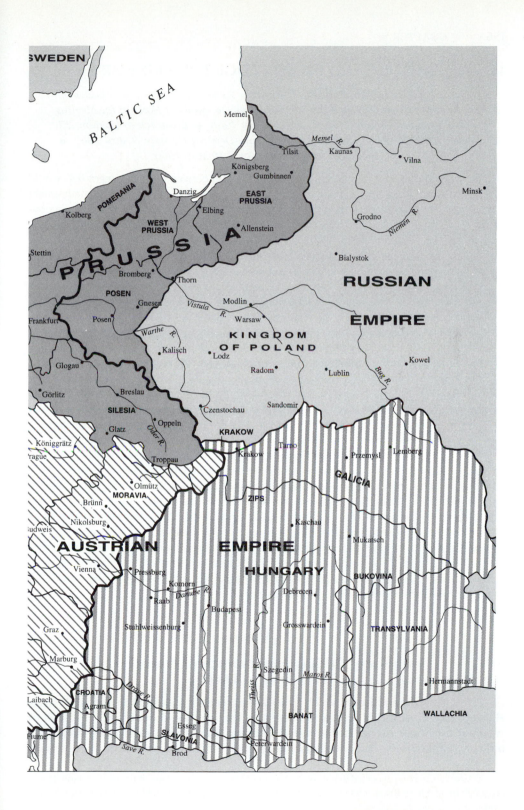

SWEDEN

BALTIC SEA

Memel

Memel R.

Tilsit

Kaunas

Vilna

Minsk

Königsberg
Gumbinnen

EAST
PRUSSIA

Danzig

Elbing

Allenstein

Grodno

Niemen R.

Kolberg

POMERANIA

WEST
PRUSSIA

Bialystok

Stettin

P R U S S I A

RUSSIAN

Bromberg

Thorn

EMPIRE

POSEN

Gnesen

Vistula R.

Modlin

Warsaw

Frankfurt

Posen

Warthe R.

KINGDOM

OF POLAND

Kowel

Glogau

Kalisch

Lodz

Radom

Lublin

Bug R.

Görlitz

Breslau

SILESIA

Czenstochau

Sandomir

Königgrätz

Glatz

Oppeln

Oder R.

KRAKOW

Tarno

Przemysl

Lemberg

Prague

Troppau

Krakow

GALICIA

Olmütz

ZIPS

Brünn

MORAVIA

Nikolsburg

Kaschau

Budweis

AUSTRIAN

EMPIRE

Mukatsch

BUKOVINA

Vienna

Pressburg

HUNGARY

Komorn

Danube R.

Debrecen

TRANSYLVANIA

Raab

Budapest

Graz

Stuhlweissenburg

Grosswardein

Marburg

Theiss R.

Szegedin

Maros R.

Hermannstadt

Laibach

CROATIA

Drave R.

Agram

BANAT

WALLACHIA

Fiume

Esseg

SLAVONIA

Peterwardein

Save R.

Brod

155

8.6   AUSTRIA AND PRUSSIA EDGE TOWARD WAR

Minutes of the Austrian Council of Ministers, 21 February 1866 • Minutes of the Prussian Crown Council, 28 February 1866 • Moltke's Notes of the Meeting of the Prussian Crown Council, 28 February 1866 • Bismarck to Usedom, 27 March 1866 • Prusso-Italian "Offensive and Defensive" Treaty, 8 April 1866 • Prokesch-Osten to Mensdorff, 18 May 1866

Bismarck was mistaken if he had hoped that the Gastein convention (Document 8.4) would usher in an era of Austro-Prussian equality in Germany or that Austria, in its aftermath, might acquiesce in Prussian leadership in the German north. Austria would not yield; Prussia continued to persist. By February 1866, the political and military leadership of both Austria and Prussia began to reckon with the likelihood of war.

Ending the Prussian crown council of 28 February, King Wilhelm paid lip service to the notion that a political solution might be found after all. But virtually in the same breath, Wilhelm ruled out further diplomatic steps while negotiations were under way with Italy for an anti-Austrian alliance. Nor was Bismarck's stance free of contradictions: in his instructions to the Prussian minister in Florence, he referred to "the course of events" as if it were an independent agent. Instead, the question might be put whether the Prusso-Italian treaty of 1866, in sandwiching Austria between these powers, created for Bismarck an opportunity of three months' duration which contributed to "the course of events" by hastening it.

On 9 April, Prussia raised the stakes by proposing that the German Confederation—hitherto a union of princes, not of their populations—should be restructured on a democratic basis, thereby guaranteeing Prussia, as the most populous state, a leadership role. This ruse was too transparent and was defeated with the votes of the midsize German states that stood to lose by it. With the momentum seemingly in its favor, Austria on 1 June submitted the future of Schleswig-Holstein to the German Confederation—in the expectation that the confederation would constitute these territories as another midsize state which, after its creation, would join the remainder in defending its privileges against Prussian encroachments. But in submitting the Schleswig-Holstein question to the German Confederation, Austria violated the Austro-Prussian alliance of 1864 and the Gastein convention (Documents 8.4a and 8.4c).[10] Prussia countered by invading Holstein and by calling for the exclusion of Austria from the confederation. On 14 June, the confederation overwhelmingly carried an Austrian motion to mobilize the armies of the member states against Prussia. In response, Prussian units invaded Hanover, Hesse-Kassel, and Saxony. Without any formal declarations of war, the struggle for supremacy in Germany moved into its final phase.

a)   Minutes of the Austrian Council of Ministers, 21 February 1866

. . . The threatening attitude which Prussia has recently assumed in the Schleswig–Holstein matter, said H.M., raises the question whether we should look on calmly or whether the honor, dignity, and security of Austria did not demand that we make such military preparations which would allow us to face even the most serious contingen-

---

[10]Austria may have expected that its renunciation of Venetia (Austro-French treaty of 12 June; Document 7.8) freed it from the specter of a two-front war; hence it was emboldened to force the issue in Germany.

cies [*Eventualitäten*]. He shared the view that although there was not sufficient cause for an event as regrettable as a collision between Austria and Prussia, one nonetheless had to take into account that the Prussian army was far more mobile in the field and that the network of railroads there greatly facilitated its deployment to strategic pressure points, whereas our army had been reduced to a peacetime footing and would require a great deal of time to be brought up to full strength. . . . H.M. concluded by saying that he was agreed to abstain from overt military preparations and to seek, through diplomatic means, the maintenance of the honor and dignity, as well as the interests, of the country. Moreover, all the preparations could be readied bureaucratically [*auf dem Papier*], and the necessary instructions had already gone to the war ministry.

—Srbik, *Quellen*, op. cit., 5i:202–4

b)   Minutes of the Prussian Crown Council, 28 February 1866

[Bismarck:] . . . It would be a humiliation if Prussia were to retreat now. Such a humiliation had to be avoided at all costs. In this event a rupture with Austria was probable. This was the question which had to be considered and decided: whether Prusssia should shy away from this obstacle—a rupture and possibly [*eventuell*] a war with Austria? . . . The whole evolution of German conditions, the hostile attitude of Austria was driving us toward a war. . . .

. . . H.M. summarized the views expressed in this meeting: if no rapprochement with Austria could be brought about, all preparations which we need to make to cope with such a contingency we should make; that suitable foreign alliances should be sought; that the Austrian government should not be left to doubt either the full seriousness of the situation or Prussia's determination not to shy away from war; so that Prussia, if there were no peaceful rapprochement, could confidently accept battle.

Finally, H.M. approved in principle the step, labelled for the present time as necessary and indispensable by the prime minister and recommended by the entire ministry, of [sending] an extraordinary mission to Florence[10a] which, without attracting atttention, should not leave any doubt about the intentions of this government but should avoid the appearance of rattling the sabre.

H.M. also agreed to the proposal of the prime minister—for now and until the mission to Florence has borne fruit—to avoid any further diplomatic steps in Vienna. . . .

—Historische Reichskommission [Rudolf Ibbeken, vol. ed.], *Die auswärtige Politik Preussens* (Berlin, 1939), 6:611–16

c)   Moltke's Notes of the Meeting of the Prussian Crown Council, 28 February 1866

. . . [Goltz:[11]] Emperor Napoleon has, since his accession, shown sympathy and benevolence towards Prussia. . . . [Bartering] the Danubian Principalities . . . might help in reach-

---

[10a]Capital of the Kingdom of Italy, 1861–1870.
[11] Robert, Count Goltz (1817–1869). Prussian ambassador in Paris. Cf. Document 8.2.

ing an accommodation in regard to the Elbe Duchies. Austria:Wallachia; Russia: Moldavia; Italy:Venice; Prussia: Schleswig-Holstein; France: Genoa;Turkey: left holding the bag. . . .

—*Auswärtige Politik Preussens*, op. cit., 6:618

d)   *Bismarck to Usedom,*[12] *27 March 1866*

. . . I would like Y.E. to remember that none of my instructions and telegrams have ever departed from the premise of what is possible [*eventuelle Charakter*][13] in our representations. We do not and cannot intend that, as a result of an arbitrary attack on Austria, we appear in the eyes of Europe as the aggressor and disturber of the peace. I have repeatedly pointed out that we had to await the further course of events and that we only wanted to reassure ourselves of the intentions of Italy in case this [course] was heading towards a war—which, in our view, will be difficult to avoid. But we have never taken the view that a war was about to commence immediately; we never said that we had already decided on mobilization. If the Italian minister had cause to assume that we wanted to begin an aggressive war at all costs, then such [an assumption] would be premature. . . .

—*GW*, 5:425–28

e) *Prusso-Italian "Offensive and Defensive" Treaty, 8 April 1866*

. . . Art. 2: If the negotiations—which H.M. the King of Prussia has opened with other German governments on a reform of the federal constitution [of the German Confederation][14] so that it meets the needs of the German nation—should fail, and if His Majesty consequently should resort to arms to give effect to his proposals, then His Italian Majesty, after the initiative has been taken by Prussia . . . will declare war on Austria.

Art. 3: . . . neither Prussia nor Italy will conclude peace or an armistice without the consent of the other.

Art. 4: This consent cannot be withheld after Austria has agreed to cede to Italy the Lombardo-Venetian Kingdom and to Prussia Austrian territories commensurate in population to this Kingdom.

Art. 5: This treaty will expire three months after its signature if within these three months the course of events depicted in Art. 2 has not transpired, that is, if Prussia has not declared war on Austria. . . .

—*GW*, 5:462; Heinrich von Sybel, *Die Begründung des Deutschen Reiches durch Wilhelm I* (rev. ed., 1908), 229

[12]Guido, Count Usedom (1805–1884). Prussian minister in Florence, 1863–1869.

[13]How valid, given the context of this document, was Bismarck's distinction between what was merely possible and what was inevitable? In any event, the reader is invited to compare the use of the term "*eventuell*" (which can be rendered to mean "possibly," "probably," or even "if necessary") here and in Document 12.9b.

[14]The next day, Prussia submitted proposals to that effect to the Diet of the German Confederation.

f)   ***Prokesch-Osten[15] to Mensdorff,[16] 18 May 1866***

Today Your Excellency is in a similar position as President Lincoln when the South took up arms against the union and wanted to secede. The moment has perhaps come for Austria to strengthen the [German] Confederation and to raise [its reputation]; it is the only possible union for Germany. . . . [A]s things are today, namely favorable—thanks to the unprincipled and unscrupulous stance of Bismarck—, and given the tremendous efforts into which Austria has already been forced, war is surely to be preferred to procrastination and one can only wish that the solution is a thorough one, one which will make it impossible for Prussia to resume this vicious game. A secure warranty for this, however, cannot consist of mere words, promises, and similar snow jobs, not in a second Olmütz,[17] but only in a reduction of Prussia's power to the point that it must abandon its desire for dominance in Germany. . . .

—Srbik, *Quellen,* op. cit., 5ii:714–15

8.7   NAPOLEON III'S SPEECH AT AUXERRE, 6 MAY 1866

Not about to let the French army's engagement in Mexico stand in the way of an active diplomacy in the German question, Napoleon III hoped to profit from the worsening Austro-Prussian crisis. A war between the German powers would allow France to sell its neutrality at a high price after the two sides had exhausted themselves. French diplomats took care not to spell out detailed demands, but it was widely assumed that France would seek territorial compensations. Napoleon's speech at an agricultural fair at Auxerre (département of Yonne) may have been intended as a signal that France would have to be reckoned with in the event of a political reorganization of Central Europe. It may also have been a rebuke to Adolphe Thiers, who, in a parliamentary speech delivered on 3 May, urged the government to take an anti-Prussian stance. This, by extension, implied an attitude sympathetic to Austria; sympathetic also to what remained of the 1815 settlement.

Napoleon may have selected Auxerre for its symbolism: it was here in March 1815 that Marshal Ney, after having pledged to Louis XVIII that he would bring Napoleon to Paris "in an iron cage," instead deserted the Bourbon cause and went over to the emperor. Be that as it may, his speech at Auxerre acquired immediate notoriety because of the passage quoted below. This passage, however, appears not to have been delivered; it was probably inserted after the fact and published in the official *Moniteur* the next day.

I see with happiness that the memories of the First Empire have not been erased from your memory. Believe that, for my part, I have inherited the feelings of the head of my

---

[15]Anton von Prokesch-Osten (1795–1876), diplomat and orientalist. Austrian minister in Berlin, 1849–1852; Frankfurt, 1852–1855; Constantinople, 1855–1867.

[16]Alexander, Count Mensdorff (1813–1871). Austrian foreign minister, 1864–1866.

[17]Cf. Document 4.13.

family for those energetic and patriotic people [*populations*] who supported the Emperor through good as well as bad fortune. I have, moreover, towards the Département of the Yonne, a debt of recognition to repay. It was one of the first to give me its support in 1848; that is, it knew, like the great majority of the French people, that its interests were mine and that I despised, just as it did, those treaties of 1815 which nowadays people [*on*] want to make the basis of our policy. I thank you for your feelings. Among you I breathe freely, because it is among the working people of the towns and the fields that I find again the true spirit of France.

—Hermann Oncken, *Die Rheinpolitik Kaiser Napoleons III* (Berlin, 1926), 1:165

8.8   PEACEMAKING, 1866

Bismarck to Wilhelm I, 24 July 1866 • Bismarck in his Memoirs on his Meeting with Wilhelm I, 25 July 1866 • Austro-Prussian Armistice of Nikolsburg, 26 July 1866 • Alliance between Prussia and Bavaria, 22 August 1866

Like the war of 1859, Prussia's war against Austria and its German allies was short and localized. One fact helps explain the other. Uncertainty about Napoleon's intentions gave Bismarck an impetus to conclude the war: the longer the war, the greater the temptation for Napoleon III to offer his mediation, to ask for "compensations," or even to adopt a warlike stance. Moreover, Bismarck had already attained his objectives. He outlined these in a report to Wilhelm I in which he persuaded his reluctant monarch to support his conception of the new political and territorial order in Germany.

Bismarck's moderation in the negotiations with Austria is all the more important as the war of 1866 brought the Habsburg monarchy closer to the brink of disaster than any event since the secession of Hungary in 1849 or even the Napoleonic period. In Bismarck's calculation, the continued vitality of Austria was not contrary to Prussia's interests; its collapse, however, would have confronted him and Prussia with a series of agonizing choices.

Bismarck's moderation in his approach to Austria was not mirrored in his dealings with the German north—clearly, the same standards and calculations did not apply. The southern German states fared considerably better: Bavaria, Württemberg, Baden, and Hesse-Darmstadt were left intact territorially but paid a political price. In Bismarck's negotiations with these states, Prussian coercion was less a factor than the specter of French restlessness. Bavaria in particular had much to fear from a French attempt to revise its border on the left bank of the Rhine, as France would almost certainly be "compensated" at the expense of the Bavarian Palatinate. Indeed, Bavaria's fear of French intentions, never mind its military helplessness vis-à-vis Prussia, left it little choice but to acquiesce to the military alliance which Bismarck made a condition for a swift peace. Prussia had already concluded identical treaties with Württemberg and Baden; a similar treaty with Hesse-Darmstadt was signed in April 1867.

a)   ***Bismarck to Wilhelm I, 24 July 1866 (with annotations by Wilhelm I)***

. . . Austria in a twofold declaration grants all substantive points which Prussia has to demand: that it leaves the German Confederation and that it permits a reconstruction of the confederation without its participation and under Prussia's leadership, and that it will recognize everything which Your Majesty deems proper in North Germany. To maintain the Kingdom of Saxony is the joint request of Austria and France [*that Sax-*

ony has been assured not only its continued existence but also its integrity is very difficult for me because Saxony is the main instigator of the war and now emerges from it without loss]. If Austria, as it seems, is willing to sacrifice its other allies in North Germany for this, then it seems wise to take the request into account; our political interests and needs will be met in a convention with Saxony in which it puts the whole strength of the country at the disposal of Your Majesty. . . . The exclusion of Austria from the confederation, with the annexation [by Prussia] of Schleswig-Holstein, Hanover, Electoral Hesse, Upper Hesse, and Nassau and with the aforementioned relationship of Saxony to Prussia can altogether be regarded as an accomplishment larger than any which could have been envisaged when the war broke out [*this is a result that could never have been predicted. . .*].

If this goal can be secured by a swift conclusion of a preliminary [peace], then in my humble view it would be a political mistake to endanger this result by attempting to obtain from Austria a few more square miles of territorial cessions or a few more million in reparations and to expose it to the uncertain fortunes of a prolonged war in which third-party intervention could not be ruled out [*agreed, but it all depends how much money or land one can obtain without jeopardizing the whole*].

The outbreak of cholera in the army, the danger—inherent in a campaign in August in this climate—of an epidemic also speaks against a continuation of military operations [*and very powerfully so*]. . . .

I feel wholly responsible to Your Majesty for rendering the advice which my office requires me to give; and I am therefore motivated to lay down officially that, even though I will faithfully represent in the upcoming negotiations every instruction of Your Majesty, [I consider] any impediment to the swift conclusion [of peace] with Austria, for the sake of peripheral advantages, contrary to my humble application and advice [*if, in spite of this conscientious report, one cannot attain from the vanquished, without endangering the main objective, what army and country are justified in expecting—namely a large reparation for the war from Austria as the main enemy or an acquisition of territory fitting to behold—then the victor at the gates of Vienna must swallow this bitter pill and leave the judgement to posterity*].

—*GW*, 6:498

b)   **Bismarck in his Memoirs on his Meeting with Wilhelm I,
25 July 1866**

. . . I replied that the task at hand was not to judge [Austria], but to pursue a German policy: Austria had been no more in the wrong in opposing our claims than we were in the right in making them. . . .

—Bismarck, *Gedanken und Erinnerungen*, op. cit., 2:46

c)   **Austro-Prussian Armistice of Nikolsburg, 26 July 1866**

Art. 1: With the exception of the Lombardo-Venetian Kingdom, the territory of the Austrian monarchy remains intact. . . .

Art. 2: His Majesty the Emperor of Austria recognizes the dissolution of the German Confederation as it has existed hitherto, and consents to a new organization of Germany without the participation of the Austrian Empire. . . .

Art. 3: . . . the Emperor of Austria transfers to . . . the King of Prussia all the rights which the Treaty of Vienna of 30th October 1864, recognized as belonging to him over the Duchies of Schleswig and Holstein, with this reservation, that the people of the northern districts of Schleswig shall again be united to Denmark if they express a desire to be so by a vote freely given. . . . [18]

Art. 5: In conformity with the wish expressed by . . . the Emperor of Austria, . . . the King of Prussia declares his willingness to let the territorial state of the Kingdom of Saxony continue in its present extent when the modifications are made which are to take place in Germany. . . .

—Hurst, 1:425–27

e)   *Alliance between Prussia and Bavaria, 22 August 1866*

Art. 1. An alliance for mutual protection and solidarity [*Schutz- und Trutz-Bündnis*] is herewith concluded between His Majesty the King of Prussia and His Majesty the King of Bavaria. The High Contracting Parties mutually guarantee the integrity of their respective states, and for this purpose commit themselves to put at one another's disposal all their forces in the event of war.

Art. 2. Should such an event arise, His Majesty the King of Bavaria will put his forces under the command of the King of Prussia. . . .

—Huber, *Dokumente*, op. cit., 2:215

8.9   THE BENEDETTI DRAFT TREATY, AUGUST 1866

Benedetti Draft Treaty, August 1866 ● *Treaty of London, 11 May 1867*

On 29 August 1866, the French ambassador to Prussia, Vincent Benedetti, presented Bismarck with a draft for a Franco-Prussian alliance. The treaty, if implemented, would reward France for its neutrality during the war of 1866. Benedetti's proposal was in fact a retreat from a French suggestion, made earlier that month, that Prussia should cede to France the border of 1814, sever any connection to Luxemburg and Limburg (both of which had been part of the German Confederation), and pressure Bavaria and Hesse-Darmstadt to surrender to France their territories west of the Rhine.[19] This earlier scheme did not mention Belgium.

Luxemburg, which had been left adrift by the dissolution of the German Confederation and was not included in the North German Confederation created by Bismarck in 1867, was likely to be the one property where Napoleon could expect least resistance. But when the Luxemburg question was aired—almost certainly at the instigation of Bismarck himself—in the parliament of the North German Confederation in early April 1867, it provoked an outburst of German national sentiment. Given the popular indignation in Germany, an international conference appeared to be the solution which would allow the powers to save face. Despite the concessions offered by Prussia, the outcome of the Luxemburg crisis did not conform to Napoleon's expectations.

---

[18]This reservation, incorporated in the definitive Peace of Prague, was set aside by an Austro-German agreement in October 1878. *SP*, 69:773. It was revived by the Versailles peace—though Denmark, a neutral in World War I, was not a signatory. As a result of the plebiscite of February 1920, about two-thirds of northern Schleswig joined Denmark.

[19]Text in Oncken (ed.), *Rheinpolitik*, op. cit., 2:245.

By putting its objectives in writing, the French government had unwittingly placed a potent weapon in Bismarck's hands. Within days of the French declaration of war on Prussia in July 1870, Bismarck published the text of the Benedetti draft in the London *Times*. He thus nipped in the bud any British expressions of sympathy for France in the early stages of the war. The attention of the British government was now focused on the neutrality of Belgium and on obtaining from the belligerents some assurance that they would respect the treaties of 1839 (Document 2.8).

a)   *Benedetti Draft Treaty, August 1866*

Art. 1: His Majesty the Emperor of the French admits and recognizes the acquisitions which Prussia has made in the course of the last war which she undertook against Austria and its allies.

Art. 2: His Majesty the King of Prussia promises to assist France in the acquisition of Luxembourg; to this effect the said Majesty will enter into negotiations with His Majesty the King of the Netherlands in order to determine how to accomplish the cession of his sovereign rights over this Duchy to the Emperor of the French by means of such compensation as shall be judged sufficient or otherwise. For his part, the Emperor of the French undertakes to assume the financial responsibilities which this transaction will incur.

Art. 3: His Majesty the Emperor of the French will not oppose a federal union of the Confederation of the North with the states of the south [*les états du Midi*] of Germany, with the exception of Austria, the union of which may be based on a common parliament, always respecting in a just measure the sovereignty of such states.

Art. 4: For his part, His Majesty the King of Prussia, in the event His Majesty the Emperor of the French would be obliged by circumstances to invade Belgium or to conquer it, will give the aid of his arms to France and will effect this with all his land and sea forces toward and against any Power which in such an event would declare war on him.

Art. 5: In order to insure the full execution of the preceding stipulations, His Majesty the King of Prussia and His Majesty the Emperor of the French agree by the present treaty to an offensive and defensive alliance which they solemnly commit themselves to maintain. Their Majesties oblige themselves, beyond this and especially, to observe in every case in which their respective states, each of which mutually guarantees the integrity of the other, would be threatened by aggression to consider themselves allies. In such an event [they will] take, without delay and not to refuse on any pretext whatsoever, the military arrangements which would be demanded by their common interests in accordance with the clauses and provisions enumerated above. . . .

—*The Times*, 25 July 1870

b)   *Treaty of London, 11 May 1867*

. . . Art. 2: The Grand Duchy of Luxemburg, within the Limits determined by the Act annexed to the Treaties of the 19th April, 1839,[20] under the Guarantee of the Courts of

[20]See Document 2.8.

Great Britain, Austria, France, Prussia, and Russia, shall henceforth form a perpetually Neutral State. . . . That principle is and remains placed under the sanction of the collective Guarantee of the Powers signing Parties to the present Treaty, with the exception of Belgium, which is itself a Neutral State. . . .

Art. 3: . . . it is agreed by common consent that the City of Luxemburg, considered in time past, from a military point of view, as a Federal Fortress [of the German Confederation], shall cease to be a fortified city.

—Hurst, 1:449–50

8.10   THE AUSTRO-HUNGARIAN COMPROMISE, 1867

The Hungarian Law XII, 12 June 1867

Ever since Austria quelled the Hungarian secession in 1849, Habsburg rule in Hungary relied on a succession of administrative expedients that shared only one common denominator—they were implemented without the constitutional assent of Hungary. Austria's defeat in 1866 made it all the more urgent that constitutional rule return to Hungary. By 1867, a complex bundle of laws enacted by both legislatures, the *Ausgleich*, restructured the Austrian empire and transformed it into the Austro-Hungarian ("Dual") Monarchy. Both the Austrian and the Hungarian halves were to have their own ministries and legislatures and would, in essence, be self-governing. There would be three joint ministries—foreign affairs, war, and finance—whose budgets were determined by the *Delegationen*, a committee composed of sixty members from each of the two legislatures. Passage of the *Ausgleich* by the Hungarian legislature finally made possible the coronation, in Budapest, of Franz Joseph as King of Hungary—nineteen years after he had assumed the title.

In later years, the *Ausgleich* laws gave rise to different interpretations of the nature of the Austro-Hungarian state, particularly whether Hungary had an identity of its own in international law. This argument, advocated with increasing tenacity by Hungarian ministries after the turn of the century, derives considerable strength from the first sentence excerpted below, which could be construed to imply a dimension of foreign affairs outside the purview of the joint ministry.

Altogether absent in the equivalent Austrian law was the phrase "with the concurrence of the ministries of both parts and with their agreement." This omission (and therefore the discrepancy between the Hungarian and Austrian law) conferred on the Hungarian prime minister, in the formulation of foreign policy, a constitutionally more privileged position than that enjoyed by his Austrian counterpart.

The Hungarian Law XII, 12 June 1867

. . . Art. 8: . . . The effective management of foreign affairs requires uniformity with regard to those foreign dealings which have a simultaneous [*együtt*] bearing on all lands under the dominion of His Majesty. Therefore the diplomatic and commercial representation of the realm [*birodalom*] in other countries, as well as the measures deriving from international treaties, are the task of the joint minister of foreign affairs [who proceeds] with the concurrence of the ministries of both parts [of the monarchy] and with their agreement. Each ministry will communicate international treaties to its own legislature. These foreign affairs Hungary too will recognize as joint and it is prepared to contribute proportionally to the cost, to be jointly determined. . . .

—Edmund Bernatzik, *Die österreichischen Verfassungsgesetze* (2nd ed., Vienna, 1911), 334, 439, 451–52

8.11   BISMARCK AND THE GERMAN SOUTH

Bismarck in the North German Reichstag, 11 March 1867 ● *Bismarck to Werthern, 26 February 1869* ● *Friesen's Recollection of a Conversation with Bismarck, Fall 1869*

Bismarck's varying assessments on the timing and the opportuneness of the union of the North German Confederation with the German south have to be understood in the context of day-to-day politics. Bismarck's initial expectation, that union could be effected from "below," soon ran aground. In February and March 1868, elections in the four southern states to a "customs parliament" (Zollparlament), a newly created forum with a mandate to discuss issues relating to the Zollverein, yielded two-to-one majorities for the opponents of union.[21] In 1869, protests against the export to the south of the Prussian system of military organization became a rallying point for antiunionists in Württemberg. On 25 November 1869, clericals and particularists triumphed in elections to the Bavarian parliament.

a)   *Bismarck in the North German Reichstag, 11 March 1867*

. . . Let us put Germany, so-to-speak, into the saddle! Surely it will be able to ride [lively applause].

—Scheler (ed.), *Bismarck. Werke in Auswahl*, op. cit. (Stuttgart, 1968), 4:46

b)   *Bismarck to Werthern,[22] 26 February 1869*

That German unity could be advanced through a resort to force, I too believe to be true. But a completely different question is having the job of bringing about a violent cataclysm and the responsibility for choosing the moment [to unleash it]. An arbitrary intervention into the course of history, determined solely on the basis of subjective criteria, has always resulted in the knocking down of unripe fruit; and that German unity at this moment is not a ripe fruit is, in my view, evident. If time moves in this direction, just as it has since the accession of Frederick the Great and namely since 1840, the year when a national movement became noticeable for the first time since the wars of liberation,[23] then we can view the future with calm and can leave the rest to our descendants. The loquacious tumult—with which those away from

---

[21]Unionists held a slim edge in Baden with eight against six seats, tied in southern Hesse-Darmstadt three against three, but were outnumbered by their opponents, twenty-six to twenty-one in Bavaria and seventeen to none in Württemberg. Pflanze, *Bismarck*, op. cit., 1:396–99.

[22]Georg von Werthern (1816–1895). Prussian minister in Munich, 1867–1888.

[23]See Document 3.9.

power search for the font of wisdom which will bring about German unity—as a rule hides a superficial and certainly impotent acquaintance with the realities [of the case] and their repercussions. . . . We can set ahead the clocks, but this will not cause time to move faster; and the ability to wait for conditions to develop is a prerequisite for practical policies. . . .

—*GW*, 6b:1327

c)   *Friesen's[24] Recollection of a Conversation with Bismarck, Fall 1869*

He viewed an early war with France as an unalterable necessity. Emperor Napoleon III, more and more unstable in his domestic position, had lost his former clear decisiveness and was making mistakes of all kinds in his domestic policies—causing dissatisfaction to spread among the French people and causing the power and influence of his opponents to grow every day, a danger for him. The emperor would have little choice but to deflect the attention of the nation from domestic to foreign politics by means of a war and to flatter the self-image of the French—who had still not forgotten his inglorious, weak conduct in 1866—possibly with a successful military campaign to strengthen anew his own position and that of his dynasty. For the North German Confederation too a war with France was not only unavoidable but also necessary, because as long as the present unstable situation vis-à-vis France endured, the development and stabilization of our own conditions would remain in limbo. He added that though the North German Confederation had to be prepared for all eventualities, it had no reason to cause or even accelerate the outbreak of a war if it were intended by France. . . . With reference to the relations between the confederation and the south German states, Bismarck stressed that it was in our interest not to trigger a war. On the basis of the treaties concluded with these states in 1866 we could expect their support with certainty if France declared war or made it unavoidable; this would hardly be the case if we were the attacking or the provoking party.

—*GW*, 7:224

8.12   ANOTHER BISMARCKIAN LEVER: THE HOHENZOLLERN CANDIDACY FOR THE SPANISH THRONE

Prince Karl Anton to Bismarck, 25 February 1870 ● Bismarck to Wilhelm I, 9 March 1870

Ever since the flight of Queen Isabella II from Spain in 1868, Bismarck had toyed with promoting the candidacy of a Hohenzollern prince for the vacant throne. Bismarck's candidate, Prince Leopold of Hohenzollern-Sigmaringen, was the scion of a Catholic branch line of the Prussian royal house; Leopold's younger brother Karl (Carol) had been elected Prince of Romania in 1866 (with, incidentally, the approval of Napoleon III). But there would be no candidacy without the acquiescence of the candidate's father, Prince Karl Anton, or, more important, the approval of King Wilhelm of Prussia, head of the Hohenzollern clan. This Bismarck sought in March 1870. He badgered his monarch with an array of arguments as bold as they were brazen: he argued the economic and dynastic benefits of a Hohenzollern on the Spanish

---

[24]Richard von Friesen (1808–1884). Foreign minister of Saxony, 1866–1876.

throne; cited the boost to "the hitherto so imperfectly satisfied need of the Germans for recognition by other countries"; asserted that Prince Leopold would face no obstacles in Spain; warned that the possibility of a Bavarian candidate, in Leopold's stead, would set back the effort for German unity; conjured up the specter, if there were no monarchical candidates at all, of a Spanish republic; ominously hinted that, if it was revealed that Wilhelm had stood in the way of the candidacy, the king would have to contend with the wrath of German public opinion. Excerpted here are passages from Bismarck's analysis of how the candidacy would affect the Franco-Prussian relationship. For now, the king's objections stalled the project, but by June, Bismarck had charmed Leopold into proceeding and Wilhelm into giving his blessing.

a)   ***Prince Karl Anton to Bismarck,***
                        25 February 1870

. . . A Hohenzoller in Spain would give rise to a wild outcry in anti-Prussian Europe and would either precipitate or defer the solution of many pending questions. . . .

—Georges Bonnin (ed.), *Bismarck and the Hohenzollern Candidature for the Spanish Throne* (London, 1959), 64

b)   ***Bismarck to Wilhelm I, 9 March 1870 (with marginalia***
                        by Wilhelm)

. . . For Germany it is desirable to have on the other side of France a country on whose sympathies [*how long would these sympathies last?*] we can rely and with whose feelings France is obliged to reckon. If, during a war between Germany and France, . . . Spain [is] sympathetic to Germany [*what potentate in Spain would be in a position to* guarantee *such a policy?*], the difference . . . in terms of the armed forces that France could put in the field against Germany may be estimated at not less than one or two French army corps. . . . [*The above marginal notes make it clear that I have strong scruples against the acceptance of the Spanish crown by the Prince of Hohenzollern. . . . Since however the latter upheld his verbal and written declaration that he could only decide on acceptance at my command and I from conviction am unable to give this command, the discussion was thereby brought to an end.*]

—Bonnin, *Hohenzollern Candidature*, op. cit., 68–73

8.13   **THE EMS DISPATCH**

Heinrich Abeken to Bismarck, 13 July 1870 ● *Bismarck's Edited Version*
of the "Ems Dispatch"

Bismarck's promotion of the candidacy of a Hohenzoller prince to the Spanish throne has been compared to holding a torch to an open gas nozzle. Whatever his motives—whether he intended to divert French attention to the Iberian peninsula, whether he intended to counter a possible Franco-Austrian rapprochement in the Eastern Question,[25] whether he intended to foster a Franco-Prussian diplomatic crisis to further his goals in Germany, or whether he intended to cause in cold blood a war between the two countries—yesterday's opportunity turned into today's defeat when the project was prematurely exposed through a clerk's error. The revelation forced Bismarck to scramble for cover and to pretend that the entire episode was a family matter outside the competence of the Prussian government. In the meantime, the French ambassador, Benedetti, secured from King Wilhelm a promise to withdraw the candidacy. Not content with this response, Benedetti again sought out the king on his holiday in the Rhenish spa of Ems. Wilhelm gave a brief written account of this encounter to Heinrich Abeken, his foreign ministry liaison; Abeken, in turn, telegraphed what had come to pass to Bismarck in Berlin.

Bismarck now sensed that he held in his hands the device with which he could turn the tables on the French government. The edited and shortened version of the dispatch which he published in the Berlin press made Wilhelm's dismissal of Benedetti appear far more brusque than it actually was. Blinded by this insult, Eugénie and other members of the war party in Paris gained the upper hand and prevailed on Napoleon to declare war on Prussia on 19 July.

a) Heinrich Abeken to Bismarck, 13 July 1870

b) Bismarck's Edited Version of the "Ems Dispatch"

His Majesty the King writes to me: "M. Benedetti intercepted me on the promenade in order to demand of me most insistently that I should authorize him to telegraph immediately to Paris that I shall obligate myself for all future time never again to give my approval to the candidacy of the Hohenzollern should it be renewed.

I refused to agree to this, the last time somewhat severely, as it is neither right or possible to assume such obligations *à tout jamais.* Naturally, I informed him that I had received no news as yet and since he was informed about Paris and Madrid sooner than I, he could clearly see that my government once more had no hand in the matter."

Since then, His Majesty has received a dispatch from the prince [Karl Anton

After the reports of the renunciation by the prince of Hohenzollern had been officially transmitted by the royal government of Spain to the imperial government of France, the French ambassador presented to His Majesty the King at Ems the demand to authorize him to telegraph to Paris that His Majesty the King would obligate himself for all future time never again to give his approval to the candidacy of the Hohenzollern should it be renewed.

His Majesty the King thereupon refused

---

[25]Cf. Document 8.2. In 1870, the aftermath of a revolt in Crete might have supplied the appropriate coat hanger for a Franco-Austrian combination.

writing on behalf of his son]. As His Majesty had informed Count Benedetti that he was expecting news from the prince, His Majesty himself, in view of the above-mentioned demand and in consonance with the advice of [the court chamberlain] Count Eulenburg and myself, decided not to receive the French envoy again but to inform him through an aide-de-camp that His Majesty had now received from the prince confirmation of the news which Benedetti had already received from Paris, and that he had nothing further to say to the ambassador. His Majesty leaves it to the judgment of Your Excellency whether or not to communicate at once the new demand by Benedetti and its rejection to our ambassadors and to the press.

to receive the French envoy again and informed him through the aide-de-camp on duty that His Majesty

had nothing further to say to the ambassador.

—GW, 6b:1612

8.14   WAR *À OUTRANCE*

Helmuth to Adolf von Moltke, 27 October 1870 ● *Morier to Lord Arthur Russell, 16 January 1871*

The armies of the Second Empire collapsed only weeks after the French declaration of war on Prussia; Napoleon himself was taken prisoner at the battle of Sedan on 2 September. Within hours, the Second Empire faded away and a republican "Government of National Resistance" took its place. In response to insinuations in Germany that peace could be had only at the price of French territorial cessions, the "Government of National Resistance" proclaimed on 6 September that France would not yield "an inch of her soil or a stone of her fortresses" and, in fulfillment of this pledge, set about to raise a people's army. While the new republican army was being constituted, the government's most articulate spokesman, Léon Gambetta, untiringly invoked the memory and spirit of 1792. Rallying the nation by exhorting the revolutionary nationalism of the First Republic was one thing, but Gambetta went further: he encouraged civilians behind the German lines to take up arms against the invader. These franc-tireurs, as they came to be called, were in essence guerrillas; like all nonuniformed irregulars, they were not covered by the laws of war when captured by the enemy.

a)   *Helmuth to Adolf von Moltke, 27 October 1870*

...through lies and patriotic slogans, the [French] government continues to incite the local population to further resistance, which then, in turn, must be squashed by destroying entire cities. The pinpricks of the franc-tireurs must be answered by bloody repressive measures, and the war becomes more and more odious. It's bad enough that the armies are tearing one another apart. But siccing entire peoples on one another—that's not progress; that's a relapse into barbarism. How little a levée en masse, even that of a brave nation such as this, manages to accomplish against a small but well-trained contingent of troops—that is an object lesson which our Liberals, who have preached the arming of the people, might take to heart. For as long as there is no effective authority in France, recognized by the nation, we have little choice but to spread the devastations of war to an ever larger part [of the country]. . . .

—Helmuth von Moltke, *Gesammelte Schriften und Denkwürdigkeiten* (Berlin, 1891), 4:205

b)   *Morier[26] to Lord Arthur Russell,[27] 16 January 1871*

. . . A war *à outrance* . . . is being waged because, in reply to Germany's declaration that a cession of territory must form one of the conditions of peace, France has replied that she will never cede an inch of territory or the stone of a fortress. . . . In the advanced Liberal code, in the international cosmogony of the future, there is, I quite admit, no room for a transfer of territory against the will of the human units settled thereon (and that as individuals we should subscribe to this idea, and preach it as part of the political millenium we desire to establish in the world, is what I altogether approve of). But in judging a great international contest like the present, we have not only no right, but we are guilty of a great wrong in judging either the one side or the other by an ideal code which has never been practically established. Now to say that Germany is to be held accursed because she claims to end the war in the way that, without exception, every European war has ended, that is, by the transfer of territory and fortresses from the vanquished to the victor, and because she does not subscribe to a new code of international morality on the strength of the one precedent of the Abyssinian war,[28] is to be guilty of this injustice. . . .

We have so completely yielded ourselves prisoners to the "phrases" with which France appears to have the power of fascinating the world, that we entirely forget that war is an operation which must in the very nature of things go on until it is put a stop to by peace. . . . But if France refuses to ask for peace, who is to ask for it? . . .

In my opinion, they who are to be held accursed are two. First, the *maîtres de ballet* who possessed themselves of authority when the Empire broke down, and prepared the melodramatic *mise en scène* with which Europe was to be regaled when the curtain drew up on Republican France, and the pose in which poor, bleeding, mangled Paris was to show herself off to the public when the ruffians of the piece

---

[26]Sir Robert Morier (1826–1893). British minister to Hesse-Darmstadt, 1868–1874; ambassador in Petersburg, 1884–1893.

[27]Arthur, Lord Russell (1825–1892), nephew of the Earl of Russell. Arthur Russell had married into the French high aristocracy; his father-in-law had held various cabinet portfolios under Charles X.

[28]An allusion to the British campaign against the Negus Theodore (Ras Kassa) in 1868. See Alan Moorehead, *The Blue Nile* (New York, 1962).

closed upon her. Second, the British gallery which, by its fanatic yells of applause, has played into the hands of these infernal dancing-masters and given them exactly what they wanted—a public before which to perform. I cannot find words to express my indignation against men, who, unless they have wholly parted with their wits, must know that England will not interfere in favor of France, and that France unaided must submit at last to the terms of Germany, yet find nothing better to do than to applaud the frantic efforts of the poor victim, and lash her on by their safe acclamations to re-newed endeavors as futile as the last. . . .

The devil who inhabits the innermost soul of the German is brutality; the devil who inhabits the innermost soul of the Frenchman is cruelty. From the evidence I have collected since the commencement of the war, there is no doubt left in my mind that very many acts of individual cruelty preceded the outburst of systematised Ger-man brutality. The assassination and mutilation of prisoners and wounded by non-combatants dated from the very first days of the war. I doubt whether any Frenchman has been mutilated or had his eyes gouged out, though thousands have been brutally shot, and whole villages systematically burnt, to punish individual acts. . . . But this must not blind us to the fact that the French, having begun a purely political war, at once gave to it the savage character of a national war. . . .

800,000 men individually and corporatively filled with a sense of invincibility and steadied by it (I mean professionally of course) are not to be got rid of unless they choose to go; you must make them choose to do so. Where is your lever? They desire ardently to be rid of the war, but, of course, they will only end as victors. To give up their demand for a cession of territory is in their minds equivalent to owning them-selves beaten: masters of the military situation, they have no hold of the political situ-ation, and are here utterly at sea. They don't know with whom to negotiate, on whom to act—in a word—this is the side where they require aid and help. . . .

—Rosslyn Wester Wemyss (ed.), *Memoirs and Letters of the Rt. Hon. Sir Robert Morier, GCB, from 1826 to 1876* (London, 1911), 2:226–37

8.15   THE CONTROL OF POLICY IN WARTIME: BISMARCK ON CIVIL-MILITARY RELATIONS

Bismarck to Wilhelm I (Draft), 18 November 1870

Castigating the "demigods" of the Prussian general staff, Bismarck wrote in his *Thoughts and Reminiscences*, "[the fact] that the general staff . . . will allow itself to be led astray into poli-cies which endanger the peace lies within the nature of the institution." In Prussia, top military commanders and the chief of the general staff had the right of direct access to the king, with-out first having to clear their views with the prime minister. This constitutional fact did little to assuage Bismarck's fear that, in war, the civilian leadership would be by-passed. Bismarck's conflict with the general staff in the Austro-Prussian war of 1866 did not bode well; indeed the civil-military struggle for the control of policy came to a head during the Franco-Prussian war. While Bismarck ultimately decided against sending the document excerpted here, it retains its value as a single cohesive summary of his complaints.

Bismarck to Wilhelm I (Draft), 18 November 1870

I have . . . encountered in the army general staff an obstinateness which does not mesh well with the norms usually observed in the contacts of higher state offices towards one another and which has repeatedly obstructed me. This has gone so far that I have only now, here in Versailles,[29] succeeded in at least getting the general staff to let me have the communiqués on the results of military operations at the same time as they are released to the Berlin press.

What is at stake for me is not a journalistic account of individual encounters and operational details, but knowledge of the general intentions of the military leadership and the opportunity to bring up political considerations when these necessarily have an impact on the conduct of the war. This is particularly true of a war such as the present one, the continuation and conduct of which depend largely on [our] relations to the neutral powers, while the form and even the opportuneness of the future peace is conditioned by the conduct of the war. The stand which Your Majesty's government will take in its political relations with other states, will be conditioned by the location of the armies and the tasks which they will confront in France.

—*GW*, 6b:1920

8.16   ## THE IMPROVEMENT OF INTERNATIONAL LAW: LONDON DECLARATION ON INTERNATIONAL TREATIES, 17 JANUARY 1871

The law of contracts suggested, and diplomatic custom followed, the notion that international treaties could be altered or abrogated only with the consent of all signatories. Though generally understood, this doctrine had never been explicitly written into an international agreement and was therefore, in a technical sense, not part of treaty law.

This omission was brought home in December 1870. Russia, taking advantage of the preoccupation of the powers with the Franco-German war, announced that it would unilaterally terminate the Black Sea clauses of the Treaty of Paris (Document 5.7). The Russian step rested on the calculation that Britain, Austria-Hungary, and particularly Prussia could ill afford to oppose it for fear that an ensuing diplomatic crisis in the east would mesh with the war in the west of Europe. Indeed, the powers shied away from this specter and, at an international conference convened in London, acquiesced in the Russian move.

In return for their consent to Russia's abrogation of the Black Sea clauses, the powers exacted a multilateral agreement on the modification of international treaties. What remained unclear, however, was how the language of the London Declaration affected the legal principle of *rebus sic stantibus* ("things remaining the same"). Widely accepted in customary law, *rebus sic stantibus* was a kind of escape clause, embodying the very opposite of the London Declaration. Under *rebus sic stantibus*, international agreements retained their validity only as long as the circumstances under which they were negotiated remained the same—thereby allowing signatories to cite altered circumstances as grounds for treaty revision.

[29]Site of Prussian headquarters in France.

London Declaration, 17 January 1871

The plenipotentiaries of North Germany, of Austria-Hungary, of Great Britain, of Italy, of Russia, and of Turkey, assembled today in conference, recognize that it is an essential principle of the law of nations that no power can liberate itself from the engagements of a treaty, nor modify the stipulations thereof, unless with the consent of the contracting powers by means of an amicable arrangement.

—Hertslet, 3:1926; Hurst, 2:459

8.17   TREATY OF FRANKFURT, 10 MAY 1871

By the standards of 1815, 1856, and 1866, Bismarck's peace with France was harsh. Most of the provisions of the Treaty of Frankfurt spelled out the financial and administrative details entailed by the transfer to Germany of Alsace-Lorraine and its assets. The second major aspect of the peace was the payment of a French indemnity. Following the example of 1815, French compliance was to be ensured by the continued presence of a German occupation force, but, unlike in 1815, the sum exacted was vast (five billion francs plus interest). To Bismarck's surprise, France met its financial obligations six months earlier than stipulated, thereby putting an end to the German occupation by September 1873.

For all its severity, the peace treaty upheld a high standard in its treatment of individual rights. For instance, the clauses on property rights, excerpted below, compare favorably to the democratic settlements of the twentieth century.

The defeat of France in 1871, however, brought with it repercussions that could not be codified by any treaty. The decline in French power, the disappearance of midsized German states that had previously enjoyed a modicum of independence, and the rise in their stead of a new center of gravity—a united Germany under Prussian leadership—could not but affect the relations of all the European Great Powers toward one another.

... Art. 2: French subjects ... shall be at liberty to preserve their immovables situated in the territory united to Germany. ...

Art. 12: All expelled Germans shall preserve full and entire enjoyment of property which they may have acquired in France. Such Germans who had obtained the authority required by French Laws to establish their domicile in France shall be reinstated in all their rights, and may consequently again establish their domicile in French territory. ... The above conditions shall be applicable in perfect reciprocity to the French subjects residing, or wishing to reside, in Germany. ...

—Hertslet, 3:1954–72; Hurst, 2:496–508

CHAPTER 9

The Search for a New International Stability, 1871–1890

The terms "international system" or "international order" often describe no more than a mix of certainties and uncertainties with which individuals have learned to reckon. When such assumptions collapse, they leave a void in which the principal actors grope for policies to guide them—a condition familiar to students of the onset of the cold war in 1945–1946 or of the recent implosion of the Soviet empire. If one looks for similar situations in the nineteenth century, one might find them in the diplomatic confusions following the Crimean War or, fifteen years later, in the general bafflement which greeted the defeat of France and the unification of Germany.

One need not accept the hyperbole of Benjamin Disraeli's statement in the House of Commons that the Franco-German war "represents the German Revolution, a greater political event than the French Revolution of last century."[1] Disraeli was, after all, leader of Her Majesty's Opposition and took advantage of the license that comes with the position. But in the diplomatic environment of 1871, the overarching question *was* German ascendancy. What place would the new German state carve out for itself? How could the European equilibrium be adjusted to accommodate a Great Power dominating the heart of the continent? Indeed, was the existence of a unified Germany compatible with the European equilibrium?[2] The answers, in large part, depended on the management skills of the German leadership—on its ability to inspire confidence in its conduct or on its success in keeping other powers from coalescing against it. Measured by these standards, one of Bismarck's first forays after the unification of Germany—the "war-in-sight" crisis of 1875—was a dismal failure. But insofar as there was a lesson to this episode, it was to show Bismarck that he had reached beyond the limits of the possible.

The Balkan crisis of 1875–1878 and the two international flashpoints of the 1880s—Egypt and Bulgaria—diverted the attention of the powers from the German problem and once again, after a hiatus of two decades, brought the Eastern Question into focus.

---

[1] 9 February 1871. *Parl. Debates*, 3rd Series, 24:81.

[2] This last question, informed by the experiences of 1914 and 1939, was kept alive by the media during the 2+4 negotiations of the reunification of Germany in the spring of 1990. The question of course assumes that the problem lies in Germany or Germanism and that factors such as the quality of leadership, *Zeitgeist*, ideology, generational differences, or the willingness to learn from the horrors of the past need not enter into the equation.

Against this backdrop, Bismarck in 1879 began to build a network of formal peacetime alliances, ultimately involving all Great Powers except France. Bismarck regarded the Eastern Question as a lever, and in retrospect its principal trouble spots, Egypt and Bulgaria, were to the 1880s what the Schleswig-Holstein and Spanish throne crises had been to the 1860s.

Bismarck's diplomatic "system" of the 1880s promoted goals easily summarized in a few catch phrases—the maintenance of the status quo; the preservation of the Habsburg monarchy; the attempt to convince Britain that the days of getting something for nothing were over, that it too had to shoulder some of the burdens which came with being a European power. Above all, the integrity and safety of Bismarck's own creation, the Second Reich, had to be assured. In A. J. P. Taylor's judgment, "he ceased to be Cavour and became Metternich. . . . Bismarck was now engaged in building a conservative system, like Metternich before him."[3] There is of course much to the analogy: both Metternich's and Bismarck's "systems" were bulwarks of the status quo; both were based on the centrality of Germany. One obvious difference lay in the function of Germany. Metternich had assigned to the German Confederation an essentially passive role in international politics, enabling it to react but not act. Bismarck, on the other hand, sought to attain for Germany a position "in which all the Powers, except France, need us."[4] By the late 1880s, he had, in the estimate of the American historian William Langer, succeeded in making "Berlin the focal point of international relations."[5]

Critics of the Bismarckian "system" point out that the alliances to which he committed Germany often contradicted other agreements which Bismarck merely sponsored. Bismarck's strategy, they claim, was to sic the powers onto one another so that Germany would reap the benefit of their antagonism. As some of the documents in this chapter show, Bismarck did indeed find useful the discomfiture of other powers and had a peculiar talent for bringing their antagonisms to bear upon one another. Certainly some of the terms (and intentions) of his treaties *were* contradictory. But Britain and Russia did not need Bismarck's encouragement to quarrel in the Near East or over Central Asia; Britain and France did not lock horns over Egypt at Bismarck's behest; Austria and Russia were rivals in the Balkans without incentives from Bismarck.

A word of caution before the reader casts Bismarck as a deceitful manipulator, or as the illusionist who explains one trick by performing another, or as a statesman imbued with a deep understanding of the unity of opposites: all generalizations need to be firmly

---

[3] *Struggle for Mastery in Europe*, 259, 272. In a later work, Taylor reversed himself: "[Bismarck] was not a 'system-maker' in the sense Metternich had been." *Bismarck*, 109. Whether the differences between the 1815 system and Bismarck's system were differences in degree or differences in kind depends on one's criteria for measurement. Of course there were some similarities: just as the diplomacy of the 1820s was rooted in differing interpretations of the 1814–1815 settlement, so too the diplomacy of the 1880s revolved around the latticework of the 1878 Treaty of Berlin. On the other hand, the 1815 system had created a new public law for all of Europe except the Near East, whereas the Berlin treaty covered only the Eastern Question and not Europe as a whole. Bismarck never intended his treaties to be normative, and none of his alliances were as encompassing as the Quadruple Alliance. The difference in their architecture might be illustrated by borrowing an image from civil engineering: if the Metternich-Castlereagh design resembled a viaduct, then Bismarck's was more akin to that of a cantilever bridge.

[4] Document 9.6c.

[5] *European Alliances and Alignments*, 459.

anchored in the context of specific issues and contingencies. It is no different in the case of Bismarck's diplomacy. Unless one understands *how* the Bismarckian edifice was constructed, one runs the danger of missing the point altogether. Bismarck's treaties did not exist in the abstract: they responded to specific circumstances and addressed limited contingencies, and left their signatories free to act as they pleased in other scenarios. To comprehend Bismarck's purpose one has to retrace his calculations, has to juggle the hypothetical combinations he conjured up, has to play the game with him. After all this is said and done, the one question that remains is whether the Bismarckian "system" could endure once the substratum on which it was built disappeared.

GENERAL READING: F. R. Bridge, *The Habsburg Monarchy among the Great Powers* (New York, 1990); Barbara Jelavich, *The Ottoman Empire, the Great Powers, and the Straits Question, 1870–1887* (Bloomington, 1973); Paul M. Kennedy, *The Rise of the Anglo-German Antagonism, 1860–1914* (London, 1980); William L. Langer, *European Alliances and Alignments* (1931; rev. ed., New York, 1951); Dwight E. Lee, *Great Britain and the Cyprus Convention Policy of 1878* (Cambridge, MA, 1934); Cedric J. Lowe (ed.), *The Reluctant Imperialists: British Foreign Policy, 1878–1902* (London, 1967); Richard Millman, *Britain and the Eastern Question, 1875–1878* (Oxford, 1979); Otto Pflanze, *Bismarck and the Development of Germany*, vols. 2 and 3 (Princeton, 1990); Norman Rich, *Friedrich von Holstein*, 2 vols. (Cambridge, 1965); Ann Pottinger Saab, *Reluctant Icon: Gladstone, Bulgaria, and the Working Classes, 1856–1878* (Cambridge, MA, 1991); Fritz Stern, *Gold and Iron: Bismarck, Bleichröder and the Building of the German Empire* (New York, 1977); B. H. Sumner, *Russia and the Balkans, 1870–1880* (Oxford, 1937); [on Egypt:] Afaf al-Sayyid-Marsot, *Egypt and Cromer* (New York, 1968); Alexander Schölch, *Egypt for the Egyptians!* (London, 1981); [on partition of Africa:] Thomas Pakenham, *The Scramble for Africa, 1876–1912* (New York, 1991); Ronald E. Robinson and John Gallagher, *Africa and the Victorians* (2nd ed., 1981); Wm. Roger Louis (ed.), *Imperialism: The Robinson and Gallagher Controversy* (New York, 1976)

9.1   FIRST THREE EMPERORS' LEAGUE

Russo-German Convention, 24 April/6 May 1873 ● *Austro-Russian ("Schönbrunn") Agreement, 25 May/6 June 1873*

Though it produced no written agreements, the meeting in Berlin in September 1872 of the emperors Wilhelm I, Franz Joseph, and Alexander II underscored the harmony among the eastern courts. When Wilhelm returned the tsar's visit in May 1873, a Russo-German military convention was signed by the chiefs of the Russian and Prussian general staffs—something of an oddity in light of Bismarck's oft-stated belief that the military should not be allowed to meddle in politics (Documents 8.15 and 9.29). But he may have calculated that a convention in this form was better than no agreement at all: its main promoter throughout had been the chief of the Russian general staff, while Gorchakov, the Russian chancellor, was averse to it. Bismarck too had reservations and considered the pact operative only if Austria joined.

At their meeting one month later, the Russian and Austrian emperors agreed only on a much vaguer understanding, expanded by the accession of the German emperor in October 1873. This Three Emperors' League probably superseded the earlier Russo-German convention. Both agreements soon faded away (Document 9.2), although they were not explicitly retired until the second Three Emperors' League of 1881 (Document 9.14).

The formation of the Three Emperors' League should be seen against the background of events in France. The memory of the Paris Commune of 1871 (and fear of similar upheavals in the future) motivated the Austrian and Russian emperors to reaffirm the principle of monarchical solidarity. In Bismarck's view, the danger was not French radicalism, paralyzing the

Third Republic for years to come, but a stable, united France. These divergent readings of the French problem may have stymied the Three Emperors' League from the start.

For Bismarck, France's ability to complete its reparation payments well ahead of schedule was a disturbing portent of French resolve to undo the results of the Franco-German war. Nor was there much solace in the assumption of the French presidency in May 1873 by Count Edme MacMahon, a Bonapartist hero of the Italian war of 1859 and the mouthpiece of a monarchist-clerical coalition.[6] French revanchism had evidently lined up with the Catholic church, the other major opponent of the new status quo; both would join forces to galvanize proclerical politicians elsewhere. Austria in particular was susceptible to the ultramontane siren song, and Bismarck, always at the mercy of an overly active imagination, already saw in his mind's eye the specter of a Franco-papal-Austrian alliance consecrated by a determination to reopen the Roman Question and fueled by anti-German sentiments. Thus the Three Emperors' League, from Bismarck's perspective, was very much a preemptive measure to keep Austria from drifting into the revisionist camp. In its Russo-German dimension, of course, the Three Emperors' League meant a return to the traditions of early nineteenth-century Prussian foreign policy. Insofar as there is an irony to this tale, it is that Bismarck, whose early career had been dedicated to preventing a revival of the Holy Alliance, now acquiesced in its reincarnation.

a)   *Russo-German Convention, 24 April/6 May 1873*

Art. 1: If one of the two empires is attacked by a European power, it will be supported as soon as possible by an army with an effective strength of 200,000 men.

Art. 2: This military convention is concluded in a spirit [harboring] no hostile intention towards any nation or any government. . . .

—*GP,* 1:127

b)   *Austro-Russian ("Schönbrunn") Agreement,*
25 May/ 6 June 1873

1. Their Majesties mutually promise, should the interests of their States diverge in respect to special questions, to take counsel together in order that these divergences may not be able to prevail over the considerations of a higher order which preoccupy them. Their Majesties are determined to prevent any one from succeeding in moving them apart on the principles [*terrain des principes*] which they regard as the only ones suitable for assuring and, if necessary, for imposing the maintenance of the peace of Europe against all upheavals, from whatsoever quarter they may come.

2. In the event that the aggression of a third Power should threaten to compromise the peace of Europe, Their Majesties mutually engage to come to a preliminary understanding between themselves, without seeking or contracting new alliances, in order to agree as to the line of conduct to be followed in common.

---

[6]The beginning of the MacMahon presidency thus coincided with the start of Bismarck's campaign against the Catholic church in Prussia, the so-called *Kulturkampf.*

3. If, as a result of this understanding, a military action should become necessary, it would be governed by a special convention to be concluded between Their Majesties.

4. If one of the High Contracting Parties, wishing to recover its independence of action, should desire to renounce the present Agreement, it must do so two years in advance, in order to give the other Party time to make whatever arrangements may be suitable.

—*GP*, 1:129; Hurst, 2:508–9 (archaic translation!)

9.2   IS WAR IN SIGHT?

Disraeli to Derby, 6 May 1875 ● *Ponsonby to Derby, 9 May 1875* ● *Victoria to
Alexander II, 10 May 1875* ● *Bismarck to Münster, 14 May 1875* ●
Marginalia by Wilhelm I, 16 May 1875

The brittleness of the first Three Emperors' League and the precariousness of Germany's position in Europe were revealed to Bismarck during April and May 1875. In an article entitled "Is War in Sight?" published on 8 April, a Berlin paper conjured up the specter of an anti-German coalition, organized by the chief opponents of the new European order—France and the Catholic church.[7] The article culminated in the thinly veiled suggestion that Germany should strike before its opponents had readied their armaments.

In subsequent weeks, the Berlin press and a number of German officials—among them Helmuth von Moltke, chief of the Prussian general staff; Georg von Kameke, the Prussian minister of war; and Joseph von Radowitz, a high-ranking diplomat—created the impression that Bismarck contemplated a preventive war against France. The French, British, and Russian governments reacted with dismay and, as is evident from the documents excerpted here, forced Bismarck to retreat.

For Bismarck, the most obvious lesson of the "war-in-sight" crisis was that neither Britain nor Russia would tolerate the destruction of France as a Great Power. But this lesson could be turned to full advantage: Bismarck could use the British and Russian intervention to show those in Berlin who advocated preventive war that they had better be prepared to fight not only France but also Britain and Russia—an undertaking which even the Prussian general staff understood to be well beyond the resources of the new German state.

a)   *Disraeli to Derby,[8] 6 May 1875*

My own impression is that we should construct some concerted movement to preserve the peace of Europe like Pa[l]m[erston] did when he baffled France and expelled the Egyptians from Syria.[9] There might be an alliance between Russia and

[7]For the text of the article in the Berlin *Post*, see Lucius von Ballhausen, *Bismarck-Erinnerungen* (Stuttgart, 1921), 531–34.
[8]Edward Stanley, Earl of Derby (1826–1893). Foreign secretary, 1866–1868; 1874–1878. Colonial secretary in Gladstone's government, 1882–1885.
[9]Cf. Document 3.8.

ourselves for this special purpose; and other powers, as Austria and perhaps Italy might be invited to accede. . . .

—W. F. Monypenny and G. E. Buckle, *Life of Benjamin Disraeli, Earl of Beaconsfield* (London, 1920), 5:422

b)   *Ponsonby[10] to Derby, 9 May 1875*

. . . it is scarcely correct to assume that no such design as making war for the recovery of the lost provinces is entertained by France, for no such intention is dreamt of at present, the Queen is sure that the wish exists in almost every Frenchman's heart, and that the Germans know this better than we do. Her Majesty therefore thinks that, while remonstrating with Germany, it becomes our duty also to warn France against aggressive movements.

—*QV*, 2nd Series, 2:393–96

c)   *Queen Victoria to Alexander II, 10 May 1875*

. . . I cannot finish this letter without expressing to you the firm hope that you will use your great influence to assure the maintenance of peace, and to dissipate the profound alarm which the language used by Berlin has caused in all Europe. . . .

—*QV*, 2nd Series, 2:393–96

d)   *Bismarck to Münster,[11] 14 May 1875*

. . . We have to draw the conclusion that England would be ready to alert [*aufzurufen*] Europe against us and in favor of the French, if we ever—which is not the case now—made military or diplomatic preparations to fend off renewed French attacks. . . .

—*GP*, 1:180

e)   *Marginalia by Wilhelm I, 16 May 1875*

. . . In order to wage a successful war, the attacker must be able to count on the sympathy of all noble individuals and countries, while public opinion must cast stones at whoever unjustly provokes war. That was the secret of the enthusiasm in Germany in 1870! Whoever unjustly takes up arms, will have public opinion against him; he will find no allies, no benevolent neutrals, probably no neutrals but only adversaries.—I

[10]Sir Henry Ponsonby (1825–1895). British general; private secretary to Queen Victoria, 1870–1895.
[11]Georg Herbert, Count zu Münster (1820–1902). German ambassador in London, 1873–1885; in Paris, 1885–1900.

told the Emperor Alexander as much, and he took both of my hands and expressed his full agreement! (Russia has experienced this in 1853/6 and Austria in 1859 and 1866).

—*GP*, 1:181

9.3   **THE BULGARIAN HORRORS**

Bulgarian Horrors and the Question of the East, *6 September 1876* •
Disraeli to Derby, 8 September 1876

In July 1875, Herzegovina rose against its Ottoman administrators. By May 1876, the insurrection spread to the Bulgarian-speaking districts of the Ottoman Empire, only to be crushed, with appalling barbarity, by Ottoman irregulars. The news of the Bulgarian atrocities left the British cabinet of Benjamin Disraeli quite unmoved but stirred general outrage among the literate public. Predictably, the chief beneficiary of this ground swell was William Ewart Gladstone, elder statesman of the Liberal opposition. In making himself a leading spokesman for this cause, Gladstone was animated by humanitarian considerations, but he also found in the Bulgarian issue the means to attack the Disraeli government. The pièce de résistance in Gladstone's campaign against both Ottoman misrule and the Disraeli cabinet was his publication, in September 1876, of a pamphlet entitled *Bulgarian Horrors and the Question of the East*. But Gladstone wavered on what was perhaps the crucial point—his prescription for the future of Ottoman rule in Europe. Nonetheless, sales of the pamphlet—200,000 copies in the first month—outpaced all other publications on the subject and dwarfed by far even Gladstone's own follow-up effort of March 1877, *Lessons in Massacre*.

In the course of the summer, the situation in the Balkans had become, if anything, more complicated. Serbia, a self-governing province of the Ottoman Empire, in June 1876 declared war against its nominal overlord, the sultan. Russian volunteers—most prominent among them General Cherniaev, the conqueror of Tashkent (Document 6.6)—flocked to Serbia but could not ward off a series of devastating defeats inflicted by the Ottoman armies. But the catastrophes that befell Serbia made it difficult for the Russian government to resist the increasing domestic outpouring of support for Serbia. In his pamphlet, Gladstone chose to ignore this factor. In any case, this development was likely to undermine his prediction that Russia would play "for the present epoch what is called the waiting game."

a)   **Bulgarian Horrors and the Question of the East,**
6 September 1876

. . . there have been perpetrated, under the immediate authority of a Government to which all the time we have been giving the strongest moral, and for part of the time even material support, crimes and outrages, so vast in scale as to exceed all modern example, and so unutterably vile as well as fierce in character, that it passes the power of heart to conceive, and of tongue and pen adequately to describe them. These are the Bulgarian horrors; and the question is, What can and should be done, either to punish, or to brand, or to prevent? . . .

Let me endeavour very briefly to sketch, in the rudest outline, what the Turkish race was and what it is. It is not a question of Mahometanism simply, but of Mahometanism compounded with the peculiar character of a race. They are not the mild Mahometans of India, nor the chivalrous Saladins of Syria, nor the cultured Moors of Spain. They were, upon the whole, from the black day when they first entered Europe, the one great anti-human specimen of humanity. Wherever they went, a broad line of blood marked the track behind them; and, as far as their dominion reached, civilisation disappeared from view. . . .

Now, as regards the territorial integrity of Turkey, I for one am still desirous to see it upheld, though I do not say that desire should be treated as of a thing paramount to still higher objects of policy. For all the objects of policy, in my conviction, humanity, rationally understood, and in due relation to justice, is the first and highest. . . .

Let the Turks now carry away their abuses in the only possible manner, namely by carrying off themselves. Their Zaptichs and their Mudirs, their Bimbashis and their Yuzbachis, their Kaimakams and their Pashas, one and all, bag and baggage, shall, I hope, clear out from the province they have desolated and profaned. This thorough riddance, this most blessed deliverance, is the only reparation we can make to the memory of those heaps on heaps of dead; to the violated purity alike of matron, of maiden, and of child; to the civilisation which has been affronted and shamed; to the laws of God or, if you like, of Allah; to the moral sense of mankind at large. . . .

—William Ewart Gladstone, *Bulgarian Horrors and the Question of the East* (London, 1876), 11–13; 51–53; 61–62

b)   ***Disraeli to Derby, 8 September 1876***

. . . Gladstone has had the impudence to send me his pamphlet, tho' he accuses me of several crimes. The document is passionate and not strong; vindictive and ill-written—that of course. Indeed in that respect, of all the Bulgarian horrors, perhaps the greatest. . . .

—Monypenny and Buckle, *Life of . . . Disraeli,* 6:60

9.4   THE OTTOMAN CONSTITUTION, 11/23 DECEMBER 1876

Article 9 of the Peace of Paris denied the powers "the right to interfere, either collectively or separately, in the relations of His Majesty the Sultan with his subjects, . . . [or] in the Internal Administration of his Empire" (Document 5.7). Notwithstanding this article, the powers responded to the slaughter in the Balkans with a spate of notes and suggestions. By November 1876, they had tired of the evasions and subterfuges of the Porte and finally ordered their ambassadors in Constantinople to meet in conference for the purpose of devising a reform project for the European provinces of the Ottoman Empire. But as the conference wound down, the Porte upstaged the powers by promulgating a constitution. Its reasoning was that the civil and political liberties envisaged in this constitution surpassed the measures contemplated by the Constantinople conference. Hence, so went the argument, such measures had become unnecessary. An even more unmistakable hint of the Porte's resolve to fight off the intervention of the Great Powers (and particularly the plans of the Constantinople conference to carve an autonomous Bulgarian region out of Turkey-in-Europe) came at the very outset of the

constitution: its first article affirmed the empire's territorial integrity and thus directly challenged any plans entertained by the Constantinople conference for pressuring the Porte into
territo-rial concessions.

No matter how defective from a stylistic or an organizational point of view, the Ottoman
constitution is of considerable interest. First, the Russo-Turkish war of 1877 gave the Porte the
excuse to suspend it. It was reinstated only in 1908 as a result of the Young Turks' revolt
against the autocracy of Sultan Abdul Hamid (Documents 11.9 and 11.11). Second, the constitution's promise of political rights to Ottoman subjects has a bearing on at least one facet of
the twentieth-century Israeli-Palestinian conflict. In the 1980s, supporters of the right-wing Is-
raeli Likud bloc asserted that Palestinians were not entitled to "political" rights, as the Balfour
Declaration, written into international law by the 1922 mandate treaty for Palestine, spoke
only of the "*civil* and *religious* rights of existing non-Jewish communities in Palestine."[12] A
closer look at the protocol of the inter-Allied conference of San Remo of April 1920, however,
suggests otherwise. At San Remo, the World War I Allies agreed on the guiding principles for
their mandates in the Middle East. Britain accepted that the mandate for Palestine "would not
involve the surrender of the rights hitherto enjoyed by the non-Jewish communities in Palestine."[13] Among "the rights hitherto enjoyed" were, of course, those bestowed by the Ottoman
constitution of 1876.

Art. 1: The Ottoman Empire comprises present countries and possessions and privileged provinces. It forms an indivisible whole from which no part may be detached
for whatever reason. . . .

Art. 8: All subjects of the empire are called Ottomans, without distinction, whatever faith they profess. . . .

Art. 17: All Ottomans are equal in the eyes of the law. They have the same rights
and owe the same duties towards their country, without prejudice to religion. . . .

Art. 42: The General Assembly is composed of two chambers: the Chamber of No-
tables or Senate, and the Chamber of Deputies. . . .

Art. 65: The number of deputies is fixed at one deputy for every 50,000 male Ottoman subjects. . . .

Art. 69: The general elections for the Chamber of Deputies shall take place every
four years. . . .

—*SP*, 67:683–95

9.5   **TREATY OF BUDAPEST, 15 JANUARY 1877**

Austro-Russian Treaty of Budapest, 15 January 1877 •
Additional Convention (18 March 1877)

For Russia, the failure of the Constantinople conference of ambassadors was the last straw. It
now embarked on a diplomatic campaign to ensure it a free hand against the Ottoman

---

[12]See, for instance, Sidney Zion, "Is Jordan Palestine? Of Course," *New York Times*, 5 October 1982.
[13]*Documents on British Foreign Policy, 1919–1939*, 1st Series (London, 1958), 8:176–77.

Empire. Any Russian strike against the Ottoman Empire, however, required that Russia first secure the support of Austria-Hungary, the power in the Balkans that would be most affected by a Russo-Turkish war and its attendant political changes.

a)   *Austro-Russian Treaty of Budapest, 15 January 1877*

Art. 1: The High Contracting Parties, considering that the Christian and Mohammedan populations in Bosnia and in Herzegovina are too much intermingled for it to be permissible to expect from a mere autonomous organization a real amelioration of their lot, are agreed with one another to ask for these provinces in the conference of Constantinople only an autonomous regime. . . . As Bulgaria is placed under more favourable conditions for the exercise of autonomous institutions, they mutually engage to demand for this province in the conference a larger autonomy, buttressed by substantial guaranties.

Art. 2: In the case that the negotiations should not succeed, and should result in a rupture followed by war between Russia and Turkey, the Imperial and Royal [= Austro-Hungarian] Government formally pledges itself to observe an attitude of benevolent neutrality in the presence of the isolated action of Russia, and by its diplomatic action to paralyze, so far as this lies in its power, efforts at intervention or collective mediation which might be attempted by other Powers.

Art. 3: If the Government of the Emperor and King is invited to assist in putting into force the treaty of April 15, 1856,[14] it will, in the event foreseen by the present convention, refuse its co-operation, and, without contesting the validity of the said Treaty, it will proclaim its neutrality. . . .

Art. 6: The Austro-Hungarian Government will not obstruct the commissioners and agents of the Russian Government in making in the limits of the Austro-Hungarian States purchases and contracts for objects indispensable to the Russian Army, with the exception of articles of contraband of war prohibited by international laws. The Government of His Imperial and Royal Majesty, however, engages in the application and in the interpretation of these laws to show the broadest good will towards Russia.

Art. 7: His Majesty the Emperor of Austria, etc., and Apostolic King of Hungary reserves to himself the choice of the moment and of the mode of the occupation of Bosnia and of Herzegovina by his troops. . . .

Art. 8: The High Contracting Parties reciprocally engage not to extend the radius of their respective military action: His Majesty the Emperor of Austria, etc., and Apostolic King of Hungary, to Rumania, Serbia, Bulgaria, and Montenegro; and His Majesty the Emperor of All the Russias to Bosnia, Herzegovina, Serbia, and Montenegro. Serbia, Montenegro, and the portion of Herzegovina which separates these two principalities are to form a continuous neutral zone, which the armies of the two Empires may not cross, and intended to preserve these latter from all immediate contact. It remains understood, however, that the Imperial and Royal Government will not oppose the combined action of Serbian and Montenegrin forces outside of their own countries with the Russian troops.

Art. 9: The consequences of war and the territorial modifications which would

[14]Document 5.7d.

result from an eventual dissolution of the Ottoman Empire shall be regulated by a special and simultaneous convention. . . .

—Hurst, 2:511–15; Sumner, *Russia and the Balkans*, 597–99

b)   ***Additional Convention (18 March 1877)[15]***

Art. 1: The two High Contracting Parties, having as their ultimate aim the amelioration of the lot of the Christians, and wishing to eliminate any project of annexation of a magnitude that might compromise peace or the European equilibrium, which is neither in their intentions nor in the interests of the two Empires, have come to an agreement to limit their eventual annexations to the following territories:

The Emperor of Austria, etc., and King of Hungary: to Bosnia and Herzegovina, with the exception of the portion comprised between Serbia and Montenegro [= Sanjak of Novibazar], on the subject of which the two Governments reserve the right to reach an agreement when the moment for disposing of it arrives;

The Emperor of All the Russias: in Europe to the regions of Bessarabia which would re-establish the old frontiers of the Empire before 1856.

Art. 2: The High Contracting Parties engage to lend each other mutual assistance in the diplomatic field, if the territorial modifications resulting from a war or from the dissolution of the Ottoman Empire should give rise to a collective deliberation of the Great Powers.

Art. 3: His Majesty the Emperor of Austria, etc., and King of Hungary, and His Majesty the Emperor of All the Russias, in the interview which took place between them at Reichstadt, came to an agreement in principle on the following points: In case of a territorial modification or of a dissolution of the Ottoman Empire, the establishment of a great compact Slavic or other state is excluded; in compensation, Bulgaria, Albania, and the rest of Rumelia might be constituted into independent states; Thessaly, part of Epirus, and the island of Crete might be annexed to Greece; Constantinople, with a territory of which the limit remains to be determined, might become a free city. Their said Majesties record that they have nothing to change in these views, and declare anew that they wish to maintain them as bases of their subsequent political action.

Art. 4: The High Contracting Parties engage to keep secret the stipulations of the present Convention. . . .

—Hurst, 2:511–15; Pribram, 2:190–203

9.6   **BISMARCK AND THE EASTERN CRISIS**

Memorandum by Bismarck, 9 November 1876 • Bismarck in the Reichstag, 5 December 1876 • Bismarck's "Kissingen Memorandum," 15 June 1877 • Bismarck in the Reichstag, 19 February 1878 • Herbert Bismarck to Bernhard Ernst von Bülow, 2 November 1878 • Bernhard Ernst von Bülow to Friedrich Wilhelm, November 1878

Bismarck's Reichstag speeches of 5 December 1876 and 19 February 1878 came to epitomize his attitude toward the Balkan crisis. Their imagery has supplied would-be pundits with staple

---

[15]Antedated to 15 January 1877.

phrases to the present day. But Bismarck's stand also needs to be understood in the context of the recent "war-in-sight" crisis (Document 9.2) and in light of a specifically Prussian nemesis that he invoked—the mid-eighteenth-century "Kaunitz coalition" of Austria, France, and Russia, which brought Prussia to the brink of ruin in 1762.

Whether the memorandum developed by Bismarck at Kissingen should be treated as a blueprint for his future policy or whether it instead expressed the stray musings of a summer afternoon, it does mark one of the rare moments when a statesman could look beyond the minutiae of the day to develop a broader perspective. His instructions to the German foreign ministry of November 1878 reveal another and less benign component of his strategy. Be that as it may, the common feature of both documents is Bismarck's sense of the precariousness of Germany's position.

a)   ***Memorandum by Bismarck, 9 November 1876***

. . . The word "Europe" is always found on the lips of those politicians who demand from other powers something which they do not dare ask of themselves: the western powers during the Crimean war and the Polish question of 1863; Thiers in the fall of 1870; and Count Beust when he described the failure of his attempts to forge a coalition against us with the words, "I can't see Europe anymore!"[16] In the present case, Russia and England are alternately trying to get us to pull the carriage of their policies—which, as they well know, we Germans have no interest in doing. . . .

—*GP*, 2:256

b)   ***Bismarck in the Reichstag, 5 December 1876***

. . . I will advise against taking an active role in these matters for as long as I fail to detect in this entire enterprise the German interest which would be—pardon the bluntness of the expression—worth the healthy bones of a single Pomeranian grenadier. I want to make clear that we should be thrifty in the expenditure of the blood of our compatriots and soldiers rather than squandering it on behalf of an arbitrary policy dictated by no compelling interest [bravo!]. . . .

—Horst Kohl (ed.), *Die politischen Reden des Fürsten Bismarck* (Stuttgart, 1892), 6:461

c)   ***Bismarck's "Kissingen Memorandum," 15 June 1877***

I wish to encourage the English, without making it too obvious, if they have intentions on Egypt. I think that it will suit our interests and be better for our future to promote a compromise between England and Russia, which may establish relations

---

[16]The Austro-Hungarian foreign minister, Friedrich von Beust, had tried to organize a league of neutrals in the first phase of the Franco-Prussian war. When it became clear that Russia, after instigating the idea, would not participate, Beust exclaimed, *"je ne vois plus d'Europe!"* Beust to Chotek, 12 October 1870. *Correspondenzen des kaiserlich-königlichen Ministeriums des Aeusseren, 1866–72* (Vienna, 1868–1872), 4:31.

between these two powers as good as they were at the beginning of this century, and which may be followed by the rapprochement of both to ourselves. Perhaps this aim cannot be realized, but that too is not certain. If only England and Russia could agree to the proposition of the one controlling Egypt, and the other the Black Sea, both might find it possible to remain content with maintaining the *status quo* for a long period. At the same time, in their chief interests they would still be rivals, which would practically preclude their joining in coalitions against us, quite apart from the domestic pressures which would dissuade England from such a combination.

A French paper recently attributed to me "le cauchemar des coalitions." This sort of bogey will for long—perhaps for ever—be quite rightly feared by all German ministers. Coalitions may be formed against us by the Western Powers, joined by Austria; or, of greater danger to us, among France, Russia, and Austria. A close rapprochement between any two of these three powers would give the third the means to exert grievous pressure on us. My anxiety in the face of these possibilities leads me to regard as desirable, not at once, but as time goes on, the following consequences of the Eastern Crisis: (1) Gravitation of the interests of Russia and Austria, and their mutual rivalries, towards the East; (2) Russia to be impelled to take up a strong defensive position in the East, and on its own shores, and to need an alliance with us; (3) For England and Russia a satisfactory *status quo* giving them the same interest which we have in the maintenance of things as they are; (4) Separation of England from France, which is still hostile to us, over Egypt and the Mediterranean; (5) Relations between Russia and Austria to be such that it is difficult for both to carry on a joint anti-German conspiracy, which in some measure attracts the clerical and centralizing elements in Austria.

If I were able to work, I could fill in and develop in greater detail the picture in my mind's eye. It is not one portraying any acquisition of territory, but rather one showing a political landscape in which all the Powers, except France, need us and are prevented, by virtue of their relations towards each other, from the possibility of coalescing against us. . . .

—*GP*, 2:294

d)   *Bismarck in the Reichstag, 19 February 1878*

. . . [Our role] in the peacemaking process [*Vermittelung des Friedens*] I do not visualize in the following manner: that, when opinions diverge, we play the referee and say, "this is the way things should be and behind this looms the power of the German Reich" [very good!], but more modestly, indeed—perhaps I can cite an analogy from everyday life—as that of an honest broker, who is chiefly interested in clinching the deal. . . . There are many in Russia who have no love for Germany and who are, fortunately, not in power, but who would be far from disconsolate should they find themselves in power [amusement]: how would they speak to their compatriots, to others, perhaps to other statesmen who up to now cannot yet be counted among our enemies? They would say: consider the sacrifices in blood, men, treasure through which we have attained a position for which Russia has striven for centuries! We were able to ward off those opponents who had a natural interest in denying us these gains: it was not Austria, with which we have coexisted for a long time; it was not England, which has a national interest openly acknowledged to be contrary to ours; but it was Germany, our close friend to whom we have rendered services in the past, from whom we could expect repayment, who has no interest in the Near East; it was Germany which unsheathed not the saber but a dagger behind our back. This is what we would hear—I have exaggerated the picture, but don't think that Russian public opinion wouldn't exaggerate—and this picture corresponds to the truth. We will never take upon ourselves the responsibility of sacrificing a secure friendship with a great and powerful neighboring nation, proven over generations, to the temptation of playing judge and jury in Europe [bravo!]. . . .

—Kohl, *Reden,* 7:92, 95–96

e)   *Herbert von Bismarck*[17] *to Bernhard Ernst von Bülow,*[18] *2 November 1878*

. . . The essential point of these documents[19] is, in brief, that a lasting peace in the Near East is not in Germany's interest: given our geographic position, the neighboring Great Powers—all of which hate us—would probably seek and find a common denominator [*Vereinigungspunkt*] with an anti-German edge as soon as their hands are free. Moreover, Austria could undergo in a surprisingly short span of time a change of government and in outlook which could bring to power anti-German and ultramontane forces, providing a cover for a rapprochement with France . . . that could lead to an alliance. For this reason, we have to nurse along our relations with Russia: [on the other hand] we have always turned down every unjustified Russian demand which transgressed the limits of friendship, thus enabling us to remain on good terms with England and Austria. It would be a triumph of our statecraft if we succeeded in keeping open the Near Eastern wound in order to prevent the other Great Powers from uniting [against us] and to secure our peace. . . .

—PA Türkei I.A.B.q. 133 secr.

f) *Bernhard Ernst von Bülow to Crown Prince Friedrich Wilhelm, November 1878*

. . . Germany's main interest is not in this or that domestic setup in the Ottoman Empire, but in the attitude of friendly powers towards us and towards one another. The question whether Germany, because of the Near Eastern troubles, will become enmeshed in a lasting dispute with Austria, England, or Russia is infinitely more impor-

---

[17]Herbert von Bismarck (1849–1904). Bismarck's oldest son; member of the foreign ministry staff from 1874 onward; state secretary, 1886–1890.

[18]Bernhard Ernst von Bülow (1815–1879). State secretary in the German foreign ministry, 1873–1879. Father of Bernhard von Bülow (cf. Chapters 10 and 11).

[19]This letter was prompted by the crown prince's request for representative documents on German policy in the Balkan crisis. The selection referred to here included the Kissingen memorandum. The crown prince was known to favor a pro-British and anti-Russian policy.

tant for our future than either the relationship of the Porte to its subjects or its relationship to the European powers or both. . . .

—PA Türkei I.A.B.q. 133 secr.

9.7   TREATY OF SAN STEFANO

Treaty of San Stefano, 19 February/3 March 1878 ●
Memorandum for the British Cabinet, 3 May 1878

The Russo-Turkish peace was signed in the Constantinople suburb of San Stefano, with the Russian advance force only a day's march from the Ottoman capital. The Russian negotiator was Count Nicholas Ignatiev, architect of the Treaty of Peking (Document 6.4d), who had served as Russia's ambassador in Constantinople between 1864 and 1877, and who now had "the chance of remodelling the Ottoman Empire according to his taste."[20] Ignatiev seized this chance with gusto. His political orientation was decidedly Pan-Slav—a liability in his relations with his own foreign ministry, given the cosmopolitan orientation of Gorchakov and the senior members of the diplomatic corps. Ignatiev's first mistake may have been to ignore Gorchakov's suggestion that for now, to avert the suspicion of the other Great Powers, he conclude only a protocol rather than a full-fledged peace treaty. But far more troubling questions were whether or how Ignatiev's treaty met Russia's obligations to Austria-Hungary under the Budapest convention (Document 9.5) and whether it allayed the fears of other powers. In Ignatiev's defense, it might be argued that the "Big Bulgaria" envisioned by the Treaty of San Stefano was to remain tributary to the Porte and hence would not be a "state" in the technical sense.

a)   Treaty of San Stefano, 19 February/3 March 1878

. . . Art. 2: The Sublime Porte recognizes definitively the Independence of the Principality of Montenegro. . . .

Art. 3: Serbia is recognized as independent. . . .

Art. 5: The Sublime Porte recognizes the Independence of Roumania, which will establish its right to an indemnity, to be discussed between the two countries. . . .

Art. 6: Bulgaria is constituted an autonomous tributary Principality, with a Christian Government and a national militia. . . .

Art. 7: The Prince of Bulgaria shall be freely elected by the population and confirmed by the Sublime Porte, with the assent of the Powers. No member of the reigning dynasties of the great European Powers shall be capable of being elected Prince of Bulgaria. In the event of the dignity of Prince of Bulgaria being vacant, the election of the new Prince shall be made subject to the same conditions and forms. . . .

Art. 8: . . . Russian troops will occupy the country. . . . This occupation will also be limited to a term approximating to two years. . . .

Art. 10: The Sublime Porte shall have the right to make use of Bulgaria for the transport by fixed routes of its troops, munitions, and provisions to the provinces beyond the Principality, and vice versa. . . .

[20]Sumner, *Russia and the Balkans*, 399.

RUSSIA

AUSTRIA-HUNGARY

Danube R.

Jassy

Bessarabia

Pruth R.

ROMANIA

Danube R.

Bosnia
(occupied by
Austria, 1878)

Belgrade

Bucharest

Sarajevo

SERBIA

Herzegovina

Novi
Pazar

Nish

Danube R.

Plevna

Bulgaria
(under Turkish
suzerainty until 1908)

Varna

MONTE-
NEGRO

Sofia

BALKAN MTS.

Dobruja

Antivari
Dulcigno
(1880)

Scutari

Eastern Rumelia
(administered by Turkey)

BLACK
SEA

ADRIATIC SEA

Albania

Philippopolis

Macedonia

Constantinople

Dedeagach

San Stefano

Salonika

IONIAN
SEA

AEGEAN

SEA

OTTOMAN
EMPIRE

GREECE

Athens

M E D I T E R R A N E A N

Crete

S E A

Legend

Gains by Montenegro		
Gains by Serbia	Ottoman boundary after the Congress of Berlin	
Gains by Greece	Bulgaria proposed by Treaty of San Stefano, 1878	
Gains by Russia	Ottoman Empire after 1878	
Gains by Romania	Independent after 1878	

MAP 7   THE BALKANS AFTER THE TREATIES OF SAN STEFANO AND BERLIN

Art. 19: The war indemnity and the losses imposed on Russia which His Majesty the Emperor of Russia claims, and which the Sublime Porte has bound itself to reimburse to him, consist of. . .

Total 1,410,000,000 roubles.

Taking into consideration the financial embarrassments of Turkey, . . . the Emperor of Russia consents to substitute for the payment of the greater part of the moneys . . . , the following territorial cessions: . . . b) Ardahan, Kars, Batoum, Bayazid, and the territory as far as the Saganlough.

—Hertslet, 4:2672ff. (with maps); Hurst, 2:528–46

b)   *Memorandum for the British Cabinet, 3 May 1878*

The objections of Great Britain to the Treaty of San Stefano rest principally on three grounds: (1) that it admits a new naval power to the coasts of the Aegean; (2) that it threatens with extinction the non-Slav populations of the Balkan peninsula; (3) that it places the Porte so much at the mercy of Russia, that it is no longer able to discharge with independence political functions which are still assigned to it, and which deeply interest other nations.

The remedy for the first two of these evils, is to push the frontier of the Slav State back from the Aegean and Macedonia. This change is essential to any agreement between England and Russia. Due securities for good government must, of course, be provided for the populations of the regions thus excluded from the autonomous State. . . .

In the first rank of importance stands the configuration of the Slav State. It runs close up to Constantinople, is separated from it by no effective or defensible frontier, and severs it from communication with the remaining European provinces [of the Ottoman Empire]. These effects must be considered, together with the influence over this State conferred upon Russia by the provisions as to government and occupation. A remedy for this evil would be in the restriction of the Slav State to the north of the Balkans, together with a limitation of the time of occupation.

In the second place come the annexations in Asia. They despoil the Porte of the only good harbor in the Black Sea; menace from the conquered line of fortresses the richest of the remaining provinces; and, by the acquisition of Kars, will alienate from Turkey the respect, and shake the fidelity, of the Mesopotamian and Syrian populations.

In the third rank stand the vague provisions of the indemnity clause, which are capable of being converted either into further annexations, or into a compulsory alliance.

And, after these, stand such provisions as the alienation of Bessarabia, the augmentation of territory given to the tributary States, and some other less prominent stipulations. . . . As it is the operation of the instrument as a whole to which England objects, so it is the result of the modifications as a whole, and not the particular form which they take, to which England looks as a condition of her assenting to any definitive Treaty founded on the Preliminaries of San Stefano.

—Sumner, *Russia and the Balkans*, 638–40

9.8   # CYPRUS CONVENTION, 4 JUNE 1878

Anglo-Russian Memorandum (No. 3), 31 May 1878 •
Anglo-Ottoman Cyprus Convention, 4 June 1878

The Marquess of Salisbury took over the Foreign Office in March 1878. His task was to pressure Russia to abandon the Treaty of San Stefano in favor of a settlement more palatable to Britain; his powers of persuasion were augmented by the presence of the British fleet at Constantinople. His bargaining position thus enhanced, Salisbury adopted a two-pronged strategy. He reached agreement with the Russian ambassador in London, Count Peter Shuvalov, on the agenda for the forthcoming peace congress in Berlin; and, insuring himself against the possibility that the congress might end in failure, devised a fall-back strategy of propping up the Ottoman Empire. The cornerstone of this latter course was the Cyprus convention of 4 June 1878: Britain pledged to defend Turkey-in-Asia in return for the right to occupy Cyprus and the sultan's promise to introduce reforms in his eastern provinces.

The Cyprus convention was the most visible manifestation of what might be called Salisbury's grand design for the defense of British interests in the Middle East. As an exercise in the containment of Russia, its scope was ambitious: over the next year, a small army of British advisers descended on Anatolia to jump-start the reforms; Cyprus, under British tutelage, was to become a model for the modernization of the mainland provinces; the British ambassador in Constantinople promoted a scheme for a railroad connecting Alexandretta with Karachi. The purpose of these projects was ostensibly to help the Ottoman Empire defend itself against further Russian encroachments, but in reality these endeavors were about to transform Turkey-in-Asia into a British sphere of influence—and were resisted by the Porte for precisely this reason. By late 1879, Ottoman intransigence and the unwillingness of British financiers to risk their capital in the political quicksands of eastern Anatolia brought down Salisbury's plan. Its sole vestige, but one that endured until 1960, was the British presence in Cyprus.

For Salisbury, the eastern crisis of 1875 to 1878 had proved wrong Palmerston's hope that the Ottoman Empire could reform itself. The lesson of the preceding decades seemed clear: only a reform program implemented by an outside power could stave off the collapse of Turkey, and only England was equipped to play this part. Salisbury may well have been motivated by altruism or the concern for the balance of power in the Middle East. But it is just as likely that his Cyprus policy rested on a far shrewder calculation. The avowed purpose of the Cyprus convention was to create a counterforce to Russian expansion in the Caucasus. Yet one week before its conclusion, Salisbury, in his secret negotiations with Shuvalov, acquiesced in Russia's retention of the major fortresses it had wrested from the Ottomans. Though the Anglo-Russian deal was clinched, the Cyprus convention kept alive the illusion that these territories might be returned. Salisbury's conduct thus resembled that of a corporate raider, who, through the skillful use of conditions created by others and through the withholding of information, turns a profit for himself with no money down.

a)   ### Anglo-Russian Memorandum (No. 3), 31 May 1878

His Majesty the Emperor of Russia having consented to return to His Majesty the Sultan the valley of Alaschkert and the town of Bayazid, and having no intention of extending his conquests in Asia beyond Kars, Batoum, and the limits imposed by the Preliminary Treaty of San Stefano and rectified by the above-mentioned retrocession, the Imperial Government is willing to conclude with the British Government a secret agreement to the end of reassuring [the latter] in this regard.

—Sumner, *Russia and the Balkans*, 649

b)   *Anglo-Ottoman Cyprus Convention, 4 June 1878*

Art. 1: If Batoum, Ardahan, Kars, or any of them shall be retained by Russia, and if any attempt shall be made at any future time by Russia to take possession of any further territories of His Imperial Majesty the Sultan in Asia, as fixed by the Definitive Treaty of Peace, England engages to join His Imperial Majesty the Sultan in defending them by force of arms.

In return, His Imperial Majesty the Sultan promises to England to introduce necessary reforms, to be agreed upon later between the two Powers, in the government and for the protection of the Christian and other subjects of the Porte in these territories.

And in order to enable England to make necessary provision for executing her engagement, His Imperial Majesty the Sultan further consents to assign the island of Cyprus to be occupied and administered by England. . . .

—Hertslet, 4:2722; Hurst, 2:546–48

9.9   SALISBURY AND SHUVALOV ON THE STRAITS

Article 63 of the Treaty of Berlin • *Salisbury at the Congress of Berlin,*
11 July 1878 • *Shuvalov at the Congress of Berlin, 12 July 1878*

In one of the last sessions of the Congress of Berlin, the second British delegate, the Marquess of Salisbury, read into the record a British declaration on the regime of the Straits. Salisbury's interpretation exasperated the Russian representatives, who on the next day countered with a declaration of their own. From the Russian vantage point, Salisbury's maneuver showed that British policy in the Straits question had become unpredictable. This concern about British intentions haunted Russian diplomacy throughout the 1880s and set the stage for the Russian insistence on addressing the Straits question in the Three Emperors' League of 1881 and the Russo-German Reinsurance Treaty of 1887 (Documents 9.14 and 9.28).

a)   *Article 63 of the Treaty of Berlin*

The Treaty of Paris of 30 March 1856, as well as the Treaty of London of 13 March 1871,[21] are maintained in all such of their provisions as are not abrogated or modified by the preceding stipulations.

—Hurst, 2:576

---

[21]Article 1 of the Treaty of London abrogated articles 11, 13, and 14 of the 1856 Paris treaty (Document 5.7). Article 2 affirmed the principle of the closure of the Straits, but "with power to His Imperial Majesty the Sultan to open the said Straits in time of peace to the vessels of war of friendly and allied powers, in case the Sublime Porte should judge it necessary in order to secure the execution of the stipulations of the Treaty of Paris." See also Documents 8.16 and 10.8.

b)   *Salisbury at the Congress of Berlin, 11 July 1878*

. . . I declare on behalf of England that the obligations of Her Britannic Majesty on the closure of the Straits are limited to an obligation to the Sultan to respect in this matter His Majesty's independent determinations in conformity with the spirit of existing treaties.

—(source attributions below)

c)   *Shuvalov[22] at the Congress of Berlin, 12 July 1878*

The Russian plenipotentiaries, without quite understanding the proposal of the Second British plenipotentiary on the closure of the Straits, for their part limit themselves to demand insertion of the following remark into the protocol: in their view, the principle of the closure of the Straits is a European principle, and the pertinent stipulations of 1841, 1856, and 1871, now confirmed by the Treaty of Berlin, are obligatory for all powers, conforming to the spirit and letter of existing treaties not only towards the Sultan but also towards all signatories of these agreements.

—Protocols 18 and 19, *SP*, 69:1070–76; Imanuel Geiss, *Der Berliner Kongress: Protokolle und Materialien* (Boppard, 1978); Hurst, 2:549–50

9.10   TREATY OF BERLIN, 13 JULY 1878

The exhaustion of Russia's armies and the opposition of Britain and Austria to the Treaty of San Stefano made the revision of that instrument at the Congress of Berlin a foregone conclusion. Above all, "Big Bulgaria"—the centerpiece of San Stefano—was to be dismantled. But what must have been particularly galling to the Russian plenipoteniaries (who themselves had no great love for the architect of San Stefano, Count Nicholas Ignatiev) was that Britain and Austria-Hungary, neither of which had expended a single soldier in the great eastern crisis, proved the real victors—Britain under the terms of the Cyprus convention, Austria-Hungary under articles 25 and 29 of the Berlin treaty.

It is tempting to see the Congress of Berlin as the final episode in the great eastern crisis of 1875–1878. Perhaps a more accurate depiction might be that the Treaty of Berlin merely shifted the crisis to a new, albeit less dangerous, plane. The powers delegated many of the details of the settlement to commissions whose work could be expected to drag on for years (for instance, the commission on the northern border of Greece only completed its task in 1881). This arrangement kept open old wounds: disagreement among the commissioners could easily cloud the relationship of governments toward one another; conversely, discord among the powers could affect the way in which each government would instruct its commissioners to vote.

[22]Peter Andreevich, Count Shuvalov (1827–1889). Russian ambassador in London, 1874–1879; second Russian delegate at the congress.

Art. 1: Bulgaria is constituted an autonomous and tributary Principality under the suzerainty of His Imperial Majesty the Sultan; it will have a Christian Government and a national militia. . . .

Art. 3: The Prince of Bulgaria shall be freely elected by the population and confirmed by the Sublime Porte, with the assent of the Powers. No member of the Reigning Dynasties of the Great European Powers may be elected Prince of Bulgaria. In case of a vacancy in the princely dignity, the election of the new Prince shall take place under the same conditions and with the same forms. . . .

Art. 13: A province is formed south of the Balkans which will take the name of "Eastern Rumelia," and will remain under the direct political and military authority of His Imperial Majesty the Sultan, under conditions of administrative autonomy. It shall have a Christian Governor-General. . . .

Art. 17: The Governor-General of Eastern Rumelia shall be nominated by the Sublime Porte, with the assent of the Powers, for a term of five years. . . .

Art. 25: The Provinces of Bosnia and Herzegovina shall be occupied and administered by Austria-Hungary. The Government of Austria-Hungary, not desiring to undertake the administration of the Sanjak of Novi-Bazar, which extends between Serbia and Montenegro in a south-easterly direction to the other side of Mitrviotza, the Ottoman Administration will continue to exercise its functions there. Nevertheless, in order to assure the maintenance of the new political state of affairs, as well as freedom and security of communications, Austria-Hungary reserves the right of keeping garrisons and having military and commercial roads in the whole of this part of the ancient Vilayet of Bosnia. To this end the Governments of Austria-Hungary and Turkey reserve to themselves to come to an understanding on the details.

Art. 26: The independence of Montenegro is recognized. . . .

Art. 29: Antivari and its sea-board are annexed to Montenegro under the following conditions: . . . [iv] Montenegro shall have neither ships of war nor flag of war; [v] The port of Antivari and all the waters of Montenegro shall remain closed to the ships of war of all nations; [vi] The fortifications situated on Montenegrin territory between the lake and the coast shall be razed, and none shall be rebuilt within this zone; . . . [viii] Montenegro shall adopt the maritime code in force in Dalmatia. On her side, Austria-Hungary undertakes to grant consular protection to the Montenegrin merchant flag; [ix] Montenegro shall come to an understanding with Austria-Hungary on the right to construct and keep up across the new Montenegrin territory a road and a railway. . . .

Art. 34: The High Contracting Parties recognize the independence of the Principality of Serbia, subject to the conditions set forth in the following article.[23]

Art. 43: The High Contracting Parties recognize the independence of Romania, subject to the conditions set forth in the two following Articles.

Art. 44: In Romania the difference of religious creeds and confessions shall not be alleged against any person as a ground for exclusion or incapacity in matters relating

---

[23]Article 35 corresponds to the first two paragraphs of article 44; for "Romania" in article 44 read "Serbia" in article 35. See Document 9.12.

to the enjoyment of civil and political rights, admission to public employments, functions, and honours, or the exercise of the various professions and industries in any locality whatsoever. . . .

Art. 45: The Principality of Romania restores to His Majesty the Emperor of Russia that portion of the Bessarabian territory detached from Russia by the Treaty of Paris of 1856. . . .

Art. 57: The Sublime Porte cedes to the Russian Empire in Asia the territories of Ardahan, Kars, and Batoum. . . .

Art. 59: His Majesty the Emperor of Russia declares that it is his intention to constitute Batoum a free port, essentially commercial.[24]

Art. 61: The Sublime Porte undertakes to carry out, without further delay, the improvements and reforms demanded by local requirements in the provinces inhabited by the Armenians, and to guarantee their security against the Circassians and Kurds. It will periodically make known the steps taken to this effect to the Powers, who will superintend their application.

Art. 62: . . . The rights possessed by France are expressly reserved, and it is well understood that no alterations can be made in the status quo in the Holy Places. . . .[25]

—Hertslet, 4:2759ff.; Hurst, 2:551–77

9.11   RESIDUAL PROBLEMS: THE OCCUPATION OF BOSNIA-HERZEGOVINA

Frommelt to Reuss, 5 August 1878 • *Radolinski to Bismarck, 14 August 1878* • *Reuss to Bismarck, 19 August 1878*

Fighting in the Balkans, albeit of a different sort, continued after the Congress of Berlin. Sporadic risings pitted Balkan Muslims against the new order: Pomaks ambushed Russian troops in the Rhodope Mountains, Albanians rebelled against the cession of Ottoman territory to Montenegro, Bosnians battled Austria's army of occupation.

The occupation of Bosnia-Herzegovina proved far more costly than Austria had expected. Austrian forces crossed into the provinces on 29 July 1878 and entered Sarajevo one month later. But skirmishes in the countryside ensured that the human toll continued to climb: by the end of the year, 1,160 Austrian soldiers had been killed in action; another 2,300 had died of disease. The Porte's insistence that Austria specify the length of the occupation (a demand flatly turned down by Austria) delayed until 21 April 1879 the Austro-Turkish convention on Bosnia[26] which had been envisaged by the Treaty of Berlin. The Ottoman foot-dragging encouraged Bosnian resistance, but, conversely, the agreement did not prevent a new flare-up in August 1879.

[24]This servitude was repudiated by Russia in July 1886, in the midst of the Bulgarian crisis. Cf. Document 9.23.

[25]France relinquished these rights at the San Remo conference in April 1920 in return for the British promise not to abridge rights "hitherto enjoyed by the non-Jewish communities in Palestine." See Document 9.4, headnote.

[26]Text in Hurst, 2:583–86.

a)   ***Frommelt*[27] *to Reuss,*[28] *5 August 1878***

Most Moslems of this city [Sarajevo] and several hundred Christians have left to fight the army of occupation. Sarajevo therefore calm on the surface but situation is no less dangerous. Ongoing anarchy. Exclusive rule of Muslim law proclaimed. Hesitation of occupation forces and continuation of resistance interpreted as signs of victory. Postal communications have ceased.

—PA Türkei I.A.B.q. 131

b)   ***Radolinski*[29] *to Bismarck, 14 August 1878***

. . . The Austrian ambassador was very agitated about the attitude of Serbia and the many emissaries which arrive from there in Bosnia to destabilize [the province]. He thinks that this kind of behavior could easily lead to an Austrian invasion of Serbia and that it would not be difficult to reach an understanding with Russia on this.

—PA Türkei I.A.B.q. 131

c)   ***Reuss to Bismarck, 19 August 1878***

. . . The strengthening of the Slav element in the [Austro-Hungarian] monarchy is something which [the advocates of a] Greater Hungary find difficult to digest. . . . Opinions in Cisleithania[29a] are different. The old conservative party, which is hostile to the government, [thinks]. . . that Count Andrassy has missed a golden opportunity and could have easily, if he had only known how, annexed these provinces with the approval of Europe—instead of carrying out, as the mandatory of Europe, an occupation the goals of which are hazy. The country will have to make sacrifices, and no-one knows whether these would not be in vain. It was undignified for the monarchy to settle on the role of a mandatory for carrying out something so fleeting, while hiding its true intentions. The time would come when the government, to obtain further loans [in the legislatures], would have to own up to its goals, but it was impossible to foresee the European situation at that juncture and whether it would permit the implementation of Austria-Hungary's wishes. . . .

—PA Türkei I.A.B.q. 131

---

[27] Felix Frommelt (1842–1886). German consul in Sarajevo, 1876–1883.

[28] Heinrich VII, Prince Reuss (1825–1906). German ambassador in Vienna, 1878–1894.

[29] Hugo Leszcyc, Count Radolinski, later Prince Radolin (1841–1917). German chargé in Constantinople; later attendant at the court of Friedrich III; German ambassador in Paris, 1900–1910.

[29a] The Leitha river formed the symbolic dividing line between the Austrian lands ("Cisleithania") and the Kingdom of Hungary ("Transleithania").

9.12   ## RESIDUAL PROBLEMS: ROMANIA

Circular by Bernhard Ernst von Bülow, 6 October 1878

The Berlin treaty, in articles 35, 44, and 45, laid down the requirements that Serbia and Romania had to fulfill in order to secure international recognition as independent states. Articles 35 (applying to Serbia) and 44 (applying to Romania) were almost identical, but the real motive force behind the two articles was the powers' revulsion at the official anti-Semitism of Romania. The only dissenter was Russia: in Gorchakov's view, eastern European Jewry constituted a "scourge" [*fléau*] for the non-Jewish populations of the Russian "pale" and the Balkans.[30]

The Romanian response was to meet the criteria for recognition by passing a constitutional amendment. But by offering citizenship to fewer than 1 percent of Romanian Jews, the Romanian legislation fell far short of the requirements of article 44. The Romanian calculation nonetheless paid off in that the powers had tired of the controversy. After the passage of the constitutional amendment, Russia and Austria-Hungary recognized Romania without delay; Italy, citing linguistic affinities, followed suit; German acquiescence was bought by Romania's willingness to settle a financial dispute with German investors on terms favorable to the latter.

Circular by Bernhard Ernst von Bülow, 6 October 1878

. . . We have learned . . . that, even recently, vexing administrative measures have been taken against the Israelites [in Romania] and it almost looks as if politicians in that country hoped to secure international recognition of Romania piecemeal and at little cost without fulfilling the stipulations of the treaty. This situation obliges us—in view also of the state of public opinion in Germany which, prompted by the Reichstag debate on the German-Romanian trade convention,[30a] has directed its attention to the unfortunate situation of the Israelites in Romania—not to rush into recognizing its independence. We will shelve recognition until Romania will give sufficient guarantees for the fulfillment of its obligations. . . .

—PA Türkei I.A.B.q. 133

9.13   ## DUAL ALLIANCE, 1879

"I should be alarmed if we sought protection from the gathering storm by tying our neat seaworthy frigate to Austria's worm-eaten battleship," Bismarck said of Prussian policy on the eve of western intervention in the Crimean War.[31] Twenty-five years later, in 1879, Bismarck did tie the new German state to the Habsburg empire in a formal peacetime alliance.

---

[30] See Protocols 8 and 17 of the Congress. See Geiss, *Berliner Kongress*, 85, 158, 252n.

[30a] Of 14 November 1877. On 14 May 1878, various speakers in the Reichstag termed unacceptable a situation in which Romania might treat German Jews differently from Germans of other faiths. *Reichstag 1878*, III:1325.

[31] Bismarck to Manteuffel, 15 February 1854, *GW*, 1:473.

What were his motives? It is probably safe to say that, for Bismarck, the alliance was not an end in itself, but the means to an end. His goal, and the wording of article 4 points in this direction, was to improve *Russo*-German relations. In 1879, the Russo-German relationship reached a new nadir—strained by Pan-Slav attacks on the Treaty of Berlin and weighted down by the general realization, in Russia, of the extent of Russia's concessions in the Near East. In repairing the damage, however, Bismarck was determined to prevent the impression that Germany could be made to buckle at the slightest hint of Russian displeasure. Not Germany but Russia should be made to change course—and the Austro-German alliance would give it the incentive to do so.

In practical terms, Bismarck offered Russia a choice: it could opt either for continuing the confrontation with both Germany and Austria (with, ultimately, little or no hope of success given that France could not and England would not champion the Russian cause) or for a general conciliation among the three eastern empires (which held out the promise of an Austro-Russian compromise). Russia would realize—so ran Bismarck's calculation—that Austria, allied to Germany, would be a more secure and hence more responsible member of the European concert; moreover, that Germany as the dominant partner in this combination could drill Austria back into line by threatening to cancel the alliance.

This threat was gauged correctly by Friedrich von Holstein, one of Bismarck's principal assistants in the German foreign ministry, in a remark made almost two decades later: "If it becomes a matter of life or death for the Austrians, we will have to intervene with or without a treaty; but as to when we feel the psychological moment has come is our secret, and through this uncertainty we oblige the Austrians to think well in advance about what they do."[32] Implicit in Holstein's remark, of course, was the unspoken assumption that Germany would remain the dominant partner in the alliance. But Holstein's interpretation of the *casus foederis* ("a matter of life or death for the Austrians") went well beyond the treaty's terms. The circumstances of 1914 may have constituted a "matter of life or death" for Austria, but it is another question altogether whether Germany's "blank check" for Austria of 5 July 1914 was mandated by the terms of the Dual Alliance (cf. Documents 12.1 through 12.3).

[Preamble:] . . . Their Majesties . . . while solemnly promising each other never to allow their purely defensive agreement to develop an aggressive tendency in any direction, have determined to conclude an alliance of peace and mutual defence. . . .

Art. 1: Should, contrary to their hope, and against the genuine desire of the two high contracting parties, one of the two empires be attacked by Russia, the high contracting parties are bound to come to each other's assistance with the whole war strength of their empires, and will accordingly conclude peace together and upon mutual agreement.

Art. 2: Should one of the high contracting parties be attacked by another power, the other high contracting party binds itself hereby, not only not to support the aggressor against its high ally, but to observe at least a benevolent neutral attitude towards its fellow contracting party. Should, however, the attacking party in such an event be supported by Russia, either in the form of active cooperation or by military measures which constitute a menace to the party attacked, then the obligation

---

[32]Holstein to Eulenburg, 9 February 1896, *HP*, 3:528.

stipulated in Art. 1 of this treaty, for reciprocal assistance with the whole fighting force, becomes equally operative, and the conduct of the war by the two high contracting parties shall in this case also be in common until the conclusion of a common peace. . . .

Art. 4: This treaty shall, in conformity with its peaceful character, and to avoid any misinterpretation, be kept secret by the two high contracting parties, and only communicated to a third power upon a joint understanding between the two parties, and according to the terms of a special agreement.[33] The two high contracting parties venture to hope, after the sentiments expressed by the Emperor Alexander at the meeting at Alexandrovo,[34] that the armaments of Russia will not in reality prove to be menacing to them, and have on that account no reason for making a communication at present; should, however, this hope, contrary to their expectations, prove to be erroneous, the two high contracting parties would consider it their loyal obligation to let the Emperor Alexander know, at least confidentially, that they must consider an attack on either of them as directed against both. . . .

—Hurst, 2:590–91 (transcription error in Art. 2); Pribram, 1:25–31

9.14 THE MAKING OF THE THREE EMPERORS' LEAGUE, 1881

Gladstone in Edinburgh, 17 March 1880 •
Three Emperors' League, 18 June 1881

Bismarck may have regarded the Austro-German Dual Alliance as a steppingstone to an improved relationship with Russia, but this sentiment was not shared in Vienna. The Austrian calculation, rather, was to rely on the Dual Alliance together with Austria's much vaguer friendship with England to advance Austrian aims in the Balkans at the expense of Russia. But the second plank in this edifice—reliance on British support—collapsed when Disraeli's Conservative ministry lost the parliamentary elections of April 1880. The attitude that the new prime minister, William Ewart Gladstone, was likely to take toward Austria had already become discernible during the election campaign. Now deprived of British backing, Austria had to choose between isolation or acquiescing in Bismarck's efforts to compose the Austro-Russian relationship; the result was the second Three Emperors' League of June 1881, renewed in 1884.

Gladstone's stance on Austria marks an important milestone in the evolution of English Liberal thinking. His position is approximately halfway between that of Palmerston, who had little love for Austria but nonetheless found it useful as a pawn in his policy toward Russia, and that of Sir Edward Grey, whose icy indifference helped seal the fate of the Habsburg monarchy in July 1914.

It is interesting to compare the commitments undertaken in the Dual Alliance with those of the Three Emperors' League. Indeed, they might be examined for the following proposition: that the Dual Alliance prescribed a maximum code of conduct (i.e., what the parties to it could expect of one another, but no more), whereas the Three Emperors' League suggested a minimum code of conduct for its signatories (i.e., the least that they could expect of one another).

[33]Communicated unofficially to Russia by Bismarck in June 1887, to Salisbury in November 1887; published in January 1888. These dates should be placed in the context of the Reinsurance Treaty and the second Mediterranean entente of 1887. See Documents 9.28 and 9.30.

[34]Summit of Alexander II and Wilhelm I on 3 September 1879.

a)   ***Gladstone in Edinburgh, 17 March 1880***

... What has that foreign policy of Austria been? ... Austria has been ever the unflinching foe of freedom in every country of Europe [cheers]. Austria trampled underfoot, Austria resisted the unity of Germany [cheers]. Russia, I am sorry to say, has been the foe of freedom too; but in Russia there is an exception—Russia has been the friend of Slavonic freedom; but Austria has never been the friend even of Slavonic freedom. Austria did all she could to prevent the creation of Belgium [cheers]. Austria never lifted a finger for the regeneration and constitution of Greece [cheers]. There is not an instance—there is not a spot upon the whole map where you can lay your finger and say, "There Austria did good" [loud cheers]. ...

—*The Times*, 18 March 1880

b)   ***Three Emperors' League, 18 June 1881***

Art. 1: In case one of the High Contracting Parties should find itself at war with a fourth Great Power, the two others shall maintain towards it a benevolent neutrality and shall devote their efforts to the localization of the conflict. This stipulation shall apply likewise to a war between one of the three Powers and Turkey, but only in the case where a previous agreement shall have been reached between the three Courts as to the results of this war. ...

Art. 2: Russia, in agreement with Germany, declares her firm resolution to respect the interests arising from the new position assured to Austria-Hungary by the Treaty of Berlin. The three Courts, desirous of avoiding all discord between them, engage to take account of their respective interests in the Balkan Peninsula. They further promise one another that any new modifications in the territorial status quo of Turkey in Europe can be accomplished only in virtue of a common agreement between them. ...

Art. 3: The three Courts recognize the European and mutually obligatory character of the principle of the closing of the Straits of the Bosporus and of the Dardanelles, founded on international law, confirmed by treaties, and summed up in the declaration of the second Plenipotentiary of Russia at the session of 12 July of the Congress of Berlin (Protocol 19).[35] They will take care in common that Turkey shall make no exception to this rule in favour of the interests of any Government whatsoever, by lending to warlike operations of a belligerent Power the portion of its Empire constituted by the Straits. In case of infringement, or to prevent it if such infringement should be in prospect, the three Courts will inform Turkey that they would regard her, in that event, as putting herself in a state of war towards the injured Party, and as having deprived herself thenceforth of the benefits of the security assured to her territorial status quo by the Treaty of Berlin.

Art. 4: The present Treaty shall be in force during a period of three years, dating from the day of the exchange of ratifications. ...

[35]See Document 9.9.

Art. 6: The secret Conventions concluded between Austria-Hungary and Russia and between Germany and Russia in 1873 are replaced by the present Treaty. . . . [36]

[Separate Protocol:] 1. Bosnia and Herzegovina: Austria-Hungary reserves the right to annex these provinces at whatever moment she shall deem opportune. . . .

4. Bulgaria: The three Powers will not oppose the eventual reunion of Bulgaria and Eastern Rumelia within the territorial limits assigned to them by the Treaty of Berlin, if this question should come up by the force of circumstances. . . .

—Hurst, 2:603–7; Pribram, 1:36–49

9.15   THE AUSTRO-SERB TREATY, 16/28 JUNE 1881

Austro-Serb Treaty, 16/28 June 1881 ●
Austro-Serb Declaration, 13/25 October 1881

Throughout the nineteenth century, Russia's cozy relationship with Serbia and Serb-speaking Montenegro had been predicated on sentiment—the Serbs were a fellow Orthodox and Slavic people—and by the uses of Serbia as a thorn in the Ottoman flank. Russian volunteers had flocked to Serbia's side in the Serb-Ottoman war of 1876; one year later, Serbia benefited from Russian exertions in the Russo-Turkish war.

But at San Stefano and Berlin, Russia lavished its affection on Bulgaria rather than on its traditional Balkan ally. The beneficiary of the lingering resentment in Belgrade was Austria, which in 1881 induced the Serb ruler, Milan Obrenovic, to conclude an alliance. The measure of the Austrian coup lies not just in the fact that Austria stole a march on Russia, but in the provisions of the treaty text: in article 2, Serbia undertook to curb Serb irredentism against the dual monarchy, while article 4 practically reduced it to the status of an Austrian protectorate.

The treaty was not without its inherent weaknesses. Milan had negotiated it over the head of his horrified ministers, who secured a modification to article 4 in a subsequent Austro-Serb declaration. Bluntly put, Milan's stake in the treaty was that in return for his willingness to abide by its terms, he could expect Austrian subsidies to keep him solvent. But Austria's largesse had its drawbacks, as Milan's and his son (and successor) Peter's eccentricities could also backfire on their patron. The periodic embarrassments that sprang from being too closely associated with the Obrenovic dynasty help explain why, when the treaty lapsed in 1895, its passing was viewed with little regret in Vienna.

a)   *Austro-Serb Treaty, 16/28 June 1881*

. . . Art. 2: Serbia will not tolerate political, religious, or other intrigues, which, taking her territory as a point of departure, might be directed against the Austro-Hungarian Monarchy, including therein Bosnia, Herzegovina, and the Sanjak of Novibazar. Austria-Hungary assumes the same obligation with regard to Serbia and her dynasty, the maintenance and strengthening of which she will support with all her influence. . . .

[36]See Document 9.1.

Art. 4: Austria-Hungary will use her influence with the other European Cabinets to second the interests of Serbia. Without a previous understanding with Austria-Hungary, Serbia will neither negotiate nor conclude any political treaty with another Government, and will not admit to her territory a foreign armed force, regular or irregular, even as volunteers. . . .

Art. 7: If, as a result of a combination of circumstances whose development is not to be foreseen at present, Serbia were in a position to make territorial acquisitions in the direction of her southern frontiers (with the exception of the Sanjak of Novibazar), Austria-Hungary will not oppose herself thereto, and will use her influence with the other Powers for the purpose of winning them over to an attitude favourable to Serbia.

—Hurst, 2:601–2; Pribram, 1:50–55

b)   *Austro-Serb Declaration, 13/25 October 1881*

. . . Article 4 cannot impair the right of Serbia to negotiate and to conclude treaties, even of a political nature, with another Government. It implies for Serbia no other engagement than that of not negotiating and of not concluding any political treaty which would be contrary to the spirit and the tenor of the said secret Treaty. . . .

—Pribram, 1:60–61

9.16   THE TRIPLE ALLIANCE, 22 MAY 1882

The Treaty of Bardo of May 1881[37] established a French protectorate in Tunis—an area geographically close to Italy, home to a large number of Italian residents, and hitherto tributary to the Ottoman Empire. The French move on Tunis created an immediate backlash in Italy and propelled the government of Agostino Depretis to seek closer ties to the Dual Alliance. Just as the formation of the Gladstone government in 1880 had inadvertently assisted Bismarck in forging the Three Emperors' League one year later, so the French bid for Tunis now played midwife to the Triple Alliance of Italy, Austria-Hungary, and Germany of 1882.

The Italian initiative was welcome to Bismarck for a variety of reasons. First, the Austro-Italian component of the alliance would bolster Austria by making unlikely an Italian attack against Austria's rear in the event of a Balkan crisis; at the very least, the agreement could be used to hold the Italian government accountable for any anti-Austrian outbursts by the irredentist lobby. Second, a defensive alliance between Germany and Italy would retard any French desire for a war of revanche against Germany, as France would have to divert some of its forces to guard its Alpine border with Italy. Third, the Triple Alliance would lend Germany leverage in its dealings with Russia, for Germany might now be able to neutralize or even deliver the Italian vote, along with its own and that of Austria, in international questions in which Russia had a stake.

[37]Text in Hurewitz, 1:441–42; *SP*, 72:247; Hertslet II, 3:1187–90.

. . . Art. 2: In case Italy, without direct provocation on her part, should be attacked by France for any reason whatsoever, the two other Contracting Parties shall be bound to lend help and assistance with all their forces to the Party attacked. This same obligation shall devolve upon Italy in case of any aggression without direct provocation by France against Germany.

Art. 3: If one, or two, of the High Contracting Parties, without direct provocation on their part, should chance to be attacked and to be engaged in a war with two or more Great Powers nonsignatory to the present Treaty, the *casus foederis* will arise simultaneously for all the High Contracting Parties.

Art. 4: In case a Great Power nonsignatory to the present Treaty should threaten the security of the states of one of the High Contracting Parties, and the threatened Party should find itself forced on that account to make war against it, the two others bind themselves to observe towards their Ally a benevolent neutrality. Each of them reserves to itself, in this case, the right to take part in the war, if it should see fit, to make common cause with its Ally. . . .

Art. 6: The High Contracting Parties mutually promise secrecy as to the contents and existence of the present Treaty. . . . [38]

[Additional Declaration by Italy, 22 May 1882:] The Royal Italian Government declares that the provisions of the secret Treaty concluded on 20 May 1882 between Italy, Austria-Hungary, and Germany, cannot, as has been previously agreed, in any case be regarded as being directed against England.

—Hurst, 2:611–13; Pribram, 1:65–73

9.17 TREATY BETWEEN AUSTRIA-HUNGARY AND ROMANIA, 30 OCTOBER 1883

Memories of the manner in which the Russian army had barged across Romanian territory during the Russo-Turkish war of 1877 again exercised the imagination of Romanian politicians six years later. Romania's renewed concern was triggered by the knowledge that the rapport between the new prince of Bulgaria, Alexander of Battenberg (Document 9.23), and his erstwhile Russian sponsors had broken down so completely that the dispatch of a Russian army to Bulgaria—to chastise Battenberg and to reestablish Russian influence in that country— seemed entirely possible. Its route would have been the same as in 1877. This quandary led Romania to conclude a defensive alliance with Austria—an instrument that at the very least gave Romania some leverage in the event that Russia demanded passage through its territory. Germany acceded instantly; Italy associated itself with the alliance in the heyday of the Mediterranean entente (Document 9.30) in May 1888.

It is intriguing to contrast the Austro-Romanian treaty with the Austro-Serb convention of 1881 (Document 9.15). Unlike the treaty with Serbia, the Romanian alliance did not include an anti-irredentist clause—such as, for example, a promise by the Romanian government to stifle Romanian irredentists coveting Transylvania. But the Austro-Romanian alliance resembled

---

[38]The treaty's existence, but not its terms, was acknowledged after its renewal in February 1887.

the Serb treaty in its form: it was chiefly a dynastic arrangement with King Charles (Carol) and his chief ministers, while the remainder of the Romanian cabinet was kept in the dark. This secretive feature was retained when the treaty was renewed in 1892, 1902, and 1913.

The Austro-Serb and Austro-Romanian treaties, coupled with Battenberg's anti-Russian drift, catapulted Austria to the height of its influence in the Balkans. It is little wonder then that Austria turned a deaf ear to Bismarck's repeated entreaties that, in order to compose its differences with Russia, Austria should consent to a division of the Balkans into a western (Austrian), and an eastern (Russian), sphere of influence.[39]

The importance of the Austro-Romanian-German treaty went beyond the Balkans. If Russia attacked Romania and Austria honored its treaty commitment by striking back at Russia, Germany would have to intervene on Austria's side against Russia—even though Austria, in a purely bilateral Austro-Russian context, was the *attacking* party. This scenario expanded Germany's commitment under the Austro-German Dual Alliance (Document 9.13) and, moreover, contradicted Bismarck's oft-stated assurance that Germany had no interests—certainly none worth a Russo-German war—in the Balkans.

. . . Art. 2. If Rumania, without any provocation on her part, should be attacked, Austria-Hungary is bound to bring her in ample time help and assistance against the aggressor. If Austria-Hungary be attacked under the same circumstances in a portion of her states bordering on Rumania, the *casus foederis* will immediately arise for the latter.

Art. 3. If one of the High Contracting Parties should find itself threatened by an aggression under the above mentioned conditions, the respective Governments shall put themselves in agreement as to the measures to be taken with a view to cooperation of their armies. . . .

—Hurst, 2:630–32; Pribram, 1:79–89

9.18   **CONVENTIONS OF PRETORIA AND LONDON**

Pretoria Convention, 3 August 1881 •
London Convention, 27 February 1884

In 1880–1881, a Boer revolt sought to undo the British annexation of the Transvaal of 1877. The Boer insurgents were remarkably successful and, in February 1881 at Majuba Hill, handed a British force a devastating defeat. Rather than fight on to reverse this fiasco, the Gladstone government agreed to redefine the status of the Transvaal in a convention signed in August 1881 at Pretoria, the capital of this Boer republic. After the Pretoria convention, the Transvaal—a landlocked quasi state under the "suzerainty of Her Majesty"—continued to be at the mercy of Britain, but the Boers sought to overcome the constraints imposed on them by geography by expanding into Bechuanaland to the west and toward the Indian Ocean. Both efforts were frustrated by the British. In the London convention of 1884, the Boers at least managed to trade their territorial claims to Bechuanaland for an improvement of their legal

---

[39]Cf. Bismarck's instructions and marginalia of June and July 1884. *GP*, 3:636–39.

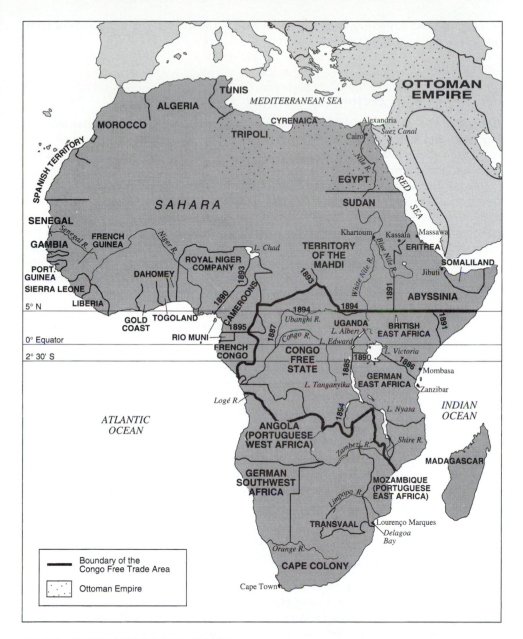

MAP 8   THE PARTITION OF AFRICA

status. In omitting any mention of the "suzerainty of Her Majesty" over the Transvaal, the London convention on the surface appeared as a victory for the Boers. But by nullifying Boer territorial claims, the convention made illusory the possibility, however remote, of a territorial link between the Transvaal and German South-West Africa (Document 9.20). The Boers' attempt to reach the Indian Ocean also came to naught: British opposition blocked expansion through Zululand; similarly, all hope of establishing a a joint border with the colonial outpost of a sympathetic power evaporated when, in March 1885, the German government relinquished to Britain its claims on St. Lucia Bay.

a)   *Pretoria Convention, 3 August 1881*

[Preamble:] . . . [C]omplete self-government, subject to the suzerainty of Her Majesty, her heirs and successors, will be accorded to the inhabitants of the Transvaal Territory, upon the following terms and conditions, and subject to the following reservations and limitations: . . .

Art. 2: Her Majesty reserves to herself, her heirs, and successors, *(a)* the right from time to time to appoint a British resident in and for the said state, with such duties and functions as are hereinafter defined; *(b)* the right to move troops through the said state in time of war, or in case of the apprehension of immediate war between the suzerain power and any foreign state, or native tribe in South Africa; and *(c)* the control of the external relations of the said state, including the conclusion of treaties, and the conduct of diplomatic intercourse with foreign powers, such intercourse to be carried on through Her Majesty's diplomatic and consular officers abroad. . . .

—*SP*, 72:900–11

b)   *London Convention, 27 February 1884*

. . . Art. 4: The South African Republic will conclude no treaty or engagement with any state or nation other than the Orange Free State, nor with any native tribe to the eastward or westward of the Republic, until the same has been approved by Her Majesty the Queen. Such approval shall be considered to have been granted if Her Majesty's Government shall not, within six months after receiving a copy of such treaty (which shall be delivered to them immediately upon its completion), have notified that the conclusion of such treaty is in conflict with the interests of Great Britain, or any of Her Majesty's possessions in South Africa. . . .

—Hertslet II, 1:233

9.19   THE EGYPTIAN QUESTION, 1876–1885

Khedival Decree, 2 May 1876 • Khedival Decree (Goschen-Joubert Proposals), 18 November 1876 • Law of Liquidation, 17 July 1880 • Self-Denying Protocol of Britain, Austria-Hungary, France, Germany, Italy, and Russia, 25 June 1882 • Granville Circular, 3 January 1883 • Granville to Baring (Cromer), 4 January 1884 • Cromer on his Position in Egypt • Gladstone to Granville, 6 January 1884 • Bismarck to Wilhelm I, 21 August 1884 • Herbert von Bismarck to Bismarck, 6 October 1884 • Proceedings of the British Cabinet, 12 March 1885 • London Convention, 18 March 1885 • Gladstone to Granville, 1 June 1885

In 1876, the Egyptian question concerned mainly bankers and financiers. By 1882, it had evolved into the central, and most perplexing, foreign policy preoccupation of the British government, and in its various manifestations shaped Britain's relations with the other European Great Powers.

In these six years, the Egyptian question became baffling in its complexity. The technical details of the Egyptian debt problem were almost a science unto themselves. No less intricate was the behind-the-scenes maneuvering of nationalist politicians and their sympathizers to escape the vise of foreign financial control. Finally, the instability of Egypt impaired its control of the Sudan, which, by the early 1880s, succumbed to a rebellion of Islamic fundamentalists and slave traders against westernized (i.e., Egyptian) rule. The warriors of Mohammed Ahmed (acclaimed as the "Mahdi" by his followers) eventually defeated an Anglo-Egyptian force in 1883 and captured Khartoum in 1885, killing General Charles Gordon, who had been hired by the Egyptian government to organize the defense of the city. Britain took no action to reverse this debacle: stymied by squabbles over how to finance the reconquest of the Sudan, it was content to abandon the region to its own fate.

Interesting though these aspects of the Egyptian question certainly are, they lie beyond the scope of the present book. The documents excerpted here focus on Britain's legal predicament after its occupation of Egypt in 1882 and examine Britain's position in the context of rights that other powers claimed in that country.

In 1876, the Khedive Ismail warded off the holders of Egyptian bonds by creating a *caisse* of the public debt under the direction of one French, one Austrian, and one Italian commissioner. In the view of the bondholders, Ismail's reorganization of Egyptian finances did not go far enough, and he was forced to accept the conclusions reached by a commission chaired by the British financier George Goschen and his French counterpart Edmonde Joubert. The Goschen-Joubert proposals added an English commissioner to the *caisse* and subordinated the Egyptian budget to two controllers, one English and one French, who were charged with the supervision, respectively, of revenues and expenditures—the so-called Dual Control of Egyptian finances.

In increasing taxation and slashing public expenditures, the Dual Control relied on measures only too familiar to students of the present-day third world debt crisis. By 1879, Ismail sought to undo the new financial regime, but his decision to dismiss the controllers recoiled on him. The European powers now pressured the Porte to depose its unruly viceroy and to appoint a more pliable successor, the Khedive Tewfik. In the wake of this decision, yet another international financial commission took up its work and by July 1880 codified the various khedival decrees on the debt question into a coherent Law of Liquidation.

But the social fallout of the Dual Control, which Ismail had already discerned, spread further. The principal spokesman for the antiforeign movement was Arabi (U'rabi) Pasha, minister of war in Tewfik's cabinet. Arabi probably did not instigate the Alexandria riots of June 1882, which caused the loss of European lives and property, but his hand was nonetheless forced by them. The subsequent British shelling of and landing in Alexandria caused even greater property damage and threw the gauntlet down to Arabi, who felt compelled to resist. His poorly equipped army was no match for the British expeditionary force, and after the decisive engagement at Tell-el-Kebir in the Nile Delta and a few mopping-up operations, Britain found itself master of Egypt.

Britain had quite literally stumbled into its new role in Egypt in a fit of absence of mind. As the crisis gathered momentum in the summer of 1882, the Gladstone government had repeatedly emphasized that it considered the Egyptian question to have an international character. Its attempt to find a solution to the Egyptian crisis by working through the Constantinople conference of ambassadors attests to this conviction, as does the British request that France, which had joined England in the naval demonstration off Alexandria, participate in the bombardment and landing as well. The French government, in the midst of a parliamentary crisis at home, declined the invitation, thereby leaving Britain to act alone. In the light of subsequent events, it is difficult to say which of the two countries—France or Britain—regretted more the French decision to stay out.

The British occupation of Egypt in 1882 gave Britain physical control of that country, but created a host of new dilemmas. Foremost among these was the question of whether Britain should annex Egypt. Given that Egypt was still an Ottoman province, to do so would have further weakened the Ottoman Empire and tempted other powers to clamor for compensations (Russia in Armenia, France in Syria, Italy in Libya and Albania, Austria in Bosnia). From a fiscal point of view too, annexation was undesirable: British sovereignty in Egypt would make *Britain* liable for Egypt's debt—an ironic and surely unintended coda to six years of diplomatic efforts to get *Egypt* to meet its own financial obligations. Last but not least, annexation could not be reconciled with the self-denying protocol to which the powers had agreed just before the British military intervention.

If Britain did not want to be held responsible for the Egyptian debt, it—as the power that had restored order in Egypt—was nonetheless under an obligation to ensure that Egypt would generate the revenues necessary for servicing the debt. To meet this obligation, the Gladstone cabinet attempted a patchwork reorganization of Egyptian finances. Britain did not tamper with the *caisse*, probably for fear that under the Law of Liquidation any infringement of the rights of the *caisse* could be appealed to Egypt's Mixed Courts—which would in all likelihood have ruled in favor of the *caisse*. More problematic was the British decision to abolish the Dual Control. In Gladstone's eyes, the Dual Control had been the root cause of the 1882 crisis. Termination of the Dual Control, however, meant a unilateral revision of the Law of Liquidation and, to be legal, would require the retroactive sanction of the powers. Given its military control of Egypt, Britain was in a position to blaze ahead and to ignore the powers—had it not been for the fact that Egypt required a substantial loan to pump-prime its economy. But third powers—France or Germany, for instance—were under no obligation to open their markets to such a loan and, as a precondition, could be expected to insist that they first approve the termination of the Dual Control.

Egypt's need for a fresh infusion of money before it could service its debt gave France—the principal victim of the abolition of the Dual Control—the opportunity to delay and even obstruct British plans for the reorganization of Egyptian finances. An international conference, convened in London between June and August 1884, came to naught. Agreement was reached only in March 1885 at a second conference, also held in London, which sanctioned an Egyptian loan of up to nine million pounds, guaranteed by the powers, and expanded the *caisse* to include a German and a Russian member.

a)   ***Khedival Decree, 2 May 1876***

. . . 1. A *Caisse* of the Public Debt is established which will receive the funds necessary to service the interest payments and the amortization of the debt and those destined exclusively for that object. . . .

—*SP*, 67:1014

b)   *Khedival Decree (Goschen-Joubert Proposals),*
18 November 1876

. . . 7. Two controllers will be named, one a controller of receipts; the other controller of the public debt. . . .

13. One of the two controllers will be English, the other French. . . .

18. The Commission of the Public Debt will be permanent until the complete amortisation of the debt. . . .

20. An English commissioner will become a member of the Commission. . . .

—*SP,* 67:1028–30

c)   *Law of Liquidation, 17 July 1880*

. . . Art. 38: The commissioners of the debt, as legal representatives of the bondholders, shall be empowered to bring suit in the Mixed Courts [*tribunaux de la réforme*] against the financial administration represented by our minister of finance in regard to the implementation of measures concerning revenue, interest on the debt, the treasury guarantee, and generally all obligations falling upon our government as a result of the present law regarding the service of the debts.

Art. 39: All of the measures of the decress of 2 May and 18 November 1876 concerning the jurisdiction of the Commission of the Public Debt which are not in violation of the present law are upheld. . . .

Art. 55: The executive council [*conseil supérieur*] will be composed of our minister of finance, two controllers, and the commissioners. . . . The executive council will be empowered to vote the budget, to accept and approve the annual accounts of the administration, to authorize loans, alienations, rents . . . , to fix the total amounts of current accounts, and to determine the investment of reserve funds. . . .

—*SP,* 71:557–75

d)   *Self-Denying Protocol of Britain, Austria-Hungary, France,*
Germany, Italy, and Russia, 25 June 1882

The governments . . . pledge . . . not to seek any territorial advantage, nor any concession of exclusive privileges, nor any commercial advantage for their subjects other than those which all other states can obtain equally.

—Hurst, 2:613–14; *SP,* 73:1179

e)   *Granville Circular, 3 January 1883*

The course of events has thrown upon Her Majesty's Government the task, which they would willingly have shared with other Powers, of suppressing the military rebellion in Egypt, and restoring peace and order in that country. The object has happily been accomplished; and although for the present a British military force remains in Egypt for the preservation of public tranquillity, Her Majesty's Government are desirous of withdrawing it as soon as the state of the country, and the organization of proper means for the Khedive's authority, will admit of it. . . .

. . . I enclose . . . a copy of a note officially delivered by the Egyptian Government to the British and French Agents in Egypt on the 7th November, containing a proposal for the abolition of the [Dual] Control. . . . Her Majesty's Government are prepared to accede to the proposal of the Egyptian Government. In this measure they earnestly desire the concurrence of France. . . .

—*PP 1883*, 83:38–40

f)   *Granville to Baring (Cromer), 4 January 1884*

. . . It is essential that in important questions affecting the administration and safety of Egypt, the advice of Her Majesty's Government should be followed, as long as the provisional occupation continues. Ministers and Governors must carry out this advice or forfeit their offices. The appointment of English ministers would be most objectionable, but it will no doubt be possible to find Egyptians who will execute the Khedive's orders under English advice. . . .

—Earl of Cromer [Sir Evelyn Baring], *Modern Egypt* (New York, 1908), 1:382

g)   *Cromer on his Position in Egypt*

. . . I never received any general instructions for my guidance during the time I held the post of British Consul-General in Egypt [1883–1907]. . . . I had not, indeed, to govern Egypt, but to assist in the government of the country without the appearance of doing so and without any legitimate authority over the agents with whom I had to deal. . . .

—Cromer, *Modern Egypt*, op. cit., 2:323–26

h)   *Gladstone to Granville, 6 January 1884*

. . . if the dilemma comes, and Egypt has no Government, will there not be a necessity of laying the matter before the powers? The Treaty of Paris still makes Egypt, as part of the Ottoman Empire, a matter of common interest and concern. It would be a grave mischief at the best to become provisionally administrators of the country: I suppose bastinadoed fellaheen would be reported to parliament at the rate of a hundred cases a week. . . .

—Agatha Ramm, *The Political Correspondence of Mr. Gladstone and Lord Granville, 1876–86,* (London, 1962), 2:1208

i)   *Bismarck to Wilhelm I, 21 August 1884*

. . . On the Egyptian Question, the Austrian minister shares my view that the legal situation remains unchanged after the London conference, that the Law of Liquidation remains binding for all powers, and that the indemnity for the bombardment of Alexandria, if it is not paid by Egypt, will have to be paid by England. . . .

—*GP*, 3:643

j)   *Herbert von Bismarck to Bismarck, 6 October 1884*

. . . the Eastern treaties are a cohesive whole: if England started unilaterally to abrogate portions of these, then other powers might follow this precedent. Moreover, England would lose all trust: this kind of practice—breaking treaties whenever these caused discomfort—might continue and would put into question the whole basis of today's state system. . . .

—*GP*, 3:694

k)   *Proceedings of the British Cabinet, 12 March 1885*

. . . it would consequently be imprudent to do anything which would practically extend our obligations in that quarter [the Sudan], as it is the entanglement of the British forces in Sudanese operations which would most powerfully tempt Russia to adopt aggressive measures [against Afghanistan].[40]

—*QV*, 2nd Series, 3:623

l)   *London Convention, 18 March 1885*

With a view to facilitate the conclusion by the Egyptian Government of a loan intended partly to provide for the Alexandria indemnities, the payment of which is especially urgent, and as regards the remainder, to settle the financial situation and secure the payment of certain extraordinary expenditure, the Governments of Great Britain, Germany, Austria-Hungary, France, Italy, Russia, and Turkey have, by common consent, agreed upon the following provisions . . . : 7. . . . [they] undertake to guarantee jointly and severally, or to ask authority from their parliaments, to guarantee jointly and severally, the regular payment of the annuity of £315,000. . . .

—*PP 1884–1885*, 88:815–35

[40]Cf. Document 9.22.

m)   **Gladstone to Granville, 1 June 1885**

. . . O for the day when we shall escape from the consequences of the original folly there.

—Ramm, *Granville,* 2:1676

9.20   **BISMARCK'S BID FOR COLONIES**

Derby to Ponsonby, 29 June 1883 • Merriman to Mills, 31 January 1884 •
Note by Bismarck, 25 May 1884 • Diary Entry by Holstein, 6 June 1884 •
Ampthill (Russell) to Granville, 16 August 1884 • Herbert von Bismarck to
Holstein, 5 September 1884 • Diary Entry by Holstein, 19 September 1884 •
Herbert von Bismarck to Bismarck, 7 March 1885 • Swaine to Sanderson,
28 March 1885

Bismarck had long turned a deaf ear to the plea of lobbyists and colonial enthusiasts that Germany too should acquire an overseas empire. In 1884, however, Bismarck changed his mind and laid the foundation for German colonies in Angra Pequeña (South-West Africa), the Cameroons, Tanganyika, and New Guinea. But several years later, his ardor now cooled, he again reversed himself. In a remark that has come to symbolize his attitude toward colonial empire, he told the German promoter Eugen Wolf in December 1888, "Your map of Africa is very nice, but my map of Africa is in Europe. Here is Russia and . . . here is France, and we are in the middle: that is my map of Africa."[39a]

Bismarck's colonial undertaking of the mid-1880s carried with it the price of considerable Anglo-German friction. The episode made a lasting impression on junior officials in the British Foreign Office, who, after attaining positions of real influence almost a quarter-century later, harked back to the Anglo-German crisis of 1884–1885 to support their contention that heavy-handedness and duplicity were hallmarks of the German style of diplomacy (Document 11.7).

This none-too-benign legacy naturally piqued the interest of historians writing in the aftermath of the First World War. Their investigations of the topic soon began to focus on Bismarck's motives and launched a scholarly debate that continued into the 1970s. Perhaps no single explanation will do justice to this issue and in a debate of such complexity the reader might be well advised to treat the interpretations of various historians not as exclusive but as complementary.

Economic determinists are likely to find Bismarck's motives in the search for markets and raw materials, and to see his quest for colonies as a belated response to the Great Depression that had gripped European economies since 1873. Historians who would give pride of place to political rather than economic processes argue that Bismarck's colonial policy was a device to cement his own power. Basic to this interpretation is the assumption that the octogenarian Wilhelm I would soon be replaced by his son and that the new emperor would pursue a liberal agenda at home, follow an Anglophile foreign policy under the tutelage of his English-born wife, and serve notice on Bismarck that the new regime no longer required his steward-

[39a]*GW* 8, p. 646.

ship. This equation would be undercut by Germany's acquisition of an overseas empire, with its attendant fallout for Anglo-German relations.

Those who believe that the European state system had its own momentum are apt to place Bismarck's colonial policy in the larger context of his European diplomacy, particularly his relations with Britain and France. For its reorganization of Egyptian finances (preceding document), Britain needed to secure the assent of the powers. France for one could be expected to jockey for a restoration of the Dual Control and perhaps a British evacuation from Egypt. The Anglo-French deadlock, it will be remembered, lasted for two and a half years. It allowed third powers—foremost Germany, ironically the power with the least direct interest in the Eastern Question—to play a pivotal role by supporting one side or the other. Bismarck was perfectly conscious that he wielded an instrument of extortion, but the Gladstone cabinet was rather slow to realize that other powers might demand or were entitled to a payback for their services.

For its part, the Gladstone government was afflicted by bureaucratic gridlock. The Foreign and Colonial Offices each marched to a different drummer and between them left unanswered for six months Bismarck's query of November 1883 as to whether Britain had a claim to Angra Pequeña—an evasion as impolitic as it was impolite. The Gladstone cabinet's search for a coherent policy was further complicated by the demands of Britain's self-governing overseas territories: German claims to South-West Africa affected the government of the Cape Colony, while German claims to New Guinea irritated the Australian governments.

a)   *Derby to Ponsonby, 29 June 1883*

. . . The Australian agents have lately come to me from their Governments, with a request that we would annex, or at least undertake the protectorate of (1) New Guinea, (2) the New Hebrides, (3) Samoa, (4) all the islands lying north and north-east of New Guinea. These last are mostly unexplored, in all bigger than France or Germany, and peopled by cannibals.

I asked them whether they did not want another planet all to themselves and they seemed to think it would be a desirable arrangement, if only feasible. The magnitude of their ideas is appalling to the English mind. . . . It is hardly too much to say that they consider the whole Southern Pacific theirs *de jure*; the French possession of New Caledonia they regard as an act of robbery committed on them. It certainly is hard for four millions of English settlers to have only a country as big as Europe to fill up. . . .

—*QV*, 2nd Series, 3:432–33

b)   *Merriman[41] to Mills,[42] 31 January 1884*

. . . Get some member [of Parliament] to put a question on the Angra Pequeña business. It is another opportunity for Lord Derby to be kicked into a reputation for statesmanlike prescience and manly firmness. We must have a Monroe Doctrine. . . .

—Phyllis Lewsen (ed.), *Selections from the Correspondence of J. X. Merriman*, 4 vols. (Capetown, 1960–1969), 1:163n

---

[41]John Xavier Merriman (1841–1926). Commissioner of crown lands and public works in the Scanlen cabinet, 1881–1884; Cape prime minister, 1908–1910.

[42]Charles Mills (1825–1895). Cape agent-general in London, 1882–1895.

c)   ### Note by Bismarck, 25 May 1884

. . . I have today admonished Count Münster no longer to speak of Helgoland,[43] because we can only articulate this kind of wish to a government which is a secure friend. This is not the case with the present English government, as is proven by [its] boundless claims against us in colonial matters: African Monroe Doctrine! Our wishes vis-a-vis Helgoland are without legal foundation and, if they were linked to our rightful overseas claims, would tarnish the justness of the latter. . . .

—*GP*, 4:742n

d)   ### Diary Entry by Holstein, 6 June 1884

. . . The colonial question, now in its early stages, may bedevil our relations with England for a considerable period, even though an actual conflict is out of the question. The problem is likely to pass over unresolved into the new reign. But should a conflict arise, no other question is so liable to put the future Empress, with her Anglophile tendencies, in a false position vis-à-vis the German nation. For it is precisely the liberals and democrats who want colonies. . . .

—*HP*, 2:155

e)   ### Ampthill (Russell) to Granville, 16 August 1884

. . . The newspaper quarrel over "Angra Pequeña" borders on the ridiculous! The *Times* lectures Bismarck for his "passing fit of ill humour"; the *Norddeutsche Allgemeine* replies that the "passing fit may become eternal as regards England"; the *National Zeitung* thinks Germany strong enough to disregard English annexations and to take what she pleases in Africa; whilst the *Standard* proposes "to return blow for blow"! All this might be amusing if it were not "too stupid." Of course Bismarck knows what he is about and he is taking advantage of a national craze that England opposes Germany's colonial aspirations, as an election cry, which may finally secure him the working majority in the coming elections. . . .

—Paul Knaplund (ed.), *Letters from the Berlin Embassy, 1871–1874, 1880–1885* (Washington, 1944),
339–40

f)   ### Herbert von Bismarck to Holstein, 5 September 1884

. . . I am entirely of your opinion, we must for the moment at all costs make common cause with France and against Gladstone, until he is brought down.

—*HP*, 3:124

[43]Bismarck had proposed that Britain might consider ceding that North Sea island to Germany as part of a larger territorial swap. See Document 10.3.

g)   *Diary Entry by Holstein, 19 September 1884*

Prince Bismarck told Tsar Alexander in Skierniewice that the sole aim of German colonial policy was to drive a wedge between the Crown Prince and England. The Tsar, who had just been saying how anxious he was about the fate of Russo-German relations after the death of Kaiser Wilhelm, remarked: "Voilà qui est intelligent." I think for my part that all this colonial policy was undertaken simply as an election stunt. . . . Prince Bismarck said recently . . . : "All this colonial business is a fraud, but we need it for the elections. . . . "

—*HP,* 2:161

h)   *Herbert von Bismarck to Bismarck, 7 March 1885*

. . . after our earlier substantial assistance in Egypt, we expected England's willing co-operation in colonial matters. To our disappointment we got nothing but words. Therefore we found it necessary to exert pressure on England in a place where it is vulnerable, to get it to realize what difference German friendship or hostility can make. . . .

—*GP,* 4:760

i)   *Swaine[44] to Sanderson,[45] 28 March 1885*

. . . Germany though generally represented by us allegorically as a student drinking beer we should be making a great mistake if we consequently handled her à la student in our dealings with her. Far from being as rough in her feelings as she appears outwardly when represented drinking & smoking, she in reality has all the delicate little vanities of a woman, & the Englishman who deals with the German should be a veritable Don Juan in his delightful & insinuating manner, & in irresistible powers of persuasion. . . .

—Knaplund, *Berlin Embassy,* op. cit., 393–94

9.21   THE BERLIN WEST AFRICA CONFERENCE AND ITS AFTERMATH

General Act of the Berlin West Africa Conference, 25 February 1885 • *Charter of the National African Company, 10 July 1886* • *Charter of the Imperial British East Africa Company, 3 September 1888* • *Charter of the British South Africa Company, 29 October 1889*

In their scramble for colonies, concessions, and protectorates in Africa, the imperialist powers advanced a myriad of conflicting territorial claims. Perhaps because the confusion was so

[44]Leopold V. Swaine (1840–1931). English major-general; military attaché in Berlin, 1882–1889; 1891–1896.

[45]Sir Thomas H. Sanderson (1841–1923). Private secretary to Granville, 1880–1885; permanent under-secretary in the Foreign Office, 1894–1906. See also Document 11.7.

widespread, the powers had little trouble in agreeing that they needed criteria by which their claims could be evaluated and settled. Negotiating these criteria became the task of a conference convened in Berlin between November 1884 and February 1885. The Berlin conference dealt primarily with the Niger and Congo river basins and laid down some general guidelines for claims on the African coastline. The division of the interior was left for the powers to settle among themselves, and the student of the partition of Africa should think of this phenomenon as a process that took over twenty years to complete: in West Africa, for instance, English and French border commissions were at work as late as 1906, while in East Africa the borders between the Belgian, German, and British possessions were finalized only in 1910.

The positions taken by the European powers at the Berlin conference have to be appreciated in the context of other pending issues. When the conference convened, France's quarrel with Britain over the latter's abolition of the Dual Control in Egypt had not yet been composed (Document 9.19); the Anglo-German dispute over German colonial claims continued to simmer (Document 9.20); and Russia's advance in Turkmenistan made Anglo-Russian relations unpredictable (Document 9.22). It is little wonder then that Britain was particularly vulnerable and that the conference became a showcase for the Franco-German entente so assiduously promoted by Bismarck and the French premier Jules Ferry.

More important from an African point of view was that the Berlin conference provided European governments with an impetus to sponsor chartered companies for the penetration of the interior of the continent and for the exploitation of the new colonies. Although these companies formally eschewed commercial monopolies, in practice their powers were vast—an atavistic reminder of the mercantilist practices of the seventeenth and eighteenth centuries. The most notorious of these enterprises, the *Association Internationale du Congo* (in reality neither an association, nor international, nor actually responsible to the Belgian government, but a front for the greed of the Belgian king Leopold II), actually predated the conference and, on its sidelines, secured recognition as the representative of a sovereign Congo Free State. But in the wake of the conference, other chartered companies—soon instrumental in shaping the fortunes of large tracts of the African interior—were founded: the Royal Niger Company, the Imperial British East Africa Company, Cecil Rhodes's British South Africa Company, and a host of similar French and German ventures, albeit on a smaller scale.[46]

a)   *General Act of the Berlin West Africa Conference, 25 February 1885*

... Art. 34: Any Power which henceforth takes possession of a tract of land on the coasts of the African continent outside of its present possessions, or which, being hitherto without such possessions, shall acquire them, as well as the Power which assumes a Protectorate there, shall accompany the respective act with notification thereof addressed to the other Signatory Powers of the present Act, in order to enable them, if need be, to make good any claims of their own.

Art. 35: The Signatory Powers of the Present Act recognize the obligation to

---

[46]For an illustration of how this system of concessions operated in practice, see the map of French Equatorial Africa reproduced in L. H. Gann and Peter Guignan (eds.), *Colonialism in Africa, 1870–1960* (Cambridge, 1969), 1:188, or Roland Oliver and G. N. Sanderson (eds.), *The Cambridge History of Africa* (Cambridge, 1985), 6:306.

insure the establishment of authority in regions occupied by them on the coasts of the African Continent sufficient to protect existing rights, and, as the case may be, freedom of trade and of transit under the conditions agreed upon. . . .

—Hertslet II, 2:468–87

b)   *Charter of the National African Company, 10 July 1886*

[Preamble:] . . . the Kings, Chiefs, and peoples of various territories in the basin of the River Niger, in Africa, fully recognizing, after many years' experience, the benefits accorded to their countries by their intercourse with the Company and their predecessors, have ceded the whole of their respective territories to the Company. . . .

[Art. 1:] . . . [the Company] is hereby authorized and empowered to hold and retain the full benefit of the several cessions aforesaid, or any of them, and all rights, interests, authorities, and powers for the purposes of government, preservation of public order, protection of the said territories, or otherwise of what nature or kind soever, under or by virtue thereof, or resulting therefrom, and ceded to or vested in the Company in, over, or affecting the territories, lands, or property in the neighborhood of the same, and to hold, use, enjoy, and exercise the same territories, lands, property, rights, interests, authorities, and powers. . . .

—Hertslet II, 1:125–27; *SP*, 77:1022–29 (full text)

c)   *Charter of the Imperial British East Africa Company,*
3 September 1888

[Art. 1:] . . . [the Company] is hereby authorized and empowered to hold and retain the full benefit of the several Grants, Concessions, Agreements, and Treaties [thereafter as for National African Company above]. . . .

—Hertslet II, 1:345–50; *SP*, 79:641–50 (full text)

d) *Charter of the British South Africa Company, 29 October 1889*

[Art. 1:] The principal field of the operations of the British South Africa Company . . . shall be the region of South Africa lying immediately to the north of British Bechuanaland, and to the north and west of the South African Republic, and to the west of the Portuguese Dominions. . . .

[Art. 20:] Nothing in Our Charter shall be deemed to authorize the Company to set up or grant any monopoly of trade; provided that the establishment of or the grant of concessions for banks, railways, tramways, docks, telegraphs, waterworks, or other similar undertakings or the establishment of any system of patent or copyright approved by Our Secretary of State, shall not be deemed monopolies for this purpose. . . .

[Additional Conditions, 5 March/2 April 1891:] The Charter of the British South Africa Company shall extend over the territory under British influence north of the

Zambesi and south of the territories of the Congo Free State and the German sphere
[except Nyasaland]. . . .

—Hertslet II, 1:271–79; *Hertslet's Commercial Treaties*, 18:133–43 (full text)

9.22   **THE PENDJEH CRISIS, 1885**

*Gladstone's Notes of a Cabinet Meeting, 24 March 1885 • Gladstone to
Queen Victoria, 25 March 1885 • Diary Entry by Hamilton, 25 April 1885 •
Granville to Gladstone, 26 April 1885 • Queen Victoria to Granville,
28 April 1885 • The Duke of Argyll in the House of Lords, 11/12 May 1885 •
Dufferin to Churchill, 30 July 1885 • Currie to Herbert von Bismarck and
Salisbury, 4 August 1885 • Directive by Bismarck, 13 November 1885 •
Hatzfeldt to Herbert von Bismarck, 5 December 1885*

The establishment of a Russian protectorate over Merv in 1884 and a subsequent skirmish
between Russian and Afghan forces at Pendjeh seemed to open the way for a Russian advance on Herat, an area that the Amir of Afghanistan considered part of his dominions. A
Russian presence in western Afghanistan, however, would have jeopardized British efforts to
position this country as a buffer separating Russian Central Asia from British India and the
Persian Gulf.

The diplomatic showdown between Britain and Russia over Pendjeh and Herat commenced in earnest in March 1885. The quarrel was remarkable for the speed with which it
was settled, though the Anglo-Russian compromise struck on 10 September 1885[47] came too
late to shore up Gladstone's government and was concluded by a Conservative cabinet under Salisbury. The crisis may have been short, but its intensity can be judged by a stray remark of the Duke of Argyll (who confessed to "Mervousness"),[47a] by the British seizure of Port
Hamilton off the South Korean coast as an advance base for operations against the Russian
Maritime Province, and by the willingness of parliament to vote the government a credit of
eleven million pounds (10 percent of the annual budget) to be utilized in the event of mobilization.

The Pendjeh crisis showed how the "men on the spot" could increase the discomfiture of
metropolitan governments by creating faits accomplis; illustrates the "carrot-and-stick" approach by which an imperialist crisis might be resolved; and underscored the risks, even for
Britain, of alienating too many Great Powers at once.

a)   ***Gladstone's Notes of a Cabinet Meeting, 24 March 1885***

. . . 2. . . . c) Acquaint Russia in substance—her going against Herat will be a *casus
belli*. . . .

—H. C. G. Matthew (ed.), *The Gladstone Diaries* (Oxford, 1968–1994), 11:312

[47] Text of Anglo-Russian protocol in *PP 1885*, 87:75–76 [= new pagination, 314–16] (C. 4389).
[47a]H. C. G. Matthew, *The Gladstone Diaries* (Oxford, 1968–1994), 10:lxvi.

b)   *Gladstone to Queen Victoria, 25 March 1885*

. . . The Cabinet also thought that Lord Granville should communicate with the Russian Ambassador and point out to him the necessary consequence of any design upon Herat, in bringing about a case of war between the two countries, according to the policy of the British Empire, as it has now been understood and established for nearly half a century: maintaining at the same time an unbroken friendliness of tone with respect to the proposed negotiation for an Afghan frontier.

—*QV*, 2nd Series, 3:630

c)   *Diary Entry by Hamilton,*[48] *25 April 1885*

. . . This Central Asian question, like many other questions, would never have given rise to present difficulties had the Government looked ahead a little more in time. But the fact is the interests of the Empire are so diverse that Ministers can only live on a "hand to mouth" policy. They can merely deal with burning questions. They have not the time to attend to those that do no more than smoulder. This is a very serious matter; and one which will become more and more aggravated as time goes on. . . .

—Dudley W. R. Bahlman (ed.), *The Diary of Sir Edward Walter Hamilton* (Oxford, 1972), 2:848

d)   *Granville to Gladstone, 26 April 1885*

We have announced to the Chinese, Japanese & the Coreans, that we have occupied temporarily Port Hamilton. . . .

—Ramm, *Granville*, 2:1639

e)   *Queen Victoria to Granville, 28 April 1885*

. . . [The Queen] thinks nothing but firmness will do with Russia. The danger of delay, if we cannot agree, is very serious. We are without friends. Mr. Gladstone has alienated all other countries from us, by his very changeable and unreliable policy—unintentionally no doubt. . . .

—*QV*, 2nd Series, 3:643

[48]Sir Edward Walter Hamilton (1847–1908). Private secretary to Gladstone, 1880–1885.

f)   *The Duke of Argyll in the House of Lords, 11/12 May 1885*

. . . We are about to enter upon a great General Election under entirely new conditions as regards the constituencies of this country.[49] I do not wish to make any forecast as to the effect of the new democracy upon the foreign policy of this country; but this I must say—that democracies are not generally of an eminently pacific character. They are not, perhaps, so inclined to undertake wars for ambition as great conquering sovereigns; but, on the other hand, they are more apt to get into war out of mere sentiment and emotion. . . . There is one great comfort I find with regard to these advances of Russia—namely, that our own annexations during that period have been far larger, far richer, far more important. . . . The real truth of the matter is this—and it is a very formidable one—we have lost in Asia our hitherto insular position. We hardly realize in this country how completely hitherto our position has been insular, not only in England, but all over the world. . . .

—*Parl. Debates*, 3rd Series, 298:111, 118–19, 305

g)   *Dufferin[50] to Churchill,[51] 30 July 1885*

. . . I have often had misgivings as to the wisdom of the engagements into which we entered with the Amir under the auspices of my predecessor. . . . [52] Under this stipulation, we are bound to assist the Amir to the best of our ability, though in whatever manner we may think expedient, in the event of the integrity of his dominions being threatened by a foreign power. Now, what are his dominions? A range of thinly populated and open frontier many hundred miles in length, destitute of strategical positions, and of defenders skilful enough to use them to advantage if they did exist, exposed at all points to the excursions of every neighbor. . . . Even supposing that the ruler himself were to prove as docile and subservient as we could desire, his subjects consist of a conglomeration of divided and insubordinate tribes, or else of subservient and alien races hating his rule, and ready to welcome the first comer who will advance to their liberation, while most of the subordinates through whom he administers his provinces are either incompetent, disobedient, corrupt, or disloyal, and sometimes all these things at once. . . . It would be a thousand pities if, through any impatience or unreasonable demands, we should revive the bitter ill-feeling between ourselves and the Afghans which successive invasions of their country have very naturally created, but which might, by skilful management on our part, be made readily to disappear. We have everything to gain and nothing to lose by being friends with

---

[49]A reference to the Franchise Act of 1884, which had increased the British electorate from about three to about five million.

[50]Frederick Blackwood, Marquess of Dufferin (1826–1902). British ambassador in Constantinople, 1881–1884; viceroy of India, 1884–1888.

[51]Lord Randolph Churchill (1849–1895). Secretary for India in Salisbury's cabinet, 1885–1886.

[52]Ripon to Amir Abd al-Rahman, 16 June 1883; text in Hurewitz, 1:431.

them, whereas their declared enmity and their cooperation with Russia would force upon us a policy which, though perhaps not disadvantageous in its ultimate result, should, if possible, be avoided, or at all events be postponed to the last moment, on account of the fierce political controversies it would excite in England, as well as on account of the great strain it would impose on our resources here. . . .

—Lowe, *Reluctant Imperialists*, 312–14

b) Currie[53] to Herbert von Bismarck and Salisbury, 4 August 1885

. . . In order to avert this calamity [of an Anglo-Russian collision], the only plan seems to be to make an appeal to Prince Bismarck to mediate between the two countries. . . . If he were to effect this, he would secure for himself and his country the lasting gratitude of England, and he would be laying the foundations of a closer and more intimate alliance between the two countries. . . .

—Rose L. Greaves, *Persia and the Defence of India, 1884–92: A Study in the Foreign Policy of the Third Marquis of Salisbury* (London, 1959), 240–41

i)   Directive by Bismarck, 13 November 1885

. . . Lord Salisbury should not interpret it as a lack of courtesy towards England if, given our geographic location in Europe and our historical experience, we above all sought to prevent European coalitions against us. Lord Salisbury says that he has to take into account English public opinion in the making of his foreign policy: exactly this reason makes it difficult for us to calculate with any certainty England's policy in the future. [This results from] Gladstone's attempt—contrary to all English tradition—to incline towards France and Russia against Germany and Austria, without provocation from the latter powers. . . . The possibility of a sudden change in the English position must make us very cautious. . . .

—GP, 4:787

j)   Hatzfeldt[53a] to Herbert von Bismarck, 5 December 1885[54]

. . . [Lord Randolph Churchill's] wish, as you know, is an alliance with Germany. . . . "Between the two of us we could have ruled the world [*not good enough*]. But you didn't want to." I tried to explain to him that no German statesman could risk incurring the enmity of Russia and also a French attack. . . . [Also] in what position would

---

[53] Sir Philip Currie (1834–1906). Assistant under-secretary in the Foreign Office.
[53a] Paul von Hatzfeldt (1831–1901). German ambassador in London, 1885–1901.
[54] With annotation by Bismarck.

we be if the chancellor, as a result of his correspondence with Salisbury, entered into an alliance and then Gladstone will be returned to power after the upcoming elections? . . .

—GP, 4:788

9.23   BATTENBERG IN BULGARIA

Battenberg's Notes of a Conversation with Bismarck, 12 May 1884 ● *Queen Victoria to Battenberg, 4 September 1886* ● *Battenberg to Queen Victoria, 6 September 1886* ● *Diary Entry by Holstein, 31 March 1888*

The election as prince of Bulgaria of Alexander of Battenberg, a descendant of a branch line of the house of Hesse-Darmstadt but also a cousin of Tsar Alexander III and a one-time officer in the Russian army, seemed to confirm Russia's preponderance in the new Balkan quasi state. But soon after arriving in Bulgaria, Battenberg showed that he had no intention of slavishly following Russian directives and raised the specter, from the Russian point of view, that he would altogether take Bulgaria out of the Russian orbit.

Further aggravating tensions between Battenberg and his Russian patrons was the fact that the prince, only twenty-two at the time of his election in 1879, was one of Europe's most eligible bachelors. Both Queen Victoria and her eldest daughter, Crown Princess Victoria of Germany, sought to interest Battenberg (who went by the nickname of "Sandro" at the English court) in the hand of the latter's sixteen-year-old daughter, also named Victoria. Whether the two elder Victorias promoted the marriage because of a lack of imagination—Battenberg's second brother Henry married Queen Victoria's youngest daughter in 1885; his oldest brother Louis married one of her granddaughters in 1884—is difficult to say, but from a Russian perspective, the marriage project was likely to draw Bulgaria into Queen Victoria's web of dynastic diplomacy, thereby transforming it before long into a British satellite.

Battenberg now found the way paved with difficulties. After an insurrection in Eastern Rumelia allowed Battenberg to fuse this province with Bulgaria in 1885, Russia—reversing the stand that it took at the Congress of Berlin when it had agreed only reluctantly to the separation of these two territories—proved a formidable adversary. Russian hostility to Battenberg culminated in his kidnapping by Russian agents in August 1886. Although an international outcry forced his abductors to return him to Bulgaria, Battenberg by now had had quite enough and abdicated voluntarily.

In Germany, the Battenberg marriage project was kept alive by Victoria during the ninety-nine-day reign of her husband, Friedrich III. But Friedrich was already terminally ill with throat cancer when he ascended the throne, and shortly after his death, Wilhelm II, now head of the Hohenzollern dynasty, forbade the marriage. Princess Victoria consoled herself by marrying the elderly prince of Schaumburg-Lippe and took up residence in Bonn. Never quite able to extricate herself from the lure of things Bulgarian, Victoria, several years after the prince's death, became infatuated with a Bulgarian exotic dancer, who gambled away most of her fortune at the gaming tables. Her villa in Bonn, the Palais Schaumburg, has, since 1949, housed the offices of the German chancellor.

The documents below show the keen interest of the two Victorias in Battenberg. They also show Bismarck's determination not to have the Battenberg problem cloud his relationship with Russia. Bismarck no doubt derived genuine pleasure from frustrating the plans of the crown princess, one of his most dedicated and dangerous opponents. Nor were Battenberg's chances of a sympathetic hearing from the German chancellor helped by the fact that the rumors of his romance first reached Bismarck at the height of his colonial quarrel with Britain—the very moment when his struggle against the crown prince and crown princess was at its height (Document 9.20).

a)   *Battenberg's Notes of a Conversation with Bismarck, 12 May 1884*

. . . I, as Imperial Chancellor, have informed His Majesty [Wilhelm I] that Germany has no interest in Bulgaria, our interest is: peace with Russia. To insure that, it is absolutely necessary that Russia is convinced that we have no interests in the Near East. On the day a Prussian princess becomes Princess of Bulgaria, Russia will become suspicious and will no longer believe this assurance, hence this marriage would interfere with my political plans. This I will not allow and I have informed His Majesty that so long as I am chancellor, this marriage will not take place. . . . I would advise you to marry an Orthodox millionairess; that would stabilize your position in Bulgaria, for ruling in the East means greasing palms and that requires money. There, one can't get anywhere with morals. Anyhow, I think it is time you made up your mind whether you are German or Bulgarian. Up to now you have been a German, but that will lead to your exit. If I were in your place I too might have remained a German, for I can understand that it must be repugnant to an honest, upright character like yours to have to deal with Levantines. But if you wish to remain in Bulgaria you must throw yourself at Russia's mercy: if you need to, take an anti-German position! In any case I consider the permanent existence of Bulgaria to be problematical. Some day it will become an object for compensations, and sooner or later—but the day will certainly come—you will sit by the fireside and remember your stormy youth. . . . I myself have high regard for you, but I am the chancellor of forty-five million Germans whose interests I cannot sacrifice for one individual German. . . .

—Egon Caesar Corti, *Alexander von Battenberg: Sein Kampf mit den Zaren und Bismarck*
(Vienna, 1920), 165–67

b)   *Queen Victoria to Battenberg, 4 September 1886*

I have not the words to describe my feelings and deep worry since that horrible 21st of August! Your parents could not have been more worried and afraid than I; and no one rejoiced more than I, when, on the third day, the news of the counterrevolution arrived telling of the close, warm devotion of your people and the great enthusiasm everywhere.

But how much you, poor dear Sandro, must have suffered—emotionally more than physically. My indignation and anger against your barbaric, Asiatic-like, tyrannical cousin are so great that I cannot trust myself to write about them. He has, however, damaged himself, thank God! and in Germany, Austria (particularly there) and, of course, here the horror is tremendous. My government will try everything to influence the powers against Russia and for you. . . .

—Corti, *Battenberg*, op. cit., 165–67

c)   ***Battenberg to Queen Victoria, 6 September 1886***

. . . My remaining any longer would only cause a civil war, as, being betrayed by all, I could only maintain myself by suspending the constitution and decreeing summary executions. As soon, however, as blood flows, Russia will yield to public opinion, and occupy Bulgaria, which Europe will not be able to prevent. My only choice, therefore, is to abdicate of my free will. . . .

—*QV*, 3rd Series, 1:200

d)   ***Diary Entry by Holstein, 31 March 1888***

The Battenberg struggle is in full swing. When the chancellor arrived at Charlottenburg [palace] today for an audience, the Kaiser [Friedrich III] told him (or wrote down) that he wished to give Battenberg an army post and confer on him the *Pour le Mérite,* as the first of several measures he had in mind for the prince.

The chancellor explained to him that such a procedure would strain our relations with Russia so severely that he would refuse to accept the responsibility; he, the chancellor, would resign if that happened. The Kaiser gave in and instructed Radolinski to send Battenberg a telegram requesting him not to come here the day after tomorrow as arranged. The Kaiserin, who had been waiting at the door for the chancellor to go, came in just as Radolinski was receiving these instructions. Then the sparks flew. "But that's outrageous, it will be the death of my poor child," and so on. The poor helpless Kaiser wrote down: "I cannot plunge this country into a war with Russia on account of her marriage." She became more and more violent. Radolinski said to her: "But, Your Majesty, I implore you to think of the Kaiser's health." She did not even hear him, she kept talking. The Kaiser rent his clothes, wept, tore his hair, gasped for breath, but stood firm about Battenberg's visit. . . .

—*HP*, 2:366

9.24   **THE BOULANGIST PHENOMENON**

Paul Deroulède's Preface to Avant la bataille, *1886* •
Boulanger in the Chamber, 4 June 1888

The domestic backlash in France against the policy of accommodation with Germany pursued by the Freycinet and Ferry governments went hand in hand with the growth of the *Ligue des patriots,* a right-wing lobby as anti-German as it was critical of the constitutional order of the Third Republic. Headed by Paul Deroulède (1846–1914), popular poet and protégé of Gambetta, the league became an umbrella group for a wide cluster of patriotic organizations and sponsored a lively nationalist agitation.

The league's most visible contribution to the politics of the Third Republic was its promotion of the career of General Georges Boulanger. Boulanger, minister for war from January

1886 to May 1887, came to personify the spirit of revanche so assiduously stoked by the *Ligue des patriots*. The dashing figure he cut on a black charger at the military review on Bastille day in 1886 set him apart from his drab colleagues—his appearance may have bordered on exhibitionism, but it made him a household name almost overnight. While Boulanger was lionized by an adoring public, his fellow ministers became increasingly concerned about the possibility of a coup organized by him and his followers. Upon the formation of a new government by Maurice Rouvier in May 1887, Boulanger was excluded from the cabinet, reassigned to garrison duty, and ultimately even relieved of his command.

The last decision hardly put an end to the Boulangist specter, for the general was now free to seek election to the chamber. From the floor of parliament, Boulanger launched unsparing attacks on the government. The insults traded between him and the prime minister, Charles Floquet, on 12 July 1888, led the two men to fight a duel the next morning. The wound inflicted on Boulanger by the elderly but agile civilian might have derailed his career, but Boulanger's popularity continued to surge. He capped his political rise in January 1889 by winning a seat from the Seine prefecture (i.e., Paris), hitherto deemed a republican and radical bastion. Although his followers had apparently prepared the ground for a coup d'état in the event of his victory in this by-election, Boulanger failed to seize the moment and instead spent the night with his lover, Marguerite de Bonnemains. The phenonemon that had gripped France for three years thus began to unravel: evading an official investigation, Boulanger fled France in April 1889 and, in a gesture befitting his flair for the melodramatic, killed himself two years later on the grave of his mistress.

The first passage below is from Paul Deroulède's preface to the book *Avant la bataille*, published by Hippolyte Barthélemy, another disciple of Gambetta, in April 1886. Its title, "before the battle," in itself suggested a program.

a) *Paul Deroulède's Preface to* Avant la bataille, *1886*

. . . Governments, preoccupied above all with maintaining their impotent power, accept all advice, hasten to comply with all orders, propose all surrenders, flaunt their deference, care as little about the revival so necessary to us as they care about our vital dignity. . . .

Oh! chief heretics of the Fatherland! with what satisfied nods do they reveal to you their dogmas:"All bloodshed is murder. War is barbarism, repudiated by all intelligent democracies. Germany and France have common interests that make their rapprochement useful and necessary. What good is it to nurture dangerous hatreds? Let time heal all wounds."

. . . These partisans of slavery cloak themselves in the veils of wisdom and the mantle of humanity. Let us uncover their shameful ideas, let us articulate for them what they perhaps do not dare to say themselves:"France should stay defeated; bloodshed will not change anything; democracy is incapable of valor; it is dangerous to hate what one cannot defeat; shame that has been forgotten is not shameful." These are surely their secret blasphemies. . . .

Yes, surely, the rapprochement of France and Germany is necessary, but by arms; yes, certainly, it will be useful and productive, but through victory. . . . If then a war of revenge is only a war of honor and of [national] interest, then it should be necessary to pursue it for national interest and honor. But it is also a war of justice.

With what heart could we leave that million and half of our fellow citizens in the hands of the enemy in contradiction of all that is right, dispossessed by the cruelest injustice?. . . In staying faithful to our grief; in keeping intact and permanent the claim to Alsace and Lorraine; in rejecting and repelling any possible alliance between victorious Prussia and mutilated France; in exposing with rightful indignation this military complacence that will make us the lackeys of tyrants; we not only act as a brake on the shame of our Fatherland, but on the division of the world.

—Hippolyte Barthélemy, *Avant la bataille* (Paris, 1886)

b)   *Boulanger in the Chamber, 4 June 1888*

[Boulanger:] France grows weary to the point of disgust with a regime that is only empty agitation, disorder, corruption, lies and sterility. It must be reformed, and it will be reformed by transforming the seat of power from top to bottom [commotion]. . . . Such are the fundamental points, I believe. . . [laughter]

[from various benches:] "I!" Always "I!"

[Pelletan:][55] This is a symphony in "I-major!"

[Boulanger:] . . . on which revision of the constitution should rest. . . . And France, with stable and regular governments finally restored . . . [exclamations and prolonged commotion].

[From the left]: Order! Order!

[Pelletan:] That's how they argue abroad. You talk like Tisza![56]

[Floquet:] Go to Berlin to say that!

[Goblet:][57] Don't talk that way! Those are not the words of a Frenchman. . . .

[Boulanger:] Then France, strong in its military institutions which themselves have been brought peacefully to the last degree of perfection, [can] at the same time offer foreign governments the continuity and steadiness [exclamations] . . .

[Goblet:] Don't touch on these questions [stirring on the right]. . . .

[Boulanger:] . . . which are the beginning of long and fruitful ententes: France, honored and powerful, would find itself to be the surest guarantor of peace, which is her most ardent vow and her foremost need, and by this alone she would give others an awareness of the perils of aggression. These reforms, as desirable and pressing as they appear to be, cannot be realized by the present Parliament. They should be the work of a constituent assembly charged by the nation with an express mandate. . . .

—*Annales de la Chambre des Députés: 1888*, 3 [n.s. 25]:446–49

9.25   THE BISMARCKIAN SYSTEM UNDER ATTACK: KATKOV

Katkov in the Moscow Vedomostei, *7/19 March 1887* •
Schweinitz to Bismarck, 2 September 1887

Within Russia, the most dedicated opponent of alliance with Germany and Austria-Hungary was Mikhail N. Katkov, editor of the influential Moscow *Vedomostei*. Though on previous

---

[55]Camille Pelletan (1846–1915). Radical journalist and deputy.
[56]Kálmán Tisza von Borosjenö (1830–1902). Hungarian prime minister, 1875–1890.
[57]René Goblet (1828–1905). Foreign minister in the Floquet cabinet, 1888–1889.

occasions Katkov had enjoyed the patronage of Tsar Alexander III, his editorial of 7/19 March 1887 aroused the tsar's ire. Only a few weeks earlier, a leak from within the Russian foreign ministry had allowed Katkov to publish the terms of the Three Emperors' League; now, his editorial attacked Russia's ties to Berlin and Vienna, pilloried its foreign policy establishment, implicitly criticized its concessions in Bulgaria, and insinuated that Russia ought to improve its relations with France.

The excerpt below reveals Katkov not as much a Pan-Slav as a champion of a specific Russian mission on behalf of Eastern Orthodoxy. But what made Katkov dangerous, from Bismarck's perspective, was that his articles, holding out as they did the expectation of a change in Russia's foreign policy, provided fodder for French revanchists. Equally disturbing were the contacts which Katkov maintained with Paul Deroulède. For his part, Deroulède paid his last respects to Katkov by traveling to Moscow to attend Katkov's funeral in August 1887.

a)   *Katkov in the Moscow* **Vedomostei,** *7/19 March 1887*

. . . Russia has been losing its identity as an independent power. It has been pushed out of the East [Balkans] step by step. Meanwhile, there appeared signs of Russia's intent to escape from this predicament . . . which has been so detrimental to Russia's vital interests. These signs were that Russia intended to restore its freedom, to establish equally good relations with all European powers while staying free of secret conspiracies. . . . Our allies used everything imaginable—cajolery and lures, cheating and sophistry, a charade of principles, psychological pressure, the cosmopolitan orientation of our diplomacy, the illiteracy of our politics, and the threat of [hostile] coalitions. . . . We see with great concern that, due to the Three Emperors' League, Russia's authority was shaken; that its policies, injurious to Russia, and to which Russia contributed on its own, alienated from Russia those countries for whose independence Russia shed so much of its own blood—an independence dear to Russia, provided this independence is in harmony with and not in opposition to Russia's interests. The co-religious peoples of the East are part of the same system [of beliefs] as Russia and can preserve the very foundations of their national existence only in close alliance with Russia. Russia can restore its importance in the East only by being itself. . . .

—M. N. Katkov, *Sobranie Peredovykh Statei Moskovskikh Vedomostei: 1887g.* (Moscow, 1898), 124–26

b)   *Schweinitz[58] to Bismarck, 2 September 1887[59]*

. . . But neither the love of peace nor, more generally, the personal attributes of the Tsar can remove the justifiable mistrust which is caused by the insincerity of Russian policy—a policy which is determined not by a government certain of its goals, but is influenced by eddies and countercurrents far more so than in most constitutionally governed states. These can have a lasting quality and can be dangerous, long before the monarch recognizes and corrects them; this is something which the experience

[58]Hans Lothar von Schweinitz (1822–1901). Prussian general; German ambassador in Petersburg, 1876–1892.
[59]With marginalia by Bismarck.

with Katkov taught us. One question is whether the will of the tsar, in the future, will suffice to stem forces more profound than mere journalism. His predecessor, in the fall of 1876, did not prevail.

A peculiar phenomenon, which sets Russia apart from party politics in other states, is that in Russia civil servants and government employees work against the government's very own policy [*as was the case with us before 1848*]. There is no unitary or homogenous ministry, functioning under a prime minister [*nor does this exist here*]; there are only ministers who [individually] solicit the Emperor's permission on important matters, often without the knowledge of their colleagues. This explains why one bureaucracy can come to oppose another. . . .

—*GP*, 6:1216

9.26   RENEWAL OF THE TRIPLE ALLIANCE, FEBRUARY 1887

German-Italian Treaty, 20 February 1887

The Triple Alliance was renewed in 1887, 1891, 1902, and 1912. The supplementary articles inserted in 1887 make interesting reading in light of Bismarck's diplomacy toward France and Russia in the course of that year: in William L. Langer's judgment, "the Italian-German pact [of 1887] . . . changed the very nature of the alliance, for it transformed what was a strictly defensive treaty into one with a distinct offensive tinge."[60] But these articles became integral parts of the treaty text in subsequent renewals of the alliance. Used by Italy to fortify its claim to Libya, they created not a little embarrassment for Germany and Austria-Hungary in 1911, when Italy provoked war with the Ottoman Empire to seize this North African province (Document 11.14).

German-Italian Treaty, 20 February 1887

Art. 1:[61] The High Contracting Parties, having in mind only the maintenance, so far, as possible, of the territorial status quo in the Orient, engage to use their influence to forestall, on the Ottoman coasts and islands in the Adriatic and Aegean Seas, any territorial modification which might be injurious to one or the other of the powers signatory to the present Treaty. . . .

Art. 3:[62] If it were to happen that France should make a move to extend her occupation, or even her protectorate or her sovereignty, under any form whatsoever, in the North African territories, *whether in the Vilayet of Tripoli or in the Moroccan sultanate*[63] and that in consequence thereof Italy, in order to safeguard her position in the Mediterranean, should feel that she must herself undertake action in the said North African territories, or even have recourse to extreme measures in French territory in Europe, the state of war which would thereby ensue between Italy and France

---

[60]*Alliances and Alignments*, 395.
[61]Identical to article VI of the Triple Alliance of 1891, 1902, 1912.
[62]Identical to article X of the Triple Alliance of 1891, 1902, 1912.
[63]The phrase in italics was omitted in 1891 and thereafter.

would constitute *ipso facto*, on the demand of Italy and at the common charge of the two Allies, the *casus foederis* with all the effects foreseen by Article 2 and 4 of the aforesaid Treaty of 20 May 1882 as if such an eventuality were expressly contemplated therein. . . .

—Hurst, 2:641–43, Pribram, 1:111–15

9.27 FIRST "MEDITERRANEAN ENTENTE," FEBRUARY 1887

Italian Note to the British Government, 12 February 1887 ● *British Note to the Italian Government, 12 February 1887* ● *Spanish Note to Italy, 4 May 1887*

The aloofness, and hence isolation, of Britain from the European alliance system was modified by an Anglo-Italian exchange of notes in February 1887, to which Austria acceded in March and Spain in May.

This "Mediterranean entente" needs to be understood in the broad context of the international fault lines of the late 1880s. The specter of Boulangism had revived Franco-German frictions (Document 9.24); Katkov's brand of Pan-Slavism strained Russia's relations with Germany and Austria-Hungary (Document 9.25); in the ongoing Bulgarian crisis, Russia's interests clashed with those of Austria-Hungary and Britain (Document 9.23); and the Egyptian problem continued to define the Anglo-French antagonism (Document 9.19). The question was how these conflicts would intersect and how they might coalesce into a pattern of alignments among the powers. The sum of these issues seemed to divide the powers into two groups—on one hand, Britain and the Triple Alliance; on the other, France and Russia. But this is too facile an equation: it needs to be rethought in light of, first, Bismarck's refusal to join any anti-Russian coalition (while being content to promote such a grouping among others) and, second, the tsar's deep misgivings about making common cause with that fount of political radicalism, the French republic.

The commitments undertaken in the Anglo-Italian-Austrian exchange of notes fell far short of the much more specific obligations which were a feature of the other alliances of the 1880s. Indeed, the vagueness of the notes made them so elastic that they could be defined or redefined as it suited the signatories, but—despite this defect—the new alignment nonetheless signaled an intent to act in certain contingencies. The Mediterranean entente confirmed Austria's abandonment of the Three Emperors' League and its drift into the British camp—a change in the diplomatic lineup that from the British vantage point translated into a net gain. In return, Austria received an assurance of some form of support in the Near East, an area in which—as Bismarck had made clear again and again—it could expect no backing from Germany.

Britain was now aligned, however vaguely, with two of the powers of the Triple Alliance. Most important from the British perspective, the Mediterranean entente provided a modicum of support against Russia in the event that the Bulgarian crisis flared up again, and against France, which obstructed ongoing Anglo-Ottoman negotiations defining the terms of the British occupation of Egypt.[64] In fact, the Anglo-Italian note had an anti-French origin, resting

---

[64]The draft convention—concluded on 22 May 1887 and named after Sir Henry Drummond Wolff, the British negotiator—was abandoned by the sultan under pressure from the French and Russian ambassadors. The French position was that an Anglo-*French* understanding should have preceded any Anglo-Ottoman instrument.

on Britain's wariness of French intentions in Egypt and Italy's suspicion of French aims in the Red Sea.

Perhaps the real winner in this arrangement was Italy, which, in the competitive environment of 1887, found its bargaining power much enhanced. Since the mid-1880s, Italy had enjoyed the active support of England in colonizing Eritrea—in the British calculation, the Italian presence in the Red Sea made for a useful counterweight to France's efforts to expand its own East African foothold in Djibouti. For Italy, the Mediterranean entente upgraded what had hitherto been a rather informal cooperation. Though the British note to Italy evaded any explicit reference to Tripoli (and stopped short of the much farther-reaching pledges made by Italy's partners in the Triple Alliance [Document 9.26]), Italy could boast for the first time the stature in international affairs that it had sought since its emergence as a unified state.

a)   *Italian Note to the British Government, 12 February 1887*

. . . 3. Italy is entirely ready to support the work of Great Britain in Egypt. Great Britain in her turn is disposed, in case of encroachments on the part of a third Power, to support the action of Italy at every other point whatsoever of the North African coast districts, and especially in Tripolitania and Cyrenaica. . . .

—Hurst, 2:635–36; Pribram, 1:94–97

b)   *British Note to the Italian Government, 12 February 1887*

. . . Her Majesty's Government wish to act in the closest concert and agreement with that of Italy. Both powers desire that the shores of the Euxine [Black Sea], the Aegean, the Adriatic and the northern coast of Africa shall remain in the same hands as now. If, owing to some calamitous events, it becomes impossible to maintain the absolute status quo, both powers desire that there shall be no extension of the domination of any other Great Power over any portion of those coasts. . . .

—Hurst, 2:636; Pribram, 1:96–97

c)   *Spanish Note to Italy, 4 May 1887*

1. Spain will not lend herself as regards France, in so far as the North African territories among others are concerned, to any treaty or political arrangement whatsoever which would be aimed directly or indirectly against Italy, Germany, and Austria, or against any one of these Powers. . . .

—Hurst, 2:643–45; Pribram, 1:116–23

9.28   THE REINSURANCE TREATY, 18 JUNE 1887

Bismarck to Reuss, 15 May 1887 • *Reinsurance Treaty, 18 June 1887* •
Bismarck to Wilhelm I, 28 July 1887

The Three Emperors' League was due for renewal in 1887. But Russia, miffed at the seemingly endless Austro-Russian competition for influence in Bulgaria, was in no mood to continue an arrangement whose spirit, in its view, had been continually violated by Austria. The Russian foreign minister, Nicholas Giers, nonetheless continued to promote a Russo-German treaty *à deux*, perhaps in the hope of prying Germany away from Austria. For Bismarck too the continuation of the Russo-German treaty arrangement was desirable, if only as a counterforce to the lobbying of Boulangists and Katkovites for a Franco-Russian league.

The Russo-German Reinsurance Treaty, concluded on 18 June 1887, is the most controversial of Bismarck's treaties. On the surface, it seemed to contradict the letter and the spirit of the Austro-German Dual Alliance (Document 9.13); the Triple Alliance (Documents 9.16 and 9.26); the Mediterranean notes of that month (Document 9.27); and—in the event of a Russian invasion of Bulgaria by land—the German commitment to the Austro-Romanian alliance (Document 9.17).

Or did it? It will be recalled that although Bismarck promoted the Mediterranean notes, Germany was not a party to them. Moreover, the Reinsurance Treaty, like all of Bismarck's treaties, was *not* all-encompassing: it covered specific scenarios only and left its signatories free to act as they pleased in other contingencies. Any kind of judgment of the Reinsurance Treaty thus depends on an article-by-article and clause-by-clause juxtaposition of it with the texts of Bismarck's other alliances.

The Reinsurance Treaty and the negotiations leading up to it reflect many of Bismarck's assumptions about the nature of the diplomatic game. All the major players were essential to the "system"; international commitments should be dictated neither by ideology nor by boundless or absolute promises. Accordingly, Germany should be able to cooperate with Russia in Bulgaria, with France in North or West Africa, and intermittently with England in Egypt. This view of international relations may strike some as unprincipled, while others will praise it for its elasticity. In any case, it is interesting to contrast Bismarck's conception of international politics with that of Palmerston before him or with that of Grey later on.

a)   *Bismarck to Reuss,[65] 15 May 1887*

. . . I told him [Shuvalov[66]] . . . that there can be no questioning the validity of the premise, articulated in 1876, that the existence of Austria as well as Russia as independent European Great Powers is indispensable for the European equilibrium and in particular for Germany's future therein. If this equilibrium were jeopardized in regard to Austria, it would be impossible for us to sit things out until this friendly power were so disabled that it, in its turn, could not assist us in maintaining this equilibrium. . . .

—*GP*, 5:1078

b)   *Reinsurance Treaty, 18 June 1887*

Art. 1: In case one of the High Contracting Parties should find itself at war with a third Great Power, the other would maintain a benevolent neutrality towards it, and would devote its efforts to the localization of the conflict. This provision would not apply to

[65]Heinrich VII, Prince Reuss (1825–1906). German ambassador in Vienna, 1878–1894.
[66]Paul Andreievich, Count Shuvalov (1830–1908). Russian ambassador in Berlin, 1885–1894. Brother of Peter Shuvalov.

a war against Austria or France in case this war should result from an attack directed against one of these two latter Powers by one of the High Contracting Parties.

Art. 2: Germany recognizes the rights historically acquired by Russia in the Balkan Peninsula, and particularly the legitimacy of her preponderant and decisive influence in Bulgaria and in Eastern Rumelia. The two Courts engage to admit no modification of the territorial status quo of the said peninsula without a previous agreement between them, and to oppose, as occasion arises, every attempt to disturb this status quo or to modify it without their consent.

Art. 3: [identical to Art. 3 of the Three Emperors' League of 18 June 1881].[67]

Art. 4: The present Treaty shall remain in force for the space of three years, dating from the day of the exchange or ratifications.

Art. 5: The High Contracting Parties mutually promise secrecy as to the contents and the existence of the present Treaty and of the Protocol annexed thereto.[68]

Additional and Very Secret Protocol: . . .

1. Germany, as in the past, will lend her assistance to Russia in order to reestablish a regular and legal government in Bulgaria. She promises in no case to give her consent to the restoration of the Prince of Battenberg.

2. In case His Majesty the Emperor of Russia should find himself under the necessity of assuming the task of defending the entrance of the Black Sea in order to safeguard the interests of Russia, Germany engages to accord her benevolent neutrality and her moral and diplomatic support to the measures which His Majesty may deem it necessary to take to guard the key of His Empire. . . .

—Pribram, 1:274–81; *GP*, 5:1092; Hurst, 2:645–47

c)   **Bismarck to Wilhelm I, 28 July 1887**

. . . For us the main purpose of our German-Russian treaty is that for three years we have the assurance that Russia will remain neutral if we are attacked by France. Now as before, my view is that the most likely disturbance of the peace in Europe will be a French attack on Germany caused by domestic conditions and developments in France; this is far more likely than a Russian war in the Near East.

—*GP*, 5:1100

9.29   MANAGING THE "SYSTEM"

Marginalia by Bismarck, 24 October 1887 • *Rantzau to the German Foreign Ministry, 12 November 1887* • *Bismarck to Reuss, 27 December 1887*

Bismarck would have rejected any suggestion that his diplomacy had manufactured a "system" of international relations. His own musings, marginalia, and instructions show that he regarded his diplomacy, even at its zenith, as frail, fraught with uncertainties, and at the mercy of events he could not control. The extracts below highlight some of the constants that per-

---

[67]Cf. Document 9.14.

[68]Intending to embarrass the regime of Wilhelm II, Bismarck after his dismissal revealed in a Hamburg newspaper the existence and scope of the treaty, but not its text or the protocol. The article in the *Hamburger Nachrichten* of 24 October 1896 is reprinted in Huber, *Dokumente*, 1:313.

meated Bismarck's thinking in the late 1880s: doubts about the steadiness of British policy, aversion to preventive war and the general staffs, and—always—the *cauchemar des coalitions.*

Of the excerpts below, the first captures his response to the news that Britain and France had agreed on language for a Suez Canal users treaty[69] and was earmarked for transmission to Vienna and Rome, Britain's partners in the Mediterranean entente. The second is from a directive for a memorandum for Wilhelm I to prepare him for his summit, in November 1887, with Tsar Alexander III. The third was penned in response to Austrian attempts to expand the Dual Alliance and to fashion it into an offensive instrument.

a)   ***Marginalia by Bismarck, 24 October 1887***

An admonition to be cautious: for the pursuit of any kind of energetic policy, England clearly does not have its "battlestations ready."

—PA Aegypten 8

b) ***Rantzau[70] to the German Foreign Ministry, 12 November 1887***

. . . he, the Reich chancellor, no longer trusted the tsar: it was simply impossible for the tsar to pursue a policy like the one presently pursued by Russia unless he harbored the intention of expanding Russian armaments in order to ambush us at a moment of his choosing. His Highness said further that the memorandum [to be prepared] for [Wilhelm's] conversation with the tsar should be expanded to contain the following notion: "the avoidance of great wars was nowadays in the interest of the great monarchies because each nation, if defeated in war, would hold its government responsible and would seek to change it. In France, Napoleon fell; Austria traded in a monarchic for a parliamentary form of government after the unsuccessful war [of 1866]; in Italy or Spain, an unsuccessful war would bring down the government; even in Germany . . . the prospects of a republic and democracy would increase considerably in the event of a defeat. . . . " The chancellor remarked that if the tsar were given the pill in this form, he might be able to draw his own conclusion of how an unsuccessful war might affect his fate. . . .

—PA Deutschland 131 *secr.*

c)   ***Bismarck to Reuss, 27 December 1887***

. . . I cannot fend off the impression that certain military circles in Vienna intend to transform our defensive alliance; therefore, I again stress that it was not concluded for any aggressive purposes. Count Kálnoky[71] completely agrees with me on this. But both of us have to be on our guard that the responsibility to give our monarchs

---

[69]Text in Hurst, 2:910–13; *SP*, 79:18.
[70]Kuno von Rantzau (1843–1917). Foreign ministry official; Bismarck's son-in-law.
[71]Gustav, Count Kálnoky von Köröspatak (1832–1898). Austro-Hungarian foreign minister, 1881–1895.

political advice does not slip away from us and is arrogated by the general staffs. . . .

That the outbreak of a Russo-German war will for us immediately be followed by a war against France is not doubtful: if such a war, contrary to our expectations, does not occur automatically, then it would be more or less in our interest to bring it about without delay. We cannot give our full effort to a war in the east far beyond our borders, as long as we have France's power, undiminished and ready to attack, in our rear. We do not know what the situation in France would be if such an event came to pass, but if the peace there then is no more secure than it is today, it may be imperative for us to respond to the outbreak of an Austro-Russian war with our declaration of war on France, in order to secure our western border and then to have available our full resources against Russia. . . .

For now I do not think that war is imminent and I will do my utmost to avoid it. Emperor Franz Joseph shares my peaceable intentions. But in order to strengthen the prospects for peace it is necessary that Austria follow our example and that it stay armed, perhaps more heavily than at present. Otherwise it will offer Russia a temptation to attack. The size of the calamity which would befall the peoples of Austria-Hungary and Germany in a war with France and Russia, whatever its results may be, imposes on us the duty to prevent, if at all possible, its outbreak—or at least not to interfere with divine providence by provoking it before it is thrust upon us. Time works more in our favor than in our opponents'. Conditions in France and Russia are far more tense than ours and can lead to domestic developments which would relieve us from a struggle of such gigantic dimensions. On the other hand, in two or three years we hope to be stronger than today, at home and abroad. But we can activate the full power of the German people only for a defensive war, to counter an attack. The argument that we have to fight now because war will break out later anyhow and that conditions are more favorable today than at a later time will convince not even parliaments, much less the people. No one can predict whether success will bear out the claim that the present is the right moment for striking the blow. . . .

—*GP*, 6:1186

9.30   SECOND MEDITERRANEAN AGREEMENT, 1887

Salisbury to Lumley, 28 October 1887 ● *Austrian Note to Britain, 12 December 1887* ● *British Reply to the Austrian Note, 12 December 1887*

The Bulgarian throne had remained vacant since the abdication of Alexander von Battenberg in September 1886 (Document 9.23). In July 1887, the Bulgarian assembly elected as his successor Ferdinand of Saxe-Coburg-Koháry—another German princeling, a distant relative of Queen Victoria, and a former officer in the Austro-Hungarian army. It is difficult to explain the choice of Ferdinand other than as a deliberate slap in the face of Russia, and particularly Russia's effort to reestablish its influence in Bulgaria. Taking up the gauntlet, Russia not only refused to recognize Ferdinand but went one step further: it tried to pressure the sultan, Bulgaria's nominal suzerain, into voiding the election altogether.

Russia's display of muscle in Constantinople moved the Bulgarian problem into a new phase and kept it in the forefront of European politics. In contemplating countermeasures, Austria, Italy, and Britain now agreed to reinvigorate the Mediterranean agreement of February 1887 (Document 9.27) and to substitute more specific language for the original text. Overriding his Austrian and Italian counterparts, Salisbury insisted that the new notes, like their predecessors, be kept secret. He argued that those members of his cabinet (such as Randolph Churchill) in favor of accommodating rather than counterbalancing Russia opposed a public declaration as too provocative but would countenance a secret agreement. But Salisbury, like Bismarck (Document 9.29c), may have wanted to cool the ardor of the Austrian and Italian leadership, and, like Bismarck, may have wanted to assure Vienna and Rome of passive support while making clear that he could or would not back an active policy against Russia.

Nonetheless, the Mediterranean notes of December 1887 entailed a firmer and more formal promise of British support than any held out by a British government since the Crimean War. But it would be mistaken to view Britain as the only party prepared to give under the agreement, and the notes might be read as formally completing Austria's reversal from the Near Eastern policy to which Bismarck had harnessed it in the Three Emperors' League. It might even be argued that the language of the Mediterranean entente fleshed out Salisbury's declaration on the Straits at the Congress of Berlin nine years earlier (Document 9.8) and tied both Austria and Italy to his reading of the international law on the status of the Straits.

Be that as it may, the Bulgarian problem and the Mediterranean entente drifted apart in the 1890s; both petered out within months of each other. Tsar Nicholas II finally recognized Ferdinand as prince of Bulgaria in 1896, after the Bulgarian crown prince, Boris, was baptized in the Orthodox faith—an event that enraged the Austrians. Britain's show of support for Greece rather than the Ottoman Empire in the Greco-Turkish war of 1897 similarly gnawed away at the raison d'être for the Mediterranean entente, and Austria now thought that accommodation with St. Petersburg, instead of London, provided a better safeguard for Austrian interests in the Near East (Document 10.8e).

Some writers stress that the Mediterranean agreements of 1887 entailed, on the part of England, a far more specific commitment than the Anglo-French entente of 1904 and its Anglo-Russian counterpart of 1907.[72] This conclusion is entirely warranted if one is content to do no more than compare the language of these instruments. But it downplays the fact that the *texts* of the Anglo-French and Anglo-Russian engagements were to the *policy* of the ententes what the tip is to the iceberg: the Anglo-French and Anglo-Russian ententes spawned parallel agreements (such as the Anglo-French-Spanish "Mediterranean entente" of May 1907) and a myriad of military undertakings, wholly absent from the Mediterranean agreements of 1887 (cf. Chapter 11). Whether intended or not, the conclusion described above prettifies the record of British diplomacy after 1906—did not Salisbury, so goes the argument, enter into much farther-reaching commitments than Grey?[72a] If this was so, then Salisbury's game was far more dangerous than Grey's, and the latter's diplomacy is exonerated from having played its part in the collapse of the state system in 1914.

a)   *Salisbury to Lumley,*[73] *28 October 1887*

. . . The two powers, Austria and Italy, have made a proposal for telling Turkey that, if she resists Russia, she will be supported, but if she makes herself Russia's vassal, she will be invaded. The language is more diplomatic, but that is the drift. Germany is ostensibly no party to this project. In secret she patronizes and presses it, in public she stands aloof,—and no doubt privately expresses her horror of it at St. Petersburg. England may find it necessary to adhere rather than break up the alliance. But the step in the interests of peace is an unwise one, though very useful doubtless to Bismarck for

[72] For example, Taylor, *Struggle,* 312; Lowe, *Reluctant Imperialists,* 120; Bridge, *Habsburg Monarchy,* 221.

[72a]Sir Edward Grey (1862–1933). Foreign secretary, 1905–1916.

[73] Sir John Savile Lumley (1818–1896). British ambassador in Rome, 1883–1888.

taking the strain off his eastern frontier. But for us it commits the blunder of building on the Sultan's fitful and feeble disposition. . . . [I]f the arrangement gets out, it will back up the Panslavic feeling at Moscow which is a genuine force. . . .

—Cecil, *Salisbury*, 4:69–70

b)   *Austrian Note to Britain, 12 December 1887*

. . . [Austria-Hungary] has come to an agreement with the government of Italy to propose to the British government the adoption of the following points. . . .

1. The maintenance of peace and the exclusion of all policy of aggression.

2. The maintenance of the status quo in the Near East, based on treaties, to the exclusion of all policy of compensation.

3. The maintenance of the local autonomies established by these said treaties.

4. The independence of Turkey, as guardian of important European interests (independence of the Caliphate, the freedom of the Straits, etc.), from all foreign preponderating influence.

5. Consequently, Turkey can neither cede nor delegate her suzerain rights over Bulgaria to any other power, nor intervene in order to establish a foreign administration there, nor tolerate acts of coercion undertaken with this latter object, under the form either of a military occupation or of the despatch of volunteers. Likewise Turkey, constituted by the treaties guardian of the Straits, can neither cede any portion of her sovereign rights, nor delegate her authority to any other Power in Asia Minor. . . .

8. Should the conduct of the Porte, however, in the opinion of the three Powers, assume the character of complicity with or connivance at any such illegal enterprise, the three Powers will consider themselves justified by existing treaties in proceeding, either jointly or separately, to the provisional occupation by their forces, military or naval, of such points of Ottoman territory as they may agree to consider it necessary to occupy in order to secure the objects determined by previous treaties.

9. The existence and the contents of the present Agreement between the three Powers shall not be revealed, either to Turkey or to any other Powers who have not yet been informed to it, without the previous consent of all and each of the three Powers aforesaid.

—Pribram, 1:125–27; Hurst, 2:648–49

c)   *British Reply to Austrian Note, 12 December 1887*

. . . The eighth point provides against a contingency which, without technical illegality, may frustrate the object of the treaties altogether. It is necessary, however, to avoid a premature publicity which might precipitate the lapse of Turkey into that state of vassalage from which it is the aim of the three Powers to protect her. In view of these considerations, . . . H.M. Government . . . communicate to the Austro-Hungarian Government their entire adhesion to the nine points. . . .

—Pribram, 1:128–30; Hurst, 2:649–51

CHAPTER 10

Equivocation and Imperialism, 1890–1904

Bismarck's "system" did not long survive his fall. The lapse of the Reinsurance Treaty in 1890 and the conclusion of the Franco-Russian alliance between 1892 and 1894 signaled a steady deterioration in Germany's diplomatic position vis-à-vis the other powers. This process, however, was masked by the preoccupation of all powers with expanding their overseas empires. In the competition for empire and influence, the Franco-Russian alliance seemed to operate as much against England—France's rival in Africa and Russia's in Asia—as against Germany. As the Anglo-French and Anglo-Russian contests unfolded, Germany's flip-flops between a pro-British and a pro-Russian orientation further muddied the waters; at the same time, these reversals gave German policy a well-deserved reputation for aimlessness and inconsistency. In sum, the diplomacy of the 1890s—characterized as it was by fleeting combinations of the powers—can be said to mark the interval between the dissolution of one state "system" and the formation of another.

With their energies focused on East Asia, the Nile valley, or South Africa, the powers tended to ignore the more traditional arenas of European diplomacy. For instance, the Greco-Turkish War of 1897, had it taken place in an earlier or later period, might well have triggered a major European crisis, but—occurring when it did—was widely regarded as a bothersome distraction from the more pressing business of imperial expansion. The real issue at hand, or so it seemed to the foreign offices of the day, was to establish control over the remaining parcels of overseas real estate and, in so doing, to jockey for position in the Great Power rivalries. These endeavors were accompanied by a search for allies, but in practice this search resembled an elaborate shell game in which the objective was to bribe or browbeat other powers into pursuing ostensibly common goals while in reality shifting disproportionate risks and burdens onto the shoulders of the prospective partner.

Except in the western hemisphere, the colonial crises and rivalries of the turn of the century by and large ended on terms favorable to Britain. Even in that country there emerged a tacit understanding that the limits of imperial growth had been reached; that the consolidation, rather than expansion, of empire was the new fashion; and that imperial consolidation, in its turn, required the trading of claims or spheres of influence. Holding the upper hand in this game of colonial barter, Britain could force asymmetrical exchanges—receiving tangible assets while giving only promises of support for the future. But once contracted, obligations are obligations, and the penalty for default can be a ruined reputation and a reopening of old rivalries. Maintaining these colonial agreements thus became an objective in itself, and the parties to them, eager to demonstrate their good faith, began to cooperate with their new partners in other areas as well. The implications for the European equilibrium were perhaps best understood by Théophile Delcassé, French foreign minister between 1898 and 1905. One of the side benefits of his colonial ententes with Italy, Britain, and Spain was the shifting of the European diplomatic scene to the detriment of Germany.

The diplomatic history of the period 1890 to 1904 can be written from a variety of perspectives. The emergence of new players—the rise of Japan and the United States as Great Powers or Germany's desire to play a global role—added a new element to a game hitherto dominated by the established contestants. From a "systemic" point of view, the importance of the years 1890 to 1904 lies in the interplay between the diplomacy of imperialism and the European equilibrium: it could, for example, be measured by how the Sino-Japanese, Spanish-American, Boer, and Russo-Japanese wars shaped the relations and expectations of the Great Powers. If the tale were told from the perspective of the catastrophe of 1914, its focus might be on "missed opportunities," that is, moments at which the story could have taken a different turn. Whether upon closer inspection some of these missed opportunities did or did not exist and whether it is not more accurate to speak of a "myth" of missed opportunities has been debated ad nauseam, but the reader may arrive at a preliminary answer by perusing the documents that follow.

GENERAL READING: Bridge, *Habsburg Monarchy* (ch. 9); Christopher Andrew, *Théophile Delcassé and the Making of the Entente Cordiale* (New York, 1968); J. A. S. Grenville, *Lord Salisbury and Foreign Policy* (London, 1963); George F. Kennan, *The Fateful Alliance: France, Russia, and the Coming of the First World War* (New York, 1984); Kennedy, *Anglo-German Antagonism* (cf. ch. 9); William L. Langer, *The Diplomacy of Imperialism* (1935; reprint New York, 1951); Rich, *Holstein* (cf. ch. 9); [East Asia:] Ramon Meyers and Mark Peattie (eds.), *The Japanese Colonial Empire* (Princeton, 1984); Ian Nish, *The Origins of the Russo-Japanese War* (New York, 1985); Rosemary Quested, *The Russo-Chinese Bank* (Birmingham, 1977); [Nile valley:] G. N. Sanderson, *England, Europe, and the Upper Nile* (Edinburgh, 1965); [South Africa:] Thomas Pakenham, *The Boer War* (New York, 1979); Peter Warwick (ed.), *The South African War* (Harlow, 1980); [Americas:] Raymond Esthus, *Theodore Roosevelt and the International Rivalries* (Waltham, MA, 1970); Ernest R. May, *Imperial Democracy* (1961; reprint: New York, 1973); Robert F. Smith, *The United States and the Latin American Sphere of Influence*, 2 vols. (Malabar, FL, 1981)

10.1   THE TWO-POWER STANDARD

Hamilton in the House of Commons, 7 March 1889 ● *Hamilton in the House of Commons, 19 December 1893* ● *Balfour in the House of Commons, 19 December 1893* ● *Dilke in the House of Commons, 19 December 1893*

When the naval maneuvers of 1888 exposed shortcomings in the organization and technological capabilities of the British fleet, the Salisbury government came under pressure to find a remedy. The Naval Defense Act, passed by parliament in May 1889, was calculated to give the British fleet superiority over the combined navies of the next two strongest naval powers, France and Russia. This two-power standard, as it came to be known, required more than a simple equivalent in firepower. Naval strategists estimated that Britain would need to retain a 5:3 ratio to secure the seas or bottle up the enemy in port. In the latter scenario, the wear and tear of blockade duty and the need to revictual vessels required a superiority in numbers.

How real was the Franco-Russian threat? In 1887, France and Russia had used their influence in Constantinople to scuttle the Drummond-Wolff convention, an Anglo-Ottoman agreement defining the terms of the British occupation of Egypt. France was hostile to the British presence in Egypt (Documents 9.19 and 9.27); the Anglo-Russian relationship faced an uncertain future over Bulgaria and Afghanistan. Under these circumstances, the Franco-Russian intervention in Constantinople seemed to presage further cooperation between these two powers. But it was unlikely that France, in view of its antagonism to Germany, would allow a diplomatic confrontation to turn into a military showdown. Moreover, geography was a powerful impediment to any concerted Franco-Russian naval assault against British forces. Whether the Naval Defense Act was an expression of pragmatism or a response to a form of hysteria peculiar to Britain, its passage enabled Britain to realize two objectives: to match the French and Russian fleets and to remain aloof from the Triple Alliance.

Excerpted below are passages from the parliamentary debate on the Naval Defense Act and from a subsequent debate on the Naval Estimates for 1894–1895. In August 1892, the Conservative Salisbury cabinet had given way to a Liberal government under Gladstone. In 1893, another naval scare, similarly animated by fear of the French and Russian fleets, was used by Conservative members of parliament to attack the Gladstone government and to reflect on the purposes of the 1889 Naval Defense Act. Quoted here are Lord George Hamilton, first lord of the Admiralty in 1889 and the main opposition spokesman on naval affairs in 1893; Salisbury's nephew Arthur Balfour, future prime minister (1902–1905) and foreign secretary (1917–1922); and Sir Charles Dilke, a one-time Liberal hopeful for the prime ministership and a prolific writer on naval and colonial issues.

a)   Hamilton in the House of Commons, 7 March 1889

. . . [T]he leading idea has been that our [naval] establishment should be on such a scale that it should at least be equal to the naval strength of any two other countries. . . .

—*Parl. Debates*, 3rd Series, 333:1210

b)   Hamilton in the House of Commons, 19 December 1893

. . . it is admitted to be a cardinal part of the policy of this country that the minimum standard of security which the country demands and expects is that our fleet should be equal to the combination of the two next strongest navies in Europe. Having thus cleared the ground, it is just to make a comparison between our fleet and the fleets of the two strongest naval powers in Europe—namely France and Russia. . . . A great proportion of the expenditure of foreign nations upon their fleets is not upon cruisers or vessels to protect their commerce, but rather upon battleships which can be intended for one purpose alone—that is, to challenge the naval supremacy of this country. . . . If any nation, or any combination of nations, were to attempt to deprive us of the command of the sea and fail, the consequences to them might be inconvenient, but nothing more. If, on the other hand, they succeeded in their attempt, the result to us would be national and imperial ruin. We have made a very good use of our time since we became masters of the sea. We have built up at the other end of the world the largest and most populous empire of which history, I think, has record; we have planted colonies in all parts of the world, and we have monopolised the sea-carrying trade of the world. We have done something more. Possessing the command of the seas, we have built up here at home the largest and most compact system of industrial employment that this world has ever seen; and if we lose the command of the sea we not only lose empire over the sea, we not only lose our connection with the colonies beyond the sea, and our commerce upon the sea, but undoubtedly a very large portion of the great system and structure of our industrial employment at home would come tumbling down upon our heads. I know there are gentlemen in this House who are so impressed with the social problems and labour problems which the density of the population of this country suggest that they have no time to think about external matters or about such a simple affair as the supremacy of the British navy. But I would ask anyone of them, from their own standpoint, what would be the position of any one of the questions in which they are interested if we lost the command of the sea? . . .

—*Parl. Debates*, 4th Series, 19:1774, 1786–1787

c)   *Balfour in the House of Commons, 19 December 1893*

. . . I can assure him [Mr. Gladstone] that we consider it a very small matter who governs this empire as compared with the question whether there shall be an empire to govern, and that there is no question of domestic policy, however deeply we may think upon it, however profoundly it may move us, which we for one moment place in comparison to the tremendous issue raised by this resolution. . . .

—*Parl. Debates*, 4th Series, 19:1812

d)   *Dilke in the House of Commons, 19 December 1893*

. . . We have no army at all in the modern sense, we have no rapidity of mobilization, no security against invasion, for the protection of our trade and for our colonies, except that which an overwhelming fleet can give. . . . There is no ground for believing that either upon a masking policy or upon a blockading policy can we hope to contend against our enemy in time of war with a less supremacy than five battleships to three. A great many think on this matter that in time of war we shall not stand alone, but should have friends and allies. There are such things as dangerous illusions, and the most dangerous illusion that any inhabitant of the United Kingdom can have is that we are a popular power. We are probably the most unpopular of the Great Powers, and I think the most unpopular of all the powers, great and small, with the possible exception of China. . . . This country has deliberately rejected the policy of alliance, and if we are to stand alone we must be prepared to make the sacrifice which that position involves. . . .

—*Parl. Debates*, 4th Series, 19:1817; 1820

10.2   **LAPSE OF THE REINSURANCE TREATY**

Memorandum by Caprivi, 22 May 1890

Leo von Caprivi replaced Bismarck as German chancellor in March 1890. His first foreign policy decision was to respond to repeated pleas from the Russian foreign minister, Count Nicholas Giers, to renew the Reinsurance Treaty of 1887. In a memorandum prepared for the Kaiser, Caprivi summarized the arguments that persuaded him and his advisers to turn down the Russian overtures. Caprivi's memorandum lacks the crisp, clear style of his predecessor and shows him to be very much the novice in foreign policy.

The memorandum needs to be understood against the background of the unresolved situation in Bulgaria.[1] Russia refused to recognize the legitimacy of the new prince elected by the Bulgarian assembly, Ferdinand of Saxe-Coburg, and attempted to regain its influence in the country. Caprivi feared that a revived Reinsurance Treaty would chain Germany to Russia's ambitions and would alienate Germany from the signatories of the Mediterranean ententes—Britain, Austria, and Italy.

Caprivi's objectives were a closer alignment between England and Germany and an upgrading of Germany's relationship to its partners in the Triple Alliance, Austria and Italy. For Caprivi, the Reinsurance Treaty was a hindrance to these plans. But as one historian has suggested, Caprivi failed to foresee the possibility of two parallel consequences of his "new course."[2] Closer ties to Austria and Italy would, paradoxically, defeat his long-range goal of intimate relations between Germany and England: if Germany shored up its partners in the Triple Alliance, there would be no need for England to do so. Rather than having to expend its own energy in containing Russia, England could luxuriate in its isolation while Germany did the job. Second, Caprivi underestimated the danger of a Franco-Russian alliance which would increase Germany's dependence on Austria and Italy, allow these two powers to extort an even greater price for their alliance with Germany, and leave Germany with fewer chips to bring to a future round of Anglo-German bargaining.

Memorandum by Caprivi, 22 May 1890

. . . because the world can expect a disturbance of the peace only from Russia: there is no "Bulgarian danger" if Russia does not will it.

Of all the Russian intimations, the one which least ensnares us is the recreation of a League *à trois* among Russia, Austria, and Germany. But Russia had reason not to suggest as much in 1887. This reason, now latent, will resurface, as conditions in the Balkans have increased the antagonism between Russia and Austria. Germany would run the danger of some day having to decide between Austria and Russia. If we decided in favor of Austria, we would have the same situation as we have today, except that at that point we would not have good relations with Italy or England. If we decided in favor of Russia, we would tie ourselves to its good graces but leaving it free to woo France or Austria against us if it so desired.

Giers's other intimations all suggest a secret agreement, be it a treaty, an exchange of notes, or an exchange of letters between our monarchs. But such a secret would be

[1] Cf. Document 9.30, headnote.
[2] Rich, *Holstein*, 1:307–24.

tantamount to placing a land mine under the Triple Alliance, a land mine which Russia can explode whenever it pleases.

Even if this were not so, we could not commit ourselves, not even orally, to a change in the status of Bulgaria or the Straits. As before, we consider the existing condition in Bulgaria to be illegal, but also view it as better than expected. We will not ignore the personal interest which the Russian Emperor takes in Bulgarian affairs, but it is not in our interest either to change these and we have to take into account Austria's interest in the present status quo.

Nor do we have a direct interest in the Straits. We have even less of an interest in maintaining Article III of the Reinsurance Treaty which might force us to oppose England and Italy at the Straits. . . .

We therefore have no reason to change the status quo in the East. But it follows from Russia's repeated efforts that it has the opposite interest. Russia feels isolated, but would like—perhaps because the situation in Bulgaria is consolidating too rapidly—to make a move on Constantinople. Russia's embarrassment is that it can only make this move across the Black Sea. . . . But the way across the sea can be barred by the English. Hence: let's close the Straits—that is the thrust of Giers's last proposal.

A German-Russian rapprochement would alienate our allies, damage England, and would not be understood and not greeted with approval by our own population which has become more and more accustomed to the idea of the Triple Alliance.

What would we gain to offset these disadvantages? How valuable would it be if Russia, as Schweinitz[3] says, would remain quiet in the first weeks after a French attack on us? This calm would not be so total that we could afford not to deploy a part of our army at the Russian border. We would not be able to move against France with all of our forces, and there would be no *casus foederis* for Austria.

Further, one cannot ignore the question: what is the value of alliances if they are not founded on a community of interest between nations? Unlike in the days of the Seven Years' War, nations are now governed by their own interests and moods when it comes to questions of war and peace. Consequently, the value of an alliance between governments is much reduced if this alliance is not supported by public opinion. Whether German public opinion can be induced to cherish a bond with Russia is questionable; that Russian public opinion would not accept us as an equal partner is without question. Irrespective of whether Giers or anyone else is in charge of Russia, no one can give us the guarantee that our alliance with Russia would not at the critical moment become a victim of popular pressure. The most insecure kind of alliance is the one where the *casus foederis* is only given after one of the parties has been attacked. It is possible to taunt an opponent with pinpricks until he strikes back at his tormentor: does that constitute a *casus foederis* [for the ally]? Years ago Russian public opinion and Prince Gorchakov left no doubt that they did not value alliances. . . .

As for the possibility that Russia will seek elsewhere the alliance to which we are not willing to commit—that leaves only France and England. But for supporting the kind of move which Russia now seems to be contemplating—a move short of a general war—, an alliance with France is of no value, as the British Mediterranean fleet can neutralize it. Whereas Russia was hoping to obtain an alliance with us at no cost to itself, this kind of alliance with England could only be obtained by Russia in

[3]See note 58 in Chapter 9.

exchange for compensations elsewhere (Asia?) and would loosen Russia's rapport with France. Finally, given what British interests are in the Mediterranean, an alliance with both England and France is unlikely.

As before, we wish to maintain a good relationship with Russia and will not do anything to upset it. But we have to show so much consideration for our allies that even when circumstances arise in which we cannot or do not want to support them (be it in Bulgaria or Bizerta), we will at least not create difficulties for them. . . .

—*GP*, 7:1379

10.3   QUEEN VICTORIA ON
THE HELIGOLAND-ZANZIBAR TREATY

Queen Victoria to Salisbury, 9 June 1890 • *Salisbury to Queen Victoria, 10 June 1890* • *Queen Victoria to Salisbury, 11 June 1890* • *Salisbury to Queen Victoria, 12 June 1890* • *Queen Victoria to Salisbury, 12 June 1890*

The lapse of the Reinsurance Treaty (cf. preceding document) gave a first indication of the Anglophile bent of the "new course" in German foreign policy. The second was the conclusion of the Heligoland-Zanzibar Treaty (signed 1 July 1890).[4] Under its terms, Britain ceded the North Sea island of Heligoland to Germany; Germany relinquished Zanzibar and extensive territorial claims to the East African mainland. Heligoland controlled access to the entire German North Sea coastline but was of little commercial value; Zanzibar was the leading entrepôt on the East African coast. Although both sides benefited from this exchange of real estate, Britain made the better territorial bargain. The treaty provides a classic illustration of how the intentions of the contracting parties can diverge: while the British government evaluated the treaty on its inherent merits, the German leadership hoped that it would serve as a stepping-stone to a broader Anglo-German accord.

The documents reproduced here also offer insight into the constitutional relationship between the British monarch and prime minister; into the attitude of both toward self-determination in the British Empire; and the depth of Queen Victoria's scorn for Germany.

a)   *Queen Victoria to Salisbury, 9 June 1890*

. . . [A]bout Heligoland[:] 1st. The people have been always very loyal, having received my heir with enthusiasm; and it is a shame to hand them over to an unscrupulous despotic Government like the German without first consulting them. 2nd. It is a very bad precedent. The next thing will be to propose to give up Gibraltar; and soon nothing will be secure, and all our Colonies will wish to be free.

I very much deprecate it and [am] anxious not [to] give my consent unless I hear that the people's feelings are consulted and their rights are respected. I think it a very dangerous proceeding. It seems to me that we are always changing, and often thereby may upset things.

—*QV*, 3rd Series, 1:612

[4]Text in Hertslet II, 3:899–906.

b)   ***Salisbury to Queen Victoria, 10 June 1890***

. . . [T]he Cabinet . . . are of opinion that in any agreement arrived at with Germany the rights of the people of Heligoland should be carefully reserved. That has been done: no actual subject of your Majesty living now will be subject to naval or military conscription. The existing customs tariff will be maintained for a period of years, and every person wishing to retain his British nationality will have the right to do so. The Cabinet thought it was impracticable to obtain the formal consent of the 2,000 people who live there: anything like a plebiscite would be very dangerous as admitting the right of the inhabitants of an imperial post to decide for themselves as to the political disposal of that post. It might be used by discontented persons in Gibraltar, Malta, Cyprus, and even India. But the information the Cabinet get is that the population, which is not British but Frisian, would readily come under the German Empire if protected from conscription. The Cabinet unanimously and earnestly recommend this arrangement to your Majesty under these conditions.

The equivalent for Heligoland will be the protectorate over the islands of Zanzibar and Pemba and 150 miles of coast near the Sultanate of Monastir Witu, and the islands of Manda and Patta,[5] and the abandonment of all claim to the interior behind it by Germany. Under this arrangement the whole of the country outside the confines of Abyssinia and Gallaland will be under British influence up to Khan, so far as any European competition is concerned. On the other hand, we could not without this arrangement come to a favourable agreement as to the Stevenson road,[6] and any indefinite postponement of a settlement in Africa would render it very difficult to maintain terms of amity with Germany, and would force us to change our systems of alliance in Europe. The alliance of France instead of the alliance of Germany must necessarily involve the early evacuation of Egypt under very unfavourable conditions.

—*QV*, 3rd Series, 1:613–14

c)   ***Queen Victoria to Salisbury, 11 June 1890***

The conditions you enumerate are sound and the alliance of Germany valuable; but that any of my possessions should be thus bartered away causes me great uneasiness, and I can only consent on receiving a positive assurance from you that the present arrangement constitutes no precedent.

—*QV*, 3rd Series, 1:614

---

[5] The three locations are near or off the coast of present-day Kenya.

[6] The "Stevenson road" connected Karonga on Lake Nyasa (Malawi) with Hore Bay on Lake Tanganyika. It was retained in its entirety by Britain.

d)   ***Salisbury to Queen Victoria, 12 June 1890***

Lord Salisbury quite understands and so do his colleagues that this case is not and cannot be a precedent. It is absolutely peculiar. The island is a very recent conquest. It became a British possession by Treaty in 1814. Why it was retained at the general settlement we do not certainly know; but most probably because it was geographically a dependency of Hanover which was then ruled by the British Sovereign. Now that Hanover has gone it has no connection with us. No authority has ever recommended that it should be fortified, and no House of Commons would pay for its fortification. But if it is not fortified, and we quarrelled with Germany, it would be seized by Germany the day she declared war, and it is so near her great arsenals that she could fortify it impregnably in three or four days; unless we are prepared to arm it, we are merely incurring a certain humiliation if ever we are at war with Germany. Yet a war with Germany is the only contingency in which any possible advantage could arise from it. There is no danger of this case being made a precedent, for there is no possible case like it.

—*QV*, 3rd Series, 1:615

e)   ***Queen Victoria to Salisbury, 12 June 1890***

Your answer respecting Heligoland forming no possible precedent I consider satisfactory. I sanction the proposed cession or almost exchange: but I must repeat that I think you may find great difficulties in the future. Giving up what one has is always a bad thing.

—*QV*, 3rd Series, 1:615

10.4   # THE FRANCO-RUSSIAN ALLIANCE

Memorandum by Obruchev, 7/19 May 1892 ●
The Franco-Russian Alliance, 10 August 1892–4 January 1894

A Franco-Russian exchange of letters on 27 August 1891[7] paved the way for the chiefs of the French and Russian general staffs to negotiate a military convention between the two countries. Drafted by August 1892, it was not ratified until January 1894. The motivations of the signatories, however, remained disparate. Russia, increasingly preoccupied with East Asia, had little taste for a confrontation with Germany. Consequently, Russia and France found limited cooperation against England a more satisfying common denominator. This anti-English

---

[7]Not reproduced here. See Hurst, 2:662–65, or *DDF*, 1st Series, 8:514, 517. For an analysis of the letters and the circuitous route of the subsequent negotiations, see Kennan, *Fateful Alliance*.

edge masked the original intent of the convention—that is, the creation of a counterforce to Germany and the Triple Alliance—in the decade after its inception.

A shared element of all alliances of this period was their claim to serve defensive purposes. Nonetheless, it is instructive to contrast the Franco-Russian alliance with Bismarck's treaties. Article 2 of the Dual Alliance (Document 9.13) and article 4 of the Triple Alliance (Document 9.16) contained veiled references to the possibility of mobilization by third parties. But the Franco-Russian alliance spelled out a more explicit *casus foederis* and stipulated, in a far more detailed manner than Bismarck's alliances, the obligations of the contracting parties in peacetime as well as war. Whether these provisions made the Franco-Russian alliance a bird of a very different feather is, of course, a matter for debate. Particularly striking is the contrast between, on one hand, Bismarck's method of dealing with specific and limited contingencies and, on the other, General Obruchev's insistence, in the conclusion of his memorandum to Tsar Alexander, that Russia "retain . . . an absolute freedom of action."

a)   ***Memorandum by Obruchev,[8] 7/19 May 1892***

. . . Success on the battlefield now depends (other things being equal) on the most rapid possible deployment of the greatest possible mass of troops and on beating the enemy to the punch. Whoever first concentrates his forces and strikes against a still unprepared enemy has assured himself of the highest probability of having the first victory, which facilitates the successful conduct of the entire campaign. The undertaking of mobilization can no longer be considered as a peaceful act; on the contrary, it represents the most decisive act of war. . . . [T]he side that delays for even as much as twenty-four hours can pay for this bitterly. . . . The impossibility of delaying the actual opening of war means that at the moment of the declaration of mobilization no further diplomatic hesitation is permissible. . . .

. . . The French are talking not about a treaty of alliance but only a military convention that would provide for simultaneous mobilization of the French and Russian armies and for a plan of their operations, agreed upon in advance. This procedure seems advantageous to them, because the conclusion of a treaty of alliance, like a declaration of war, requires parliamentary ratification, whereas the mobilization of the army can be declared by the President of the Republic, bypassing the parliament, not wasting time on the debates of the parliament, which, instead, will have to deal with an accomplished fact. This way of looking at the question seems entirely reasonable. By having to deal only with the French government we protect the agreement from the influence of the political parties. . . .

We have to retain for ourselves an absolute freedom of action, and for this reason it will be best, in questions of joint action with the French, to bind ourselves only by the general obligation: in case of an attack upon France by one of the parties to the Triple Alliance, to mobilize our army immediately and to begin military obligations against the nearest to us of the powers of that alliance—Germany or Austria—while demanding a similar obligation of the French.

—Kennan, *Fateful Alliance,* 264–68

[8]Nikolai Nikolaevich Obruchev (1830–1904). Chief of the Russian general staff, 1881–1897.

b) *The Franco-Russian Alliance, 10 August 1892–4 January 1894*

France and Russia, being animated by an equal desire to preserve peace, and having no other object than to meet the necessities of a defensive war, provoked by an attack of the forces of the Triple Alliance against the one or the other of them, have agreed upon the following provisions:

1. If France is attacked by Germany, or by Italy supported by Germany, Russia shall employ all her available forces to attack Germany. If Russia is attacked by Germany, or by Austria supported by Germany, France shall employ all her available forces to fight Germany.

2. In case the forces of the Triple Alliance, or of one of the Powers composing it, should mobilize, France and Russia, at the first news of the events and without the necessity of any previous concert, shall mobilize immediately and simultaneously the whole of their forces and shall move them as close as possible to their frontiers.

3. The available forces to be employed against Germany shall be, on the part of France, 1,300,000 men; on the part of Russia, 700,000 or 800,000 men. These forces shall engage to the full, with all speed, in order that Germany may have to fight at the same time in the East and in the West.

4. The General Staffs of the Armies of the two countries shall cooperate with each other at all times in the preparation and facilitation of the execution of the measures above foreseen. They shall communicate to each other, while there is still peace, all information relative to the armies of the Triple Alliance which is or shall be within their knowledge. Ways and means of corresponding in times of war shall be studied and arranged in advance.

5. France and Russia shall not conclude peace separately.

6. The present Convention shall have the same duration as the Triple Alliance.

7. All the clauses above enumerated shall be kept rigorously secret.

—*DDF*, 1st Series, 9:461 and 11:7

10.5   CONSEQUENCES OF THE SINO-JAPANESE WAR OF 1894–1895

Anglo-Japanese Treaty of Commerce and Navigation, 16 July 1894 • Treaty of Shimonoseki, 17 April 1895 • Japanese Proclamation in Response to the "Triple Intervention," 10 May 1895 • Mutsu's Reflections on the Triple Intervention, 31 December 1895 • Sino-Russian ("Li-Lobanov") Treaty, 22 May/3 June 1896 • Russo-Japanese ("Lobanov-Yamagata") Treaty, 28 May/9 June 1896 • Sino-Japanese Commercial Treaty, 21 July 1896 • Contract between the Russo-Chinese Bank and China, 27 August/8 September 1896

Korea had been a tributary kingdom of China since 1637 but was recognized by Japan as an independent state in 1876. Intrigues between Chinese and Japanese factions at the Korean court came to a head in April 1894 and led to war between the two countries. Japan's military victory over China was sealed in the Treaty of Shimonoseki in April 1895.

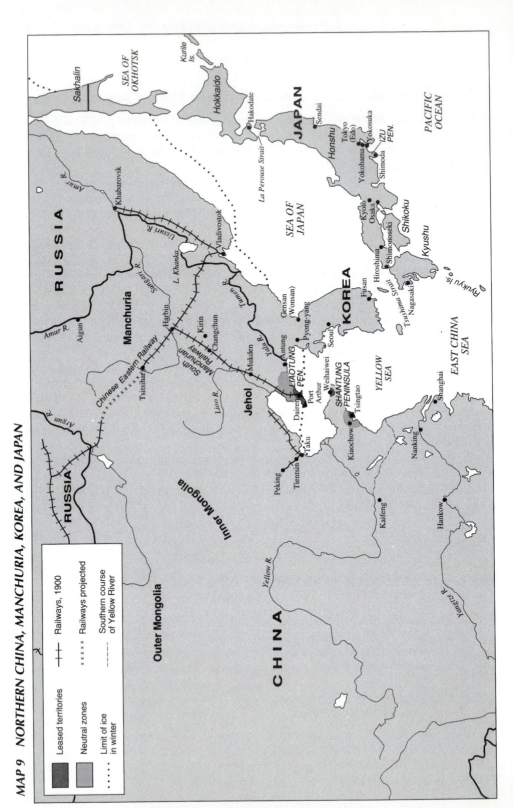

MAP 9   NORTHERN CHINA, MANCHURIA, KOREA, AND JAPAN

Legend:

Leased territories
Neutral zones
Limit of ice in winter

Railways, 1900
Railways projected
Southern course of Yellow River

Labels:

RUSSIA
Manchuria
Sakhalin
SEA OF OKHOTSK
Kurile Is.
Hokkaido
Hakodate
JAPAN
Honshu
Sendai
Tokyo (Edo)
Yokosuka
IZU PEN.
Yokohama
Shimoda
Kyoto
Osaka
Shikoku
Hiroshima
Shimonoseki
Kyushu
Tsushima Strait
Nagasaki
Ryūkyū Is.
La Perouse Strait
SEA OF JAPAN
Amur R.
Khabarovsk
Ussuri R.
Vladivostok
L. Khanka
Sungari R.
Harbin
Aigun
Amur R.
Manchuria
Kirin
Changchun
Tumen R.
Chinese Eastern Railway
Tsitsihar
South Manchurian Railway
Mukden
Liao R.
Jehol
Yalu R.
Antung
Gensan (Wonsan)
Pyong-yang
Seoul
Fusan
KOREA
YELLOW SEA
EAST CHINA SEA
Shanghai
Argun R.
RUSSIA
Inner Mongolia
LIAOTUNG PEN.
Dairen
Port Arthur
Weihaiwei
SHANTUNG PENINSULA
Tsingtao
Kiaochow
Peking
Tientsin
Taku
Nanking
Kaifeng
Hankow
Outer Mongolia
CHINA
Yellow R.
Yangtze R.
PACIFIC OCEAN

From the vantage point of the European powers, the most important feature of the treaty was China's cession to Japan of the southern part of the Liaotung peninsula. Control of the peninsula poised Japan to take a commanding position in north China and establish itself as Russia's main rival in the region. Russia's displeasure with the peace of Shimonoseki in turn brought into play the European alliance system: it gave France the opportunity to demonstrate to Russia the value of the new Franco-Russian alliance. The prospect of active Franco-Russian cooperation in East Asia naturally raised German fears that such cooperation would soon spill over into European politics to the detriment of Germany. So Germany joined the Franco-Russian protest against the Treaty of Shimonoseki in what now became a Triple Intervention; in fact, the German minister in Tokyo used far more brusque language than his French and Russian counterparts. Under duress, Japan retroceded the peninsula to China.

If the German purpose was to woo Russia away from the Franco-Russian alliance by trying to outbid France, it failed miserably. To the contrary: Germany's sudden willingness to please convinced the Russian leadership that the alliance gave Russia the leverage it had previously lacked in its dealings with Germany. As a consequence, the Triple Intervention improved Russia's position in Europe. Russia also reaped a windfall in East Asia: its treaties with both China and Japan in the aftermath of the East Asian war indicate that it was well positioned to exploit China's weakness and Japan's bewilderment at the Triple Intervention.

For Japan, the years 1894–1895 were milestones in its quest for equality with the western powers.[9] The Anglo-Japanese treaty of 1894, coincidentally concluded on the eve of the war, was one measure of Japan's new importance. Within the year, its victory against China— notwithstanding the setback suffered at the hands of Russia, France, and Germany—established Japan as an imperialist power in its own right. The commercial treaty that Japan exacted from China in 1896 makes for an instructive comparison with the Anglo-Japanese treaty of 1894; when juxtaposed, both treaties capture the change in Japan's international status.

a) Anglo-Japanese Treaty of Commerce and Navigation, 16 July 1894

. . . Art. 18: . . .The several foreign settlements in Japan shall be incorporated with the respective Japanese communes, and shall thenceforth form part of the general municipal system of Japan. . . .

Art. 20: . . . from the date it [the present treaty] comes into force . . . [earlier] Conventions, Treaty, Arrangements, and Agreements shall cease to be binding, and, in consequence, the jurisdiction then exercised by British courts in Japan, and all the exceptional privileges, exemptions, and immunities then enjoyed by British subjects as part of or appurtenant to such jurisdiction, shall absolutely and without notice cease and determine, and thereafter all such jurisdiction shall be assumed and exercised by Japanese courts.

Art. 21: The present treaty shall not take effect until at least five years after its signature. . . .

—CTS 180:257–72; SP 86:39; also F. C. Jones, *Extraterritoriality in Japan and the Diplomatic Relations Resulting in its Abolition, 1853–1899* (New Haven, 1931), 175–86

[9]For the origins of the unequal treaties with Japan, cf. Document 6.3.

b)   *Treaty of Shimonoseki, 17 April 1895*

Art. 1: China recognizes definitively the full and complete independence and autonomy of Korea, and, in consequence, the payment of tribute . . . shall wholly cease. . . .

Art. 2: China cedes to Japan in perpetuity and full sovereignty the following territories, together wih all fortifications, arsenals, and public property thereon: a) The southern portion of the province of Fêng-Tien [Liaotung peninsula]. . . . b) The island of Formosa [Taiwan], together with all islands appertaining or belonging to the said island of Formosa. c) The Pescadores Group. . . .

Art. 4: China agrees to pay to Japan as a war indemnity the sum of 200,000,000 Kuping taels. . . .

Art. 6: . . . The Treaties, Conventions, and Regulations now subsisting between China and European Powers shall serve as a basis for the said Treaty [of Commerce and Navigation to be concluded] . . . between Japan and China. . . . The Japanese Government, its officials, commerce, navigation, frontier intercourse and trade, industries, ships, and subjects shall, in every respect be accorded by China most-favored-nation treatment. . . .

—Hertslet III, 1:362–69

c)   *Japanese Proclamation in Response to*
the "Triple Intervention," 10 May 1895

. . . [W]e, out of our regard for peace, do not hesitate to accept their [the three governments'] advice. Moreover, it is not our wish to cause suffering to our people, or to impede the progress of the national destiny by embroiling the Empire in new complications, and thereby imperilling the situation and retarding the restoration of peace. . . .

—Hertslet III, 1:369–70

d)   *Mutsu's[10] Reflections on the Triple Intervention,*
31 December 1895

. . . The reader may well ask, then, why we proceeded to demand territories from China which we already knew might be necessary to retrocede. . . . It was a time when the entire nation seemed delirious with victory, when ambitions and vain hopes ran to a fever pitch. Imagine how chagrined the public would have felt if the peace treaty had omitted that one clause relating to the cession of the Liaotung

---

[10]Mutsu Munemitsu (1844–1897). Japanese foreign minister, 1892–1897, and member of the Japanese delegation at Shimonoseki.

peninsula, an area taken at the cost of so much Japanese blood! The nation's feelings might well have run beyond chagrin; quite possibly the prevailing spirit of the moment would have prohibited the implementation of such a treaty. . . .

Many incidents in world history have been reminiscent of the domestic and international tribulations we experienced during this period. There is, for example, the case of the San Stefano treaty.[11] . . . As in our case more recently, the Russian government found its options limited by internal and external circumstances and probably had little alternative to doing what it did. . . . In considering the revisions made in the Treaty of Shimonoseki, it may appear from today's perspective that Japan, like Gorchakov, caved in to foreign pressures. But actually, our problems arose because we had to give prior concern to *domestic* pressures. . . .

—Mutsu Munemitsu, *Kenkenroku: A Diplomatic Record of the Sino-Japanese War, 1894–95*, ed. by Gordon Mark Berger (Tokyo, 1982), 251–54

e)   Sino-Russian ("Li-Lobanov") Treaty, 22 May/3 June 1896

Art. 1: . . . all the provisions prescribed in it [this treaty] become immediately operative in the event of a Japanese invasion of the territory of Russia in East Asia, the territory of China, or the territory of Korea. In such an event, both of the contracting powers shall dispatch all the military and naval forces that can be mobilized at the moment to assist each other. . . .

Art. 4: . . . the Chinese government agrees to let Russia build a railroad through the Chinese territory of Heilungkiang and Kirin [northern Manchuria] to reach Vladivostok. . . .

—*CTS* 182:425; also Dun J. Li (ed.), *China in Transition, 1517–1911* (New York, 1969), 189–90

f)   Russo-Japanese ("Lobanov-Yamagata") Treaty, 28 May/9 June 1896

Art. 1: Intending to ameliorate the financial difficulties of Korea, the governments of Japan and Russia will advise the Korean government to limit all unnecessary expenditures and to attempt to balance revenues and expenditures. Should it become necessary, as a result of substantial and official reforms, for Korea to take out a foreign loan, the two governments will extend their assistance to Korea after reaching bilateral agreement. . . .

Art. 3: To facilitate its communications with Korea, the Japanese government will exercise control over the telegraph lines presently in its possession. Russia has the right to construct a telegraph between Seoul and its own borders. Korea will be entitled to acquire the said telegraph lines as soon as it is in a position to do so. . . .

—*CTS* 182:455–57; *SP* 88:471

[11]Document 9.7.

g)   *Sino-Japanese Commercial Treaty, 21 July 1896*

... Art. 9: ... In no case shall Japanese subjects be called upon to pay in China other or higher import or export duties than are or may be paid by the subjects or citizens of the most-favored-nation; ...

Art. 20: Jurisdiction over the persons and property of Japanese subjects in China is reserved exclusively to the duly authorized Japanese authorities, who shall hear and determine all cases brought against Japanese subjects or property by Japanese subjects. ...

[Additional Protocol, 19 October 1896, Art. 1:] It is agreed that settlements to be possessed exclusively by Japan shall be established at the towns and ports newly opened to trade. The management of roads and local police authority shall be vested solely in the Japanese consuls. ...

—Hertslet III, 1:373–82

h)   *Contract between the Russo-Chinese Bank and China,*
27 August/8 September 1896

... The Chinese government, having decided on the construction of a railroad line establishing direct communication between the town of Chita and the Russian railroad of the South Ussuri, entrusts the construction and establishment of this railroad to the Russo-Chinese Bank under the following conditions:

1. ... The statutes of this Company shall conform to Russian usages for railroad companies. The stock of this Company can only be acquired by Chinese or Russian subjects. ...

6. ... Property belonging to the Company shall be exempt from all state taxes [*impôt foncier*]. The Company shall have the absolute and exclusive right of administration of its property. The Company shall have the right to undertake on its property construction of all types, and also to construct and to establish a telegraph for the needs of the line. Also, the revenues of the Company, all its receipts and tariffs for the transport of persons and merchandise, shall be exempt from all taxes and duties. An exception is made for mines, for which there will be a special arrangement. ...

9. Travellers who are not Chinese subjects, if they wish to leave the property of the railroad, must be in possession of Chinese passports. The Company is responsible for seeing that travellers who are not Chinese subjects do not leave the railroad's property if they have no Chinese passports.

—China. The Maritime Customs, *Treaties, Conventions, etc., between China and Foreign Countries*
(1917; reprint: New York, 1973), 1:208–11

10.6   CLEVELAND'S MESSAGE TO CONGRESS,
17 DECEMBER 1895

In the course of the drawn-out border dispute between Venezuela and British Guiana, the Salisbury government argued that the United States did not have legal standing in this conflict because the Monroe Doctrine (Document 2.7) did not apply. The Cleveland administration rose to this challenge in a message to Congress. Although his defense of the Monroe Doctrine's standing in international law was ingenuous at best, President Cleveland left no doubt about the determination of the United States to play a role in the settlement of the dispute. Whether Cleveland's language constituted an ultimatum is debatable. A comparison of the message with the contemporaneous Kruger Telegram (Document 10.7)—which mapped out no conditions or course of action for the future—is instructive, as is a contrast with the "ultimatum" Germany served Russia at the height of the Bosnian crisis in March 1909 (Document 11.12).

Cleveland's Message to Congress, 17 December 1895

Practically, the principle for which we contend has peculiar, if not exclusive, relation to the United States. It may not have been admitted in so many words to the code of international law, but since in international councils every nation is entitled to the rights belonging to it, if the enforcement of the Monroe Doctrine is something we may justly claim, it has its place in the code of international law as certainly and as securely as if it were specifically mentioned. . . .

The course to be pursued by this Government, in view of the present condition, does not appear to admit of serious doubt. Having labored faithfully for many years to induce Great Britain to submit this dispute to impartial arbitration, and having been now finally apprised of her refusal to do so, nothing remains but to accept the situation, to recognize its plain requirements, and deal with it accordingly. Great Britain's present proposition has never thus far been regarded as admissible by Venezuela, though any adjustment of the boundary which that country may deem for her advantage and may enter into of her own free will can not of course be objected to by the United States. Assuming, however, that the attitude of Venezuela will remain unchanged, the dispute has reached such a stage as to make it now incumbent upon the United States to take measures to determine with sufficient certainty for its justification what is the true divisional line between the Republic of Venezuela and British Guiana. The inquiry to that end should of course be conducted carefully and judicially, and due weight should be given to all available evidence, records, and facts in support of the claims of both parties.

In order that such an examination should be prosecuted in a thorough and satisfactory manner, I suggest that the Congress make an adequate appropriation for the expenses for a commission, to be appointed by the Executive, who shall make the necessary investigation and report upon the matter with the least possible delay. When such report is made and accepted, it will, in my opinion, be the duty of the United States to resist, by every means in its power, as a willful aggression upon its rights and interests, the appropriation by Great Britain of any lands or the exercise of governmental jurisdiction over any territory which, after investigation, we have determined of right belongs to Venezuela.

In making these recommendations I am fully alive to the responsibility incurred, and keenly realize all the consequences that may follow.

—*Congressional Record*, 54th Congress, 1st Session
(Washington, 1896), 28i:191

10.7   **THE KRUGER TELEGRAM**

Wilhelm II to President Kruger, 3 January 1896 • *Queen Victoria to Wilhelm II,*
5 January 1896 • *Queen Victoria to the Prince of Wales, 11 January 1896* •
Holstein to Hatzfeldt, 12 April 1897

About five hundred British raiders, led by Dr. Leander Starr Jameson, crossed from the Cape
Colony to the Transvaal on 29 December 1895. Jameson was an administrator of the British
South Africa Company and a long-time intimate of the Cape prime minister, Cecil Rhodes. The
pretext for Jameson's raid was to support an uprising of British residents ("uitlanders") in the
Transvaal. When the uprising did not materialize, Rhodes tried to call off the venture, but
Jameson, ignoring this last-minute reversal, went ahead. He and most of his followers were
captured by the Boers on 2 January. Turned over to British authorities by the Transvaal government, Jameson was charged with "preparing a military expedition" against a "friendly
state" and sentenced to fifteen months in an English prison. He was released after five and
served as Cape prime minister from 1904 to 1908.

   The failure of the raid led to Rhodes's resignation and a mild censure by a parliamentary
committee. As a member of the committee, Colonial Secretary Joseph Chamberlain skillfully
covered his own tracks. For his part, Rhodes avoided implicating Chamberlain even though
there was little love lost between the two men. Chamberlain used his influence to repay the
debt: the committee neither revoked the charter for Rhodes's South Africa Company nor recommended that his name be struck from the list of Her Majesty's privy councilors.

   The news of Jameson's capture gave Wilhelm II the opportunity he had been seeking to
embarrass the Salisbury government. On a visit to Cowes the preceding summer, Wilhelm had
received the impression that he had been stood up by Salisbury. Probably the result of a misunderstanding, the incident was nonetheless interpreted by the Kaiser as a deliberate snub; in
any case, Wilhelm had been hoping to even the score ever since. The vehicle he chose was a
congratulatory telegram to the president of the Transvaal, Paul Kruger.

   The Kruger Telegram unleashed a storm of indignation in Britain, all the more severe because of the pent-up frustration over President Cleveland's invocation, on 17 December 1895,
of the Monroe Doctrine in the boundary dispute between Venezuela and British Guiana (Document 10.6).

a)   ***Wilhelm II to President Kruger, 3 January 1896***

I express to you my sincere congratulations that you and your people, without appealing to the help of friendly powers, have succeeded, by your own energetic action
against the armed bands which invaded your country as disturbers of the peace, in
restoring peace and in maintaining the independence of the country against outside
attacks.

                                                              —*GP*, 11:2610

b)   ***Queen Victoria to Wilhelm II, 5 January 1896***

My Dear William, . . .As your Grandmother to whom you have always shown so much
affection and of whose example you have always spoken with so much respect, I feel

I cannot refrain from expressing my deep regret at the telegram you sent President Kruger. It is considered very unfriendly towards this country, which I feel sure it is not intended to be, and has, I grieve to say, made a very painful impression here. The action of Dr. Jameson was of course very wrong and totally unwarranted; but considering the very peculiar position in which the Transvaal stands towards Great Britain,[12] I think it would have been far better to have said nothing. Our great wish has always been to keep on the best of terms with Germany, trying to act together, but I fear your Agents in the Colonies do the very reverse, which deeply grieves us. Let me hope that you will try and check this. . . .

I hope you will take my remarks in good part, as they are entirely dictated by my desire for your good.

—*QV*, 3rd Series, 3:8–9

c)   *Queen Victoria to the Prince of Wales, 11 January 1896*

Dearest Bertie, . . . It would not do to have given him [Wilhelm] "a good snub." Those sharp, cutting answers and remarks only irritate and do harm, and in Sovereigns and Princes should be most carefully guarded against. William's faults come from impetuousness (as well as conceit); and calmness and firmness are the most powerful weapons in such cases. . . .

—*QV*, 3rd Series, 3:18–20

d)   *Holstein to Hatzfeldt,[13] 12 April 1897*

. . . It is my firm conviction that we must get out of the position in which the Krüger Telegram placed us. For what practical results can we expect from the Krüger Telegram policy? No sensible person can expect Germany to establish herself in Delagoa Bay or its vicinity, with Madagascar on one side and the Cape Colony on the other. But if we don't want that, what business have we to be there at all? We can't burden ourselves with the luxury of England's antipathy simply for the sake of the Boers, who like all Dutchmen are full of mistrustful antagonism towards Germany.

I admit that I agreed last year to the Krüger Telegram and that I knew of its contents before it was dispatched. I remained silent because Marschall[14] told me on his return from the conference with the Kaiser, Chancellor, and various military and naval officers: "You have no idea what proposals were made there, this is still the mildest." At that moment I did not suspect *how* harmful the effect of that telegram would be for what I regard as German interests. . . .

England interpreted the Krüger Telegram in all seriousness as a military challenge. All signs point to that. . . . To him [the Kaiser] the Krüger Telegram was not a prelude to war—at most he thought of a war on land in South Africa in which the

---

[12]See Document 9.18.

[13]Paul von Hatzfeldt (1831–1901). German ambassador in London, 1885–1901.

[14]Adolf Marschall von Bieberstein (1842–1912). State secretary in the German foreign ministry, 1890–1897; ambassador in Constantinople, 1897–1912; ambassador in London, 1912.

fleets would be onlookers!—but as an argument for bringing the German navy up to the strength of the English. This is still the Kaiser's guiding political idea which takes precedence over all others, and it is not impossible that he will be afraid that his plans for the fleet will lose in urgency the moment our relations with England are again somewhat better. However, "money talks." A political offer—that is, a casual remark by Lord Salisbury that, for example, he would have no objection to an occupation of Amoy and its hinterland—would in my opinion still be very effective. Moreover the Kaiser, despite his naval hobby horse, is too open-minded not to see how greatly Germany's political power would be increased if we, without sacrificing our good relations with Russia, were to restore our relations with England. . . .

—HP, 4:608

10.8   FROM GRIDLOCK TO DISENGAGEMENT: THE POWERS, THE ARMENIAN MASSACRES, AND THE MEDITERRANEAN, 1894–1897

Holstein to Radolin, 21 December 1895 ● Salisbury to Iwan-Müller,
31 August 1896 ● Salisbury's Circular, 20 October 1896 ●
Meeting of the Russian Crown Council, 23 November/5 December 1896 ●
Muraviev to Liechtenstein, 5/17 May 1897

The Porte's pledge, in article 61 of the Treaty of Berlin (Document 9.10) and in the Cyprus convention (Document 9.8), to sponsor reforms in the Armenian vilayets remained a dead letter. But between 1894 and 1896, the European public was jolted out of its complacency by successive massacres of Armenians at the hands of Turks and Kurds—first in Armenia proper and, subsequently, in Constantinople. Some of the outrages were deliberately provoked by members of the Armenian Revolutionary Federation in the hope of spurring the intervention of the powers on behalf of Armenian liberties. This expectation, however, was not fulfilled.

Whether one, several, or all of the powers should intervene—and, if so, how—became a recurring question in European diplomacy for the better part of three years. In an atmosphere rife with mutual recriminations, Britain was widely suspected of favoring a partition of the Ottoman Empire as long as others bore the brunt of the ensuing conflagration. But Salisbury in fact shied away from a go-it-alone policy. Fearing a Russian counterstrike against the Bosporus if Britain sent a fleet to the Dardanelles, the Salisbury cabinet resigned itself to proposing no more than a joint démarche in Constantinople.

The frustrations of the Armenian question prompted Salisbury to reexamine British policy. His conclusions ranged from a scathing critique of previous British administrations to the realization that the defense of the Straits was no longer a vital British interest. He thus acknowledged a trend that had been in the making ever since Britain acquired control of the Suez canal, Cyprus, and Egypt (Documents 9.8 and 9.19). Britain's indifference to the fate of the Straits was a consequence of its occupation of Egypt; but disengagement from the Straits in turn demanded that Britain further consolidate its presence on the Nile (Document 10.14).

The Russian government similarly preferred inaction. The Russian ambassador to Constantinople, Alexander Nelidov, traveled in vain to Petersburg in December 1896 to persuade the tsar's crown council to approve a *coup de main* against the Bosporus. The opposition to Nelidov's scheme was led by Sergei Witte, the Russian minister of finance. Witte feared a larger conflagration in which Russia could not count on French support and that would dissipate resources he intended for East Asia (cf. Document 10.5). Like the British cabinet, the Russian crown council feared that a unilateral expedition against the Straits would provoke the formation of a European coalition; Russia, like Britain, preferred to channel its energies toward ventures that held out greater promise.

The relative ease with which the powers, in 1897, contained the Greco-Turkish war and the Cretan question showed how the Eastern Question had receded from their collective consciousness. The diplomatic aftermath of a state visit to Russia by Emperor Franz Joseph further testified to this phenomenon: in an exchange of notes, both Austria-Hungary and Russia agreed to set aside their rivalry in the Balkans.

a)   **Holstein to Radolin,[15] 21 December 1895**

. . . Our attitude towards England is at the moment mistrustful; for we don't want a war, but we suspect that England is planning a big war not only for herself—this idea we would tolerate—but one that would involve Austria and Italy, in other words something that would seriously endanger our after-dinner nap. That the latter have consistently rejected recent English proposals was our doing. . . .

I think that Salisbury is untruthful. . . .

If Russia is cautious in pressing towards the Mediterranean, if it focused its attention there, we will undoubtedly succeed in restraining Austria, despite the howls of Hungary, and also Italy. As long as these two are out of it and not in danger of being demolished, we can be indifferent to everything else. Marschall today told the English ambassador: "Even if another hundred thousand Armenians are killed, their death still concerns us less than that of two hundred thousand Germans. . . ."

—HP, 3:514

b)   **Salisbury to Iwan-Müller,[16] 31 August 1896**

. . . There is no such thing as a fixed policy because policy, like all organic entities, is always in the making. I do not know that I can sum up the present trend of English policy better than by saying we are engaged in slowly escaping from the dangerous errors of 1846–1856. Palmerston was a disciple of Canning, and with him believed that foreign policy should follow your political proclivities. France was Liberal, Russia and Austria despotic,—therefore, in his mind, it was our policy to shake off the Russian and Austrian alliance and cultivate that of France. Such a policy is obviously unsound,—similarity of political faith is no more indicative of a useful ally than similarity of religious faith would be.

Politics is a matter of business: our allies should be those who are most likely to help or not to hinder the interests of which we, as a government, are the trustees.

---

[15]Hugo Leszczyc, Prince von Radolin (1841–1917). German ambassador in Constantinople, 1892–1895; in Petersburg, 1895–1900; in Paris, 1900–1910.

[16]Ernest Iwan-Müller (1853–1910), English Tory. Foreign policy columnist for the London *Daily Telegraph*, 1896–1910.

Now the interests of France clashed with ours on almost every coast; those of Russia only on the Afghan-Perso frontier, those of Austria nowhere. Therefore it was our policy to maintain the friendship with Russia and Austria which had existed during the first half of the century, and by its help to keep France within bounds.

But Palmerston would be guided by common sympathies instead of by common interests. He made war with Russia; he insulted Austria; and he ostentatiously made friends with France. In order to baulk and baffle Russia he, and his school, set up as a political faith the independence and integrity of the Ottoman Empire.

Forty years have passed away, and look at the results. We have not kept France,—she is more our enemy than ever. But the feud with Russia remains. Austria has become of less importance, because out of the fragments of her dominions or her followings Germany and Italy have been created; and we have to find in the nominal alliance of these two last what consolation we can for the necessity of coping, practically alone, with the alliance of France and Russia. If we had only listened to the Emperor Nicholas when he spoke to Sir Hamilton Seymour, what a much pleasanter outlook would meet us when we contemplate the continent of Europe.[17]

It is much easier to lament than to repair. It may not be possible for England and Russia to return to their old relations. But it is an object to be wished for and approached as opportunity offers. At all events efforts should be made to avoid needless aggravation of the feud between them which governments and not the nations have made. The French and German *people* both hate us; the Russian people do not. It is not possible to stop the impulse which past mistakes have given. The generation whose political beliefs were molded by the passions of the Crimean War is only now dying out. We may, without any fault of our own, find ourselves opposed to Russia on this question or that, in consequence of past commitments. All we can do is to try to narrow the chasm that separates us. It is the best chance for something like an equilibrium of Europe.

There is no reason why Germany, under steady guidance, should not go with us, but steadiness is not the note of its government just now.

—BD, 6, p. 780

c)   *Salisbury's Circular, 20 October 1896*

. . . These attacks [on Armenians] may possibly in some cases have originated in disturbances commenced by Armenian agitators, but it is impossible not to hold the Turkish authorities, civil and military, mainly responsible for them and their effects. . . . I propose that the Six Powers should instruct their representatives [in Constantinople] to consider and report to their governments what changes in the government and administration of the Turkish Empire are, in their judgement, likely to be most effective in maintaining the stability of the Empire, and preventing the recurrence of the frightful cruelties by which the last two years have been lamentably distinguished. But before those instructions are given, Her Majesty's Government are of opinion that provision ought to be made that any resolution to which the Powers may, in consequence, unanimously come should be carried into operation. It is an ob-

[17]See Document 5.2.

ject of primary importance that the concert of Europe should be maintained; and as long as any of the Powers, or any one Power, is not satisfied with the expediency of the recommendations that are put forward, no action in respect to them can be taken. But if any recommendations made by the ambassadors should approve themselves to all the Powers as measures suitable for adoption, it must not be admitted, at the point which we have at present reached, that the objections of the Turkish government can be an obstacle to their being carried into effect. . . .

—*PP 1897* 51:279–83; Bourne, 442–46

d)   *Meeting of the Russian Crown Council, 23 November/5 December 1896*

[Witte:[18]] Capture of the Upper Bosporus, at the present time and under present conditions, without prior agreement with the Great Powers, is extremely risky and may have dire consequences. . . .

—V. Khvostov, "Pro'ekt zakhvata Bosfora v 1896g," *Krasny Arkhiv* 47/48 (1931), 64–70

e)   *Muraviev[19] to Liechtenstein,[20] 5/17 May 1897*

. . . It was agreed that, in case, in spite of all our efforts, the present status quo of the Balkan peninsula can no longer be maintained, "Russia and Austria-Hungary discard in advance all idea of conquest; and they are decided to make this principle respected by every other power which should manifest contrary designs." As Russia is unable to admit the least infringement of the provisions relative to the closing of the Straits of the Bosporus and of the Dardanelles, as sanctioned by existing treaties, Austria-Hungary "recognizes from the outset the perfect legitimacy of this principle." On the other hand, "the establishment of a new order of things in the Balkan peninsula, in case it should occur, would give rise to a special stipulation between Austria-Hungary and Russia."

Count Goluchowski,[21] in his note of 8 May, fixed, henceforth, as a basis of such an understanding, the four following points:

a. "The advantages accorded to Austria Hungary by the Treaty of Berlin [Document 9.10] are and remain acquired by her." In subscribing to this principle, we deem it necessary to observe that the Treaty of Berlin assures to Austria-Hungary the right of military occupation of Bosnia and Herzegovina. The annexation of these two provinces would raise a more extensive question, which would require special

---

[18]Sergei Lu Witte (1849–1915). Minister of finance, 1892–1903.

[19]Michael Nikolaevich, Count Muraviev (1845–1900). Russian foreign minister, 1896–1900.

[20]Franz, Prince von und zu Liechtenstein (1853–1938). Austro-Hungarian ambassador to Russia, 1894–1898; reigning prince of Liechtenstein, 1929–1938.

[21]Agenor, Count Goluchowski (1849–1921). Austro-Hungarian foreign minister, 1895–1906. The contents of Goluchowski's note of 8 May, not reproduced here, can be inferred from this extract.

scrutiny at the proper times and places. As to the Sanjak of Novibazar, there would also be the necessity to specify its boundaries, which, indeed, have never been sufficiently defined.

It seems to us that points *b* and *c*, having regard to the eventual formation of a principality of Albania and to the equitable partition of all the territory to be disposed of between the different small Balkan states, touch upon questions of the future which it would be premature and very difficult to decide at present.

As to point *d*, providing: "having finally recorded that our two cabinets have no other objective in the Balkan peninsula than the maintenance, the consolidation, and the pacific development of the small states established there, we agreed to pursue in the future in this field a policy of perfect harmony, and to avoid in consequence everything which might engender between us elements of conflict or of mistrust"—this point answers entirely to the views of the Emperor [Nicholas II], my August Master. . . .

—Pribram, 1:191–95

10.9   SALISBURY PROPOSES ENGLISH AND RUSSIAN SPHERES IN ASIA, 25 JANUARY 1898

Salisbury to O'Conor, 25 January 1898

The scramble for territorial concessions in China (Document 10.10), set off by the German seizure of Kiaochow in November 1897, reached an acute stage in the winter and spring of 1898. Foremost among the contestants, Russia sought to lease Port Arthur and Dairen, hoping to secure a stranglehold on Manchuria and the approaches to Peking (Bejing). Fearing that the Chinese government would give in to the Russian demands, Salisbury sought an agreement with Russia that would ensure the latter's economic preponderance in north China, thereby obviating the need for territorial concessions. There can be no question that his proposal reflected the frustrations and "lessons" of the Armenian crisis (Document 10.8). In Russia, the leading proponent of purely economic expansion in Asia, finance minister Sergei Witte, may well have favored an agreement embodying Salisbury's suggestions, but the tsar turned it down.

Salisbury to O'Conor,[22] 25 January 1898

Our idea was this. The two Empires of China and Turkey are so weak that in all important matters they are constantly guided by the advice of Foreign Powers. In giving this advice Russia and England are constantly opposed, neutralizing each other's efforts much more frequently than the real antagonism of their interests would justify; and this condition of things is not likely to diminish, but to increase. It is to remove or lessen this evil that we have thought than [sic] an understanding with Russia might benefit both nations.

[22]Sir Nicholas O'Conor (1843–1908). British minister in Peking, 1892–1895; ambassador in St. Petersburg, 1895–1898, Constantinople, 1898–1908.

We contemplate no infraction of existing rights. We would not admit the violation of any existing treaties, or impair the integrity of the present empires of either China or Turkey. These two conditions are vital. We aim at no partition of territory, but only a partition of preponderance. It is evident that both in respect to Turkey and China there are large portions which interest Russia much more than England and *vice versa*. Merely as an illustration, and binding myself to nothing, I would say that the portion of Turkey which drains into the Black Sea, together with the drainage valley of the Euphrates as far as Bagdad, interest Russia much more than England: whereas Turkish Africa, Arabia and the Valley of the Euphrates below Bagdad interest England much more than Russia. A similar distinction exists in China between the Valley of the Hoango [sic] with the territory north of it and the Valley of the Yangtze.

Would it be possible to arrange that where, in regard to these territories our counsels differ, the Power least interested should give way to and assist the other? . . .

—BD, 1:9

10.10   SLICING THE CHINA MELON, 1898

Chinese Notes to the British Government, 11 and 13 February 1898 ●
Chinese Lease of Kiaochow to Germany, 6 March 1898 ● *Chinese Lease of
Port Arthur to Russia, 15/27 March 1898* ● *Chinese Lease of Kuang-chou wan
to France, 10 April 1898* ● *Chinese Note to Japan, 26 April 1898* ●
Chinese Lease of Kowloon to Britain, 9 June 1898 ● *Chinese Lease of
Weihaiwei to Britain, 1 July 1898* ● *Chinese Note to the Russian Government,
20 May/1 June 1899*

The Sino-Japanese war of 1894–1895 once again drew the attention of the Great Powers to China. In the contest for commercial concessions in the aftermath of the war, the undisputed victor was Russia (Document 10.5). But the rivalry among the powers entered a new phase in 1897 when the murder of two German missionaries in Shantung province gave the German government the excuse to extract a coaling station from the Chinese government.

The German seizure of Kiaochow led all Great Powers to jockey for position in China. In their scramble for concessions, the powers looked beyond the acquisition of naval bases and sought to carve out spheres of influence in which they would receive preferential treatment in railroad building, mining, and the construction of public works. As before, Russia wrested the farthest-reaching concessions from China.

Much of the subsequent history of imperialism in China is intertwined with the territorial features of the 1898 treaties. As a result of Japan's victory against Russia in 1905, the lease of the Kwantung peninsula with Port Arthur was transferred to Japan.[23] Japan sought a similar arrangement after its capture of Kiaochow in the First World War but was pressured by the United States to retrocede the Shantung peninsula to China in 1922. As Hong Kong's urban sprawl expanded into Kowloon, the colony became inseparable from its New Territories. Anticipating the expiration of the Kowloon lease in 1997, the British government in a treaty concluded with the People's Republic of China in 1985 arranged for the transfer to the latter not only of Kowloon but of Hong Kong in its entirety.

---

[23]Article 5 of the Treaty of Portsmouth, 5 September 1905. French text in Hertslet III, 1:608–14.

MAP 10   SOUTHERN CHINA AND SOUTHEAST ASIA

a)   ***Chinese Notes to the British Government,***
11 and 13 February 1898

[11 February 1898:] . . . the Chinese government[,] . . . aware of the great importance
that has always been attached by Great Britain to the retention in Chinese possession
of the Yang-tze region . . . observe[s] that the Yang-tze region is of the greatest impor-

tance as concerning the whole position of China, and it is out of the question that territory (in it) should be mortgaged, leased, or ceded to another power. . . .

[13 February 1898:] The Yamên [Chinese foreign ministry] . . . observe that British trade with China exceeds that of all other countries, and . . . that as in the past, so in the future, an Englishman shall be employed as Inspector-General [of Maritime Customs]. But if at some future time the trade of some other country at the various Chinese ports should become greater than that of Great Britain, China will then of course not be bound to necessarily employ an Englishman as Inspector-General. . . .

—Hertslet III, 1:120; John V. A. MacMurray (ed.), *Treaties and Agreements with and Concerning China, 1894–1919* (reprint: New York, 1973), 1:106

b)   *Chinese Lease of Kiaochow to Germany, 6 March 1898*

Part I, . . .Art. 2: . . . the Emperor of China cedes to Germany on lease, provisionally for ninety-nine years, both sides of the entrance to the Bay of Kiaochow. . . .

Part II, Art. 1: The Imperial Chinese Government grants Germany the concession for the following railroads in the province of Shantung. . . .

Art. 4: Within a distance of 30 li along the said railways . . . German entrepreneurs will be permitted to engage in the exploitation of coal deposits and in other enterprises, and to construct the necessary public works. . . .

Part III, Single Article: When in the province of Shantung for whatever purpose there will be need for foreign individuals, capital, or materials, the Chinese Imperial Government commits itself to offer these projects and requests for materials to German industrialists and merchants occupied in such trades. . . .

—Hertslet III, 1:350–54; binding German and Chinese text in Maritime Customs, *Treaties*, op. cit., 2:208–14

c)   *Chinese lease of Port Arthur to Russia, 15/27 March 1898*

Art. 1: In order for the protection of the Russian fleet, and (to enable it) to have a secure base on the north coast of China, His Majesty the Emperor of China agrees to lease to Russia Port Arthur, Talienwan [Dairen], and the adjacent waters. But this lease is to be without prejudice to Chinese sovereign rights in that territory. . . .

Art. 3: The term of the lease is fixed as twenty-five years. . . .

Art. 5: To the north of the territory leased there shall be left a piece of [neutralized] territory. . . . This piece is to be entirely left to Chinese officials, but no Chinese troops are to enter it, except after arrangement with Russian officials.

Art. 6: . . . as Port Arthur is solely a naval port, only Russian and Chinese vessels are to be allowed to use it, and it is to be considered a closed port as far as the war and merchant vessels of the other powers are to be concerned. As to Talienwan, with the exception of a part within the port which, like Port Arthur, is to be reserved for the use of Russian and Chinese men-of-war, the remainder is to be a trading port, where the merchant vessels of all countries can freely come and go. . . .

[Additional Agreement, 25 April/7 May 1898:] Art. 3:The Russian government consents that the terminus of the branch line connecting the Siberian railway with the Liaotung Peninsula shall be at Port Arthur and Talienwan, and at no other port in the said peninsula. It is further agreed in common that railroad privileges in districts traversed by this branch line shall not be given to the subjects of other Powers. . . .

Art. 5: The Chinese government agrees 1. That without Russia's consent no concession will be made in the neutral ground for the use of subjects of other powers; 2. That the ports on the seacoast, east and west of the neutral ground, shall not be opened to the trade of other Powers; 3. And that without Russia's consent no road and mining concessions, industrial and mercantile privileges shall be granted in the neutral territory.

—Hertslet III, 1:505–9; binding Russian and Chinese text in: Maritime Customs, *Treaties*, op. cit., 1:219–32

d)   *Chinese Lease of Kuang-chou wan to France, 10 April 1898*

Art. 1: The Chinese Government, because of its friendship for France, leases Kuang-chou wan to the French Government for 99 years for the establishment of a naval base and a coaling station. . . .

[Separate French Note:] . . . [T]he Government of the [French] Republic would attach particular value to receiving from the Chinese government an assurance that it will not cede to any other power all or a part of the territory of those provinces . . . [bordering on Tonkin].

[Separate Chinese Note:] Our Yamên considers that the Chinese provinces bordering on Tonkin, being important frontier points which interest her in the highest degree, must always be administered by China and remain under her sovereignty. There is no reason that they should be ceded or leased to any power.

—Hertslet III, 1:329–31; MacMurray, *Treaties*, op. cit., 1:123

e)   *Chinese Note to Japan, 26 April 1898*

. . . [T]he Province of Fukien . . . China will never cede or lease to any other power whatsoever. . . .

—MacMurray, *Treaties*, 1:126

f)   *Chinese Lease of Kowloon to Britain, 9 June 1898*

Whereas it has for many years past been recognized that an extension of Hong Kong territory is necessary for the proper defence and protection of the colony, it has now been agreed . . . that the limits of British territory shall be enlarged under lease. . . . The term of this lease shall be 99 years. . . .

—Hertslet III, 1:120–22

g)   *Chinese Lease of Weihaiwei to Britain, 1 July 1898*

In order to provide Great Britain with a suitable naval harbor in North China, and for the better protection of British commerce in the neighboring seas, the Government of His Majesty the Emperor of China agree to lease . . . Weihaiwei, in the province of Shantung, and the adjacent waters, for so long a period as Port Arthur shall remain under the occupation of Russia.

—Hertslet III, 1:122–23; MacMurray, *Treaties*, 1:207–8, 335–36

h)   *Chinese Note to the Russian Government,*
20 May/1 June 1899

. . . if railways are in future built from Peking to the north or to the northeast towards the Russian border, China reserves the right to construct such roads with Chinese capital and under Chinese supervision, but if it is proposed to have such construction undertaken by any other nation, the proposal shall be first made to the Russian government or to the Russian [Chinese Eastern Railroad] syndicate to construct the railway, and under no consideration will any other government or a syndicate of any other nationality be allowed to construct the railway. . . .

—MacMurray, *Treaties*, 1:207–8, 335–36

10.11   SALISBURY AND CHAMBERLAIN ON IMPERIALISM AND ISOLATION

Salisbury's "Dying Nations" Speech, 4 May 1898 •
Chamberlain at Birmingham, 13 May 1898

Founded in 1884 and named in deference to Disraeli's botanical tastes, the Primrose League became one of England's principal proimperial lobbies. Its annual meeting of 1898 gave Salisbury the opportunity to launch a spirited defense of his foreign policy. The speech was notable for its unabashed application of Social Darwinist arguments to the world of foreign affairs and caused consternation among the representatives of some lesser states accredited to the Court of St. James.

Salisbury's "Dying Nations" speech has to be understood against the background of Russia's seizure of Port Arthur (Document 10.10) and Britain's reaction—the impending lease of Weihaiwei from China. His approach to the problems of imperial defense, however, was challenged immediately by his colonial secretary, Joseph Chamberlain. Not to be outdone, Chamberlain developed *his* vision before his home constituency on 13 May. The speech reflected all the recurring themes in Chamberlain's thinking: closer integration of the dominions with the mother country, an understanding with the United States, and, in a direct challenge to his own prime minister, abandonment of the policy of isolation.

a)   ***Salisbury's "Dying Nations" Speech, 4 May 1898***

. . . Do not imagine that this imbroglio that has taken place in China is exceptional in its character, or that similar things will not recur. If we could look simply upon the world as it presents itself to us, if we could merely count our colonies and our possessions and our growing enormous trade, we might, indeed, look forward to the future without disquietude. We know that we shall maintain against all comers that which we possess, and we know in spite of the jargon about isolation, that we are amply competent to do so [cheers]. But that will not secure the peace of the world.

You may roughly divide the nations of the world as the living and the dying. On one side you have great countries of enormous power growing in power every year, growing in wealth, growing in dominion, growing in the perfection of their organization. Railways have given to them the power to concentrate upon any one point the whole military force of their population, and to assemble armies of a magnitude and power never dreamt of in the generations that have gone by. Science has placed in the hands of those armies weapons ever growing in the efficacy of destruction, and therefore, adding to the power—fearfully to the power—of those who have the opportunity of using them. By the side of these splendid organizations, of which nothing seems to diminish the force and which present rival claims which the future may only be able by a bloody arbitrament to adjust—by the side of these there are a number of communities which I can only describe as dying, though the epithet applies to them of course in very different degrees and with a very different amount of certain application. They are mainly communities that are not Christian, but I regret to say that is not exclusively the case, and in these States disorganization and decay are advancing almost as fast as concentration and increasing power are advancing in the living nations that stand beside them. Decade after decade they are weaker, poorer, and less provided with leading men or institutions in which they can trust, apparently drawing nearer and nearer to their fate and yet clinging with strange tenacity to the life which they have got. In them misgovernment is not only not cured but is constantly on the increase. The society, and official society, the administration, is a mass of corruption, so that there is no firm ground on which any hope for reform or restoration could be based, and in their various degrees they are presenting a terrible picture to the more enlightened portion of the world—a picture which, unfortunately, the increase in the means of our information and communication draws with darker and more conspicuous lineaments in the face of all nations, appealing to their feelings as well as to their interests, calling upon them to bring forward a remedy. How long this state of things is likely to go on, of course, I do not attempt to prophesy. All I can indicate is that that process is proceeding, that the weak States are becoming weaker and the strong States are becoming stronger. It needs no speciality of prophecy to point out to you what the inevitable result of that combined process must be. For one reason or for another—from the necessities of politics or under the pretence of philanthropy—the living nations will gradually encroach on the territory of the dying, and the seeds and causes of conflict amongst civilized nations will speedily appear. Of course, it is not to be supposed that any one nation of the living nations will be allowed to have the profitable monopoly of curing or cutting up these unfortunate patients [laughter] and the controversy is as to who shall have the privilege of doing so, and in what measure he shall do it. These things may introduce causes of fatal difference between the great nations whose mighty armies stand opposite threatening each other. These are the dangers, I think, which threaten us in the period that is coming on. It is a period which will tax our resolution, our tenacity, and imperial instincts to the utmost. Undoubtedly we shall not allow England to be at a disadvantage in any re-arrangement that may take place [cheers]. On the other hand, we shall not be jealous if desolation and sterility are removed by the aggrandizement of a rival in regions to which our arms cannot extend. . . .

—*The Times*, 5 May 1898

b)   *Chamberlain at Birmingham, 13 May 1898*

The other day . . . Lord Salisbury [cheers] made a powerful and an eloquent speech, in which he urged the people of this country to apply this same method of testing by results to the foreign policy of the Government. . . .

Since the Crimean War, nearly fifty years ago, the policy of this country has been a policy of strict isolation. . . . But now . . . a new situation has arisen, and it is right the people of this country should have it under their consideration. All the powerful States of Europe have made alliances, and as long as we keep outside these alliances, as long as we are envied by all, and suspected by all, and as long as we have interests which at one time or another conflict with the interests of all, we are liable to be confronted at any moment with a combination of Great Powers so powerful that not even the most extreme, the most hotheaded politician would be able to contemplate it without a certain sense of uneasiness [hear, hear]. . . . What is the first duty of a Government under these circumstances? I say, without hesitation, that the first duty is to draw all parts of the Empire closer together [loud and prolonged cheers], to infuse into them a spirit of united and of Imperial patriotism [cheers]. . . .

What is our next duty? It is to establish and to maintain bonds of permanent amity with our kinsmen across the Atlantic [loud cheers]. They are a powerful and a generous nation. They speak our language, they are bred of our race [loud cheers]. Their laws, their literature, their standpoint upon every question are the same as ours; their feeling, their interest in the cause of humanity and the peaceful development of the world are identical with ours [cheers]. . . . And I even go so far as to say that, terrible as war may be, even war itself would be cheaply purchased if in a great and noble cause the Stars and Stripes and the Union Jack should wave together [loud and prolonged cheers] over an Anglo-Saxon alliance. . . .

Everybody has foreseen, everybody has known—not for the last few months, but for many, many years—that it was the persistent ambition and the continuous policy of Russia to extend her Eastern dominions southward, to have an ice-free port for her trade, and an ice-free harbour for her safety. . . .

The expected happened, and Russia did go down to Port Arthur and to Ta-lien-wan. As to the way in which Russia secured that occupation, as to the representations which were made and repudiated as soon as they were made, as to the promises which were given and broken a fortnight afterwards, I had better perhaps say nothing except I have always thought that it was a very wise proverb, "Who sups with the Devil must have a long spoon" [laughter]. . . . We obtained the cession of Weihaiwei, and we obtained commercial privileges for ourselves and the whole of the world, the importance of which I believe will be fully recognized at no short distance of time [cheers]. . . . Now, what does history show us? It shows us that unless we are allied to some great military power, as we were in the Crimean War, when we had France and Turkey as our allies, we cannot seriously injure Russia, although it may be true that she cannot seriously injure us [hear, hear]. . . . It is not a question of a single province; it is a question of the whole fate of the Chinese Empire, and our interests in China are so great, our proportion of the trade is so enormous, and the potentialities of that trade are so gigantic that I feel that no more vital question has ever been presented. . . . One thing appears to me to be certain. If the policy of isolation, which has hitherto been the policy of this country, is to be maintained in the future, then the fate of the Chinese Empire may be, probably will be, hereafter decided without reference to our wishes and in defiance of our interests. If, on the other hand, we are determined to enforce the policy of the open door, to preserve an equal opportunity for trade with all our rivals, then we must not allow jingoes to drive us into a quarrel with all the world at the same time, and we must not reject the idea of an alliance with those Powers whose interests most nearly approximate to our own [cheers].

—*The Times,* 14 May 1898

10.12   **THE FUTURE OF THE PORTUGUESE COLONIAL EMPIRE**

Anglo-German Agreement, 30 August 1898

Part of the British strategy in South Africa was to ensure the geographic and diplomatic isolation of the Boer republics. These considerations explain the willingness of the British government to conclude, on 30 August 1898, an Anglo-German agreement on the future of the Portuguese colonies. In the event of a breakup of the Portuguese colonial empire, Britain would acquire southern Mozambique. With it came physical control of the Delagoa Bay railway, the Boer republics' only link to the outside world that did not run through British territory. Germany, by abandoning any legal claims it may have had to southern Mozambique, in effect also abandoned any pretense of rendering assistance to the Boer republics. In return Germany was to receive northern Mozambique, most of Angola, and Portuguese Timor.

Anglo-German Agreement, 30 August 1898

In view of the possibility that Portugal may require financial assistance from some foreign Power or Powers . . . the undersigned . . . have agreed[:]

[Art.] 1. Whenever either the British or the German Government is of opinion that it is expedient to accede to a request for an advance of money to Portugal on the security of the customs revenues or other revenues of Mozambique, Angola, and the Portuguese part of the island of Timor, it shall communicate the fact to the other government, and the other government shall have the right to advance a portion of the total sum required. . . .

[Art.] 2. Of the customs revenues, referred to in Article 1, those of the province of Mozambique south of the Zambezi . . . and . . . of . . . portions of the province of Angola . . . shall be assigned to the British loan. The customs revenues of the remaining

MAP 11 SOUTHERN AFRICA AND THE ANGLO-GERMAN PARTITION AGREEMENT

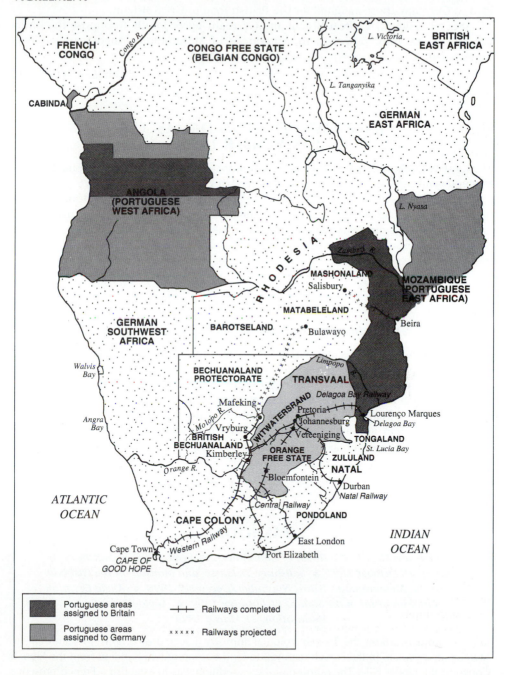

FRENCH CONGO

CONGO FREE STATE (BELGIAN CONGO)

Congo R.

L. Victoria

BRITISH EAST AFRICA

CABINDA

L. Tanganyika

GERMAN EAST AFRICA

ANGOLA (PORTUGUESE WEST AFRICA)

L. Nyasa

R H O D E S I A

Zambezi R.

MASHONALAND
Salisbury

MOZAMBIQUE (PORTUGUESE EAST AFRICA)

GERMAN SOUTHWEST AFRICA

MATABELELAND

BAROTSELAND

Bulawayo

Beira

Walvis Bay

Limpopo

BECHUANALAND PROTECTORATE

TRANSVAAL

Delagoa Bay Railway

Angra Bay

Mafeking

Molopo R.

Vryburg

WITWATERSRAND

Pretoria
Johannesburg
Vereeniging

Lourenço Marques
Delagoa Bay

BRITISH BECHUANALAND

ORANGE FREE STATE

TONGALAND
St. Lucia Bay

Kimberley

ZULULAND

Orange R.

Bloemfontein

NATAL

Durban
Natal Railway

ATLANTIC OCEAN

Central Railway

PONDOLAND

CAPE COLONY

East London

INDIAN OCEAN

Cape Town
CAPE OF GOOD HOPE

Western Railway

Port Elizabeth

Portuguese areas assigned to Britain

+++ Railways completed

Portuguese areas assigned to Germany

xxxxx Railways projected

parts of the provinces of Mozambique and Angola and the customs revenues of Portuguese Timor shall be assigned to the German loan. . . .

[Art.] 4. In case of default in the payment of the interest or sinking fund of either loan, the administration of the various customs-houses in the two provinces and in Portuguese Timor shall be handed over by Portugal; those assigned for the German loan to Germany, those assigned for the British loan to Great Britain. . . .

[Secret Articles:] 1. Great Britain and Germany agree jointly to oppose the intervention of any third power in the provinces of Mozambique, Angola, and in Portuguese Timor . . . .

—*GP*, 14i:3872; *BD*, 1:90, 91

10.13   KAISER WILHELM II IN DAMASCUS, 8 NOVEMBER 1898

The Kaiser's off-the-cuff remarks at public appearances always attracted widespread notice. But on several occasions his impetuousness came back to haunt him.

Visiting Damascus at the conclusion of a tour of the Holy Land, Wilhelm responded to a dinner speech by one of the city's Muslim dignitaries. Once the Anglo-German relationship had soured, the German emperor's expression of friendship for the "three hundred million Muslims" was resurrected as alleged evidence of Germany's boundless ambition and its ill will toward England, which ruled over millions of Muslims in its Indian empire and elsewhere.

Wilhelm II in Damascus, 8 November 1898

. . . Deeply touched by this overwhelming display, and at the same time moved by the thought of standing at the spot where one of the most chivalrous rulers of all times, the great Sultan Saladin, dwelled, a knight without fear and beyond reproach, who often had to teach his opponents what chivalry really was, I seize with joy the opportunity first of all to thank the Sultan Abdul Hamid for his hospitality.

May the Sultan, and may the three hundred million Muslims living dispersed on this earth who honor him as their khalif, be assured that the German Kaiser is their friend at all times. . . .

—Johannes Penzler (ed.), *Die Reden Kaiser Wilhelms II in den Jahren 1898–1900* (Leipzig, 1904), 2:127

10.14   FASHODA

Sir Edward Grey in the House of Commons, 28 March 1895 • Salisbury to Currie, 19 October 1897 • Salisbury, Delcassé, and Monson on the Fashoda Crisis • Memorandum Faure, November/December 1898 • Anglo-Egyptian Condominium in the Sudan, 11 January 1899 • Anglo-French Sudan Declaration, 21 March 1899

On 24 February 1896, the French colonial ministry issued instructions to Jean-Baptiste Marchand, a captain in the French marines, to lead a troop of two hundred from the French Congo to the Upper Nile. The purpose of the expedition was to establish a French presence

MAP 12 NORTHERN AFRICA AND THE NILE WATERSHED

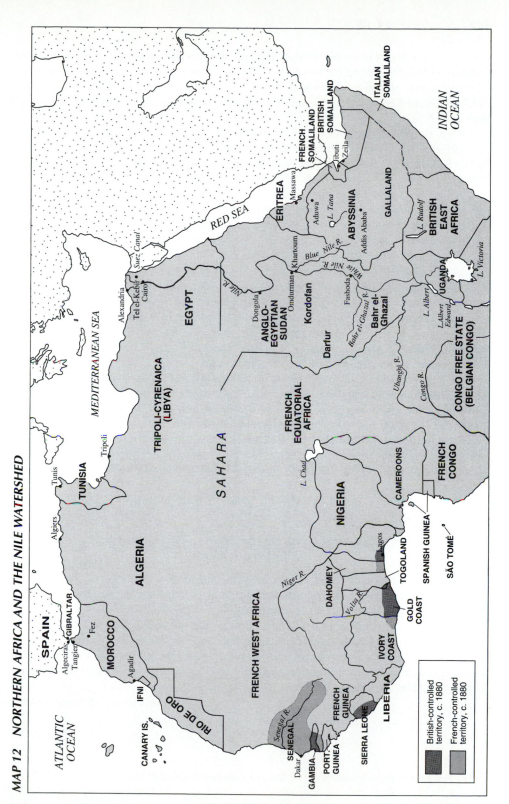

ATLANTIC OCEAN

CANARY IS.

SPAIN

GIBRALTAR
Algeciras
Tangier
Fez
MOROCCO
Agadir

IFNI

RIO DE ORO

MEDITERRANEAN SEA

Algiers
Tunis
TUNISIA
Tripoli

ALGERIA

TRIPOLI-CYRENAICA
(LIBYA)

S A H A R A

EGYPT

Alexandria
Tel el-Kebir
Cairo
Suez Canal
Nile R.

RED SEA

Massawa
ERITREA

FRENCH SOMALILAND
BRITISH SOMALILAND
ITALIAN SOMALILAND
Jibuti
Zeila

ABYSSINIA
Aduwa
L. Tana
Addis Ababa
Khartoum
Omdurman
Blue Nile R.
White Nile R.

GALLALAND

L. Rudolf

BRITISH EAST AFRICA

INDIAN OCEAN

ANGLO-EGYPTIAN SUDAN
Dongola
Kordofan
Darfur
Fashoda
Bahr el-Ghazal R.
Bahr el-Ghazal

UGANDA
L. Albert
L. Albert Edward
L. Victoria

Ubangi R.
Congo R.

CONGO FREE STATE
(BELGIAN CONGO)

FRENCH EQUATORIAL AFRICA

FRENCH CONGO

CAMEROONS

L. Chad

NIGERIA

SPANISH GUINEA
SÃO TOMÉ

FRENCH WEST AFRICA

Niger R.

DAHOMEY
TOGOLAND
Volta R.
GOLD COAST
Lagos

IVORY COAST

LIBERIA

SIERRA LEONE
FRENCH GUINEA
PORT. GUINEA
GAMBIA
SENEGAL
Senegal R.
Dakar

British-controlled
territory, c. 1880

French-controlled
territory, c. 1880

on the White Nile that could be parlayed into an international conference on the future of the Sudan or even used as a lever to reopen the Egyptian question. After sailing up the Congo and Ubanghi rivers, portaging its packets around cataracts, and crossing the Ubanghi/Bahr-el-Ghazal watershed, Marchand's party reached the former Egyptian outpost of Fashoda on the Upper Nile in July 1898.

It will be recalled (Document 9.19, headnote) that as of the early 1880s an insurrection in the northern Sudan had ended Egyptian rule there. Since its occupation of Egypt in 1882, Britain had made two halfhearted attempts to reconquer the Sudan but each time had suffered defeat at the hands of Mohammed Ali (the "Mahdi"). Unable and unwilling to finance another expedition from Egyptian revenues, Britain was content to let the matter rest there. But British officialdom was roused from its complacency in the waning days of the Rosebery administration by persistent reports of a French move on the Upper Nile from the Congo basin. The frustrations suffered by Rosebery's successor, Salisbury, in the Armenian crisis and his subsequent reevaluation of British strategic interests (Document 10.8) in the Middle East provided a further impetus for the reconquest of the Sudan. By September 1898, an Anglo-Egyptian force had defeated the Mahdists, taken Khartoum, and dispatched two river steamers to secure the upper reaches of the White Nile. On 19 September, the Anglo-Egyptian force reached Fashoda, where it was welcomed by Marchand "in the name of France."

The selections below chronicle the subsequent Anglo-French showdown over the Upper Nile. The French predicament has to be appreciated in light of the fact that Marchand was outnumbered and outgunned, and that his only effective means of communicating with Paris was via the Omdurman-Cairo telegraph—at British sufferance. It also has to be viewed in light of the chronic instability of the Third Republic: since Marchand first proposed his mission in September 1895, three French governments had come and gone. The new foreign minister, Théophile Delcassé, had been at his desk only since June 1898. Although Delcassé had headed the colonial ministry between April 1893 and January 1895 and had at that time advocated an aggressive policy on the Upper Nile, his recent arrival at the Quai d'Orsay had not given him sufficient time to prepare the ground for a full-fledged confrontation with Britain.

a)   ***Sir Edward Grey in the House of Commons,***
28 March 1895

. . . [I]n consequence of these claims of ours, and in consequence of the claims of Egypt in the Nile valley, the British and Egyptian spheres of influence covered the whole of the Nile waterway. . . . I cannot think it is possible that these rumors [of a French expedition][24] deserve credence, because the advance of a French expedition under secret instructions right from the other side of Africa, into a territory over which our claims have been known for so long, would be not merely an inconsistent and unexpected act, but it must be perfectly well known to the French Government that it would be an unfriendly act.

—*Parl. Debates*, 4th Series, 32:405–6

---

[24]Possibly the abortive mission of P.-L. Monteil, canceled in October 1894.

b)   ***Salisbury to Currie,[25] 19 October 1897***

. . . I confess that since, some two years back,[26] the Cabinet refused me leave to take the fleet up the Dardanelles, because it was impracticable, I have regarded the Eastern Question as having little serious interest for England. . . . We have really no hold on— and therefore no interest in—any of the Sultan's territories except Egypt. On the other hand our interest in Egypt is getting stronger. . . . [T]he Concert of Europe has conclusively shown that it can never be trusted with even the slenderest portion of executive authority. It follows that either Egypt must be given back to the Muslims— which no one except the Muslims would approve; or we must use for the purpose of maintaining peace and order there, the authority with which we have been invested by the victory of Tel-el-Kebir.[27] This is the only policy which it seems to me is left to us by the Cabinet's decision to which I have referred—to strengthen our position on the Nile (to its source) and to withdraw as much as possible from all responsibilities at Constantinople. . . .

—Bourne, 452; Lowe, *Reluctant Imperialists*, op. cit., 377–78; extracts in J. A. S. Grenville, *Lord Salisbury and Foreign Policy* (London, 1963), 94

c)   ***Salisbury, Delcassé, and Monson[28] on the Fashoda Crisis***

[Salisbury to Monson, 9 September 1898:] . . . I request you to point out to him [Delcassé] that, by the military events of last week,[29] all the territories which were subject to the Khalifa passed to the British and Egyptian Governments by right of conquest. . . .

[Monson to Salisbury, 28 September 1898:] . . . He [Delcassé] reiterated that it is the desire of the present French Government to make a friend of England, adding that between ourselves he would much prefer an Anglo-French to a Franco-Russian alliance. . . .

[Monson to Salisbury, 7 October 1898:] . . . In spite of the critical nature of other questions of international importance now occupying the attention of the civilized world, it is no exaggeration to say that all those questions are dwarfed into insignificance by the possibility of a rupture between the two great Maritime Powers of Western Europe. . . .

[Delcassé to Geneviève Delcassé,[30] 7 October 1898:] . . . I trust that the desire for an understanding with England I have freely expressed ever since taking over the ministry, is understood to spring not from any sense of weakness, but from a general conception of policy, and that I must not be placed officially in an obligation to say

[25]Sir Philip Currie (1834–1906). British ambassador in Constantinople, 1894–1898.
[26]During the Armenian massacres. See Document 10.8.
[27]Cf. Document 9.19.
[28]Sir Edmund Monson (1834–1909). British ambassador in Paris, 1896–1905.
[29]The Anglo-Egyptian victory at Omdurman.
[30]His wife.

"No" [to a possible British ultimatum]. I hope also further reflection has brought the conviction that England's real interest lies in fostering the friendship of France, and that for this friendship a sacrifice of exclusive claims is reasonable. . . .

[Delcassé to Geneviève Delcassé, 22 October 1898:] The problem is, how to combine the demands of honor with the necessity of avoiding a naval war which we are absolutely incapable of carrying through, even with Russian help. I could not wish my worst enemies, if I have any, to have this situation facing them.

[Delcassé to Geneviève Delcassé, 23 October 1898:] . . . I have let it be known—"recognize an outlet for us on the Nile and I shall order Marchand's withdrawal." The arrangement would be honorable, and would reach the goal which I assigned myself when I first held the colonial portfolio in 1893.

[Delcassé to Geneviève Delcassé, 24 October 1898:] The hapless Marchand still goes on asking for the relief he has so often, and always vainly, requested. He draws a vivid picture of his plight in the swamps and mud under endless rains and envisages his return through Egypt, his communications with our Congo possessions being cut. So my line is clear. If England does not accept my proposal, I publish Marchand's journal and recall the heroic little band. I will not murder them out there, with no gain to the country.

[Monson to Salisbury, 3 November 1898:] . . . Foreign Minister has expressed to me his hope that Her Majesty's Government will give them every facility to accomplish this [evacuation of Marchand from Fashoda]. The mission has ceased to have any political character and must henceforth be considered a simple inoffensive troop armed only for its own defence against native attack. . . .

—*BD*, 1:189, 198, 204; André Maurois, *King Edward and His Times* (London, 1933), 71–72; *BD*, 1:226

d)   *Memorandum by Faure,*[31] *November/December 1898*

. . . Does anyone think that we are the only ones who will open the Egyptian question? Should we thus make ourselves the policeman of Europe? Can we believe that missions like those of Marchand, Bonchamps and Bonvalot,[32] etc., are going to lead the English to make concessions to us? . . .

We have been like fools in Africa, led by irresponsible people—the colonial [lobby]. For what purpose is Africa divided among us until the present, and why this exaggerated ambition? We do not exploit our colonies, we can trade in foreign colonies. Africa won't be an economic power for two centuries. In two centuries, what will the political map of the world look like? Our actions in any case exceed our maritime power. England can actually cut off our colonies as it wishes, especially if it is in agreement with Germany. Let us thus understand not only how to moderate ourselves, but even to abandon what is not worth much to us and what will cause us serious difficulties if we do not watch out. Algeria, Tunisia, Senegal, the Congo, create for

[31]Félix Faure (1841–1899). French president, 1895–1899.
[32]Bonvalot and his deputy Bonchamps tried to reach the White Nile via Abyssinia in 1897. Accompanying an Ethiopian expedition, two members of Bonchamps's party penetrated to the confluence of the White Nile and the Sobat south of Fashoda in June 1898—unbeknownst to Marchand, who passed through the same spot two weeks later. G. N. Sanderson, *England, Europe, and the Upper Nile*, 293–95.

us a sufficient domain in Africa. Madagascar, Indochina,—there is enough to allow France to take a role in the opening of China in the next century. The Germans don't trouble us. Neither do the English. If we were to abandon our ridiculous protectionist policy, we would not have any friction with England that could disrupt the stability of the world and place France in a completely secondary position. Be that as it may, we have been able to avoid the English ultimatum on Fashoda, but British public opinion, urged on by an irresponsible and venal press, has shown itself in a nervous and very aggressive mood. The American successes [in the Spanish-American War] have raised spirits in England notably. . . . And we know that the naval power of Russia is nearly nil; we would have been led to promise maritime action in the Far East and there things will boil over before long. . . .

—Félix Faure, "Fachoda (1898)," *Revue d'histoire diplomatique* 69 (1955), 29–39

e)   *Anglo-Egyptian Condominium in the Sudan, 11 January 1899*

. . . Art. 3: The supreme military and civil command in the Sudan shall be vested in one officer, termed the "Governor-General of the Sudan." He shall be appointed by Khedival decree on the recommendation of Her Britannic Majesty's Government. . . .

—*SP*, 91:19–22; Hurewitz, 1:473–75; Hertslet II, 2:620–22

f)   *Anglo-French Sudan Declaration, 21 March 1899*[33]

Art. 1: . . . Her Britannic Majesty's Government engages not to acquire either territory or political influence to the west of . . . and the Government of the French Republic engages not to acquire either territory or political influence to the east of the same line.

Art. 2: The line of frontier shall start from the point where the boundary of the Congo Free State and French territory meets the water-parting between the watershed of the Nile and that of the Congo and its affluents. It shall follow in principle that water-parting. . . .

—Hertslet II, 2:796–97

10.15   THE AFTERMATH OF THE
SPANISH-AMERICAN WAR, 1898

Spanish-American Treaty of Paris, 10 December 1898 ●
Spanish-German Treaty of Madrid, 12 February 1899

The outcome of the Spanish-American War not only fortified the American position in the Caribbean but established the United States, almost in a fit of absence of mind, as a major player in East Asia. Reproduced below are the territorial provisions of the peace with Spain.

[33]Annexed to article 4 of the Anglo-French convention of 14 June 1898 (Hertslet II, 2:785–96) on spheres of influence in west and central Africa.

MAP 13   IMPERIALISM IN ASIA

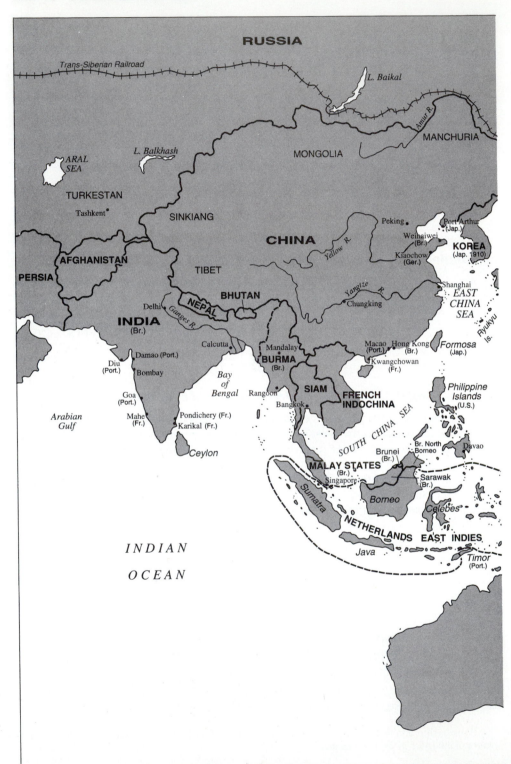

RUSSIA

Trans-Siberian Railroad

L. Baikal

Amur R.

MANCHURIA

MONGOLIA

ARAL
SEA

L. Balkhash

TURKESTAN

Tashkent

SINKIANG

CHINA

Peking

Port Arthur
(Jap.)

Weihaiwei
(Br.)

KOREA
(Jap. 1910)

AFGHANISTAN

Yellow R.

Kiaochow
(Ger.)

PERSIA

TIBET

Shanghai

EAST
CHINA
SEA

BHUTAN

Yangtze R.

Chungking

Ryukyu Is.

Delhi

NEPAL

Ganges R.

INDIA
(Br.)

Calcutta

Mandalay

Macao Hong Kong
(Port.) (Br.)

Formosa
(Jap.)

Damao (Port.)

BURMA
(Br.)

Kwangchowan
(Fr.)

Diu
(Port.)

Bombay

Bay
of
Bengal

Rangoon

SIAM

**FRENCH
INDOCHINA**

Philippine
Islands
(U.S.)

Goa
(Port.)

Arabian
Gulf

Mahe
(Fr.)

Pondichery (Fr.)

Karikal (Fr.)

Bangkok

SOUTH CHINA SEA

Br. North
Borneo

Davao

Ceylon

Brunei
(Br.)

Sarawak
(Br.)

MALAY STATES
(Br.)

Singapore

Sumatra

Borneo

Celebes

NETHERLANDS EAST INDIES

INDIAN
OCEAN

Java

Timor
(Port.)

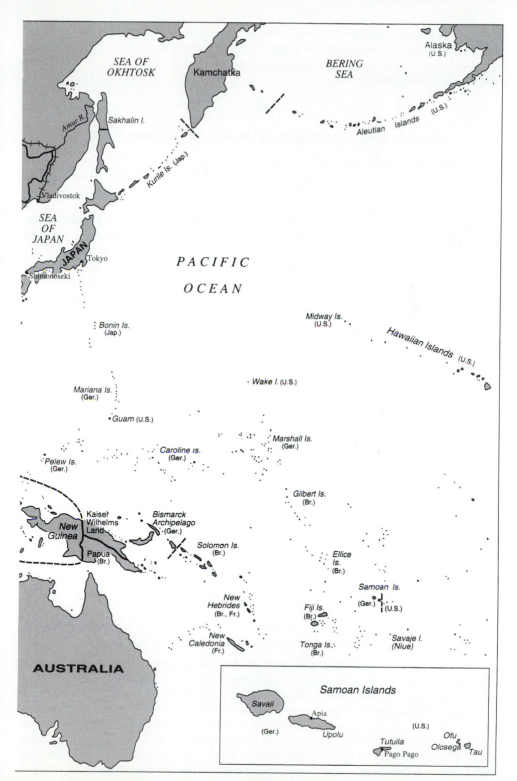

SEA OF OKHTOSK

Kamchatka

BERING SEA

Alaska (U.S.)

Amur R.

Sakhalin I.

Aleutian Islands (U.S.)

Kurile Is. (Jap.)

Vladivostok

SEA OF JAPAN

JAPAN

Tokyo

Shimonoseki

PACIFIC OCEAN

Bonin Is. (Jap.)

Midway Is. (U.S.)

Hawaiian Islands (U.S.)

Wake I. (U.S.)

Mariana Is. (Ger.)

Guam (U.S.)

Caroline Is. (Ger.)

Marshall Is. (Ger.)

Pelew Is. (Ger.)

Gilbert Is. (Br.)

Kaiser Wilhelms Land

Bismarck Archipelago (Ger.)

New Guinea

Papua (Br.)

Solomon Is. (Br.)

Ellice Is. (Br.)

Samoan Is. (Ger.) (U.S.)

New Hebrides (Br., Fr.)

Fiji Is. (Br.)

New Caledonia (Fr.)

Tonga Is. (Br.)

Savaje I. (Niue)

AUSTRALIA

Samoan Islands

Savaii

Apia

(U.S.)

Ofu Olosega Tau

Tutuila

(Ger.)

Upolu

Pago Pago

277

The collapse of Spain gave Germany, another colonial have-not, the opportunity to bid for the remnants of the Spanish empire in the Pacific. In terms of square miles, the real estate transacted was minute, but it was scattered over an expanse of ocean nearly as vast as the continental United States.

a)   *Spanish-American Treaty of Paris, 10 December 1898*

Art. 1: Spain relinquishes all claim of sovereignty over and title to Cuba. . . . [T]he United States will, so long as such occupation shall last, assume and discharge the obligations that may under international law result from the fact of its occupation, for the protection of life and property.

Art. 2: Spain cedes to the United States the island of Puerto Rico and other islands now under Spanish sovereignty in the West Indies, and the island of Guam in the Marianas or Ladrones.

Art. 3: Spain cedes to the United States the archipelago known as the Philippine Islands. . . . The United States will pay to Spain the sum of twenty million dollars ($20,000,000) within three months after the exchange of the ratifications of the present treaty. . . .

—Bevans, *Treaties*, 11:615–21

b)   *Spanish-German Treaty of Madrid, 12 February 1899*

. . . [T]he government of Spain agrees to cede to Germany the Caroline islands with Pelew as well as the Marianas (Guam excepted). The total pecuniary indemnity is 25 million pesetas. . . .

[Secret Article:] The Spanish government promises that if in the future it considers the cession of the island of Fernando Po [in Spanish Guinea] for a financial indemnity to be in its best interests, it shall give the right of first refusal to Germany, provided that the [German] offer is at the same level as the highest offer made by any other party.

—*GP*, 15:4188, 4197

10.16   SOUTH AFRICA AT THE BRINK

*Milner to Rendel, 21 July 1899 • Milner to Chamberlain, 30 August 1899 •
Smuts's Memorandum for the Transvaal Government, 4 September 1899*

It is uncanny when political adversaries, motivated by diametrically opposed interests, arrive at almost identical conclusions about the issues that divide them, about the surface manifestations that obscure the real nature of these issues, and about the road ahead. The second and third documents excerpted below were penned within the same week, independently of one another, by two of the principals in the Anglo-Boer confrontation. Sir Alfred Milner (1854–1925), the chief British administrator in South Africa from 1897 to 1905, and Jan Smuts (1870–1950) came face to face with one another at the Bloemfontein conference, called in May 1899 to settle the Anglo-Boer quarrel over the citizenship laws of the Transvaal. The failure of the Bloemfontein negotiations and the subsequent diplomatic gridlock ultimately set the stage for armed confrontation.

The Jameson raid (Document 10.7) had transformed Jan Smuts, a Boer from the Cape and formerly an admirer of Cecil Rhodes, into a critic of British policy in South Africa and prompted him to move to the Transvaal. Appointed state attorney of the Transvaal in 1897, Smuts resisted British demands that the Boer republic alter its citizenship laws to accommodate British residents ("uitlanders"). In Smuts's view, acquiescence to the British demands would have amounted to a surrender of the Transvaal's legislative sovereignty.[34] Moreover, he was convinced that the uitlander question did little more than mask the real motivations of the Cape government: "the franchise has nothing to do with the situation and even if we [gave in] . . . , England would still seek and find a cause for hostilities in other points of dispute."[35]

By September 1899, Smuts's views had hardened. His memorandum to his colleagues in the Transvaal government, excerpted below, did not by itself decide the policy of the Boer republics. But in all likelihood it reflected the sentiments of the Transvaal leadership; it deserves to be quoted for this reason and as a cogent statement of the Boer cause.

Attacking British Natal and the Cape on 12 October, the Boers retained the initiative until February 1900. By September of that year, both the Orange Free State and the Transvaal were overrun by British forces. The Boers' recourse to guerrilla warfare (cf. Document 10.24), however, held up the conclusion of peace until May 1902. By the end of the war, British forces numbered about 300,000 (including contingents from Canada, Australia, and New Zealand); the Boers managed to field about seventy thousand men.

a)   ***Milner to Rendel,*[36] *21 July 1899***

. . . Of course England may give us away—probably will—not from cowardice but from simple ignorance of the situation and the easy-going belief that you have only to be very kind and patient and magnanimous, and *give away your friends to please your enemies,* in order to make the latter love you forever. She may give us away. *It is the last time she will have the chance.* But there will always be, when I return to my books in Duke Street, the recollection of the time when I had done all the man on the spot could do to recover the position. . . . I have brought into the field *scores,* who have long been sulking in their tents, and vowed long ago never to trust G. Britain or any of her emissaries again. . . .P.S.—Joe [Chamberlain] has stuck to me *magnificently.* If he throws me over after all, or, worse still, retreats under a garbled version of my advice to him, I shall know it is only because he could not help it.

—Cecil Headlam (ed.), The Milner Papers (London, 1931), 1:473

b)   ***Milner to Chamberlain, 30 August 1899***

. . . It is evident that, as someone said to me long ago, Kruger will "bluff up to the cannon's mouth." The big expedition, which would be so costly, is necessary to get him down on his knees, with or without fighting. I know what such an expedition means

[34]W. K. Hancock, *Smuts: The Sanguine Years, 1870–1919* (Cambridge, 1962), 101.

[35]Smuts to Willem Leyds, 30 April 1899, *Smuts Papers,* 1:229.

[36]James Meadows Rendel (b. 1854). Barrister; Milner's roommate at Balliol in the mid-1870s.

for *you*; it may be more than Great Britain can be got to rise to even for this big object, for of course if we send an army we should settle once for all the question of paramountcy and obtain once for all, equal rights. But of course I fight to the last for the position in South Africa and I know well how bad the position would be for us if this bout were to end in a draw. . . . I have not yet had an answer from Pretoria to our last message, but if I know them rightly, it will be the old story; not a point-blank refusal, and not a frank acceptance. If we don't bring matters to a head on that, there will be a break-away of our people shortly. . . .

—Headlam, *Milner Papers*, op. cit., 1:499–500

c)   *Smuts's Memorandum for the Transvaal Government, 4 September 1899*

. . . The capture of Natal by a Boer force, together with the cutting of the railway-line between the Cape Colony and Rhodesia, will cause an immediate shaking of the British Empire in very important parts of it: the British Government would under these circumstances not be able to dream of weakening their forces in India, Egypt, or elsewhere. . . .

Thus all considerations, not only of a military but also of a political nature, indicate the great desirability of the South African Republic taking the offensive against England while her forces in South Africa are still weak and can be defeated without great difficulty.

It is true that our people are always loath to attack first or to fire the first shot, as they express it; but when we are once convinced that all diplomatic means have been used in vain and when the impossibility of reaching a solution in a peaceful way has become clear, then there is no longer a political question but only a military one. . . . [T]here is a chance that by a war the Afrikaner people will maintain and strengthen its position of leadership. With the spreading of the industrial and money spirit among our people our position also will be weakened. It must also not be overlooked that through the encirclement of the two Republics by British territory and through their exclusion from the sea, their position as independent states will become more and more untenable and weak. . . .

—W. K. Hancock and Jean van der Poel (eds.), *Selections from the Smuts Papers*
(Cambridge, 1966), 1:313–30

10.17   GLOBAL IMPLICATIONS OF THE BOER WAR

Bülow to Wilhelm II, 6 August 1899 ● *Anglo-Portuguese Secret Convention,*
14 October 1899 ● *Bülow to Wilhelm II, 8 November 1899*

Control of the sea lanes, together with the inaccessibility of South Africa, allowed Britain to localize the Boer war and to spurn an early peace. Unencumbered by the task of having to seek a negotiated settlement, British diplomacy was free to secure strategic advantages and to keep third powers at bay. On both of these counts, it was remarkably successful—Joseph Chamberlain's jitters (Document 10.18) and Britain's deference to the United States in the western hemisphere (Document 10.22) notwithstanding.

The excerpts below make clear that Germany was eager to profit from Britain's entanglement in South Africa, though ultimately the new German foreign secretary, Bernhard von Bülow, had very little to show for his labors. In the 1898 Anglo-German agreement on the Portuguese colonies (Document 10.12), Germany held out for a larger reward in exchange for renouncing its claims to Delagoa Bay. But the British government, acting on the belief that a weak Portugal made for a better neighbor in South Africa than an augmented German colonial empire, shrewdly affirmed the integrity of Portugal's overseas possessions in a secret Anglo-Portuguese convention. Concluded only two days after the outbreak of the Boer war, this accord coopted Portugal, secured important tactical benefits for Britain, and further undercut the Boer position. Its terms may not have contradicted the letter of the earlier Anglo-German agreement but were certainly at variance with its spirit. In any case, the text of the Anglo-Portuguese treaty was revealed to the German foreign ministry only in January 1914.[37]

Farther afield, the Boer war hastened the conclusion of an Anglo-German-American treaty on the future of the Samoan islands. This treaty replaced the tridominium that the three powers had maintained on Samoa since 1889 and divided the islands between the United States and Germany.[38] Britain, now excluded from Samoa, gave way—albeit with bad grace and only after having secured the neighboring Tonga archipelago in a prior Anglo-German agreement (14 November 1899).

a)   *Bülow to Wilhelm II, 6 August 1899*

There is probably no other person in Europe who incenses me as much as the fat English prime minister. Never will I forgive him the annoyance which he caused Your Majesty in the Samoan matter. . . . Odysseus did not reveal his intentions to his enemies. If Your Majesty—by applying Your extraordinary skills in the treatment of Englishmen—can win over Salisbury and maintain passable relations with him until our fleet has gotten over the worst, then that would be a masterly coup. . . . If Your Majesty will continue to nurse along Your personal relationship to Russia and England, it will deny the advocates of revanche in Paris the chance to manipulate one or the other of these world powers against us and then *la belle France* will become pocket change in Your Majesty's hands. . . .

—Stiftung Preussischer Kulturbesitz, Rep. 53J Lit. B No. 16a

b)   *Anglo-Portuguese Secret Convention, 14 October 1899*

[The two governments] . . . equally affirm the final article of the treaty of the 23rd June, 1661, of which the first part runs as follows:—

" . . . Charles [II] . . . shall promise and oblige himself as by this present article he doth, to defend and protect all conquests or colonies belonging to the crown of Portugal against all his enemies, as well future[39] as present."

[37]Cf. *GP*, 37i:14695.
[38]Text in Bevans, *Treaties*, 1:276–77.
  [39]As the Portuguese colonial empire in 1899 covered a larger acreage than in 1661, the reiteration of the phrase here actually expanded the earlier British commitment.

The government of His Most Faithful Majesty [of Portugal] undertakes not to permit, after the declaration of war between Great Britain and the South African Republic, or during the continuance of the war, the importation and passage of arms, and of munitions of war destined for the latter.

The Government of His Most Faithful Majesty will not proclaim neutrality in the war between Great Britain and the South African Republic.

—*BD*, 1:118

c)   ***Bülow to Wilhelm II, 8 November 1899***

Your Majesty maintains a free hand vis-à-vis all sides. It is a great success for Your Majesty to solve in a satisfactory manner the most difficult colonial question [Samoa] which stood between Your Majesty and England on the very day on which Tsar Nicholas II appears for his first visit in Your Majesty's residence in Potsdam. . . .

—Stiftung Preussischer Kulturbesitz, Rep. 53J Lit. B No. 16a

10.18   CHAMBERLAIN AT LEICESTER, 30 NOVEMBER 1899

Bülow accompanied the Kaiser on a visit to England in November 1899, six weeks after the outbreak of the Boer war. On this occasion, Bülow encouraged Joseph Chamberlain to promote in public his vision of an Anglo-American-German alliance. Bülow created the expectation that a public statement would give him the opportunity to second the idea in Germany. So encouraged, Chamberlain went ahead. But Bülow, in his major parliamentary address of 11 December (Document 10.19), took no notice of this overture, thereby giving Chamberlain the impression that he had been duped.

Chamberlain—whose portfolio as colonial secretary gave him a leading role in the politics of the South African crisis—may have viewed the proposed alliance as a prophylactic measure designed to neutralize Great Power opposition to Britain's war effort. Though Chamberlain lavished praise on the foreign policy of the Salisbury cabinet, the very nature of his proposal ran counter to Salisbury's defense of British isolation and can be interpreted as yet one more challenge to the prime minister's leadership in foreign affairs.

Chamberlain's "personal interest" in close cooperation with the United States was no doubt a reference to the fact that his third wife was American. He had married the daughter of William Endicott, secretary for war in the first Cleveland administration, whom he had met during his first visit to the United States in 1887.

Chamberlain at Leicester, 30 November 1899

. . . I rejoice—it is perhaps natural that I should take a personal interest in the matter—in the friendly feeling, which I hope is now a permanent feeling, between two great branches of the Anglo-Saxon race [cheers]. . . . I may point out to you that at bottom the character, the main character, of the Teutonic race differs very slightly indeed from the character of the Anglo-Saxon [cheers], and the same sentiments which bring us into close sympathy with the United States of America may also be evoked to bring us into closer sympathy and alliance with the Empire of Germany. What do we find? We find our system of justice, we find our literature, we find the very base and foundation on which our language is established the same in the two countries, and if the union between England and America is a powerful factor in the cause of peace, a new Triple Alliance between the Teutonic race and the two great branches of the Anglo-Saxon race will be a still more potent influence in the future of the world [cheers]. I have used the word "alliance" sometimes in the course of what I have said, but again I desire to make it clear that to me it seems to matter little whether you have an alliance which is committed to paper or whether you have an understanding which exists in the minds of the statesmen of the respective countries. . . .

—*The Times*, 1 December 1899

10.19   THE SECOND GERMAN NAVAL LAW, 1900

Tirpitz's Notes on his Meeting with the Kaiser, 28 September 1899 •
Bülow in the Reichstag, 11 December 1899

The appointment in 1897 of Alfred von Tirpitz as state secretary in the German naval office and of Bernhard von Bülow as state secretary in the foreign ministry constitutes a major turning point in the history of the Second Reich. The two men were expected to implement the Kaiser's craving to build a sizable navy, a wish heretofore scuttled by the German parliament. While Tirpitz's task was to persuade the Reichstag of the technical and financial feasibility of a fleet, Bülow's was to create the political and diplomatic cover for Germany's emergence as a major naval power. The Reichstag approved a first naval law in March 1898, but the decisive role played by the navies of other powers in the Spanish-American War, the Fashoda crisis, and the South African conflict allowed Tirpitz and Bülow to make the case for a further expansion of the fleet.

In a meeting with Wilhelm II about two months before the introduction of the second naval law in the Reichstag, Tirpitz rehashed the rationale for the German navy. In so doing, he revealed the fundamentals of his "risk principle": Britain would not risk an Anglo-German war over the naval issue for fear of the damage that Germany would inflict on the British fleet. Faced with a strong German fleet, England would opt for accommodation rather than confrontation and so the fleet would ultimately *enhance* Germany's value as an ally. Tirpitz clung with tenacity to these notions, claiming—as late as 1915!—that "the war did not disprove the risk principle."[40] Tirpitz's notes of his meeting with the Kaiser reveal not only the flimsy premises and shallowness of his reasoning but also render inescapable the conclusion that sloppy writing is a sign of sloppy thinking.

Bülow introduced the proposed legislation to the Reichstag on 11 December 1899. A master in the art of political packaging, he gave respectability to the very ideas that in Tirpitz's graceless prose appeared naive and turbid. Quarrying the Social Darwinism of the age, he, like Tirpitz, referred to Salisbury's "Dying Nations" speech (Document 10.11); like Tirpitz, Bülow played on the fear that Germany would be left empty-handed in any future distribution of territorial spoils unless it built a fleet and pursued a "world policy" (*Weltpolitik*).

[40]Tirpitz to Bethmann Hollweg, January 1915, Bundesarchiv-Militärarchiv N253/174.

a)   ***Tirpitz's Notes on his Meeting with the Kaiser,***
28 September 1899

. . . 9) When goal has been reached, Your Majesty will have an effective strength of 45 battleships plus all accessories. Strength so great, that only England will be superior. Even vis-à-vis England we have a good chance [of success] because of geographic location, military system, mobilization, torpedo boats, tactical training, structured planning, unified leadership by the monarch. Aside from the fact that the conditions for battle are not too unfavorable for us, England will lose any inclination to attack us for reasons of a general political nature as well as sober businessman-like considerations and will therefore concede to Your Majesty a considerable measure of naval influence [*Seegeltung*] and will enable Your Majesty to carry out a great overseas policy.

10) . . . [T]he creation of an efficient fleet is for Germany such a necessity that Germany would face ruin without it.

Four world powers. Russia, England, America, and Germany. Because two of these powers are only accessible by sea, so power at sea has to be a priority.

Salisbury's assessment: the great states are growing larger and stronger, the small ones smaller and weaker; this also my view.

According to modern development, a system of trusts. Because German naval power is particularly backward, it is an existential question for Germany, as a world power and a great cultural nation, to make up for lost time. . . .With the development of trade and industry, there arise areas of contact and conflict with other nations; therefore, naval power is necessary if Germany does not want to experience a rapid decline. Not to mention here [its value for] political speculations, alliances. . . .

—Volker R. Berghahn and Wilhelm Deist (eds.), *Rüstung im Zeichen der wilhelminischen Weltpolitik: Grundlegende Dokumente, 1890–1914* (Düsseldorf, 1988), 160–61

b)   ***Bülow in the Reichstag, 11 December 1899***

. . . On one point there can be no doubt: world affairs are in a state of flux which no-one could have predicted two years ago [commotion]. Gentlemen, it has been said that in every century a struggle, a whole-sale liquidation takes place which redistributes influence, power, and possessions across the globe: in the sixteenth century Spaniards and Portuguese divided the New World, in the seventeenth the Dutch, the French, and the English entered the competition—while we were busy bashing in our own heads [laughter]—in the eighteenth century the Dutch and the French lost most of what they had won to the English. In this nineteenth century of ours, England has expanded its colonial empire—the greatest empire which the world has seen since the Romans—farther and farther, the French have made inroads in North and East Africa and have created a new empire in Indochina, Russia is running its victory lap in Asia, which has taken it from the altitudes of the Pamir to the Pacific Ocean. The Sino-Japanese War four years ago, the Spanish-American war barely a year and a half ago have brought further changes, have brought about great, incisive, far-reaching decisions, have shaken old empires, have brought about new and serious ferment. No-one can say what kind of consequences will come in the wake of the war which is presently engulfing South Africa in flames [hear! hear!]. The English prime minister said some time ago that the strong states will become stronger and that the weak ones will become weaker. Everything which has happened since proves the correctness of those words. . . .

When the English speak of a Greater Britain, when the French speak of a nouvelle France, when the Russians open up Asia for themselves, then we too can claim a greater Germany [bravo! on the right; laughter left], not in the sense of making conquests, but in the sense of the peaceful expansion of our trade and its bases. Gentlemen, your laughter confuses me. We cannot tolerate nor do we want to tolerate that others will then proceed to business as usual, disregarding the German people [stormy applause right; interjections from the left; call to order]. . . .

We must be secure from surprises not only on land but also at sea. We have to create a fleet strong enough to prevent the attack of any power. I emphasize the word "attack": because of our peacefulness, for us it is always only a question of defense. . . . I wish to stress that in reality things are not quite so simple and smooth as they might appear to someone with a lively and boundless imagination. It is not difficult to sit in one's study, atlas in hand and a cigar clenched between the teeth, contemplating new coaling stations, protectorates, and colonies [laughter]. In real life, this is trickier: acquiring Kiauchow, the Carolines, the Marianas, Samoa for Germany was not quite so simple. . . .

Gentlemen, why is it that all other states are strengthening their fleets? Surely not because of the sheer pleasure of spreading money around [laughter on the left]. Despite its financial difficulties, Italy is willing again and again to make sacrifices for its fleet. In France, the government can barely keep up with parliamentary requests for naval expenditures. Russia has doubled its naval construction. America and Japan are making a mighty effort, and England, which has the world's most powerful fleet, is continually adding to it. . . . I say that unless we build a fleet which is capable of protecting our commerce, our compatriots abroad, our missions, and the security of our coasts, we endanger the vital interests of our country. . . .

There are individuals and interest groups and political currents and perhaps also peoples who have found that dealing with Germans was more comfortable and that the German was for his neighbors more pliable in those earlier days when, despite our accomplishments in education and despite our culture, in the political and economic sphere foreigners looked down on us the way haughty noblemen look down on humble family tutors [quite right!—laughter]. Those days of political impotence and economic and political meekness shall not return [applause]. We will not be the menials of mankind. But we will maintain our position only if we realize that there is no commonweal without power, without a strong army and a strong navy [correct! on the right; dissent on the left]. Gentlemen, the means by which a people of sixty million—inhabiting the center of Europe and sending out economic feelers in all directions—can prevail in the struggle for survival without strong armaments on land and sea, those means have not yet been found [correct! on the right]. In the coming century, the German people will either be hammer or anvil. . . .

Gentlemen, I want to sum up: our policy, our overseas policy, our foreign policy, our entire policy is peaceful, honest, independent. We will not apprentice ourselves; we only conduct German policy. If and whether, how and where we might be induced to cast aside our reserve to maintain our position, that, gentlemen, depends on the course of events, on the general course of events which no power can determine on its own, which no-one can predict with exactitude. . . .

—Reichstag, 168:3292–95; Johannes Penzler, *Fürst Bülows Reden* (Berlin, 1907), 1:88–97

10.20   BÜLOW ON GERMANY'S RELATIONS WITH ENGLAND AND RUSSIA

Bülow to Eulenburg, 28 September 1895 ● *Bülow to Wilhelm II, 19 August 1898*
● *Bülow to Wilhelm II, 24 August 1898* ● *Bülow to Wilhelm II, 6 August 1900*
● *Bülow to Waldersee, 13 August 1900*

Bülow owed his appointment as state secretary in the foreign ministry in 1897 and German chancellor in 1900 to the Kaiser's belief that he would be a reliable agent of Wilhelm's " personal rule," faithfully translating the Kaiser's every wish into policy. The letters excerpted here support the notion that, at least in his correspondence with Wilhelm, Bülow willingly pandered to the Kaiser's moods. The record of his chancellorship, however, raises the question of whether Bülow was too ambitious or duplicitous to serve as a mere fig leaf for his master's pretensions. In any case, these letters offer an interesting glimpse of the constitutional relationship between Kaiser and chancellor, at least as interpreted by Bülow. Their tone makes for an instructive contrast to the exchanges between Queen Victoria and Salisbury (Document 10.3).

Bülow's long-term goal was to establish Germany as a world power, on a par with England and Russia, through the construction of a fleet. Germany's opportunity to do so lay in the continuation of the Anglo-Russian antagonism, one of the constants in the diplomacy of the previous century. Germany needed to take care not to sell its services to either side, as it would incur the wrath of one party if it were too closely associated with the other. In theory, Germany should cultivate a policy of the "free hand," maintaining friendly but not intimate relations with both powers. Once the fleet was completed, Germany could dictate its price as an ally at a moment of its choosing. This remarkably static conception of the relationship among the Great Powers discounted the possibility of a general realignment among them and took no heed of what Bismarck termed the "imponderabilia" of politics.

The excerpts below span a period of five years. They appear here in a group for the purpose of illustrating policy rather than the specific events that spawned them. Bülow's contemporary musings on the Boer war are featured in Documents 10.17, 10.19, and 10.22; his later adherence to the policy outlined below can be found in Documents 10.26 and 10.27.

a)   *Bülow to Eulenburg,*[41] *28 September 1895*

. . . The political part of your so informative and interesting letter leads me to believe that the clouds on the domestic and foreign horizons, despite the occasional flash of lightning, will not produce a thunderstorm quite so soon. But this is no excuse for the fire department to fall asleep at the clutch. We have to take advantage of the respite to install as many lightning rods as possible. . . .

[41]Philip zu Eulenburg-Hertefelt (1847–1921). Intimate of Wilhelm II, promoter of Bülow's early career; German ambassador in Vienna, 1894–1902.

Consequently, we should not tie ourselves in advance to any side, but should take care not to pick fights either. In spite of all the Muscovite bad manners . . . I would stay cool vis-à-vis the Russians. It is in their nature that whenever they feel on top of things—which for a number of reasons is now the case—they will become overbearing and impudent. It possibly won't be long before Russia offends the English, Austrians, possibly even the French; we just have to avoid putting ourselves into the path of the coarse muzhik.—The greater the antagonism between Russia and England, the better for us:"St. Florian, protect our house, set fire to the others.'"[42]

—John C. G. Röhl (ed.), *Philipp Eulenburgs politische Korrespondenz* (Boppard, 1976–1983), 3:1139

b)   ***Bülow to Wilhelm II, 19 August 1898***
                        [with annotations by Wilhelm II]

In my view, the possibility of war between England and Russia is still remote [*right*], but it is not impossible that John Bull won't vent his anger in one direction or another.

Our ideal remains the position outlined by Your Majesty—firm and independent between England and Russia, independent of both, but with the option that—as soon as Your Majesty desires—to make common cause with one or the other [*yes*]. That it is difficult to join in an eternal league with Russia is proven by the agitation of the Russian press against us. The liberties which the Russian government permits the Russian press against us are a measure for the real intentions of Russia and its real inclinations. . . .

—Stiftung Preussischer Kulturbesitz, Rep. 53J Lit. B No. 16a

c)   ***Bülow to Wilhelm II, 24 August 1898***

. . . What Your Majesty told Sir Frank Lascelles[43] about England's relationship to Russia was, in my humble opinion, first-rate. Your Majesty has therewith defused any English suspicion that we wanted to drive them into a war with Russia. That this war will come one day is an elemental necessity, and it will come all the sooner if neither party thinks that we desire it. On the other hand, Your Majesty has in this manner prevented our relationship with Russia from being damaged, a relationship which, above all, is decisive for the security of the Reich. . . .

—*GP*, 14i:3867

d)   ***Bülow to Wilhelm II, 6 August 1900***

It is really difficult to get down to business with these people, but it is in our interest to stay in touch with Russia on East Asian affairs, not only in view of the geographic

[42]This letter should be interpreted in the context of the rivalry between England and Russia in east Asia (Document 10.5) and in the Eastern Question (Document 10.8).
[43](1841–1920). British ambassador in Berlin, 1895–1908.

position of Shantung and the unreliability of the English, but also because the Russians will be persuaded by a friendly attitude on our part to move more and more troops from west to east, which is a useful thing for Your Majesty's eastern provinces.

The English cloven foot of their reckless egotism is becoming more and more visible. . . . How true it is that in the reign of Your Majesty the British play the same role as the French in the reign of the Great Elector and the Austrians in the reign of the great king [Frederick II]. Dealing with the English is infinitely laborious, infinitely difficult, requires infinite patience and skill. But just as the Hohenzollern griffin beat off the double-headed Austrian eagle and clipped the wings of the Gallic rooster, so too it will with God's help and through Your Majesty's strength and wisdom handle the English leopard. . . .

—Stiftung Preussischer Kulturbesitz, Rep. 53J Lit. B No. 16a

e)   *Bülow to Waldersee,*[44] *13 August 1900*

. . . that particularly in East Asia we should not maneuver ourselves into an antagonism with Russia. At the same time, given the state of our naval forces, we cannot risk a conflict with England. Consequently, we will indulge Russia's political preponderance north of the Hoang Ho,[45] while in the Yangtze valley we will sic the others on John Bull.

—Stiftung Preussischer Kulturbesitz, Rep. 53J Lit. B No. 16a

10.21   THE BOXER REBELLION

Hay's Circular of 3 July 1900 • *Wilhelm II in Bremerhaven, 27 July 1900* •
Anglo-German Agreement on China, 16 October 1900

Large-scale antiforeign violence finally erupted in China in June 1900. The secret society of the "Righteous and Harmonious Fists" (dubbed "Boxers" by foreigners), with the encouragement of the imperial court, was the principal instigator of the revolt. After cutting the Peking-Tientsin road and telegraph, the Boxers laid siege to the foreign legations in Peking. A Japanese official and the German minister were murdered by the mob.

Attending the embarkation of German marines for China almost one month later, the Kaiser gave free rein to his outrage. His fiery send-off was part of an impromptu speech but, like his earlier remarks in Damascus, attracted immediate notice.

The Boxer rebellion elicited an altogether different reaction from the American secretary of state, John Hay. In the preceding year, Hay had responded to the scramble for concessions in China (cf. Document 10.10) by trying to coax the powers into at least paying lip service to an "'Open Door' policy to insure the commerce of the world in China equality of treatment."[46]

---

[44]Alfred von Waldersee (1832–1904). Vice-chief of the Prussian general staff, 1882–1888; chief, 1888–1891; nominal commander of the international expeditionary force against the Boxers, 1900. See Document 10.21.

[45]Also: Yellow River.

[46]Hay to Choate, 6 September 1899, *Foreign Relations of the United States, 1899*, 131. See Document 10.10.

Having received only lukewarm replies to these "Open-Door notes," Hay restated the American position after the outbreak of the Boxer rebellion. Hay's circular of 3 July 1900 differed from the 1899 notes in form (it did not expect any responses) and in its scope (in its principal passage toward the end, it went considerably further than his earlier initiative). Hay did not say how American or any power's treaty rights in China could be reconciled with "Chinese territorial and administrative entity"—though he certainly intended this phrase to signal a new departure in American policy. But if evaluated in the context of the American acquisition of the Philippines and the extension of American tariffs to this archipelago, Hay's Open-Door notes appear far less altruistic. Seen in this light, they must have struck contemporaries as a manifestation of the principle "what is mine, is mine; what is yours, is negotiable."

The essence of Hay's policy was replicated in an Anglo-German exchange of notes in October 1900. Both signatories, however, pursued disparate motives. While Britain, bogged down in South Africa, sought German assistance in blocking further Russian encroachments on China, Bülow conversely hoped to add to Britain's difficulties by embroiling it with Russia (Documents 10.20 and 10.23, introduction).

a)   ## Hay's Circular of 3 July 1900

. . . The purpose of the President is, as it has been heretofore, to act concurrently with the other powers, first, in opening up communication with Peking and rescuing the American officials, missionaries, and other Americans who are in danger; secondly, in affording all possible protection everywhere in China to American life and property; thirdly, in guarding and protecting all legitimate American interests; and fourthly, in aiding to prevent a spread of the disorders to the other provinces of the Empire and a recurrence of such disasters. It is, of course, too early to forecast the means of attaining this last result; but the policy of the Government of the United States is to seek a solution which may bring about permanent safety and peace to China, preserve Chinese territorial and administrative entity, protect all rights guaranteed to friendly powers by treaty and international law, and safeguard for the world the principle of equal and impartial trade with all parts of the Chinese Empire.

—*Foreign Relations of the United States 1900*, 299

b)   ## Wilhelm II in Bremerhaven, 27 July 1900

Great tasks overseas have been thrust upon the new German Empire, tasks which are greater than many of My countrymen expected. . . . One great task awaits you: to avenge the great injustice which happened. The Chinese have overthrown international law; they have in a fashion unknown in world history scorned the sanctity of the envoy, the obligations of hospitality. This is all the more shocking in that this crime was committed by a nation proud of its ancient culture. Maintain the old Prussian efficiency, show yourselves to be Christians in the joyous bearing of suffering, may honor and glory follow your flags and arms, give the world an example of your discipline.

You know well you will fight against a brave, well-armed, cruel enemy. If you meet him, know: there will be no pardon! Prisoners will not be taken! A thousand years ago the Huns under king Attila made a name for themselves which in history and legend still stands for power. May your actions insure that the word German is similarly looked upon in China for a thousand years so that never again will a Chinaman even dare to look askance at a German. Keep discipline.

God's blessing with you; the prayers of a whole people, my wishes, accompany you, each and every one of you. Pave the way for culture once and for all.

—Johannes Penzler (ed.), *Die Reden Kaiser Wilhelms II in den Jahren 1898–1900* (Leipzig, 1904), 2:210–12; Bernd Sösemann, "Die sogenannte Hunnenrede Wilhelms II," *Historische Zeitschrift* 222 (1976), 342–358

c)   *Anglo-German Agreement on China, 16 October 1900*

1. It is a matter of joint and permanent international interest that the ports on the rivers and littoral of China should remain free and open to trade and to every other legitimate form of economic activity for the nationals of all countries without distinction; and the two governments on their part to uphold the same for all Chinese territory as far as they can exercise influence.

2. . . . [the Contracting Parties] will not, on their part, make use of the present complication to obtain for themselves any territorial advantages, in Chinese dominions, and will direct their policy towards maintaining undiminished the territorial condition of the Chinese empire.

3. In case of another power making use of the complications in China in order to obtain under any form whatever such territorial advantages, the two Contracting Parties reserve to themselves to come to a preliminary understanding as to the eventual steps to be taken for the protection of their own interests in China. . . .

—Hertslet III, 1:591ff.

10.22   THE UNITED STATES IN THE WESTERN HEMISPHERE

Bülow to Wilhelm II, 11 August 1899 ● Selborne to the British Cabinet, 17 January 1901 ● Platt Amendment, 25 February 1901 ● Roosevelt to Spring Rice, 3 July 1901 ● (Second) Hay-Pauncefote Treaty, 18 November 1901 ● Roosevelt to Hinman, 29 December 1902 ● Roosevelt to Hay, 22 April 1903 ● Roosevelt to Kermit Roosevelt, 4 November 1903 ● Isthmian Canal (Hay-Buneau Varilla) Convention, 18 November 1903 ● Roosevelt's Fourth Annual Message to Congress, 6 December 1904 ● Roosevelt's Fifth Annual Message to Congress, 5 December 1905 ● Sir Henry Mortimer Durand, Annual Report for 1906 ● Hardinge to Knollys, 15 May 1906 ● Second Hague Conventions (No. II), 18 October 1907

The extracts reproduced below afford a glimpse of the vigorous efforts by the United States to consolidate and even expand its informal empire in the Americas. Residual border issues with Canada, the future of Cuba, the Isthmian canal project, and the growing inability of Caribbean and Latin American states to meet their foreign debt provided the backdrop for American policy.

MAP 14   THE CARIBBEAN AREA

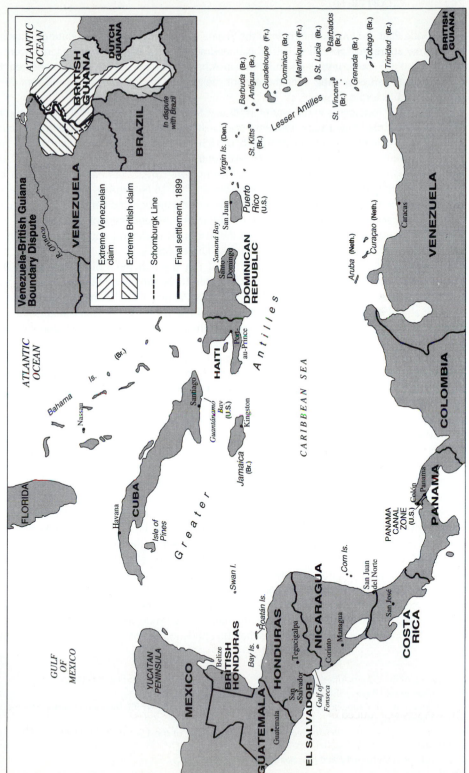

Venezuela-British Guiana Boundary Dispute

Extreme Venezuelan claim	
Extreme British claim	
Schomburgk Line	
Final settlement, 1899	

ATLANTIC OCEAN

DUTCH GUIANA

BRITISH GUIANA

BRAZIL

In dispute with Brazil

VENEZUELA

R. *Orinoco*

Barbuda (Br.)

Antigua (Br.)

Guadeloupe (Fr.)

Dominica (Br.)

Martinique (Fr.)

St. Lucia (Br.)

Barbados (Br.)

St. Vincent (Br.)

Grenada (Br.)

Tobago (Br.)

Trinidad (Br.)

Lesser Antilles

St. Kitts (Br.)

Virgin Is. (Den.)

San Juan

Puerto Rico (U.S.)

Samaná Bay

Santo Domingo

DOMINICAN REPUBLIC

Port-au-Prince

HAITI

Antilles

Caracas

Curaçao (Neth.)

Aruba (Neth.)

VENEZUELA

BRITISH GUIANA

ATLANTIC OCEAN

Bahama Is. (Br.)

Nassau

Santiago

Guantánamo Bay (U.S.)

Kingston

Jamaica (Br.)

Greater

CUBA

Havana

Isle of Pines

CARIBBEAN SEA

COLOMBIA

Swan I.

Corn Is.

San Juan del Norte

San José

Colón

Panama

PANAMA

PANAMA CANAL ZONE (U.S.)

COSTA RICA

NICARAGUA

Managua

Corinto

HONDURAS

Tegucigalpa

Roatán Is.

Bay Is.

Belize

BRITISH HONDURAS

YUCATAN PENINSULA

GULF OF MEXICO

MEXICO

FLORIDA

GUATEMALA

Guatemala

San Salvador

EL SALVADOR

Gulf of Fonseca

291

Orville Platt (R-Conn.), chairman of the Senate Committee on Cuban Relations, attached to the army appropriations bill of 1901 the amendment that bears his name. Its terms were inserted into the Cuban constitution and a Cuban-American treaty; they in essence ensured that Cuba, though self-governing after the end of the American occupation, would remain an American protectorate.[47]

Buoyed by its success in the war of 1898 and taking advantage of Britain's embroilment in South Africa, the United States reopened the question of a canal traversing Central America. The Anglo-American (Clayton-Bulwer) treaty of 1850 had stipulated that neither country "will ever obtain or maintain for itself any exclusive control" over a canal across Nicaragua.[48] This agreement was set aside by the second Hay-Pauncefote[49] treaty (an earlier treaty draft had been amended by the Senate and rejected by Britain)[50] of 18 November 1901, which cleared the way for the United States' unilateral operation of a transoceanic canal. The British cabinet's acquiescence to this treaty—and to the Alaskan border settlement of January 1903—was rooted in the realization that Britain lacked the resources to defend imperial interests in the western hemisphere against the opposition of the United States.

The shortest route for a transoceanic canal ran through the Colombian province of Panama. A French canal company initially sponsored by Ferdinand de Lesseps[51] failed amidst a major financial scandal in 1889. Although the New Panama Canal Company was formed in 1894, it abandoned work on the project five years later. The New Panama Canal Company's single most valuable asset was its concession from the Colombian government, and it was this which the Roosevelt administration sought to purchase under the terms of the Hay-Herran treaty with Colombia of 22 January 1903. The treaty, however, was scuttled by the Colombian senate on 12 August. Undeterred by this failure, Roosevelt and Hay now encouraged the secession of Panama from Colombia and recognized the new republic two days after insurgents declared its independence. The new Panamanian government immediately authorized Philippe Buneau Varilla, a partner in the New Panama Canal Company with a considerable financial stake in its sale, to conclude the treaty excerpted below.

In December 1902, the inability of Venezuela to service its foreign debt led to a blockade of Venezuelan ports by Britain, Germany, and Italy. Sensing American opposition to this show of force, the British government soon withdrew its ships. The British move caused the German government to wonder whether any operation could be conducted in tandem with Britain but, more immediately, left Germany as the principal target of Roosevelt's wrath. The quarrel was settled with an agreement to submit the debt question to the Hague tribunal and an American assurance, if necesssary, to hold Venezuela to the terms set by the tribunal.

The Latin American debt crisis was the trigger for the so-called Roosevelt corollary to the Monroe Doctrine, announced by the president in his annual message to Congress in December 1904. Less well known is the Latin American reaction to the Venezuela blockade. To counteract the threat of naval intervention by European powers (and also to forestall measures on their behalf by the United States), the Argentine foreign minister, Luis Maria Drago, sought to establish in international law the rule that the collection of debts by force was impermissi-

---

[47]Text of the Cuban-American treaty of 22 May 1903 in Bevans, *Treaties*, 6:1116–19.

[48]Text of the Clayton-Bulwer treaty in Bevans, *Treaties*, 12:105–8.

[49]Julian, Baron Pauncefote (1828–1902). British minister, 1889–1893; then ambassador, 1893–1902, to the United States.

[50]Text in Christian L. Wiktor (ed.) *Unperfected Treaties of the United States* (Dobbs Ferry, 1976–), 3:337–40.

[51]Cf. Documents 4.12 and 6.5, headnote.

ble. The United States, in part to humor the Latin American republics, endorsed a watered-down version of the Drago doctrine (now recast as the "Porter proposition")[52] at the Second Hague Peace Conference of 1907—but in subsequent years honored this convention in the breach.

a)   *Bülow to Wilhelm II, 11 August 1899*

. . . As long as we do not get on America's bad side, John Bull will confront the alternative of either having to abandon Canada or having to risk a fatal collision with Uncle Sam. . . .[53]

—Stiftung Preussischer Kulturbesitz, Rep. 53J Lit. B No. 16a

b)   *Selborne[54] to the British Cabinet, 17 January 1901*

. . . Hitherto the policy of this country [Britain] has been stated to be so to build battleships as to maintain an equality of numbers with the combined battleships of the two powers possessing for the moment the largest fleets. It does not seem to me that this basis of calculation is one that will any longer serve, considering that within the last five years three new navies have sprung into existence—those of the United States, Germany, and Japan. It is certain that it would be a hopeless task to attempt to achieve an equality with the three largest navies; but I go further, and say that, if the United States continue their present naval policy and develop their navy as they are easily capable of developing it if they choose, it will be scarcely possible for us to raise our navy to a strength equal to that both of France and the United States combined. I propose therefore to consider our position almost exclusively from its relative strength to that of France and Russia combined. . . .

—George Monger, *The End of Isolation: British Foreign Policy, 1900–1907* (London, 1963), 11; Bourne, 461–62

[52]After Horace Porter (1837–1921). American ambassador to France, 1897–1905, and delegate to the Second Hague Peace Conference.

[53]It is likely that Bülow referred to the smoldering dispute between the United States and Britain over the Alaskan boundary. This issue was ultimately submitted to an Anglo-American tribunal. In five of seven "questions" put to the tribunal, the English member of the British Empire delegation assured an American victory by voting with the Americans against his Canadian colleagues. For the text of the convention of 24 January 1903, see Hurst, 2:743–51, or Bevans, *Treaties*, 12:263–68. Between 1905 and 1912, this convention was followed by a spate of notes and conventions on other U.S.-Canadian border and fisheries issues. For texts, see Bevans, *Treaties*, vol. 12. For the connection between the Isthmian canal and the Alaskan-Canadian boundary dispute, see Kenneth Bourne, *Britain and the Balance of Power in North America, 1815–1908* (Berkeley, 1967), 347, 372–401. British preoccupations with the Boer war explain the British retreat on both issues.

[54]William Waldegrave, Lord Selborne (1859–1942). First Lord of the Admirality, 1900–1905.

c)   *Platt Amendment, 25 February 1901*

Art. 1: . . . the government of Cuba shall never enter into any treaty or other compact with any foreign power or powers which will impair or tend to impair the independence of Cuba, nor in any manner authorize or permit any foreign power or powers to obtain by colonization or for military or naval purposes or otherwise lodgment in or control over any portion of said island. . . .

Art. 3: . . . the government of Cuba consents that the United States may exercise the right to intervene for the preservation of Cuban independence. . . .

Art. 7: . . . to enable the United States to maintain the independence of Cuba, and to protect the people thereof, as well as for its own defense, the government of Cuba will sell or lease to the United States lands necessary for coaling or naval stations. . . .

—*Congressional Record*, 56th Congress, 2nd Session, 34:2954

d)   *Roosevelt to Spring Rice,[55] 3 July 1901*

. . . The more I have heard of the Kaiser the more my respect for him has grown, and though I do not think the Czar is much of a man, still I think he is a good fellow in his way too. The German press at times makes me so angry that I feel a cordial desire to try a fall with Germany. But as a matter of fact I think it would be most unfortunate if Germany could not continue to get along well with both the United States and England. . . . I explained to the German ambassador that I did not want to see America get a foot of territory at the expense of any one of the South American states, and that I did not want her to get a commercial advantage over Germany or any other European power save as it was obtained by fair competition by the merchants or by the ordinary form of treaty; but that I most emphatically protested against either Germany or any other power getting new territory in America—just as I am certain England would object to seeing Delagoa Bay becoming German or French instead of Portuguese. . . .

—Elting E. Morison et al. (eds.), *The Letters of Theodore Roosevelt*
(Cambridge, MA, 1951), 3: 2091

e)   *(Second) Hay-Pauncefote Treaty, 18 November 1901*

[Preamble: The United States and Great Britain are] desirous to facilitate the construction of a ship canal to connect the Atlantic and Pacific Oceans, by whatever route may

---

[55]Sir Cecil Arthur Spring Rice (1859–1918), British diplomat in Washington, 1886–1895. In 1901, Spring Rice was British commissioner of the Egyptian debt. After serving in a variety of European and Middle Eastern posts, Spring Rice returned to Washington as British ambassador, 1913–1918.

be considered expedient, and to that end to remove any objection which may arise out of the . . . Clayton-Bulwer Treaty. . . .

Art. 2: It is agreed that the canal may be constructed under the auspices of the Government of the United States. . . .

Art. 3.2: . . . The United States, however, shall be at liberty to maintain such military police along the canal as may be necessary to protect it against lawlessness and disorder. . . .

Art. 4: It is agreed that no change of territorial sovereignty or of the international relations of the country or countries traversed by the afore-mentioned canal shall affect the general principle of neutralization. . . .

—Bevans, *Treaties*, 12:258–60

f)   ***Roosevelt to Hinman,*** [56] ***29 December 1902***

. . . In this Venezuela situation I knew exactly what I wanted. I was bound that we should not be put in the position of preventing the collection of an honest debt. I was also bound that there should be no territorial aggrandizement by any European power under cover of the collection of such a debt. . . .

—Morison, *Letters*, op. cit., 3:2539

g)   ***Roosevelt to Hay, 22 April 1903***

. . . Both the Dutch and the Danish possessions in America will be constant temptations to Germany unless, or until, we take them. The way to deliver Germany from the temptation is to keep on with the upbuilding of our navy. . . .

—Morison, *Letters*, 3:2638

h)   ***Roosevelt to Kermit Roosevelt, 4 November 1903***

. . . For half a century we have policed that isthmus in the interest of the little wildcat republic of Colombia. Colombia has behaved infamously about the treaty for the building of the Panama Canal; and I do not intend in the police work that I will have to do in connection with the new insurrection any longer to do for her work which is not merely profitless but brings no gratitude. Any interference I undertake now will be in the interest of the United States and the people of the Panama isthmus themselves. There will be some lively times in carrying out this policy. . . .

—Morison, *Letters*, 3:2856

---

[56]George Wheeler Hinman (1864–1927). Editor of the Chicago *Inter Ocean*, 1898–1912.

i)   *Isthmian Canal (Hay-Buneau Varilla) Convention,*
18 November 1903

Art. 1: The United States guarantees and will maintain the independence of the Republic of Panama.

Art. 2: The Republic of Panama grants to the United States in perpetuity the use, occupation and control of a zone of land and land under water for the construction, maintenance, operation, sanitation and protection of said Canal of the width of ten miles extending to the distance of five miles on each side of the center line of the route of the Canal. . . .

Art. 8: The Republic of Panama . . . authorizes the New Panama Canal Company to sell and transfer to the United States its rights, privileges, properties and concessions. . . .

—Bevans, *Treaties*, 10:663–72

j)   *Roosevelt's Fourth Annual Message to Congress,*
6 December 1904

. . . Chronic wrongdoing, or an impotence which results in a general loosening of the ties of civilized society, may in America, as elsewhere, ultimately require intervention by some civilized nation, and in the western hemisphere the adherence of the United States, however reluctantly, in flagrant cases of such wrongdoing or impotence, to the exercise of an international police power. If every country washed by the Caribbean Sea would show the progress in stable and just civilization which with the aid of the Platt amendment Cuba has shown since our troops left the island, and which so many of the republics in both Americas are constantly and brilliantly showing, all question of interference by this nation with their affairs would be at an end. . . . We would interfere with them only in the last resort, and then only if it became evident that their inability or unwillingness to do justice at home and abroad had violated the rights of the United States or had invited foreign aggression to the detriment of the entire body of American nations. . . . In asserting the Monroe Doctrine, in taking such steps as we have taken in regard to Cuba, Venezuela, and Panama, and in endeavoring to circumscribe the theater of war in the Far East, and to secure the open door in China, we have acted in our own interest as well as in the interest of humanity at large. . . .

—*Congressional Record*, 58th Congress, 3rd Session, 39:19

k)   *Roosevelt's Fifth Annual Message to Congress,*
5 December 1905

. . . The previous rulers of Santo Domingo had recklessly incurred debts, and owing to her internal disorders she had ceased to be able to provide means of paying the debts. The patience of her foreign creditors had become exhausted. . . . [Under] a temporary arrangement . . . the Dominican government has appointed Americans to all the important positions in the customs service. . . . [S]tability and order and all the benefits of peace are at last coming to Santo Domingo, danger of foreign intervention has been suspended, and there is at last a prospect that all creditors will get justice. . . .

—*Congressional Record*, 59th Congress, 1st Session, 40:98

l)   *Sir Henry Mortimer Durand,*[57] *Annual Report for 1906*

. . . [The president's] early prejudices were strongly anti-English and he has no love for England now . . . but his cooler judgement and the influence of the late John Hay have, I think, convinced him that it is to the interest of the U.S. to keep on good terms with England. . . . I regard him as a man who might at any time be extremely dangerous, for neither his temper nor his honesty can be trusted. . . .

—FO, 371/357

m)   *Hardinge*[58] *to Knollys,*[59] *15 May 1906*

. . . [Roosevelt's letters] have amused Grey and me greatly. These are extraordinarily childish for a man, who, as he says, has been to Harvard and who is undoubtedly a big man in America. . . .

—Royal Archives, Windsor, W 49/17

n)   *Second Hague Conventions (No. II), 18 October 1907*

Art. 1: The Contracting Powers agree not to have recourse to armed force for the recovery of contract debts claimed from the government of one country by the government of another country as being due to its nationals. This undertaking is, however, not applicable when the debtor state refuses or neglects to reply to an offer of arbitration, or, after accepting the offer, prevents any "compromis" from being agreed on, or, after the arbitration, fails to submit to the award.

—Bevans, *Treaties*, 1:614; William M. Malley (ed.), *Treaties, Conventions, International Acts, Protocols, and Agreements between the USA and Other Powers* (Washington, 1910), 2:2248–55

[57](1850–1924). British ambassador in Washington, 1903–1905; recalled because of his incompatibility with Roosevelt.

[58]Sir Charles Hardinge (1858–1944). Permanent under-secretary in the British Foreign Office, 1906–1910.

[59]Francis, Lord Knollys (1837–1924). Private secretary to King Edward VII.

10.23   **SALISBURY ON THE VIRTUES OF ISOLATION, 29 MAY 1901**

Neither Salisbury nor Bülow favored a general Anglo-German alliance in 1901. This idea was nonetheless vigorously promoted by Friedrich von Holstein and other senior figures in the German foreign ministry who had been misled by the German chargé in London, Baron Hermann von Eckhardstein, into believing that the British government was in fact eager to explore the prospects for an alliance.

Holstein had been converted from his earlier doubts about the merits of a general Anglo-German alliance. None of the colonial agreements between the two countries had led to the improvement in Anglo-German relations that he desired. The effusive welcome accorded to a British squadron visiting Lisbon in December 1900 had aroused German suspicions about British sincerity in seeing through the Anglo-German deal on the Portuguese colonies (Document 10.12). Conversely, the British expectation that the Anglo-German agreement of 16 October 1900 (Document 10.21c) on China could serve as a basis for a broader accord had been dashed by Bülow's announcement in the Reichstag on 15 March 1901 that "the Anglo-German agreement did not apply to Manchuria. . . . As to the fate of Manchuria: yes, gentlemen, I don't know of anything that could leave us more indifferent."[60] With these limited agreements in tatters, Holstein may have reasoned that a general alliance provided one last hope for ending the cycle of mutual suspicions and recriminations between the two countries. The essence of Holstein's proposal—as communicated to Salisbury by Paul von Hatzfeldt, the German ambassador—was a defensive treaty between England and the Triple Alliance, activated by an attack on the signatories by two or more powers. Salisbury's response is reproduced below; it should be understood in the context of Britain's success in localizing the Boer war and in staving off diplomatic intervention by other powers. Above all, Britain avoided paying the price that any foreign commitment entailed—in itself a triumph for Salisbury's policy of isolation.

. . . Count Hatzfeldt speaks of our "*isolation*" as constituting a serious danger for us. *Have we ever felt that danger practically?* If we had succumbed in the revolutionary war, our fall would not have been due to our isolation. We had many allies, but they would not have saved us if the French Emperor had been able to command the Channel.

Several times during the last sixteen years Count Hatzfeldt has tried to elicit from me, in conversation, some opinion as to the probable conduct of England, if Germany or Italy were involved in war with France. I have always replied that no English minister could venture such a forecast. The course of the English Government in such a crisis must depend on the view taken by public opinion in this country, and public opinion would be largely, if not exclusively, governed by the nature of the *casus belli*.

—*BD*, 2:86

10.24   **THE CHAMBERLAIN-BÜLOW CONTROVERSY**

Chamberlain in Edinburgh, 25 October 1901 ● *Bülow in the Reichstag, 8 January 1902* ● *Bülow in the Reichstag, 10 January 1902* ● *Chamberlain at Birmingham, 11 January 1902*

The British policy of interning Boers in concentration camps during the last stage of the South African war aroused widespread criticism at home and abroad. Adding his voice to the

---

[60]Penzler (ed.), *Bülows Reden*, 1:202–3.

chorus of disapproval, the Liberal leader in the Commons and future prime minister, Sir Henry Campbell-Bannerman, castigated British practices as "methods of barbarism." Joseph Chamberlain's defense of the government, however, featured an injudicious aside that further inflamed public sentiment in Germany against Britain. Commenting on this uproar in the German Reichstag, Bülow failed to extinguish the fire and instead reopened the debate. A subsequent speech by the Pan-German deputy Liebermann von Sonnenberg outdid all by commenting that "[t]his Chamberlain, who dares to attack the German army, is the most villainous knave on God's earth" and added the insult, "The English army in South Africa is barely more than a mob of thieves and robbers." Liebermann's remarks were censured by the Reichstag president, and Bülow rose to repudiate them. But Bülow's reply was judged in England to be insufficient, prompting his senior foreign policy adviser to comment that "Bülow's speech against Chamberlain is the Krüger telegram on a small scale."[61]

a)   ***Chamberlain in Edinburgh, 25 October 1901***

. . . I go on to a complaint which perhaps is more serious, a complaint that we, the Government, have not pressed forward this war with sufficient vigour. . . . I think that the time has come—is coming—when measures of greater severity may be necessary ["hear, hear," and cheers], and if that time comes we can find precedents for anything that we may do in the action of those nations who now criticize our "barbarity" and "cruelty," but whose example in Poland, in the Caucasus, in Almeria, in Tonkin, in Bosnia, in the Franco-German war, whose example we have never even approached [cheers]. . . .

—*The Times*, 26 October 1901

b)   ***Bülow in the Reichstag, 8 January 1902***

. . . I think we are all agreed and I think that all conciliatory people in England agree with us that, when a minister is forced to justify his policies—this sort of thing happens now and then [laughter]—, he is well advised to leave out references to other countries [quite right]. . . .This is all the more regrettable when this happens towards a country which has always maintained with his own . . . good and friendly relations, the undisturbed continuation of which is in the mutual interest of both parties [very true]. It was certainly understandable that in a people which is so closely intertwined with its glorious army as the German people . . . there was a general revulsion against the attempt and the appearance to distort the heroic character and moral basis of our national struggle for unity. The standing of the German army however is much too high and its shields are too spotless for it to be affected by slanted judgments [bravo]. To this applies what Frederick the Great once said when he was told that someone had attacked him and the Prussian army: "Let the man be and don't get excited, he's biting on granite. . . ."

—Penzler, *Bülows Reden*, op. cit., 1:241–47

[61]Diary entry by Holstein, 14 January 1902. *HP*, 4:794.

c)   **Bülow in the Reichstag, 10 January 1902**

Gentlemen, after the President has censured a remark of the previous speaker, I will not dignify this remark by challenging it. I simply want to say that I believe that I am in agreement with a large, very large majority of this House when I express the hope that it will not become a habit to insult foreign ministers from the speaker's platform of the German parliament [lively approval]. . . . If we are sensitive to any attack against the honor of our own army, then we should not insult other armies in whom there are also people who know how to die [lively approval]. . . . The previous speaker has revealed a lack of responsibility [correct]. A few days ago I left no doubt that it was justified when our public opinion decidedly rejected the attempt or even the appearance that the honor of our army had somehow been besmirched. But if this rejection was to serve as a pretext to force upon us a different attitude towards the South African war or a pretext to bring about unfriendly, hostile relations between our people and the people who has never been our enemy and with whom we are connected through manifold and weighty interests, then I want to leave no doubt that I will not participate in this [bravo]. Speeches, resolutions, and popular assemblies cannot dictate to us the direction of our foreign policy [very good]. This will be determined by the real and permanent interests of the country, and this requires us, while preserving our independence, while upholding our dignity and honor, to maintain peaceful and friendly relations with England. . . .

—Penzler, *Bülows Reden*, 1:241–47

d)   **Chamberlain at Birmingham, 11 January 1902**

. . . I understand a good party fight; I myself am a party man; when I am struck I try to strike back again [loud laughter]; but I cannot appreciate the position of those who are influenced by party passion and not content with fighting the battle here at home on fair and reasonable lines but must go out of their way to impute methods of barbarism to our soldiers in the field [shame!], to imply that His Majesty's ministers, who are Britons like themselves, can by any possibility be guilty of deliberate cruelty and inhumanity, and who laud the Boers while they slander the Britons [hear, hear], and then profess to be astonished and surprised at the growing hostility of foreign nations [cheers]. They have helped to create the animosity which we all deplore [hear, hear]. I am well aware that in some quarters this animosity is attributed to another cause. It is said to be due to the indiscreet oratory of the Colonial Secretary [laughter]. Gentlemen, what I have said I have said [loud cheers]. I withdraw nothing [much cheering]. I qualify nothing [renewed cheers]. I defend nothing. As I read history, no British minister has ever served his country faithfully and at the same time enjoyed popularity abroad [cheers]. I make allowance, therefore, for foreign criticism. I will not follow an example that has been set to me. I do not want to give lessons to a foreign minister ["hear, hear," and cheers] and I will not accept any at his hands [loud cheers]. . . .

—*The Times*, 13 January 1902

10.25　　　　　　　# THE ANGLO-JAPANESE ALLIANCE

Anglo-Japanese Alliance, 30 January 1902 ●
Franco-Russian Declaration, 3/16 March 1902

After Germany had cold-shouldered British attempts to forge an anti-Russian coalition in East Asia, Britain turned to Japan. The Anglo-Japanese alliance, signed on 30 January 1902 and published twelve days later, satisfied a range of mutual needs. The prospect of a coordinated Anglo-Japanese policy in East Asia would encourage Russia to halt its expansion in north China and bring that power to the negotiating table. In the event of war, the signatories would seek to localize the conflict, coming to one another's direct aid only when a fourth power joined the adversary. The treaty language was remarkably vague: it did not differentiate among various scenarios that might lead to war ("if either Great Britain or Japan . . . *should become involved* in war with another power" [emphasis added]), nor did it spell out whether the war, if it engulfed both signatories, would remain a regional event or would be prosecuted on a global scale.

According to the preamble and its first article, this was an alliance to "safeguard" British interests in China and Japan's in China and Korea. Pointing to the regional character of the alliance, some historians have argued that it was consistent with Britain's earlier policy of isolation, as in theory it allowed Britain to remain aloof from European commitments.[62] If this was so, the events that the alliance helped set in motion led to an outcome different from the one intended by its makers.

a)　　　　　　## *Anglo-Japanese Alliance, 30 January 1902*

. . . Art. 2: If either Great Britain or Japan, in defence of their respective interests as above described, should become involved in war with another Power, the other High Contracting Party will maintain a strict neutrality, and use its efforts to prevent other Powers from joining in hostilities against its ally.

Art. 3: If, in the above event, any other Power or Powers should join in hostilities against that ally, the other High Contracting Party will come to its assistance, and will conduct the war in common, and make peace in mutual agreement with it.

—*BD*, 2:125; Hertslet III, 1: 597–98

b)　　　　　## *Franco-Russian Declaration of 3/16 March 1902*

. . . [O]bliged to consider the case in which either aggression of third Powers or new troubles in China threaten the integrity and the free development of that Power [and in turn] threaten their own interests, the two allied Governments reserve for themselves [the right] to consider the means to safeguard them.

—Hertslet III, 1:599

[62]Taylor, *Struggle for Mastery*, 440; Lowe, *The Reluctant Imperialists*, 249.

THE FRANCO-ITALIAN RAPPROCHEMENT, 1898–1902

Barrère to Visconti-Venosta, 14 December 1900 ●
Visconti-Venosta to Barrère, 16 December 1900 ● *Bülow to Metternich,*
18 December 1901 ● *Bülow in the Reichstag, 8 January 1902* ●
Prinetti to Barrère, 30 June (1 November) 1902 ● *Barrère to Delcassé,*
20 July 1902

A Franco-Italian commercial agreement, concluded in November 1898 at the height of the Fashoda crisis (Document 10.14), may have rested on its own merits. Both events, though co-incidental, served as steppingstones for Delcassé's policy toward Italy.

The geographic connection between the Anglo-French settlement on the Congo/Nile watershed of 21 March 1899 (Document 10.14f) and the Franco-Italian notes of 1900 is readily apparent from the text of the latter. More important, the debacle at Fashoda showed that the tactics of the 1880s and early 1890s were out of date: a successful colonial policy now required that the antics of the men-on-the-spot be preceded by a diplomatic campaign aimed at neutralizing the rival claims of other powers. This insight was all the more important given the fact that the imperialist land grab in Africa of earlier decades had left few territories into which expansion was still possible.

The lesson of Fashoda, if applied to Delcassé's ambition to transform Morocco into a French protectorate, suggested that any such venture could be realized only through prior agreements with other powers. Beginning with Italy, this was precisely the task Delcassé set himself. While purchasing Italy's support for French aims in Morocco, he discovered that the coordination of colonial claims could blossom into a broader political rapprochement. He thereby—unwittingly, if his biographer is to be believed[63]—set in motion a process with far-reaching consequences for the European alliance system.

Both the German and French documents suggest that Delcassé may have originally aimed the Franco-Italian entente as much at Britain as at Germany. The last excerpt below speaks to this motive, but it is also possible that Delcassé encouraged this belief to cover his own tracks and to mislead Bülow.

a) *Barrère[64] to Visconti-Venosta,[65] 14 December 1900*

. . . while leaving the vilayet of Tripoli outside the spheres of influence sanctioned by it, the [Anglo-French] convention of 21 March 1899 sets, for the French sphere of influence in relation to Tripolitania-Cyrenaica, a limit which the government of the Republic has no intention of exceeding. . . .

—*DDF*, 2nd Series, 1:17

[63]Andrew, *Delcassé*, 140, 190.

[64]Camille Barrère (1851–1940). French ambassador in Rome, 1897–1924.

[65]Emilio, Marchese Visconti-Venosta (1829–1914). Italian foreign minister, 1863–1864; 1866–1867; 1869–1876; 1896–1898; 1899–1901.

b)   *Visconti-Venosta to Barrère, 16 December 1900*

. . . So far as concerns Morocco more particularly, it appeared from our conversations that the action of France has as its purpose the exercise and the safeguarding of the rights which are the result for her of the proximity of her territory with that empire. So defined, I recognized that such action is not in our view of a nature to prejudice the interests of Italy as a Mediterranean power. It has also been agreed that if there should come about a modification of the political or territorial status quo of Morocco, Italy would reserve the right, as a measure of reciprocity, to develop her influence with regard to Tripolitania-Cyrenaica. . . .

—*DDF*, 2nd Series, 1:17

c)   *Bülow to Metternich,*[66] *18 December 1901*

. . . Germany is not directly affected by these Mediterranean questions. Nowadays we no longer have to figure, as we had to in the first years after our French war, that we will be the target of a concentric attack. The great objects of today's global politics— the Mediterranean, Persia, East Asia—are questions in which the freedom of decision remains with us. If one of them is set into motion, then the states most immediately affected will presumably inquire at the outset as to Germany's stand. . . .

—*GP*, 18ii:5835

d)   *Bülow in the Reichstag, 8 January 1902*[67]

. . . The Triple Alliance does not prohibit its participants from maintaining good relations with other powers, and I would not think it right for even a small part of the German press to show disquiet because of the Franco-Italian agreements. In a happy marriage the husband need not blush with embarrassment when his wife allows another man to waltz her innocently across the dance floor [hilarity]. The main thing is that she doesn't run off; and she won't bolt if she is in fact better off with him [very good!]. . . .

—Penzler, *Bülows Reden*, op. cit., 1:243

---

[66]Paul, Count Wolff-Metternich (1853–1934). German ambassador in London, 1901–1912.
[67]Earlier portions of this speech are reproduced above in Document 10.24.

e)   ***Prinetti*[68] *to Barrère, 30 June (1 November) 1902*[69]**

... [E]ach of the two powers [Italy and France] can freely develop its sphere of influence in the above mentioned regions [Tripolitania-Cyrenaica and Morocco respectively] at the moment it deems opportune, and without the action of one of them being necessarily subordinated to that of the other....

In case France should be the object of a direct or indirect aggression on the part of one or more powers, Italy will maintain a strict neutrality.

The same should hold good in case France, as the result of a direct provocation, should find itself compelled, in defense of its honor or of its security, to take the initiative of a declaration of war. In that eventuality, the government of the [French] Republic shall previously communicate its intention to the Royal [Italian] Government, which will thus be enabled to determine whether there is really a case of direct provocation.

... I am authorized further to confirm to you that on the part of Italy no protocol or military provision in the nature of an international contract which would be in disagreement with the present declaration exists or will be concluded by it....

—*DDF,* 2nd Series, 2:329

f)   ***Barrère to Delcassé, 20 July 1902***

... Prinetti said that he would consider as constituting a direct provocation those resulting from the direct relations of foreign powers with the signatory governments [France and Italy]. And he gave as examples the following cases:

1) The publication of the dispatches edited by Prince Bismarck in 1870 [and] the refusal of King Wilhelm to receive M. Benedetti;[70]

2) the Schnaebele incident;[71]

3) certain vicissitudes [*péripéties*] during the Fashoda affair.

In contrast, he cited [examples of] "indirect provocations" which would not fall within the purview of the Italian declarations: the candidacy of the Prince of Hohenzollern for the throne of Spain[72] and any indirect initiative in the affairs of the Far East

---

[68]Giulio Prinetti (1851–1908). Italian foreign minister, 1901–1903.

[69]Originally: 30 June 1902. The date on this letter and Barrère's reply of the same day were changed at Prinetti's insistence. The minister apparently feared that the timing of this exchange, only two days after the renewal of the Triple Alliance, would appear tactless if the letters were ever made public. Barrère's letter, which simply reiterated Prinetti's note, is not reproduced here.

[70]Document 8.13.

[71]Schnaebele, a French customs inspector, was arrested in Germany in April 1887 under suspicion that he maintained a spy network in Lorraine. He was released after he proved that he crossed into Germany at the invitation of his German counterpart to discuss local border issues. Large segments of French public opinion, though not the government, thought Bismarck planned the incident to provoke France into a declaration of war. Cf. Document 9.24.

[72]Document 8.12.

that does not directly involve [*viserait*] one of the contracting Powers, even if that initiative is displeasing to them and might appear to them contrary to their direct interest.

—*DDF*, 2nd Series, 2:340

10.27   BÜLOW AND HOLSTEIN ON GERMANY BETWEEN BRITAIN AND RUSSIA

*Bülow to Wilhelm II, 31 March 1903 • Bülow to Holstein, 3 April 1903 •
Holstein to Bülow, 16 April 1903*

The question of whether or not the British government should back the German-dominated Bagdad railroad company unleashed a storm of controversy in the British press in March and April 1903 (Document 10.28, headnote). The uproar mirrored the general deterioration of the Anglo-German relationship; it also ran parallel to an improvement in Anglo-French relations. The latter was most visibly underscored by King Edward VII's state visit to Paris scheduled for early May 1903.

The Kaiser speculated that the increasing Anglo-French intimacy would drive a wedge between France and Russia, Britain's principal adversary in East Asia; Russia would then seek closer ties with Germany. Neither Bülow nor Holstein shared this expectation. Like his earlier communications on the subject of Russo-German relations (Document 10.20), Bülow's letter to the Kaiser may have deliberately exaggerated the point to calm down the effusive monarch.

The second excerpt shows that Bülow put far more stock in the Russo-German relationship than he was willing to admit to the Kaiser. On this occasion too (cf. Document 10.26d) he cavalierly assumed that the premises of his policy still held. His use, in this dispatch, of the word "*pomadig*" conveys a certain irony: pomade being a powdery, greasy substance, the adjective *pomadig* is descriptive of Bülow himself and brings to mind Holstein's assessment of Bülow as "clean-shaven and pasty, with a shifty look and an almost perpetual smile. Intellectually plausible rather than penetrating."[73]

In his assessment of the international situation, Holstein counseled caution and may have wanted to use this opportunity to impress on Bülow, whom he had long suspected of being too pro-Russian, the folly of an alignment with that power. Unwittingly, his dispatch of 16 April 1903 offers a devastating critique of Germany's aspiration to pursue *Weltpolitik*.

The documents excerpted here reveal the divisions within Germany's leadership but are equally interesting for another reason. They demonstrate that German officialdom, like its British counterpart (Document 10.22), began to acknowledge the United States as a factor in world politics and speculated on the advantages this development might offer.

a)   *Bülow to Wilhelm II, 31 March 1903*

... It is very useful from time to time to let the Russians know that Your Majesty is on better terms with England and with America than they seem to think in

[73]Diary entry of 8 April 1885. *HP*, 2, 188.

Petersburg. . . . The English global empire has gotten so big that it can no longer be maintained on its own strength. It requires an ally and would give a lot for a firm alliance with America. . . . Such a commitment would be contrary to American tradition and inclinations. America is too egotistical not to realize that it will fare better with a policy of the free hand than with a business deal with an overfed and equally egotistical John Bull. . . . To deflect English attention from its own expansionist plans, Russia, with all the traditional methods of its cunning and machiavellian diplomacy, is seeking to sic England on Germany. . . . [We] should seek to arouse neither English, nor Russian, nor American mistrust. . . .

—Stiftung Preussischer Kulturbesitz, Rep. 53J Lit. B No. 16a

b)   *Bülow to Holstein, 3 April 1903*

. . . Delcassé's coquetry with England will become worrisome for us only if the French minister succeeds in bringing about a rapprochement between England and Russia as well, therewith [creating] the Anglo-French-Russian entente pursued by Gambetta[74] in the seventies. If not, then his wooing of England will cast in an even more favorable light our policy in Petersburg—friendly, stable, and supportive of Russia in all questions which Russia considers important—and will fortify Count Lamsdorff[75] in his conviction that the old Three Emperors' League represents, all in all, the best deal for Russian autocracy. But the present alignments will not change overnight, and in my view we simply cannot take things nonchalantly [*pomadig*] enough. . . .

—*GP,*18ii:5911

c)   *Holstein to Bülow, 16 April 1903*

. . . The Russian cover was sufficient for Germany as long as the latter pursued Central European policies. In today's world politics, a Russian rapprochement with Germany . . . would be advantageous only for Russia. If Germany acts as its coast guard in the Baltic, Russia is capable of occupying all areas from Scutari[76] to Korea without getting its feet wet. Germany, however, can seek expansion only across the sea, but there, identified as the collaborator of Russia, it will face the concentric jealousies of England and America.

---

[74]Léon Gambetta (1838–1882). Cf. Document 8.13, headnote. Gambetta served as prime and foreign minister in 1881–1882. Barrère (cf. Document 10.26) and Delcassé started their political careers as columnists for Gambetta's paper, *La Republique française*—a fact that may explain their shared ideals and lifelong friendship. The connection between Gambetta and Delcassé may well have been the only correct observation in these remarks.

[75]Vladimir, Count Lamsdorff (1845–1907). Russian foreign minister, 1900–1906.

[76]Unclear whether Holstein meant Scutari in Albania or the suburb of Constantinople on the eastern shore of the Bosporus.

. . . Russia would gradually absorb those parts of Asia it finds appealing, but we would have to consider ourselves lucky if Russia's advances would not ricochet on us and, identified as its ally, we wouldn't become entangled in a world war which would yield no desirable results. Any expansion overseas would come about not as a result of victory on land but of success at sea, and I shouldn't think that our navy—even if we continued to build ships with all our efforts for years—in league with Russia could hope to defeat England and America. Our commerce at sea would be ruined for at least a generation; Russia has no seaborne commerce which could be ruined. As a result, Russia could survive a blockade far longer than we. Therefore final result of a rapprochement: for Russia a certain hegemony and its choice of territories in Asia, for Germany no recognizable gain, but lots of contingencies, one more unpleasant than the others. . . .

I think it is out of the question that things will come to a comprehensive or even limited treaty with Russia. Even a "coast guard in the Baltic"—which will create the prospect of incalculable entanglements and might just torpedo the Triple Alliance— would require, as a minimum prerequisite for Germany, a mutual guarantee of the status quo. Russia, out of consideration for France, will balk. But even without a treaty, our coquetting with Russia will be welcome to England because England knows no greater yearning than to sidle up to America—the trip which Mr. Chamberlain allegedly plans to take there probably only has that one objective. It would not be practical if we supplied him with arguments to assist him in this quest. . . .

—*GP*,18i:5421

10.28   THE RUSSO-JAPANESE CONFRONTATION
IN MANCHURIA

Russian Imperial Decree, 30 July/12 August 1903 •
Sino-Japanese Supplementary Commercial Treaty, 8 October 1903

The issue that continued to dominate the regional politics of East Asia in the aftermath of the Anglo-Japanese alliance (Document 10.25) was the continued presence of Russian forces in Manchuria—a legacy of the Russian effort to restore law and order during the Boxer rebellion. A Sino-Russian agreement of 26 March/8 April 1902[77] finally provided for the phased withdrawal of these units, but local Russian authorities devised a myriad of excuses not to budge. At the same time, Russia sought to consolidate its informal empire in Manchuria by securing further railroad concessions (cf. Documents 10.5d, 10.5g, and 10.10h).[78] Within the Russian government, the advocates of a go-slow approach or a *penetration pacifique* lost out to those who promoted a more overt policy in East Asia. The ouster of the cautious Sergei Witte from the finance ministry on 16/29 August 1903 and the creation, just a fortnight earlier, of two new institutions—a vice-royalty for the Far East, headed by the hard-liner Eugenii Alexeiev, and a special committee for Far Eastern affairs on which the like-minded Alexei Abaza served as secretary—signaled the triumph of the expansionists.

[77]Text in Hertslet III, 1:511.

[78]A coal mining concession of the Russian-controlled Chinese Eastern Railroad (1/14 January 1902) is of some cultural interest ("any grave plot which shall not contain more than ten graves may be removed"). MacMurray, *Treaties*, 1:661–62. Other concessions (of 28 June/11 July and 2/15 October 1902) in ibid., 1:629–31 and 1:356–67.

Faced by a combination of Russian intransigence and pressure, the Chinese government had little choice but to play the barbarians against one another. In October 1903, it submitted to Japanese and American demands to open further treaty ports in Manchuria. The prospect of Japanese commercial expansion into Manchuria probably stiffened the Russian hard-liners in their determination to press their claims on the Manchurian-Korean border and their refusal to yield ground in Manchuria proper. The ensuing gridlock set the stage for the next phase of the Russo-Japanese confrontation: before Russia could complete the last segment of the Trans-Siberian railroad around Lake Baikal (and thereby improve its logistics for all of north-east Asia), the Japanese navy launched a torpedo attack on the Russian fleet at Port Arthur on 8 February 1904.

a)   *Russian Imperial Decree of 30 July/12 August 1903*

. . . recognizing the necessity of forming a Special Lieutenancy to include all the provinces now under the rule of the Governor-General of Pri-Amur and the Kwan-tung Province, it is decreed as follows:

1. The Imperial Lieutenant of the Far East is invested with the supreme power in respect to the civil administration over those provinces and is independent of different ministries. He is also given the supreme authority regarding the maintenance of order and security in the localities appropriated for the benefit of the Chinese Eastern Railway. . . .

3. All diplomatic relations with neighboring powers in regard to affairs arising in those provinces of the Far East shall be concentrated in the hands of the Imperial Lieutenant.

4. The command of the naval forces in the Pacific and of all military forces stationed in the territories assigned to him is given to the Imperial Lieutenant.

5. In order that the action of the chief authority of the Far East shall conform with the general policy of the Empire and the activities of the Ministers, a special committee under Our [the tsar's] presidency shall be instituted. . . .

6. General Adjutant Alexeiev, who is appointed as the Imperial Lieutenant of the Far East, is charged with the development of this Imperial Decree. . . .

—MacMurray, *Treaties,* 1:122

b)   *Sino-Japanese Supplementary Commercial Treaty,*
8 October 1903

Art. 10: . . . upon the exchange of the ratifications of this treaty, Mukden and Tatungkow, both [situated] in . . . [Manchuria],[79] will be opened by China. . . .

—MacMurray, *Treaties,* 1:414; Hertslet III, 1:387

---

[79]Article 12 of a Sino-American commercial treaty concluded on the same day provided for the opening of Mukden and Antung. Herstlet III, 1:574. In September 1902, Britain had secured the opening of five further treaty ports—none of them, however, in Manchuria. Hertslet III, 1:180.

10.29   FURTHER ADJUSTMENTS IN BRITISH STRATEGY

Précis by Hardinge, 16 November 1906, of an Opinion on the Straits by the Committee of Imperial Defense, 13 February 1903 • Lansdowne on the Persian Gulf in the House of Lords, 15 May 1903 • Cabinet Memorandum by Selborne on the German Navy, 26 February 1904

The conclusion of the Boer war hastened an assessment of Britain's overall strategic position. With regard to the Straits, the Committee of Imperial Defense, a deliberative body of cabinet ministers and military experts, in February 1903 confirmed the conclusion that Salisbury had already reached in 1896–1897.[80]

In May 1903, the British foreign secretary, Lord Lansdowne, reiterated the British determination to remain the preponderant power in the Persian Gulf, most recently expressed in 1899 when Britain established a protectorate over the sheikdom of Kuwait. Lansdowne's declaration was directed at Russian plans for the construction of a railroad linking the Caucasus with the gulf. But this statement of policy came only weeks after the British government reneged, on 23 April, on an earlier assurance that it would open the London market for shares of the German-dominated Bagdad Railway company. The railway was expected to be built as far as Basra or Kuwait, but the company had yet to determine the actual route and still needed to secure the requisite permissions from the Porte. Although Lansdowne himself did not oppose the railroad, his successor in the Foreign Office, Sir Edward Grey, in 1906 justified his hostility to the German-sponsored project by referring to Lansdowne's declaration as if Lansdowne had specifically objected to the railroad.

In April 1902, the Earl of Selborne, first lord of the Admiralty in Salisbury's cabinet, for the first time raised the question whether the German naval program was a greater threat to Britain than the navies of France or Russia. Writing to Selborne, Arthur Balfour—who would succeed his uncle Lord Salisbury as prime minister three months later—thought "it extremely difficult to believe that we have, as you seem to suppose, much to fear from Germany—in the immediate future at all events. It seems to me so clear that, broadly speaking, her interests and ours are identical."[81] But Selborne remained unconvinced; by February 1904 his apprehensions had hardened into firm belief.

a)   *Précis by Hardinge, 16 November 1906, of an Opinion on the Straits by the Committee of Imperial Defense, 13 February 1903*

. . . "What difference would it make to the balance of power in the Mediterranean if Russia were to obtain, through possession of Constantinople, free egress from the Black Sea through the Dardanelles, these remaining closed, as at present, against other Powers?

"The answer to this question unanimously accepted by the Committee was that, while Russia would no doubt obtain certain naval advantages from the change, it would not fundamentally alter the present strategic position in the Mediterranean." . . .

---

[80]See Document 10.8, 10.14b.
[81]Balfour to Selborne, 5 April 1902, in Boyce, *Imperial and Naval Papers of . . . Selborne*, 142.

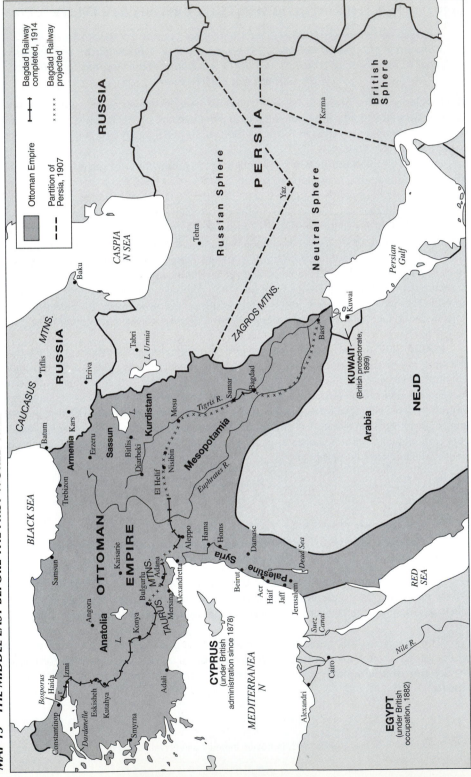

MAP 15   *THE MIDDLE EAST BEFORE THE FIRST WORLD WAR*

Legend:
- Ottoman Empire
- Partition of Persia, 1907
- Bagdad Railway completed, 1914
- Bagdad Railway projected

RUSSIA

PERSIA

Russian Sphere

Neutral Sphere

British Sphere

Kerma

Yaz

Tehra

CASPIAN SEA

Baku

Persian Gulf

Kuwai

KUWAIT
(British protectorate, 1899)

NEJD

Arabia

Tabri

L. Urmia

Basr

ZAGROS MTNS.

Tiflis

Eriva

CAUCASUS MTNS.

RUSSIA

Bagdad

Samar

Tigris R.

Mosu

Kurdistan

Mesopotamia

Kars

Batum

Armenia

Erzeru

Sassun

Bitlis

Diarbeki

Nisibin

El Helif

Euphrates R.

Trebizon

BLACK SEA

OTTOMAN

EMPIRE

Anatolia

Samsun

Angora

Kaisarie

Bulgurlu

Aleppo

Hama

Homs

Damasc

Syria

Dead Sea

RED SEA

Konya

TAURUS MTNS.

Adana

Mersina

Alexandretta

Beirut

Acr

Haif

Jaff

Palestine

Jerusalem

Suez Canal

Nile R.

Eskisheh

Kutahya

Smyrna

Adali

Haida

Bosporus

Dardanelle

Constantinop

Izmi

CYPRUS
(under British administration since 1878)

MEDITERRANEAN

Alexandri

Cairo

EGYPT
(under British occupation, 1882)

"It may be stated generally that a Russian occupation of the Dardanelles, or an arrangement for enabling Russia to freely use the waterway between the Black Sea and the Mediterranean, such as her dominating influence can extract from Turkey at her pleasure, would not make any marked difference in our strategic dispositions as compared with present conditions."

From these extracts it is evident that it is, if desirable, possible to make an important concession to Russia in relation to the Dardanelles without fundamentally altering the present strategic position in the Mediterranean.

—*BD*, 4:59–60

b)   *Lansdowne[82] on the Persian Gulf in the House of Lords, 15 May 1903*

. . . The noble Lord[83] asked me for a statement of our policy with regard to the Persian Gulf. . . . It seems to me that our policy should be directed in the first place to protect and promote British trade in those waters. In the next place I do not think that he suggests, or that we should suggest, that those efforts should be directed towards the exclusion of the legitimate trade of other Powers. In the third place—I say it without hesitation—we should regard the establishment of a naval base, or of a fortified port, in the Persian Gulf by any other Power as a very grave menace to British interests, and we should certainly resist it with all the means at our disposal. I say that in no minatory spirit, because, so far as I am aware, no proposals are on foot for the establishment of a foreign naval base in the Persian Gulf. I at least have heard of none; and I cannot help thinking that the noble Lord waxed almost unnecessarily warm at the idea of such a foreign intrusion, with which, so far as I am aware, we are not at present threatened. . . .

—*Parl. Debates*, 4th Series, 121:1348

c)   *Cabinet Memorandum by Selborne on the German Navy, 26 February 1904*

. . . 3. It is an errror to suppose that the two–power standard adopted by this country some fifteen years ago, ratified by every government since, and accepted as an article of faith by the whole nation, has ever had reference only to France and Russia. It has always referred to the two strongest naval powers at any given moment, and it has been identified in many minds with France and Russia only because France and Russia have for some years past possessed the two most powerful navies next to our own. If the Russian navy does emerge from the present [Russo-Japanese] war materially weakened, the result will be that the two–power standard must hereafter be

---

[82]Henry Fitzmaurice, Marquess of Lansdowne (1845–1927). Viceroy of India, 1888–1894; foreign secretary, 1900–1905.

[83]Charles Baillie, Baron Lamington (1860–1940). Governor of Queensland, 1895–1901; of Bombay, 1903–1907.

MAP 16   THE MOROCCO QUESTION

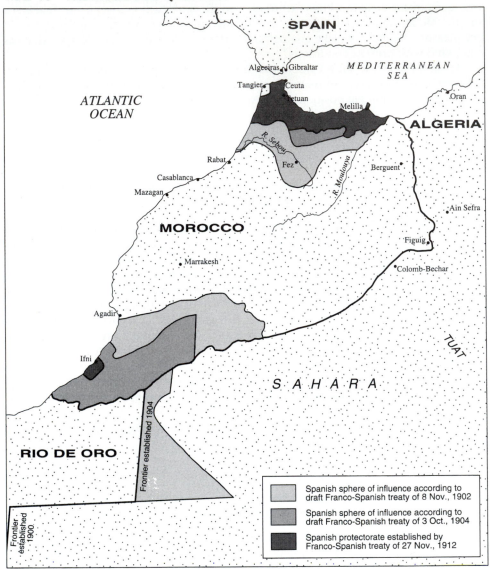

calculated with reference to the navies of France and Germany, instead of those of France and Russia. . . .

. . . [T]he great new German navy is being carefully built up from the point of view of a war with us. This is also the opinion of Sir Frank Lascelles, and he has authorized me to say so. The more the composition of the new German fleet is examined the clearer it becomes that it is designed for a possible conflict with the British fleet. It cannot be designed for the purpose of playing a leading part in a future war between Germany and France and Russia. The issue of such a war can only be decided by armies and on land, and the great naval expenditure on which Germany has embarked involves a deliberate diminution of the military strength which Germany might otherwise have attained in relation to France and Russia. . . .

—D. George Boyce (ed.), *The Crisis of British Power. The Imperial and Naval Papers of the Second Earl of Selborne, 1895–1910* (London, 1990), 170–73

10.30   THE ANGLO-FRENCH ENTENTE, 8 APRIL 1904

The Anglo-French entente was a bilateral settlement of outstanding colonial issues, concluded against the backdrop of the Russo-Japanese war. French fears of being drawn into this conflict speeded the last phase of the negotiations. The entente was global in its scope: it delineated colonial borders in West Africa, settled conflicting claims in Newfoundland, envisaged an Anglo-French condominium in the New Hebrides, and reallocated the British and French spheres of influence in Siam.[84] Its centerpiece, however, was a declaration dealing with Egypt and Morocco. Reversing a policy pursued for twenty-two years, France agreed to cooperate with the British occupation of Egypt in exchange for a British promise of support in Morocco. In its eagerness to conclude the negotiations, France gave more than it received: whereas the British now had a clear mandate to administer Egypt, Morocco was still the subject of the Convention of Madrid of 1880, which guaranteed Morocco's independence and, in article 17, provided for the open door in that country. The incompatibility of the entente with the Convention of Madrid was apparently lost on the signatories.

Art. 1: His Britannic Majesty's Government declare that they have no intention of altering the political status of Egypt. The Government of the French Republic, for their part, declare that they will not obstruct the action of Great Britain in that country by asking that a limit of time be fixed for the British occupation[85] or in any other manner. . . .

Art. 2: The Government of the French Republic declare that they have no intention of altering the political status of Morocco. His Britannic Majesty's Government, for their part, recognise that it appertains to France, more particularly as a Power whose dominions are coterminous for a great distance with those of Morocco, to preserve order in that country, and to provide assistance for the purpose of all administrative, economic, financial, and military reforms which it may require. They declare that they will not obstruct the action taken by France for this purpose, provided that such action shall leave intact the rights which Great Britain, in virtue of Treaties, Conventions, and usage, enjoys in Morocco. . . .

[84]The British and French zones in Siam were originally delineated in a convention dated 15 January 1896. *SP*, 88:13. The condominium in the New Hebrides was established by an Anglo-French convention of 20 October 1906. *SP*, 99:229.

[85]Cf. Document 9.19e.

Art. 4: . . . [T]he Government of the French Republic reserve to themselves in Morocco, and His Britannic Majesty's Government reserve to themselves in Egypt, the right to see that the concessions for roads, railways, ports, etc., are only granted on such conditions as will maintain intact the authority of the State over these great undertakings of public interest. . . .

Art. 9: The two Governments agree to afford to one another their diplomatic support, in order to obtain the execution of the clauses of the present Declaration regarding Egypt and Morocco.

—Hurst, 2:760–64; Hertslet II, 2:820; secret articles in *SP*, 101:1053;
PP 1911, 103:162–68 [new pagination: 354–60]

CHAPTER 11

The Narrowing Margin, 1905-1914

In exploring the origins of the First World War, the student of the subject faces a bewildering choice of long-term or structural explanations. Among contemporaries, Lenin indicted imperialism as the principal cause of the war,[1] Woodrow Wilson saw the culprit in secret diplomacy,[2] Wilhelm II blamed an anti-German conspiracy directed by England,[3] the British foreign secretary Sir Edward Grey in his memoirs faulted the arms race.[4] In drafting the Versailles treaty, the victorious Allies bluntly asserted Germany's responsibility. From retirement, the British wartime prime minister, David Lloyd George, assailed the "weak men" who had been charged with the making of foreign policy in 1914.[5] Beginning in the 1920s and 1930s, historians have vied with one another to show the crucial role played by the war plans of the powers, by nationalist passions and an irresponsible press, by the strength (or, conversely, by the fear of an imminent collapse) of the alliance system.

In the 1960s, the German scholar Fritz Fischer and his students attributed the war to Germany's "grasp for world power."[6] Hotly contested in Germany, this view soon became the new orthodoxy in Britain and the United States. But among American dissenters, Norman Rich wondered why Germany, if its aims had indeed been so single-minded, did not start the war earlier and under auspices more favorable to it than those of 1914; German unpredictability, argued Rich, was a far greater threat to the European

---

[1] *Imperialism, the Highest Stage of Capitalism* (1916).

[2] Point 1 of Wilson's Fourteen Points of January 1918 sought a remedy in "open convenants of peace, openly arrived at. . . ."

[3] See Document 12.11f.

[4] *Twenty-Five Years* (New York, 1925), 2:53. Grey of course was not alone in hoping to prettify his own record by laying the blame elsewhere.

[5] Unfortunately, his timing was not always flawless. See the record of his conversation with Hitler in Berchtesgaden in September 1936, reprinted in Martin Gilbert, *The Roots of Appeasement* (London, 1967), 197–211.

[6] *Griff nach der Weltmacht* (Düsseldorf, 1961; translated as *Germany's Aims in the First World War*, New York, 1967). Also by the same author: *War of Illusions: German Policies from 1911 to 1914* (New York, 1975); *World Power or Decline: The Controversy over Germany's Aims in the First World War* (New York, 1974); "Twenty-Five Years Later: Looking Back at the 'Fischer Controversy' and its Consequences," *Central European History* 21 (1988), 207–23.

equilibrium than German purposefulness.[7] Joachim Remak reminded his readers that the shots of Sarajevo had been preceded by a Balkan crisis of two years' duration and that the Austrian ultimatum to Serbia needed to be understood in this context.[8] Paul Schroeder pointed to the utter indifference with which the French, Russian, and—primarily—British leadership had come to regard the Habsburg monarchy, thereby undermining not just Austria-Hungary but the entire European equilibrium.[9]

All of these explanations have merit, and many are complementary. But any inquiry into why the European powers in 1914 so willingly jettisoned an international order that had served all of them reasonably well in the past must begin with the question of whether or not fundamental changes, tectonic shifts perhaps, had taken place in the international system in the prewar decade. Indeed the years 1905 to 1914 were shaped by several themes that set them apart from the previous period (1895–1904) of imperialism and overseas crises: by the renewed prominence of the Balkans; by a succession of crises centered on Europe that, in their cumulative impact, narrowed the range of options available to the statesmen of 1914; and by the questions "what was the nature of German policy?" and "what, after 1906, was the nature of the ententes?"—two questions that, as will be seen, describe flip sides of the same issue.

First, the reemergence of the Balkans as an international flashpoint was almost a natural consequence of Russia's military defeat by Japan. In search of a diplomatic victory to compensate for the East Asian disaster, Russia redirected its attention to the Balkans. This Russian effort in turn kindled Britain's desire to turn the Balkans into a proving ground for the fledgling Anglo-Russian entente. Anglo-Russian cooperation in the Near East signified a diplomatic revolution in its own right, but also provoked Germany's fear that unless it showed some support for Austria in the Balkans, Austria would have no choice but to accommodate the Anglo-Russian camp and leave Germany in complete isolation. After 1912, France too abandoned its earlier reserve and sought to cement the Franco-Russian alliance by viewing Balkan developments through the Russian lens.

Second, the statesmen of 1914 found that they operated in an environment with far less room for maneuver than a decade earlier. The cumulative effect of the four crises that roiled the European equilibrium in the years 1905 to 1914 was to rob the European "system" of much of its former elasticity. The first of these, the Moroccan crisis of 1905–1906, completed a diplomatic revolution from which emerged, for the first time, the alignments later seen in the First World War. At the Algeciras conference on Morocco, Germany was supported only by Austria-Hungary and was outvoted by what soon thereafter became known as the Triple Entente—Britain, France, and Russia—a grouping that on this occasion was joined by Italy, the United States, and several lesser states. The memory of being outnumbered at Algeciras made itself felt during the Bosnian crisis three years later: despite lip service to the contrary, Germany successfully opposed a conference. The Bosnian crisis also created its own legacy—the retreat of Russia in March 1909, even more humiliating than that of Germany at Algeciras, increased the determination of the Russian cabinet never again to be caught ill prepared and translated into the so-called "great program" of Russian military expenditure and increased armaments. In the aftermath of the third major crisis of the prewar decade—a Second

[7] *Holstein*, 2:745.

[8] "1914—The Third Balkan War: Origins Reconsidered," *Journal of Modern History* 43 (1971), 353–66.

[9] "World War I as Galloping Gertie: A Reply to Joachim Remak," *Journal of Modern History* 44 (1972), 319–45.

Moroccan crisis in 1911—both the French and German governments came under fire at home from a newly militant right for allegedly having buckled under pressure. The net result was to make the search for compromise even more difficult. Finally, during the Balkan crises of 1912–1913, Austria-Hungary concluded that the European concert was too timid to enforce its own decisions, that this spinelessness encouraged the Serb government to continue its taunts, that Austria was on its own in containing the Serb challenge, and that the only language understood in Belgrade was that of the ultimatum. Austria's newfound certainty that only threats would carry the day in itself reflected a dangerous escalation from the norms of everyday discourse between states. If, on the other hand, Serbia could portray itself as the victim of Austrian bullying, then it was only a question of time before the sympathies of its patron, Russia, were aroused and before Russia, making the Serb cause its own, would feel that the limits of its endurance had been reached. The sum total then of the crises of 1905–1906, 1908–1909, 1911, and 1912–1913 was this: given a diplomatic environment in which governments were as a rule quick to take offense, how many more retreats, real or perceived, could Germany, Russia, France, or Austria afford before reaching the conclusion that the only defense was to lunge forward?

Third is the question of whether German aims were shaped by the desire to establish preeminence on the continent and a commensurate colonial empire or whether German policy was reactive, dictated by the fear of being encircled by a coalition of hostile powers. If it is true that Germany was driven by aggressive instincts, then of course Britain, France, and Russia were justified in preparing their defenses, justified too in strangling, so to speak, the baby gorilla in its crib before it grew too powerful. If instead Germany found itself in a vise or, put more gently, excluded from a role in setting the agenda of Great Power politics, then it is imperative that we investigate the evolution of Britain's ententes with France and, after 1907, with Russia. Were the ententes ends in themselves, animated by the principle that in the politics of overseas empire, good fences make good neighbors?[10] Was Britain reluctantly dragged into supporting the European aspirations of its partners in order to maintain its ententes? Or were the ententes on the contrary designed to serve Britain's European interests, to egg on France and Russia to join Britain in an anti-German coalition with Morocco, Persia, or the Balkans as the down payment?

Whatever the answers to these questions may be, a number of puzzles remain. Why did Germany's efforts to break the Triple Entente yield no more than momentary victories? Why was Britain so reluctant to apply to Germany, for the purpose of coopting or managing it in Europe, the very formula that had brought about an improvement in Anglo-French and Anglo-Russian relations, namely, a colonial compromise in Africa or the Middle East?

GENERAL READING: (also introduction to Chapter 10 and footnotes 6–10, above) Richard Bosworth, *Italy, the Least of the Great Powers* (Cambridge, 1979); Timothy W. Childs, *Italo-Turkish Diplomacy and the War over Libya* (Leiden, 1990); John W. and Peter F. Coogan, "The British Cabinet and the Anglo-French Staff Talks," *Journal of British Studies* 24 (1985), 110–31; Andreas Hillgruber, *Germany and the Two World Wars* (Cambridge, MA, 1981); F. H. Hinsley (ed.), *British Foreign Policy under Sir Edward Grey* (Cambridge, 1977); Konrad Jarausch, "From Second to Third Reich: The Problem of Continuity in German Foreign Policy," *Central European History* 12 (1979), 68–82; James Joll, *The Origins of the First World War* (London, 1984); Gerd Krumeich, *Armaments and Politics in France* (Leamington Spa, 1984);

[10]Cf. Keith M. Wilson, *The Policy of the Entente: Essays on the Determinants of British Foreign Policy, 1904–1914* (Cambridge, 1985). Wilson, however, errs in downplaying the hostility of the Foreign Office toward Germany.

Wolfgang Mommsen, "Domestic Factors in German Foreign Policy," *Central European History* 6 (1973), 3–43; Zara Steiner, *Britain and the Origins of the First World War* (New York, 1977); idem, *The Foreign Office and Foreign Policy, 1898–1914* (1968; reprint: London, 1986); Samuel R. Williamson, Jr., *Austria-Hungary and the Origins of the First World War* (New York, 1991); idem, *The Politics of Grand Strategy* (1969; reprint: Atlantic Highlands, 1991)

11.1   GERMANY AND THE FIRST MOROCCAN CRISIS

Directive by Bülow, 24 March 1905 ● *Schoen to the German Foreign Ministry, 31 March 1905* ● *Bülow to Sternburg, 3 April 1905* ● *Holstein to Bülow, 5 April 1905* ● *Bülow to Sternburg, 30 May 1905*

As already noted, fear of being dragged into the Russo-Japanese war increased the desire of France (Russia's ally) and Britain (Japan's ally) to settle their outstanding differences by concluding the *entente cordiale* (Document 10.30). But any gains that France might have realized under this agreement had to be weighed against the fact that the East Asian conflict severely damaged the Franco-Russian alliance: Russia's preoccupation with the war precluded it from exerting any military or diplomatic pressure on Germany. Temporarily freed from the specter of having to prepare for a two-front war, Germany had considerable room to maneuver and could even hope to reverse its deteriorating position among the powers.

Bülow's vehicle for doing so was to target the centerpiece of Delcassé's diplomacy. Delcassé regarded the French conquest of Morocco as an end in itself, but, beyond this, he appreciated that his agreements on Morocco with Italy, Britain, and Spain brought with them the additional benefit of underscoring the isolation of Germany. By challenging Delcassé's Moroccan policy, Bülow could therefore strike at the French statesman's European diplomacy. Bülow's objective was to prove that France would require German assent to realize its ambitions in Morocco; that, conversely, German obstructionism could undo all of Delcassé's efforts; and, hence, that Delcassé policy of ignoring Germany was misguided.

Certainly the defects in Delcassé's Moroccan diplomacy played into Bülow's hands: Delcassé had neglected to notify the German government of the Franco-Spanish accord of October 1904 (an omission, that, though not illegal, was discourteous); French representatives, in their dealings with the sultan of Morocco, were giving the erroneous impression that France was acting on behalf of all powers; most important, Delcassé was seemingly oblivious to the legal fact that any alteration in the status of Morocco had to be sanctioned by all signatories of the 1880 Convention of Madrid, including Germany.

Bülow and Holstein could not have devised a more visible challenge to France's ambitions in Morocco than by inducing the Kaiser, en route to a Mediterranean cruise, to go ashore in Tangier. On his visit to this Moroccan port, Wilhelm was supposed to stress Germany's desire for equal commercial opportunity in Morocco, to refer to the sultan's independence only in the context of free trade, and to ignore the French chargé. But when the latter seemed to welcome Wilhelm to Tangier in the name of the French foreign minister, the Kaiser went considerably further.

By stressing the international character of the Moroccan quandary, the Kaiser seemed to suggest that it required an international solution. The question was how Germany could compel or persuade the other signatories of the Madrid convention to take the same view. In Holstein's opinion, the other powers would follow Germany's lead if an appropriate framework for resolving the Moroccan question could be found, while Bülow's prescription was to keep the other powers guessing to what lengths Germany would be prepared to go to get its way. But this kind of sibylline approach suffered from a drawback: it was now easy for others to attribute to Germany the most sinister intentions and to suspect it of wanting to launch a Franco-German war.

a)   *Directive by Bülow, 24 March 1905*

Should foreign diplomats inquire about Tangier and Morocco, please give no answer but put on a serious and impassive face. Our demeanor should resemble that of the sphinx which, when beleaguered by curious tourists, also refuses to give anything away.

—*GP*, 20i:6573

b)   *Schoen[11] to the German Foreign Ministry, 31 March 1905*

. . . With French chargé at first also indifferent [conversation]. When chargé conveyed Delcassé's respects and greetings and seemed to welcome His Majesty to Morocco in [the minister's] name, [H.M.] replied: His visit meant that His Majesty demanded for Germany free trade and complete equality with other nations; when Count Chérisey wanted to concede this, His Majesty remarked that he would treat the Sultan as an equal, as a free ruler of an independent country; that he would know how to have his legitimate demands respected; and that he expected that these would be respected by France also. Count Chérisey turned pale, wanted to reply, but was prevented from so doing by being asked to take leave. . . .

—*GP*, 20i:6589

c)   *Bülow to Sternburg,[12] 3 April 1905*

. . . Please point out to President [Roosevelt] the connection between the Chinese and the Moroccan questions. Germany acts on behalf of the Open Door in Morocco, that is, it defends the interest of all peoples carrying on commerce against the special interests of France. . . .

—*GP*, 19ii:6302

d)   *Holstein to Bülow, 5 April 1905*

. . . Contractual collectivity is a principle on which we can take a firm stand without ourselves appearing to harbor aggressive intentions. Moreover this idea has the

[11]Wilhelm von Schoen (1851–1933). German foreign ministry liaison in the Kaiser's entourage; state secretary in the German foreign ministry, 1907–1910.

[12]Hermann Speck von Sternburg (1857–1908). German ambassador to Washington, 1903–1908.

advantage that while affecting French interests, it does not affect French pride, just as the collective victories of 1814 were not so great an insult to the French as the German victory, gained alone, in 1870. If France refuses the conference, she puts herself in the wrong, shows that she has a bad conscience and evil intentions. If the conference is held, it will, whatever the result, definitely not hand Morocco over to the French. These are the advantages of the conference idea, unique in character. . . .

—*HP*, 4:882

e)   **Bülow to Sternburg, 30 May 1905**

. . . The Moroccan question is not an isolated one, but can become the point of departure for a realignment among the powers. . . . If France, at the instigation of England, rejects a conference then we face this alternative: either a war against France or an understanding with France, an understanding which the French government indicated it would be willing to reach and which could then lead to the creation of a large European grouping. . . . [We] hope not to have to confront this alternative—it would however be imposed on us if the conference were rejected. As the French government shows little inclination for a war and as Petersburg will probably influence it to be accommodating, it would probably propose separate bilateral negotiations and conditions which would make possible a separate deal. We however believe that it is in the interest of Germany and America if we continue to maintain our independent stance. Whether we are able to do so or not depends on President Roosevelt, because whether the conference will become a reality depends on him. All he needs to do is to unequivocally support the conference. . . . Leave the president in no doubt that the creation of a powerful European group of states which would include Germany is for us a last resort which would become attractive only if English opposition and American indifference wrecked our selfless program of upholding the status quo, the Open Door, and the equality of all signatories. . . .

—*GP*, 20ii:6668

11.2   THE SCOPE OF THE ANGLO-FRENCH ENTENTE, 1905

Lansdowne to Paul Cambon, 25 May 1905 • *Metternich to the German Foreign Ministry, 28 June 1905*

To the German government and to many of his own colleagues in the French cabinet, Delcassé personified an anti-German policy. But in the context of April and May 1905, a hard-line approach—that is, a confrontational or even evasive response to the German demand for an international conference on Morocco—harbored the risk of a Franco-German war that France could ill afford without effective help from its allies. Delcassé argued that under these circumstances Britain would be found on the side of France. The credibility of this claim was, however, open to question, as Delcassé was not able to secure a formal alliance from the British cabinet. His colleagues now fully appreciated the dangers to which France would be exposed if Delcassé were allowed to persist in his course, and he was consequently dropped from the ministry on 6 June.[13]

Any assessment as to whether Delcassé's sang-froid was justified or whether his colleagues panicked prematurely depends on one's interpretation of the assurances that Delcassé did manage to elicit from the British foreign secretary, Lord Lansdowne. These were spelled out in a letter that Lansdowne gave Paul Cambon, the French ambassador in London, on 25 May. According to one student of this episode, "the precise import of the letter of 25 May depended on the preoccupations of the reader."[14] Certainly the meaning of the letter hinges on the reader's interpretation of the phrase "discuss any contingencies by which we might in the course of events find ourselves confronted."

a)   ***Lansdowne to Paul Cambon, 25 May 1905***

. . . [T]he moral of all these incidents seemed to be that the French and British Gov[ernmen]ts should continue to treat one another with the most absolute confidence, that we should keep one another fully informed of everything which came to our knowledge, and so far as possible discuss any contingencies by which we might in the course of events find ourselves confronted, and I cited as showing our readiness to enter into such timely discussion the communication recently made to the French Gov[ernmen]t by Sir F. Bertie[15] at a moment when the idea prevailed that Germany might be about to put pressure on France in order to obtain the cession of a Moorish port.

I do not know that this account differs from that which you have given to M. Delcassé, but I am not sure that I succeeded in making quite clear to you our desire that there should be full and confidential discussion between the two Gov[ernmen]ts, not so much in consequence of some acts of unprovoked aggression on the part of another Power, as in anticipation of any complications to be apprehended during the somewhat anxious period through which we are at present passing.

—*BD,* 3:95

b)   ***Metternich to the German Foreign Ministry, 28 June 1905***

. . . Lord Lansdowne replied that I surely knew that the French government had been assured diplomatic support within the limits of the Anglo-French agreement. . . . But the question of an alliance with France was never discussed in the cabinet, nor had an

---

[13]It was convenient for both Delcassé and his prime minister, Maurice Rouvier, to blame Delcassé's dismissal on German pressure. This rendition flattered the German leadership into believing that Germany had scored a triumph of the first order by its ability to dictate to the French government who should be its foreign minister; it established Delcassé's reputation as an injured innocent who had become a victim of German brutality; and it obscured Delcassé's blistering fight with Rouvier on whether to advance any more money to Russia before a peace settlement had been reached in East Asia.

[14]George Monger, *The End of Isolation. British Foreign Policy, 1900–1907* (London, 1963), 198.

[15]Sir Francis Bertie (1844–1919). British ambassador in Paris, 1905–1918.

alliance ever been offered to the French government: not now, not at any earlier point. But he did not want to conceal from me that if Germany lightheartedly[16] provoked a war with France—a possibility he thought altogether unlikely—, [he] would not be able to foretell to what extent English public opinion would pressure the government to support France. . . .

—*GP*, 20ii:6860

11.3   BIDDING FOR RUSSIA, 1905–1906

Russo-German Treaty of Björkoe, 24 July 1905 ● *Second Anglo-Japanese Alliance, 12 August 1905* ● *Holstein to Bülow, 19 September 1905* ● *Wilhelm II to Nicholas II, 26 September 1905* ● *Witte to Kokovzev, 5 January 1906* ● *Boutirond to Rouvier, 11 January 1906*

Defeated in war and beset by revolution at home, Russia nonetheless continued to play a pivotal role in the calculations of the remaining European powers. Britain, France, and Germany expected Russia's weakness to be temporary but speculated that the commitments undertaken by Russia in the interim would govern the outlook of the Russian leadership once the country had recovered its strength.

In this contest for Russia's favor, Britain was motivated by the desire to improve its relationship with Russia in Central Asia. This goal was advanced by the renewal of the Anglo-Japanese alliance in August 1905. The alliance was renegotiated on its own merits, but its terms—published on 27 September 1905—demonstrated to Russia the futility in continuing the Anglo-Russian antagonism in Asia. The alternative to confrontation was, of course, mutual accommodation.[17]

The paramount aim of French diplomacy toward Russia was to repair the Franco-Russian alliance. In the view of the Rouvier government, the litmus test of Russian goodwill was support for the French position at the upcoming international conference on Morocco.

The German government had debated the merits of an alliance with Russia at the height of the Russo-Japanese war but soon shelved this project for fear that such an alliance would antagonize England into launching a preemptive strike against the fledgling German fleet. The idea surfaced again in July 1905: during their meeting in Björkoe bight, the Kaiser induced the tsar to sign a defensive alliance. The treaty of Björkoe was supposed to broaden the split in the Franco-Russian alliance or to transform it altogether. But Russia's foreign minister, Count Vladimir Lamsdorff, opposed the treaty precisely on these grounds and prevented its implementation. Nonetheless, the German government clung to the vain hope that, because of the Björkoe treaty, Russia would at the very least support Germany at the forthcoming Morocco conference.

Throughout the Moroccan crisis, the Kaiser's personal diplomacy complicated the German position. Wilhelm in his speech at Tangier went further than Bülow had counseled; he inserted the restrictive term *"en Europe"* into the text of the Björkoe treaty without prior consultation with Bülow (thereby causing a constitutional crisis within the German government);

---

[16]This word is in English in the original.
[17]The new instrument differed substantially from the original alliance (cf. Document 10.25) in its definition of the *casus foederis* and in its geographic range.

believing that Germany's objectives had already been secured by the fall of Delcassé, he intimated to French, Russian, and British visitors and relatives that he would not risk war over Morocco (thereby exposing Bülow's bluff that Germany should leave other powers guessing how far it was prepared to go).[18]

Russia's choice among the various hands seemingly proffered was dictated by its need for a major foreign loan. The purpose of the loan was to cushion Russia's government from the domestic crisis of 1905, but also to render it independent, at least initially, from the power of the purse to be wielded by the Duma, Russia's first national parliament, which was to meet in the spring of 1906. By turn-of-the-century standards, the amount (2,250,000,000 francs) was staggering—only the London and Paris markets were sufficiently large to accommodate it. But in return for opening their financial markets, the British and French governments demanded that Russia support their position at the Morocco conference.

a)   *Russo-German Treaty of Björkoe, 24 July 1905*

1. In the event that one of the two empires will be attacked by a European power, its ally will come to its assistance in Europe with all of its land and sea forces.

2. The high contracting parties pledge not to conclude a separate peace with any common enemy.

3. The present treaty will come into force as soon as peace between Russia and Japan has been made, and will remain valid unless notice is given one year in advance.

4. His Majesty the Emperor of all the Russias will take, once this treaty has come into effect, the necessary steps to acquaint France with its terms and will request [France] to join in as an ally.

—*GP*, 19ii:6220

b)   *Second Anglo-Japanese Alliance, 12 August 1905*[19]

[Preamble:] The Governments of Great Britain and Japan, being desirous of replacing the agreement concluded between them on the 30th of January, 1902, by fresh stipulations, have agreed upon the following articles, which have for their object:

a) The consolidation and maintenance of the general peace in the regions of Eastern Asia and of India.

b) The preservation of the common interests of all powers in China by insuring the independence of and integrity of the Chinese Empire and the principle of equal opportunities for the commerce and industry of all nations in China.

---

[18]The Kaiser conveyed as much to General Henri de Lacroix, the French representative at the wedding of the German crown prince in June 1905; to the Marquis de Laguiche, the French military attaché in Berlin; to the Prince of Monaco; to the tsar; to Witte, who stopped at the imperial hunting lodge of Rominten on his return to Russia from the Portsmouth peace conference in September 1905; to the English financier Alfred Beit; and, in a letter dated 1 February 1906, to Edward VII.

[19]Published on 27 September 1905.

c) The maintenance of the territorial rights of the high contracting parties in the regions of Eastern Asia and of India, and the defence of their special interests in the said regions. . . .

Art. 2: If by reason of unprovoked attack or aggressive action, whenever arising, on the part of any other power or powers, either contracting party should be involved in war in defence of its territorial rights or special interests mentioned in the preamble of this agreement, the other contracting party will at once come to the assistance of its ally, and will conduct the war in common, and make peace in mutual agreement with it.

Art. 3: Japan possessing paramount political, military, and economic interests in Korea, Great Britain recognises the right of Japan to such measures of guidance, control, and protection in Korea as she may deem proper and necessary to safeguard and advance those interests, provided always such measures are not contrary to the principle of equal opportunities for the commerce and industry of all nations. . . .

—Hurst, 2:770–72

c)   *Holstein to Bülow, 19 September 1905*

. . . I had heard that . . . the Moroccan position which the German government had been defending against France had been surrendered to the French long ago by the Kaiser. . . . It . . . illustrates a state of affairs which I do not want to describe as normal. It happens often enough that a monarch who feels that he is absolute conducts his own policy. But it is something quite new in the history of diplomacy for a constitutional sovereign to keep secret from his own government the concessions which he had made to a foreign government. . . . We must face the fact that this sort of thing may occur again. We must therefore count with the possibility of finding ourselves, without any means of preventing it, in impossible situations. . . .

—*HP*, 4:913

d)   *Wilhelm II to Nicholas II, 26 September 1905*[20]

[Witte][21] is a firm advocate of a Russo-German-France alliance which as he tells me will be gladly "cotoygé" [gone along with] by America—for the maintenance of the peace & the statu quo in the world, the balance of which has been disturbed by the Anglo-Japanese treaty. He was consequently very agreeably surprised when I told him of our work at Björkoe. It is the grouping of powers which is the most natural—they being the representants of the "continent"—& will have the consequence of drawing all the other lesser powers in Europe into the orbit of this great block. America will stand on the side of this "combination." Firstly from the "racial" point of view, they are decidedly "white" anti-yellow. . . . The "continental combine" flanked by America is the sole & only manner to effectively block the way to the whole world becoming John Bull's private property, which he exploits at his hearts content after having, by

---

[20]In English in the original.
[21]Principal Russian negotiator at the peace talks with Japan in Portsmouth, NH.

lies & intrigues without end, set the rest of the civilized nations by each others ears for his own personal benefit. We see this pernicious principle at work now in the Morocco question, in which John Bull is equally doing his best to set the French dead against us. . . . Witte kindly gave the French advice about Morocco to take reason & I have ordered Radolin to be as "conciliant" as possible, so that I hope we shall come to terms in a few days. . . .[22]

—N. F. Grant (ed.), *The Kaiser's Letters to the Tsar* (London, 1920), 210–12

e)   ***Witte to Kokovzev,[23] 5 January 1906***

You are authorized by His Majesty the Emperor [Nicholas II] to declare to M. Rouvier that the Imperial Government will lend (in the Moroccan question) its moral support in exerting an influence on the German government. In general, His Majesty, in view of the ties of friendship and alliance, is always disposed to lend support to the French government. . . .

—*DDF*, 2nd Series, 8:327

f)   ***Boutirond[24] to Rouvier, 11 January 1906***

. . . Count Lamsdorff assures you that His Majesty the Emperor "has acted, acts and will continue to act" in the way you ask. . . . Count Lamsdorff took advantage of the occasion to reassure me of the solidity of our alliance despite the constant effort even up until recently of Germany to break the tie and particularly to emphasize the firmness of His Sovereign's confidence in the Franco-Russian system. . . .

—*DDF*, 2nd Series, 8:381

11.4   GREY ON THE TASKS OF BRITISH DIPLOMACY, 1906

Grey to Lascelles, 1 January 1906 • *Memorandum by Grey, 20 February 1906*

Sir Edward Grey became foreign secretary in the new Liberal cabinet formed on 11 December 1905. Grey had previously served Rosebery's government as permanent under-secretary in the Foreign Office and had since been chief opposition spokesman in the Commons on foreign affairs.

Grey's first task was to define the British position in the upcoming international conference on Morocco, held in the Spanish port of Algeciras between January and April 1906. The two excerpts below show him to be more lachrymose and far less self-assured than Salisbury or Lansdowne, but with an uncanny ability to impute to others motives and sentiments they

---

[22]Although the French government consented to the principle of an international conference on Morocco on 8 July, Germany and France reached agreement on its agenda only on 28 September 1905.

[23]Vladimir Nicolaevich Kokovzev (1853–1943). Principal Russian negotiator for the loan of 1906; minister of finance, 1904–1911; prime minister, 1911–February 1914.

[24]French chargé in Petersburg.

may not have had: the American and Japanese governments had criteria other than Morocco by which to judge Britain's performance; the Russian government thought of Morocco as a hindrance obstructing its frantic search for loans in Europe's financial markets; the Porte would have opposed Britain's territorial claims on the Sinai peninsula no matter how the Moroccan issue was resolved. One further characteristic of Grey's approach was a propensity to listen selectively to the signals emanating from Berlin—screening out, for example, Wilhelm II's protestations that he wished to put Morocco behind him. But in January 1906 Grey sanctioned Anglo-French military conversations to coordinate a British landing in northern France, as a "precaution" and provided that these conversations "did not commit either government."[25] They could have hardly done so from a constitutional point of view, as Grey withheld his decision from the cabinet as a whole—which was not informed until 1911.[26]

Of paramount interest is Grey's prescription for dealing with the aftermath of the conference. He had previously made the case for an Anglo-Russian entente on its own merits,[27] but his memorandum of 20 February 1906 shows that he now advocated such an understanding on different grounds. In Grey's defense, it might be said that his musings were jotted down before the Anglo-French victory at Algeciras was sealed, but one can question whether this strategy was suited to repair the damage wreaked by the Moroccan crisis, whether it could reestablish a concert among the powers, and whether it did not in fact worsen the confrontation with Germany against which he ostensibly sought to guard.

It is intriguing to speculate on whether Grey did no more than amplify the policy established by Lansdowne (Document 11.2) or whether he went beyond the bounds set by his predecessor. Lansdowne had shied away from military conversations, but he too (and Salisbury before him) had entertained a rapprochement with Russia. Lansdowne's conduct nevertheless leaves the impression that he thought of the combinations among powers as fleeting. The Moroccan crisis, while undesirable, was part of the normal give-and-take among the powers. Lansdowne seemed to suggest that there was nothing exceptional in the spectacle of powers probing and challenging the system, their subsequent rebuttal and retreat, and that the minuet could begin thereafter with a chastened adversary. The question rather is whether this kind of mental elasticity was as native to Grey as it was to Lansdowne.

a)   ***Grey to Lascelles, 1 January 1906***

. . . The danger of speaking civil words in Berlin is that they may be used or interpreted in France as implying that we shall be lukewarm in our support of the Entente at the Conference. I think it is essential to guard against this danger, even at the risk of sending a little shudder through a German audience. . . .

—FO, 800/61

b)   ***Memorandum by Grey, 20 February 1906***

If there is war between France and Germany it will be very difficult for us to keep out of it. . . . If th[e] expectation [of British intervention] is disappointed the French

---

[25]*BD*, 3:215, 216.

[26]Document 11.14.

[27]For instance in a speech to the London City on 20 October 1905. Text in *The Times*, 21 October 1905.

will never forgive us. There would also I think be a general feeling in every country that we had behaved meanly and left France in the lurch. The United States would despise us, Russia would not think it worthwhile to make a friendly arrangement with us about Asia, Japan would prepare to re-insure herself elsewhere, we should be left without a friend and without the power of making a friend and Germany would take some pleasure, after what has passed, in exploiting the whole situation to our disadvantage, very likely by stirring up trouble through the Sultan of Turkey in Egypt. As a minor matter the position of any Foreign Secretary here, who had made it an object to maintain the entente with France, would become intolerable. On the other hand the prospect of a European war and of our being involved in it is horrible. . . . I have also a further point in view. The door is being kept open by us for a rapprochement with Russia; there is at least a prospect that when Russia is re-established we shall find ourselves on good terms with her. An entente between Russia, France and ourselves would be absolutely secure. If it is necessary to check Germany it could then be done. The present is the most unfavourable moment for attempting to check her. . . .

—*BD*, 3:299

11.5   GENERAL ACT OF THE ALGECIRAS CONFERENCE, 7 APRIL 1906

By endorsing the predominance of France and Spain in Morocco, the Algeciras conference handed Germany a resounding diplomatic defeat. Even so, the Algeciras Act conferred on France and Spain only a limited mandate. More striking—and adding further to its sense of incompleteness—was the absence of a mechanism to review, renegotiate, prolong, or terminate its most contentious articles upon their expiration.

The restrictions on French authority gave the German government a juridical lever to reopen the Moroccan question almost at its discretion. In 1907 and 1908, German charges that France had overstepped its mandate kept Franco-German tensions simmering. In a Franco-German agreement concluded in February 1909, Germany renounced any political aims in Morocco. But the 1909 accord did not prevent it from citing the Algeciras Act when it protested French troop movements into that North African country two years later, which set off a series of events that culminated in the second Moroccan crisis of 1911 (Document 11.14).

. . . Art. 2: The police shall be under the sovereign authority of His Majesty the Sultan. It shall be recruited by the maghzen [Moroccan government] from Moorish Mohammedans, commanded by Moorish kaids, and distributed in the eight ports open to commerce.

Art. 3: In order to aid the Sultan in the organization of this police, Spanish officers and noncommissioned officers as instructors, and French officers and noncommissioned officers as instructors, shall be placed at his disposal by their respective governments. . . .

Art. 4: These officers and noncommissioned officers for a period of five years, to date from the ratification of the act of the conference, shall give their service. . . .

Art. 30: In the region bordering on Algeria, the enforcement of the regulation on the contraband of arms shall be the exclusive concern of France and Morocco. Similarly, the enforcement of the regulation on the contraband of arms in the Rif and in general in the regions bordering on the Spanish possessions shall be the exclusive concern of Spain and Morocco. . . .

Art. 33: The bank shall, to the exclusion of every other bank or establishment of credit, discharge the duty of the treasury-paymaster of the [Moroccan] Empire . . . .

Art. 51: Each of the following institutions, the Bank of the German Empire, the Bank of England, the Bank of Spain, and the Bank of France, shall, with their governments' approval, appoint an auditor for the State Bank of Morocco. . . .

—*FRUS 1906*, 2:1495–1511; Hurst, 2:772–805

11.6   HOLSTEIN ON THE LESSONS OF ALGECIRAS

Holstein to Brandt, 10 April 1906

The real importance of the Algeciras conference lay not in the specifics of its Final Act, but in the fact that on all substantive issues Germany was supported only by Austria-Hungary and Morocco. Outvoted and isolated, Germany nonetheless preferred retreat to defiance. Neither the Kaiser nor Bülow had the stomach for the fall-back strategy recommended by Holstein, briefly summarized below. His policy undercut by his superiors' lack of nerve, Holstein resigned from the German foreign ministry—a tactical error that allowed others to cast him as the scapegoat for the Moroccan debacle. This letter analyzes the "lessons" of Algeciras for Germany and castigates the German response to the conference: the introduction in the Reichstag of another naval appropriations bill. This supplementary bill provided for the construction of several cruisers; more important, it was designed to cover the heavy expenditures entailed by the German decision to upgrade future battleship construction to match the new British *Dreadnought* class.

Holstein to Brandt,[28] 10 April 1906

. . . In the Morocco question, the chancellor, the state secretary, the undersecretary, and I all took the point of view that we should wait calmly until the neutrals in need of money and peace—Russia, Italy, etc.—came up with mediation proposals. It would not have taken much longer. However, His Majesty ordered the retreat and thereby justified the prediction of King Edward and Luzzatti[29] that Germany would lose her nerve. Out of this retreat there arises an indefinite danger of war, because the pressure method which succeeded in Morocco, may be applied against us at the next opportunity.

[28]Maximilian von Brandt (1835–1920). German minister to Peking, 1875–1893.
[29]Luigi Luzzatti (1841–1927), Italian banker. Minister of finance, 1903–1904; prime minister, 1910–1911.

Among the questions of the future, the most interesting is that of the fleet; I refer to the international limitations on armaments. . . .[30]

What will our position be if the question should one day be firmly pushed into the foreground? What can we achieve by continuing our naval armaments? Could we ever challenge *both* England and France at sea? Can we expect that England will ever separate herself from France as long as there is the danger of a German invasion? Is a German fleet that is unable to cope with an Anglo-French fleet an asset in war or a liability? Would the fear of a German land army, no matter how strong, but without a fleet, be great enough to cause England to take part in a Franco-German or a Franco-Russian-German war?

—*HP*, 4:959

11.7   # THE CROWE MEMORANDUM

Memorandum by Crowe, 1 January 1907 ● *Countermemorandum by Sanderson, 21 February 1907*

The "Memorandum on the Present State of British Relations with France and Germany" created an uproar among German historians when it was first published in the *British Documents on the Origins of the War* in 1928. Here was tangible evidence of the hostility of the prewar British Foreign Office toward Germany—the "smoking gun," so to speak, that British diplomacy had taken such great pains to conceal.

The memorandum came from the pen of Eyre Crowe, senior clerk in the Foreign Office—an expert on Germany, fluent in its language, married to a German-born wife, son of a German-born mother. Taking the Moroccan crisis as his point of departure, Crowe traced the transformation of the *entente cordiale* from a purely colonial agreement into an enduring, if vague, instrument for Anglo-French diplomatic cooperation. Crowe then moved on to his main purpose: a review of Anglo-German relations since the Bismarck era. Long on Britannia's benevolence to others, Crowe's arguments echoed the classic Whig sentiment that the interests of England and humanity coincided. At the same time, he left no doubt whom he considered the culprit of the piece: German actions and motives, by and large, were cast in lurid colors. Although Crowe seasoned the narrative with some grudging praise for German achievements, his references to German industry and efficiency only heightened the effect by making the German threat appear ever more menacing.

Of interest here is not Crowe's skill as a historian or his acuity as a therapist, but his prescription for the future of Anglo-German relations. Crowe ruled out an Anglo-German entente on the curious grounds that the differences between Britain and Germany were not sufficiently concrete or serious to warrant an understanding patterned on the Anglo-French agreement. But neither were these differences superficial, nor could they easily be settled. Germany should be resisted, except in the exercise of its legitimate aspirations—though Crowe evidently felt it unnecessary to specify whose standards should apply in determining what was legitimate and what was not. Surprisingly, Crowe did not regard the German navy as the primary threat to Britain, an assessment that most of his countrymen would not have shared.

Crowe's memorandum elicited meager but approving comments from his superiors in the Foreign Office. A more critical rejoinder came from Lord Sanderson, who had served as permanent under-secretary in the Foreign Office from 1894 to 1905 and had been a direct participant in some of the events recounted by the memorandum. Working from memory and

---

[30]The reference is to the Second Hague Peace Conference of 1907.

without the benefit of Foreign Office documentation, Sanderson nonetheless found Crowe's reconstruction defective. Crowe, his pique very much in evidence, attempted a defense in the margins of Sanderson's countermemorandum and enlisted a Foreign Office coworker, Louis Mallet, to corroborate his views.

In the judgment of one historian, the Crowe memorandum was "perhaps the only Foreign Office memorandum to have become a classic state paper."[31] But the Crowe memorandum did not lead to any policy initiatives; indeed it could be argued that its very purpose was to inhibit a rapprochement with Germany. Though its arguments surfaced again in several Foreign Office deliberations on the merits of an Anglo-German understanding between 1907 and 1912, the importance of the memorandum lay elsewhere. The fact that neither the foreign secretary, nor the under-secretaries, nor any other top official took issue with its findings and that it was left to a retiree to voice his discomfort pointed to the profound generational change that had taken place in the top hierarchy of the Foreign Office.

a)   ***Memorandum by Crowe, 1 January 1907***

. . . The danger [of a general combination of powers against England] can in practice only be averted—and history shows that it has been so averted—on condition that the national policy of the insular and naval state is so directed as to harmonize with the general desires and ideals common to all mankind, and more particularly that it is closely identified with the primary and vital interests of a majority, or as many as possible, of the other nations. Now, the first interest of all countries is the preservation of national independence. It follows that England, more than any other non-insular power, has a direct and positive interest in the maintenance of the independence of nations, and therefore must be the natural enemy of any country threatening the independence of others, and the natural protector of the weaker communities. . . .

England has, by a sound instinct, always stood for the unhampered play and interaction of national forces as most in accord with nature's own process of development. No other state has ever gone so far and so steadily as the British Empire in the direction of giving free scope to the play of national forces in the internal organization of diverse peoples gathered under the King's scepter. . . .

The immediate object of the present inquiry was to ascertain whether there is any real and natural ground for opposition between England and Germany. It has been shown that such opposition has, in fact, existed in an ample measure for a long period, but that it has been caused by an entirely one-sided aggressiveness, and that on the part of England the most conciliatory disposition has been coupled with never-failing readiness to purchase the resumption of friendly relations by concession after concession. . . .

There is then, perhaps, another way of looking at the problem: it might be suggested that the great German design is in reality no more than the expression of a vague, confused, and unpractical statesmanship, not fully realizing its drift. A charitable critic might add, by way of explanation, that the well-known qualities of mind

---

[31]Perhaps so, if this definition covers internal memoranda and excludes position papers for the cabinet or circulars to British embassies. The reader is invited to test this assertion against Castlereagh's memoranda (Documents 2.1d and 2.3a) or Salisbury's circular on the Straits (Document 10.8c).

and temperament distinguishing for good or for evil the present ruler of Germany may not improbably be largely responsible for the erratic, domineering, and often frankly aggressive spirit which is recognizable at present in every branch of German public life, not merely in the region of foreign policy; and that this spirit has called forth those manifestations of discontent and alarm both at home and abroad with which the world is becoming familiar; that, in fact, Germany does not really know what she is driving at, and that all her excursions and alarums, all her underhand intrigues do not contribute to the steady working out of a well-conceived and relentlessly followed system of policy, because they do not really form part of any such system. This is an hypothesis not flattering to the German government, and it must be admitted that much might be urged against its validity. But it remains true that on this hypothesis also most of the facts of the present situation could be explained. . . .

If, merely by way of analogy and illustration, a comparison not to be intended to be either literally exact or disrespectful be permitted, the action of Germany towards this country since 1890 might be likened not inappropriately to that of a professional blackmailer, whose extortions are wrung from his victims by the threat of some vague and dreadful consequences in case of refusal. To give way to the blackmailer's menaces enriches him, but it has long been proved by uniform experience that, although this may secure for the victim temporary peace, it is certain to lead to renewed molestation and higher demands after ever-shortening periods of amicable forbearance. The blackmailer's trade is generally ruined by the first resolute stand made against his exactions and the determination rather to face all risks of a possibly disagreeable situation than to continue in the path of endless concessions. But, failing such determination, it is more than probable that the relations between the two parties will grow steadily worse. . . .

It cannot be good policy for England to thwart such a process of development where it does not directly conflict either with British interests or with those of other nations to which England is bound by solemn treaty obligations. If Germany, within the limits imposed by these two conditions, finds the means peacefully and honorably to increase her trade and shipping, to gain coaling stations or other harbors, to acquire landing rights for cables, or to secure concessions for the employment of German capital or industries, she should never find England in her way.

Nor is it for the British governments to oppose Germany's building as large a fleet as she may consider necessary or desirable for the defense of her national interests. . . . [N]othing is more likely to produce in Germany the impression of the practical hopelessness of a never-ending succession of costly naval programs than the conviction, based on ocular demonstration, that for every German ship England will inevitably lay down two, so maintaining the present relative British preponderance. . . .

It is not unlikely that Germany will before long again ask, as she has so often done hitherto, for a "close understanding" with England. To meet this contingency, the first thing to consider is what exactly is meant by the request. The Anglo-French entente had a very material basis and tangible object—namely, the adjustment of a number of actually-existing serious differences. The efforts now being made by England to arrive at an understanding with Russia are justified by a very similar situation. But for an Anglo-German understanding on the same lines there is no room, since none could be built up on the same foundation. It has been shown that there are no questions of any importance now at issue between the two countries. . . .

[T]here is one road which, if past experience is any guide to the future, will most certainly not lead to any permanent improvement with any power, least of all Germany, and which must therefore be abandoned: that is the road paved with graceful British concessions—concessions made without any conviction either of their justice or of their being set off by equivalent counter-services. The vain hopes that in this manner Germany can be "conciliated" and made more friendly must be definitely given up. . . .

—*BD*, 3: app. A

b)   *Countermemorandum by Sanderson, 21 February 1907*[32]

. . . 3. I cannot agree in the description of the inception of German colonial policy, nor of the acts of "direct and unmistakable hostility to England" by which it is said to have been pursued [*I believe it to be a fact that the acts were considered at the time so hostile that the question of resisting them by force was seriously considered by the cabinet*]. . . . 9. My recollection of the Samoan negotiations[33] is not very precise but my impression is that we have not an absolutely clear record, and that Lord Salisbury while conceding any claims on our part did his best to rouse the opposition of the United States. [*I have been unable to confirm this statement. Perhaps it is another instance of Lord Salisbury's action by private letter?*][34] It is not likely that the German gov[ernment]t were unaware of this. They certainly always contended that we had not treated them fairly and some of our own diplomatists were inclined to share this view [*So far as I know only Sir C[harles] Eliot can be said ever to have been so inclined. His opinion and judgment would hardly carry any great weight. The history of German proceedings in Samoa show the German gov[ernmen]t probably in its very worst light*]. . . . 24. I have written these notes, partly because the circumstances themselves are of considerable interest, partly because they tend to show that the history of German policy towards this country is not the unchequered record of black deeds which the Memorandum seems to portray [. . . *My object . . . was not at all to portray a record of black deeds, but to show that the line of action followed by England with amiable persistency for 20 years did not in the end secure what she expected and bargained for: Germany's friendship and political support*]. There have been many occasions on which we have worked comfortably in accord with Germany, and not a few cases in which her support has been serviceable to us [*Lord Sanderson does not quote these cases*]. There have been others in which she has been extremely aggravating, sometimes unconsciously so, sometimes with intention. The Germans are very tight bargainers, they have earned the nickname "les Juifs de la diplomatie." The German foreign office hold to a traditional view of negotiation that one of the most effective methods of gaining your point is to show how intensely disagreeable you can make yourself if you do not [*This is what I have illustrated by the analogy of the blackmailer*]. . . . If the mere acquisition of territory were in itself immoral, I conceive that the sins of Germany since 1871 are

---

[32]With annotations by Crowe.
[33]Cf. Document 10.17.
[34]For a corrective to this view, see Grenville, *Lord Salisbury and Foreign Policy*, 12–14.

light in comparison to ours, and it must be remembered that, from an outside point of view, a country which looks to each change as a possible chance of self-aggrandizement is not much more open to criticism than one which sees in every such change a menace to its own interests, existing or potential, and founds on this theory continued claims to interference or compensation. It has sometimes seemed to me that to a foreigner reading our press the British Empire must appear in the light of some huge giant sprawling over the globe, with gouty fingers and toes stretching in every direction, which cannot be approached without eliciting a scream. . . . I do not think it can be justly said that "Germany" is ungrateful for friendly support. [*Gratitude among nations had better not be expected. We have for our continuous "friendly support" not only received from Germany no gratitude, but are undoubtedly the most detested of her neighbors. With the rest of the concluding paragraph I quite agree. I have said practically the same in my memorandum*]. It is at all events unwise to meet her with an attitude of pure obstruction, such as is advocated by part of our press. A great and growing nation cannot be repressed. It is altogether contrary to reason that Germany should wish to quarrel with us though she may wish to be in a position to face a quarrel with more chances of success, than she can be said now to have. But it would be a misfortune that she should be led to believe that in whatever direction she seeks to expand she will find the British lion in her path. . . .

—*BD*, 3: app. B

11.8   BÜLOW AND TSCHIRSCHKY ON *WELTPOLITIK*, 1907

Bülow to Tschirschky, 29 August 1907 ● *Tschirschky to Bülow, 4 September 1907*

In the spring and summer of 1907, Germany's isolation was highlighted by a spate of agreements among other powers (Britain and France with Spain; France with Japan; Japan with Russia), culminating in the Anglo-Russian entente of 31 August 1907.[35] This last accord destroyed Bülow's theory, developed in the 1890s, of the "elemental necessity"[36] of the Anglo-Russian antagonism under the cover of which Germany could pursue *Weltpolitik*. The Anglo-Russian entente neither mentioned Germany nor touched on Germany's treaty rights, but its central feature—the division of Persia into Russian, British, and "neutral" spheres—at the very least affected Germany's interests in that country. Even more significantly, the entente harbored the danger that Britain and Russia might extend their cooperation to other areas.

An Anglo-French-Italian agreement of 13 December 1906[37] had distributed similar prerogatives among its signatories in Abyssinia. It will be recalled (Document 11.5) that the Algeciras conference established a Franco-Spanish preponderance, albeit limited, in Morocco. These agreements hemmed in German influence in supposedly independent states; they also cemented their signatories' relationship to one another. The letters excerpted here underscore

[35]The Anglo-French-Spanish notes can be found in *DDF*, 2nd Series, 10:499; the Franco-Japanese entente in Hertslet III, 1:618–19; the public articles of the Russo-Japanese entente in MacMurray, 1:657–58, its secret articles in Ernest B. Price, *The Russo-Japanese Treaties of 1907–1916 Concerning Manchuria and Mongolia* (Baltimore, 1933), 107–8; the Anglo-Russian entente in Hurst, 2:805–9.

[36]See Document 10.20c.

[37]Text in Hertslet II, 2:436–44.

the dilemmas of German policy after 1906, provide some clues to the nature of *Weltpolitik*, and speak to the subject of an overseas versus a continental policy.

a)   *Bülow to Tschirschky,[38] 29 August 1907*

. . . It would not be uninteresting someday to determine the extent of German economic interests in Persia, Morocco, Abyssinia. We in Germany are gradually becoming susceptible to a mood as if we had interests everywhere in the world and had to stand up for them everywhere with drums beating and trumpets sounding. This could eventually lead to a general defensive coalition against [us as] an all too bothersome competitor. . . .

—PA Asservat 185

b)   *Tschirschky to Bülow, 4 September 1907*

. . . In my opinion, [the question] is not how much we have invested in these countries up to the present, but how to keep our future options open. We must put our eggs into the baskets of others, as our own production far outstrips our baskets. It is clear that our entire *Weltpolitik*—insofar as it is conducted outside of Europe—is for the main part *Prestige-Politik*: a precarious and difficult brand of politics because our global interests exceed the means by which we can protect them. But we cannot turn back. And when the European basis of our commercial interests in the world is no longer broad enough, then we will broaden it. In my view, it should be our objective to strive for this through peaceful means for as long as possible. . . .

—PA Marokko 4 Nr. 2

11.9   THE REVAL SUMMIT, JUNE 1908

Memorandum by Hardinge, 12 June 1908

Soon after taking charge of the Foreign Office, Grey hoped that a meeting between the English and Russian monarchs would spur along a rapprochement between the two countries. The continuing unrest in Russia's Baltic provinces in the summer of 1906 forced the postponement of the king's visit until some semblance of domestic tranquillity had been restored in the tsarist empire. In the interim, the Anglo-Russian relationship was cemented by the entente of 31 August 1907 and by increasing Anglo-Russian cooperation in the Balkans. Its original purpose superseded, the visit finally took place at Reval in June 1908. Grey now went to considerable lengths to belittle the Reval summit's importance, for fear that it might lend substance to the

[38]Heinrich von Tschirschky und Bögendorff (1858–1916). State secretary in the German foreign ministry, 1906–1907; ambassador in Vienna, 1907–1916.

German complaint of being encircled by a hostile Anglo-French-Russian coalition. But the inclusion in Edward VII's entourage of Jack Fisher, the First Sea Lord, and Sir John French, inspector of the British territorial army, made it difficult to explain away this visit as a purely dynastic affair.

As on previous voyages, King Edward was accompanied by Sir Charles Hardinge, undersecretary in the Foreign Office and formerly British ambassador in St. Petersburg (1904–1906). Hardinge's conversations at Reval linked the Anglo-Russian relationship with the prominent issues of the day. Foremost among these was the agitation in England spawned by yet another German naval amendment, passed by the Reichstag in January 1908. Less visible was the British effort to replace Austria-Hungary as Russia's cosponsor of a far-reaching program of judicial reform for Ottoman Macedonia, a project denounced by the Porte as an unwelcome intrusion in Ottoman domestic affairs.

The Anglo-Russian reform project became a victim of the Young Turk revolt of July 1908. The revolutionaries' seizure of power in Constantinople, their initial Anglophilia, and their promise to restore the Ottoman constitution of 1876[39] caused Britain and Russia to shelve the reform. In retrospect, the importance of the Macedonian project lies not in its practical results—there were none—than in the fact that it served as a vehicle for increasing Anglo-Russian intimacy beyond the terms of the entente of 31 August 1907.

Memorandum by Hardinge, 12 June 1908

. . . Although the attitude of His Majesty's Government towards Germany was, and had been, absolutely correct, it was impossible to ignore the fact that, owing to the unnecessarily large increase in the German naval program a deep distrust in England of Germany's future intentions had been created. This distrust would be still further accentuated with the progress of time, the realization of the German program, and the increase of taxation in England entailed by the necessary naval counter-measures. In seven or eight years' time a critical situation might arise, in which Russia, if strong in Europe, might be the arbiter of peace, and have much more influence in securing the peace of the world than at any Hague conference. For this reason it was absolutely necessary that England and Russia should maintain towards each other the same cordial and friendly relations as now exist between England and France, which in the case of England and Russia are, moreover, inspired by an identity of interests of which a solution of the Macedonian problem was not the least. . . .

—BD, 5:195

11.10   THE *DAILY TELEGRAPH* INTERVIEW, 1908

The London *Daily Telegraph* on 28 October 1908 printed an interview with Wilhelm II in which the Kaiser tried to put to rest English fears about Germany's intentions. The Kaiser's remarks and his generalizations about the attitude of the German public toward England re-

---

[39]See Documents 9.4 and 11.11.

mained without tangible effect on Anglo-German relations[40] but unleashed a severe constitutional crisis in Germany that culminated in Bülow's assurance to parliament that Wilhelm would exercise restraint in the future. These tactics allowed Bülow to stay in office for the time being with the backing of virtually all parliamentary parties, but Wilhelm's disgust at Bülow's self-serving performance made his ultimate fall a foregone conclusion.

"You English," he [Wilhelm] said, "are mad, mad, mad as March hares. What has come over you that you are so completely given over to suspicions quite unworthy of a great nation? What more can I do than I have done? I declared with all the emphasis at my command, in my speech at Guildhall,[41] that my heart is set upon peace, and that it is one of my dearest wishes to live on the best of terms with England. Have I ever been false to my word? Falsehood and prevarication are alien to my nature. My actions ought to speak for themselves, but you listen not to them, but to those who misinterpret and distort them. That is a personal insult which I feel and resent. To be for ever misjudged, to have my repeated offers of friendship weighed and scrutinised with jealous, mistrustful eyes, taxes my patience severely. I have said time after time that I am a friend of England, and your press—or, at least, a considerable section of it—bids the people of England refuse my proffered hand, and insinuates that the other holds a dagger. How can I convince a nation against its will?"

"I repeat," continued his Majesty, "that I am the friend of England, but you make things difficult for me. My task is not of the easiest. The prevailing sentiment among large sections of the middle and lower classes of my own people is not friendly to England. I am, therefore, so to speak, in a minority in my own land, but it is a minority of the best elements, just as it is in England with respect to Germany. . . .

"Just at the time of your Black Week [during the Boer war] . . . I bade one of my officers procure for me as exact an account as he could obtain of the number of combatants in South Africa on both sides, and of the actual position of the opposing forces. With the figures before me, I worked out what I considered to be the best plan of campaign under the circumstances, and submitted it to my General Staff for their criticism.[42] Then I despatched it to England, and that document, likewise, is among the state papers at Windsor Castle, awaiting the serenely impartial verdict of history. And, as a matter of curious coincidence, let me add that the plan which I formulated ran very much on the same lines as that which was actually adopted by Lord Roberts, and carried by him into successful operation. Was that, I repeat, the act of one who wished England ill? Let Englishmen be just and say!"

"But, you will say, what of the German navy? . . . Germany looks ahead. Her horizons stretch far away. She must be prepared for any eventualities in the Far East. Who can foresee what may take place in the Pacific in the days to come, days not so distant as some believe, but days, at any rate, for which all European Powers with Far Eastern

[40]For a second interview which, despite Bülow's successful effort to keep it out of the press, did affect Anglo-German relations, see Ralph R. and Carol Bresnahan Menning, "'Baseless Allegations': Wilhelm II and the Hale Interview of 1908," *Central European History* 16 (1983), 368–97.

[41]During Wilhelm's state visit to England in November 1907.

[42]The essence of these remarks is confirmed in *QV*, 3rd Series, 3:421–22, and by Lady Susan Townley, *'Indiscretions' of Lady Susan* (New York, 1922), 64–67.

interests ought steadily to prepare? Look at the accomplished rise of Japan; think of the possible national awakening of China; and then judge of the vast problems of the Pacific. Only those Powers which have great navies will be listened to with respect, when the future of the Pacific comes to be solved; and if for that reason only Germany must have a powerful fleet. It may even be that England herself will be glad that Germany has a fleet when they speak together on the same side in the great debates of the future."

—*Daily Telegraph*, 28 October 1908

11.11   THE BUCHLAU MEETING, 16 SEPTEMBER 1908

Izvolski to Charykov, 3/16 September 1908

Implicit in the Young Turks' reinstatement of the Ottoman constitution (Documents 9.4 and 11.9) was the convening of an Ottoman parliament, a body widely expected to issue a proclamation affirming the territorial integrity of the Ottoman Empire. In so doing, the Ottoman parliament would draw attention to the fact that Bosnia and Herzegovina, though occupied and administered by Austria-Hungary under article 25 of the Treaty of Berlin (Document 9.10), were by law Ottoman territories. First and foremost, this reminder was bound to set back Austria-Hungary's efforts to assimilate both provinces into the Habsburg monarchy.

The Young Turk revolt hardened the resolve of the Austro-Hungarian foreign minister, Alois Lexa von Aehrenthal, to do away with the awkwardness of Austria's position in Bosnia and Herzegovina: because Austria-Hungary was not sovereign in the provinces it could not introduce a provincial constitution (in itself a sovereign act), while the very absence of a constitution served as a reminder to the Serbs, Croats, and Muslims of Bosnia-Herzegovina that they enjoyed fewer rights than the inhabitants of the Dual Monarchy or of neighboring Serbia—a fact not lost on the irredentist propaganda emanating from Belgrade.

Any change in the legal status of Bosnia and Herzegovina, however, meant a revision of the Treaty of Berlin. Aehrenthal had the option to secure the consent of all signatories or to plead that the near-anarchic conditions in Turkey-in-Europe allowed him to invoke the *rebus sic stantibus* exception to this rule. He chose a middle course, tipping off his German and Italian counterparts that a change in the status of the provinces was imminent, and then proceeded to canvass the Russian foreign minister, Alexander Izvolski, at a meeting at Buchlau estate in Moravia on 16 September 1908.

Izvolski's report of the Buchlau meeting to N. V. Charykov, his deputy in the Russian foreign ministry, belies his later claim that the Austrian annexation of Bosnia-Herzegovina caught him unawares. Similarly, it shows that both Aehrenthal and Izvolski were less than candid in their later attempts to cover up advance knowledge of Bulgaria's proclamation of independence. While Aehrenthal made good on his promise to withdraw the Austrian garrison from the Sanjak of Novibazar, it was the height of naïveté on Izvolski's part to assume that Austria or any other power could be charmed into granting the compensations which he sought. In particular, his demand for a change in the status of the Straits put Britain in a quandary. British support for an alteration in the law of the Straits, as envisaged by Izvolski, would render Britain suspect in the eyes of the Young Turks and would undercut British efforts to profit from what appeared to be a geopolitical opportunity: on ideological grounds, the

Young Turks were expected to draw closer to Britain while distancing themselves from Germany, now in disfavor as the leading foreign sponsor of the ousted autocratic regime of Sultan Abdul Hamid.

Izvolski to Charykov, 3/16 September 1908

. . . First of all, I found out with complete certainty that the Austro-Hungarian government [sic] has irrevocably decided on the annexation of Bosnia and the Herzegovina. . . . It is very possible that Baron Aehrenthal will make the announcement of the annexation in the Delegations,[43] which open about 6 October. . . . He agreed in general terms to the following conditions:

1. Simultaneously with the announcement of the annexation of Bosnia and the Herzegovina an announcement will be made as well about the evacuation of the Sanjak of Novibazar and the final renunciation of all rights and intentions in the province. This renunciation, in Aehrenthal's opinion, ought to serve in the eyes of Russia and the Balkan states as sufficient guarantee of the absence in Austria of any desires whatever for Macedonia and Salonica. In addition to this, Aehrenthal does not see any obstacle to our explaining confidentially to Serbia and Montenegro that from this there follows for them the possibility under certain conditions—i.e., in the event of a liquidation of the Turkish Empire—of restoring in that province the frontiers of the Treaty of San Stefano. . . .[44]

2. Aehrenthal is prepared even now, i.e., without waiting for the liquidation of the Turkish Empire, to accept our formula about the Straits, namely, such an alteration of the existing legal position as would allow all the ships of Russia and the other coastal states to enter and leave the Black Sea through the Straits, while preserving the principle of their closure to warships of other nations. He would like to introduce into this formula some sort of reservation to deprive it of any aggressive character as regards Turkey, which seems to me quite feasible. He also agreed to support our demand at Berlin.

3. With regard to Bulgaria, he agrees to the proclamation of independence [from the Ottoman Empire] and of the royal title [for Prince Ferdinand].

4. With regard to Serbia, he was least of all inclined to concessions and compensations, pointing to the hostile attitude assumed by her in recent times towards Austria-Hungary. In his view, the renunciation of the Sanjak of Novibazar ought to satisfy her completely. He is not in agreement with any kind of frontier rectification in the direction of Bosnia and the Herzegovina, and as his furthest concession is only prepared to admit Serbia (and also Bulgaria) to the Riparian Danube Commission. . . .

In conclusion, I think it is necessary to direct your special attention to the necessity of preparing, and at the decisive moment of directing, our press and public opinion, which can very easily get on to the wrong track. . . . Our agreement with Austria must, of course, be kept completely secret, and the matter should be put across thus: Austria, for one reason or another, decided to annex Bosnia and the Herzegovina. We

---

[43]Cf. Document 8.10.
[44]Cf. Document 9.7.

learned of this in good time. We, of course, immediately pointed out to her the dangerous consequences, and thanks to our exhortations she agreed to the evacuation of the Sanjak. But what more can be done? To confine ourselves to a futile protest? Not, indeed, to declare war. From here there is a direct transition to compensations and guarantees in favor of Russia and the Balkan states. I am fully aware of the enormous difficulty of guiding our press on to this track. . . .

—F. R. Bridge, "Izvolsky, Aehrenthal, and the End of the Austro-Russian Entente, 1906–8," *Mitteilungen des österreichischen Staatsarchivs* 29 (1976), 348–51

11.12   THE BOSNIAN CRISIS, OCTOBER 1908–MARCH 1909

Diary Entry by Goschen, 10 November 1908 • *Kiderlen to Holstein, 17 March 1909* • *Kiderlen to Pourtalès, 21 March 1909* • *Tschirschky to Bülow, 28 March 1909* • *Bülow in the Reichstag, 29 March 1909* • *Five-Power Memorandum to the Serb Government, 30 March 1909*

The crisis ushered in by Austria-Hungary's annexation of Bosnia and Herzegovina on 4 October 1908 lasted almost six months. In its first phase, Austria-Hungary faced Russia, Britain, and the Ottoman Empire; the second phase of the crisis was characterized by a showdown between Austria-Hungary, backed by Germany, and both Russia and Serbia.

Aehrenthal's critics were quick to point out that the annexation unilaterally abrogated article 25 of the Treaty of Berlin (Document 9.10) without the formal consent of its signatories. But legal arguments aside, Russia and Britain had political reasons for opposing the annexation. In Russia, Pan-Slav protests on behalf of Serbia forced Izvolski to retreat from the accommodating stance he had taken at Buchlau (Document 11.11). The British government opposed the annexation not only out of deference to Russia, but also because it hoped to strengthen its influence with the Young Turk regime—which was, after all, the principal victim of Aehrenthal's move.

Faced with Russia's and Britain's refusal to recognize the annexation, Aehrenthal went to what was—allegedly—the heart of the grievance: if Aehrenthal could persuade the Porte to acquiesce in the annexation, Britain's and Russia's objections would lose much of their force. In February 1909, the Ottoman government accepted the annexation in return for a cash payment, and it was reasonable for Aehrenthal, now that he had indemnified Turkey, to expect that the other signatories of the Treaty of Berlin would declare themselves content. He was mistaken.

The focus of the crisis now shifted to Serbia. Citing its ethnic kinship with the Serb minority and its linguistic affinity with other Slavs in Bosnia and Herzegovina, Serbia demanded territorial compensation. Serbia's legal armor, however, was defective: it had no standing in the crisis, as it was not a signatory to the Treaty of Berlin. Aehrenthal turned a deaf ear to Serbia but found to his dismay that Russia would continue to withhold recognition of the annexation unless Austria met some of the Serb demands.

However, Izvolski had overreached himself and, in an embarrassing climb-down, had to abandon Serbia. Russia's military weakness ruled out armed intervention on behalf of the Serbs in the event of an Austro-Serb war. Moreover, the Franco-Russian alliance was immobilized even as a diplomatic instrument: French bondholders controlled 40 percent of the Turkish debt and were thus loath to see a Balkan conflagration that might still draw in the Ottoman Empire; French financiers feared for their investments in Russia in the event of military catastrophe and domestic turmoil; French public opinion had just been coopted by a

Franco-German declaration on Morocco.[45] Last but not least, the attitude of Germany made Izvolski's position completely untenable.

German policy throughout the crisis was shaped by Bülow and the acting state secretary in the foreign ministry, Alfred von Kiderlen-Wächter. Its objective was to shore up the Austro-German alliance; to demonstrate the frailty of the Franco-Russian alliance and the Triple Entente, thereby showing Izvolski the error of his ways; and to even the score for the Algeciras debacle.

Kiderlen's message to the Russian government of 21 March 1909 resolved the Bosnian crisis on Germany's and Austria's terms. Implicit in Kiderlen's démarche was the suggestion that Germany would not restrain Austria from disciplining Serbia unless Russia recognized the annexation. Izvolski (and British diplomats) later claimed that the démarche contained a thinly veiled ultimatum, a charge denied by Kiderlen (cf. Document 11.18). Whether it did or did not hinges on one's reading of the pivotal phrase—"we would then withdraw and let events take their course"—a phrase that could be construed to mean that Germany would not check Austria if it wanted to crush Serbia on the battlefield.

The last three documents reproduced here have considerable bearing on the July crisis of 1914. First, Bülow's speech to the Reichstag of 29 March 1909 laid down Germany's conditions for attending a conference of the powers—an event that did not come to pass. These conditions reflected the lessons of Algeciras and were presumably still part of the mindset of the German foreign ministry five years later (cf. Document 12.8). Second, the memorandum of 30 March, drafted by the Great Powers and agreed to by Serbia, was designed to regulate the Austro-Serb relationship. If Serbia violated its tenets, Austria would have grounds for complaint, perhaps even a mandate for action—a consideration that loomed large in the thinking of the Austro-Hungarian foreign ministry after the Sarajevo assassination. Finally, from the perspective of 1914, it may be tempting to regard the Bosnian crisis as a missed opportunity for Austria. But such regrets should be weighed against the objections to an Austro-Serb war raised by Aehrenthal himself on 28 March.

a)   *Diary Entry by Goschen,[46] 10 November 1908*

. . . It is extraordinary that the two questions which have of late caused so much excitement and even created fears of general war—have been such trifles. A general war because of a few deserters from the French Foreign Legion in Morocco[47]—or because Serbia is refused compensation for having lost nothing but a dream—would look pretty silly when history came to be written! . . .

—Christopher H. D. Howard (ed.), *The Diary of Edward Goschen, 1900–1914* (London, 1980), 178–79

[45]Of 9 February 1909. Text in *GP*, 24:8490–92, or Hurst, 2:811–12.

[46]Edward Goschen (1847–1924). British ambassador in Vienna, 1905–1908; in Berlin, 1908–1914.

[47]On 25 September, French-led police in the port of Casablanca arrested several deserters from the French Foreign Legion (all former Austrian or German subjects) who were being whisked aboard an outbound vessel by agents of the German consulate. After considerable legal wrangling, France and Germany submitted the case to the Permanent Court of Arbitration. The arbitrator–Knut Hjalmar Hammarskjöld, father of the later U.N. secretary-general—ascertained that French officials had acted within their jurisdiction but found fault with the manner in which these officials had exercised their duty.

b)   ***Kiderlen to Holstein, 17 March 1909***

. . . This time the others appear to be caving in. . . .

—PA Nl. Holstein 57

c)   ***Kiderlen to Pourtalès, 21 March 1909***

. . . Please tell Mr. Izvolski that we were ready to propose to the Austro-Hungarian government that it should seek the approval of the powers—on the basis of the Austro-
Turkish [indemnification] agreement[48] of which they have already been apprised—to
suspend Article 25 of the Treaty of Berlin. But before we make this proposal to Austria-
Hungary, we have to know with certainty that Russia would accept the Austrian note
and that it will agree, without reservations, to suspend Article 25. Please tell Mr.
Izvolski categorically that we expect a precise answer—yes or no. Any evasive, hedged,
or unclear answer we would have to regard as a rejection. We would then withdraw
and let events take their course. The responsibility for all further events would then
have to be borne by Mr. Izvolski. This is a last sincere effort on our part to be helpful to
Mr. Izvolski and to resolve the situation in a manner acceptable to him . . . .

—GP, 26ii:9460

d)   ***Tschirschky to Bülow, 28 March 1909***

. . . [Austrian] military circles . . . were in favor of the military subjugation of this
restive and unreliable neighbor. He, Baron Aehrenthal, agreed that for all intents and
purposes a victorious campaign would have had a good effect on the Austro-Hungarian
army and would have also benefited the internal development of the monarchy. But
after weighing all options, he preferred the peaceful solution of the Serb question,
now seemingly attained. A war against Serbia would have cost 600 to 800 million
crowns. Even though an amount in this order would have noticeably increased taxes,
the country would have shouldered this burden without complaint if the campaign
had held out the promise of a decisive advantage. Such an advantage, however, was
not within reach. The idea of an incorporation of Serbia into the monarchy or its partition among Austria-Hungary, Romania, and Bulgaria was, upon closer examination,
impractical given the general European situation and even from the vantage point of
the present interests of the monarchy. This brand of power politics is difficult to justify in our century; it would have mortgaged the future with a dangerous amount of
combustible material. One should allow matters in the Slavic south to develop slowly

---

[48]Text of Austro-Ottoman protocol of 26 February 1909 in *OeU*, 2:1522, or *SP*, 102:180.

and should proceed cautiously, step by step, given the difficulties posed by the monarchy's dualism and the fact that conditions in the annexed provinces have not yet been consolidated. . . .

—*GP,* 26ii:9493

e)   *Bülow in the Reichstag, 29 March 1909*

. . . Gentlemen, somewhere I saw a derisive reference to our alleged vassalage to Austria-Hungary. What a foolish statement! [correct!; amusement] This is not a quarrel over rank like the one between the two queens in the Nibelungen saga; but the loyalty of the Nibelungen[49] is a feature of our relationship to Austria-Hungary [lively shouts of bravo!]; this both of us will want to uphold [renewed applause]. . . . That the agreement of Serbia [to altering article 25] too should be required—that, gentlemen, is a demand which Austria-Hungary has rightfully scorned from the outset [correct!], no matter the form—be it compensations or other requests—in which it has been advanced. The Serbs have no legal claim [correct! on the right]. The Serb armaments are a dangerous game. It is intolerable to think that the peace of Europe could be endangered because of Serbia. But it does not necessarily follow that therefore Austria-Hungary or Turkey should be pressured to give in to the unjustifiable political or territorial aspirations of the Serbs. Rather, a heavy responsibility would have to be borne by those who have, in whatever fashion, encouraged the Serb aspirations. These are not worth a war, let alone a global conflagration. . . . Our attitude towards the question of a conference has not changed. We have no fundamental objections to such a conference, provided that all European powers participate, that these powers reach agreement on the disputed points in advance, and that the conference agenda is fixed and delineated with precision. . . .

—Reichstag, 236:7802–3

f)   *Five-Power Memorandum to the Serb Government,*
30 March 1909

The ministers of Germany, England, France, Italy, and Russia invite, with urgency, the Serb government to address to the Austro-Hungarian government a note, with the following text. . . . It is essential that this note is transcribed word for word and is sent without delay.

"Serbia recognizes that its rights have not been violated by the fait accompli in Bosnia-Herzegovina and will, consequently, comply with the decision to be reached by the powers in regard to Article 25 of the Treaty of Berlin. Following the advice of the Great Powers, Serbia pledges to abandon its attitude of protest and opposition to the annexation which it has exhibited since last fall. It also pledges to change the thrust of its policies toward Austria-Hungary and will subsequently live with the latter on the basis of good neighborliness.

---

[49] As usual, Bülow's literary reference was far from clear. He may have meant to evoke the exploits of Siegfried. But given the outcome of the epic—the destruction of the Nibelungen in an orgy of violence—the allusion was less than felicitous.

In conformity with these declarations and trusting the peaceful intentions of Austria-Hungary, Serbia will return its army to the organizational, deployment, and manpower levels of the spring of 1908. It will disarm and discharge its volunteers and its bands and will prevent the formation of new units of irregulars on its territory.". . .

. . . [The] ministers are authorized to inform the Serbian government that the Imperial and Royal Minister of Foreign Affairs, in conversations in Vienna with the representatives of England, France, Italy, and Russia, has declared that Austria-Hungary wishes neither to pressure Serbia or to limit the normal development of its armed forces, and that he has formally pledged that the Austro-Hungarian government neither plans to attack Serbia, provided it disarms, nor has any intention to infringe on its independence, its free development, its security, or its territorial integrity.

—*GP*, 26ii:9497 annex; *OeU*, 2:1425 (excerpt)

11.13 A SHOCK TO THE SYSTEM: THE ITALO-OTTOMAN WAR, 1911–1912

Guicciardini in the Chamber of Deputies, 7 June 1911 • *Foscari in the Chamber of Deputies, 8 June 1911* • *San Giuliano's Ultimatum to the Porte, 26 September 1911* • *Italo-Ottoman Treaty of Lausanne (Ouchy), 18 October 1912*

The colossal monument to Victor Emmanuel II, dedicated in June 1911, commemorated the fiftieth anniversary of the *risorgimento*. Its location on the edge of the Roman Forum intended to associate the new Italian state with the glory of ancient Rome but instead underscored the disparity between Italy's self-image as a Great Power and its actual performance. This disparity became the subject of an impassioned attack, in the Italian nationalist press, on the lackluster policy of the Giolitti government. In the Italian parliament, the verbal assault on Giolitti's foreign minister, Antonino di San Giuliano, was spearheaded by Francesco Guicciardini[50] and Piero Foscari,[51] the former an ex-foreign minister and scion of a family famous for its contributions to the Florentine Renaissance, the latter a descendant of a clan that had supplied the Venetian republic with perhaps its most famous doge. If nothing else, both names evoked a more glorious past.[52]

Fortunately for San Giuliano, the Second Moroccan crisis (Document 11.14) gave him the chance to silence his domestic critics. The prospect that France would now be free to establish a protectorate in that North African country brought within reach the fulfillment of the Franco-Italian deal of 1900 (Document 10.26); all that was left to do was to strong-arm the Ottoman Empire into surrendering Libya.

This, however, was more easily contemplated than accomplished. Preferring war to surrender, the Porte ceded Libya only when the larger threat of a Balkan alliance threatened the very survival of Turkey-in-Europe (Document 11.17). In the interim, the Ottoman garrison in Libya, aided by the local Senussi tribes, offered fierce resistance; elsewhere, the Ottoman Empire endured an Italian naval demonstration at the Dardanelles and the occupation of the Dodecanese. Though the Treaty of Lausanne of 18 October 1912 transferred Libya to Italy, sporadic Senussi revolts against Italian rule continued until 1930.

[50](1851–1915). Italian foreign minister, 1906; 1909–1910.
[51](1865–1923). President of the irredentist Trento and Trieste Society; under-secretary for colonies, 1914–1917.
[52]Cf. Felix Gilbert, *Machiavelli and Guicciardini: Politics and History in Sixteenth-Century Florence* (Princeton, 1965); Frederick C. Lane, *Venice: A Maritime Republic* (Baltimore, 1973).

The Lausanne treaty also required Italy to evacuate the Dodecanese once Ottoman forces had left Libya. But the turmoil of the Balkan wars (Documents 11.17 to 11.22) allowed Italy to evade the implemention of this article, so that by the outbreak of the First World War, Italy still held the Dodecanese in fact though not in law.

a)   *Guicciardini in the Chamber of Deputies, 7 June 1911*

. . . the fiftieth anniversary celebration would be nothing more than a vain show of pride if to the list of accomplishments achieved and possessions obtained there was not added some idea of the accomplishments that remain to be realized, of the possessions that remain to be obtained, and an indication of the shortcomings of our national life. . . .

It is obvious that after the loss of Tunisia and after the renunciation of the position that we had managed to acquire in Morocco, the question of Mediterranean Africa is, for us, reduced to the issue of Tripolis. It is also obvious that our political and economic interests demand that this region not be relinquished, either territorially or economically, to the advantage of another power. . . . I cannot hide that I share the opinion that circumstances demand, at certain moments, more energetic and resolute action. . . .

—*Atti Parlamentari*, Legislatura 23, Camera dei Deputati, 15348–56

b)   *Foscari in the Chamber of Deputies, 8 June 1911*

. . . Thus, after the loss of this primacy in the Mediterranean, and also of the control over the entire northern coast of Africa which was predicted by Giuseppe Mazzini, when Italy did not even yet exist, the only thing remaining is that precious and valuable strip of Tripolitania; there remains this shred of northern Africa that has been for thirty years our dream and towards the attainment of which our diplomacy has for thirty years been predicated, and we have acquiesced in many other concessions in the meantime because our mortgage on this region was recognized by the other powers. . . .

It is enough for me to summarize the agricultural value as a colony for settlement of that which we commonly call Tripolitania, keeping in mind that we are speaking of a region several times Italy's size, and whose cultivated and cultivatable areas are as large as Italy and have only a million inhabitants. Given these conditions and the sad state of our emigration, it seems to me beyond debate that no people in Europe has more right or a greater duty to set up there a colony of settlement, because our destiny cannot be that described yesterday by my esteemed colleague Caetani, to put our beautiful women and our great virility into the service of procreating for other nations. This is not the ideal for a great people, honorable Caetani! [Commotion] In any case it is an ideal that will bring us to this end: that we will continue to give all our precious human production to the enlargement and enrichment of all other races and nations, and within fifty years if we do not provide ourselves with a true colony of our own, we will be nothing more than a heraldic remnant of a noble race, just as the Greeks are today. . . .

—*Atti Parlamentari*, Legislatura 23, Camera dei Deputati, 15405–15

c)   *San Giuliano's Ultimatum to the Porte, 26 September 1911*

Throughout a long series of years the Italian Government has never ceased to represent to the Porte the absolute necessity that the state of disorder and neglect in which Tripoli and Cyrenaica are left by Turkey should come to an end, and that these regions should be allowed to enjoy the same progress as that attained by other parts of northern Africa. This transformation, which is required by the general exigencies of civilization, constitutes, as far as Italy is concerned, a vital interest of the very first order, by reason of the small distance separating these countries from the coasts of Italy. . . .

The Italian Government, therefore, finding itself forced to consider the guardianship of its dignity and its interests, has decided to proceed to the military occupation of Tripoli and Cyrenaica. This solution is the only one Italy can decide upon, and the Royal [Italian] Government expects that the Imperial [Ottoman] Government will in consequence give orders so that it may meet with no opposition from the present Ottoman representatives, and that the measures which will be the necessary consequence may be effected without difficulty. Subsequent agreements would be made between the two Governments to settle the definitive situation arising therefrom. The Royal Ambassador in Constantinople has orders to ask for a peremptory reply on this matter from the Ottoman government within 24 hours from the presentation of the present document, in default of which the Italian government will be obliged to proceed to the immediate execution of the measures destined to ensure the occupation.

—Sir Thomas Barclay, *The Turco-Italian War and its Problems* (London, 1912), 109–11

d)   *Italo-Ottoman Treaty of Lausanne (Ouchy), 18 October 1912*

. . . Art. 2: The two governments pledge, immediately after the signature of the present treaty, to order the return of their officers, their troops, and also their administrative personnel, namely the Ottoman government from Tripolis and Cyrenaica, and the Italian government from the islands which it has occupied in the Aegean Sea. The effective evacuation from the above-mentioned islands of Italian officers, troops, and administrative personnel will take place immediately after Tripolis and Cyrenaica have been evacuated by Ottoman officers, troops, and administrative personnel.

—*Atti Parlamentari*, Legislatura 23, Senato, 9642–44

11.14   THE SECOND MOROCCAN CRISIS, 1911

Anglo-French Military Agreement, 20 July 1911 • Lloyd George at the Mansion House, 21 July 1911 • Diary of C. P. Scott, July 1911–January 1912 (Extracts) • Wilhelm II to Bethmann, 30 September 1911 • Bethmann in the Reichstag, 10 November 1911 • Journal of Viscount Esher, 24 November 1911

In April 1911, the French government responded to antiforeign rioting in Morocco by dispatching troops. This measure caused Germany to charge that France exceeded its mandate under the Algeciras Act (Document 11.5). Subsequent negotiations between France and Germany to resolve the Moroccan problem once and for all quickly bogged down over the question of what Germany might consider adequate compensation for acquiescing to a French protectorate in Morocco.

Trying to force the pace of the Franco-German talks, the German state secretary, Alfred von Kiderlen-Wächter, sent the German gunboat *Panther* to Agadir on the southern Moroccan coast. The official explanation—that the *Panther's* mission was to protect German interests against Moroccan antiforeignism—rang hollow in light of the fact that only a few Germans resided in that part of the sherifian kingdom. For their part, the British Foreign Office and Admiralty were quick to suspect that Germany pursued a different objective altogether, namely the acquisition of a coaling station on Morocco's Atlantic coast. Whether or not Grey and Churchill were correct in imputing this motive to Germany, there can be no question that they were piqued not only by the dispatch of the *Panther*, but also by France's failure to keep the Foreign Office apprised of the details of the Franco-German negotiations. The irritation felt in the Foreign Office adds to the tale a somewhat ironic twist, given the usual Foreign Office lament about *Germany's* pathological desire to insert itself in questions where, in the considered judgment of the Foreign Office, it had no interests.

Speaking at the annual lord mayor's banquet at the Mansion House, the British Chancellor of the Exchequer, David Lloyd George, signaled the displeasure of the British government at this state of affairs. The speech jolted the ongoing Franco-German negotiations—one historian has spoken of "epic mistiming"[53]—but it left unclear which of the two countries, France or Germany, was its principal target. Nonetheless, the German government took umbrage, and thus what had been a bilateral Franco-German dispute over Morocco was transformed into an *Anglo*-German crisis. A last, and unforeseen, consequence of the speech was that it raised questions within the British cabinet about the nature of the British commitment to France; these, in turn, forced Grey to reveal to the entire cabinet that staff talks between the two countries had been conducted since 1906. Coincidentally, these talks—on the day before Lloyd George's speech—had yielded an agreement that "came close to a military alliance and was far more detailed than parallel Franco-Russian or German-Austrian arrangements."[54]

Each of the principals in the Second Moroccan crisis came under attack at home. In England, the sagacity of Grey's leadership at the Foreign Office was increasingly questioned by his colleagues in the cabinet; in Germany, the perception that the government had retreated under British pressure was grist for the mills of its right-wing critics and led Wilhelm II and Tirpitz to contemplate further naval increases; in France, the widespread belief that the Caillaux government had given in to German bullying spurred a right-wing revival in the national elections of January 1912.

[53]Oron J. Hale, *The Great Illusion, 1900–1914* (New York, 1971), 270, note 11.
[54]Zara S. Steiner, *Britain and the Origins of the First World War* (London, 1977), 198.

a)   ***Anglo-French Military Agreement, 20 July 1911***

. . . Important modifications were applied in 1911 to the early plan, the English government wishing to give more breadth to its future military cooperation on the continent and to make it more effective in expediting the arrival of the English army to the theater of operations. . . . [After] the conference which took place on 20 July 1911 at the Ministry of War in Paris between General Dubail, Chief of Staff of the Army and General Wilson, Director of Military Operations in the War Office . . . a memorandum summarizing the bases of the military entente was signed by these two high military authorities.

It is, moreover, stipulated in this document that the talks undertaken are "devoid of any official character and cannot tie on any issue the English and French governments."

The general dispositions provided by the conference of 20 July 1911 have been rendered precise and completed by the frequent communication that the French chief of staff has had with the War Office through our military attaché. . . .

1. . . . The English expeditionary army['355   s] . . . total numbers will be approximately: 6,900 officers; 165,000 men; 69,500 horses; 492 cannon. . . .

2. . . . The landing of combatants will begin on the fourth day and will end on the thirteenth day of English mobilization. . . .

—*DDF*, 3rd Series, 2:272

b)   ***Lloyd George at the Mansion House, 21 July 1911***

. . . And there is only one circumstance that could possibly interfere at this moment with the continued flow of that stream of prosperity whose fertilizing influence is spreading over the whole world, and that circumstance would be anything which would disturb international peace. Peace is the first condition of continued prosperity. Fortunately there is no reason to fear that such a catastrophe is imminent, although there are of course constant questions which arise between Governments which produce discussion and sometimes irritation. . . . Britain should at all hazards maintain her place and her prestige amongst the Great Powers of the world [cheers]. Her potent influence has many a time been in the past, and may yet be in the future, invaluable to the cause of human liberty. It has more than once in the past redeemed continental nations, who are sometimes too apt to forget that service, from overwhelming disaster and even from national extinction. I would make great sacrifices to preserve peace. I conceive that nothing would justify a disturbance of international good will except questions of the gravest national moment. But if a situation were to be forced upon us in which peace could only be preserved by the surrender of the great and beneficent position Britain has won by centuries of heroism and achievement, by allowing Britain to be treated where her interests were vitally affected as if she were of no account in the cabinet of nations, then I say emphatically that peace at that price would be a humiliation intolerable for a great country like ours to endure [cheers]. . . .

—*The Times*, 22 July 1911

c)   *Diary of C. P. Scott,*[55] *July 1911–January 1912 (Extracts)*

22 July: Breakfast with Lloyd George. . . . On the whole he was strongly in favor of proceeding in the most conciliatory manner possible but of insisting unflinchingly that no
change in the status quo in Morocco should take place without our being made parties
to it. Asquith[55a] was quite conscious of the anti-Germanism of the Foreign Office staff
and was prepared to resist it. But neither he nor Grey nor himself (Lloyd George) would
consent to hold office unless they were permitted to assert the claim of Great Britain to
have her treaty rights and her real interests considered and to be treated with ordinary
diplomatic civility as a Great Power. The whole correspondence would have hereafter
to be published and it would be fatal even to our [Liberal] party interests if it should be
found that we had not maintained the clear rights and the dignity of the country.

I of course agreed with him [Lloyd George] about this. I did not think it conceivable that Germany should resist such a demand temperately pressed, but the question
was what interests had we for which in the last resort we were prepared to go to war
and was the prevention of a German naval base at Agadir one of them. I got no clear
answer to this. . . . The impression I got was that he is not immune from the microbe
of Germanophobia. . . .

Churchill's only contributions to the discussion . . . were his highly rhetorical de-
nunciations repeated at intervals of the insolence of Germany and the need of asserting ourselves and teaching her a lesson. Every question with him becomes a personal
question. . . .

25 July: . . . Grey also told me that the [German] negotiation with France was
being conducted under the pledge of secrecy—i.e. that France was not at liberty to
inform us of its progress. A new point to me and a rather grave one was the general
contention[,] which I understood from Grey to be put forward by Germany[,] that
by our agreement giving France a free hand politically in Morocco we had estopped
ourselves from interfering in any direct political negotiations into which she might
enter with another power, just as France would be estopped from interfering under
similar circumstances in Egypt. It was this I gathered which made him so anxious that
it should be at once and clearly understood in Germany that we should regard the
presence of a great naval power like Germany on the Atlantic coast of Morocco as
constituting a new situation and giving us a right which we meant to assert to be considered and consulted. He did not wish Germany through ignorance of our real intentions to commit herself so far that she could not withdraw, as happened with Russia
before the Crimean War.[56]

7 November: [In the view of Sir Frank Lascelles,] the Germans are an extremely
sensitive people. As Lord Salisbury put it to [him], "They are like a jealous woman."
"But tell them," he added[,] "we are not monogamists; we are polygamists. . . ." . . .
Sir F. Lascelles' own opinion about Agadir is that it was a mistake—"ever since
[Bethmann[56a]] came into office," he said, "he has in my opinion made a series of mis-
takes and he has shown his cleverness chiefly in getting out of their consequences"—

[55]Charles Prestwich Scott (1847–1932), editor and publisher of the *Manchester Guardian.*
[55a]Herbert Henry Asquith (1852–1928). British prime minister, 1908–1916.
[56]To gauge the accuracy of this contention, cf. Documents 5.1, 5.2, and 5.3.
[56a]Theobald von Bethmann Hollweg (1856–1921). German chancellor, 1909–1917.

but its importance was greatly exaggerated. It was just a move in the game and need not greatly have alarmed us. . . . Speaking generally he deprecated English nervousness in regard to Germany as uncalled for and undignified. The gross error in regard to German naval construction for which McKenna[56b] was responsible last year [sic for 1909] and which had never been confessed as it ought to have been was probably due to this cause. A more recent example was the scare (of which he happened to have information though a friend in the navy) that we were on the point (a month ago) of being attacked by Germany which had no better foundation than that the Admiralty had lost sight of two German gunboats. . . .

7 January 1912: [Conversation with Loreburn[57]]. Germany for years has been trying to make friends. "Incredible" the way she has been repulsed. For 3 years have been pressing for information. Questions constantly evaded sometimes with actual falsehoods. . . .

—Trevor Wilson (ed.), *The Political Diaries of C. P. Scott, 1911–1928* (Ithaca, 1970), 47–61

d)   *Wilhelm II to Bethmann, 30 September 1911*

. . . A naval amendment is to be introduced [in the Reichstag] later in the fall of 1912.[58] We are undeniably at an important turning point in the history of our fatherland. We have recognized the adversary, were nearly humiliated by him, and had to endure this gritting our teeth. Our friendship does not interest him. That is because we are not yet strong enough. He is impressed only when confronted by power and strength, when he faces incontrovertible facts. Our people expect a government that can act, not just negotiate. There must be a national purpose [*Tat*], which directs the enthusiasm of Germans along the right path without giving the opponent cause to act. That is the path sketched by me, i.e. giving notice [that we aim for] a 2:3 ratio of the German to the British fleet. . . .

—Alfred von Tirpitz, *Politische Dokumente* (Stuttgart, 1924), 1:217–18

e)   *Bethmann in the Reichstag, 10 November 1911*

. . . Herr Bassermann[59] said that instead of sending a ship to Agadir, we should have taken measures on our western border. Well, gentlemen, what kind of measures? troop movements perhaps? Gentlemen, troop movements on our western border in the midst of a crisis are the beginning of a mobilization [correct! left and center], and a mobilization in a crisis means war [correct! left]. I doubt whether such a measure would have been seen in France as an invitation to sit down with us and to start bargaining [laughter—correct!]. . . . Herr von Heydebrand[60] . . . said that we had heard, in a speech based on consultations with the entire British cabinet, language both humiliating and constituting a warlike challenge to the German people and which I supposedly dismissed with slight-of-hand as an "after-dinner speech." . . . Gentlemen, I regret that our relations with a state with which we have normal relations are

[56b]Reginald McKenna (1863–1943). First Lord of the Admiralty, 1908–1911.

[57] Robert, Baron Loreburn (1846–1923). Lord chancellor, 1906–1916.

[58] Advanced to 22 March. See Document 11.15.

[59] Ernst Bassermann (1854–1917). Floor leader of the National Liberal party.

[60] Ernst von Heydebrand und der Lasa (1851–1924). Floor leader of the Conservative party.

discussed in this house in a tone which might have its uses in election rallies [good! left] but which is not customary for a parliament aware of its responsibility [applause, left]. When I—conscious of my responsibility—refer in guarded terms to the speeches of foreign statesmen, this is supposed to and intended to lead to an improvement in our foreign relations. Passionate and excessive language such as that of Herr von Heydebrand [correct; hear! hear! on the left] may serve the interests of political parties—but to the German Reich they do nothing but damage [lively applause and hear! hear! on the left and among the Social Democrats]. . . . If newspapers and the press present things as if our fatherland was in distress, as if we were faced with the collapse of the nation, then this does not square with the facts. But to bring national passions to the boiling point for the sake of utopian plans of conquest or for the sake of party interests—now that compromises patriotism and squanders a valuable asset [lively applause left and center, scattered applause among the Free Conservatives].

—Reichstag, 268:7755–56

f)   ***Journal of Viscount Esher,[61] 24 November 1911***

A Cabinet cabal against the entente with France and the Defence Committee. The original fault lay with that imprudent summoning of a packed Defence Committee in August to settle the immediate form of action if war had to be declared war against Germany.[62] . . . There has been a serious crisis. Fifteen members of the Cabinet against five. The entente is decidedly imperilled. The Cabinet so far is intact. . . .

—Oliver Viscount Esher (ed.), *Journals and Letters of Reginald Viscount Esher* (London, 1938), 3:74

11.15   THE HALDANE MISSION, FEBRUARY–APRIL 1912

Metternich to Wilhelm II, 10 January 1912 • British Memorandum, Presented to the German Government by Sir Ernest Cassel, 29 January 1912 • German Memorandum for the British Government, 29 January 1912 • "Observations" by Churchill, 31 January 1912 • Nicolson to Bertie, 8 February 1912 • Churchill in Glasgow, 9 February 1912 • Bethmann's and Haldane's "Sketch of a Conceivable [Anglo-German] Formula," 10 February 1912 • Minute by Crowe, 12 February 1912 • German Memorandum, 6 March 1912 • British Proposal for a British Declaration on Anglo-German Relations, 14 March 1912 • Churchill in the House of Commons, 18 March 1912 • Beresford in the House of Commons, 18 March 1912 • Bethmann to Metternich, 21 March 1912 • British Countermemorandum to the German Government, 25 March 1912, with Annotations by Wilhelm II, 31 March • Churchill, Attending Sea Trials, to Clementine Churchill, 25 March 1912 • Bertie to Nicolson, 28 March 1912 • Minute by Nicolson, 4 April 1912 • Minute by Grey, 6(?) April 1912 • Goschen to Nicolson, 20 April 1912 • Grey to Goschen, 27 June 1912

[61]Reginald, Viscount Esher (1852–1930). Constable of Windsor Castle, 1901–1928; editor of the *Letters of Queen Victoria*; member of the Committee of Imperial Defense, 1905–1918. Declined appointments as under-secretary for colonies (1899) and war (1900), governor of the Cape Colony (1900), and viceroy of India (1908).

[62]On 23 August 1911. For an account of the Committee of Imperial Defense meeting, see Ernest R. May (ed.), *Knowing One's Enemies: Intelligence Assessment before the two World Wars* (Princeton, 1986), 12ff.

The opportunity to repair the Anglo-German relationship, so heavily damaged by the second Moroccan crisis, presented itself in early 1912 when two businessmen—the director of the Hamburg-America line, Albert Ballin, and the German-born British financier Sir Edward Cassel—paved the way for Lord Haldane, the British secretary for war, to visit Berlin. From the point of view of the British Foreign Office, Haldane was in Berlin to talk about having talks. But his extensive political conversations with the German chancellor, Theobald von Bethmann Hollweg, and the Kaiser (as well as Tirpitz) gave the talks an asymmetrical quality. The German government was now committed on a higher plane than the British and, in the event the talks went awry, would have correspondingly greater difficulties in saving face and extricating itself.

Haldane returned to London with a "sketch" for a political and a colonial understanding. Bethmann and Haldane agreed that this accord should include no explicit mention of a new naval amendment to the existing German naval program, provided that the German government would ultimately build only two of the three dreadnoughts envisaged by this bill.

The proposed German naval amendment hardly seemed to fit the spirit of Anglo-German détente or the premises for an Anglo-German accord initially communicated to the German government by Cassel. But the question of whether or not to proceed with the naval legislation also caused a crisis within the German government. Bethmann hoped that the prospect of an Anglo-German political accord would make the amendment unnecessary, whereas Tirpitz, with the backing of the Kaiser, considered the amendment, in the form in which it had been discussed with Haldane, to be nonnegotiable. After the momentum of the Anglo-German talks had slowed to a crawl, Bethmann realized that they could not be revived unless the naval amendment were to be further reduced in scope. But British approval of the political formula with which Haldane had returned to London constituted the only chance—and a remote one at that—that the Kaiser would agree to a further scaling back of the naval amendment. Perhaps Bethmann was oblivious to the fundamental incompatibility of the optimum British position (neither a German naval amendment nor a political formula, i.e., the defense of the status quo) with the optimum German position (both a naval amendment and a political formula, i.e., a redefinition of the Anglo-German relationship), perhaps he believed that he could stake out a middle ground. But above all, Bethmann needed to play for time: to compel the Kaiser to again postpone publication of the naval amendment, he submitted his resignation. Three days later, Tirpitz threatened to resign if publication was in fact postponed, and, with this threat, carried the day.[63]

No matter how melodramatic the contest between Bethmann and Tirpitz, the German negotiators collectively blundered when they gave Haldane a copy of the proposed legislation to take back to England.[64] The very fact that there would be an amendment played into the hands of those in England who had opposed the Haldane mission in principle. But with an advance copy in hand, the British Admiralty now had the opportunity to discover in its fine print

---

[63]Text of Bethmann's letter of resignation in Ernst Jäckh (ed.), *Kiderlen-Wächter. Der Staatsmann und Mensch* (Stuttgart, 1924), 2:159–61, and Alfred von Tirpitz, *Politische Dokumente* (Stuttgart, 1924), 1:318–20. For Tirpitz's threat, see ibid., 323.

[64]The official announcement on 8 February, the eve of Haldane's visit, that a naval amendment would be presented to the Reichstag was a political victory for Tirpitz. Bethmann, however, delayed publication of the text of the amendment until 22 March. But giving a foreign cabinet a copy of draft legislation before it was published was a procedure hardly consonant with constitutional practice. Further complicating matters from the constitutional point of view was the fact that Churchill alluded to the principal features of the German legislation when he introduced the British naval estimates in the House of Commons on 18 March, four days before the amendment's publication in Germany.

ample reason for doubting Germany's probity. Its new first lord, Winston Churchill, concluded in a cabinet memorandum that the amendment's increases in manpower and smaller vessels "practically amounted to putting four-fifths of the German navy permanently on a war-footing."[65] Whether the pointed references to Germany in Churchill's public speeches improved or worsened the Anglo-German climate became—and remains—subject to debate. Equally subject to debate are Churchill's motives. He may have felt that his new cabinet post necessitated a public disavowal of his previous reputation as a cabinet radical widely suspected of pro-German sympathies. Or it may have been that the institution molded the man: that Churchill, chameleonlike, took on the Admiralty's bureaucratic outlook once he was at its head.

Even aside from the naval question, the deck was stacked against Haldane. Grey regarded the mission as little more than a sop to his critics in the cabinet. He was careful to dissociate himself from the talks in their most delicate phase—with the curious excuse (curious at least for a foreign secretary) that an impending strike in the British coal industry had a greater claim on his time. Consequently, the negotiations were left in the hands of Sir Arthur Nicolson,[65a] one of the architects of the Anglo-Russian entente and one of the Foreign Office's foremost Germanophobes. Like Grey, Nicolson realized that the cabinet radicals would only be reconciled to the failure of the talks (and perhaps would become more amenable to an expansion of the Triple Entente) if Germany could be blamed for their collapse.

In a cacophony of mutual recrimination, the talks ground to a halt in late March 1912. Only the search for a colonial agreement continued, leading the German government and the British colonial secretary—in spite of the ill-disguised hostility of the Foreign Office—to labyrinthine negotiations to revise the 1898 Anglo-German treaty on the Portuguese colonies (Document 10.12).

While it is easy to discern the reasons for the failure of the Haldane mission, it is more difficult to come to terms with the larger questions posed by this episode: How realistic was Bethmann's expectation that Britain, given its evasion of similar entreaties from its French ally, would acquiesce to a German request for an open-ended political assurance? Did the Foreign Office's inability to find language to please both the French and the Germans indicate a lack of imagination? Or was this inability merely a manifestation of a larger phenomenon: of Britain's diplomats working overtime to discover for France the full benefit of the doubt, but applying an altogether different standard to Germany? For the sake of argument, the reader is invited to try the following substitutions in Bertie's report to Nicolson of 28 March (Document 11.15p below): Austria-Hungary for "Russia"; Russia for "Germany"; Germany for "France." With these substitutions in place, Bertie's scenario comes close to describing the July crisis of 1914. Bertie would have been aghast at the analogy. But the fact that neither he nor Nicolson bothered to test their hypotheses for general applicability shows their limited vision and their unwillingness—or incapacity?—to think in terms of the European "system" as a whole. Similarly, the last document excerpted here shows the contortions that Grey willingly performed to justify his policy. In speaking to Marschall, the new German ambassador to London, Grey further rationalized Crowe's previous musings (Document 11.7) about the undesirability of an Anglo-German agreement and exhibited once again what one student of his diplomacy called "a curious talent for convincing himself that what he wanted to believe really was the truth."[66]

[65] 9 March. Text in Randolph S. Churchill, *Winston S. Churchill*, companion vol. 2iii (London, 1969), 1525–26.

[65a](1849–1928). British plenipotentiary at the Algeciras conference, 1906; ambassador to Russia, 1906–1910; undersecretary in the Foreign Office, 1910–1916.

[66] Monger, *End of Isolation*, 244.

Finally, the question deserves to be raised whether the Haldane mission was a missed opportunity. The answer here depends on the perspective of the observer. From the vantage point of the Balkan crises of 1912–1913 and that of the July crisis of 1914, there can be no doubt. At the very least, an Anglo-German understanding would have built mutual confidence, might have established a consultative mechanism, and might have even gone some distance toward reestablishing the European concert. But in the context of 1912, there was no opportunity to miss. If Wilhelm II, Tirpitz, Grey, Nicolson, Goschen, and Crowe shared a character trait, it was that they were men of a single idea—be it German naval power or the strengthening of the Triple Entente—rigid in their thinking, oblivious to the dangers to which they exposed their countries, and only too ready to pay the price of confrontation in a system that they expected to work for them but in which they were unwilling to invest.

a)   *Metternich to Wilhelm II, 10 January 1912*

. . . the [British] government is determined to answer a German naval amendment with an unusually energetic increase in its own sea power. . . . A naval amendment will push England again and immediately into the French camp which it will then not leave. . . . We should carry on a careful naval policy and should not resort to measures which do not involve existential issues for our fleet but will alarm and irritate our opponent before our strength is sufficient to fend him off . . . We can no longer deceive ourselves that the English system of ententes and England's hostile policy is based primarily on its fear of our growing power at sea. [England's] mistrust may be wrong and without cause, but we have to take into account the fact that it exists. . . . Several state secretaries and [Prussian] ministers share my views. . . . But I can do no other than to decline responsibility—before Your Majesty, before history, before my conscience—for the serious consequences which will arise at this time for the Reich because of this amendment. . . .

—Count Paul Metternich, "Meine Denkschrift über die Flottennovelle vom 10. Januar 1912," *Europäische Gespräche* 4 (1926), 57–76

b) *British Memorandum, Presented to the German Government by Sir Ernest Cassel, 29 January 1912*

1. Fundamental. Naval superiority recognized as essential to Great Britain. Present German naval program and expenditure not to be increased but if possible retarded and reduced.

2. England sincerely desires not to interfere with German colonial expansion. To give effect to this she is prepared forthwith to discuss whatever the German aspirations in that direction may be. England will be glad to know that there is a field or special points where she can help Germany.

3. Proposals for reciprocal assurances debarring either power from joining in aggressive designs or combinations against the other would be welcome.

—*GP*, 31:11347

c)   **German Memorandum for the British Government,
29 January 1912**

1. Fundamental. The German Government . . . is in full accord with the terms proposed in the draft submitted by Sir E. Cassel with the following exception: that this
year's (1912) estimates must be included in the "present German naval program" in as
much as all the arrangements have already been completed. . . .

—GP, 31:11347

d)   **"Observations" by Churchill, 31 January 1912**

. . . In order to meet the new German squadron we are contemplating bringing home the Medit[erranea]n battleships. This means relying on France in the
Medit[erranea]n. . . .

—Randolph S. Churchill, Winston S. Churchill, companion vol. 2iii (London, 1969), 1504

e)   **Nicolson to Bertie, 8 February 1912**

This is a private line for your eyes only—as it expresses my personal views which are
not quite in accordance with those of the Cabinet. . . . I do not myself see why we
should abandon the excellent position in which we have been placed, and step down
to be involved in endeavors to entangle us in some so-called "understandings" which
would undoubtedly, if not actually impair our relations with France and Russia, in any
case render the latter countries somewhat suspicious of us. Moreover, is it likely that
we shall be able to obtain from Germany an undertaking of a really formal and binding character that she will not increase her naval program—and will always be content to leave us in undisputed and indisputable supremacy? . . .

—C. J. Lowe and M. L. Dockrill (eds.), The Mirage of Power: British Foreign Policy, 1902–22,
3 vols. (London, 1972), 3:451

f)   **Churchill in Glasgow, 9 February 1912**

. . . We have no thoughts, and we have never had any thoughts, of aggression—and we
attribute no such thoughts to other Great Powers. There is, however, this difference between the British naval power and the naval power of the great and friendly empire—
and I trust it may long remain a great and friendly Power—of Germany. The British navy
is to us a necessity and, from some points of view, the German navy is to them more in
the nature of a luxury. Our naval power involves British existence. It is existence to us;
it is expansion to them. We cannot menace the peace of a single continental hamlet,

nor do we wish to do so no matter how great and supreme our navy may become. But, on the other hand, the whole fortunes of our race and Empire, the whole treasure accumulated during so many centuries of sacrifice and achievement would perish and be swept utterly away if our naval supremacy were to be impaired. It is the British navy which makes Great Britain a Great Power. But Germany was a Great Power, respected and honored all over the world, before she had a single ship. . . .

—*The Times* , 10 February 1912; also Robert Rhodes James (ed.), *Winston S. Churchill: His Complete Speeches, 1897–1963*, 8 vols. (New York, 1974), 2:1910

g) *Bethmann's and Haldane's "Sketch of a Conceivable [Anglo-German] Formula," 10 February 1912*

Notes by Nicolson

1. The high contracting powers assure each other mutually of their desire of peace and friendship.

2. They will not, either of them, make any unprovoked [or prepare to make any (unprovoked)][67] attack upon the other or join in any combination or design against the other for purposes of aggression, or become party to any plan or naval or military combination alone or in conjunction with any other power directed to such an end. [And declare not to be bound at present by any such engagement].[67a]

3. If either of the high contracting parties becomes entangled in a war with one or more powers in which it cannot be said to be the aggressor, the other will at least observe towards the power so entangled a benevolent neutrality and use its utmost endeavor for the localization of the conflict. [If either of the high contracting parties is forced to go to war by obvious provocation from a third party they bind themselves to enter into an exchange of views concerning their attitude in such a conflict.][67b]

1. Could certainly stand.

2. Could be improved by omitting the words after "aggression"—if we engage to abstain from entering into *any naval or military combination* involving a possible offensive line of action, we should be debarred from any arrangements which are "defensive" in policy but "offensive" in the strategical sense.

3. We have, I believe, always consistently maintained that there is no such thing as a "*benevolent* neutrality" as it involves a contradiction in terms. If a country is neutral it is neutral and nothing else—*benevolence* towards one party is distinctly a violation of that neutrality. Who can say, further, who is in reality the aggressor? A country, and history furnishes many examples, may be forced by the political action of her adversary to assume the role of an apparent aggressor. To use "best endeavors" for localizing a war might conceivably involve belliger-

[67,67a,67b]These additional phrases were suggested in a second German proposal of 12 March 1912. *GP* 31:11395.

4. The duty of neutrality which arises from the preceding article has no application in so far as it may not be reconcilable with existing agreements which the high contracting parties have already made. . . .

ent operations. I should omit the whole of No. 3.

No. 4 has no meaning without No. 3, and is open to the objection that it permits the Triple Alliance to act as it may think fit, but definitely precludes us from entering into any engagements of the same nature. I would therefore omit No. 4. . . .

—*BD*, 6:506, 507

b)   *Minute by Crowe, 12 February 1912*

. . . The essential thing is that if we are to have no naval agreement, and a political agreement is nevertheless decided upon, then there should be an overwhelming advantage for us in any merely political agreement. For public opinion in this country will be seriously disappointed at the failure to get a naval agreement and will naturally look askance at any political bargain not including such an agreement. If, in addition, the new pact is not favorable to this country on its merits, the feeling against Germany will inevitably become more bitter than it already is, which clearly ought at any reasonable cost, to be avoided.

—*BD*, 6:506

i)   *German Memorandum, 6 March 1912*

. . . The Imperial Government have accepted Lord Haldane's offers. . . . [I]t amounts to a shifting of the basis on which the negotiations have so far been conducted, that the British Government should now criticize the increases of personnel provided for in the naval amendment and in the additional funds demanded for submarines. . . . Above all, the simultaneous arrival at an understanding respecting the proposed neutrality agreement has always formed, in the eyes of the Imperial Government, the indispensable preliminary to any agreement respecting the rate of construction under the naval bill.

If, nevertheless, the Imperial Government are prepared to abide by the bargain proposed to Lord Haldane and are ready to restrict their demand for the construction of the new battleships under the Navy Bill to the years 1913 and 1916, that is, a third of a ship for each year, and altogether to refrain from indicating at present any year for the construction of the third ship, they are inspired with the hope that the British government will come forward with a proposal as regards the political understanding agreed to in principle. . . .

—*BD*, 6:529

j) *British Proposal*[68] *for a British Declaration on Anglo-German Relations, 14 March 1912*

England will make no unprovoked [*what constitutes the provocation? who gets to decide?*] attack upon Germany and pursue no aggressive policy towards her.

Aggression upon Germany is not the subject and forms no part of any treaty, understanding or combination to which England is now a party, nor will she become a party to anything that has such an object.

—*GP*, 31:11401

k) *Churchill in the House of Commons, 18 March 1912*

. . . The actual standard in new construction—I am not speaking of men or establishment—which the Admiralty has, in fact, followed during recent years, has been to develop a 60 per cent superiority in vessels of the Dreadnought type over the German navy on the basis of the existing [German] fleet law. There are other and higher standards for the smaller vessels. . . . Applying the standard which I have outlined . . . and guarding ourselves very carefully against developments in other countries which cannot now be foreseen . . . we framed the estimates which are now presented to the House of Commons. If we are now, as it would seem, as I fear it is certain to be, confronted with an addition of two ships to German construction in the next six years . . . we should propose to meet that addition upon a higher ratio of superiority . . . .

—*Parl. Debates*, 5th Series, 35:1555–57

l) *Beresford*[68a] *in the House of Commons, 18 March 1912*

. . . I say the language used by the right hon. Gentleman was very provocative, and it will bring about the state of affairs which evidently the right hon. Gentleman wishes to avoid. . . .

—*Parl. Debates*, 5th Series, 35:1592

m) *Bethmann to Metternich, 21 March 1912*

Although Mr. Churchill's speech has complicated matters considerably, I have not yet given up hope that an agreement might after all be attained. But, judging from your

---

[68] With annotation by Wilhelm II.
[68a] Sir Charles Beresford (1846–1919). British admiral; member for Portsmouth, 1910–1916.

last conversation with Sir E. Grey, I don't think that the British government has a clear picture of how things are over here. It is not a question whether the present cordial relations can continue if a neutrality formula cannot be obtained—this continuation is self-evident, provided there is reciprocity. Rather, only a far-reaching neutrality agreement can [allow us to] meet British wishes in the question of [naval] armaments. Sir E. Grey seems to overlook the fact that a neutrality agreement is not a unilateral English gift to us, but is no less valuable to England as it is for Germany. Instead England continually speaks of limitations on our armaments, and even reserves the right—according to Churchill's explanations—to increase its armaments in the event other powers do so. Consequently, we—located, as we are, between France allied to Russia—are tied down but England is not, [and all this] without even guaranteeing us its benevolent neutrality. . . .

—*GP*, 31:11415

n) *British Countermemorandum to the German Government, 25 March 1912, with Annotations by Wilhelm II, 31 March*

. . . The British Government therefore hopes that in light of what has been above stated, the Imperial Government will see that there has been no desire to shift the basis on which the conversations were conducted in Berlin. . . . *Nevertheless it has been shifted & dropped. . . . Haldane came as a facilitator* [Unterhändler], *instructed to find a basis for later negotiations. This basis was found . . . . It was even incorporated into our* [naval] *amendment. Now everything is being watered down, questioned, and Haldane is being disavowed. [This is] a completely vacuous document which is supposed to veil a pitiful retreat. In a sneering manner, we are being laughed at because we took these proposals and this talk seriously, or even considered it binding. I myself had a hunch and therefore had for months urged to publish our defense legislation, independently of these events. My diplomats were of a different opinion, against me; took everything that emanated from London at face value, as certain and conclusive. . . . I hope that my diplomats have learned the lesson to pay greater heed to their master and his commands and wishes than hitherto, especially when anything is to be accomplished with the British, with whom they do not know how to deal, whereas I understand them well! . . . One can reconstruct the plan of the English government, which lay at the basis of this entire episode, from the above document and the course of the negotiations themselves: through Haldane's conversations the German government was to be moved to drop the naval amendment in exchange for England's offer to endow us with an African transcontinental colonial empire, consisting of territories belonging not to England but to other nations whose desire to divest themselves of these so that we can acquire them is not known or vouchsafed. At the same time, the neutrality clause was rejected outright because it was too difficult to define. . . . I saw through him* [Haldane] *and his fine fellows in time and thoroughly spoiled their game. I have saved the German people their right to sea power and self-determination in arms matters. Have shown the British that they bite on granite when they start fussing about our armaments, and have perhaps fed their hatred but also earned their respect, which may at the proper time persuade them to continue negotiations in a more modest tone and with a more favorable outcome.*

—*GP*, 31:11422

o)   *Churchill, Attending Sea Trials, to Clementine Churchill,* *25 March 1912*

. . . Unluckily there are no Germans to be found. Tiresome people—but their turn will come. . . .

—*Churchill*, companion vol. 2iii:1530

p)   *Bertie to Nicolson, 28 March 1912*

. . . The formula would tie our hands and consequently diminish our value to France. Attack is often the best means of self-defense. If Russia were occupied in such matters as prevented her from rendering useful military aid to France and the German government were pressing some question on the French government, a question which though not one of importance to England was vital to France, the German government might make every military preparation for war and move troops towards the frontier with the evident intention of attack if the German demands were not conceded. If in such circumstances the French government convinced that France was about to be attacked gave the order for the French troops to cross the frontier so as to gain a military advantage so essential to success, given the French temperament, who would be the real aggressor, Germany or France? I say Germany. . . .

—*BD*, 6:556

q)   *Minute by Nicolson, 4 April 1912*

. . . Let us definitely abandon formulas, which are at best dangerous and embarrassing documents, and the signature of which would apparently, in present circumstances, affect our relations with France. Were we to continue to endeavor to find words which would satisfy Germany, we should gradually be led into signing a document restrictive of our liberty of action, and which would thereby remove, to my mind, one of the best guarantees of peace. So long as Germany cannot rely on our abstention or neutrality, so long will she not be disposed to disturb the peace. . . .

—*BD*, 6:566

r)   *Minute by Grey, 6(?) April 1912*

. . . on the other hand it has to be borne in mind that Russia and France both deal separately with Germany and that it is not reasonable that tension should be permanently greater between England and Germany than between Germany and France or Germany and Russia.

—*BD*, 6:564

s)   *Goschen to Nicolson, 20 April 1912*

. . . I need hardly tell you that I feel great relief at the idea that the formula question is in the process of interment; it has always been my dream to be on cordial relations with Germany *without* any definite political understanding, and if, as I hope, the recent conversations have that result no one will be more pleased than I. They have tried hard to bustle us into a hampering formula and I rejoice that they have failed. You have been foremost in this good work. I heartily agree with you also about the conversations which are now going on about cessions and exchanges in Africa: and it rather makes my blood run cold when we talk to Germany about the shortcomings of our Portuguese allies. Is it quite playing the game? Of course it is *quite* true what we say about them—but is it quite right or even politic to say it to the Germans? . . .

—*BD,* 6:579

t)   *Grey to Goschen, 27 June 1912*

As I thought that Marschall would like to begin making the acquaintance of some of my colleagues, I asked him to lunch at my house yesterday with the Prime Minister and Haldane. . . . When he instanced what he considered the exceedingly good relations between Russia and Germany as being perfectly compatible with the Franco-Russian alliance, we pointed out that the alliance had precedence of any agreement which Russia might make with Germany, that it necessarily remained definite and intact, and that Russia could therefore go further perhaps than we could go, for our relations with France were much more vague; and, if we entered into an agreement with Germany more definite than any which we had with France, the agreement with Germany would necessarily tend to supersede our good understanding with France. . . .

—*BD,* 6:592

11.16   RELOCATION OF THE BRITISH MEDITERRANEAN FLEET

Nicolson to Grey, 6 May 1912 • The Debate in the House of Lords, 2 July 1912
• Letters of Viscount Esher, July 1912 • Anglo-French Naval Conventions,
January/February 1913

Introducing the 1912–1913 naval estimates in the Commons on 18 March 1912 (Document 11.15), Churchill proposed to shift the bulk of the British Mediterranean fleet from Malta to Gibraltar. This radical departure from existing Admiralty practice attracted little notice at first but soon made Churchill's proposal a target of blistering criticism. Heading the opposition were Lord Kitchener, the British consul-general in Egypt; Lord Esher in the Committee of Imperial Defense; and the advocates of empire in the House of Lords. Though the government hastened to modify Churchill's original scheme, the principal objection of his critics was borne out by subsequent events: in the Mediterranean, Britain became increasingly dependent on French goodwill.

The Anglo-French naval conventions of January and February 1913 confirmed this state of affairs. As these agreements in turn allowed France to shift most of its Atlantic fleet to the Mediterranean, France's Channel ports would now have to be protected by the British navy, and one wonders whether the specter of a French coastline denuded of its own fleet increased Britain's moral obligation to assist France in a continental crisis, no matter its exact cause. Equally so, one wonders to what degree these conventions in their details, not reproduced here, created a mutual strategic and political dependency and whether this dependency did not nullify the disclaimer that the conventions would become effective only upon the conclusion of an Anglo-French alliance.

a)   ***Nicolson to Grey, 6 May 1912***

. . . If the Admiralty consider that it is essential to concentrate all their naval forces in the Channel and North Sea, and that therefore the naval force in the Mediterranean must be very materially reduced, I can conceive only three alternative courses open to us.

A. to increase the Naval Budget so as to enable an additional squadron to be created for permanent service in the Mediterranean. This solution would presumably be ruled out as imposing too heavy a charge on the Estimates.

B. to come to an alliance with Germany so as to free a large portion of the fleets at present locked up in home waters for the purpose of watching Germany. Such a measure would

    (1) place us in an inferior naval position to Germany who would be then very much the predominant partner, and able to put unendurable pressure upon us whenever she thought it necessary. Moreover the safety of our vital parts would be left dependent on the favour of Germany.

    (2) It would throw the three Scandinavian countries, Belgium and Holland into the arms of Germany who would in general estimation be the dominating Power.

    (3) It would cause France and Russia to be at least cold and unfriendly—and our position throughout the mid–East and on the Indian frontier and elsewhere would be seriously shaken and imperilled. These are three indisputable facts. I do not allude to the probabilities of German pressure on France and the risk of a European war, and the loss of our prestige throughout the world who would regard us as having been compelled to make terms with Germany and become practically dependent on her. I would therefore rule out this solution.

C. An understanding with France whereby she would undertake, in the early period of a war and until we could detach vessels from home waters, to safeguard our interests in the Mediterranean. She would naturally ask for some reciprocal engagements from us which it would be well worth our while to give. This to my mind offers the cheapest, simplest and safest solution.

—BD, 10ii:385

b)   *The Debate in the House of Lords, 2 July 1912*

[Crewe:[69]] . . . The word "inevitable" has sometimes a rather unhappy significance. History points to a number of inevitable wars, of inevitable partitions, of inevitable combinations of states in which in some instances the term has merely served either to gloss over unsuccessful diplomacy or to mask sinister ambitions of aggression or of acquisition. . . .

[Ellenborough:[70]] . . . Mr. Churchill . . . has evidently assimilated the teaching of the naval officers with whom he has come into contact; but I am afraid that he has been hampered by other members of the Cabinet—by men who have seldom looked at a globe, and whose geographical studies since they left school have been limited to an examination of the boundaries of constituencies. . . .

[Lansdowne:] . . . My Lords, what will be the effect of this policy upon our great Colonies, upon the Dominions who at this very moment are considering what they can do to help us to meet our Imperial obligations, when they find that while we are making these proposals to them we are—I am afraid it will so seem to them—shirking the old obligations which until now we have always honourably fulfilled? Then what of the effect which will be produced in India? What will the people of India think when they find that we are unable to hold the great highway which connects India with the British Isles? We were told not long ago in connection with the creation of a new capital in India that one of the recommendations of the step was that it was an intimation to the people of India that we intended to remain there. . . . What kind of an impression will be produced, for example, upon the mind of our allies in Japan, a maritime Power keen and quick to appreciate any failure of maritime strength on our part. . . . What of our position with regard to the Balkan Peninsula and in Asia Minor? What of the part we have taken in the affairs of Crete? Surely in regard to all these matters there is all the difference in the world between a diplomacy which is supported by a sufficient force at sea and one which is not. . . .

—*Parl. Debates*, 5th Series, Lords, 12:311, 322, 334–35

c)   *Letters of Viscount Esher, July 1912*

[To Arthur Balfour, 1 July:] . . . This Mediterranean question is the vital essence of our being. . . .

[To Lord John Fisher, 9 July:] . . . I mean to see our country keep a sixty percent margin in our home waters, and an independent fleet in the Mediterranean! Whatever the cost may be it is cheaper than a conscript army and any entangling alliance.

—*Journals and Letters of Reginald, Viscount Esher*, op. cit., 3:98–101

[69]Robert, Marquess of Crewe (1858–1945). Secretary of state for India, 1910–1915.
[70]Cecil Henry, Lord Ellenborough (1849–1931).

d)   *Anglo-French Naval Conventions, January/February 1913*[71]

[23 January:] The British navy will take the responsibility of defending the Straits of Dover . . . in the event of being allied with the French government in a war with Germany. . . .

     [10 February:] 1. In case of an alliance with the British government in a war against Germany, the French navy has the responsibility of defending the Channel west [of a line] from the Cotentin [Cherbourg] peninsula to the English coast. . . .

     [10 February:] 1. In the event of a war in which Great Britain and France are allied against the Triple Alliance, the two powers will endeavor to cooperate in the Mediterranean as elsewhere to the best of their respective abilities as far as the general situation will permit. The North Sea will be the decisive theater of naval operations, and it is absolutely essential to ultimate success in all quarters that Great Britain should have complete freedom to concentrate such forces in that area as are necessary to defeat the enemy. The British government therefore cannot enter into any arrangement specifying that the British Mediterranean squadron shall be kept at any permanently fixed standard. But it will be the aim of British policy in practice to maintain in peace and war such force in the Mediterranean as should be able with reasonable chances of success to deal with the Austrian fleet should it emerge from the Adriatic. . . .

—*DDF*, 3rd Series, 5:397

11.17   CONVERGING TRACKS, I: THE BALKAN CRISIS AND THE STRENGTHENING OF THE FRANCO-RUSSIAN ALLIANCE, 1912

Serb-Bulgarian Alliance, 29 February/13 March 1912 • *Greek-Bulgarian Alliance, 16/29 May 1912* • *Franco-Russian Naval Convention, 3/16 July 1912* • *Sazonov to Nicholas II, 4/17 August 1912* • *Serb-Montenegrin Alliance, 23 September/6 October 1912*

Ever since the height of the Bosnian crisis, Russia had promoted the idea of a Balkan league of Slav and/or Orthodox states. Its efforts finally bore fruit in March 1912: an alliance between Serbia and Bulgaria seemingly put to rest the long-standing rivalry between these two neighbors. But the genie was now out of the bottle, and both Serbia and Bulgaria, largely leaving their Russian mentor in the dark, set about to forge a larger Balkan coalition encompassing Greece and Montenegro as well. With the annihilation of Turkey-in-Europe as their objective, the four Balkan allies were confident of an easy success against a tottering Ottoman Empire whose European provinces they had surrounded on all sides and whose strength had been sapped by a yearlong war with Italy (Document 11.13).

     In France, the nationalist backlash in the wake of the Second Moroccan crisis catapulted to the prime ministership Raymond Poincaré, a native of Lorraine and a die-hard nationalist.

---

[71]These conventions were rounded out on 27 January by an agreement to cooperate in Asian waters. For précis, see *DDF*, 3rd Series, 3:170 and 5:303.

MAP 17   MACEDONIA AND THE BALKAN WARS

Legend:
- Serbian-Greek treaty of alliance, 1913
- Serbian-Greek military convention, 1913
- Boundaries established after the Balkan Wars
- Romanian gains from Bulgaria, 1913
- Treaty of London, 1913
- Ottoman Empire, 1912
- Serbian-Bulgarian contested zone, 1912

BLACK SEA

Constanza

Dobruja

Varna

Bosporus

SEA OF MARMARA

Midia

Constantinople

TURKEY (OTTOMAN EMPIRE)

Dardanelles

Burgas

Adrianople

Thrace

Enos

Samothrace

Tenedos

Imbros

Lemnos

Ploesti

Bucharest

ROMANIA

BALKAN MTNS.

BULGARIA

Silistria

Maritza R.

Dedeagach

Thasos

AEGEAN SEA

RHODOPE MTNS.

Sofia

Kavala

Macedonia

Struma R.

Salonika

Salonika

Vardar R.

Nish

Morava R.

SERBIA

KOSSOVO

Uskub (Skoplje)

Monastir

Monastir (Bitolje)

L. Prespa

GREECE

Thessaly

Belgrade

Save R.

Novi Pazar

Sanjak of Novi Pazar

Prizren

SHAR MTNS.

Proposed Serbian sphere of influence

Ochrid

L. Ochrid

L. Scutari

MONTENEGRO

Cetinje

Scutari

Antivari

Bay of Cataro

ALBANIA

Tirana

Durazzo

Valona

Bay of Saseno

Proposed Greek sphere of influence

Janina

Epirus

Corfu

AUSTRIA-HUNGARY

Bosnia

Herzegovina

Sarajevo

Dalmatia

ADRIATIC SEA

ITALY

Appalled by what he considered French weakness during the Second Moroccan crisis, Poincaré set out to strengthen France's diplomatic and military armor. He therefore welcomed a Franco-Russian naval convention—negotiated, incidentally, under the patronage of Delcassé, who had returned to the French cabinet as minister of the navy in March 1911. To further underscore his commitment to the Franco-Russian alliance, Poincaré paid a state visit to Russia in August 1912, the first ever by a French prime minister.

On his visit to Petersburg, Poincaré was shown the text of the Serb-Bulgarian pact by Sergei Sazonov, the new Russian foreign minister. Undeterred by Sazonov's disclaimer about the purposes and scope of the Balkan alliance, Poincaré immediately realized its full import. But even if Poincaré hedged his support for Russia with qualifications, his remarks signaled a departure from previous French policy. His predecessors sought to safeguard French investments in the Ottoman Empire by conserving its territorial integrity; Poincaré's policy on the other hand was determined not by tradition, financial interests, or the dynamics of the Eastern Question, but by his view of the requirements of the Franco-Russian alliance and the Franco-German antagonism.

a)   *Serb-Bulgarian Alliance, 29 February/13 March 1912*

[Secret Art. 1:] In the event of internal troubles arising in Turkey which might endanger the state or the national interests of the contracting parties, or of either of them; or in the event of internal or external difficulties of Turkey raising the question of the maintenance of the status quo in the Balkan peninsula, the contracting party which first arrives at the conclusion that, in consequence of all this, military action has become indispensable must make a reasoned proposal to the other party, which is bound immediately to enter into an exchange of views and, in the event of a disagreement, must give to the proposing party a reasoned reply.

Should an agreement favorable to action be reached, it will be communicated to Russia, and if the latter power is not opposed to it, military operations will begin as previously arranged, the parties being guided in everything by the sentiment of solidarity and community of their interests. In the opposite case, when no agreement has been reached, the parties will appeal to the opinion of Russia, which . . . will be binding. . . .

—Hurst, 2:819–22

b)   *Greek-Bulgarian Alliance, 16/29 May 1912*

Art. 1: If, notwithstanding the sincere wish of the two high contracting parties and efforts of their governments to avoid all aggression or provocation against Turkey, one of the parties should be attacked by Turkey, either on its territory or through systematic disregard of its rights, based on treaties or on the fundamental principles of international law, the two contracting parties undertake to assist each other with all their armed forces, and not to conclude peace except by joint agreement.

—Hurst, 2:825–27

c)   ***Franco-Russian Naval Convention, 3/16 July 1912***

Art. 1: The naval forces of France and Russia shall cooperate in all eventualities to which the alliance applies and in which it stipulates joint action by the land armies.

Art. 2: The cooperation of the naval forces will be prepared [in advance] in peacetime. . . .

—Hurst, 2:827–28; *DDF,* 3rd Series, 3:206

d)   ***Sazonov to Nicholas II, 4/17 August 1912***

. . . We informed, in confidence, the French government of the Serb-Bulgarian treaty. M. Poincaré showed some concern about its existence. Though he welcomed the treaty as contributing to the military power of these Balkan states, he considers it to have more of an aggressive than a defensive character and sees in this a strong danger, as complications in the Balkans are possible at any moment. . . .

M. Poincaré felt bound to emphasize that French public opinion would not permit the French government to commit itself to military measures on behalf of purely Balkan affairs, unless Germany were involved and its initiatives would bring about a *casus foederis.* In the latter case we could of course count on France meeting its obligations punctiliously and completely.

For my part I explained to the French prime minister that we are always ready to stand decisively at the side of France in circumstances for which our alliance provides, but that we could not justify to our public opinion active participation in military operations caused by some colonial, extra-European matter, unless France's vital interests in Europe were affected. . . .

—Friedrich Stieve (ed.), *Der diplomatische Schriftwechsel Iswolskis, 1911–1914* (Berlin, 1926), 2:401

e)   ***Serb-Montenegrin Alliance, 23 September/6 October 1912***

. . . Art. 2: . . . the Kingdom of Serbia and the Kingdom of Montenegro pledge to aid each other with their entire strength should Austria-Hungary attempt to annex, occupy or even temporarily hold with its army a part of Turkey-in-Europe, and should one of the contracting parties regard this as contrary to its vital interests. . . .

Art. 4: Inasmuch as the governments of the Kingdom of Serbia and the Kingdom of Montenegro regard the present situation in Turkey and general conditions in Europe as very favorable for action aimed at the liberation of Serbs under the Turkish yoke, they have agreed that war should be declared upon Turkey at the latest by 1 October [o.S.] of the current year. . . .

—Hurst, 2:828–30

11.18   **CONVERGING TRACKS, II: THE BALKAN CRISIS, THE AUSTRO-GERMAN ALLIANCE, AND THE STRENGTHENING OF THE ANGLO-FRENCH ENTENTE, NOVEMBER-DECEMBER 1912**

Wilhelm II to Kiderlen, November 1912 ● *Grey to Cambon, 22 November 1912* ● *Bethmann in the Reichstag, 2 December 1912* ● *Lichnowsky to Bethmann, 3 December 1912* ● *Lichnowsky to Bethmann, 4 December 1912* ● *Gwynne's Notes of a Briefing at the Foreign Office, 4 December 1912* ● *Kiderlen to Lichnowsky, 6 December 1912*

The collapse of Turkey-in-Europe in the first weeks of the Balkan war aggravated the tension, already acute, between Austria and Russia. The remaining Great Powers were captives of the general temptation to see in the twin Balkan and Austro-Russian crises the litmus test of their alliances; because of this self-inflicted pressure, none could evade taking a stance. The danger of a larger conflagration, however, was reduced when the powers agreed on a conference of their ambassadors to convene in London on 17 December 1912.

The diplomatic activity of the powers in the fall of 1912 was rounded off by an Anglo-French exchange of notes on 22 November. In themselves, and when viewed in the isolated framework of Anglo-French relations, these notes take on an almost anodyne quality; only when they are considered in the larger context of the eastern European crisis does their significance—that is, the interpretation that Grey was about to give them—become fully apparent.

These three intertwined problems—the Balkans, the Austro-Russian crisis, and the Anglo-French notes—require some further elucidation. In the Balkans, the most pressing issue was the Serb occupation of the central Albanian coastline. For Austria, the Serb presence at the mouth of the Adriatic raised the specter of a Serb port at the very spot where Austria's maritime vulnerability was greatest. To bar Serbia from the sea, Austria—otherwise no champion of the self-determination of peoples—insisted on the creation of an independent Albania incorporating as many Albanians as possible. The Austrian demand was made more palatable for Serbia by Austria's acquiescence in the Serb annexation of Kossovo province, which, though primarily inhabited by Albanians, was the focal point of Serb nationalism.[72] Austria was also resigned to the partition of the Sanjak of Navibazar (which it had garrisoned from 1878 to 1908) between Serbia and Montenegro, thereby giving these two Serb-speaking states a common border.

The haggling over the future of the western Balkans unfolded against the backdrop of a deepening Austro-Russian crisis. A Russian "trial mobilization" in the Warsaw military district in September was followed by Austria's decision to increase its military strength in Dalmatia and Bosnia-Herzegovina. In early November, Russia postponed the scheduled release of 375,000 conscripts; on 21 November, Austria responded with a mobilization of its forces in Galicia. The cycle of escalation came to an end when, in a session of the Russian crown council on 23 November, Prime Minister Kokovzev resisted pressure from the Russian military to order a partial mobilization in the military districts adjoining Austria-Hungary but could not rescind the earlier Russian measures.

In Germany, the Kaiser and Bethmann arrived at rather different conclusions as to how Austria-Hungary would be affected by the events in the Balkans. While the Kaiser's attitude was remarkably dispassionate, Bethmann felt the need to allay Austrian doubts about Germany's fidelity in a speech to the Reichstag on 2 December. Bethmann's remarks drew

[72]As a result of the battle of Kossovo in 1389, the kingdom of Serbia became an Ottoman vassal state.

immediate notice in England, and both Haldane and Grey referred to the speech in separate conversations with the German ambassador. Both ministers' warnings about the European implications of the Balkan crisis were notable for their mix of precision and imprecision: Grey and Haldane were firm about Britain's attitude if France became involved in a European war originating from a conflict in the Balkans but showed little concern about how, under what circumstances, or at whose beckoning France might enter the fray.

These remarks give insight into Grey's and Haldane's understanding of the range of contingencies covered by the Anglo-French notes of 22 November. Grey's letter to Paul Cambon, the French ambassador in London, was a belated response to Cambon's attempts, pursued with fine consistency ever since the First Moroccan crisis, to get the Foreign Office to render more precise the British commitment to France. Because the letter was written with the approval of the cabinet—a departure from previous practice—and because the wording avoided a specific commitment, Grey's critics in the cabinet fancied that they had scored a victory. But they erred in this assumption, for the letter, in its last paragraph, expanded rather than reduced Britain's political commitment to its French ally.

Did the British government retain all of its options? First, the assumption that the Anglo-French staff talks and naval convention (Documents 11.14 and 11.16) were somehow nonpolitical or did not express policy is naive at best or, at worst, aims to deceive. Second, the question can be answered with reference to Haldane's and Grey's conversations with the German ambassador. Third, one can only wonder whether it was judicious to time this exchange of notes so that it would coincide with the height of the Austro-Russian tension over the Balkans.

a) *Wilhelm II to Kiderlen, November 1912*

[7 November:] . . . There is no question that for Vienna many of the changes in the Balkans brought about by the war are uncomfortable and even undesirable, but none is so radical that because of it we have to expose ourselves to the danger of becoming embroiled in war—that is something for which I could not answer to my people or my conscience. It was completely different in 1908—at issue then was an integral part [sic!] of Austria, which had long been joined to it. . . .

[9 November:] . . . under no circumstances will I march on Paris and Moscow for Albania and Durazzo. Have suggested: an independent Albania ruled by a Serb prince with the freedom to enter alliances with the four [Balkan] allies, with permission [for Serbia] to use a port. . . .

—*GP*, 33:12339, 12348

b) *Grey to Cambon, 22 November 1912*

From time to time in recent years the French and British naval and military experts have consulted together. It has always been understood that such consultation does not restrict the freedom of either Government to decide at any future time whether or not to assist the other by armed force. We have agreed that consultation between experts is not, and ought not to be regarded as an engagement that commits either Government to action in a contingency that has not arisen and may never arise. The disposition, for instance, of the French and British fleets respectively at the present moment is not based upon an engagement to co-operate in war.[73]

You have, however, pointed out that, if either Government had grave reason to expect an unprovoked attack by a third Power, it might become essential to know whether it could in that event depend upon the armed assistance of the other.

I agree that, if either Government had grave reason to expect an unprovoked attack by a third Power, or something that threatened the general peace, it should immediately discuss with the other, whether both Governments should act together to prevent aggression and to preserve peace, and if so what measures they would be prepared to take in common. If these measures involved action, the plans of the General Staffs would at once be taken into consideration, and the Governments would then decide what effect should be given to them.

—*BD*, 10ii:416

c)   ***Bethmann in the Reichstag, 2 December 1912***

. . . When we realized that the [Balkan] struggle was inevitable, we sought to localize it. This has up to now been accomplished and I can express the certain hope that this will continue to be the case [bravo!]. The events in the Balkans do not affect us directly, and in some ways our interests take second place to those of other powers. But we, like the other powers, are entitled to take part in determining the new order which will emerge from the present war, for we very much have a direct interest in the economic future of the Balkans [quite correct!]: I refer to upholding the guarantees for the bondholders of the Turkish debt. In addition, we will add our voice to that of our allies in the settling of various questions [quite correct!]. . . . If, in the process, there arise irreconcilable differences—which is something we hope will not occur—it will be a matter for those powers most directly affected to look after their own interests. This holds true also for our allies. But if, contrary to all expectations, they are attacked by third powers as they assert their interests, and are thereby threatened in their existence, then we will have to be true to our obligations and will in a determined manner take their side [lively applause, right, in the Center, and among the National Liberals]. And in so doing we would fight for the maintenance of our own position in Europe, for the defense of our own future and security [bravo! right, in the Center and among the National Liberals]. . . .

—Reichstag, 286:2471–72

d)   ***Lichnowsky[74] to Bethmann, 3 December 1912[75]***

. . . [Haldane argued that] England was certainly peaceable and noone here wanted war, at the very least for economic reasons. But in the event of a general European

---

[73]See Document 11.15.
[74]Karl Max, Prince Lichnowsky (1860–1928). German ambassador in London, 1912–1914.
[75]With annotations by Wilhelm II.

confusion which could result from an Austrian invasion of Serbia if Serbia did not voluntarily evacuate its forces from the Adriatic coast, it would not be probable that Great Britain could remain a silent spectator [*Expected by noone. They will help the Gauls*].

I replied that I did not want to ask him directly whether this meant that England would then proceed against us in a hostile manner [*of course*]. He replied that this would not be an inevitable but a probable consequence of a war between the two continental groupings. The roots of English policy, he said, could be found in the impression which was widespread here that the balance between the groups had to be pretty much maintained [*this will change!*]. Therefore, England could under no circumstances tolerate the annihilation of the French [*they may not have a choice*]. . . . Should Germany be dragged into the conflict by Austria and would thus get into a war with France, currents would be created in England which no government could resist and which would lead to incalculable results [*right; already counted on by us*]. The theory of the balance of groups after all was an axiom [*it is an imbecility! and will make England our enemy, eternally*] of England's foreign policy and has led to its association with France and Russia. He could vouchsafe that the best relations with Germany were desired [*completely futile in light of these conceptions*]. . . .

—*GP*, 39:15612

e)   ***Lichnowsky to Bethmann, 4 December 1912***

. . . He [Grey] feared that the chancellor's speech—which he was surprised to say at this early stage referred to the possibility of a war between the continental groupings—, . . . led him to ask me whether I had the impression that it could be interpreted to mean that we will give our backing to Austria-Hungary in all eventualities and for all steps which it believed it had to take to safeguard its interests, issuing it, so-to-speak, a blank cheque. He feared that such far-reaching support for Austrian policies would endanger our joint goal, the maintenance of peace and moderation on both sides, and would fortify Austria's desire to resist. . . . [Grey] said that he was concerned that the situation of 1909[76] would not be repeated. He was convinced, and he repeated this sentence twice with special emphasis, that Russia would prefer to take up arms rather than beat a second retreat. Therefore everything in the question of a Serb port hinged on things turning out in such a way that neither of the two Great Powers would be forced to give in . . . . If a European war were caused by an Austrian intervention against Serbia and if [Russia] were forced—by its public opinion and to avoid a humiliation like the one of 1909—to invade Galicia which would cause us to assist [Austria], then the involvement of France was unavoidable and the further consequences could not be foretold. . . .

—*GP*, 33:12481

[76]See Document 11.12.

f)   ***Gwynne's***[77] ***Notes of a Briefing at the Foreign Office,***
4 December 1912

As things are at present, Russia while not being ready for war, has been backing Serbia very strongly and in consequence making Austria angry. What our people fear is that Austria may become menacing and that Germany will go to St. Petersburg and propose holding Austria in, if Russia will leave the entente. This is the real danger of the situation—not a conflict of the powers. We are sincerely afraid lest out of the hurly burly of the crisis Russia should emerge on the side of the [Triple] Alliance.

Our policy therefore is to try and make Austria and Russia settle matters between them without any interference from outside. This, however, is difficult because Sazonov is a fool. He created a Frankenstein—in the shape of the Balkan League—and now cannot control it.

If we can succeed in getting the two powers to settle matters themselves, we are prepared to keep the ring for them and to be very strong in doing so. Grey has Cabinet permission to tell Germany that if she bumps in, it will mean war! And Lloyd George is heart and soul in this policy!

Meanwhile all the Powers are working very nicely together. Failing—at any rate for the present—to secure cooperation between Austria and Russia, England has prevented the powers from falling into Alliance and Entente lines. . . .

—Keith M. Wilson, "The British Démarche of 3 and 4 December 1912: H. A. Gwynne's Note on Britain, Russia, and the First Balkan War," *Slavonic and East European Review* 62 (1984), 556–57

g)   ***Kiderlen to Lichnowsky, 6 December 1912***

. . . Sir Edward Grey still seems to think that we had used threats to force Russia to retreat in the Bosnian crisis. This assertion has long been proven wrong and this would be public fact if Izvolski had not consistently refused publication of all documents, which at the time we repeatedly requested.

Now as then noone contemplates forcing Russia to retreat. The dealings of the Danube Monarchy are exclusively with Serbia, where, as its immediate neighbor, it has the kind of special interests which France in its day claimed in Morocco by virtue of its possession of Algeria; England in Syria or Arabia by virtue of its Egyptian interests. Grey himself has recognized the patience and moderation with which Austrian government asserts its interests despite continuing Serb provocations. It has tolerated [the Serb] occupation of the Sanjak, conquest of Macedonia, military advance to the Adriatic. . . . Russia is not expected to sacrifice interests or prestige. But it can also be expected that tsarist empire will not hinder Austria in the defense of its existence and prestige. This kind of natural reserve would be tantamount to a retreat only if Russia had already committed itself to backing, in an anti-Austrian sense, exaggerated Serb demands. This is not the case according to credible assurances from the Petersburg

[77]Howell Arthur Gwynne (1865–1950). Editor of the conservative *Morning Post,* 1911–1937.

cabinet. If it were the case, then the onus of provocation would surely not rest on Austria.

—*GP*, 33:12482

11.19   HEIGHTENED GERMAN ANXIETIES: WILHELM II'S "WAR COUNCIL," 8 DECEMBER 1912

Diary Entry by Admiral von Müller, 8 December 1912 • *Bethmann to Eisendecher, 20 December 1912* • *Eisendecher to Wilhelm II, 23 December 1912*

Haldane's and Grey's remarks (preceding document) to the German ambassador in London—and a similar comment by King George V to the Kaiser's brother, Prince Henry of Prussia—left Wilhelm shaken. Deeply impressed by what he read, he summoned Tirpitz; the chief of the Prussian general staff, Moltke; and the chief of his naval cabinet to a conference, an event that Bethmann (who had been excluded from this gathering), with a touch of sarcasm, dubbed a "war council."

Historians continue to debate whether the conference of 8 December 1912 presents conclusive evidence for the Kaiser's determination to wage war. Certainly this view derives strength from what the Kaiser actually said; moreover, there is an uncanny coincidence between Tirpitz's remark that the navy would not be ready for war for another year and a half (i.e., after the widening of the Kiel canal, completed in June 1914) and the outbreak of war in August 1914. But it can also be argued that the meeting neither reflected a settled purpose nor set government policy. The conference was not attended by Bethmann, Kiderlen, or Josias von Heeringen, the Prussian minister of war; its prescriptions were vague and fell short of the kind of detailed planning an imminent war would require; and, finally, Wilhelm's previous (Document 11.18) and subsequent vacillation (Documents 11.21 and 11.22) on the merits of a war over the Balkans sheds doubt on the firmness of his resolve.

The historiographical debate on the "war council" focuses not just on the meeting itself but also on Bethmann's policy in the aftermath of this conference. There is general agreement that Bethmann's exertions on behalf of an army bill and his fight against further appropriations for the navy once again signaled his desire for closer Anglo-German relations. But historians differ on whether he pursued an Anglo-German rapprochement on its own merits or solely for the purpose of detaching Britain from the Franco-Russian alliance (against which German land armaments were directed). Whether either strategy was feasible of course hinged on the attitude of the Foreign Office (Documents 11.18 and 11.21b). In light of the documents in this chapter, the question deserves to be raised whether the Kaiser's assessment of the Anglo-German relationship—at least for the duration of Grey's tenure in the Foreign Office—was not, after all, more realistic than Bethmann's.

a)   *Diary Entry by Admiral von Müller[78], 8 December 1912*

Sunday. Called to His Majesty at 11 a.m. with Tirpitz, Heeringen (vice-Admiral), and General von Moltke. H.M [discusses] telegraphic report of the ambassador in London,

---

[78]Georg Alexander von Müller (1854–1940). German admiral; chief of Wilhelm II's naval cabinet, 1906–1918.

Prince Lichnowsky, about the political situation.[79] Haldane, as Grey's mouthpiece, told Lichnowsky that if we attacked France, England would unconditionally assist France because England could not tolerate that the balance of power in Europe would be disturbed. H.M. welcomes this communication as a desirable clarification of the situation for the benefit of those who had felt sure of England due to the recent friendliness of the press.

H.M. has sketched the following situation: Austria must deal energetically with the foreign Slavs (the Serbs), otherwise it will lose control over the Slavs of the Austro-Hungarian monarchy. If Russia supports the Serbs—which it evidently does (Sazonov's declaration that Russia will immediately invade Galicia if Austria does the same to Serbia), then war would be unavoidable for us too. But we could hope to have on our side Bulgaria and Romania and also Albania, possibly also Turkey. Bulgaria has already offered an alliance to Turkey. We have encouraged the Turks in this direction. H.M. had recently tried to encourage the crown prince of Romania, who was passing through on his way from Brussels, to come to an understanding with Bulgaria. If these states join Austria, then we are free to wage war against France with full force. Of course the navy has to be prepared for a war against England. The scenario discussed by the Chief of the Admiralty Staff in his last report, [i.e.] a war against Russia alone, is—after Haldane's statement—no longer a possibility. Therefore immediate submarine warfare against English troop transports in the Scheldt or near Dunkirk, mine warfare in the Thames. To Tirpitz: accelerated construction of U-boats, etc. Recommends a conference of all interested naval authorities. General von Moltke: "I think a war to be unavoidable [and the sooner the better].[80] But we should through the press better lay the groundwork for popularizing a war against Russia, in the vein of the Kaiser's analysis." H.M. confirms this and told the state secretary [Tirpitz] to use some of his means [for influencing] the press in this direction. Tirpitz observes that the navy would prefer to see the great struggle postponed by about one and one half years. Moltke said that the navy would not be ready even then and the situation for the army was getting more and more unfavorable because our opponents were arming more rapidly than we, as we were very short of money.

That was the end of the meeting. The result was about zero.

The chief of the general staff [Moltke] says: war the sooner the better, but he does not draw the logical conclusion from this, which is to present Russia or France or both with an ultimatum which unleashes the war with right on our side. . . .

Wrote in the afternoon to the chancellor about the influencing of the press.

—John C. G. Röhl, "An der Schwelle zum Weltkrieg: Eine Dokumentation über den 'Kriegsrat' vom 8. Dezember 1912," *Militärgeschichtliche Mitteilungen* 10 (1977), 100

b)   *Bethmann to Eisendecher,[81] 20 December 1912*

. . . Haldane's explanation to Lichnowsky was not all that serious. He only repeated what we already knew: that England now, as before, pursues a balance of power pol-

[79]Document 11.18d.
[80]The words in brackets were inserted later by Müller.
[81]Karl von Eisendecher (1841–1934). German admiral; Prussian minister to Baden, 1884–1914.

icy and will therefore side with France if the latter is in danger of being annihilated in a war with us. H.M.—who, despite the policy which he pursues, demands that England embrace us—got terribly agitated; immediately held a war council with his loyal followers from army and navy, of course behind my and Kiderlen's back; ordered the preparation of an army *and* a *navy* appropriations bill; and trumpeted all that far and wide, including a fantastically embellished [version of the] Haldane conversation. Indeed, I suspect that a consequence of this year's naval amendment was—apart from the Canadian dreadnoughts—an even closer cooperation between England and France. If H.M., in unison with Tirpitz, wants to make that bond even more indestructible, he will have no difficulty in accomplishing this by way of a new naval amendment. But if we pursue a skilled policy I don't see anything threatening in Haldane's remarks. In the present [Balkan] crisis, England has worked very loyally and cordially with us and has had a calming influence, particularly with Russia. It does not want a continental war in which it might get caught up, but it would prefer not to have to fight one. In this vein there might even be something positive in its obligations toward France. But we should not carry on a nervous jerky policy [*Hampelmannpolitik*], because there is always a chance that the patience of the others may snap. . . .

—Röhl, "Dokumentation," 124–25

c)   ***Eisendecher to Wilhelm II, 23 December 1912***

. . . I cannot share Your Majesty's view that England wants to be our enemy and that, accordingly, we have to take special precautions. On the contrary, Haldane's remarks, now that I have gotten to know their content, do not strike me as hostile. Just now we seem to have a good chance to get a normal relationship underway; we are well along and should develop this further. Sooner or later the two great Germanic nations of Europe will have to stand together, or the Slavs, Yankees, and finally the yellow race are destined to get the upper hand. The time should soon come for all of western Europe to unite, led by Germany and England. The Triple Alliance and the Triple Entente are a fact for the time being, but are also transitory and in part not very logical phenomena.

. . . [A] new German naval amendment would probably be the most suitable way of bringing about a conflict and to transform the entente into a real alliance. Noone will object if we flesh out the gaps in our naval construction program and especially if we make the additions to our army which are necessary in light of the enormous military development of France, but I think a new large expansion of the fleet is justified only if we want a war. . . .

—Röhl, "Dokumentation," 127

11.20   # THE ARMS RACE ON LAND, 1913

Izvolski to Sazonov, January–February 1913 ● *The Introduction of the Three-Year Law in the French Chamber, 6 March 1913* ● *Izvolski to Sazonov, 28 February/13 March 1913* ● *Esher to Brett, March 1913* ● *Note by Bethmann, 17 March 1913* ● *Bethmann in the Reichstag, April 1913* ● *French Aide-Mémoire to the Russian Foreign Ministry, 11/24 August 1913* ● *Ninth Franco-Russian Staff Conference, August 1913*

In May 1912, the Reichstag voted to increase the German army by twenty-nine thousand. Six months later, the collapse of the Ottoman Empire in the first days of the Balkan war, Russia's "trial mobilization" in the Warsaw military district, and its decision to delay the scheduled discharge of about 400,000 recruits all convinced the German military of the need for a larger increase. The Kaiser's panic in December 1912 (Document 11.19) gave a further impetus to proceed. By early March 1913, the internal squabbling between the general staff (which had demanded 300,000 additional troops) and the Prussian ministry of war (which was content with 138,000) was resolved in favor of the latter; nonetheless, the proposed increase was the largest ever. The Reichstag acted speedily on the pertinent legislation (introduced on 7 April) and passed it on 30 June.

The French national revival in the wake of the Second Moroccan crisis has already been noted (Document 11.17). It was epitomized by the formation of a government under Raymond Poincaré in January 1912 and his subsequent election, in January 1913, to the French presidency. The strategic counterpart to this electoral phenomenon was the decision by the French general staff to abandon the defensive orientation of Plan XVI in favor of an offensive strategy, to be embodied in the next plan. Approved by the war ministry in May 1913, Plan XVII depended on simultaneous Franco-Russian offensives against Germany and a quantitative edge on the Franco-German border. An increase in German manpower, however, would undo this second premise. As the French army already drafted a high percentage of eligible nineteen-year-olds (83 percent as opposed to Germany's 58 percent), any increase in the German army could only be offset by raising the term of service for French conscripts from two to three years. Anticipating the formal announcement of the German army increases, the government of Aristide Briand[82] proposed the three-year law to the chamber on 6 March 1913. After an acrimonious rite of passage that bitterly divided the French left, it was approved by the chamber on 19 July and by the senate on 7 August.

Given that the "class" of 1913 was the first to be affected, the law's impact on the peace-time strength of the French army would not be felt until 1915–1916. But the parliamentary elections of April–May 1914 put even this outcome in doubt: while the nationalist revival fizzled, the parties hostile to the law scored a resounding victory. Much of Poincaré's time during his visit to Russia in July 1914 (Document 12.6) was apparently spent reassuring Russian statesmen that they need not fear a repeal.

The large-scale Russian military reorganization that followed the Bosnian crisis (Document 11.12) was to be capped by the "Great Program" of 1913. A legislative package was approved by Tsar Nicholas II on 4 November 1913; the Duma, however, was slow to act and passed the relevant laws only on 7 July 1914 (cf. Document 12.3). The objectives of the "Great Program" became apparent in the meetings of the chiefs of the French and Russian general staff in August 1913. Equally apparent on this occasion was the French role in prodding Russia along, of which the most visible public manifestation had been Delcassé's appointment as ambassador in Petersburg, a post he held from March 1913 to January 1914.

Finally, in evaluating the documents below, the reader is invited to correlate the escalating arms race of 1913 with the ongoing crisis in the Balkans (Documents 11.21 and 11.22).

---

[82]Aristide Briand (1862–1932). French prime minister, 1909–1911, 1913, 1915–1917, 1921–1922, 1925–1926, 1929; foreign minister, 1925–1932. Principal French advocate of a policy of reconciliation with Germany in the 1920s.

a)   *Izvolski[82a] to Sazonov, January–February 1913*

[17/30 January:] The election of M. Poincaré to the highest office in the republic signifies a decisive victory of political moderation over the extreme radicalism which has always been so hostile to Russia and the Franco-Russian alliance. . . . From long conversations with [Poincaré and Jonnart[83]], I have reached the following conclusions: the French government is determined to fulfill its obligations under the alliance to their fullest extent and admits consciously and in cold blood that the results of the present complications may bring about the necessity of France's participation in a general war. The moment when France will draw its saber are specified by the Franco-Russian military convention and in this regard there is not the least doubt or hesitation among the French ministers. On the other hand, the French government has to take into account the mood in parliament and of public opinion; both of these consider the events on the Balkan peninsula to be alien, touching upon the vital interests of France only indirectly. . . . [T]he French government in no way wants to deprive Russia of its freedom of action or to question its moral obligations to the Balkan states. Consequently, Russia can count not only on the armed support of France in the circumstances specified by the Franco-Russian convention, but also on its most effective and energetic diplomatic assistance for all measures of the Russian government on behalf of these states. . . .

[14/27 February:] According to [Poincaré], the events of the last eighteen months have brought about a sudden reversal in French public opinion, a new patriotic sentiment, the likes of which have not been experienced here for a long time. In this respect, the "coup of Agadir" had provided an immense service to France. The increase in the German army will have a perhaps equally beneficial effect, as it will prove the inconsistencies in the theories of the pacifists and the necessity for a more effective organization of the French army. . . . England was not bound to France by any specific engagements, but the tone and the character of the assurances given by the London cabinet permitted the French government to count, in the event of a conflict with Germany under the present circumstances, on England's armed support. The plans for Anglo-French military and naval[84] cooperation had been worked out in the most minute details. . . . On Balkan matters, M. Poincaré assured us again of his fullest support. . . .

—René Marchand (ed.), *Un livre noir* (Paris, n.d.), 2:18–22, 32–33; Friedrich Stieve (ed.),
Der diplomatische Schriftwechsel Iswolskis (Berlin, 1926), 3:711, 747

b)   *The Introduction of the Three-Year Law in the French Chamber, 6 March 1913*

[Étienne:[85]] I have the honor of presenting to the Chamber a piece of legislation aimed modifying the Law of 21 March 1905 [lively exclamations on the extreme left; repeated applause in the center, on the right; scattered applause on the left].

[82a]In 1910, Izvolski and Sazonov had switched posts, Izvolski becoming Russia's ambassador to France.
[83]Charles Jonnart (1857–1927). Minister of public works, 1893–1894. Replaced Poincaré as foreign minister (January–March 1913) after the latter's election to the presidency.
[84]Documents 11.14 and 11.16.
[85]Eugène Étienne (1844–1921), French colonial advocate. Minister of the interior, 1905; of war, 1906, 1913.

[Speaker:] Gentlemen! [commotion]

[Vaillant[85a]: We protest this criminal act! [dissent on the left, in the center, and on the right]

[Jaurès:[86]] This is folly!

[Colly:[86a]] Down with reactionaries! [commotion]

[de Gailhard-Bancel[86b]]: Vive la France!

[Plichon:[86c]] Down with the Commune!

[Vaillant:] This is a mortal blow aimed at the republic! [lively approval on the extreme left—commotion]

[Étienne:] You are the republicans and we are the reactionaries, that is understood [lively approval on the left, in the center, and on the right—interruptions and prolonged commotion on the extreme left].

[Jaurès:] This is a crime against the republic and against France! [approval on the extreme left—noise in the center, to the right, and scattered throughout the left]

[On the extreme left:] Down with war!

[Colly:] Down with reactionaries! Down with the provocateurs! [exclamations and noise in the center and on the right]

[In the center:] Order!

[Speaker:] Gentlemen, these interruptions are intolerable [commotion on the extreme left]. Listen to the minister of war!

[Étienne:] I have the honor of presenting to the Chamber a piece of legislation aiming to modify the Law of 21 March 1905, especially concerning the length of service in the active army [lively approval in the center, on the right, and scattered throughout the left—noise on the extreme left].

[Driant:[86d]] Vive la France!

[Several voices:] Read! read! [commotion on the extreme left]

[Speaker]: Now, gentlemen, allow the minister of war to read the proposal [lively approval on the left, in the center, and on the right].

[Jaurès:] Down with the Empire! [commotion]

[Colly:] Vive la république! Down with the reactionaries! [prolonged commotion on the extreme left]

[Speaker:] This is not the appropriate way to protest [lively interruptions and commotion on the extreme left]. If this tumult continues, I will be obliged to adjourn this sitting, and the responsibility will be yours! [approval—new interruptions from the extreme left]

[On the extreme left:] Vive la république!

[Émile-Dumas:[86e]] Down with Empire! Down with War!

[Speaker:] It is impossible for me . . . [lively interruptions on the extreme left and shouts: down with war!] Will you let me speak?! It is impossible for me to control these group outbursts [commotion on the extreme left]; but if they continue, certainly the Chamber will support me in assigning the responsibility for adjourning this

[85a]Edouard Vaillant (1840–1915). Socialist member from Seine.

[86] Jean Jaurès (1859–1914). French socialist leader and founder of L'Humanité. Assassinated on 31 July 1914.

[86a]Jean Colly (1858–1929). Socialist member from Seine.

[86b]Hyacinthe de Gailhard–Bancel (1869–1936). Right-wing member from Ardèche.

[86c]Jean Plichon (1863–1936). Right-wing member from the Nord.

[86d]Émile Driant (1855–1916). Member for Action liberale from Meurthe-et-Moselle; ex-major.

[86e]Émile Dumas (1873–1932). Socialist from Cher.

sitting to those who are carrying out these disturbances [lively approval on the left, in the center, and on the right—prolonged commotion on the extreme left].

[On the left and in the center:] No! no! No adjournment!

[On the extreme left:] Vive la république! Death to the Empire!

[In the center and on the right:] Introduce the bill! [commotion and interruptions on the extreme left]

[Étienne:] You will tire of this before I do, gentlemen [approval on the left, in the center, and on the right—commotion on the extreme left]. I will read the reasons for the bill [approval on the left, in the center, and on the right].

[Scattered voices:] Yes! yes! read! read!

[Étienne:] Gentlemen, it is the foremost duty of a responsible government to submit to you [lively interruptions on the extreme left—commotion] to submit to you, with the solutions that it requires, the military problem which France is presently facing [commotion on the extreme left].

[Colly:] War against War!

[Émile-Dumas:] War against draft evaders and shirkers!

[On the extreme left:] Reactionaries! Reactionaries! [commotion]

[On the right:] Treason! Treason!

[Speaker:] No, gentlemen, let the country hear them! [lively approval on the left, in the center, and on the right]

[On the extreme left:] Vive la république!

[Albert-Poulain:[86f]] We are republicans!

[Étienne:] You—republicans?? Yesterday's reactionaries! [approval on the left and in the center—commotion]

[Speaker:] Minister, please continue reading.

[Étienne, reading:] "In the present state of Europe. . ."

[Émile-Dumas:] Let's make war on the bourgeois who are never soldiers! Down with shirkers! Down with draft evaders! [commotion]

[Rognon:[86g]] Down with the Empire!

[Vaillant:] Down with the government! Down with war!

[In the center:] Vive la France!

[Étienne:] . . . [T]he peacetime strength must be such that it can meet all contingencies, especially those which may arise at the beginning of a modern war [interjections from the extreme left—good! good! on the left, in the center, on the right]. . . . This army needs veteran trained soldiers, and a suffecent number of them. . . . [C]ontrary to our hope, two years are not enough to allow recruits to acquire the necessary instruction and training [commotion on the extreme left]. . . . There is only one solution to the problem, namely: the simultaneous presence of three classes under the colors which will give France a peacetime strength which is necessary for our protection and for our security while mobilizing. . . . Once the three-year service is in effect, we will be able to increase peacetime strength by about 160,000. . . .

Art. 1: . . . "provides for 28 years [of service]. . . ."

Art. 12: . . . "Every Frenchman called to military service will successively participate in: the active army for three years; the active army reserve, eleven years; the territorial army, seven years; the reserve territorial army, seven years. . . ."

—Chambre des députés, *Journal officiel* du 6 mars 1913, 815–18

[86f]Albert Poulain (1866–1916). Socialist from the Ardennes.
[86g]Etienne Rognon (b. 1869). Socialist from Rhône.

c)   ***Izvolski to Sazonov, 28 February/13 March 1913***

As you know, M. Delcassé is particularly well versed not only in questions of foreign policy but also in everything which concerns naval and military matters. According to our military attaché, he has been instructed to convince our military authorities of the necessity to expand our strategic railroads in order to accelerate the deployment of our army on the western border. . . . He is also authorized to offer Russia the necessary financial support. . . .

—Stieve, *Schriftwechsel*, 3:762

d)   ***Esher to Brett,[86h] March 1913***

[12 March:] . . . You see that the Prime Minister denied yesterday[87] that there was an "arrangement" with France. Of course there is no treaty or convention, but how we can get out of the commitments of the General Staff with honor, I cannot understand. It seems all so shifty to me.
    [13 March:] . . . The mood of the French has changed. Delcassé at Petersburg. Poincaré at the Élysée. All this makes the situation a bit of a strain.

—*Journals and Letters of Reginald, Viscount Esher*, op. cit., 3:122

e)   ***Note by Bethmann, 17 March 1913***

. . . On 13 October 1912 H.M. demanded a military appropriations bill but desisted when the minister of war and the chief of the general staff objected. The two military authorities changed their mind after the collapse of Turkey. On 2 December 1912, the minister of war—without a direct order from H.M., but with my concurrence—asked [his ministry] to draw up the outlines of a military bill. . . . On 5 January, I suggested to H.M. that we proceed later in the spring with a large increase for the army, on condition that there would be no naval bill and provided that by then the Balkan crisis has simmered down. H.M. expressly agreed with both [conditions].

—*GP*, 39:15634

f)   ***Bethmann in the Reichstag, April 1913***

[7 April:] . . . I have every reason to believe that the present French government wants to live in a state of good neighbourly peace with us. . . . No-one can even imagine the dimension of a global conflagration, the destruction and the misery that it

---

[86h]Maurice Brett, Esher's younger son.
[87] See Document 11.24d.

will visit on all peoples. All wars of the past will be child's play in comparison [correct! among the National Liberals]. No responsible statesman will frivolously put the fuse to the powderkeg. The inclination to do so has decreased. But what has increased is the power of public opinion and within public opinion the pressure exercised by those who are the most vocal. These tend to be in the minority, not majority [correct! among the National Liberals]. . . . Beyond the Vosges, there exists a chauvinistic literature which speaks with justifiable pride of this [French] army, but does so for the purpose of comparing it with the German army [and] in order to demonstrate our inferiority in a future war. While bragging about the superiority of French artillery, the lead of French aviators, the better training of the French footsoldier, these [writers] really visualize in their mind's eye masses of Russian cavalry and infantry overwhelming our country. Gentlemen, in all this there is much illusion. But hostage to such illusions, France once started a war against us . . . Together with the astounding development of the economy of Russia—a giant country with inexhaustible resources [correct! on the right]—, there is taking place a reorganization of the army never before experienced in Russia, in terms of numbers, equipment, organization, speed in the transition from peacetime to wartime strength [hear! hear! on the right]. France has long surpassed us in terms of utilizing the conscript potential of its population. For years it has been drafting every last man and now France is poised to strengthen itself more through the introduction of a three year term of service. I do not see this as a challenge, just as our legislation is not supposed to be a provocation of our western neighbor [correct! on the right and among the National Liberals]. . . .

[9 April:] . . . I want to counter the way in which some speakers have interpreted my remarks about German-Slav differences. I spoke of Pan-Slav currents: I could not avoid doing so, as they play a marked role in the present Balkan crisis [correct! on the right]. From these [currents], some writers have inferred a future conflagration between Slavs and Germans. I am vehemently opposed to this slogan. I have often warned against its use, and I again repeat my warning today with the greatest of emphasis [very good! on the right]. The slogan . . . does damage to the policy which I intend to pursue and which has as its object good neighbourly relations with Russia. . . .

—Reichstag, 289:4512–14, 4521, 4609

g)   *French Aide-Mémoire to the Russian Foreign Ministry,*
11/24 August 1913

. . . The conditions under which the Imperial [Russian] government can obtain annual loans of four to five hundred million francs in the form of state loans or loans guaranteed by the state for a program of railroad construction throughout the empire are:

1) The construction of strategic lines, which will be undertaken in agreement with the French general staff, will commence immediately.

2) The peacetime strength of the Russian army will be increased considerably. . . .

—*Livre noir*, 2:442–43; Stieve, *Schriftwechsel*, 3:1030

b)   ***Ninth Franco-Russian Staff Conference, August 1913***

. . . Art. 3: . . . The putting into effect of the German military law of 1913 will have for its principal consequence to shorten the delays in the mobilization of the German army. This army can then have more time than in the past to operate against France before turning against Russia. The Allies' plan ought then to be to strive to attack simultaneously on both sides at once, while exercising the maximum of combined efforts. General Joffre declares that France will engage on her northeastern frontier nearly all her forces, of which the number will exceed by more than 200,000 that stipulated in the text of the Convention [1,300,000; cf. Document 10.4]; that the deployment of the troops on the frontier will be ended, for the most part, on the tenth day of mobilization; and that the offensive operations of these forces will begin on the eleventh day in the morning. General Zhilinskii declares that Russia will engage against Germany a group of forces of at least 800,000, of which the deployment on the Russo-German frontier will be completed for the most part on the fifteenth day of mobilization, and that the offensive operations of this group of forces will begin immediately after the fifteenth day. At the end of the year 1914 the completed deployment will be advanced by about two days. . . .

It is then essential that the French armies should have a marked numerical superiority over the German forces in the west. These conditions will easily be realized if Germany is under the obligation of guarding her eastern frontier with more forces. General Joffre states that, in light of these considerations, it would be advantageous for both armies if the Russian forces in the Warsaw district were already deployed in peacetime in such a manner that they formed a direct threat to Germany. General Zhilinskii states that the new organizational plan for the Russian army envisages the creation of an army corps for the Warsaw region. . . .

—*DDF*, 3rd Series, 8:79; *Livre noir*, 2:435–37

11.21   HEIGHTENED AUSTRIAN ANXIETIES, I: THE SCUTARI CRISIS

Wilhelm II to Franz Ferdinand, 26 February 1913 ● *Grey to Cartwright, 1 May 1913* ● *Sazonov to Hartwig, 23 April/6 May 1913*

The ambassadors of the Great Powers met in London on 17 December 1912 to deal with the problems created by the collapse of Ottoman rule in Europe. The goal of the conference was, first and foremost, to negotiate a new territorial order for the Balkans and, ultimately, to determine what portion of the Ottoman debt should be assigned to the successor states.

For the western Balkans, the conference sanctioned the Austro-Serb compromise that had been taking shape since late November 1912 (Document 11.18): in a rough exchange for Serbia's pledge to withdraw from central Albania, Austria acquiesced to the Serb annexation of Kossovo and the division of the Sanjak of Novibazar between Serbia and Montenegro. Moreover, this compromise allowed Austria and Russia to reach agreement on 11 March to demobilize their armies.

But the Balkan détente did not extend to the siege of Scutari, where an Ottoman garrison still held out against a combined Serb and Montenegrin force. When the London conference assigned Scutari to the nascent state of Albania, neither the Serb nor the Montenegrin government took notice, and the siege continued. The conference's decision to respond with a multinational naval blockade of the Montenegrin coast caused Serb forces to withdraw, but King Nikita of Montenegro could not yet be swayed to abandon Scutari. Its fall on 23 April 1913 and annexation by Montenegro six days later brought the issue to a head: Austria now announced its intent to act unilaterally if Montenegro continued to defy the conference. Anticipating an Austrian ultimatum, King Nikita on 5 May placed the fate of Scutari in the hands of the powers.

The documents excerpted here illustrate the stance taken by Germany, Britain, and Russia at various stages of the crisis. The Kaiser's letter to Archduke Franz Ferdinand raises the question of whether his outburst at the "war council" of 8 December (Document 11.19) did or did not reflect a settled purpose. The second excerpt shows that Grey's policy toward Britain's partners in the Triple Entente was endowed with the very consistency the Kaiser lacked and reveals once again the degree to which Grey was beholden to Russia and France.

The last excerpt looks beyond the Scutari crisis to the looming confrontation between Serbia and Bulgaria about their respective spoils in Macedonia. This dispute threatened to break apart the Balkan alliance that Russia had so laboriously forged in the spring of 1912 (Document 11.17). Within weeks, Bulgaria's preemptive attack on Serbia again embroiled the Balkans in war, as Greece, Romania, and even Turkey entered the fray on the side of the Serbs. Sazonov's advice to the Serb government should be seen in the context of the growing Serb-Bulgarian tension but is included here because of the clues which it offers about his long-term goals.

a)   *Wilhelm II to Franz Ferdinand, 26 February 1913*

. . . The present situation means a true calamity for the vast majority of people in Europe and environs. . . . I ask myself often whether the issues at stake here—for example the pastures for the goats of Scutari and similar things—are really important enough to justify you and Russia still facing each other half mobilized. . . .

—Robert A. Kann, "Emperor William II and Archduke Francis Ferdinand in Their Correspondence,"
American Historical Review 57 (1951/52), 345–46

b)   *Grey to Cartwright,[88] 1 May 1913*

. . . Whether separate action by Austria in the last resort, limited to action in Albania and the expulsion of the Montenegrins from Scutari, could be agreed to without breaking up the concert, I could not say. All I could do, if the time came when there was no alternative to separate action, would be to discuss the matter with France and Russia, to ascertain if there was any form of separate action to which it was possible to get Russia to agree. . . . It might be the spark that created a European conflagration, and if that occurred the question of Scutari, which would be the spark, would be completely lost sight of in the other issues that would be raised. In such an event, we

---

[88]Sir Fairfax Cartwright (1857–1928). British ambassador in Vienna, 1908–1913.

and other powers should have to consider, not the merits of the question of Scutari, but what our own interests required us to do in a European crisis. . . .

—*BD*, 9ii:926

c) **Sazonov to Hartwig,**[89] **23 April/6 May 1913**

. . . Serbia has only passed through the first phase of its historic destiny, and to reach its goal, it will yet need to sustain a terrible struggle which might put into question its entire existence. Serbia's promised land is in the territory of today's Austria-Hungary, not in what it now covets and where the way is blocked by the Bulgars. Under these circumstances it is in Serbia's vital interest to maintain the alliance with Bulgaria on one hand, and, on the other, to attain a state of readiness through persistent and patient work for the unavoidable struggle of the future. Time works for Serbia and towards the ruin of its enemies which are already marked by telltale signs of disintegration.

Explain all this to the Serbs! . . . A rupture between Bulgaria and Serbia is a triumph for Austria. This would postpone its agony by many years. . . .

—Milosh Bogicevic, *Die auswärtige Politik Serbiens* (Berlin, 1930), 2:807

11.22   HEIGHTENED AUSTRIAN ANXIETIES, II: SERBIA AND THE ALBANIAN CRISIS, OCTOBER 1913

Stolberg to the German Foreign Ministry, 15 October 1913 ● Zimmermann to Wedel, 16 October 1913 ● Berchtold to Storck, 17 October 1913 ● Stolberg to the German Foreign Ministry, 18 October 1913 ● Laffert to Bethmann, 22 November 1913

Bulgaria's defeat in the Second Balkan War, as sealed by the Treaty of Bucharest, put considerable strain on the Austro-German alliance. The Austro-Hungarian foreign minister, Count Leopold Berchtold, hoped to revise the Bucharest settlement in favor of Bulgaria, but the German foreign ministry blunted his initiative, arguing that intervention by one Great Power would set a precedent for the others to do the same. Moreover, Germany cared little for Bulgaria and preferred to cultivate Romania and Greece, both beneficiaries of the Bucharest peace.

This flutter in Austro-German relations subsided when another crisis over Albania pointed to an Austro-Serb showdown. Albanian bands had entered Kossovo to aid an insurgency of the local Albanian population against the transfer of their homeland from Ottoman to Serb rule. In hot pursuit of the Albanian bands, Serb forces seized territory that the London conference of ambassadors had already allocated to the new Albanian state. This fact allowed Austria, as it protested the renewed presence of Serb troops in Albania, to claim that it was merely acting on behalf of the powers represented at the London conference. The Austrian protests brought forth assurances from the Belgrade government that the Serb army would be

---

[89]Nicholas von Hartwig (d. 1914). Russian minister in Belgrade, 1911–1914.

withdrawn, but these rang hollow when it became clear that Serb forces showed no inclination to budge. Berchtold, his patience at an end, on 18 October forced the issue with an ultimatum that Serbia grudgingly accepted six days later.

Berchtold had scored a victory for the Habsburg monarchy, albeit at a price. The Serb, British, Russian, French, and Italian governments were all incensed, and even the German foreign ministry found fault with his procedure. But Berchtold's success in October 1913 may have convinced him, in the words of one recent historian, that Serbia "would only understand force."[90] In this sense, the Albanian crisis confirmed the lessons of Austria-Hungary's earlier dispute with Montenegro over Scutari (Document 11.21) and may well have provided a model for handling future Austro-Serb collisions.

a)   Stolberg[91] to the German Foreign Ministry, 15 October 1913

[Berchtold] wanted to tell me that Austria-Hungary was determined not to yield. According to the information he has received, Serbia apparently wants to force Austria-Hungary, by way of a Franco-Russian intrigue, to modify [Albania's] border in [Serbia's] favor. This would be a first step in Serbia's advance to the Adriatic and would endanger the creation of a viable Albania, which has already proven so difficult; the existence of Albania was necessary to contain the Slavs and to maintain the accord between Austria and Italy. Moreover, Austria-Hungary's yielding would be tantamount to its complete abdication; it would be fatal with regard to its own Southern Slavs, as a weakening of the monarchy would strengthen their centrifugal aspirations. In the event of Serbia's rejection, he would have to resort to extreme measures [*zum Aeussersten gehen müssen*] and had secured for this the unanimous agreement of the Austrian and Hungarian governments and also the concurrence of His Majesty the Emperor Franz Joseph. . . .

—*GP*, 36:14160

b)   Zimmermann[92] to Wedel,[93] 16 October 1913

. . . Enforcing decisions reached in London by Europe is a European matter. The English government, under whose chairmanship the London conference of ambassadors has been convened, has a prominent role to play when it comes to enforcing the decisions of the conference of ambassadors. Hence, it is desirable to air this matter without further delay in London and to urgently invite the English government to participate in the demarche to be made in Belgrade in order to prevent a unilateral Austrian step which may bring about European complications. It will be sufficient merely to inform Paris and Petersburg of the events which have come to pass. . . .

—*GP*, 36:14161

[90]Williamson, *Austria-Hungary and the Origins of the First World War*, 155.
[91]Wilhelm, Prince Stolberg-Wernigerode (1870–1931). German chargé in Vienna, 1912–1919.
[92]Arthur Zimmermann (1864–1940). Under state secretary in the German foreign ministry, 1911–1916; state secretary, 1916–1917.
[93]Botho, Count Wedel (1862–1943). Foreign ministry representative in the entourage of Wilhelm II.

c)   ***Berchtold to Storck,*** [94] ***17 October 1913***

The [Austro-Hungarian] I[mperial] and R[oyal] legation [in Belgrade] has had the honor of drawing, more than once, by order of its government the attention of the Royal [Serb] minister of foreign affairs to the necessity of strictly respecting the decision of the London conference of ambassadors and to abstain from all military action in the territory specified by the will of the powers in Albania. This point of view of the I. and R. government is, moreover, more justified given that the London conference has already taken into account, in a very broad sense and to the detriment of Albania, the desires formulated by Serbia on the subject of the border in question.

Austria-Hungary thus cannot consent that the international decision on the borders of Albania be further modified in favor of Serbia.

The last response given on this subject by the Royal Serb government to the I. and R. legation is no more satisfactory than the contents of the note given to the I. and R. ministry of foreign affairs by the Serb minister. In effect, the order that requires the Serb troops to halt their march cannot be considered sufficient. In the eyes of the I. and R. government it is indispensable that the Serb government proceed with the immediate recall of the troops which have crossed the borders fixed by the London conference and which, as a result, are occupying territories belonging to Albania. The I. and R. government is pleased to hope that the Serb government will not delay in proceeding to effect the complete evacuation of Albanian territory within eight days. In the event of non-observance, the I. and R. government will, to its great regret, have recourse to the appropriate means of assuring compliance [*réalisation*] with its demand.

—*OeU*, 7:8850

d)   ***Stolberg to the German Foreign Ministry, 18 October 1913*** [95]

. . . The strong stance taken by Germany . . . confirmed him [Berchtold] in his expectation that Serbia would comply with the eight-day time limit and would not allow matters to get beyond the brink. [*That would be very regrettable! Now or never! Order and calm must somehow be established down there!*]

—*GP*, 36:14176

e)   ***Laffert*** [96] ***to Bethmann, 22 November 1913***

. . . The Serbs are policing the border with a dense line of pickets who prevent all Albanians from returning. As soon as one crosses the border [into Albania], one en-

---

[94]Wilhelm von Storck (1868–1928). Austro-Hungarian chargé in Belgrade 1913–1914.
[95]With minute by Wilhelm II.
[96]German member of the military commission charged by the London conference with establishing the borders of northern Albania.

counters Albanians who plead with the commission to help them return to their villages, which is something we are regrettably not empowered to do. Dibra, only recently a town of 30,000 people, is completely deserted. Only a small Serb section is still inhabited. The buildings have not been destroyed, but all has been plundered.

The Serbs were very lucky that the Albanians staged their fateful insurrection. In declaring every Albanian a rebel and in gunning down without mercy everyone, armed or not, they caused this incredible panic which, at one fell swoop, allowed them to dispose of a burdensome population of 100,000. With ruthless intent and caring not one with about the philanthropic outcry of Europe, they drew what was from their vantage point the only right conclusion. . . .

—GP, 36:13999

11.23   HEIGHTENED RUSSIAN ANXIETIES: THE LIMAN VON SANDERS CRISIS

Contract between the Ottoman Government and Liman von Sanders, 27 November 1913 • Franco-Russian Protocols, 17/30 December 1913 • Sazonov to Nicholas II, 23 December 1913/5 January 1914 • Minutes of the Russian Cabinet, 30 December 1913/12 January 1914 • Memorandum by P. N. Durnovo, February 1914 • Pourtalès to Bethmann, 11 March 1914

Of all the Great Powers, Russia was most affected by the Italian decision in March 1912 to force an end to the Italo-Turkish war with a naval demonstration at the Dardanelles (Document 11.13). The subsequent closure of the Dardanelles by Turkey held up Russian seaborne grain exports; it also alerted Russian statesmen to the vulnerability of the Straits. Russian anxieties were again aroused by the Bulgarian threat to Constantinople—fleeting though it was—during the First Balkan War. Finally, Russian sensibilities were offended when the Ottoman government offered the command of the Constantinople army corps to the Prussian lieutenant-general Otto Liman von Sanders. The subsequent crisis in Russo-German relations was defused only when the Kaiser in January 1914 promoted Liman to full general, thereby making him ineligible to command a mere corps.

Interestingly enough, Russian pleas for diplomatic support fell on deaf ears in London and Paris. An English admiral occupied a post in the Turkish navy analogous to Liman's in the Turkish army, and a French general was similarly charged with the reorganization of the Turkish police. Joining the Russian protest against the Liman mission would have left the British and French governments open to charges of hypocrisy.

For Russia, the moral of the Liman affair was clear: it needed to further strengthen its military, if only to lessen its dependence on its allies. But to accomplish this long-range goal, Russia for the time being had to bow to French terms for the loan package it had been seeking since the summer (Document 11.20). At the same time, a keen appreciation of Russia's present weakness caused Prime Minister Kokovzev to avert confrontation with Germany. His dismissal in February 1914, the result of a court intrigue, removed an advocate of caution from the corridors of power. Just as Kokovzev's policy was at variance with the emotional anti-German campaign waged with fever-pitch intensity in the Russian press, so were the recommendations urged on the tsar by P. N. Durnovo, a member of the crown council and a conservative who otherwise had little in common with Kokovzev.

a)   *Contract between the Ottoman Government and Liman von Sanders, 27 November 1913*

Art. 1: The Royal Prussian Lieutenant-General Liman von Sanders, Excellency, will be in the employ of the Imperial Ottoman Army for a duration of five years with the rank of a General of Cavalry and with the titles, rights, and obligations as Chief of the Military Mission and will also command the First Army Corps. The above-mentioned is a member of the Highest War Council. Accordingly, his views will be considered on the following matters, though decisions on them will require a majority vote: general questions of discipline; promotions; awards and punishments; organisation; reorganisation, exercises, and training; equipment, armaments, clothing; commissariat and logistics; medical, veterinary, and equestrian issues; levies and recruiting; mobilization and fortifications; statistics; railways, telephone and telegraphs; matters pertaining to traffic, rails, aircraft, and dirigibles. In addition, the above-mentioned general heads all military academies, military cadets, training regiments, training grounds, and all foreign officers in the Imperial Ottoman Army. . . .

—Carl Mühlmann, *Deutschland und die Türkei, 1913–1914* (Berlin, 1929), 88–92

b)   *Franco-Russian Protocols, 17/30 December 1913*

1. The Imperial [Russian] Government may borrow per annum, for five successive years, a maximum sum of 500 million francs on the Paris market, in the form of state loans or bonds guaranteed by the state to pursue its railroad [construction] program.

   2. The construction program, the necessity of which was recognized by the French and Russian general staffs during their meetings in August 1913, shall commence as soon as possible so that it will be completed within four years. . . .

—*DDF*, 3rd Series, 8:698, app. II

c)   *Sazonov to Nicholas II, 23 December 1913/5 January 1914*

. . . Should Russia treat such an essential question as the command of a German general over an army corps in Constantinople as an accomplished fact, then our acquiescence will be tantamount to an important political defeat and can harbor the most dangerous consequences. Above all, our acquiescence will not safeguard us from the growing aspirations of Germany and its allies, which have adopted a more and more unyielding tone in all questions that touch upon their interests. On the other hand, the dangerous conviction will take root in England and France that Russia is prepared to make any concession for the sake of peace. If this kind of conviction becomes engrained in our friends and allies, the coherence of the entente, already loose, will fall apart and each of the powers will seek other guarantees for its interests, by way of accords with powers in the opposite camp. Such a result is probably intended by Germany which, under cover of all sorts of strange premises, has objected to the compensations which we have proposed—such as the transfer of the English admiral from Constantinople to another place. The cabinet in Berlin may figure on reaching an understanding with England at our expense. . . . Should these assumptions hold true, Russia would be politically isolated. . . .

—Evgenii A. Adamov, *Die europäischen Mächte und die Türkei während des Weltkriegs* (Dresden, 1930), 1:77–80

d)   *Minutes of the Russian Cabinet, 30 December 1913/ 13 January 1914*

[Kokovzev:] cites the measures enumerated in the foreign ministry memorandum, namely: financial boycott, recall of diplomatic representatives, and military measures. He remarks that, although Turkey will be the immediate target of these measures, their ultimate purpose is the cancellation of the agreement between the Porte and Germany. As Germany's interests will be affected, will these measures bring about its intervention?

[Sazonov:] draws the attention of the meeting to the possibility of effecting a success through energetic and, at the same time, careful and joint action by the three [Triple Entente] powers, which, in the view of the minister would not inevitably lead to a war with Germany. . . . In connection with the measures [debated here], the imperial government, before it takes decisive steps, would have to secure the support of the London cabinet, whose active participation, in the view of the minister, cannot be taken for granted. If, however military events turn against France and Russia, there will be no doubt about the intervention of Great Britain. . . .

[Kokovzev:] thinks that such measures [Russian seizure of Trebizond] will inevitably lead to war with Germany and poses the question: is war with Germany desirable and can Russia sustain it?

[Sazonov:] agrees with Kokovzev's view that in principle a war with Germany is not desirable. The question whether Russia is at present capable of fighting Germany is outside the minister's sphere of competence.

[Sukhomlinov[97] and Zhilinskii:[98]] categorically state the complete readiness of Russia for a one-on-one with Germany, not to mention a one-on-one with Austria. Neither contingency, however, was to be expected; rather, we would have to deal with the Triple Alliance.

[Kokovzev:] wishes to return to a consideration of those steps that can be taken without incurring what is to him an unacceptable risk. . . .

—Mikhail Pokrovskii, *Drei Konferenzen* (Berlin, 1920), 40–42

e)   *Memorandum by P. N. Durnovo,[99] February 1914*

. . . [W]hat can we gain from a victory over Germany? Posen, or East Prussia? But why do we need those regions, densely populated as they are by Poles, when we find it dif-

---

[97]Vladimir Alexandrovich Sukhomlinov (1848–1926). Russian minister of war, 1909–1915.
[98]Yacob Grigorevich Zhilinskii (1853–1918). Chief of the Russian general staff, 1911 to March 1914.
[99]Peter Nicholaevich Durnovo (1844–1915). Russian minister of the interior, 1905–1906.

ficult enough to manage our own Russian Poles? . . . And Germany is in exactly the same situation with respect to Russia. She could seize from us, in case of a successful war, only such territories as would be of slight value to her, and because of their population, would prove of little use for colonization; the Vistula territory, with a Polish-Lithuanian population, and the Baltic provinces, with a Lettish-Estonian population, are all equally turbulent and anti-German. . . . [A] general European war is mortally dangerous both for Russia and Germany, no matter who wins. It is our firm conviction, based upon a long and careful study of all contemporary subversive tendencies, that there must inevitably break out in the defeated country a social revolution which, by the very nature of things, will spread to the country of the victor. . . . If the war ends in victory, the putting down of the Socialist movement will not offer any insurmountable obstacles. . . . But in the event of defeat, the possibility of which in a struggle with a foe like Germany cannot be overlooked, social revolution in its most extreme form is inevitable. . . . Germany, likewise, is destined to suffer, in case of defeat, no lesser social upheaval. The effect of a disastrous war upon the population will be too severe not to bring to the surface destructive tendencies, now deeply hidden. . . . Defeated, Germany will lose her world markets and maritime commerce, for the aim of the war—on the part of its real instigator, England—will be destruction of German competition. . . . [T]he [pro-] English orientation of our diplomacy is essentially wrong. We do not travel the same road as England; she should be left to go her own way, and we must not quarrel on her account with Germany.

The Triple Entente is an artificial combination, without a basis of real interest. It has nothing to look forward to. The future belongs to a close and incomparably more vital rapprochement of Russia, Germany, France (reconciled with Germany), and Japan (allied to Russia by a strictly defensive union). A political combination like this, lacking all aggressiveness toward other states, would safeguard for many years the peace of the civilized nations, threatened, not by the militant intentions of Germany, as English diplomacy is trying to show, but solely by the perfectly natural striving of England to retain at all costs her vanishing domination of the seas. . . .

—Frank Alfred Golder (ed.), *Documents of Russian History, 1914–1917* (New York, 1927), 3–23

f) **Pourtalès[100] to Bethmann, 11 March 1914[101]**

. . . The peaceful intentions of Emperor Nicholas are beyond any doubt [*as are his absolute unreliability and spinelessness in face of all influence-peddling*]. That there are some Russian generals who would look forward to a war, together with France, against us and Austria is no less in doubt—just as there are bellicose elements in any army [*typical phrase of the piqued twentieth-century diplomat*]. To predict how things will look in three or four years strikes me as a risky undertaking unless one has the ability to peer into the future [*this ability is said to exist! in monarchs every once in a while, in statesmen rarely, in diplomats almost never*]. . . . The weakness [*of the Russian government*], duly exploited by the French, is at present a

---

[100]Friedrich, Count Pourtalès (1853–1928). German ambassador in St. Petersburg, 1907–1914.
[101]With annotations (excerpts) by Wilhelm II.

far greater source of danger than are the alleged plans by the leading statesmen for preparing a war of aggression.

GP, 39:15844

11.24   AN ANGLO-RUSSIAN NAVAL CONVENTION, MAY/JUNE 1914?

Buchanan to Nicolson, 16 April 1914 • Benckendorff to Sazonov, 7/20 May 1914 • Grey to Bertie, 21 May 1914 • Grey in the House of Commons, 11 June 1914

As foreign secretary, Grey traveled abroad only once: to accompany King George V on a state visit to Paris in April 1914. On this occasion, the French prime minister, Gaston Doumergue, urged Grey to explore with the Russian government the prospects for an Anglo-Russian naval accord modeled on the Anglo-French military and naval conventions of 1911 and 1913 (Documents 11.14 and 11.16). On his return to London, Grey informed the Russian ambassador, Count Benckendorff, of the willingness of the British government to engage in naval conversations with Russia.

The second secretary in the Russian embassy, Benno von Siebert, leaked Grey's decision to the German foreign ministry, which, without revealing its source, induced a Berlin paper, the liberal *Berliner Tageblatt*, to speculate on an impending Anglo-Russian naval accord. The revelations of the *Tageblatt* resulted in a flurry of articles in the German press. In the House of Commons, two members of parliament questioned Grey on the proposed agreement. Whether Grey's reply was sincere or not hinges on a second question: Was Grey's depiction of Britain's commitment to the ententes an accurate synopsis not only of Britain's legal obligations but also of the moral and political engagements that Britain had entered upon?

In Germany, Bethmann was profoundly disturbed. Not only did Grey's statement in parliament strike him as untruthful, but greater Anglo-Russian intimacy threatened to undo his efforts to pry England and Russia apart. He gloomily confided to his assistant, Kurt Riezler, that an Anglo-Russian naval accord would signify the "last link in the chain" forged by the ententes.[102]

a)   *Buchanan*[103] *to Nicolson, 16 April 1914*

. . . What the Emperor and Sazonov apparently want is a written agreement which would make it clear to the world that in the event of Russia being involved in a defensive war, England would give her armed support. They argue that the publication of an agreement of this character would secure the peace of Europe, as the Germans would never force a war on Russia did they know that they would have to deal with the British fleet as well as with the Russian army; but as such an agreement would virtually amount to a defensive alliance I do not imagine that there is much chance of His Majesty's Government agreeing to it. The naval agreement of which the Emperor

---

[102]Diary entry, 7 July 1914. Karl Dietrich Erdmann (ed.), *Kurt Riezler. Tagebücher, Aufsätze, Dokumente* (Göttingen, 1972), 182.

[103]Sir George Buchanan (1854–1924). British ambassador in St. Petersburg, 1910–1918.

spoke as an alternative to an alliance is perhaps more feasible, as without binding our-selves to support Russia at sea in the event of her being at war, we might enter into an interchange of views with regard to a combined naval plan of campaign, should a war break out in which both countries had become involved. The two fleets would then be in a position to co-operate effectively with one another without having to wait till the naval staffs had been able to consult together after the outbreak of hostilities.

Another way might be to extend by an exchange of notes the scope of the Anglo-Russian Agreement of 1907, which is the only official record of our understanding, so as to ensure Anglo-Russian co-operation in Europe as well as Asia. The difficulty here would be to find a formula which would not, on the one hand, commit us to a regular alliance and which would not, on the other, be of so platonic a character as to leave things virtually as they are at present. . . .

I fully realize all the difficulties in the way of an agreement of this nature, but I can't help feeling that we shall be running a great risk if we do nothing to consolidate our understanding. . . . Russia is rapidly becoming so powerful that we must retain her friendship at almost any cost. If she acquires the conviction that we are unreliable and useless as a friend, she may one day strike a bargain with Germany and resume her lib-erty of action in Turkey and Persia. Our position then would be a very parlous one. . . .

—*BD*, 10ii:538

b)   *Benckendorff[104] to Sazonov, 7/20 May 1914*

. . . Despite the elasticity of the formulas and the imprecise vocabulary, we are talking about active cooperation. The spirit of the Triple Entente harbored this principle, even though it remained latent. . . . Guided by these strong convictions about the value of the entente, Sir Edward Grey did not hesitate for a moment. . . . There can be no doubt that there has been a détente in England's relationship to the powers of the Triple Alliance, that in fact it has improved. The present decision of the English gov-ernment proves that it has decided to pursue such an improvement only within the bounds set by the principles of the Triple Entente. Therefore I hold that one has to strike while the iron while is hot, and that the [Russian] admiralty should be con-tacted as soon as possible, without delay. . . .

—*ZI*, 3:39

c)   *Grey to Bertie, 21 May 1914*

. . . I said that Count Benckendorff would see from the letters that the French and British Governments were not bound to each other by an alliance, and remained free to decide in any crisis whether they would assist each other or not, but that there had taken place between the Naval and Military Staffs certain conversations, which, should the Governments decide to assist each other in a crisis, would enable them to

---

[104]Alexander, Count Benckendorff (1849–1917). Russian ambassador in London, 1903–1917.

do so. The reason for these conversations had been that, unless something of the kind was arranged beforehand, however anxious the two Governments might find themselves in a crisis to assist each other, they would be unable to do so when the time came. . . . We thought, however, that the Russian Government might be informed of what had passed between the French and British Naval Staffs. They would then see what scope there was for conversations between the Russian and British Naval Staffs, and we should be prepared that such conversations should take place: on the footing of the letter that I had written to M. Cambon. . . .

—*BD*, 10ii:543

d)   *Grey in the House of Commons, 11 June 1914*

Mr. King[105] asked whether any naval agreement has been recently entered into between Russia and Great Britain; and whether any negotiations, with a view to a naval agreement, have recently taken place or are now pending between Russia and Great Britain?

Sir William Byles[106] asked the Secretary of State for Foreign Affairs whether he can make any statement with regard to an alleged new naval agreement between Great Britain and Russia; how far such agreement would affect our relations with Germany; and will he lay Papers?

Sir Edward Grey: The hon. Member for North Somerset asked a similar question last year with regard to military forces, and the hon. Member for North Salford asked a similar question also on the same day, as he has again done to-day.[107] The Prime Minister then replied that, if war arose between European Powers, there were no unpublished agreements which would restrict or hamper the freedom of the Government or of Parliament to decide whether or not Great Britain should participate in a war.[108] That answer covers both the questions on the Paper. It remains as true to-day as it was a year ago. No negotiations have since been concluded with any Power that would make the statement less true. No such negotiations are in progress, and none are likely to be entered upon so far as I can judge. But if any agreement were to be concluded that made it necessary to withdraw or modify the Prime Minister's statement of last year, which I have quoted, it ought, in my opinion, to be, and I suppose that it would be, laid before Parliament.

—*Parl. Debates*, 5th Series, 63:457–58

[105]Joseph King (1860–1943). Member for North Somerset.

[106](1839–1917). Member for North Salford.

[107]On 24 March 1913. See *Parl. Debates*, 5th Series, 50:1316–17. These interpellations came within weeks of the Anglo-French naval accords of January 1913. Cf. Document 11.16.

[108]Grey here omitted Asquith's next sentence: "The use that would be made of the naval or military forces if the Government and Parliament decided to take part in a war is, for obvious reasons, not a matter about which public statements can be made beforehand."

CHAPTER 12

❧

The Collapse of Diplomacy, July 1914

By the middle of the twentieth century, the debate on the causes of the First World War was overshadowed by the horrors of the Second and by the tensions of the Soviet-American Cold War. Mesmerized by concerns more immediate to their daily lives, historians and the interested public alike accepted the dictum first popularized by the British wartime prime minister David Lloyd George that in 1914 the European Great Powers had "slithered" into war.[1] One implication of this notion was that all powers had played their part in bringing about or at least in not preventing the war; hence all were responsible.

This consensus was shattered in the 1960s by the German scholar Fritz Fischer and his followers.[2] Fischer assigned the major responsibility for the war to Germany, arguing that the domestic tensions between left and right propelled the German leadership to embark on a successful war to silence its domestic critics and to shore up the traditional elites. According to Fischer and his students, Germany had willed war in order to "grasp for world power."[3] In Germany, Fischer's contentions split the historical profession into hostile camps; in Britain and the United States, the assumptions of the "Fischer school" were enthusiastically received by a majority of historians.[4]

Whether or not one agrees with all of Fischer's hypotheses, his findings made untenable the earlier commonplace that the German chancellor, Theobald von Bethmann Hollweg, was an injured innocent at the mercy of events he was unable to control. Early on in the crisis, Bethmann weighed the risk of war and concluded that he preferred to take the plunge into war rather than accept diplomatic defeat. What does remain subject

---

[1]David Lloyd George, *War Memoirs* (Boston, 1933), 1:49.

[2]For Fischer's most important works, see Chapter 11, note 6. Of special relevance for the present chapter is the one-volume compilation of documents by Imanuel Geiss, one of Fischer's students, published as *July 1914* (New York, 1967). The user should keep in mind that Geiss's purpose was to bolster Fischer's arguments and that this criterion determined his selection of documents. Of the twenty-two excerpts found in the first five subsections of the present chapter, only three were published in Geiss's collection. Moreover, several of Geiss's translations are marred by serious errors (two of the more glaring ones are corrected in Documents 12.2f and 12.8b below).

[3]In German: *Griff nach der Weltmacht*, the title of the German edition of *Germany's Aims in the First World War*.

[4]For the views of American dissenters, see the introduction to Chapter 11.

MAP 18   EUROPE IN 1914

to debate, however, are the exact definitions of these terms. What situation constituted a diplomatic success or defeat for Germany? What kind of a war was Bethmann willing to contemplate: a local Austro-Serb war? a continental war of Austria and Germany against the Franco-Russian alliance? a world war with Britain among Germany's adversaries?

These questions have guided the selection of documents in this chapter. The official document collections, published in the 1920s and 1930s, proceed chronologically; to reduce the bewilderment of the reader trying to follow half a dozen themes unfolding simultaneously, the present chapter has arranged most documents topically while moving within a general chronological framework. In the last stages of the July crisis, several of the subsections overlap, and the reader might need to note even the time of day when a particular telegram was sent or received.

In boiling down the thousands of items on the July crisis published by the various foreign ministries, I have paid little heed to the Italian,[5] Romanian,[6] Bulgarian,[7] and Turkish[8] dimensions of the crisis, although these aspects occupied a far greater share of the attention, especially of the German and Austro-Hungarian leadership, than is evident here. Moreover, any situation where the pace of events becomes increasingly frenetic is a spawning ground for dis- and misinformation. These gaffes have also been omitted, including the erroneous report by the German ambassador in London on 1 August that Britain might after all remain neutral in a continental war.[9] Finally, most of the communications among the monarchs themselves have not been included; though the Willy-Nicky and Willy-Georgie exchanges are heart-stirring and of great human interest, these letters and telegrams add little to the positions already taken by their governments.

GENERAL READING: (cf. also Chapter 11, introduction with notes, and note 2 above): R. J. W. Evans and Hartmut Pogge von Strandmann (eds.), *The Coming of the First World War* (rev. ed., Oxford, 1990); H. W. Koch (ed.), *The Origins of the First World War* (2nd ed., London, 1984); John W. Langdon, *July 1914: The Long Debate, 1918–90* (New York, 1991); Gregor Schöllgen (ed.), *Escape into War?* (Oxford, 1990); Fritz Stern, "Bethmann Hollweg and the War: The Limits of Responsibility" in Leonard Krieger and Fritz Stern (eds.), *The Responsibility of Power* (Garden City, NY, 1969); Wayne C. Thompson, *In the Eye of the Storm: Riezler and the Crisis of Modern Germany* (Iowa City, 1980); Keith Wilson (ed.), *Decisions for War, 1914* (London, 1995).

12.1   AUSTRIA-HUNGARY'S DILEMMAS

*Statutes of "Union or Death," (*Ujedinjenje ili Smrt*), 1911 ● Szápáry to Berchtold, 8 May 1914 ● Czernin to Berchtold, 22 June 1914 ● Bunsen to Grey, 29 July 1914 ● Affidavit by "Apis," 28 March/11 April 1917*

Tsar Alexander II in 1882, the French president Sadi Carnot in 1894, Empress Elisabeth of Austria in 1899, King Umberto of Italy in 1900, President McKinley in 1901, King Carlos of Por-

---

[5]Because Germany declared war on Russia and France, Italy maintained on 3 August that the *casus foederis* of the Triple Alliance did not apply. *DD*, 4:755, 756. See Document 9.16. Italy joined the Allies in May 1915.

[6]Citing the position taken by Italy, Romania maintained that the *casus foederis* of the 1883 Austro-Romanian treaty did not apply. *DD*, 4:868. See Document 9.17. Romania joined the Allies in August 1916.

[7]A draft for an alliance between Austria-Hungary and Bulgaria was in place by 19 July. *OeU*, 8:10389. Bulgaria joined the Central Powers in October 1915.

[8]An Ottoman-German treaty, with a *casus foederis* contingent on that of the Austro-German Dual Alliance, was signed on 2 August. *DD*, 3:726, 733. As the German declaration of war on Russia did not fall within the *casus foederis* of the Dual Alliance (Document 9.13), Turkey hesitated before entering the war on Germany's side in October 1914.

[9]*DD*, 3:570.

tugal in 1908, the Russian prime minister Stolypin in 1911, King George of Greece in 1913: judging from this list of victims, assassinations were a staple of the turn-of-the-century political scene. But they remained without international repercussions—with the exception perhaps of the murder in 1903, by army officers, of the Serb royal couple in Belgrade. Appalled by the brutal circumstances of the regicide (the conspirators tossed the dismembered bodies of King Alexander Obrenovic and Queen Draga from the palace balcony), European governments temporized before extending recognition to the new Serb king, Peter I, of the rival Karageorgevic clan. The nature of the crime particularly offended the sensibilities of Edward VII, and England consequently became the longest holdout among the powers.

The murder in Sarajevo on 28 June 1914 of the Austrian heir and his wife, Archduke Franz Ferdinand and Countess Sophie Chotek, differed from most of its predecessors in that it spawned not a domestic but an international crisis, even though the assassins were Bosnian Serbs and hence subjects of the Habsburg monarchy. The Habsburg government could have chosen to treat the assassination as a domestic event, essentially opting to do nothing and in the process proving correct those who had been convinced of the atrophy of the monarchy, emboldening other restive nationalities, and perhaps bringing onto itself further terrorist acts. The alternative was to use the murder both to settle the score with Serbia and to give warning to any neighboring state with an irredentist lobby or to restive national minorities within Austria-Hungary that all speculation about the impending demise of the monarchy was premature.

In the course of July 1914, the Austrian police investigation of the Sarajevo crime tried to prove that the assassins had been equipped and funded by a Serb secret society with close ties to the Serb army and government. The purpose of the investigation was twofold: to build a case against the Belgrade government and to justify Austrian countermeasures. But in trying to court the sympathies of third parties, the Habsburg government may have been prone, in A. J. P. Taylor's words, to the "peculiarly Austrian illusion" that the justice of its case would become self-evident if the facts were allowed to speak for themselves.[10]

One document the Austrian investigation failed to uncover was the charter, excerpted below, of the Serb secret society "Union or Death," also called "Black Hand." Moreover, the discovery of a paper trail (Document 12.1e below) linking the chief of "Union or Death" to the Sarajevo assassination came only in the midst of the *Second* World War. Thus, in July 1914, much of the Austrian evidence was circumstantial—but, as was shown by the report of the British ambassador of 29 July, the assumption that Serbia aimed at detaching the southern Slav provinces from the Dual Monarchy was almost a commonplace within the diplomatic community.

a)   *Statutes of "Union or Death" (*Ujedinjenje ili Smrt*), 1911*

This organization is created for realizing the national ideal: the union of all Serbs. . . .

2. The organization prefers terrorist action to intellectual propaganda, and for this reason must be kept absolutely secret. . . .

4. To accomplish its purpose, the organization will:

[10]For Taylor's brilliant juxtaposition of July 1914 with similar Austrian appeals to the "conscience of Europe" in 1859 and 1938, see *Origins of the Second World War* (1961), 139–40 (cited from 1983 Atheneum ed.).

i) exert influence on government circles, on the various social classes, and on the entire social life of Serbia, which [we] regard [to the Southern Slav movement] as Piedmont [was to Italy];[11]

ii) organize revolutionary action in all territories inhabited by Serbs;

iii) beyond the borders of Serbia, use all means to fight the enemies of the Serb national idea. . . .

5. A Central Committee, having its headquarters in Belgrade, is at the head of this organization. . . .

26. Within the organization, the members are designated by numbers. Only the Central Committee in Belgrade knows their names. . . .

31. Once having entered the organization, no one may ever leave it, and no one has the authority to accept a member's resignation. . . .

33. When the Central Committee in Belgrade has pronounced a death sentence, the only matter of importance is that the execution takes place without fail. . . .

—Milos Bogicevic, *Kriegsschuldfrage [Berliner Monatshefte]* 4 (Sept. 1926), 664–89

b)   ***Szápáry[12] to Berchtold, 8 May 1914***

. . . Has not Germany, in the era Bethmann Hollweg, surrendered all of its positions vis-à-vis Russia? The "neo-German policy of nonviolent confrontation for the securing of economic-cultural spheres of activity" is what this system is called in the jargon of German officialdom. For years now, accommodation and retreat have been the hallmarks of the German "drive to the east.". . . There is cause for concern when a power of Germany's stature—misjudging the realities of power in a way which is becoming characteristic of its psychological state—sacrifices a good part of its Asian[13] and African[14] aspirations "nonviolently" just to placate others; when it meets the Serb danger by burying its head in the sand, thereby permitting the flank of its ally to become exposed. In view of a policy which treats the continental bulwarks of the Reich according to methods which might be appropriate for the partitioning of fever-infested Portuguese colonies, the question emerges where this German state of mind might lead when the next unpleasant situation vis-à-vis Russia renders attractive another "nonviolent confrontation"? . . .

—*OeU*, 8:9656

[11]For the role of Piedmont in the unification of Italy, see Chapter 7. Though "Union or Death" was a secret society, it began publishing a periodical, tellingly named *Pijemont*, in September 1911.

[12]Friedrich, Count Szápáry (1869–1935). Austro-Hungarian ambassador in Petersburg, 1913–1914.

[13]On 15 June 1914, Britain and Germany initialed an agreement on the Bagdad railroad, in which Germany renounced its claims to building the portion of the line between Basra and the Persian Gulf. In addition, Germany agreed to British participation in public works projects (irrigation and harbor works) and virtually condoned British dominance in river shipping and oil. Text in *BD*, 10ii:249; *GP*, 37i:14907. The Anglo-German agreement followed a Franco-German accord on the railway of 15 February 1914. *GP*, 37ii:14996. Also cf. Document 10.29.

[14]In 1913, Britain and Germany renegotiated their 1898 agreement on Angola and Mozambique (Documents 10.12 and 10.17). A dispute over publication prevented its signing. Text in *BD*, 10ii:366; *GP*, 37i:14682. The German ambassador was to resume negotiations on 27 July (!) 1914; on 30 July, he received plenipotentiary powers to sign the accord on the Bagdad railway. It is tempting to conclude that in both cases the German government was grasping at straws to slow or even prevent England's drift into war.

c)   ### Czernin[15] to Berchtold, 22 June 1914

. . . As of last year—a result of the stance taken by the [Austro-Hungarian] monarchy during the [Balkan] war—the firm belief has taken root here [Bucharest] and also in other places in Europe that the monarchy is headed for collapse and dissolution, that with the partition of Turkey we have inherited from this state nothing but its fate, that in other words the Habsburg monarchy will soon be up for auction. This is where the subversive activity of the Russians and French sets in; this train of thought is nourished continuously with rumors and selective information hawked in an atmosphere rife with infamy, mendacity and perfidy: "don't cling to a moribund body"; "leave the sinking ship while there is still time"; "don't tie your fate to that of the monarchy as Vienna will cause you untold harm while the entente, when the distribution of the spoils is at hand, will reward you with Transylvania.". . . In front of our very eyes there takes place—in plain daylight, transparently, openly and clearly, with a shameless impertinence, step by step—the encirclement of the monarchy. Under Franco-Russian patronage, a new Balkan league is being fused whose purpose today may be difficult to discern but which will soon become evident with flabbergasting simplicity: against the monarchy!. . . Why couldn't a special emissary travel to Berlin to enlighten the German Kaiser . . .? The Germans should understand that they too will be in serious danger if our entire army is tied up by Romania and Serbia, and they would face a fight with Russia and France all by themselves. Once Germany has been brought around . . ., then it should be possible—together with Berlin or, better yet, through Berlin—at last to confront Romania with a categorical "either-or.". . .

—*OeU*, 8:9902

d)   ### Bunsen[16] to Grey, 29 July 1914

. . . French ambassador . . . is convinced by admissions of Serbian minister, with whom he was in close contact till minister departed 26 July, that growing condition of unrest in Southern Slav provinces of Dual Monarchy was such that Austro-Hungarian government were compelled either to acquiesce in separation of those provinces or make a desperate effort to retain them by reducing Serbia to impotency. Serbian minister always said that time was working for Serbia, and he told French ambassador that within three years Southern Slav provinces would be ready to rise against Austria-Hungary without Serbia having to raise her little finger. Austria-Hungary realizes she could wait no longer, and determined on war, from which it looks as if nothing would now deter her. French ambassador thinks this shows that conflict is not due to German instigation and that it does not necessarily show that Germany desires European war, as is thought by many in France.

—*BD*, 11:265

---

[15]Ottokar, Count Czernin (1872–1932). Austro-Hungarian minister in Bucharest, 1914–1916; foreign minister, 1916–1918. Protégé of Archduke Franz Ferdinand.

[16]Sir Maurice de Bunsen (1852–1932). British ambassador in Vienna, 1912–1914.

e)   *Affidavit by "Apis,"[17] 28 March/11 April 1917*

... I thus engaged the services of Rade Malobabic to organize the plot of Sarajevo. Malobabic followed my orders and organized the plot. Before I made the final decision to proceed, I enquired from Colonel Artamonov[18] what (Russia would do) if Austria attacked us, Serbia. Artamonov answered that Russia would not abandon us. I asked for this assurance because Austria might notice our cooperation and might then use this as a pretext to attack us—I did not[19] communicate to him my intentions about the plot. The participants in the plot were all my agents and received small sums of money which I sent them via Rade. Some of their receipts are in Russian hands, as at first I received money for such activities from abroad from General Artamonov at a time when the [Serb] general staff did not yet have funds. ...

—Hans Uebersberger, "Das entscheidende Aktenstück zur Kriegsschuldfrage 1914," *Auswärtige Politik* 10 (July 1943), 429–38

12.2   GERMANY'S "BLANK CHECK," 5–6 JULY 1914

Franz Joseph to Wilhelm II, 5 July 1914 • Austro-Hungarian Memorandum, 5 July 1914 • Szögyény to Berchtold, 5 July 1914 • Szögyény to Berchtold, 6 July 1914 • Bethmann to Tschirschky, 6 July 1914 • Protocol of the Austro-Hungarian Council of Ministers, 7 July 1914

The Austro-Hungarian foreign minister, Count Leopold Berchtold, on 5 July sent a high-ranking foreign ministry official on a special mission to Berlin. Count Alexander Hoyos was to deliver to the German government two documents, a handwritten letter from Emperor Franz Joseph to the German Kaiser and a memorandum on Austria's predicament in the Balkans, prepared even before the Sarajevo assassination and hastily brought up-to-date by the addition of the final paragraph excerpted here.

Neither document specified the military measures to be taken. In their principal passages, the Austrian documents were so ambiguous and imprecise that they not only allow for a variety of interpretations, but they also raise the question of what exactly Berchtold hoped to accomplish by sending Hoyos. A second question centers on the reaction of Wilhelm and Bethmann to the Austrian documents: Did Germany simply promise support for whatever

[17]"Apis" was the nom de guerre of Colonel Dragutin Dimitrijevic (1878–1917), a leading participant in the 1903 coup and chief of the intelligence department of the Serb general staff, 1909–1915. "Apis" was accused in December 1916 of plotting against the Serb crown prince and was subsequently tried and executed by the Serb army, then deployed outside of Salonika, in June 1917. This document formed part of his defense at the Salonika trial; it was discovered after the Nazi conquest of Yugoslavia in 1941 and published in Nazi Germany in 1943.

[18]Victor Alexeivich Artamonov, Russian military attaché to Serbia, 1909–1917.

[19]In order to conform to Nazi ideological strictures (see note 17 above), this phrase was rendered in the affirmative (and hence falsified) when the document was first published in 1943. In all other essentials, the 1943 version conforms to Vladimir Dedijer's translation of this text in *The Road to Sarajevo* (New York, 1966), 398, 514 note 33. The second sentence in this excerpt (1943 version) appears after the phrase "pretext to attack us" in Dedijer's translation.

measures Austria contemplated against Serbia, or did Germany in fact push Austria into war? If the former is a correct rendition, then Germany either shared responsibility with Austria or even took a back seat to Austria as the latter contemplated its next move; if the latter version accurately captures what transpired on 5 and 6 July, then the responsibility for war (but for what kind of a war?) was primarily Germany's. Common to both interpretations is the view that the commitment undertaken by Germany was akin to issuing a "blank check" that Austria could fill out for any amount it pleased.[20]

In reporting to his government, the Austrian ambassador waxed more enthusiastic about the German reaction than Bethmann in his account to the German ambassador in Vienna. Whether German enthusiasm was in fact an issue might be debated in light of the deliberations undertaken by the Austro-Hungarian council of ministers on 7 July: two ministers pointed out that whatever Germany's stance, the principal decision had to be taken by Austria.

To some historians, Germany's insistence, in the conversations of 5 and 6 July, that Austria act quickly is evidence of aggressive intent. Others argue that the central German concern was that Austria seize the moment before the sympathy aroused abroad by the assassination evaporated. Moreover, time was working for Serbia, as the armament programs of the Triple Entente would make it far more difficult in the future for the Austro-German alliance to assert itself.

One feature common to all the documents excerpted below is their detailed analysis of Balkan alliance patterns, in particular the reliability of Romania as an ally (cf. Document 9.17) and whether Germany should drop its resistance to bringing Bulgaria into the Triple Alliance (cf. Document 11.22, headnote). These often lengthy passages have been omitted here.

a)   ***Franz Joseph to Wilhelm II, 5 July 1914***

. . . The plot against my poor nephew was the direct result of an agitation carried on by Russian and Serb Pan-Slavs, an agitation whose sole object is the weakening of the Triple Alliance and the destruction of my realm.

So far, all investigations have shown that the Sarajevo murder was not perpetrated by one individual, but grew out of a well-organized conspiracy, the threads of which can be traced to Belgrade. Even though it will probably be impossible to prove the complicity of the Serb government, there can be no doubt that its policy, aiming as it does at the unification of all Southern Slavs under the Serb banner, encourages such crimes, and that the continuation of such conditions constitutes a permanent threat to my dynasty and my lands. . . .

This will only be possible if Serbia, which is at present the pivot of Pan-Slav policies, is put out of action as a factor of political power in the Balkans.

You too are [surely] convinced after the recent frightful occurrence in Bosnia that it is no longer possible to contemplate a reconciliation of the antagonism between us and Serbia and that the [efforts] of all European monarchs to pursue policies that preserve the peace will be threatened if the nest of criminal activity in Belgrade remains unpunished.

—*DD*, 1:13; *OeU*, 8:9984

---

[20]The expression "blank check" (*Blankovollmacht*) may have been coined by the Bavarian chargé in Berlin. See his report of 18 July, Document 12.5 below. Also cf. Document 11.18e.

b)   *Austro-Hungarian Memorandum, 5 July 1914*

. . . Austria-Hungary has not been lacking in good faith in trying to establish a tolerable relationship with Serbia. But recent events have shown that these efforts were in vain and that in the future the monarchy will have to reckon with the tenacious, irreconcilable, and aggressive enmity of Serbia.

The necessity for the monarchy to tear apart decisively the threads which its opponents want to weave into a web is thus all the more imperative.

—*DD*, 1:14; *OeU*, 8:9984 annex

c)   *Szögyény[21] to Berchtold,[22] 5 July 1914*

. . . [Wilhelm II] assured me that he had expected a serious move on our part against Serbia, but he had to confess that the arguments of our Emperor drew his attention to the possibility of serious European complications and that he could give no definitive answer before having consulted the chancellor.

After lunch, when I again emphasized the seriousness of the situation, the Kaiser authorized me to inform our Emperor that we could in this case too count on Germany's full support. As stated earlier, he first had to hear the chancellor's views, but he did not doubt in the least that Bethmann Hollweg would completely agree with him. This was especially true concerning our move against Serbia. In his (Kaiser Wilhelm's) opinion this move must not be delayed. Russia's attitude will certainly be hostile, but for this he had prepared for years, and should it come to a war between Austria-Hungary and Russia, we should be certain that Germany, with its customary fealty, would stand at our side. Moreover, as things stood today, Russia was in no way prepared for war, and would think twice before it took up arms. But it will stir up the other powers of the Triple Entente against us and fan the flames in the Balkans. He understands well that it will be difficult for our Emperor, given his well-known love for peace, to march on Serbia, but if we had really recognized the necessity of military action against Serbia, he (Kaiser Wilhelm) would regret it if we did not make use of the present moment, which is so favorable to us. . . .

—*OeU*, 8:10058

d)   *Szögyény to Berchtold, 6 July 1914*

. . . In the further course of the conversation, I ascertained that the chancellor, like the Emperor, considers our immediate move [*Einschreiten*] against Serbia as the most radical and the best solution to our difficulties in the Balkans. From the point of view

---

[21]Ladislas, Count Szögyény (1841–1916). Austro-Hungarian ambassador in Berlin, 1892–1914.
[22]Leopold, Count Berchtold (1863–1942). Austro-Hungarian foreign minister, 1911–1915.

of international [politics], he considers the present moment as more favorable than some later time; he agrees with us that we need inform neither Italy nor Romania beforehand of a possible move against Serbia. On the other hand Italy should even now be informed, by the German government and our own, of the intention to bring Bulgaria into the Triple Alliance. . . .

—*OeU*, 8:10076

e)   *Bethmann to Tschirschky,*[23] *6 July 1914*

. . . Finally, as far as Serbia is concerned, it is within the nature of things that H.M. [Wilhelm II] cannot take a stand on the questions pending between Austria-Hungary and that country, as [this is a matter] outside his competence. The Emperor Franz Joseph may, however, rest assured that H.M. will faithfully stand at the side of Austria-Hungary in accordance with his obligations as an ally and his ancient friendship.[24]

—*DD*, 1:15

f)   *Protocol of the Austro-Hungarian Council of Ministers,*
7 July 1914

[Berchtold:] . . . The conversations in Berlin have led to a very satisfactory result, in that both Emperor Wilhelm and [chancellor] Bethmann Hollweg had assured us emphatically of Germany's unconditional support [*unbedingte Unterstützung*] in the event of military complications with Serbia. . . . It was clear to him that a military conflict with Serbia might bring about war with Russia. . . .

[Tisza:[25]] . . . We should decide what our demands on Serbia will be [but] should only present an ultimatum if Serbia rejected them. These demands must be hard but not so that they cannot be complied with. If Serbia accepted them, we could register a noteworthy diplomatic success and our prestige in the Balkans would be enhanced. If Serbia rejected our demands, then he too would favor military action. But he would already now go on record that we could aim at the down-sizing but not the complete annihilation of Serbia because, first, this would provoke Russia to fight to the death and, second, he—as Hungarian premier—could never consent to the monarchy's annexation of a part of Serbia. Whether or not we ought to go to war with Serbia was not a matter for Germany to decide. . . .

[Berchtold:] remarked that the history of the past years showed that diplomatic successes against Serbia might enhance the prestige of the monarchy temporarily, but that in reality the tension in our relations with Serbia had only increased. Neither our success in the Bosnian crisis, nor the creation of Albania, nor Serbia's later climb-down as a consequence of our ultimatum last fall had changed anything. . . .[26]

[23]Heinrich von Tschirschky (1858–1916). State secretary in the German foreign ministry, 1906–1907; ambassador in Vienna, 1907–1916.

[24]The additional words "in all circumstances" were struck from the original draft by Bethmann.

[25]Istvan, Count Tisza (1861–1918). Hungarian prime minister, 1903–1905; 1913–1917.

[26]Cf. Documents 11.12, 11.18, 11.21, and 11.22.

[Stürgkh:[27]] . . . agreed with the Royal Hungarian Prime Minister that we and not the German government had to determine whether a war was necessary or not . . . [but] Count Tisza should take into account that in pursuing a hesitant and weak policy, we run the risk later on of not being so sure of Germany's unconditional support. . . .

[Bilinsky:[28]] . . . The Serb understands only force; a diplomatic success would make no impression at all in Bosnia and would be harmful rather than beneficial. . . .

[Krobatin:[29]] is of the opinion that a diplomatic success would be worthless. Such a success would only be interpreted as weakness. . . .

[Berchtold:] . . . in his opinion, Romania could not be brought back into the fold for as long as the Pan-Serb agitation continued to exist, as it also fed a Pan-Romanian agitation that Romania would be able to check only after it sensed its isolation once Serbia was annihilated. . . .

—*OeU*, 8:10118; Miklós Komjáthy (ed.), *Protokolle des Gemeinsamen Ministerrats der Oesterreichisch-Ungarischen Monarchie, 1914–1918* (Budapest, 1966), 141–50

12.3   GERMANY'S DILEMMAS

Lerchenfeld to Hertling, 4 June 1914 ● *Riezler Diary, 7 and 8 July 1914*

The first document below focuses on Germany's predicament a few weeks before the Sarajevo assassination. Its author was the Bavarian representative in Berlin; its recipient the Bavarian prime minister. The second reproduces a selection from the diary of Kurt Riezler, penned shortly after Hoyos's mission to Berlin. Riezler was a foreign ministry aide to Bethmann during much of July 1914; his diary is regarded by some historians as the best source on Bethmann's thinking during that month. But the diary, published only in 1972, became the subject of a historiographical controversy in the 1980s amidst charges that Riezler's brother and the editor had sanitized it before publication. Be that as it may, this excerpt—like the Bavarian document preceding it—emphasizes not only Germany's position among the powers but also the difficulties Bethmann encountered in German domestic politics.

One event not specifically noted in Riezler's diary but no doubt part of his frame of mind was the Duma's approval, on 7 July, of the Russian "Great Program" of armaments (cf. Documents 11.20g and h; 11.23b).

a)   *Lerchenfeld[30] to Hertling,[31] 4 June 1914*

. . . [T]he chancellor . . . spoke also about the political situation in general and, I want to emphasize, this time definitely not in an optimistic vein. . . . I cannot quite stifle the criticism that the principal maker of our policy [in the past] often inclined to an

[27]Karl, Count Stürgkh (1859–1916). Austrian prime minister, 1911–1916.

[28]Leo von Bilinsky (1846–1923). Austro-Hungarian finance minister, 1912–1915; Polish finance minister, 1919.

[29]Alexander von Krobatin (1849–1933). Austro-Hungarian minister of war, 1912–1917.

[30]Hugo, Count Lerchenfeld (1871–1944). Bavarian minister in Berlin, 1880–1919.

[31]Georg, Count Hertling (1843–1919). Bavarian prime minister, 1912–1917; German chancellor, November 1917 to September 1918.

unjustified credulity. One sometimes had the impression that every assurance of friendliness was accepted by the chancellor at face value, and that understandings on minor issues were overestimated as having significant repercussions on the big picture. Sometimes there was even the confidence that it would be possible to revamp completely our relations to England and Russia.

One cannot deny the chancellor a certain degree of success in improving relations. In place of the almost tense relationship to those states, on which much depends now, German policy is now characterized by a greater sense of calm than in the era Holstein; normal and correct relations are the result of the trust which the personality of our leading statesman has earned everywhere. But Bethmann has not been able to alter the fundamental thrust of English and Russian policy towards us. This has been shown every time when questions have emerged which affect the deeper political interests of these states. Despite repeated attempts, Bethmann never succeeded in concluding a neutrality treaty with England; as far as Russia is concerned, its attitude to the commissioning of General Liman by Turkey[32] showed how little consideration Germany can expect when Russian core concerns are at stake. . . .

The conversation then turned to the preventive war demanded by so many military men. I expressed the view that the right moment had already been missed. The chancellor confirmed this by identifying the military situation of 1905 as the one in which we had the greatest chances. But the Kaiser did not wage a preventive war [then], and will not do so [now]. There are, however, circles in the Reich which expect a war to effect a turnabout favorable to the conservative cause in Germany's domestic conditions. He, the chancellor, thought that on the contrary a world war with unpredictable consequences would increase the power of the Social Democrats, because they preached peace, and would topple many a throne. . . .

—P. Dirr (ed.), *Bayerische Dokumente zum Kriegsausbruch* (Munich, 1922), 111–13; Ernst Deuerlein (ed.), *Briefwechsel Hertling-Lerchenfeld* (Boppard, 1973) 1:97

b)   *Riezler Diary, 7 and 8 July 1914*

[7 July:] . . . The classified reports which he [Bethmann] shared with me add up to a disturbing picture. He views the Anglo-Russian negotiations—on a naval convention, a landing in Pomerania—with much concern, as the last link in the chain. Lichnowsky[33] far too gullible. He allows himself to be tricked by the English. Russia's military power growing rapidly; the situation untenable if strategic [infrastructure in Russian] Poland is developed. Austria continuously weaker and more immobile; its undermining from the north and the south-east progresses steadily. In any event [it is] incapable of going to war for a German cause as our ally. The entente knows this, hence we are completely paralyzed. I am quite astonished, didn't think [things] were so bad. One doesn't have access to classified information unless one is part of the inner circle [*Zunft*]—and all political matters, particularly all military matters, are "top secret."

The chancellor speaks of difficult decisions. Murder of Franz Ferdinand. In-

---

[32]Cf. Document 11.23.
[33]Karl Max, Prince Lichnowsky (1860–1928). German ambassador in London, 1912–1914.

volvement of official Serbia. Austria about to pull itself together. Mission sent by Franz Joseph to inquire about *casus foederis.*[34] Our old dilemma as with all Austrian moves in the Balkans. If we encourage them, they will say that we pushed them into it; if we dissuade them, it will be that we left them in the lurch. Then they will drift towards the western powers whose arms are open, and we will lose the last ally. This time it is worse than in 1912,[35] because this time Austria is on the defensive against the Russo-Serb machinations. A move against Serbia could lead to a world war. The chancellor expects that a war, no matter how it ends, will overturn everything existing now. Existing [conditions] are out of fashion, devoid of ideas. Heydebrand[36] has said that a war would strengthen patriarchal order and sentiment. The chancellor indignant at this kind of nonsense. Everywhere delusion, heavy fog over the people. In all of Europe the same. The future belongs to Russia, which grows and grows and becomes an ever greater nightmare. The chancellor very pessimistic about intellectual conditions in Germany. Miserable decline of the political elite [*Oberfläche*]. Individuals [are becoming] smaller and more insignificant, no greatness or straight talk anywhere. Failure of the intellectuals, the professors. I object: this a time of [individual] specialization, but collective greatness. . . . The chancellor a child of the first half of the nineteenth century and a product of a superior education. Strange that with the old humanitarian outlook, his seriousness, his incapacity for pretense, he could come to power in the new German milieu and could hold his own against parliamentarians and con men [*Schieber*]. But he is not unequivocal. His slyness is probably as great as his clumsiness. Both are intertwined and alternate with one another.

[8 July:] . . . If the war comes from the East, so that we go to war on behalf of Austria-Hungary and not vice-versa, we have a prospect of winning. If there is no war—if the tsar doesn't want [it] or if France, confounded, counsels peace—we still have a chance to maneuver apart the entente.

—Karl-Dietrich Erdmann, *Kurt Riezler: Tagebücher, Aufsätze, Dokumente* (Göttingen, 1972),182–84

12.4   GERMANY'S BID FOR ENGLISH SUPPORT

Grey to Rumbold, 6 July 1914 ● *Minute by Nicolson, 9(?) July 1914* ●
Lichnowsky to the German Foreign Ministry, 14 July 1914 ● *Jagow to
Lichnowsky, 15 July 1914* ● *Lichnowsky to Jagow, 15 July 1914*
(with Annotation by Zimmermann)

While the Austrian leadership was still debating how to proceed against Serbia, the German foreign ministry hoped that Britain would remain neutral if the Austro-Serb conflict escalated into a general crisis among the European Great Powers. To some historians, particularly those of the "Fischer school," the hope that Britain might remain neutral is further evidence of Bethmann's aggressive design: British neutrality in an ensuing diplomatic crisis would have allowed Germany to face down Russia and France; in a continental war, British neutrality would have given Germany the chance to crush these powers. This theory should be meas-

---

[34]See Documents 9.13 and 12.2.
[35]See Documents 11.18, 11.21, and 11.22.
[36]Ernst von Heydebrand und der Lasa (1851–1924). Parliamentary leader of the Conservative party.

ured against the intimations, received by the German government over the years, to the effect that Britain would not remain neutral in the event of a Franco-German war.[37]

But Bethmann's reasoning might have been more complex. If the Austro-Serb conflict could be "localized," that is, limited to the Balkans, then Austria's military victory was well-nigh assured. In its turn, Germany would receive credit for having kept France and Russia at bay. As a result, Austria would be shored up, the Triple Alliance revived, and Russia motivated to examine whether its goals might not be more easily attained through cooperation rather than confrontation with Germany. The key to such an outcome, however, was the attitude of Britain during the current crisis. British neutrality would have given Russia and France pause, caused these powers to hesitate before expanding to a European plane what had hitherto been a Balkan dispute, and hence localized the Austro-Serb war. The problem in this logic—if this was indeed Bethmann's reasoning—was that he expected Britain to perform a service for Germany at a considerable cost to itself, namely at the price of weakening the Anglo-Russian relationship on which Grey, Hardinge, and Nicolson had lavished so much time and energy.

The corollary to this argument also merits consideration. If Britain abandoned all pretense of neutrality in the Balkans (an area where vital British interests were not at stake), then the Triple Entente would have proved its solidity and Germany's position would have correspondingly become untenable. Checkmated in diplomacy, Germany would have no hope of scoring a success unless it rattled the saber. But this route was fraught with dangers: Germany's ability to deliver a credible military threat was eroding in the face of the French and Russian armament programs. If this equation held—first Germany's diplomatic, then its military strangulation by the Triple Entente—then Germany would be well advised to strike while it still enjoyed some prospect of success.

a)   ***Grey to Rumbold,[38] 6 July 1914***

. . . he [Lichnowsky] knew for a fact, though he did not know details, that the Austrians intended to do something and it was not impossible that they should take military action against Serbia.

I said surely they did not think of taking any territory?

The Ambassador replied that they did not wish to take territory, because they would not know what to do with it. He thought their idea was that they must have some compensation in the sense of some humiliation for Serbia. The situation was exceedingly difficult for Germany; if she told the Austrians that nothing must be done, she would be accused of always holding them back and not supporting them; on the other hand if she let events take their course there was the possibility of very serious trouble. The Ambassador earnestly hoped that, if trouble came, we would use our influence to mitigate feelings in St. Petersburg.

A second thing which caused anxiety and pessimism in Berlin was the apprehension in Germany about the attitude of Russia, especially in connection with the recent increase of Russian military strength. . . . A third thing was the idea that there was some naval convention between Russia and England. . . .

—*BD*, 11:32

---

[37]Cf. Documents 9.2 and 11.18.

[38]Sir Horace Rumbold (1869–1941). British chargé in Berlin, 1913–1914; later ambassador, 1928–1933.

b)   *Minute by Nicolson, 9(?) July 1914*

I have my doubts as to whether Austria will take any action of a serious character and I expect the storm will blow over. . . .

—*BD*, 11:40

c)   *Lichnowsky to the German Foreign Ministry, 14 July 1914*

. . . It will be difficult to brand the entire Serb nation as a people of evildoers and murderers in order to deny it the sympathies of civilized Europe; it will be even more difficult to put the Serbs on the same level as the Arabs in Egypt and in Morocco or the Indians in Mexico.[39] It can be expected that the sympathies here will embrace Serbdom immediately and in a lively fashion as soon as Austria will use force, that the murder of the heir (who enjoyed little popularity here, possibly because of his clerical leanings) will only be [seen as] a pretext for intervening against a troublesome neighbor. British opinion, particularly that of the Liberal party, has mostly sided with the principle of nationality—in the fight of the Italians against Austrian, Papal, or Bourbon rule; and during crises in the Balkans it has backed the Slavs. . . .

—*DD*, 1:43

d)   *Jagow[40] to Lichnowsky, 15 July 1914*

. . . What it all turns on is an eminently political question, perhaps the last opportunity under reasonably favorable circumstances to sound the death knell to the Pan-Serb [idea]. If Austria lets slip this opportunity, then its prestige will vanish and it will be an even weaker partner in our group. England's intimate relationship with Russia precludes a different course for our policy: it is in our vital interest to maintain the position [*Weltstellung*, sic!] of the Austrian ally. Y. E. knows how important England's attitude will be for us in the event of further consequences of this conflict.

—*DD*, 1:48

e)   *Lichnowsky to Jagow, 15 July 1914 (with Annotation by Zimmermann[41])*

. . . I am convinced that the minister [Grey] will do his utmost in the event of an Austro-Serb quarrel to restrain Russia. But I do not think that, unlike in Paris, he will be in a position to exercise a decisive influence [*I am convinced of the opposite*]. . . .

—*DD*, 1:52

---

[39]Possibly an allusion to the American punitive expedition of April 1914 to Veracruz.

[40]Gottlieb von Jagow (1863–1935). State secretary in the German foreign ministry, 1913–1916.

[41]Arthur Zimmermann (1858–1940). Assistant state secretary in the German foreign ministry, 1911–1916; state secretary, 1916–1917.

12.5   **SAZONOV'S BID FOR BRITISH SUPPORT**

Buchanan to Nicolson, 9 July 1914 • *Memorandum by Bertie, 16 July 1914* •
Grey to Buchanan, 20 July 1914 • *Minutes by Nicolson, 20(?) and*
25(?) July 1914

As the Austro-Serb crisis gathered momentum, Britain found itself wooed not only by the German government but also by the Russian foreign minister. Whether Sazonov's thinking was driven by foresight—namely, the need to secure British support for Russia in the event of Balkan complications—is difficult to ascertain, but there can be no question that his initiative, outlined below, was in harmony with his earlier efforts on behalf of closer Anglo-Russian cooperation (Document 11.24).

Grey's reaction testifies to his frame of mind on the eve of the Austrian ultimatum to Serbia. Grey was far less militant in his support for Russia than Sir Arthur Nicolson, the permanent under-secretary in the Foreign Office. But Grey too showed himself enamored of Sazonov's initiative. His reaction is notable for the absence of "systemic" considerations—that is, an assessment of what Sazonov's proposal might mean for the *European* equilibrium. In Grey's mind, the merits of the proposal outweighed any concern he might have had about Russia's growing strength in Europe.

a)   ***Buchanan[42] to Nicolson, 9 July 1914***

Sazonov is always reproaching me with the inveterate suspicion with which Russia is regarded in India and in certain circles in England. . . . He suggested that a formula might be found under which we mutually guarantee the inviolability of each other's Asiatic possessions. On my replying that our Allies, the Japanese, might regard such a guarantee on our part as directed against themselves, Sazonov said that there was no reason why they should not be brought in also. They would be very flattered by such a proposal, and the guarantee would then have a triple instead of a dual character. . . .

—FO 800/74; also *BD*, 11: p. xi

b)   ***Memorandum by Bertie,[43] 16 July 1914***

Grey says that whereas hitherto Germany has feigned alarm at the encircling policy against Germany falsely attributed to H.M. Government under the inspiration of King Edward, and has made it an excuse for largely increasing her navy, she is now really frightened at the growing strength of the Russian army, and she may make another military effort additional to the recent large expenditure to meet which [*sic*] the special capital tax was instituted, or bring on a conflict with Russia at an early date before the increases in the Russian army have their full effect and before the completion of the Russian strategic railways to be constructed with French money. . . .

—C. J. Lowe and M. L. Dockrill, *The Mirage of Power: British Foreign Policy, 1902–22*
(London, 1972), 3:488

---

[42]Sir George William Buchanan (1854–1924). British ambassador in Petersburg, 1910–1917/1918.
[43]Sir Francis Bertie (1844–1919). British ambassador in Paris, 1905–1918.

c)   ***Grey to Buchanan, 20 July 1914***

I am personally attracted by idea of triple guarantee, and am very glad that Minister for Foreign Affairs has made it a serious proposal. I will consult Prime Minister and, if he approves, the Cabinet as soon as the Parliamentary and Irish situation gives them time.[44]

—FO 800/74; *BD*, 11: p. xi

d)   ***Minutes by Nicolson, 20(?) and 25(?) July 1914***

[20? July:] Russia is a formidable power and will become increasingly strong. Let us hope our relations with her will continue to be friendly.

[25? July:] . . . Our attitude during the crisis will be regarded by Russia as a test and we must be careful not to alienate her.

—*BD*, 11:66, 101

12.6   THE AUSTRIAN ULTIMATUM TO SERBIA

Tschirschky to Bethmann, 14 July 1914 (with Marginalia by Wilhelm II) ●
Bunsen to Grey, 16 July 1914 ● *Crackanthorpe to Grey, 17 July 1914* ● *Schoen to Hertling, 18 July 1914* ● *Protocol of the Austro-Hungarian Council of Ministers, 19 July 1914* ● *Berchtold to Giesl, 20 July 1914*

The Austrian ultimatum to Serbia finally took shape in mid-July. The documents here trace its genesis, explain the considerations that led Austria to present it on 23 July, and give a glimpse of Austria's intentions, that is, its war aims. After the Austrian government made the text available to the other Great Powers, they claimed that the note took them by surprise or altogether denied that they had advance knowledge of it. The other powers may not have been privy to the actual text, but the German and British protestations of innocence ring hollow in light of the excerpts below: the German government had a very clear idea, the British government was reasonably well apprised, and even Serbia had an inkling of the thrust of Austria's intentions.

a)   ***Tschirschky to Bethmann, 14 July 1914 (with Marginalia***
by Wilhelm II)

. . . [Tisza says that] the note will be worded in such a manner that its acceptance is well-nigh impossible. . . . According to Berchtold, there was unanimity in today's con-

---

[44]The refusal of Ulster Protestants to accept Irish Home Rule rendered Irish politics increasingly volatile. On 24 April, at Larne, the Ulster Volunteers landed about thirty thousand rifles. A similar gun-running on 26 July, but by the (proindependence) Irish National Volunteers, was partially foiled by police and soldiers. Later the same day, in a scuffle in Dublin, British troops killed three and wounded thirty-eight.

ference [between Tisza and Berchtold] that it would be advisable to await the departure of M. Poincaré from Petersburg[45] [*pity!*] before taking the step in Belgrade [*!*]. If at all possible it was to be avoided that [Franco-Russian] fraternity should be fêted in Petersburg [encouraged] by champagne and influenced by Poincaré, Izvolski, and the [anti-German] Grand Dukes, all of which would then influence and might even determine the position taken by these powers. . . .

—*DD*, 1:49, 50

b)   *Bunsen to Grey, 16 July 1914*

. . . My informant[46] states that the Serbian government will be required to adopt certain definite measures in restraint of nationalist and anarchist propaganda, and that Austro-Hungarian government are in no mood to parley with Serbia, but will insist on immediate unconditional compliance, failing which force will be used. Germany is said to be in complete agreement with this procedure, and it is thought that the rest of Europe will sympathize with Austria-Hungary in demanding that Serbia shall adopt in future more submissive atttitude. . . . My informant said that he presumed that Russia would not wish to protect racial assassins, but in any case Austria-Hungary would go ahead regardless of results. She would lose her position as a Great Power if she stood any further nonsense from Serbia. . . .

—*BD*, 11:50

c)   *Crackanthorpe[47] to Grey, 17 July 1914*

. . . General feeling is that a demand on the part of the Austro-Hungarian government for appointment of a mixed commission of enquiry, for suppression of nationalist societies or for censorship of press, could not be acceded to, since it would imply foreign intervention in domestic affairs and legislation. . . .

—*BD*, 11:53

d)   *Schoen[48] to Hertling, 18 July 1914*

. . . The step which the Vienna cabinet has decided to take at Belgrade, and which will consist of the presentation of a note, will take place on the 25th. The reason for the postponement of this measure to that date is that it has been deemed desirable to await the departure of Messrs. Poincaré and Viviani[49] from St. Petersburg, in order

---

[45]Poincaré left France on 15 July, arrived in Petersburg on 20 July, departed at 11 p.m. on 23 July, and returned to Dunkirk via the Scandinavian capitals, arriving on the morning of 29 July.

[46]Heinrich, Count Lützow (1852–1935). Austro-Hungarian ambassador in Rome, 1904–1910.

[47]Dayrell Crackanthorpe (1871–1950). British chargé in Serbia, 1912–1915.

[48]Hans von Schoen (1876–1969). Bavarian chargé in Berlin.

[49]René Viviani (1863–1925). French prime minister, 1914–1915. Viviani accompanied Poincaré on the state visit to Russia.

not to facilitate an agreement between the Dual Alliance powers on possible counter-measures. By granting leave simultaneously to the Minister of War and the Chief of the General Staff, the government in Vienna has clad itself in the mantle of peaceful intentions; and it has succeeded in influencing the press and the stock exchange. It is thought here that the Vienna cabinet has proceeded cleverly in this matter. . . .

According to Zimmermann, as things stand now the note will contain the following demands:

1. The issuing of a proclamation by the King of Serbia which shall state that the Serb Government has nothing to do with the Pan-Serb movement, and fully disapproves of it.

2. The initiation of an inquiry to discover those implicated in the Sarajevo murder, and the participation of an Austrian official in this inquiry.

3. Measures against all who take part in the Pan-Serb movement.

A deadline of forty-eight hours will be set for the acceptance of these demands. That Serbia cannot accept any such demands, which are incompatible with her dignity as a sovereign state, is readily apparent.

Hence the result would be war.

Here there is agreement that Austria should take advantage of this favorable opportunity, even at the risk of further complications. But whether Vienna will actually rise to the occasion still seems doubtful to Messrs. Jagow and Zimmermann. The assistant secretary said that Austria-Hungary, because of its indecision and its desultoriness, had really replaced Turkey as the sick man of Europe, that its partition was awaited by the Russians, Italians, Romanians, Serbs, and Montenegrins. A powerful and successful move against Serbia would make it possible again for Austrians and Hungarians to behave as the power in the state, would revive the economy, and would set back for years the aspirations of outsiders. . . .

The view here is that Austria is facing its moment of truth, and for this reason it was stated here without hesitation, in reply to an inquiry from Vienna, that we would agree to any measure on which they might decide, even at the risk of a war with Russia. The blank check that was given to Count Berchtold's chief of cabinet, Count Hoyos, who came here to deliver a personal letter from the Emperor together with a detailed memorandum,[50] went so far as to authorize the Austro-Hungarian Government to negotiate with Bulgaria for its admission to the Triple Alliance! Vienna does not seem to have expected such unconditional support of the Danube Monarchy by Germany, and Zimmermann has the impression that it is almost embarrassing to the always timid and indecisive authorities at Vienna not to be admonished by Germany to exercise caution and self-restraint. The extent of Vienna's equivocation is shown by the fact that Count Berchtold, three days after his enquiries about the alliance with Bulgaria, telegraphed that he still had doubts about closure with Bulgaria.

The preference here would have been not to wait this long with the measure against Serbia, therewith denying the Serb government the chance—perhaps as the result of Franco-Russian pressure—to [appear to] offer satisfaction voluntarily.

It is thought here that the attitude of the other powers toward an armed conflict between Austria and Serbia will essentially depend on whether Austria will be con-

---

[50]Cf. Document 12.2.

tent with chastising Serbia, or whether it will demand territorial compensations. In the former case, it should be possible to localize the war; the latter case would make larger entanglements unavoidable.

Immediately after the presentation of the Austrian note in Belgrade, the [German] government will launch an initiative with the other Great Powers to localize the war. It will claim that the Austrian action has been just as much of a surprise to it as to the other Powers, pointing out the fact that the Emperor is on his Nordic cruise and that both the Prussian minister of war and the chief of the general staff are on vacation. (I take the liberty to add here that not even the Italian government has been informed.) It will stress that it is in the interest of all monarchies to uproot "the Belgrade nest of anarchists" once and for all; and it will seek to persuade the powers to take the view that the quarrel between Austria and Serbia is a matter for these two states alone. The mobilization of German troops is to be avoided, and, working through our military authorities, [we will] seek to prevent Austria from mobilizing her entire army—especially not those troops deployed in Galicia—in order to avoid bringing about an automatic Russian counter-mobilization which would force first us and then France to take similar measures, thereby conjuring up a European war.

What will decide the question whether the attempt to localize the war will succeed will be, first and foremost, the attitude of Russia.

Unless Russia is bent on war against Austria and Germany, it can—and that is the most attractive feature of the present situation—remain passive, and justify its conduct to the Serbs that, like other civilized states, it does not approve of bombs and revolvers as a means by which to settle disputes. This [would work] as long as Austria does not threaten the national independence of Serbia.

Zimmermann expects that England and France—which, at the present time, would find war undesirable—would prevail on Russia to remain peaceable; moreover, he assumes that "bluffing" is one of the favorite tools of Russian policy—that Russia likes to rattle the saber but, in the decisive moment, does not draw it for the benefit of others.

England will not prevent Austria from holding Serbia accountable. But it will not permit the destruction of that country; rather—true to its tradition—it will support the principle of national [self-determination]. A war between the [Franco-Russian] Dual Alliance and the Triple Alliance at the present time should not be welcome to England because of the situation in Ireland.[51] It is thought here that should [a war erupt] nonetheless, we are likely to find our English cousins on the side of our enemies, given England's fear that France, in the event of a new defeat, would sink to the level of a second-class power: this would upset the "balance of power," the maintenance of which England considers to be essential. . . .

—*DD*, 4, app. IV:2; Dirr, *Bayerische Dokumente*, 4–13

e)   ***Protocol of the Austro-Hungarian Council of Ministers,
19 July 1914***

[Berchtold:] . . . [I]t is not likely that our step will become known before the departure of the French president from Petersburg, but even if this were the case, he would

---

[51]Cf. note 44 above.

not see this as a disadvantage, as we had observed the norms of courtesy by waiting until the end of the visit. But because of diplomatic considerations, he was absolutely against further delay, as Berlin was beginning to get nervous and reports about our intentions had been leaked to Rome. . . .

In light of this declaration by the chairman, it is unanimously agreed that the note will be presented on 23 [July] at 5 o'clock in the afternoon....

[Tisza] says that he . . . must insist, in view of his responsibilities as Hungarian prime minister, that his position be unanimously adopted by the council. He demands this not only for reasons of domestic politics, but especially because he is convinced that Russia would fight à outrance if we insisted on the complete annihilation of Serbia. He thought that one of our strongest cards for improving our international position was to notify the powers imminently that we did not wish to annex any territory. . . .

[Stürgkh:] notes that even if the annexation of Serb territory was out of the question, it would still be possible to make Serbia dependent on the monarchy—by deposing its dynasty, by way of a military convention, and through similar measures. . . .

The Council of Ministers resolves, at the suggestion of the Royal Hungarian Prime Minister, to notify foreign powers immediately at the start of the war that the monarchy will not wage a war of conquest and does not intend the incorporation of the kingdom [of Serbia]. Of course this resolution will not preclude strategic border rectifications deemed necessary; the down-sizing of Serbia in favor of other states; or, if necessary, the temporary occupation of parts of Serb territory.

—*OeU*, 8:10395

f)   ***Berchtold to Giesl,[52] 20 July 1914***

You are asked to present the following note to the Royal [Serb] Government on the afternoon of 23 July, not later than between four and five o'clock:

On 31 March 1909 the Royal Serb Minister at the court of Vienna by order of his Government made the following declaration before the Imperial and Royal [Austro-Hungarian] Government:[53]

"Serbia recognizes that its rights have not been violated by fait acompli in Bosnia and Herzegovina and will consequently comply with the decision to be reached by the powers in regard to article 25 of the Treaty of Berlin.[54] Following the advice of the Great Powers, Serbia pledges to abandon its attitude of protest and opposition to the annexation which it has exhibited since last fall. It also pledges to change the thrust of its policies towards Austria-Hungary and will subsequently live with the latter on the basis of good neighborliness."

The history of later years and especially the grievous events of 28 June have given proof of a subversive movement in Serbia, whose ultimate aim it is to disjoin certain

[52]Wladimir von Giesl (1860–1936). Austro-Hungarian minister in Belgrade, 1913–1914.
[53]Document 11.12f.
[54]Document 9.10.

portions from the territory of Austria-Hungary. This movement, which has developed under the eyes of the Serb Government, has resulted in acts of terrorism outside the frontier lines of the kingdom, in a series of attempts at murder and in murders.

Far from keeping the formal promises given in the declaration of 31 March 1909, the Royal Serb Government has done nothing to suppress this movement. . . .

The depositions and confessions of the criminal perpetrators of the plot of 28 June prove, that the murder of Sarajevo was prepared in Belgrade, that the murderers had received the weapons and bombs with which they were armed from officers and officials, belonging to the *Narodna Odbrana* and that the conveyance of criminals and weapons to Bosnia had been prepared and carried through by Serbian frontier organs.

The above-quoted results of the judicial inquest do not permit the I. and R. Government to keep up its attitude of patient observation, maintained for years in the face of criminal dealings, which emanate from Belgrade and thence spread to the territory of the Monarchy. These results make it the duty of the I. and R. Government to put an end to such doings, which are constantly threatening the peace of the Monarchy.

To attain this end, the I. and R. government finds itself obliged to demand from the Serb Government an official assurance that it condemns the propaganda directed against Austria-Hungary. . . .

With a view to giving these assurances a solemn character, the Royal Serb Government will publish the following declaration on the first page of its official *journal* of 26/13 July:

"The Royal Serb Government condemns the propaganda directed against Austria-Hungary, that is the entirety of the ambitions, whose ultimate aim it is to disjoin parts of the territory belonging to the Austro-Hungarian Monarchy and regrets sincerely the horrible consequences of these criminal ambitions.

"The Royal Serb Government regrets that Serb officers and officials have taken part in the propaganda above-mentioned and thereby imperiled the friendly and neighbourly relations, which the Royal Government had solemnly promised to cultivate in its declaration of 31 March 1909.

"The Royal Government . . . considers it a duty to warn officers, officials and indeed all the inhabitants of the kingdom [of Serbia], that it will in future use great severity against such persons who may be guilty of similar doings, which the Government will make every effort to suppress."

This declaration will at the same time be communicated to the Royal army by an order of His Majesty the King, and will besides be published in the official bulletin of the army.

The Royal Serb Government will moreover pledge itself to the following:

1. to suppress every publication likely to inspire hatred and contempt against the Monarchy or whose general tendencies are directed against the integrity of the latter;

2. to begin immediately dissolving the society called *Narodna Odbrana*; to seize all its means of propaganda and to act in the same way against all the societies and associations in Serbia, which are busy with the propaganda against Austria-Hungary. The Royal Government will take the necessary measures to prevent these societies continuing their efforts under another name or in another form;

3. to eliminate without delay from public instruction everything that serves or might serve the propaganda against Austria-Hungary, both where teachers or books are concerned;

4. to remove from military service and from the administration all officers and officials who are guilty of having taken part in the propaganda against Austria-Hungary, whose names and proof of whose guilt the I. and R. Government will communicate to the Royal Government;

5. to consent to the cooperation of I. and R. officials in Serbia in suppressing the subversive movement directed against the territorial integrity of the Monarchy;

6. to open a judicial inquest [*enquête judiciaire*] against all those who took part in the plot of 28 June, if they are to be found on Serbian territory; the I. and R. Government will delegate officials [*organes*] who will take an active part in these and associated inquiries [*recherches y relatives*];

[Points 7–10 omitted here]

The I. and R. Government expects the answer of the Royal government to reach it not later than Saturday, the 25th, at six in the afternoon. . . .

—*BD*, 11: app. A; English translations: Austro-Hungarian *Red Book*, no. 8; Sidney B. Fay, *The Origins of the World War* (1928; reprint: New York, 1966) 2:269–73

12.7   RECEPTION OF THE AUSTRIAN ULTIMATUM

Grey to Bunsen, 24 July 1914 • Daily Journal of the Russian Ministry for Foreign Affairs, 11/24 July 1914 • Special Journal of the Russian Council of Ministers, 12/25 July 1914 (with Annotation by Nicholas II) • Buchanan to Grey, 24 July 1914 (with Minutes by Crowe, Nicolson, and Grey, 25 July) • Szögyény to Berchtold, 25 July 1914 • Serb Note, 12/25 July 1914 • Nicolson to Grey, 27 July 1914 (with Minutes by Clerk and Crowe, 28 July) • Marginalia by Wilhelm II, 28 July 1914 • Austro-Hungarian Note, 28 July 1914

Grey's reaction to the Austrian ultimatum might be measured against the record of his own administration in its dealings with Morocco, Ethiopia, and Persia; or in light of the various coercive measures contemplated by him and his predecessors against the Ottoman Empire; or even in the broader context of nineteenth-century British diplomacy toward China. But far more formidable than Grey's reaction was the response of Sergei Sazonov, the Russian foreign minister. Under Sazonov's leadership, the Russian cabinet pursued a three-pronged strategy: first, it urged Serbia to give a conciliatory reply, perhaps in the hope that Austria might after all declare itself content, but most certainly to gain time and to capture the moral high ground in the eyes of third powers. Doing so would facilitate Russia's second objective, namely to internationalize the crisis. Third, Russia would lend muscle to these efforts by setting into motion a partial mobilization of its armed forces.

The wisdom of the last move can be debated on several levels. The sources are silent on how the mobilization of either the Baltic or the Black Sea fleet might have corresponded to the intention of the Russian cabinet to direct its measures solely against Austria. Moreover, it can be argued that Russia would have held a far stronger hand had it bided its time: Austria would be at its most vulnerable once it had committed most of its forces to a Serbian campaign, thereby leaving only few units to protect the Austro-Russian border.

a)   ***Grey to Bunsen, 24 July 1914***

. . . the note seemed to me the most formidable document I had ever seen addressed by one State to another that was independent. . . .

—*BD*, 11:91

b)   ***Daily Journal of the Russian Ministry for Foreign Affairs,*
11/24 July 1914

. . . the news made a very strong impression on the minister, who immediately exclaimed: "c'est la guerre européenne.". . . Sazonov telephoned the tsar to report on Austria's ultimatum to Serbia. His Majesty exclaimed "this is disgraceful!" and gave orders to be kept up to date. . . .

At three o'clock, a meeting of the Council of Ministers . . . approved the proposal of the foreign minister to: 1) ask Austria, in conjunction with the other Great Powers, to extend the deadline which it had set for Serbia's answer; 2) advise Serbia to avoid battle with the Austro-Hungarian troops and withdraw its forces while appealing to the powers for mediation. At the same time, it was decided in principle to mobilize four military districts (Odessa, Kiev, Moscow, and Kazan) as well as both fleets (Black Sea and Baltic) and to take further military measures if these were warranted. It was pointed out that all military preparations had to be made emphatically and solely for the event of a conflict with Austria-Hungary and should not be construed as hostile actions against Germany. . . .

—*ZI*, 5:25

c) ***Special Journal of the Russian Council of Ministers, 12/24 July***
1914 (with Annotation by Nicholas II)

. . . the Council of Ministers now considers it expeditious to put into effect for the entire territory of the empire the order pertaining to the "period preparatory to war" according to both schedules[55] and it simultaneously authorizes the minister of war to obtain the permission of His Majesty to take military measures beyond those specified in the above-mentioned schedules which he thinks justified by circumstances and to be later communicated to the Council of Ministers. . . . [*Agreed*.]

—*ZI*, 5:42

[55]Not reproduced here. See *ZI*, 5:80.

d)   *Buchanan to Grey, 24 July 1914 (with Minutes by Crowe, Nicolson, and Grey, 25 July)*

... The French ambassador gave me to understand that France would not only give Russia strong diplomatic support, but would, if necessary, fulfil all the obligations imposed on her by the [Franco-Russian] alliance.... From French ambassador's language it almost looked as if France and Russia were determined to make a strong stand even if we declined to join them. Language of [Russian] minister for foreign affairs, however, was not so (? decided) on this subject. ...

[Minute by Crowe:] The moment has passed when it might have been possible to enlist French support in an effort to hold back Russia.

It is clear that France and Russia are decided to accept the challenge thrown out to them. Whatever we may think of the merits of the Austrian charges against Serbia, France and Russia consider that these are the pretexts, and that the bigger cause of Triple Alliance versus Triple *Entente* is definitely engaged.

I think it would be impolite, not to say dangerous, for England to attempt to controvert this opinion, or to endeavour to obscure the plain issue, by any representation at St. Petersburg and Paris.

The point that matters is whether Germany is or is not absolutely determined to have this war now.

There is still the chance that she can be made to hesitate, if she can be induced to apprehend that the war will find England by the side of France and Russia.

I can suggest only one effective way of bringing this home to the German Government without absolutely committing us definitely at this stage. If, the moment either Austria or Russia begin to mobilize, His Majesty's Government give orders to put our whole fleet on an immediate war footing, this may conceivably make Germany realize the seriousness of the danger to which she would be exposed if England took part in the war.

It would be right, supposing this decision could be taken now, to inform the French and Russian Governments of it, and this again would be the best thing we could do to prevent a very grave situation arising as between England and Russia.

It is difficult not to agree with M. Sazonov that sooner or later England will be dragged into the war if it does come. We shall gain nothing by not making up our minds what we can do in circumstances that may arise tomorrow.

(a) Either Germany and Austria win, crush France, and humiliate Russia. With the French fleet gone, Germany in occupation of the Channel, with the willing or unwilling co-operation of Holland and Belgium, what will be the position of a friendless England?

(b) Or France and Russia win. What would then be their attitude towards England? What about India and the Mediterranean?

Our interests are tied up with those of France and Russia in this struggle, which is not for the possession of Serbia, but one between Germany aiming at a political dictatorship in Europe and the Powers who desire to retain individual freedom. If we can help to avoid the conflict by showing our naval strength, ready to be instantly used, it would be wrong not to make the effort.

Whatever therefore our ultimate decision, I consider we should decide *now* to

mobilize the fleet as soon as any other Great Power mobilizes, and that we should announce this decision without delay to the French and Russian Governments.

[Minute by Nicolson:] The points raised by Sir Eyre Crowe merit serious consideration, and doubtless the Cabinet will review the situation. Our attitude during the
crisis will be regarded by Russia as a test and we must be most careful not to alienate
her.

[Minute by Grey:] Mr. Churchill told me today that the fleet can be mobilized in
twenty-four hours, but I think it is premature to make any statement to France and
Russia yet.

—*BD*, 11:101

e) *Szögyény to Berchtold, 25 July 1914*

. . . I would like to remark that it is taken for granted here [Berlin] that in response to
a probable rejection by Serbia, our declaration of war will follow immediately
together with military operations. Here they see great danger in any delay of military
operations as other powers might interfere. We are advised urgently to proceed immediately and to present the world with a fait accompli. I share entirely this view of
the foreign ministry.

—*OeU*, 8:10656

f) *Serb Note, 12/25 July 1914*

The Royal Serbian Government have received the communication of the Imperial and
Royal Government of the 10th [O.S.], and are convinced that their reply will remove
any misunderstanding which may threaten to impair the good neighbourly relations
between the Austro-Hungarian Monarchy and the Kingdom of Serbia. . . .

. . . Serbia has several times given proof of her pacific and moderate policy during
the Balkan crisis, and it is thanks to Serbia and to the sacrifice that she has made in the
exclusive interest of European peace that peace has been preserved. The Royal Government cannot be held responsible for manifestations of a private character, such as
articles in the press and the peaceable work of societies. . . .

. . . [T]he Royal Government have been pained and surprised at the statements,
according to which members of the Kingdom of Serbia are supposed to have participated in the preparations for the crime committed at Sarajevo; the Royal Government
expected to be invited to collaborate in an investigation of all that concerns this
crime, and they were ready, in order to prove the entire correctness of their attitude,
to take measures against any persons concerning whom representations were made
to them. Falling in, therefore, with the desire of the Imperial and Royal Government,
they are prepared to hand over for trial any Serbian subject, without regard to his situation or rank, of whose complicity in the crime of Sarajevo proof is forthcoming, and
more especially they undertake to cause to be published on the first page of the *Journal officiel*, on the date of 26 July, the following declaration:

"The Royal Government of Serbia condemn all propaganda which may be directed against Austria-Hungary, that is to say, all such tendencies as aim at ultimately detaching from the Austro-Hungarian Monarchy territories which form part thereof, and they sincerely deplore the baneful consequences of these criminal movements. The Royal Government regret that, according to the communication from the Imperial and Royal Government, certain Serbian officers and officials should have taken part in the above-mentioned propaganda" [thereafter as in Austro-Hungarian note, Document 12.6f]. . . .

This declaration will be brought to the knowledge of the Royal Army in an order of the day, in the name of His Majesty the King, by his Royal Highness the Crown Prince Alexander, and will be published in the next official army bulletin.

The Royal Government further undertake:

1. To introduce at the first regular convocation of the Skupstina [parliament], a provision into the press law providing for the most severe punishment of incitement to hatred or contempt of the Austro-Hungarian Monarchy, and for taking action against any publication the general tendency of which is directed against the territorial integrity of Austria-Hungary. The Government engage at the approaching revision of the Constitution to cause an amendment to be introduced into article XXII of the Constitution of such a nature that such publication may be confiscated, a proceeding at present impossible under the categorical terms of article XXII of the Constitution.

2. The Government possess no proof, nor does the note of the Imperial and Royal Government furnish them with any, that the *Narodna Odbrana* and other similar societies have committed up to the present any criminal act of this nature through the proceedings of any of their members. Nevertheless, the Royal Government will accept the demand of the Imperial and Royal Government and will dissolve the *Narodna Odbrana* society and every other society which may be directing its efforts against Austria-Hungary.

3. The Royal Serbian Government undertake to remove without delay from their public educational establishments in Serbia all that serves or could serve to foment propaganda against Austria-Hungary, whenever the Imperial and Royal Government furnish them with facts and proof of this propaganda.

4. The Royal Government also agree to remove from military service all such persons as the judicial enquiry may have proved to be guilty of acts directed against the integrity of the territory of the Austro-Hungarian Monarchy, and they expect the Imperial and Royal Government to communicate to them at a later date the names and the acts of these officers and officials for the purposes of the proceedings which are to be taken against them.

5. The Royal Government must confess that they do not clearly grasp the meaning or the scope of the demand made by the Imperial and Royal Government that Serbia shall undertake to accept the collaboration of officials of the Imperial and Royal Government on their territory, but they declare that they will admit such collaboration as agrees with the principle of international law, with criminal procedure, and with good neighbourly relations.

6. It goes without saying that the Royal Government consider it their duty to open an enquiry against all such persons as are, or eventually may be implicated in the plot of 28 June, and who happen to be within the territory of the kingdom. As regards the participation in this purpose by the Imperial and Royal Government, the Royal Government cannot accept such an arrangement, as it would be a violation of

the Constitution and of the law of criminal procedure; nevertheless, in concrete cases communications as to the results of the investigation in question might be given to the Austro-Hungarian agents. . . .

If the Imperial and Royal Government are not satisfied with this reply, the Serbian Government, considering that it is in the common interest not to rush the solution of this question, are ready, as always, to accept a pacific understanding, either by referring this question to the decision of the International Tribunal of The Hague, or to the Great Powers which took part in the drawing up of the declaration made by the Serbian Government of 31 March 1909.

—*BD*, 11: app. B; *OeU*, 8:10648 annex; *DD*, 1:271

g)   *Nicolson to Grey, 27 July 1914 (with Minutes by Clerk[55a] and Crowe, 28 July)*

. . . [S]o far as I could gather from a simple perusal, it [the Serb reply] practically concedes all the Austrian demands, and it is difficult to see how Austria can honestly proceed to hostile operations when Serbia has yielded so much. . . .

[Minute by Clerk:] . . . As regards [point] 5, Serbia asks for a more precise definition of what is wanted. Point 6 contains the only direct refusal, namely, to admit Austrian participation in a criminal enquiry on Serbian soil, for reasons which are at least good arguments. . . . Otherwise, with the addition of a plea for reference to The Hague or the Powers, the Serbian note meets Austria's demands.

[Minute by Crowe:] The answer is reasonable. If Austria demands absolute compliance with her ultimatum it can only mean that she wants a war. For she knows perfectly well that some of the demands are such as no State can accept, as they are tantamount to accepting a protectorate.

—*BD*, 11:171

h)   *Marginalia by Wilhelm II, 28 July 1914*

Given the deadline of 48 hours, a brilliant accomplishment. This is more than one might have expected! A great moral success for Vienna. This removes all cause for war, and Giesl should have after all remained in Belgrade! After this, *I* would have never ordered mobilization!

—*DD*, 1:271

i)   *Austro-Hungarian Note, 28 July 1914*

The Royal Serb Government . . . deliberately and arbitrarily shift the ground on which our *demarche* was based, as we did not maintain that they and their agents have taken any official action in their direction.

[55a]Sir George Clerk (1874–1951). Senior clerk in the Foreign Office, 1913–1918.

Our charge, on the contrary, is to the effect that the Serb Government, notwithstanding the obligations undertaken in the above-quoted note, have neglected to suppress the movement directed against the territorial integrity of the Monarchy. . . .

Our demand ran:

"The Royal Government of Serbia condemn the propaganda directed against Austria-Hungary. . . ."

The alteration made by the Royal Serbian Government in the declaration demanded by us implies that no such propaganda directed against Austria-Hungary exists, or that they are cognizant of no such propaganda. This formula is insincere and disingenuous, as by it the Serbian Government reserve for themselves for later use the evasion that they had not by this declaration disavowed the then existing propaganda, and had not admitted that it was hostile to the Monarchy, from which they could further deduce that they had not bound themselves to suppress propaganda similar to that now being carried on.

The wording demanded by us ran:—

"The Royal Government regret that Serbian officers and functionaries . . . participated. . . ."

By the adoption of this wording with the addition "according to the communication from the Imperial and Royal Government" the Serbian Government are pursuing the object that has already been referred to above, namely, that of preserving a free hand for the future. . . .

Our demand was quite clear and did not admit of misinterpretation. We desired:

(1) The opening of a judicial inquest (*enquête judiciaire*) against accessories to the plot.

(2) The collaboration of representatives of the Imperial and Royal Government in the investigations relating thereto ("*recherches*" as opposed to "*enquête judiciaire*").

It never occurred to us that representatives of the Imperial and Royal Government should take part in the Serb judicial proceedings; it was intended that they should collaborate only in the preliminary police investigation, directed to the collection and verification of the material for the inquest.

If the Serbian Government misunderstand us on this point they must do so deliberately, for the distinction between "*enquête judiciaire*" and simple "*recherches*" must be familiar to them. . . .

This answer is disingenuous. . . .

—BD, 11: app. B; *OeU*, 8:10860 annex (German text)

12.8   THE BRITISH ATTEMPT AT MEDIATION

Buchanan to Grey, 25 July 1914 • *Nicolson to Grey [26 July 1914]* • *Szögyény
to Berchtold, 27 July 1914* • *Bethmann to Tschirschky, 27 July 1914* •
Circular by Yanushkevich, 14/27 July 1914

The Russian strategy is the aftermath of the Austrian ultimatum, it will be recalled, was to "internationalize" the Austro-Serbian conflict, that is, to move it from a Balkan to a European level. Sazonov's rationale was that—by virtue of the wording of the Serb declaration of March 1909 (Document 11.12f)—the European Great Powers collectively had legal standing in the crisis. Whether Sazonov's interpretation is in fact borne out by the text of this document is best left for the reader to decide.

The British Foreign Office did not find fault with this premise; indeed it might be argued that the British suggestion of 25/26 July that Britain, France, Italy, and Germany mediate between Austria and Russia acknowledged the international character of the affair. But it is another question whether the British attempt at mediation was "the only possibility of avoiding general war"[56] or whether the attempt itself was inherently defective. Certainly the British suggestion is interesting for what it did *not* contain; it said nothing about Austria being the aggrieved party. The very open-endedness of the British proposal could be intepreted in Vienna and Berlin to mean that everything was negotiable at the conference table—a defect that made the British initiative unacceptable to Austria and Germany and might have doomed it from the outset. In this context, it is worth observing that neither Grey nor Bethmann nor any of their subordinates paid heed to (or remembered) the terms set by Bülow in March 1909 for Germany's participation in a conference in which it deemed its vital interests to be at stake (cf. Document 11.12e).

It is intriguing to speculate whether the British proposal might have been more palatable to Austria and Germany if the Foreign Office had taken a somewhat different approach: if, for instance, it had proposed a conference with only a limited mandate, one that would have taken for granted the liability of Serbia for the murder of the archduke and, with this point of departure firmly in place, would have had as its sole task the assessing of the damages to which Austria was entitled. For starters, this maneuver would have allowed Austria to save face. Thereafter Britain (and others) could have taken the view that justice had been served and that the indemnification should be symbolic rather than punitive (a process analogous to a jury finding for the plaintiff but awarding damages in the amount of a single dollar).

Rather than endorsing the British initiative, the German government merely passed it on to Vienna. Bethmann changed his stance, however, when Grey repeated the British offer on 27 July: now fully aware of the explosiveness of the situation, Bethmann recommended that the Austro-Hungarian government take the British overture seriously. But, on the 27th, Jagow and Bethmann gave contradictory advice to Vienna, itself perhaps an indication of the increasing confusion within the German leadership.

a) *Buchanan to Grey, 25 July 1914*

. . . [According to Sazonov] obligations taken by Serbia in 1908 [sic for 1909] to which reference is made in Austrian ultimatum were given to powers and not to Austria, and he would like to see question placed on international footing. Were Serbia to appeal to powers, Russia would be quite ready to stand aside and leave question in hands of England, France, Italy, and Germany. It was possible, he added, that Serbia might propose to submit question to arbitration.

Minister for Foreign Affairs then told us that at Council of Ministers held under his presidency this morning, Emperor had sanctioned drafting of imperial ukaze, which is only to be published when Minister for Foreign Affairs considers moment come for giving effect to it, ordering mobilization of 1,100,000 men. Necessary pre-

---

[56]Lichnowsky's paraphrase of Nicolson and Sir William Tyrell, Grey's private secretary, on 26 July. *DD*, 1:236.

liminary preparations for mobilization would, however, be begun at once. On my expressing earnest hope that Russia would not precipitate war by mobilizing until you had had time to use your influence in favor of peace, His Excellency assured me that Russia had no aggressive intentions, and she would take no action until it was forced on her. . . .

—BD, 11:125

b)   ### Nicolson to Grey [26 July 1914]

I think that the only hope of avoiding a general conflict would be for us to take advantage at once of suggestion thrown out by Sazonov . . . and that you should telegraph to Berlin, Paris, Rome, asking that they shall authorize their Ambassadors here to join you in a Conference to endeavour to find an issue to prevent complications and that abstention on all sides from active military operations should be requested of Vienna, Serbia and St. Petersburg pending results of conference. This tel. to be repeated to Vienna, Belgrade and St. Petersburg for communication to M[inistries of] F[oreign] A[ffair]s with instructions to endeavour to obtain suggested engagements as to military questions on which assurance assembling of Conference must necessarily depend. . . .

—BD, 11:139

c)   ### Szögyény to Berchtold, 27 July 1914

State Secretary [Jagow] in strictest privacy informed me that very shortly a probable English proposal of mediation would be communicated to Your Excellency through the German government.

The German government assures in the most decided way that it does not identify itself with these propositions, that on the contrary it advises us to disregard them, but it must pass them on, to satisfy the English government. . . .

—OeU, 8:10793

d)   ### Bethmann to Tschirschky, 27 July 1914

. . . Given that we have already rejected the first British proposal for a conference, it is impossible for us to reject this one out of hand. If we rejected every mediation proposal, we would be held responsible by the whole world for the conflagration and would be portrayed as the real instigators of the war. This would also make impossible our own position at home, where we have to be seen as being forced into war. Our situation is all the more difficult as Serbia seems to have yielded a lot. We can thus not play deaf to playing the role of the mediator and must present the English proposal to Vienna. . . .

—DD, 1:277

e)   *Circular by Yanushkevich,*[57] *14/27 July 1914*

You are ordered to consider 14 [27] July as the starting date for the "period preparatory for war" in the [following] military districts: Caucasus, Turkestan, Omsk, and Irkutsk. . . .

—*ZI*, 5:156

12.9   "HALT IN BELGRADE"?

Wilhelm II to Jagow, 28 July 1914 • Bethmann to Tschirschky, 28 July 1914 • Szápáry to Berchtold, 29 July 1914 • Buchanan to Grey, 30 July 1914 (dispatched 1:15 p.m.; received 3:15 p.m.) • Circular by Sazonov, 17/30 July 1914 • Grey to Buchanan, 30 July 1914 (7:35 p.m.) • Wilhelm II to Franz Joseph, 30 July 1914 (sent 7:15 p.m.) • Bienerth to Conrad, 30 July 1914 (sent 7:40 p.m.) • Franz Joseph to Wilhelm II, 31 July 1914 • Berchtold to Szögyény, 31 July 1914 • Circular by Sazonov, 18/31 July 1914 • Goschen to Nicolson [1 August 1914]

Wilhelm II returned to Germany from his Nordic cruise on 28 July. He now saw, for the first time, the Serb reply to the Austrian ultimatum and, as has been seen (Document 12.7h), concluded that Serbia had met the essence of the Austrian demands. In the Kaiser's opinion, Austrian prestige had been preserved, and, consequently, Austria should declare itself content, provided it received some kind of security that Serbia would honor the pledges it had given. This insight became the foundation for Bethmann's last-ditch effort to prevent the crisis from spiraling out of control.[58]

Could other powers be sold on the idea? Just as Bethmann at this late stage recognized the dangers in not checking Austria, so too the dangers of not checking Russia began to dawn on Grey. Now grafting the German conditions onto his own mediation proposal (preceding document), Grey counseled moderation in Petersburg. Whether the language employed by Bethmann in Vienna and by Grey in Petersburg was sufficiently forceful, given the gravity of the situation, is another question altogether.

But in both Vienna and Petersburg, the impulse to point an accusing finger at one another seemed to outweigh the desire for a speedy resolution of the crisis. Sazonov narrowed the gap between the two adversaries by ostensibly agreeing to the new proposal when it was presented to him by the British ambassador, but he did not use his influence to order an end to the Russian mobilization (Document 12.7), a condition on which this overture—and, incidentally, Grey's earlier mediation proposal—had been predicated. Moreover, the direct exchanges between Petersburg and Vienna were remarkable for the lack of enthusiasm exhibited on both sides: on 31 July, for instance, the Austro-Hungarian ambassador noted that he had not even bothered to seek out Sazonov for want of instructions to do so.[59]

---

[57]Nikololai Nikolaievich Yanushkevich (1868–1918). Chief of Russian general staff, 1914.

[58]Albertini maintains that Bethmann "carried on a diplomatic activity at complete variance with the letter and spirit of his Sovereign's orders" (*Origins*, 2:471); Geiss claims that Bethmann "falsified" Wilhelm's instructions (*July 1914*, 223).

[59]*OeU*, 8:11174.

The last document, Goschen's report of 1 August, is included here as a summary of the fate of the "halt-in-Belgrade" proposal. Because of the rapid and confusing pace with which events now unfolded, it is essential that the reader correlate the documents below with those in sections 12.10 and 12.11.

a)   ***Wilhelm II to Jagow, 28 July 1914***

After reading over the Serb reply, which I received this morning, I am convinced that on the whole the wishes of the Danube Monarchy have been acceded to. . . . [A]s a result, every cause for war falls to the ground.

Nevertheless, the piece of paper, like its contents, can be considered as of little value so long as it is not translated into deeds. The Serbs are Near Easterners, therefore liars, tricksters, and masters of evasion. In order that these beautiful promises may be turned into truths and facts, a *douce violence* must be exercised. This should be so arranged that Austria would receive a hostage (Belgrade), as a guarantee for the enforcement and carrying out of the promises, and should occupy it until the *petita* had actually been complied with. This is also necessary in order to give the army, now unnecessarily mobilized for the third time, the external *satisfaction d'honneur* of an ostensible success in the eyes of the world, and to make it possible for it to feel that it had at least stood on foreign soil. . . . I propose that we say to Austria: Serbia has been forced to retreat in a very humiliating manner, and we offer our congratulations. Naturally, as a result, every cause for war has vanished. But a guarantee that the promises will be carried out is unquestionably necessary. That could be secured by means of the temporary military occupation of a portion of Serbia, similar to the way we kept troops stationed in France in 1871 until the billions were paid.[60] On this basis, I am ready to mediate for peace with Austria. . . .

—*DD*, 2:293

b)   ***Bethmann to Tschirschky, 28 July 1914***

. . . According to the statements of the Austrian general staff, military action against Serbia will not be possible before 12 August. As a result, the Imperial [German] government is placed in the extraordinarily difficult position of being exposed in the meantime to the mediation and conference proposals of the other cabinets and if it continues to maintain its previous aloofness in the face of such proposals, it will incur the onus of having been responsible for a world war, even, finally, in the eyes of the German people. A successful war on three fronts cannot be commenced and sustained on such a basis. It is imperative that the responsibility for the possible [*eventuelle*][61] extension of the war to those states which were at first not directly involved should definitely be incurred by Russia. . . . The Vienna cabinet [should] re-

---

[60]Documents 8.15 and 9.1.

[61]Geiss (*July 1914*, 259) errs in translating "*eventuelle*" as "eventual" rather than "possible" or even "probable." For Bismarck's definition of this term, see Document 8.6.

peat at St. Petersburg its distinct declaration that it is far from wishing to make any territorial acquisitions in Serbia, and that its military preparations are solely for the purpose of a temporary occupation of Belgrade and certain other places on Serb territory in order to force the Serb government to comply completely with its demands, and for the creation of guarantees of good conduct in the future. . . . Should the Russian government fail to recognize the justice of this point of view, it would have against it the public opinion of all of Europe, which is now in the process of turning away from Austria. As a result, the general diplomatic, and probably military, situation would undergo material alteration in favor of Austria-Hungary and her allies. . . . You will have to avoid very carefully giving rise to the impression that we wish to hold Austria back. The case is solely one of finding a way to realize Austria's desired aim, that of breaking the back of Pan-Serb propaganda, without at the same time bringing on a world war, and, if the latter cannot be avoided in the end, of improving the conditions under which we shall have to wage it, in so far as is possible. . . .

—*DD*, 2:323

c)   ***Szápáry to Berchtold, 29 July 1914***

[10 a.m.:] . . . Our territorial disinterestedness, the announcement of which he [Sazonov] doubtlessly expected, did not make much of an impression on him . . . .

[11 p.m.:] . . . I stated that we did not wish to infringe on Russian interests, did not have the intention to take Serb territory, and were not about to violate the sovereignty of Serbia. . . .

—*OeU*, 8:10999, 11003

d)   ***Buchanan to Grey, 30 July 1914 (dispatched 1:15 p.m.;***
received 3:15 p.m.)

[Sazonov] had replied that though territorial integrity might be respected Serbia would inevitably become vassal of Austria just as Bukhara,[62] though its territory had been left intact, was a vassal of Russia. Were Russia to tolerate this, there would be a revolution in country. . . . [Sazonov] then read out text of French [language] formula given by him to [German] ambassador . . . :

"If Austria, recognizing that her conflict with Serbia has assumed character of question of European interest, declares herself ready to eliminate from her ultimatum points which violate principle of sovereignty of Serbia, Russia engages to stop all military preparations.

If Austria rejects this proposal, preparations for a general mobilization will be proceeded with and European war will be inevitable. . . .

—*BD*, 11:302

[62]See Document 6.6d.

e)   *Circular by Sazonov, 17/30 July 1914*

Until receipt of completely satisfactory answer from Austria, via German government, we will continue military measures.

—ZI, 5:279

f)   *Grey to Buchanan, 30 July 1914 (7:35 p.m.)*

. . . Russian ambassador has told me of condition laid down by Sazonov, as quoted in your telegram . . . and fears that it cannot be modified; but if Austrian advance were stopped after occupation of Belgrade, I think Russian minister for foreign affairs' formula might be changed to read that the powers would examine how Serbia could fully satisfy Austria without impairing Serbian sovereign rights or independence.

If Austria, having occupied Belgrade and neighboring Serbian territory, declares herself ready, in the interest of European peace, to cease her advance and to discuss how a complete settlement can be arrived at, I hope that Russia would also consent to discussion and suspension of further military preparations, provided that other powers did the same. . . . [63]

—BD, 11:309

g)   *Wilhelm II to Franz Joseph, 30 July 1914 (sent 7:15 p.m.)*

I did not think I could turn down the personal plea of the tsar to undertake an attempt at mediation in order to prevent a global conflagration and to preserve world peace; through my ambassador I have made proposals to your government yesterday and today. Among others, these are that Austria, after the occupation of Belgrade or other sites, announce its conditions. . . .

—DD, 2:437

h)   *Bienerth[64] to Conrad, 30 July 1914 (sent 7:40 p.m.)[65]*

Moltke says that he considered situation critical if Austria-Hungary did not at once mobilize against Russia. . . . England's renewed step at preserving peace to be re-

---

[63]Similarly, George V to Henry of Prussia, 30 July. *DD,* 2:452.

[64]Karl von Bienerth (1872–1941). Austro-Hungarian military attaché in Berlin, 1908–1914.

[65]In comparing this telegram with Wilhelm's simultaneous message to Franz Joseph, Berchtold exclaimed: *"Das ist gelungen! Wer regiert: Moltke oder Bethmann?"* A translation might read: "That beats everything! Who governs: Moltke or Bethmann?" Franz Conrad von Hoetzendorf, *Aus meiner Dienstzeit* (Vienna, 1923), 4:153. A. J. P. Taylor is not far off the mark in suggesting that the phrase stand as an epithet for Wilhelmian Germany. "The Ruler in Berlin" in *Europe: Grandeur and Decline* (New York, 1967).

jected. For the maintenance of Austria-Hungary the carrying on of a European war [is] last chance [*Mittel*]. Germany will emphatically [*unbedingt*] go along.

—Franz Conrad von Hoetzendorff, *Aus meiner Dienstzeit* (Vienna, 1923), 4:152 (cf. also *OeU*, 8:11033)

i)   *Franz Joseph to Wilhelm II, 31 July 1914*

. . . The action of my army against Serbia underway now cannot be disrupted by the threatening and challenging stance taken by Russia. A renewed rescue of Serbia due to Russian intervention would have the gravest consequences for my lands and therefore I cannot countenance such an intervention. I am aware of the scope of my decisions. . . .

—*OeU*, 8:11118

j)   *Berchtold to Szögyény, 31 July 1914*

Conrad is simultaneously wiring in reply to a question put by the chief of the German [sic for Prussian] general staff: "On the basis of Emperor's decision [*Allerböchster Entscheidung*] the following was concluded: pursuit of war against Serbia. Remainder of army to be mobilized and assembled in Galicia. First day of mobilization 4 August . . . ."

—*OeU*, 8:11119

k)   *Circular by Sazonov, 18/31 July 1914*

I answered [the British ambassador] that I agreed to the English [sic] proposal. . . .

—*ZI*, 5:342

l)   *Goschen to Nicolson [1 August 1914]*

. . . the German case, to put it in a nutshell, is that while the Emperor at the Czar's request was working at Vienna—Russia mobilized—or rather ordered mobilization. I did my very best and hardest last night to persuade Jagow, notwithstanding all mobilizations and ultimatums, not to relax his efforts to prevent one of the biggest catastrophes—in fact the biggest of modern times—and to work in the direction indicated by His Majesty's Government. He was sympathetic but apparently absolutely determined that nothing more could be done until Russia said she would demobilize. . . . Oh! how much easier things would be if the events of 1909 had not taken place. . . . I see the Germans have given the French 18 hours[66] to say whether they will remain neutral or not. . . . There is intense enthusiasm in the streets—and considerable depression at the Foreign Office; Zimmermann said to Cambon[67] yesterday, "This is the most tragic day for 40 years—and it happens just as we were settling down to what we thought were improved relations all around." Jagow told me that the Emperor was fearfully depressed and said that his record as a "Peace Emperor" was finished with. . . . [Zimmermann] expressed regret that Germany, France, "and perhaps England" had been drawn in—none of whom wanted war in the least and said it came from "this d—d system of alliances, which were the curse of modern times." . . .

—*BD*, 11:510

12.10   RUSSIA'S PATH TO GENERAL MOBILIZATION

Bethmann to Pourtalès, 29 July 1914 ● *Sazonov to Izvolski and Benckendorff,*
29 July 1914 ● *Daily Journal of the Russian Ministry for Foreign Affairs,*
30 July 1914 ● *Minute by Nicolson, 31 July (?) 1914*

For a generation, military planners and politicians had pointed out the advantage enjoyed by those states that could deploy their forces rapidly at the outbreak of hostilities; conversely, they had warned of the dangers of not mobilizing quickly enough (Documents 10.4; 11.14a and e; 11.20g and h). In July 1914, Serbia ordered mobilization a few hours before giving its reply to the Austrian ultimatum on the 25th; Austria ordered a partial mobilization only on 28 July, the same day it declared war on Serbia.

The Russian cabinet had approved partial mobilization (i.e., mobilization directed solely against Austria) on 24 July; one day later, it gave the minister of war the option to expand the mobilization at his discretion (Documents 12.7b and c). For as long as possible, all preparations were to proceed in secret. On 29 July, the Russian military convinced the tsar to approve an all-out general mobilization, though this order was rescinded on the same day upon receipt of a telegram from the German Kaiser promoting the "halt-in-Belgrade" initiative and direct negotiations between Vienna and Petersburg.

The tsar's hesitation reopened the debate within the Russian leadership over a partial mobilization or a general mobilization. The issue was not resolved until the next day.

a)   *Bethmann to Pourtalès, 29 July 1914*

Please point out very seriously to Sazonov that further continuation of Russian mobilization measures would force us to mobilize, and that in this event a European war could scarcely be averted.

—*DD*, 2:342

---

[66]Document 12.13.
[67]Jules Cambon (1845–1935). French ambassador in Berlin, 1907–1914. Brother of Paul Cambon (1843–1924), French ambassador in London, 1898–1920.

b)   *Sazonov to Izvolski[68] and Benckendorff,[69] 29 July 1914*

. . . As we cannot comply with the wishes of Germany, we have no alternative than to accelerate our armaments and to take into account that war is probably inevitable. Please communicate this to the French government and express our sincere gratitude for the statement of the French ambassador on behalf of his government that we can count on France's full support as an ally. . . .

—*ZI*, 5:221

c)   *Daily Journal of the Russian Ministry for Foreign Affairs, 30 July 1914*

Between 9 and 10 a.m. the Minister for Foreign Affairs spoke to the Minister for Agriculture by telephone. Both of them were greatly disturbed at the stoppage of the general mobilization, as they fully realized that this threatened to place Russia in an extremely difficult position in the event that relations with Germany became acute. S. D. Sazonov advised A. V. Krivoshein[70] to beg an audience of the tsar in order to represent to His Majesty the dangers called forth by the change.

At 11 a.m. the Minister for Foreign Affairs again met the Minister for War and the Chief of the General Staff. Information received during the night still further strengthened the opinion which they all held that it was imperative to prepare for a serious war without loss of time. Accordingly the Ministers and the Chief of the Staff adhered to the view which they had expressed yesterday to the effect that it was indispensable to proceed to a general mobilization. Adjutant-General Sukhomlinov[71] and General Yanushkevich again endeavored by telephone to persuade the tsar to revert to his decision of yesterday to permit a general mobilization. His Majesty decidedly refused to do so, and finally declared that the conversation was at an end. General Yanushkevich, who at this moment was holding the telephone receiver, only succeeded in reporting that the Minister for Foreign Affairs was there with him and asked to be allowed to say a few words to His Majesty. A somewhat lengthy silence ensued, after which the tsar expressed his willingness to hear the Minister. S. D. Sazonov requested His Majesty to receive him today, to enable him to present a report concerning the political situation which permitted no delay. After a silence, the tsar asked: "Is it all the same to you if I receive you at 3 o'clock, at the same time as Tatistchev,[72] as otherwise I have not a free minute today?" The Minister thanked His Majesty and said that he would present himself at the hour named.

The Chief of Staff warmly pleaded with S. D. Sazonov to persuade the tsar with-

---

[68]Alexander Petrovich Izvolski (1856–1919). Russian foreign minister, 1906–1910; ambassador in Paris, 1910–1917.

[69]Alexander Constantinovich, Count Benckendorff (1849–1917). Russian ambassador in London, 1903–1917.

[70]Alexander Vasilievich Krivoshein (1858–1921). Russian minister of agriculture, 1907–1915.

[71]Vladimir Alexandrovich Sukhomlinov (1848–1926). Russian minister of war, 1909–1915.

[72]Ilja Leonidovich Tatistchev, the tsar's military representative at the court of Wilhelm II, 1905–1914.

out fail to consent to a general mobilization in view of the extreme danger we would face if we were not ready for war with Germany because a partial mobilization had thrown into confusion [the deployment plans] for a general mobilization. General Yanushkevich requested that the minister, should he succeed in persuading the tsar, telephone him to that effect from Peterhof [palace], in order that he [Yanushkevich] might immediately take the necessary steps, as he would need first of all to stop as soon as possible the partial mobilization which had already commenced and substitute fresh orders for those which had been issued. "After that," said Yanushkevich, "I shall go away, smash my telephone and generally adopt measures which will prevent anyone from finding me for the purpose of giving contrary orders which would again stop our general mobilization."

On his return to the Foreign Office, S. D. Sazonov had an interview with the French Ambassador.

. . . The general state of mind was tense and the conversation was almost exclusively concerned with the necessity for insisting upon a general mobilization at the earliest possible moment, in view of the inevitability of war with Germany, which every moment became clearer. A. B. Krivoshein expressed the hope that S. D. Sazonov would succeed in persuading the tsar, as otherwise, to use his own words, we should be marching towards a certain catastrophe.

At 2 p.m. the Minister for Foreign Affairs left for Peterhof, together with Major-General Tatistchev, and both of them were received together there in the Alexander Palace by His Majesty. During the course of nearly an hour the Minister attempted to show that war was becoming inevitable, as it was clear to everybody that Germany had decided to bring about a collision, as otherwise she would not have rejected all the pacificatory proposals that had been made and could easily have brought its ally to reason. Under these circumstances it only remained to do everything that was necessary to meet war fully armed and under the most favorable conditions for ourselves. Therefore it was better to overcome the fear that our preparations would bring about a war, and to continue these preparations carefully—rather than be trapped by this fear, be caught unprepared, and be taken unawares by war.

The firm desire of the tsar to avoid war at all costs, the horrors of which filled him with repulsion, led His Majesty in his full realization of the heavy responsibility which he took upon himself in this fateful hour to explore every possible means for averting the approaching danger. Consequently he refused for a long time to agree to the adoption of measures which, however indispensable from a military point of view, were calculated, as he clearly saw, to hasten a decision in an undesirable sense.

The tenseness of feeling experienced by the tsar at this time found expression, amongst other signs, in the irritability, most unusual with him, with which His Majesty interrupted General Tatistchev. The latter, who throughout had taken no part in the conversation, said in a moment of silence: "Yes, it is hard to decide." His Majesty replied in a rough and displeased tone: "I will decide"—in order to prevent the general from intervening any further in the conversation.

Finally the tsar agreed that under the existing circumstances it would be very dangerous not to make timely preparations for what was apparently an inevitable war, and therefore gave his decision in favour of an immediate general mobilization.

S. D. Sazonov requested the Imperial permission to inform the Chief of the General Staff of this immediately by telephone, and this being granted, he hastened to the telephone on the ground floor of the palace. Having transmitted the Imperial order to General Yanushkevich, who was waiting impatiently for it, the Minister, with reference to their conversation that morning, added: "Now you can smash your telephone."

Meanwhile His Majesty still cherished the hope of finding some means of preventing the general mobilization from becoming an irrevocable *casus belli*. . . .

—*ZI*, 5:284

d)   *Minute by Nicolson, 31 July (?) 1914*

Russia is taking very reasonable and sensible precautions, which should in no wise be intepreted as provocative. Germany, of course, who has been steadily preparing now wishes to throw the blame on Russia—a very thin pretext. However comments are superfluous.

—*BD*, 11:337

12.11   THE FAILURE OF DIPLOMACY

Varnbüler to Weizsäcker, 29 and 30 July 1914 • Goschen to Grey, 29 July 1914
• Lichnowsky to the German Foreign Ministry, 29 July 1914 (with Annotations
by Wilhelm II [Excerpts]) • Grey to Goschen, 30 July 1914 • Protocol of the
Prussian State Ministry, 30 July 1914 • Note by Wilhelm II, 30 July 1914 •
Memorandum by Crowe, 31 July 1914

The weaknesses in Russia's infrastructure—particularly the underdeveloped state of railroads in Russian Poland—meant that Russian mobilization would be slow. Russia's inertia was, it will be remembered, a subject of considerable concern to the French military, for Russia's inability to deploy its armies quickly on Germany's eastern border blunted the quantitative edge of the Franco-Russian alliance. It was also a factor on which the only German war plan, named after the former chief of the Prussian general staff, Alfred von Schlieffen, was predicated. The outline of the plan was this: Germany could afford to leave its eastern border exposed while concentrating its forces in the west, would then crush France while Russia's armies were still in midmobilization, and would subsequently redeploy its forces to the east to deal with Russia.

Russia's decision to press on with mobilization threatened the very premise of the Schlieffen plan, as it confronted Germany with the prospect of a fully deployed Russian army as the crisis wore on. Every day would gnaw at the one tactical advantage that Germany possessed, namely, the speed of *its* mobilization; once Russia's armies were mobilized, the entire German recipe for a successful war (or even a successful diplomatic resolution of the crisis) was threatened.

If Russian mobilization put pressure on Berlin, the inflexibility of German military planning compounded it. The panic in Berlin, though largely self-inflicted, translated into an increasingly grotesque diplomacy. Germany's last-ditch efforts to avert a European war have an unreal air about them; they show a leadership grasping at straws, on the verge of irrationality.

a)   *Varnbüler[73] to Weizsäcker,[74] 29 and 30 July 1914*

[29 July:] . . . In his [Lerchenfeld's] judgment, the situation was "very messy" [*sehr dreckig*]. Apparently the chancellor still believed in the possibility of a peaceful resolution. But evidently the reins had begun to slip from the hands of the diplomats into those of the military [*Kriegsdepartements*]. . . .

[30 July:] General Graevenitz[75] . . . , returning from the general staff, told me this morning that, in a meeting of the highest civilian and military authorities with the Kaiser yesterday [29 July], there emerged rather strong differences of opinion: the chancellor still wanted to gain time to continue peaceful negotiations, whereas the minister of war and the chief of the general staff advocated immediate German counter-measures in view of the Russian mobilization and French military preparations. . . .

—August Bach (ed.), *Deutsche Gesandtschaftsberichte zum Kriegsausbruch 1914* (Berlin, 1937), #40, 52

b)   **Goschen to Grey, 29 July 1914**

Chancellor . . . said he was continuing his efforts to maintain peace, but that [in the event of] a Russian attack on Austria, Germany's obligation as Austria's ally might, to his great regret, render a European conflagration inevitable, and in that case he hoped Great Britain would remain neutral. As far as he was able to judge key-note of British policy, it was evident that Great Britain would never allow France to be crushed. Such a result was not contemplated by Germany. The Imperial Government was ready to give every assurance to the British government provided that Great Britain remained neutral that, in the event of a victorious war, Germany aimed at no territorial acquisitions at the expense of France.

In answer to a question from me, His Excellency said that it would not be possible for him to give such an assurance as regards [France's] colonies.

Continuing, His Excellency said he was, further, ready to assure the British government that Germany would respect neutrality and integrity of Holland as long as they were respected by Germany's adversaries.

As regards Belgium, His Excellency could not tell to what operations Germany might be forced by the action of France, but he could state that, provided that Belgium did not take sides against Germany, her integrity would be respected after the conclusion of the war.

Finally, His Excellency said that he trusted that these assurances might form basis of further understanding with England which, as you well know, had been the object of his policy ever since he had been chancellor. . . .

—BD, 11:293

[73]Axel von Varnbüler (1851–1937). Minister of Württemberg in Berlin, 1894–1918.
[74]Carl [von] Weizsäcker (1853–1926). Prime minister of Württemberg, 1906–1918. Grandfather of Richard von Weizsäcker (German president, 1984–1994).
[75]Fritz von Graevenitz (1861–1922). Württemberg's military representative in Berlin. Maternal grandfather of Richard von Weizsäcker.

c) *Lichnowsky to the German Foreign Ministry, 29 July 1914 (with Annotations by Wilhelm II [Excerpts])*

. . . The British government desired now as before to cultivate our present friendship, and it could stand aside as long as the conflict remained confined to Austria and Russia. [*This means we are to leave Austria in the lurch. Mean and Mephistophelian! But genuinely English.*] But if we and France were pulled in, the situation would change immediately and the British government would feel pressured to make quick decisions [*have already been taken*]. In this event, it could not afford to stand aside for long and wait [*i.e., they will attack us*]; "if war breaks out, it will be the greatest catastrophe that the world has ever seen." . . .

—*DD*, 2:368

d) *Grey to Goschen, 30 July 1914*

You must inform German chancellor that his proposal that we should bind ourselves to neutrality on such terms cannot for a moment be entertained. . . . And if the peace of Europe can be preserved, and this crisis be safely passed, my own endeavour would be to promote some arrangement to which Germany could be a party, by which she could be assured that no hostile or aggressive policy would be pursued against her or her allies by France, Russia, and ourselves, jointly or separately. I have desired this and worked for it, as far as I could, through the last Balkan crisis, and, Germany having a corresponding object, our relations sensibly improved. The idea has hitherto been too utopian to form the subject of definite proposals, but if this present crisis, so much more acute than any that Europe has had for generations, be safely passed, I am hopeful that the reaction and relief that will follow may make some more definite rapprochement between the powers possible than was possible before.

—*BD*, 11:303.

e) *Protocol of the Prussian State Ministry, 30 July 1914*

[Bethmann:] . . . The following reasons were instrumental for the conduct of Germany in the present crisis: it was of great importance to portray Russia as the guilty party, and this could be achieved through an Austro-Hungarian statement which would prove wrong the claims of the Russian government; further, it had to be borne in mind that the Serb reply had in fact met the Austro-Hungarian desiderata except in minor points. . . . Germany and England had taken all steps in order to prevent a European war. . . . Closing, the prime minister [Bethmann] stressed that all governments—including that of Russia—and the great majority of people were peaceable, but control [over the crisis] had been lost and the landslide is being triggered. . . .

—*DD*, 2:456

Note by Wilhelm II, 30 July 1914[76]

If [Russian] mobilization cannot be reversed—which is not true—why then did the tsar ask me to mediate three days later without as much as mentioning the mobilization order?! This shows clearly that he thought the mobilization order to be premature and that to soothe his conscience, stirred up belatedly, he went through the motions in taking this step, although he knew that he was powerless because he did not feel strong enough to stop the mobilization. Frivolity and weakness are to plunge the world into the most horrible war, which aims ultimately at the destruction of Germany. For me there can no longer be any doubt: England, Russia, and France are in collusion—after laying the foundation of the *casus foederis* through Austria—to take the Austro-Serb conflict as the pretext for waging a war of annihilation against us. Hence Grey's cynical remark to Lichnowsky "as long as the war were limited to Austria and Russia, England would sit it out, only if we and France would get involved, he would be forced to take an active stand against us." I.e.: either we disdainfully betray our ally and abandon him to Russia (thereby breaking apart the Triple Alliance), or we pay for our fidelity to him by being jointly attacked and punished by the Triple Entente, which will thus get redress for its jealousy by jointly ruining us. This is in short the real naked situation—slowly and deliberately initiated, continued, and systematically developed by Edward VII through England's conversations, denied [always], with Paris and Petersburg; ultimately concluded and put to work by George V. The noose for us is the stupidity and ineptitude of our ally. So the famous "encirclement" of Germany has become fact, despite all attempts by our politicians and diplomats to prevent it. The net has been suddenly closed over our heads and England, smiling derisively, has earned the most brilliant success of its persistent anti-German world policy, against which we have been powerless, by making our fidelity to Austria the noose of our political and economic annihilation, while we lie in the net squirming [and] isolated. A tremendous feat which brings forth admiration even in those who are ruined by it! Edward VII is stronger in death than I, who is still living! And there have been individuals who believed that England could be calmed down or won over, by this or that small favor!!! Unremittingly, relentlessly, it has pursued its goal, with notes, proposals for [naval] holidays, [naval] scares, Haldane, etc., until this point. And we walked into the net and even introduced a rate of construction of [only] one ship per year in the touching expectation to calm England down!!! All my warnings and pleas were in vain. Now we are earning England's so-called gratitude! A situation is created out of our dilemma of our fidelity to the venerable old Emperor of Austria which gives England the pretext to destroy us under the hypocritical cloak of justice, namely, of helping France on the grounds of maintaining the notorious European balance of power, that is, to sic on us all European states for the benefit of England! These machinations must now be uncovered and the mask of Christian peaceability must be torn from its face in public, and its protestations of peace, pharisaical and hypocritical, must be exposed on the pillory!! And our consuls in Turkey and India, our agents, etc., must incite the whole Muslim world to a wild revolt against this hated, lying, un-

[76]On a report by Pourtalès.

scrupulous people of shopkeepers; for if we are to bleed to death, England shall at least lose India.

—DD, 2:401

g)   *Memorandum by Crowe, 31 July 1914*

The theory that England cannot engage in a big war means her abdication as an independent State. . . . A balance of power cannot be maintained by a State that is incapable of fighting and consequently carries no weight.

The fact that British influence has on several momentous occasions turned the scale, is evidence that foreign States do not share the belief that England cannot go to war.

At the opening of any war in all countries there is a commercial panic.

The systematic disturbance of an enemy's financial organisation and the creation of panic is part of a well-laid preparation for war.

Commercial opinion is generally timid, and apt to follow pusillanimous counsels. The panic in the City has been largely influenced by the deliberate acts of German financial houses, who are in at least as close touch with the German as with the British Government, and who are notoriously in daily communication with the German Embassay.

It has been the unremitting effort of Germany to induce England to declare herself neutral in case Germany were at war with France and Russia. The object has been so transparent that His Majesty's Government have persistently declined to follow this policy, as incompatible with their duty to France and Russia and also to England herself. The proposal was again pressed upon us in a concrete form yesterday. It was rejected in words which gave the impression that in the eye of His Majesty's Government the German proposal amounted to asking England to do a dishonourable act.

If it be now held that we are entirely justified in remaining neutral and standing aside whilst Germany falls upon France, it was wrong yesterday to think that we were asked to enter into a dishonourable bargain, and it is a pity that we did not close with it. For at least terms were offered which were of some value for France and Belgium. We are apparently now willing to do what we scornfully declined to do yesterday, with the consequence that we lose the compensating advantages accompanying yesterday's offer.

The argument that there is no written bond binding us to France is strictly correct. There is no contractual obligation. But the *Entente* has been made, strengthened, put to the test and celebrated in a manner justifying the belief that a moral bond was being forged. The whole policy of the *Entente* can have no meaning if it does not signify that in a just quarrel England would stand by her friends. This honourable expectation has been raised. We cannot repudiate it without exposing our good name to grave criticism.

I venture to think that the contention that England cannot in any circumstances go to war, is not true, and that any endorsement of it would be an act of political suicide.

The question at issue is not whether we are capable of taking part in a war, but whether we should go into the present war. That is a question firstly of right or wrong, and secondly of political expediency.

If the question were argued on this basis, I feel confident that our duty and our interest will be seen to lie in standing by France in her hour of need. France has not sought the quarrel. It has been forced upon her.

—*BD*, 11:369

12.12   GERMANY'S WAR ON RUSSIA

Portalès to the German Foreign Ministry, 31 July 1914 • Bethmann to Tschirschky, 31 July 1914 • Bethmann to Pourtalès, 31 July 1914 • Circular by Sazonov, 19 July/1 August 1914 • Pourtalès to Fredericksz, 1 August 1914 • Jagow to Pourtalès, 1 August 1914 • Pourtalès to the German Foreign Ministry, 1 August 1914 • Varnbüler to Weizsäcker, 5 August 1914

Russian general mobilization was officially posted on 31 July. The German reaction is detailed below.

a)   Pourtalès to the German Foreign Ministry, 31 July 1914

General mobilization of [Russian] army and fleet ordered. First day of mobilization: 31 July.

—*DD*, 2:473

b)   Bethmann to Tschirschky, 31 July 1914

After Russian general mobilization, we have proclaimed "period preparatory to war" [*drohende Kriegsgefahr*], presumably to be followed by mobilization within 48 hours. This would unavoidably mean war. We expect from Austria immediate active participation in the war against Russia.

—*DD*, 2:479

c)   Bethmann to Pourtalès, 31 July 1914

. . . The Russian measures force us to proclaim "period preparatory to war," which does not yet mean mobilization. Mobilization must, however, follow unless Russia suspends all hostile measures against us and Austria-Hungary within 12 hours and gives us definite assurances to that effect. . . .

—*DD*, 3:490

d)   *Circular by Sazonov, 19 July/1 August 1914*

At midnight the German ambassador, at the request of his government, told me that unless we demobilized within 12 hours—that is, by Saturday noon—not only vis-à-vis Germany but also vis-à-vis Austria, the German government would be forced to order mobilization. In reply to my question whether that would mean war, the ambassador answered that that would not be the case but that we were extraordinarily close to it.

—*ZI*, 5:385

e)   *Pourtalès to Fredericksz,*[77] *1 August 1914*

. . . A war would put all monarchies in tremendous danger. Last night I received orders to tell M. Sazonov immediately that we had not yet mobilized but that unless Russia tells us unequivocally by noon today that it has suspended its military preparations against us and Austria, the order for mobilization will be given today. You know what this means for us. We cannot deny if this event comes to pass we will be a hair's breadth away from war, a war which neither you or we desire. I know that at this point it is difficult to stop a machine which is already in motion. But the Emperor of Russia is quite able to bring this about. I beseech you to do what you can to prevent this calamity.

—*DD*, 3:539

f)   *Jagow to Pourtalès, 1 August 1914*

If the Russian government has not given a satisfactory answer to our demand, Your Excellency will present it with the following declaration at 5 o'clock Central European time: . . . His Majesty, my master, will accept the challenge in the name of the Reich and considers himself in a state of war with Russia.

—*DD*, 3:542

g)   *Pourtalès to the German Foreign Ministry, 1 August 1914*

. . . I asked M. Sazonov three times whether he could give me statement demanded in telegram no. 153[78] on ceasing mobilization. After he replied in the negative three times, I, as ordered, gave him note.[79]

—*DD*, 3:588

---

[77]Vladimir Borisovich, Baron Fredericksz (1838–1927). Minister of the Russian imperial household, 1897–1917.
[78]Document 12.12c above.
[79]Document 12.12f above.

b)   ***Varnbüler to Weizsäcker, 5 August 1914***

. . . Between Austria and Russia there is a curious state of affairs: because there has been no declaration of war, no hostilities have taken place, no formal state of war exists, and the respective ambassadors are still in Petersburg and Vienna. . . .

—Bach, *Gesandtschaftsberichte*, #98

12.13   GERMANY'S WAR ON FRANCE AND BELGIUM

Bethmann to Schoen, 31 July 1914 ● *Izvolski to Sazonov, 18/31 July 1914* ●
*Schoen to the German Foreign Ministry, 1 August 1914 (with Annotations by
Wilhelm II)* ● *Bethmann to Lichnowsky, 1 August 1914* ● *Izvolski to Sazonov,
19 July/1 August 1914* ● *Jagow to Below, 2 August (29 July) 1914* ● *Below to
the German Foreign Ministry, 3 August 1914* ● *Schoen to Viviani, 3 August
1914* ● *Treutler to Bethmann, 2 August 1914*

The "logic" of the Schlieffen Plan required Germany to fight a staggered two-front war by first defeating France and then turning its armies on Russia. Its military calculations (cf. Document 12.11, headnote) were complemented by political assumptions—namely, that war would come over a crisis in western, not eastern, Europe and that France would live up to its obligations under the Franco-Russian alliance (cf. Document 12.10).

The French side of the German border, however, was heavily fortified. To outflank the French fortifications and deploy the German armies effectively, the Schlieffen Plan decreed that Germany advance through Belgium. But passage through Belgian territory was a clear violation of Belgium's neutrality, which all the Great Powers (including Prussia, the legal predecessor of Germany) had guaranteed in 1839 (Document 2.8).

Few documents in the modern history of diplomacy are as transparent or as disingenuous as the German ultimatum to Belgium (Document 12.13f below). The instructions to the German minister in Brussels were drafted by the Prussian general staff on or before 26 July and only slightly modified in the German foreign ministry before they were sent on to Brussels on 29 July. These dates are important, for they expose as fictitious the premise of the ultimatum: it charged that France was about to use Belgium as a staging area in preparation for an attack on Germany, but no French troop movements toward Belgium could have occurred or did occur by either date.

Mobilization timetables—measures originally designed to ensure victory in war, not to cause wars—had already triggered the Russo-German war; now, purely military considerations outweighed all diplomatic, political, and legal reason and unleashed an even wider war.

a)   ***Bethmann to Schoen, 31 July 1914***

. . . [German] mobilization must follow unless Russia ceases all hostile measures against us and Austria within 12 hours. Mobilization means that war is unavoidable. Please ask French government whether it will remain neutral in a Russo-German war. Answer must be received in eighteen (18) hours. Telegraph immediately after making inquiry. Secret: If contrary to our expectation, French government declares neutrality, Your Excellency will state that we must demand as security for [its] neutrality the fortresses of Toul and Verdun which we will occupy and return after end of war with Russia. . . .

—*DD*, 3:491

b)   Izvolski to Sazonov, 18/31 July 1914

From military attaché to the minister of war.—One o'clock at night. The [French] minister of war told me in an ebullient tone of the firm decision of the government on war and asked me to confirm the expectation of the French general staff that all of our efforts will be directed against Germany and that we treat Austria as a *quantité négligeable.*

—*ZI*, 5:356

c)   Schoen to the German Foreign Ministry, 1 August 1914
(with Annotations by Wilhelm II)

In response to direct question whether France will remain neutral in Russo-German war, prime minister answered hesitatingly: France would do what its interests required [*!*]. He explained uncertainty of this statement because he considered situation to have changed since yesterday. It was official here that Russia had accepted in principle [*? what does this mean?*] Sir Edward Grey's proposal [*not known to me— I have not received any*] of mutual freeze on military preparations and that Austria-Hungary had declared that it would not violate Serb territory and sovereignty.

—*DD*, 3:571

d)   Bethmann to Lichnowsky, 1 August 1914

Paris reports that France has mobilized this afternoon at 5 o'clock, that is to the hour and minute at exactly the same time as we. . . .

—*DD*, 3:605

e)   Izvolski to Sazonov, 19 July/1 August 1914

Three o'clock at night. I just returned from the president who said that the cabinet again confirmed the decision to meet to the fullest the obligations of France under the alliance. The cabinet felt that the interests of the two allies demanded that France complete its mobilization if at all possible before hostilities commence, which will require ten days. At that point the chambers [deputies and senate] will be summoned. Poincaré still fears that Germany will attack France at once in order to make more difficult its mobilization. All this is top secret.

—*ZI*, 5:412

f)   *Jagow to Below,*[80] *2 August (29 July) 1914*[81]

... Reliable reports ... leave no doubt as to the intention of France to advance against Germany through Belgian territory. The imperial government is concerned that Belgium will not be able, without assistance, to defend itself against a French advance and [achieve] the kind of success in which Germany can see a secure warranty against the threat facing it. For Germany it is a requirement of self-preservation to anticipate the enemy attack. Therefore, the German government would regret it if Belgium interpreted as a hostile act [a situation in which] Germany were forced by the action of its enemies to enter Belgian territory in self-defense.

To remove any misunderstanding, the imperial government declares:

1. Germany intends no hostilities against Belgium. If Belgium is willing to adopt a benevolent neutrality, the German government is committed, upon the conclusion of peace, to guarantee the Kingdom's territory and independence to its full extent;

2. [If] the above condition is met, Germany commits itself to evacuate the territory of the Kingdom once peace has been concluded;

3. If Belgium adopts a benevolent attitude, Germany is prepared to reach an arrangement with Belgian authorities to pay cash for supplies for its troops and to indemnify all damages caused by German troops.

Should Belgium oppose the German troops, particularly in obstructing their advance by offering resistance in the Meuse fortifications or by way of destroying railways, roads, tunnels, or other structures, Germany would regrettably be forced to treat the Kingdom as an enemy. In this event, Germany could not undertake any obligations for the benefit of the Kingdom. ...

Your Excellency will communicate this to the Belgian government in the strictest confidence and will request an unequivocal answer within 12 hours. ...

—*DD*, 2:376 (modified in *DD*, 3:648)

g)   *Below to the German Foreign Ministry, 3 August 1914*

Belgian government rejects our proposals and is prepared to meet any violation of its neutrality with force. ...

—*DD*, 4:735

---

[80]Claus von Below-Saleske (1866–1939). German minister in Brussels, 1913–1914.

[81]This instruction was sent in a sealed envelope to the Brussels legation on 29 July; it was somewhat modified on 2 August.

b)   *Schoen to Viviani, 3 August 1914*

German civil and military authorities have confirmed a number of hostile acts against German territory committed by French aviators. Several have apparently violated the neutrality of Belgium in that they have traversed the [air] space of this country. One has tried to destroy railway installations near Wesel, others were sighted near the Eifel [plateau], another threw bombs on rail tracks near Karlsruhe and Nuremberg.

I am authorized and have the honor to notify Your Excellency that in view of these attacks the German Empire considers itself in a state of war with France. . . .

—*DD*, 3:734b

i)   *Treutler[82] to Bethmann, 2 August 1914*

The military report. . . . that French aviators had dropped bombs in the vicinity of Nuremberg has not been confirmed. Only unidentified aircraft were sighted which were apparently not military planes. Nor has the dropping of bombs been verified, much less that the aviators were French.

—*DD*, 4:758

12.14 THE BRITISH DECLARATION OF WAR ON GERMANY

Diary Entry by Hobhouse [August 1914] • *Grey in the House of Commons, 3 August 1914* • *Grey to Goschen, 4 August 1914* • *Jagow to Lichnowsky, 4 August 1914* • *Goschen to Grey, 6 August 1914* • *Grey to Lichnowsky, 4 August 1914*

In violating the neutrality of Belgium, Germany broke the Treaty of London of 1839 (Document 2.8). But the London treaty did not recommend specific sanctions, reprisals, or remedies against an aggressor; instead, it left its signatories free to decide which course of action to pursue. Britain was thus under no obligation to go to war against Germany, though war was a legitimate option. Grey's speech of 3 August in the Commons, much praised by contemporaries and posterity, glossed over this point. Nor did Grey state explicitly that Britain's national interest demanded intervention on behalf of France; he instead served up a rambling and circuitous argument that the prospect of complications in the Mediterranean compelled Britain to support France now. The credibility of this argument aside, there remains the question of whether Grey's speech was consistent with his explanations to parliament on 11 June (Document 11.24) and Asquith's assurances of 24 March 1913.

Keeping verbatim minutes of cabinet meetings became standard practice in Britain only in 1916. Before the First World War the only official record of the proceedings were the short synopses that the prime minister sent to the monarch.[83] Many participants of course jotted

---

[82]Carl Georg von Treutler (1858–1933). Prussian minister in Munich, 1912–1918.
[83]Cf. Stephen Roskill, *Hankey, Man of Secrets* (London, 1970), 1:337–41.

down recollections for their private use. For the cabinet sessions of early August 1914, the notes of Sir Charles Hobhouse, postmaster-general and an interventionist himself, are particularly revealing of the divisions that beset the British ministry. As on previous occasions during Grey's tenure as foreign secretary (Documents 11.14c and f), the British cabinet as a body did not necessarily share the outlook of the Foreign Office.

a)   ***Diary Entry by Hobhouse[84] [August 1914]***

We have had daily Cabinets since Thursday last [30 July] with two on Sunday and Monday. At each we discussed what should be our attitude to France and Germany. We had and have no engagements to France and Cambon in an interview he had with E[dward] G[rey] never suggested that we in any way were bound to her. But he pleaded hard for assistance. Grey had from Lichnowsky the most definite assurances that as Germany and in particular the Emperor were working hard for peace, we ought to remain neutral, which Grey was inclined to do. But on Thursday despite the telegrams of Henry of Prussia and the Emperor William, . . . it became clear that Germany meant to invade France and violate Belgium and that to hoodwink us, she had kept Lichnowsky deliberately in the dark as to her real intentions. From that moment Grey who is sincerity itself became violently pro-French, and eventually the author of our rupture with Germany.

At first L[loyd] G[eorge][85] was very strongly anti-German, in memory no doubt of their attempts to Delcassé[86] him in 1909 [sic for 1911][87], but as the Liberal papers were very anti-war, he veered round and became peaceful. Churchill was of course for any enterprise which gave him a chance of displaying the Navy as his instrument of destruction. McKenna[88] was for war if Belgian territory was violated, but against the dispatch of any expeditionary force. Harcourt,[89] Beauchamp[90] and Simon[91] were for unconditional peace. The P.M., Haldane and I for war if there was even a merely technical breach of the Belgium treaty. Pease[92] and Runciman[93] were strongly against war but not for unconditional neutrality. Burns[94] on Sunday morning was saying that this meant either unconditional neutrality or (leaning over the table shaking his clenched fists) war with both hands, naval and military.

[84]Sir Charles Hobhouse (1862–1941). Postmaster-general, 1914–1915.

[85]David Lloyd George (1863–1945). Chancellor of the Exchequer, 1908–1916; prime minister, 1916–1922.

[86]Cf. Document 11.2.

[87]Cf. Document 11.14.

[88]Reginald McKenna (1863–1943). First Lord of the Admiralty, 1908–1911; home secretary, 1911–1915.

[89]Lewis Harcourt (1863–1922). Colonial secretary, 1910–1915.

[90]William, Seventh Earl Beauchamp (1872–1938). Lord president, 1914–1915.

[91]Sir John Simon (1873–1954). Attorney-general, 1913–1915; foreign secretary, 1931–1935.

[92]Joseph Albert Pease (1860–1943). President of the Board of Education, 1911–1915.

[93]Walter Runciman (1870–1949). President of the Board of Agriculture, 1911–1914. Headed fact-finding mission to Czechoslovakia, August–September 1938, recommending cession of the Sudetenland to Nazi Germany.

[94]John Burns (1858–1943). Resigned as President of the Board of Trade on 6 August to protest British entry into the war.

He was interrupted by McK. and Ll.G. saying "But *which* is your policy?" He hesitated, they repeated the challenge, and with a gulp said "Neutrality, under circumstances," and turned very white. John Morley[95] then said "You all know my views, those of a lifetime, I cannot renounce and if you preserve in intervention, I cannot return to this room." As he had said the same thing about once a month for 3 years, no one took this very seriously. At the end of our meeting. J.B. leant forward and in a few words of deep feeling said he must separate himself from his colleagues with whom he had lived in friendship for 9 years and from a P.M. whom he loved. He was moved to tears. J. Morley said he too could not continue. The P.M. begged them to wait at events till our evening meeting. When we met at 6:30 to continue the pros and cons of neutrality or intervention we the majority came to an understanding that E.G. should tell the H. of C. that we could not stand aside if Belgium were invaded, and that we would give France maritime protection, and so inform Germany. The minority—Burns, J. Morley, Beauchamp, Simon said they could not agree and they must retire. On Monday Aug. 3, after settling what Grey should say, the P.M. said he had the painful duty of telling us he had received the resignations of J.M., J.B. and Simon. Beauchamp leant forward and asked to be included. The P.M. whose eyes filled with tears, said it was the first time in his 6 years of leadership; they were men for whom he had regard and friendship; the party was still hesitating; the country was in danger and unity of counsel was essential. So they agreed except Burns, who had undoubtedly been trapped by Ll.G., to stay, until after Grey had spoken and the H. of C. had indicated its opinion—not very brave conduct. In Simon's case almost despicable because he pretended to a special and personal abhorrence of killing in any shape.

Grey made a very remarkable, moving and powerful speech presenting this case as I think no one else could have done. Its simplicity and sincerity, exhibiting the depth of the feeling of the speaker, contributed greatly to the effect it had on its audience. . . .

—Edward David (ed.), *Inside Asquith's Cabinet: From the Diaries of Charles Hobhouse*
(London, 1977), 179–80

b)   *Grey in the House of Commons, 3 August 1914*

. . . The French fleet is in the Mediterranean, and has for some years been concentrated there because of the feeling of confidence and friendship which has existed between the two countries. My own feeling is that if a foreign fleet engaged in a war which France had not sought, and in which she had not been the aggressor, came down the English Channel and bombarded and battered the undefended coasts of France, we could not stand aside and see this going on practically within sight of our eyes, with our arms folded, looking on dispassionately, doing nothing! . . . If we say nothing . . . let us suppose that the French fleet is withdrawn from the Mediterranean; and let us assume that the consequences—which are already tremendous in what has happened in Europe even to countries which are at peace—in fact, equally whether countries are at peace or at war—let us assume that out of that come consequences unforeseen, which make it necessary at a sudden moment that, in defence of vital British interests, we should go to

[95]John, Viscount Morley (1838–1923). Secretary for India, 1905–1910; Lord President of the council, 1910–1914. Resigned from cabinet, 6 August.

war: and let us assume—which is quite possible—that Italy, who is now neutral [hear, hear]—because, as I understand, she considers that this war is an aggressive war, and the Triple Alliance being a defensive alliance her obligation did not arise—let us assume that consequences which are not yet foreseen—and which perfectly legitimately, consulting her own interests—make Italy depart from her attitude of neutrality at a time when we are forced in defense of vital British interests ourselves to fight, what will then be the position in the Mediterranean? . . . [W]e might have exposed this country from our negative attitude at the present moment to the most appalling risk. . . .

. . . Mr. Gladstone said: "We have an interest in the independence of Belgium which is wider than that which we may have in the literal operation of the guarantee. It is found in the answer to the question whether under the circumstances of the case, this country, endowed as it is with influence and power, would quietly stand by and witness the perpetration of the direst crime that ever stained the pages of history, and thus become participators in the sin."[96] . . . If France is beaten in a struggle of life and death, beaten to her knees, loses her position as a Great Power, becomes subordinate to the will and power of one greater than herself . . . and if Belgium fell under the same dominating influence, and then Holland, and then Denmark, then would not Mr. Gladstone's words come true . . . ? . . . I do not believe for a moment, that at the end of this war, even if we stood aside and remained aside, we should be in a position, a material position, to use our force decisively to undo what had happened in the course of the war, to prevent the whole of the west of Europe opposite to us—if that were the result of the war—falling under the domination of a single power, and I am sure that our moral position would be such as to have lost us all respect. . . .

—*Parl. Debates*, 5th Series, 65:1809–27

c)   *Grey to Goschen, 4 August 1914*

. . . In these circumstances, and in view of the fact that Germany declined to give the same assurance respecting Belgium as France gave last week in reply to our request made simultaneously at Berlin and Paris, we must repeat that request, and ask that a satisfactory reply to it . . . be received here by 12 o'clock tonight. If not, you are instructed to ask for your passports and to say that His Majesty's Government feel bound to take all steps in their power to uphold the neutrality of Belgium and the observance of a treaty to which Germany is as much a party as ourselves.

—*BD*, 11:594

d)   *Jagow to Lichnowsky, 4 August 1914*[97]

. . . A French aggression into our flank on the lower Rhine would have been disastrous. We were therefore compelled to overrule the legitimate protest of the Luxem-

[96]Gladstone spoke on 10 August 1870, during the Franco-Prussian war. His warning was directed at France, rather than Prussia. France affirmed the 1839 settlement in an Anglo-French treaty signed the next day (Document 2.8, headnote). Gladstone's speech is interesting for what he did *not* say: he never openly threatened war to avenge a violation of Belgian neutrality and may once again have been content to strike a pose. *Parl. Debates*, 3rd Series, 203:1776ff.

[97]Telegram *en clair* and in English.

burg and Belgian governments. We shall repair the wrong which we are doing, as soon as our military aims have been reached. Anybody threatened as we are and fighting for his most sacred goods must only think of pulling through. . . .

—BD, 11:612; *DD*, 4:829

e)   *Goschen to Grey, 6 August 1914*

. . . I found the chancellor very agitated. His Excellency at once began a harangue which lasted for about 20 minutes. He said that the step taken by His Majesty's Government was terrible to a degree, just for a word "neutrality" a word which in wartime had so often been disregarded—just for a scrap of paper,[98] Great Britain was going to make war on a kindred nation who desired nothing better than to be friends with her. All his efforts in that direction had been rendered useless by this last terrible step, and the policy to which, as I knew, he had devoted himself since his accession to office, had tumbled down like a house of cards. What we had done was unthinkable; it was like striking a man from behind while he was fighting for his life against two assailants. He held Great Britain responsible for all the terrible events that might happen! I protested strongly against that statement and said that in the same way as he and Herr von Jagow wished me to understand that for strategical reasons it was a matter of life and death to Germany to advance through Belgium and violate her neutrality, so I would wish him to understand that it was, so to speak, a matter of "life and death" for the honor of Great Britain that she should keep her solemn engagement to do her utmost to defend Belgium's neutrality if attacked. That solemn compact simply had to be kept, or what confidence could anyone have in engagements given by Great Britain in the future? The Chancellor said "But at what price will that compact have been kept. Has the British government thought of that?" I hinted to His Excellency as plainly as I could that fear from consequences could hardly be regarded as an excuse for breaking solemn engagements, but His Excellency was so excited, so evidently overcome by the news of our action and so little disposed to hear reason, that I refrained from adding fuel to the flame by further argument. . . .

—BD, 11:671

f)   *Grey to Lichnowsky, 4 August 1914*

. . . I have the honor to inform your Excellency that in accordance with the terms of the notification made to the German government today, His Majesty's Government consider that a state of war exists between the two countries as from today at 11 o'clock p.m. . . .

—BD, 11:643

---

[98]There is some controversy as to whether Bethmann used this phrase. Goschen's first synopsis of the interview, wired on the afternoon of 4 August, did not contain it. *BD*, 11:667. For a recent résumé of this debate, see Christopher H. D. Howard (ed.), *The Diary of Edward Goschen, 1900–1914* (London, 1980), 298–302.

12.15   **THE PAST**

Berchtold to Mérey, 21 July 1914 • Pourtalès to the German Foreign Ministry,
27 July 1914 • Bertie to Grey, 28 July 1914 • Bunsen to Grey, 28 July 1914 •
Mensdorff to Berchtold, 30 July 1914 • Protocol of the Austro-Hungarian
Council of Ministers, 31 July 1914 • Ritter to Hertling, 31 July 1914 •
Goschen to Grey, 1 August 1914 • Bethmann in the Bundesrat, 1 August 1914

At the outset of the July crisis, it was only natural for the Austrian leadership to place the Sarajevo assassination in the broader context of Austro-Serb relations over the past decade. But it is interesting to examine whether the men of 1914, as the crisis wore on, ignored the "lessons" of history or whether they were all too aware of historical precedent. Certainly the Russian leadership cast to the winds the notion that mobilization meant war; the British Foreign Office took no notice of the fact that freewheeling conferences were anathema to Germany and Austria; the German foreign ministry may have worshiped the icon of Bismarckian statecraft but in 1914 left no doubt that it did not comprehend even the most elementary axioms of Bismarck's diplomacy. Yet other moments in the recent past loomed large. How the events of 1909 and 1912 were remembered helped to shape the July crisis of 1914, though the memory of how and why peace had been preserved in those years seemed to have been lost.

a)   ***Berchtold to Mérey,*[99] *21 July 1914***

. . . because of the diplomatic "successes" of 1909 and 1912—which did not benefit us in the long run but only aggravated our relationship to Serbia—I am extremely skeptical of yet another peaceful triumph. . . .

—OeU, 8:10459

b)   ***Pourtalès to the German Foreign Ministry, 27 July 1914***

. . . [I told Sazonov that] in any event, an end had to be put to the provocations of Serbia which had now for the third time in five years brought Europe to the threshold of war. . . .

—DD, 2:282

c)   ***Bertie to Grey, 28 July 1914***

. . . Izvolski . . . said that a promise by Austria to respect territorial integrity of Serbia would be useless if Serbia were reduced to state of vassalage, that Austria's object is to extend Germanic influence and power towards Constantinople, which Russia cannot possibly permit. He added that eventuality ought to be just as repugnant to England as

---

[99]Kajetan, Count Mérey (1861–1931). Austro-Hungarian ambassador in Rome, 1910–1915.

to Russia. His Excellency declared that to allow Austria a free hand with Serbia would be as deep a humiliation for Russia as that which he himself had had to accept in 1909; he had no choice then, as Russia was not in a position to fight, but things were very different now. His Excellency further explained that he had been much blamed in 1909 for accepting German proposal without consulting England and France, but he had done so deliberately in order that humiliation might fall on Russia alone and not on all the three Powers of the *entente*, which would have meant its collapse.

—BD, 11:216

d)   **Bunsen to Grey, 28 July 1914**

. . . Russian ambassador [in Vienna] . . . is pessimistic and thinks any German attempt to overawe Russia, as in 1909, would lead immediately to war. . . .

—BD, 11:248

e)   **Mensdorff[100] to Berchtold, 30 July 1914**

. . . Tyrrell thought . . . [that] Sazonov was under all circumstances determined not to play the role Izvolski played in 1909. . . .

—OeU, 8:11064

f)   **Protocol of the Austro-Hungarian Council of Ministers,**
31 July 1914

. . . [Stürgkh] says that the thought of a conference was so odious that he wanted to avoid even the appearnce of entertaining it. . . . [Bilinsky:] . . . The course of the London conference[101] was such a terrible memory that the public would revolt if such a spectacle would be repeated. . . .

—OeU, 8:11203

g)   **Ritter[102] to Hertling, 31 July 1914**

. . . {Izvolski said] 1909 could not be repeated. . . .

—Dirr, Bayerische Dokumente, 171

---

[100]Albert, Count Mensdorff (1861–1945). Austro-Hungarian ambassador in London. 1904–1914.
[101]Cf. Document 11.21.
[102]Lothar Ritter zu Grunstein. Bavarian minister in Paris.

b)   *Goschen to Grey, 1 August 1914*

... Oh! how much easier things would be if the events of 1909 had not taken place. ...

—*BD*, 11:510

i)   *Bethmann in the Bundesrat, 1 August 1914*

... Austria's history with Serbia has shown that mere pledges given by Serbia were worthless, and that real securities would have to be given. ...

—*DD*, 3:553

12.16   THE FUTURE

Grey to Bunsen, 23 July 1914 • *Nicolson to Grey, 26 July 1914* • *C. P. Scott to Hobhouse, 29 July 1914* • *Varnbüler to Weizsäcker, 3 August 1914*

Most, though not all, of the men of 1914 were conscious of the magnitude of the disaster in which they had had a hand. Most sensed that this war would doom the world as they knew it. Prognoses of its probable outcome were legion, but the four passages excerpted here provide particularly striking vistas of the twentieth century.

a)   *Grey to Bunsen, 23 July 1914*

... The possible consequences of the present situation were terrible. If as many as four Great Powers of Europe—let us say Austria, France, Russia, and Germany—were engaged in war, it seemed to me that it must involve the expenditure of so vast a sum of money and such an interference with trade, that a war would be accompanied or followed by a complete collapse of European credit and industry. In these days, in great industrial states, this would mean a state of things worse than in 1848, and, irrespective of who were victors in the war, many things might be completely swept away. ...

—*BD*, 11:86

b)   *Nicolson to Grey, 26 July 1914*

... Prince Henry[103] said if Russia moved there would be an internal revolution and the dynasty be upset. This is nonsense—but it shows how anxious they are to make

---

[103]Henry of Prussia (1862–1929). Younger brother of Wilhelm II. Henry cut short a visit to England on 26 July.

out that Russia will remain quiet and to spread about that we will be equally quiescent—a foolish procedure—(Prince Henry has gone back to Germany).

—*BD*, 11:144

c)   *C. P. Scott[104] to Hobhouse, 29 July 1914*

What a monstrous and truly hellish thing this war will be if it really brings the rest of Europe into it. It ought to sound the knell of all the autocracies—including that of our own Foreign Office.

—Trevor Wilson (ed.), *The Political Diaries of C. P. Scott, 1911–1928* (Ithaca, 1970), 93

d)   *Varnbüler to Weizsäcker, 3 August 1914*

Cambon has behaved in a correct and dignified fashion and has made no secret of his disapproval of a war which will tear to pieces all of Europe and which will, in the final analysis, only benefit the United States. . . .

—Bach, *Gesandtschaftsberichte*, #96

[104]Charles Prestwich Scott (1847–1932). Editor and publisher of the *Manchester Guardian*.

A BIBLIOGRAPHICAL ESSAY

How We Know What We Know

1   **BY WAY OF INTRODUCTION**

In keeping with the tenor of this book, this essay will emphasize and point out published primary sources—the correspondence, diaries, speeches, and treaty texts (though not memoirs) where the principals of the story speak for themselves, albeit sometimes only as fully as the editors of their works have seen fit to allow. Readers searching for secondary sources should consult the "General Reading" at the end of chapter headnotes or the section entitled "Bibliographies and Bibliographic Essays" below.

Any attempt to shoehorn a vast literature into categories that probably exist more in the author's imagination than in discernible reality is bound to reveal a host of inconsistencies. That caveat notwithstanding, the remainder of the present essay has grouped sources into the following subdivisions:

2. Bibliographies and bibliographic essays
3. Treaty collections
4. Constitutions and parliamentary records
5. Official and quasi-official collections (spanning several periods with which this book deals)
6. Correspondence and diaries (falling predominantly within one of the following periods)
   a) 1813–1848
   b) The western hemisphere
   c) The Eastern Question to 1841
   d) East Asia, 1842–1913
   e) 1848–1871
   f) 1871–1890
   g) 1890–1914

To make the last of these sections more manageable, I have included in it scholarly works with superior bibliographies of primary sources. These books have been identified with an asterisk (*).

In perusing this bibliography—and, for that matter, this entire book—readers should always keep in mind that they are, literally, at the receiving end of a long process of selection and filtration. The sources to which we have access may have been sifted several times: deliberately, by an author or speaker posturing for posterity; deliberately, by an editor intent on whitewashing a hero; deliberately, by an institution covering its tracks; inadvertently, by quirks of fate (water damage, fire, bombing raids, dispersion in war, accidental misshelving, and like acts of God) that destroy part of the record or cause it to vanish for generations. It is wise to treat document collections with caution or even suspicion: a good portion of any historian's trip to the archives is spent comparing the published record against the archival holdings to see whether a particular document has been yanked out of context by earlier writers and editors, and to check whether it is in fact as representative as these earlier authorities have claimed. This is not to suggest, however, that the archives contain an unbroken record—they are incomplete for essentially the same reasons as the published collections. Finally, many historians doing archival research have found to their dismay that certain decisions simply did not leave a paper trail.

Most books have their precursors, and the present volume is no exception. The study of nineteenth-century diplomacy through collections of documents used to be a staple of undergraduate history curricula, and previous exercises in this genre include Kenneth Bourne, *The Foreign Policy of Victorian England, 1830–1902* (Oxford, 1970); James Joll (ed.), *Britain and Europe. Pitt to Churchill, 1793 to 1940* (London, 1950); and Harold W. V. Temperley and Lillian M. Penson (eds.), *Foundations of British Foreign Policy from Pitt (1792) to Salisbury (1902)* (Cambridge, 1938). The authors of the first and last of these titles made available a generous number of documents that they had uncovered in their own work in the archives, and, consequently, these compilations are valuable still. Neither, however, takes the story much beyond the turn of the century. As is evident from all three titles, the focus is on the making of British foreign policy—an approach which confers some internal cohesion on these books but also risks the myopia that comes with viewing international relations solely through the lens of a single country, no matter how pluralistic it may be. The four-volume collection by Joel H. Wiener (ed.), *Great Britain: Foreign Policy and Span of Empire, 1689–1971* (New York, 1972) is difficult to use, as various chapters overlap chronologically; volumes 1, 3, and 4 all deal with portions of the nineteenth century.

René Albrecht-Carrié (ed.), *The Concert of Europe* (New York, 1968) takes an international perspective, with topics chosen to illustrate how the European concert functioned. The emphasis on international cooperation is, of course, welcome but tends to give short shrift to those moments, particularly in the 1860s and after 1890, when the concert had ground to a halt. An older compilation, W. Henry Cooke and Edith P. Stickney (eds.), *Readings in European International Relations since 1879* (New York, 1931), offers an extensive, if unexciting, selection from the official publications and memoirs available at the time of writing, with an emphasis on the origins of the First World War.

2   BIBLIOGRAPHIES AND BIBLIOGRAPHIC ESSAYS

A good starting point for any bibliographical spadework is the American Historical Association's *Guide to Historical Literature*, under the general editorship of Mary Beth Norton, 2 vols. (New York/Oxford, 1995). The *Guide* focuses on secondary, rather than primary, sources; section 47, edited by Paul W. Schroeder, covers nineteenth-century international relations. Mario Toscano, *The History of Treaties and International Politics. . . . The Documentary and Memoir Sources* (Baltimore, 1966) emphasizes the origins of the two world wars but also gives an excellent overall introduction to the published primary sources for the diplomatic history of the nineteenth century. The essays in James A. Moncure (ed.), *Research Guide to European Historical Biography*, 4 vols. (Washington, 1992) assess the quality of primary and secondary sources on some, though regrettably not all, of the most prominent political figures of the nineteenth century. Not a bibliography per se, but an excellent manual of diplomatic terminology and procedure is the handbook started by Sir Ernest Satow, *A Guide to Diplomatic Practice*, 2 vols. (1917; 5th ed., London, 1979).

Three textbooks that belong on the shelf of every serious student of international affairs—not least because of their bibliographies—are Norman Rich, *Great Power Diplomacy, 1814–1914* (McGraw-Hill, 1992); Paul W. Schroeder, *The Transformation of European Politics, 1763–1848* (Oxford, 1994); and A. J. P. Taylor, *The Struggle for Mastery in Europe, 1848–1918* (Oxford, 1954). Schroeder's and Taylor's bibliographies list a vast array of published primary sources, and—if only for reasons of space—no attempt can be made here to replicate this massive body of research. The reader does not need to share all of Taylor's views to recognize that the bibliographical essay that concludes *The Struggle for Mastery* is in itself a literary exercise of the first order, but should bear in mind that forty years have elapsed since this provocative and entertaining book first appeared and that a good number of primary sources have been published in the interval.

Nineteenth-century international relations may have been dominated by the European Great Powers, but much of the story unfolded in settings in which they were cultural outsiders. The history of the European powers' penetration of these areas, their rivalries within them, and the local responses to these intrusions often poses special linguistic and cultural challenges for the historian. The thirty-page bibliography at the end of J. C. Hurewitz, *The Middle East and North Africa in World Politics*, vol. 1: 1535–1914 (New Haven, 1975) makes accessible the literature on the Eastern Question outside of Europe. Ottoman rule in the Balkans—another area requiring special linguistic skills—is the subject of Hans-Jürgen Kornrumpf's *Osmanische Bibliographie mit besonderer Berücksichtigung der Türkei in Europa* (Leiden, 1973). Essentially a collection of historiographical essays, James Morley (ed.), *Japan's Foreign Policy, 1868–1941: A Research Guide* (New York, 1974) offers full bibliographical coverage of virtually all East Asian diplomacy between the Meiji restoration and the outbreak of the Pacific war. Excellent bibliographical essays and bibliographies of secondary sources can be found in *The Cambridge History of Africa*, vol. 5: *From c. 1790 to c. 1870* (1976), edited by John E. Flint, and vol. 6: *From 1870 to 1920* (1985), edited by Roland Oliver and G. N. Sanderson.

Research on the western hemisphere might start in the bibliographic essays in *The Cambridge History of Latin America*, vol. 3: *From Independence to c. 1870* (1985) and vol. 4: *c. 1870 to 1930* (1986), both edited by Leslie Bethell; *The Cambridge History of American Foreign Relations* (1993), vol. 1: *The Creation of a Republican Empire, 1776–1865* by Bradford Perkins, and vol. 2: *The American Search for Opportunity, 1865–1913* by Walter LaFeber.

Specialty journals that are likely to review new books are: for the diplomacy of the Great Powers, the *International History Review*; for American foreign policy, *Diplomatic History* and *Foreign Affairs*; for issues in public and private international law, the *American Journal of International Law*.

3   TREATY COLLECTIONS

Of the various collections of treaties covering the nineteenth century, the most ambitious is *The Consolidated Treaty Series* (Dobbs Ferry, NY, 1969–1986), compiled in 231 volumes by Clive Parry. The goal of the *CTS* was to reproduce in a systematic fashion all international treaties concluded between the Peace of Westphalia in 1648 and the end of the First World War in 1918—accomplishing, if you will, for this 270-year span what the *League of Nations*

Treaty Series did for the interwar period and the *United Nations Treaty Series* for the post-World War II era. Individual treaties can be located in the *CTS* by way of three indexes: the *General Chronological List*, 5 vols. (Dobbs Ferry, NY, 1979–1985), compiled by Brian H. W. Hill and Paul Irwin, essentially functions as a table of contents; the *Special Chronological List*, 2 vols. (Dobbs Ferry, NY, 1984), edited by Michael A. Meyer, covers colonial, postal, and telegraph agreements; and the *Party Index*, 5 vols. (Dobbs Ferry, NY, 1986), edited by Brian H. W. Hill, cross-references the *CTS* by signatory.

The *CTS* is far easier to use than the complicated treaty collections carried on in the name of Georg Friedrich Martens: *Nouveau recueil général des traités*, 1st Series, 20 vols. (Göttingen, 1843–1875); 2nd Series, 35 vols. (Göttingen, 1876–1908); 3rd Series, 40 vols. (Leipzig, 1909–1943). The *CTS* replaces the Martens collections, but purists may still want to rely on Martens for texts in the original treaty language, for the *CTS* opted for official, but usually non-binding, English translations whenever these could be found. The *CTS* also incorporates much of *Hertslet's Commercial Treaties*, 31 vols. in 10 (1840–1925; reprint: New York, 1970), a treasure trove of private international law, trade agreements, consular issues, taxation, nationality, extradition, navigation, fisheries, and copyright.

The *British and Foreign State Papers* [also cited as *State Papers*], 170 vols. (London, 1841–1968) includes public treaties, official statements of policy, and constitutional documents from 1812 onward. Edward Hertslet (ed.), *The Map of Europe by Treaty* [1814–1891], 4 vols. (London, 1877–1891; reprint: 1969) remains a useful companion to nineteenth-century public, though not secret, treaties. Like the *State Papers*, this collection also comprises items that were not treaties in a technical sense, such as decrees, proclamations, and policy guidelines. The secret treaties of the 1880s and 1890s were published by Alfred F. Pribram, *The Secret Treaties of Austria-Hungary, 1879–1914*, 2 vols. (Cambridge, MA, 1920), but this collection, in its turn, does not include the military protocols and commitments of the Anglo-French entente. A portable collection of major nineteenth-century treaties, drawing heavily on both the Hertslet and Pribram collections, can be found in the two-volume condensation by Michael Hurst (ed.), *Key Treaties for the Great Powers, 1814–1914* (New York, 1972).

Researchers who do not have easy access to the *CTS* or the other collections listed above might begin their quest in the indexes that follow here. The American delegation to the Paris Peace Conference of 1919 was outfitted with reference works dubbed *The Inquiry Handbooks*, of which volume 17, *Catalogue of Treaties, 1814–1918* (1919; reprint: Wilmington, 1974), identified published sources for most nineteenth-century treaties. Clive Parry and Charity Hopkins (eds.), *An Index of British Treaties, 1101–1968*, 3 vols. (London, 1970) is indispensable for British treaties. American treaties are cross-referenced in Igor I. Kavass (comp.), *United States Treaty Index 1776–1990 Consolidation*, 12 vols. (New York, 1991–1993). For Austria, there is the rather dated index prepared by Ludwig Bittner, *Chronologisches Verzeichnis der österreichischen Staatsverträge*, 4 vols. (Vienna, 1903–1917). Helmuth K. G. Rönnefarth (ed.), *Konferenzen und Verträge . . . 1492–1914* [often cited as *Vertrags-Ploetz*] (2nd rev. ed., Würzburg, 1958) is more a handbook than a systematic treaty index, but nonetheless provides a useful guide to treaties on Central Europe.

Full-length collections of U.S. treaties are David Hunter Miller (ed.), *Treaties and Other International Acts of the United States of America*, 8 vols. (Washington, 1931–1948), which takes the story to 1863; and Charles I. Bevans (ed.), *Treaties and Other International Agreements of the United States of America, 1776–1949*, 13 vols. (Washington, 1968–1976). American treaties that were negotiated between 1776 and 1918 but remained unratified are reprinted in the first four volumes of Christian L. Wiktor (ed.), *Unperfected Treaties of the United States of America, 1776–1976* (Dobbs Ferry, NY, 1976–1979).

For other countries, the standard collections of public treaties and agreements are: for France, Alexandre and Jules de Clerq, *Recueil des traités de la France*, 23 vols. (Paris, 1864–1907); for tsarist Russia, Fedor Fedorovich Martens, *Recueil des traités et conventions conclus par la Russie*, 14 vols. (St. Petersburg, 1874–1905); for Italy, Ministero degli Affari Esteri, *Trattati e convenzioni tra il regno d'Italia e gli stati esteri*, 54 vols. (Turin/Rome, 1861–1941); for the Ottoman Empire, Ignatz von Testa, *Recueil des traités de la Porte Ottomane ... [de] 1536 ... jusqu'à nos jours*, 11 vols.   (Paris, 1864–1911), or Gabriel Noradounghian, *Recueil d'actes internationaux de l'empire ottoman*, 4 vols. (Paris, 1897–1903). British treaties with Persia and Afghanistan can be found in vol. 13 of C. V. Aitchison (comp.), *A Collection of Treaties, Engagements, and Sanads Relating to India and Neighbouring Countries*, 13 vols. (Calcutta, 1931–1933).

The selection of treaties, correspondence, and policy declarations in M. S. Anderson, *The Great Powers and the Near East, 1774–1923* (London, 1970) serves as a concise companion to the same author's authoritative *The Eastern Question, 1774–1923* (London, 1966). By far the best introduction to the legal complexities of the nineteenth-century Middle East is J. C. Hurewitz, *The Middle East and North Africa in World Politics*, vol. 1: *1535–1914* (New Haven, 1975). This collection sweeps a vast acreage from the Caucasus to the Persian Gulf and from Afghanistan to Morocco; moreover, the introductions that precede each document or cluster of documents set impeccable standards of scholarship.

The heyday of western imperialism in China is covered by Godfrey E. P. Hertslet (ed.), *Treaties, etc., between Great Britain and China and between China and Foreign Powers*, 2 vols. (3rd ed., London, 1908). John V. A. MacMurray (ed.), *Treaties and Agreements with and Concerning China, 1894–1919*, 2 vols. (1921; reprint: New York, 1973) is particularly good on the predatory commercial treaties of the turn of the century. Agreements covering Korea are included in an earlier version (Washington, 1904) edited by William W. Rockhill, the architect of the Open Door Note of 1899. A distinctive hallmark of the edition prepared by the Maritime Customs of China, *Treaties, Conventions, etc., between China and Foreign States*, 2 vols. (1917; reprint: New York, 1973) is the reproduction of treaties and agreements in the original treaty languages. Ernest Batson Price, *The Russo-Japanese Treaties of 1907–1916 Concerning Manchuria and Mongolia* (Baltimore, 1933) contains the texts of these instruments and lengthy excerpts from the *travaux préparatoires*.

Finally, the European scramble for and partition of Africa is chronicled in Edward Hertslet (ed.), *Map of Africa by Treaty*, 3 vols. (3rd rev. ed., 1909; reprint: London, 1967).

4   CONSTITUTIONS AND PARLIAMENTARY RECORDS

It is of course a platitude to suggest that the purpose of constitutions is to identify the rights of the governed, to define the powers of government, and to allocate these powers within the government. But most constitutions are notoriously vague as to where the power to direct foreign policy actually lies. To complicate matters further, constitutional theory often differs sharply from constitutional practice. And finally, the constitutional prerogative of determining foreign policy varied widely among European governments: no one would dispute that Wilhelm II had far greater constitutional powers in this regard than, say, Queen Victoria. But interestingly enough, the argument cannot be turned on its head, for it does not follow that the queen never sought to leave her imprint on British foreign policy, nor would it be correct to assert that Wilhelm never bowed to the advice of his chancellors.

A racy scandal, a number of by-election victories for the opposition, chronic parliamentary instability, the failure of a legislative package—any of these can block a monarch or a prime minister from committing his or her government to a particular foreign policy. Students of the twentieth century, familiar with the Watergate effect on American foreign policy in the 1970s or with the domestic quicksands that mired French foreign policy in the Third and Fourth Republics, will be quick to recognize similar situations in the nineteenth: How did the parliamentary weakness of the Aberdeen coalition affect British diplomacy on the eve of the Crimean War? How did the constitutional dualism of Austria-Hungary condition this state's attitude toward the German problem in the critical years between 1867 and 1870? How did the parliamentary difficulties of the French government in July 1882 predetermine its response to the antiforeign riots in Alexandria (and with what consequences)? How did the fallout from the *Daily Telegraph* scandal allow Bülow to curb the Kaiser from interfering with Germany's policy in the Bosnian crisis?

Anyone seeking to anchor foreign policy in its domestic context might as well begin with the study of constitutional politics. H. J. Hanham (ed.), *The Nineteenth-Century Constitution, 1815–1914: Documents and Commentary* (Cambridge, 1969) traces the development of British constitutional practice. The *Letters of Queen Victoria* in three series of three volumes each (1st Series, *1837–1861* [London, 1907]; 2nd Series, *1862–85* [London, 1926]; 3rd Series, *1885–1901* [London, 1930]), packed as they are with insights on constitutional questions, merit inclusion in this as well as subsequent sections of this bibliography. An even fuller selection, "The Papers of Queen Victoria on Foreign Affairs," is distributed on microfilm in six series by University Publications of America. A printed guide accompanies each of the series: Russia and Eastern Europe (four reels); Germany and Central Europe (thirty-three reels); Italy (eighteen reels); Portugal and Spain (ten reels); France and Belgium (thirteen reels); Greece (three reels).

John Brooke, *The Prime Ministers' Papers, 1801–1902* (London, 1968) is a guide to archival holdings. Many of these papers are now being published in *The Prime Ministers' Papers Series* (for individual listings, see section 6 below). The relationship between Whitehall and the British dominions—with the passage of time increasingly important for British diplomacy in southern Africa and imperial defense policy in the Pacific—is traced in D. K. Fieldhouse, Frederick Madden, and John Darwin (eds.), *Select Documents on the Constitutional History of the British Empire and Commonwealth*, 6 vols. to date (Westport, CT, 1985–). The five constitutional regimes experienced in France between the fall of Napoleon and the close of the nineteenth century are introduced in Léon Cahen and Albert Mathiez (eds.), *Les lois françaises de 1815 à 1914* (4th ed., Paris, 1933). Ernst Rudolf Huber, *Dokumente zur deutschen Verfassungsgeschichte*, 3 vols. (3rd ed., Stuttgart, 1978) is important for the diplomacy of the German question between 1815 and 1871 and the constitutional politics of the Second Reich after 1871. The Habsburg monarchy is the only Great Power whose cabinet minutes are available in print: *Die Protokolle des österreichischen Ministerrats, 1848–1867* (Vienna, 1970–), edited by Gerald Stourzh et al., is now almost complete in six series; the records of the joint Austro-Hungarian council of ministers are being prepared by Istvan Dioszegi, Éva Somogyi, Miklos Komjathy, et al. under the title *Die Protokolle des gemeinsamen Ministerrates der österreichisch-ungarischen Monarchie, 1867–1918* (Budapest, 1966–). The latter series will ultimately comprise seven volumes, of which the fourth (1883–1895), fifth (1896–1907), and last (1914–1918) have appeared to date.

Statesmen who otherwise worked hard to keep their legislatures at bay were quick to appreciate that an appearance in parliament would not only give them a national audience but would also allow them to be heard abroad as well. Some of the phrases by which the policy of Palmerston or Bismarck is remembered were first uttered in parliament. Yet nineteenth-century foreign ministries were not eager to share the secrets of their trade with parliaments. The foreign secretaries, prime ministers, or chancellors of all European powers were expert in evading or deflecting questions put to them by members of parliament foolhardy enough to venture into the lofty realm of *les grandes affaires*. While governments easily brushed off these challenges, the parliamentary debates on foreign policy nonetheless stand as an instructive reminder that unanimity was the exception rather than the rule and that there was more than one answer to the question, "What is the national interest?"

The proceedings of both houses of parliament are found in Hansard's *Parliamentary Debates*. A parallel publication, the *Parliamentary Papers*, printed supporting materials for the scrutiny of members of parliament and the interested public. Foreign policy documents in the *Parliamentary Papers* usually included the text of the agreement thus submitted to parliament as well as selections from its negotiating history. Bound in pamphlets (dubbed "Blue Books" after the color of the cover), these documents of course sought to promote the version of events favored by the government of the day.

Ironically, the practice of issuing Blue Books backfired on the Foreign Office, as the fear that official correspondence might after all see the light of day in the guise of a Blue Book cautioned diplomats and the Foreign Office staff to frame their reports accordingly. In one telling episode, the Foreign Office in the spring of 1909 directed British diplomats to avoid "the expression 'Triple Entente' when referring to the joint action of England, France, and Russia," and justified this admonition by arguing that "if it appeared in a parliamentary Blue Book it would be assumed to have some special official meaning and might provoke inconvenient comment or inquiry." In reply, the assistant under-secretary wryly observed that "if it is unfit for publication, it would seem so easy for the Blue Book Department to cut it out"—an interesting verdict on the purpose of the Blue Books and also their usefulness to the historian.[1]

Nonetheless, Blue Books are often the only published primary source available for those events or years not covered by scholarly editions of Foreign Office documents (see below), and, consequently, researchers without the time or money to peruse the Foreign Office files in the Public Record Office in London may still find them helpful. A chronological listing of nineteenth-century Blue Books as they appeared in the *Parliamentary Papers*, along with superb introductions to the Blue Book policy of successive foreign secretaries, can be found in Harold V. Temperley and Lillian M. Penson, *A Century of Diplomatic Blue Books, 1814–1914* (1938; reprint: New York, 1966). Thumbnail biographical sketches of M.P.s can be found in Michael Stenton and Stephen Lees (eds.), *Who's Who of British Members of Parliament*, vol. 1: *1832–85* (London, 1976) and vol. 2: *1885–1918* (London, 1978).

The adoption by other European powers of the British practice of issuing Blue Books went hand in hand with the spread of constitutions and parliaments on the continent. Collectively, these publications (including their British precursor) became known as the "colored books"— yellow for France, white for Germany, red for Austria, green for Italy, orange for Russia.

Like the records of the British parliament, the *Journal officiel de la République française, Chambre des députés* is bifurcated in Series I: *Débats parlementaires* and Series II: *Documents parlementaires*. The proceedings in various legislatures prior to the Third Republic can be reconstructed from the government-inspired gazette, *Le Moniteur universel* (Paris, 1789–1868). Beginning in 1860, French Yellow Books were made available by the Ministère des affaires

---

[1]Circular by Sir Charles Hardinge, 30 April 1909, FO, 800/342, and minute by Walter Langley, n.d., FO,H800/193A.

étrangères under the title *Documents diplomatiques*. For Germany, the debates of the Frank-furt Parliament are recorded in Franz Wigard (ed.), *Stenographischer Bericht über die Ver-handlungen der Deutschen Constituierenden Nationalversammlung*, 9 vols. (1848–1849; reprint: Munich, 1988). The records of the subcommittee on economic affairs were edited by Werner Conze and Wolfgang Zorn as *Die Protokolle des Volkswirtschaftlichen Ausschusses* (Boppard, 1992). The proceedings of the lower chamber of the Prussian legislature, *Stenographische Berichte über die Verhandlungen des Preussischen Hauses der Abgeord-neten*, are important for the German question of the 1850s and even more so for the 1860s. After 1867, the North German Parliament and, after 1871, the German parliament published its deliberations under the title *Stenographische Berichte über die Verhandlungen des Reichs-tags* (now also available on microfiche from Microcard Editions or University Publications of America). The more important moments in both the German and Prussian legislatures are ex-cerpted in H. Schulthess, *Europäischer Geschichtskalender* (annually: 1861–1884; new se-ries, 1885–1941). M. Schwarz collected biographical information on members of the 1848–1849 Frankfurt assembly and the federal parliaments after 1867 in *MdR: Biographisches Handbuch der Reichstage* (Hanover, 1965). For Austria-Hungary, parliamentary discussion of foreign policy can best be traced in the *Stenographische Sitzungsprotokolle der Delegation des* [österreichischen] *Reichsrats*. The proceedings of the Italian parliament can be found un-der the title *Atti Parlamentari*, with separate series for the *Senato* and the *Camera dei Deputati* (most legislative sessions are available on microfilm). The debates of the Russian Duma, a late-comer among European parliaments when it was first constituted in 1906, are indexed in *Ukazatel'k stenograficheskim otchetam Gosudarstvennoy Dumy*; the debates themselves can be found under the title *Gosudarstvennaia Duma. Stenograficheskiie otchety*.

5   OFFICIAL AND QUASI-OFFICIAL COLLECTIONS OF DOCUMENTS

The Bolshevik government lost no time in discrediting its predecessors—and, for that matter, all capitalist regimes—by publishing the wartime inter-Allied treaties while Allied armies were still locked in combat against the Central Powers. The initial Bolshevik revelations were soon supplemented by more documents on tsarist misdeeds from Russian archives, released in France by René Marchand as *Un Livre noir*—a word play, with a funereal connotation, on the colored books. This collection, rearranged along chronological lines and enriched with fur-ther documentation, was translated into German by Friedrich Stieve, *Der diplomatische Schriftwechsel Iswolskis, 1910–1914*, 4 vols. (Berlin, 1924).   More Russian materials ap-peared, albeit haphazardly, in the Soviet periodical *Krasny Arkhiv* (1922–1941). Many of its articles were taken up and translated by the editors of a quasi-official German quarterly tellingly named *Kriegsschuldfrage* (1923–1938) ["War Guilt Question"; as of 1929: *Berliner Monatshefte*]. A systematic index to the *Krasny Arkhiv*, with English-language abstracts of all articles, was prepared by Leonid Rubinchek et al. (eds.), *A Digest of the Krasnyi Arkhiv*, 3 vols. (Cleveland, 1947). A more organized series of Russian documents had to await the late 1920s. Published as *Mezhdunaradnye otnosheniya v epokhu imperializma*, it is exceedingly rare and most accessible in its German translation, edited by Otto Hoetzsch, *Die internationalen Beziehungen im Zeitalter des Imperialismus*. Only the third (1911–1914) and fourth series (1914–1916) were ever published. The politics of totalitarianism intruded into this series with full force: many of its Russian editors fell victim to the Stalinist purges of the 1930s; the last German volumes appeared in print, ironically, only after the Nazi invasion of the Soviet Union. One Russian collection that does not owe its existence to the Bolshevik desire to tell all (at least about the tsarist regime), but to a White Russian renegade, is Benno von Siebert's edition of the correspondence of the last tsarist ambassador in London, *Graf Benckendorffs diplomatischer Schriftwechsel*, 3 vols. (Berlin, 1928), available in an abridged English edition under the title *Entente Diplomacy and the World War* (London, 1921).

After the First World War, the German government had a material stake in disproving article 231 of the Treaty of Versailles—the so-called war-guilt clause—which blamed Germany for the war and justified the Allied demand for reparations. To undermine the legitimacy of this aspect of the peace, the German government scrambled to present its version of the diplomacy of the prewar period to the scholarly community before other powers would have a chance to do the same—launching, in effect, a kind of academic preemptive strike. The result was two collections: a four-volume edition of documents on the July crisis of 1914 prepared by Karl Kautsky, Max Montgelas, and Walter Schücking as *Die Deutschen Dokumente zum Kriegsausbruch 1914*, 4 vols. (Berlin, 1919); and a larger forty-volume series covering the period from the Franco-German war to the spring of 1914 entitled *Die Grosse Politik der europäischen Kabinette, 1871–1914* (Berlin, 1922–1927), edited by Johannes Lepsius et al.[2] Rather than having these series compiled in colored-book fashion by anonymous bureaucrats, the German government opted for the services of scholars whose reputations, it was hoped, would bestow on these collections an air of impartiality. To cite just one example: the senior editor of the *Grosse Politik*, Lepsius, had impeccable credentials as a theologian, humanitarian, and compiler of an exposé decrying the Armenian massacres of the First World War; his father had been Germany's most famous Egyptologist. For a vigorous indictment of the German effort to manipulate the documentary record and a summary of the growing German literature on this subject, see Holger Herwig, "Clio Deceived: Patriotic Self-Censorship in Germany after the Great War," *International Security* 12 (1987), 5–44. Similar investigations have yet to be attempted for the British and French collections.

Not to be outdone in the battle for the hearts and minds of a disillusioned and increasingly skeptical public, the British government tapped Harold Temperley (the biographer of Canning) and G. P. Gooch (whose credentials included a long list of works on French and German political history, a stint as a member of parliament with a distinct lack of fondness for Grey's foreign policy, and marriage to a German-born wife) to publish the *British Documents on the Origins of the War, 1898–1914*, 11 vols. (London, 1926–1938). Only volume 11, covering the July crisis of 1914, was edited by the Foreign Office historical adviser J. W. Headlam-Morley.[3]

---

[2]Those wanting to test the selection of documents in the *Grosse Politik* against the archival record in the German foreign ministry archive should brace themselves by consulting beforehand the *Catalogue of Files and Microfilms of the German Foreign Ministry Archives, 1867–1920* (Oxford, 1959), compiled by the American Historical Association Committee for the Study of War Documents. The microfilms were prepared for the National Archives and various research universities (e.g., University of California, University of Michigan, Florida State University) and many are available on interlibrary loan. Not all holdings of the foreign ministry were microfilmed.

[3]One file on which the *British Documents* were based, FO 371 (General Correspondence) on Germany, is now available on microfilm (see section 6g below). The files in the 371 series (and this holds true also for the 371 files on countries other than Germany), however, typically do not include the more candid private letters (FO 800) that members of the Foreign Office exchanged with British diplomats abroad. The 800 series can of course be inspected at the Public Record Office in London.

The model for the "scholarly" editions on the origins of the First World War may well have been a French collection, massive in scope, on France's foreign relations between 1863 and the Franco-Prussian war. In 1910, the French foreign ministry started *Les Origines diplomatiques de la guerre de 1870/71*, which ultimately spanned twenty-nine volumes and was completed only in 1932. The French collection on the origins of the First World War, however, was slow in getting started, and the last volumes appeared only in the mid-1950s, a time when interest in the origins of the First World War was scant. The *Documents diplomatiques français* is divided into three series: *1er série 1870–1900*, 16 vols. (Paris, 1929-1959); *2èmé serie 1901–11*, 14 vols. (Paris, 1930–1955); and *3ème série 1911–14*, 11 vols. (Paris, 1929–1936). From the point of view of the user, both collections have the merit of being organized chronologically rather than by topic. The French foreign ministry archives are explained in *Les Archives du ministère des relations extérieures*, 2 vols. (Paris, 1984–1985).

Italy was the only Great Power in the 1920s to resist the general clamor that it issue a documents collection. After the Second World War, the Italian republic rectified this sin of omission by projecting an edition for the entire diplomatic history of the kingdom of Italy. Of the nine series of *I documenti diplomatici italiani* (Rome, 1953–), the first four deal with the years 1861 to 1914 and are subdivided as follows: *1a Serie: 1861–70*; *2a Serie: 1870–96*; *3a Serie: 1896–1907*; *4a Serie: 1908–1914*. More scholarly in conception than the official collections that preceded it, the Italian edition is marred by one major defect: to date, it is still too fragmented, as existing volumes do not form a cohesive whole but are scattered among the various series (for instance, only volumes 1–6, 8–14, and 21 of the second series are presently available).

Apart from the Italian series, four other official collections of diplomatic documents have been launched since the Second World War. The most impressive of these is the Dutch collection edited by C. B. Wels, Joannes Aloysius Woltring and C. Smit, *Beschieden betreffende de buitenlandse politiek van Nederland, 1848–1919* (The Hague, 1957–1974). So far, only one volume has appeared in the first series (1848–1870), but the second (1871–1898) and third series (1899–1919) are complete in six and ten volumes, respectively. The first six volumes of the *Documents diplomatiques suisses, 1848–1945* (Berne, 1981–) take the account to the First World War. Like the Dutch collection, the Swiss volumes meet exacting scholarly standards. Finally, for those who read Serbo-Croatian, the Yugoslav government released Serb documents spanning the years from the Belgrade palace coup of 1903 to the outbreak of war in 1914: Petar Popovic, Vladimir Dedijer, et al. (eds.), *Dokumenti o spoljnoj politici kraljevine Srbije, 1903–1914*, 7 vols. in 12 (Belgrade, 1980). Beginning in 1960, the Soviet government embarked on a collection that, upon completion, may well be the most ambitious edition in this genre: *Vneshniaia politika Rossi XIX i nachala XX veka. Dokumenty Rossiiskogo ministerstva inostrannykh del* (Moscow, 1960–), begun by the Soviet foreign ministry under the general editorship of Aleksei Leontevich Narochnitskii, is projected for six segments (1st Series, 1801–1815; 2nd Series, 1815–1830; 3rd Series, 1830–1856; 4th Series, 1856–1878; 5th Series, 1878–1895; 6th Series, 1895–1917). To date, the first series is complete at eight volumes; the second series has six volumes so far (also listed as volumes 9–14).

One collection defying easy classification is the *British Documents on Foreign Affairs: Reports and Papers from the Foreign Office Confidential Print* [hereafter *BD-FOCP*], under the general editorship of Donald Cameron Watt and the late Kenneth Bourne. The various series under this imprint (see next section below) cannot be described as government-inspired, for they are compiled by scholars from material no longer classified. But neither do they, to quote the editors, "constitute the 'archives in print.'" The operative words in the rather cumbersome title are "Confidential Print"—a designation for Foreign Office documents circulated to individuals or agencies in the government. These might include the monarch, cabinet ministers or cabinet committees, departmental heads within the Foreign Office, or British plenipotentiaries abroad (though, unlike the Blue Books, the Confidential Print excluded members of parliament or the general public). The purpose of the Confidential Print was to inform, but not necessarily to afford glimpses of the foreign policy process or the motivations for a particular policy. Accordingly, the goal of the *BD-FOCP* is somewhat different from that of the other document collections, including the *British Documents on the Origins of the War, 1898–1914*. The rationale for the *BD-FOCP*, rather, is to focus—albeit through the British lens—on the "domestic politics of the principal state or states covered in each area series and their relations with and policies towards countries other than Great Britain." References to each of these area series can be found in the section below.

6   CORRESPONDENCE AND DIARIES

a) **1813–1848** An excellent bibliography of primary sources can be found in *Enno E. Kraehe, *Metternich's German Policy*, vol. 2: *The Congress of Vienna, 1814–1815* (Princeton, 1983). Extensive selections have been published from the papers of most of the principals of the congress. Metternich's papers appeared simultaneously in French, German, and English editions: Richard, Prince Metternich (ed.), *Aus Metternichs nachgelassenen Papieren*, 8 vols. (Vienna, 1880–1884). The English translation, *Memoirs of Prince Metternich* (1880–1882; reprint: New York, 1970), only has five volumes and peters out in the early 1830s. The gap is partially filled by G. de Bertier de Sauvigny, *Metternich and his Times* (London, 1962), which relies on lengthy excerpts from Metternich's writings, arranged by topic. Charles Stewart, Third Marquess of Londonderry, edited his brother's papers as *Memoirs and Correspondence of Viscount Castlereagh . . .* , 12 vols. (1848–1853). *The Memoirs of the Prince de Talleyrand*, 5 vols. (New York, 1891–1892), edited by the duc de Broglie, includes entertaining selections from the correspondence of this skilled opportunist. Much heavier going are the political papers, many in French, of Wilhelm von Humboldt, in volumes 10–12 of his *Gesammelte Schriften* (1903; reprint: Berlin, 1968), edited by Albert Leitzmann and Bruno Gebhardt. Arthur Wellesley, the duke of Wellington, left eight volumes of *Despatches, Correspondence, and Memoranda* (London, 1862–1880).

Charles K. Webster (ed.), *British Diplomacy, 1813–15* (London, 1921) is an admirable collection of documents, obviously inspired by the trials of the peacemaking process of 1918–1919. Perhaps the best printed source on the Congress of Châtillon is Fedor von Demelitsch's edition of Austrian documents, "Actenstücke zur Geschichte der Coalition vom Jahre 1814," *Fontes Rerum Austriacarum* 49:2, 228–447 (Vienna, 1899).

For the postwar era, John Hall Stewart (ed.), *The Restoration Era in France, 1814–1830* (Princeton, 1968) and Mack Walker (ed.), *Metternich's Europe, 1813–1848* (New York, 1968) are two relatively recent collections of excerpted documents in translation, some of which have a bearing on foreign policy.

A good guide to the primary literature on the breakdown of the congress "system" is *Paul W. Schroeder, *Metternich's Diplomacy at its Zenith, 1820–1823* (1962; reprint: Austin, 1977). *The Speeches of the Rt. Hon George Canning*, 6 vols. (London, 1836), edited by R. Thierry, is supplemented by E. J. Stapleton (ed.), *Political Correspondence of George Canning* (London, 1888). Some of Canning's letters can be found in A. Aspinall, *Letters of George IV*, 3 vols. (Cambridge, 1938). In *The Prime Ministers' Papers Series*, John Brooke et al. have edited papers from Wellington's stint as foreign secretary as *Wellington, Political Correspondence, 1833–35,* 2 vols. (London, 1975–1986). In the same series, Roger Bullen and Felicity Strong have begun to cover Palmerston's letters: to date, there is *Palmerston,* vol. 1: *Correspondence with Sir George Villiers* [later Earl of Clarendon] (London, 1985). The irrepressible Princess Lieven carried on a strictly platonic, we are assured, exchange of letters with another fixture of Tory politics. These are edited by E. Jones Parry as *The Correspondence of Lord Aberdeen and Princess Lieven, 1832–54,* 2 vols. (London, 1938–1939). Jacques Naville edited the less platonic *Lettres de François Guizot et la Princesse de Lieven,* 3 vols. (Paris, 1964). Another well-placed observer of the July monarchy was Eurydice Dosne, Adolphe Thiers's mother-in-law, whose papers were published by Henri Malo as *Mémoires de Mme. Dosne,* 2 vols. (Paris, 1928).

On Russia, each of the four volumes of Theodor Schiemann, *Geschichte Russlands unter Kaiser Nikolaus I* (Berlin, 1904–1919) has about a hundred pages of documents, generally in French or German, appended to it. Schiemann, incidentally, was one of the few academics whose opinions were respected by Kaiser Wilhelm II and who on occasion joined the imperial entourage.

b)   The Western Hemisphere   Two selections that span almost the entire history of American foreign relations are Robert H. Ferrell (ed.), *Foundations of American Diplomacy, 1775–1872* (New York, 1968) and Howard Jones (ed.), *Safeguarding the Republic: Essays and Documents in American Foreign Relations, 1890–1991* (McGraw-Hill, 1992). The bibliography in *Ernest R. May, *The Making of the Monroe Doctrine* (Cambridge, MA, 1975) is impressive in its range. The *Memoirs of John Quincy Adams, Comprising Portions of His Diary from 1795 to 1848,* 12 vols. (Philadelphia, 1872–1877), edited by Charles Francis Adams, is a document of literary distinction with shrewd insights on Anglo-American relations. Still a standard work on the British angle is Sir Charles K. Webster (ed.), *Britain and the Independence of Latin America, 1812–1830,* 2 vols. (London, 1938). Basil Dmytryshyn et al. (eds.), *The Russian American Colonies: A Documentary Record 1798–1867* (Portland, OR, 1989) serves as a reminder that there was also a Russian context to the Monroe Doctrine.

Series C (Part I) of the *BD-FOCP* (see above, section 5), edited by Kenneth Bourne, covers *North America, 1837–1914* in fifteen volumes. While this series proceeds chronologically, Series D (Part I), *Latin America, 1845–1914,* 9 vols., edited by Harold Blakemore, is organized by country.

The first president, since the 1820s, to bring to his office broad interest in international relations was Theodore Roosevelt; his views, with all their idiosyncrasies, are well revealed in Elting E. Morison (ed.), *The Letters of Theodore Roosevelt,* 8 vols. (Cambridge, MA, 1951–1954).

c)   The Eastern Question to 1841   The documents in M. S. Anderson, *The Great Powers and the Near East,* and in J. C. Hurewitz, *The Middle East and North Africa in World Politics* (see above, sections 2 and 3) essentially approach the region from the perspective of the Great Powers, while Robert G. Landen (ed.), *Emergence of the Modern Middle East* (New York, 1970) focuses on local responses to the dilemmas of Europeanization and modernization. Alexandre Bennigsen (ed.), *Le khanat de Crimée dans les archives du Musée du Palais de Topkapi* (Paris, 1978), a volume with beautiful facsimiles of Ottoman documents, covers an eighteenth-century subject of vital importance for Russo-Turkish relations.

Douglas Dakin, *British Intelligence of Events in Greece, 1824–1827: A Documentary Collection* (vol. 13 of *Bulletin de la société historique et ethnique de la Grèce,* Athens, 1959) is somewhat bland, but there is much local color in Haim Nahoum (ed.), *Recueil de firmans impériaux ottomans adressés aux valis et aux khédives d'Égypte* (Cairo, 1934) and in the French consular reports of the same period, edited by Georges Douin as *Mohamed Aly et l'expédition d'Alger, 1829–1830* (Cairo, 1930).

d)   East Asia, 1842–1913   Ssu-Yu Teng, John K. Fairbank, et al. (eds.), *China's Response to the West: A Documentary Survey, 1839–1923* (many editions, initially Cambridge, MA, 1954) and the second volume of Wm. Theodore de Bary et al., *Sources of Japanese Tradition* (New York, 1958) give excellent introductions to the reactions of, respectively, China and Japan to western intrusion and dominance.

The period between Perry's arrival in Edo Bay and the Meiji restoration is the subject of W. G. Beasley, *Select Documents on Japanese Foreign Policy, 1853–1868* (London, 1955). For subsequent years, *James W. Morley (ed.), *Japan's Foreign Policy, 1868–1941: A Research Guide* (see section 2) is authoritative. Gordon Mark Berger has translated and edited the diary and reminiscences of Mutsu Munemitsu, a Japanese foreign minister whose term in office was defined by Japan's emergence as a Great Power, as *Kenkenroku. A Diplomatic Record of the Sino-Japanese War, 1894–95* (Tokyo, 1982). The impressions of the Belgian minister to Japan are captured by George A. Lensen in *The d'Anethan Dispatches from Japan, 1894–1910* (Tokyo, 1967). Kajima Morinosuke, *The Diplomacy of Japan, 1894–1922*, 3 vols. (Tokyo, 1976–1980) carefully steers clear of controversy but contains lengthy excerpts from the *Nihon Gaiko Bunsho.* The Japanese government started this document series in 1936 and initially intended one volume for each year covered beginning with 1865—a plan that was impossible to execute for later years. *Nihon Gaiko Nempyo oyobi Shuyo Bunsho*, 2 vols. (Tokyo, 1965) is a very condensed version.

By the mid-nineteenth century, no other power matched Britain's commercial stature in East Asia, and few outside observers of East Asian cultures were better equipped to make informed, though not necessarily impartial, judgments on the politics of the day than the British. British preeminence and the growing challenge mounted by other powers are amply borne out in the first fifteen volumes of the *BD-FOCP*, Series E (Part I), *Asia, 1860–1914*, edited by Ian Nish (ultimately projected at thirty volumes). University Publications of America is in the process of making available, on microfilm, the Foreign Office correspondence on China (FO file 371) for the period 1906 to 1919 (projected at 441 reels).

The European Diary of Hsieh Fucheng, translated by Helen H. Chien and annotated by Douglas Howland (New York, 1993), covers the years 1890 to 1894 from the perspective of a Chinese ambassador in Europe. Documents on tsarist diplomacy toward China, as revealed by the Soviet journal *Krasny Arkhiv* (see section 5), can be found in English translation in the issues of the *Chinese Political and Social Science Review* of the late 1920s and early 1930s.

e)   1848–1871   As already mentioned, *A. J. P. Taylor's *Struggle for Mastery in Europe* lists a vast array of primary sources published before the early 1950s. Added to his listings should be Series F (Part I) of the *BD-FOCP, Europe, 1848–1914*, 35 vols., edited by David Stevenson and John F. V. Keiger, and Series A (Part I), *Russia, 1859–1914*, 6 vols., edited by Dominic Lieven.

The bulk of the documents in Denis Mack Smith (ed.), *The Making of Italy, 1796–1870* (New York, 1968) is devoted to the Italian question between 1848 and 1866. A good introduction to primary sources can be found in various sections of the bibliography of *Frank J.

Coppa, *The Origins of the Italian Wars of Independence* (New York, 1992). On the Roman revolution of 1849, there are the dispatches of the correspondent of the New York *Daily Tribune*: Margaret Fuller, *"These Sad but Glorious Days." Dispatches from Europe, 1846–1850*, edited by Larry J. Reynolds and Susan Belasco Smith (New Haven, 1991).

Anglo-Prussian relations during the four-year crisis (1848–1852) over Schleswig-Holstein can be traced through the letters of the Prussian minister in London in Frances Baroness Bunsen (comp.), *A Memoir of Baron Bunsen*, 2 vols. (London, 1868). There is an expanded German-language edition, Friedrich Nippold (ed.), *Christian Carl Josias Freiherr von Bunsen*, 3 vols. (Leipzig, 1869–1871).

*Paul W. Schroeder, *Austria, Great Britain, and the Crimean War* (Ithaca, 1972) and *Norman Rich, *Why the Crimean War? A Cautionary Tale* (1985; reprint: McGraw-Hill, 1991) feature bibliographies with extensive listings of primary sources. Austrian and Prussian diplomatic documents on the Crimean War have recently been published by Winfried Baumgart (ed.), *Akten zur Geschichte des Krimkriegs*, 1st Series: *Oesterreichische Akten*, 3 vols. (Munich, 1979–1980); 2nd Series: *Preussische Akten*, 2 vols. (Munich, 1990–1991). Julius von Jasmund, *Aktenstücke zur orientalischen Frage*, 3 vols. (Berlin, 1855–1859) is a good contemporary collection of documents, mostly in German translation. These include some excerpts that are otherwise difficult to find, such as Nesselrode's reaction in September 1853 ("violent interpretation") to the Porte's refusal of the Vienna Note. Still indispensable for the Russian point of view is the internal correspondence (in French) published by A. M. Zaionchkovskii, *Vostochnaya Voina, 1853–56gg.*, supplementary vol. 1: *Prilocheniya* (St. Petersburg, 1908). The Eastern Question after the Crimean War is observed in the *BD-FOCP*, Series B (Part I), *The Near and Middle East, 1856–1914*, 20 vols., edited by David Gillard. On Russia during and after the Crimean War, there is Barbara Jelavich's edition of reports from the Bavarian legation in St. Petersburg, *Russland, 1852–1871* (Wiesbaden, 1963).

The journals kept by the English economist Nassau Senior on his visits to France, published as *Conversations with M. Thiers, M. Guizot, and other Distinguished Persons*, 2 vols. (London, 1878), are of considerable insight for the Second Empire, as are the papers of the Earl of Cowley, the British ambassador in Paris from 1852 to 1867: F. A. Wellesley (ed.), *Secrets of the Second Empire: Private Letters from the Paris Embassy* (New York, 1929). The historiography of the conspiratorial meeting between Cavour and Napoleon III is explored in *Mack Walker (ed.), *Plombières: Secret Diplomacy and the Rebirth of Italy* (New York, 1968). Of the many editions of Cavour's letters (for a full listing see *Coppa, *Origins of the Italian Wars of Independence*, op. cit.), perhaps still the most important is his correspondence with the Piedmontese minister in Paris, *Il carteggio Cavour-Nigra*, 4 vols. (Bologna, 1926–1929). Cavour was in the habit of writing in both Italian *and* French to Piedmont's envoys and even to his monarch. The standard document collections on him and his followers should be supplemented by Sergio Camerani and Gaetano Arfè (eds.), *Carteggi di Bettino Ricàsoli*, 29 vols. (Rome, 1939–1972). The unification of Italy, from the point of view of the papal government, is told in Norbert Miko (ed.), *Das Ende des Kirchenstaats*, 4 vols. (Vienna, 1964–1970), with an emphasis on the events of 1870. Documents are primarily in Italian and French, with German synopses of materials that were omitted.

The bibliographical essay and historiographical analyses in the footnotes of *George O. Kent, *Bismarck and his Times* (Carbondale, 1978) are first-rate, as is the bibliography in *Otto Pflanze, *Bismarck and the Development of Germany*, 3 vols. (Princeton, 1963–1990). *E. Ann Pottinger, *Napoleon III and the German Crisis, 1865–1866* (Cambridge, MA, 1966) has an excellent annotated bibliography. The most authoritative edition of Bismarck's writings, *Die* *gesammelten Werke*, 15 vols. (Berlin, 1924–1935; reprint: 1972), is weighted in favor of the 1850s and 1860s. More of Bismarck's reports and directives can be found in *Die Auswärtige Politik Preussens, 1858–1871*, 10 vols. (Berlin, 1932–1945), a collection that has the additional merit of including material from English, Russian, and other German (i.e., non-Prussian) archives. Bismarck's speeches are in H. Kohl, *Die politischen Reden des Fürsten Bismarck*, 14 vols. (Stuttgart, 1892–1905; reprint, 1969–1970). The documents in Helmut Böhme (ed.), *The Foundation of the German Empire* (Oxford, 1971) focus on economic determinants rather than on Bismarck's skill as a diplomat. *Lawrence D. Steefel, *The Schleswig-Holstein Question* (Cambridge, MA, 1932) reprints some documents on that vexing problem. Bismarck's Austrian opponents have their say in Heinrich von Srbik (ed.), *Quellen zur deutschen Politik Oesterreichs, 1859–1866*, 5 vols. (1934–1938; reprint: Osnabrück, 1967). The English translation of Hermann Oncken, *Napoleon III and the Rhine*, 3 vols. (New York, 1928), like its German original, is based largely on Austrian archives; the work itself needs to be understood in the context of French attempts after the First World War to revive the idea of a Rhenish buffer state. Georges Bonnin (ed.), *Bismarck and the Hohenzollern Candidature for the Spanish Throne* (London, 1957) published and translated into English documents from the files of the German foreign ministry. These documents were apparently not shown to the Harvard historian Robert H. Lord for his book *The Origins of the War of 1870. New Documents from the German Archives* (Cambridge, MA, 1924). Lord was one of the first scholars to be admitted to the German foreign ministry archive, but the files were sanitized before he was given access to them.

Among outsiders, the British minister to Hesse-Darmstadt was a well-placed observer, although, in Bismarck's view, he was tainted by too close an association with the Prussian crown prince and princess. His daughter, Rosslyn Wester Wemyss, perhaps to refute the charge from the Bismarckian camp that her father had been a Germanophobe, published selections from his correspondence as *Memoirs and Letters of the Rt. Hon. Sir Robert Morier, GCB, from 1826 to 1876*, 2 vols. (London, 1911). Queen Victoria naturally took a keen interest in the German question. Her letters (see section 3) should be supplemented by the correspondence with her eldest daughter, Crown Princess Victoria of Prussia. These letters have been edited in five volumes by Roger Fulford: *Dearest Child . . . 1858–1861* (London, 1964), *Dearest Mama . . . 1861–1864* (New York, 1968), *Your Dear Letter . . . 1865–1871* (New York, 1971), *Darling Child . . . 1871–1878* (London, 1976), and *Beloved Mama . . . 1878–1885* (London, 1981).

f) 1871–1890   A comprehensive list of primary literature that appeared before 1950 can be found in *William L. Langer, *European Alliances and Alignments, 1871–1890* (rev. ed., New York, 1950). Almost half a century later, this period—in terms of published primary sources—is still dominated by the *Grosse Politik* and the *Documents diplomatiques français* (see section 5).

Most of volume 4 of Hertslet, *Map of Europe by Treaty* (London, 1891) is devoted to the Eastern crisis of 1875–1878, its "settlement" at the Congress of Berlin, and the residual territorial and financial problems that plagued European diplomacy until 1883 (and, by some counts, beyond). The course of the congress can be reconstructed from the proceedings, now reissued in French and German by Imanuel Geiss (ed.), *Der Berliner Kongress 1878: Protokolle und Materialien* (Boppard, 1978). Alexander Novotny (ed.), *Quellen und Studien zur Geschichte des Berliner Kongresses 1878* (Graz, 1957) excerpts the correspondence between the Ballhausplatz and the Austro-Hungarian embassy in Constantinople. The often conflicting policies of various Russian statesmen are illustrated in Charles and Barbara Jelavich (eds.), *Russia in the East, 1876–1880: The Russo-Turkish War and the Kuldja Crisis as Seen through the Letters of A. G. Jomini to N. K. Giers* (Leiden, 1959). On the same subject, there is the publication of documents from the Russian embassy in London begun by R. W. Seton-Watson in the *Slavonic and East European Review* (seven installments between 1924 and 1927 on the period May 1875 to January 1878; five between 1946 and 1950, taking the story to April 1878) and resumed by W. N. Medlicott and Richard G. Weeks, Jr., in volumes 64 and 65 of the same journal (1986–1987) for the crucial months, August 1878 to May 1880, in which the Berlin settlement was implemented.

C. J. Lowe (ed.), *The Reluctant Imperialists: British Foreign Policy, 1878–1902* (New York, 1969) begins with a good overview of British policy at the Congress of Berlin. Lady Gwendolen Cecil, *Life of Robert Marquis of Salisbury*, 4 vols. (London, 1921–1932 reprint, New York, 1971), which takes the story to 1892, is still the principal published primary source on her father's foreign policy. The Gladstone ministries are well served by Agatha Ramm (ed.), *The Political Correspondence of Mr. Gladstone and Lord Granville, 1868–76*, 2 vols. (London, 1952) and *. . . 1876–1886*, 2 vols. (Oxford, 1962); Dudley W.R. Bahlman (ed.), *The Diary of Sir Edward Hamilton, 1880–1885*, 2 vols. (Oxford, 1972); and Paul Knaplund (ed.), "Letters from the Berlin Embassy. Selections from the Private Correspondence of British Representatives at Berlin and Foreign Secretary Lord Granville, 1871–1874, 1880–1885," *Annual Report of the American Historical Association for the Year 1942*, vol. 2 (Washington, 1944). Michael Foot and H. C. G. Matthew (eds.), *The Gladstone Diaries*, 14 vols. (Oxford, 1968–1994) deal primarily with domestic and imperial concerns but allow a day-by-day reconstruction of the place of foreign policy in Gladstone's thinking; the index (vol. 14) is superb.

A valuable source for the European scramble for and penetration of Africa will be Series G (Part I) of the *BD-FOCP: Africa from the Mid-Nineteenth Century to the First World War.* To be edited by David Throup, David Gillard, and Michael Partridge, this series is presently projected at twenty-five volumes. For the Niger basin and the Gold and Ivory Coasts, there is Colin W. Newbury (ed.), *British Policy towards West Africa: Select Documents, 1875–1914* (Oxford, 1971) and John D. Hargreaves, *France and West Africa: An Anthology of Historical Documents* (1969; reprint: Aldershot, 1993). The Italian presence in Eritrea is treated in Giorgio Rochat (ed.), *Il colonialismo italiano* (Turin, 1973).

g)   1890–1914   The bibliographies in *William L. Langer, *The Diplomacy of Imperialism, 1890–1902* (rev. ed., New York, 1951) are unmatched in the thoroughness of their coverage. Since Langer's work, German foreign policy has been illuminated by several first-rate collections. Norman Rich and M. H. Fisher (eds.), *The Holstein Papers*, 4 vols. (Cambridge, 1956–1963) brings to light the thinking of Friedrich von Holstein, the reclusive counselor in the German foreign ministry who was saddled with much of the blame for the mishaps of German policy. Holstein's diaries (vol. 2) and correspondence (vols. 3 and 4) are a profound source for the political intrigues that shaped German foreign policy between the late Bismarck period and Holstein's death in 1909. The papers of the senior German diplomat and long-time ambassador in London, edited by Gerhard Ebel as *Botschafter Paul Graf von Hatzfeldt: Nachgelassene Papiere, 1838–1901*, 2 vols. (Boppard, 1976), add little but offer an engaging portrait of this unusual man. Throughout the 1890s (and sporadically before he was finally brought down by a scandal in 1907), Wilhelm II's favorite was Count Philipp zu Eulenburg, whose maneuverings behind the scenes are meticulously traced in John C. G. Röhl (ed.), *Philipp Eulenburgs politische Korrespondenz*, 3 vols. (Boppard, 1976–1983). Indispensable for German constitutional politics on the federal plane is Walter Peter Fuchs, *Grossherzog Friedrich I. von Baden und die Reichspolitik, 1871–1907*, 4 vols. (Stuttgart, 1968–1980). One of the shrewdest observers of the byzantine atmosphere of the Berlin court was the widow of

Württemberg's minister in Berlin, Hildegard von Spitzemberg. Her diary was made available by Rudolf Vierhaus as *Das Tagebuch der Baronin Spitzemberg* (Göttingen, 1960); there is an abridged paperback edition entitled *Am Hof der Hohenzollern* (Munich, 1965). Wilhelm II speaks for himself in N. F. Grant (ed.), *The Kaiser's Letters to the Tsar* (London, 1920).

The genesis, at the turn of the century, of German naval armaments and the increases in land armaments after 1910 are traced by Volker R. Berghahn and Wilhelm Deist (eds.), *Rüstung im Zeichen der wilhelminischen Weltpolitik: Grundlegende Dokumente* (Düsseldorf, 1988). In focusing only on Germany, this collection unwittingly raises the question of whether these ambitions were unique to that country's leadership, or whether similar assumptions motivated British and American naval planners and French and Russian military strategists.

For Britain, volume 3 of C. J. Lowe and M. L. Dockrill, *The Mirage of Power: British Foreign Policy, 1902–22* (London, 1972) presents many documents not published by Gooch and Temperley in the official *British Documents on the Origins of the War, 1898–1914* (see section 5). For the papers of the First Lord of the Admiralty between 1900 and 1905, see D. George Boyce (ed.), *The Crisis of British Power: The Imperial and Naval Papers of the Second Earl of Selborne, 1895–1910* (London, 1990). Christopher H. D. Howard edited *The Diary of Edward Goschen, 1900–1914* (London, 1980). Goschen reveals little about his tenure as British ambassador in Vienna (1905–1908) and Berlin (1908–1914); however, he is well worth reading on the imbroglio of the powers on the Balkans. An important source on dissension within the British cabinet is Edward David's edition of the diaries of Charles Hobhouse, who joined the Asquith government in February 1914: *Inside Asquith's Cabinet* (London, 1977). Trevor Wilson (ed.), *The Political Diaries of C. P. Scott* (London, 1970) contains valuable snippets on foreign affairs from the diary of the editor of the *Manchester Guardian*, a radical critic of Grey's policy. Randolph S. Churchill's biography of Winston S. Churchill is accompanied by a very full selection from the Churchill papers. *Winston S. Churchill. Companion Volume II* comes in three parts (London, 1969). As of 1995, the Foreign Office 371 file (General Correspondence) on Germany covering the years 1906 to 1918 is available on microfilm from University Publications of America. The 371 file constitutes the bulk of Foreign Office material on the Anglo-German relationship and on German domestic affairs; selections from this file had already been published by Gooch and Temperley in the interwar years in the official *British Documents on the Origins of the War* (see section 5 above). The file itself has been available to researchers in the Public Record Office in London since the late 1960s.

For the immediate prewar years, there is John C. G. Röhl, "Admiral von Müller and the Approach of War, 1911–1914," *Historical Journal* 12 (1969), 651–73, fleshed out in "An der Schwelle zum Weltkrieg: Eine Dokumentation über den 'Kriegsrat' vom 8. Dezember 1912," *Militärgeschichtliche Mitteilungen* 10 (1977), 77–134. Imanuel Geiss, *July 1914* (New York, 1967) should be used with caution (see Chapter 12, headnote). Some new documents from the files of the German naval office were made available by Volker R. Berghahn and Wilhelm Deist, "Kaiserliche Marine und Kriegsausbruch 1914: Neue Dokumente zur Juli-Krise," *Militärgeschichtliche Mitteilungen* 3 (1970), 37–58. Extremely important for the July crisis is the diary of Bethmann Hollweg's assistant, Kurt Riezler, edited by Karl Dietrich Erdmann: *Kurt Riezler. Tagebücher, Aufsätze, Dokumente* (Göttingen, 1972). In the early 1980s, an angry debate raged in the pages of the premier German historical journal, the *Historische Zeitschrift*, as to whether the diary had been sanitized prior to publication. Also of considerable importance are the diaries and correspondence of the editor of the liberal *Berliner Tageblatt*, edited by Bernd Sösemann as *Theodor Wolff. Tagebücher, 1914–1919*, 2 vols. (Boppard, 1984).

Wolff had easy access to the sources of power and immediately after the outbreak of war sought to reconstruct how and why the catastrophe had come about.

For Austria-Hungary, a logical starting point is the up-to-date bibliography at the end of *Samuel R. Williamson, Jr., *Austria-Hungary and the Origins of the First World War* New York, 1991). Other documents that should complement Ludwig Bittner et al. (eds.), *Oester-reich-Ungarns Aussenpolitik*, 8 vols. (Vienna, 1930) are: Eurof Walters, "Unpublished Documents: Aehrenthal's Attempt in 1907 to Regroup the European Powers," *Slavonic and East European Review* 30 (1951), 213–51; Keith M. Wilson, "Isolating the Isolator: Cartwright, Grey and the Seduction of Austria-Hungary, 1908–12," *Mitteilungen des österreichischen Staatsarchivs* 35 (1982), 169–98; Francis Roy Bridge (ed.), *Austro-Hungarian Documents Relating to the Macedonian Struggle, 1896–1912* (Salonika, 1976); Ernst Rutkowski (ed.), *Briefe und Dokumente zur Geschichte der österreichisch-ungarischen Monarchie unter besonderer Berücksichtigung des böhmisch-mährischen Raumes*, 2 vols. (Vienna, 1983–1984); Keith Hitchins (ed.), *The Nationality Problem in Austria-Hungary: The Reports of Alexander Vaida to Archduke Franz Ferdinand's Chancellery* (Leiden, 1974); Robert A. Kann, "Emperor William II and Archduke Francis Ferdinand in Their Correspondence," *American Historical Review* 57 (1951/52), 323–51, expanded in *Erzherzog Franz Ferdinand Studien* (Vienna, 1976), 47–85. The trial, in Sarajevo court, of Franz Ferdinand's assassins was reconstructed in the 1950s by the Bosnian archivist Vojislav Bogicevic and has been translated and edited by W. A. Dolph Owings as *The Sarajevo Trial*, 2 vols. (Chapel Hill, 1984).

One remaining mystery of the July crisis is what exactly was said by the French president Raymond Poincaré on his state visit to Petersburg. An edition of Poincaré's diaries, edited by Gerd Krumeich, has been promised but has not yet appeared.

Index